中国人民大学“十三五”规划教材

A History of American Literature

美国文学史

（第二版）

上

主编　陈世丹　屈晓丽

编者（以姓名拼音首字母为序）

陈世丹　李金云　屈晓丽　史岩林　苏　凤

王阿芳　王桃花　吴银燕　吴泽庆　尹　宇

张东芹　张丽秀　赵　丽

中国人民大学出版社

·北京·

中国人民大学“十三五”规划教材

A History of American Literature

美国文学史（第二版）

下

主编 陈世丹 屈晓丽

编者（以姓名拼音首字母为序）

陈世丹 李金云 屈晓丽 史岩林 苏 凤

王阿芳 王桃花 吴银燕 吴泽庆 尹 宇

张东芹 张丽秀 赵 丽

中国人民大学出版社

·北京·

CONTENTS

目 录

CONTENTS

目录

前言

《美国文学史（上、下）》全面、系统地描述了自17世纪以来各个历史时期的美国文学：17世纪殖民地时期的美国文学、18世纪革命与理性时期的美国文学、19世纪浪漫主义时期的美国文学、19世纪现实主义时期的美国文学、20世纪现代主义时期的美国文学和第二次世界大战后（1945年以来）的后现代主义时期的美国文学。本书选择Washington Erving, James Fenimore Cooper, William Cullen Bryant, Edgar Allen Poe, Ralph Waldo Emerson, Henry David Thoreau, Nathaniel Hawthorne, Herman Melville 和 Henry Wadsworth Longfellow 为19世纪浪漫主义时期美国文学的代表作家；Walt Whitman, Emily Dickinson, Harriet Beecher Stowe, Mark Twain, Henry James, Edith Wharton, Jack London, Theodore Dreiser 和 Willa Cather 为19世纪现实主义时期美国文学的代表作家；Ezra Pound, Wallace Stevens, Thomas Stearns Eliot, Ernest Hemingway, William Faulkner 和 Eugene O'Neill 为20世纪现代主义时期美国文学的代表作家；Robert Lee Frost, F. Scott Fitzgerald, Arthur Miller 为20世纪现代主义文学繁荣时期仍坚持现实主义文学创作的代表作家。第二次世界大战后1945年以来的美国文学虽然有 Bernard Malamud, Saul Bellow, John Updike, Joyce Carol Oates 等著名作家仍在坚持现实主义和现代主义小说创作，但从整体上看，后现代主义文学占主导地位。因此，本书选择 Robert Lowell, Charles Olson, Joseph Heller, Kurt Vonnegut, John Barth, Donald Barthelme, Thomas Pynchon, Vladimir Nabokov 和 Toni Morrison 作为后现代主义文学的代表作家。后现代主义是西方后工业社会、后现代社会、晚期资本主义的文化现象，对于我们当时仍处在农业社会、前工业社会、前现代社会的大多数中国读者来说还是一个比较陌生的概念。这些后现代主义作家的作品表现出后现代主义的核心观念：在今天的世界里，各种各样不稳定、不确定、非连续、无序、断裂和突变现象的重要作用越来越为人们所认识并重视。在这种情况下，一种新的看待世界的观念开始深入人们的意识：它反对用单一的、固定不变的逻辑、公式和原则以及普适的规律来说明和统治世界，主张变革和创新，强调开放性和多元性，承认并容忍差异。当今的时代已放弃了制定统一的、普遍适用的模式的努力，新的范畴如开放性、多义性、无把握性、可能性、不可预见性等等，已进入后现代的语言。在后现代，彻底的多元化已成为普遍的基本观念；后现代的多元性是一切知识领域和社会生活各方面的本质。这种多元性原则的直接结论是：反对任何统一化的企图；后现代思维积极维护事物的多样性和丰富性，坚决反对任何试图将自己的选择强加于别人，使异己的事物屈服于自己意志的霸权野心；它尊重并承认各种关于社会构想、生活方式以及文化形态的选择。后现代主义文学以多元变化的不断创新的叙事技巧和多样杂糅的文本结构表现后现代人类经验，揭示现实与历史的文本性和不确定性。

编写本书的目的是为高校英语语言文学专业本科生课程“美国文学”教学服务，遵循史论结合、详略得当的编写原则，既为教师的课堂讲授和学生的自主学习提供丰富的史学知识，又给教师和学生对本门课程的教学内容建构和课堂创新性发言讨论留下足够的发挥空间。真正意义上独立的美国民族文学始自19世纪浪漫主义时期。因此，本书对“第一部分 17世纪殖民地时期的美国文学”和“第二部分 18世纪革命与理性时期的美国文学”只做一般性的、综合性的描述与评论，对每个时期中几位较有重大影响的作家予以足够详细的评述，对他们在思想文化、文学创作领域所做出的杰出贡献予以充分的肯定。而在“第三部分 19世纪浪漫主义时期的美国文学”、“第四部分 19世纪现实主义时期的美国文学”、“第五部分 20世纪现代主义时期的美国文学”和“第六部分 1945年以来的后现代主义时期的美国文学”中，则采取文学流派系统介绍、综合评述和重要作家个别介绍、专题评述相结合、史学知识传授和作品主题思想艺术手法研讨相结合的方法，详细描述各时期文学流派总体表现的世界观和历史观，讨论代表作家不同的艺术主张，揭示代表作品的高度的思想价值和艺术价值。

《美国文学史（上、下）》须和《新编美国文学选读》（第1、2册）配套使用。“美国文学”教学一般在两个学期完成，每个学期18个教学周，第一和第二部分的史学综述可由学生课外自学、教师在课堂上略讲要点的办法处理；第三、第四、第五和第六部分各重点研讨9位代表作家及其代表作品，每学期完成18位代表作家及其代表作品的研讨，两个学期共重点讨论36位代表作家及其代表作品。教师可根据学期实际长短情况选讲其中的32或34位作家及其作品，其余作家及其作品留给学生课外自学。

本书的内容和体例是按讲义形式设计的，特别适合师生课前共同备课、合作建构教学内容，课上教师抛砖引玉引发学生创新思考、教师自我消解权威让学生充分展示才华的培养学生创新能力的启发式、讨论式课堂教学模式，有很大的实用性。

主　编

2019年4月

PART I

AMERICAN LITERATURE IN THE COLONIAL PERIOD

(1607–1700)

Historical Introduction

The 15th century was a time for great geographic discoveries. In October 1492, Christopher Columbus (1451–1506) discovered the new continent called America. In fact, before the so-called "America" existed, the large area of land was home to many groups of people of different cultures. The first settlers in America were the Asians known as the ancestors of American Indians or Native Americans, who were following animals across Siberia and infused new life to the uninhabited continent several thousand years before Christopher Columbus. These people were the first "natives" on the American continent. The discovery of America by Columbus led to the rush of European immigrants into this fascinating and strange continent. In the early sixteenth century, the colonists, English and European explorers, arrived in the vast new continental area. Therefore the European powers began the exploration of the new continent and competed against each other in occupying the New World. It was not until early in the seventeenth century that the English began their settlement of the North American continent. These groups have helped establish this place we call "America." The period of colonization covered the years from 1607 to 1776, that is, from the first settlement of English colonists to the independence of the United States.

Thanks largely to war with Spain and a great expansion of sea trade in the reign of Elizabeth I (1558–1603), Englishmen attempted to establish permanent colonies in America. The English settlement in America began in 1607, when Captain Christopher Newport anchored his three storm-beaten ships near the mouth of Chesapeake Bay. The English settlers laid out Jamestown as their first permanent settlement in America, and then in rapid succession other English colonies emerged one after another. In order to solve the problem of labor, the settlers turned their attention to slaves. Slavery had existed in North America even before the Europeans arrived. Many Native-American tribes enslaved those captured in battle from other tribes. In the middle of the fifteenth century the slave trade began, thousands of Africans were shipped as slaves to America where they were sold into captivity. In 1619, the first African slaves were brought to Jamestown and sold to the plantation owners. By 1775, there were about half a million slaves in the thirteen colonies in North America.

British mercantilism resulted in the eventual shift from an agricultural and tribal society to a slave-holding plantation economy in the South. Such a social transformation demanded a high price to pay for it. A number of laws of the late seventeenth century were intended to compel the settlers to sell to the mother country all their raw materials and agricultural exports. As to the policy, there was no exception to the northern colonies. The natural conditions in the northern area favored commerce and manufactures, but British exploitation in time became intolerable, and provided one of the deep-rooted reasons for the Revolution.

The English immigration and settlement in America was not only the result of economic motives but also that of religious ones. The early settlers were so-called Pilgrims and Puritans, who managed to escape to the New World to avoid the religious persecution. The Pilgrims were a small group of believers who had migrated from England to Holland in 1608, during a time of persecutions. They were a congregation of "Separatists" or non-conformists who had already endured hardness for the sake of conscience before they had ever left the old home. For ten years, this community of Englishmen had lived peacefully in the Dutch city of Leyden, but they felt themselves aliens in a foreign land, and saw that their children were destined to lose their English birthright. After long deliberation, they determined to seek "as Pilgrims" in the new continent a home where they might still possess their cherished freedom of worship, while living under English laws and following the customs and traditions of their motherland. They finally set sail by *Mayflower* on September 16, 1620. The band of Pilgrims landed at Plymouth in December, 1620. Only about half of the one hundred plus passengers on the *Mayflower* survived that first winter. After the Pilgrim's arrival, their establishment became the first successful British colony in New England to last over a year and one of the first several colonies of British Colonial America, following Jamestown, Virginia. Although the Plymouth settlement faced great hardships and earned few profits, it enjoyed a positive reputation in England and might have sown the seeds for further immigration.

The companies of settlers who followed the Pilgrims within the next few years were Puritans. The Puritans were members of the Church of England who at first wished to reform or "purify" its doctrines, however, their own firm belief and disconformities with the Church finally led to their withdrawal from it and a great Puritan exodus. Before long, however, the Pilgrims were surrounded and absorbed by the Puritans of the "Great Migration" of 1628–1640.

From the very beginning, European colonists had been striving for their own geographical expansion and growth of power and interests, therefore, all sorts of collisions between them were inevitable. During the sixteenth and seventeenth centuries, when Britain launched a series of wars against Spain, Holland and France and became triumphant in control of the continent, the English colonists, who had gradually outnumbered their European counterparts, greatly promoted their American colonies in geography and economic power, and enhanced their impact on the developing continent in terms of politics, commerce, education, art and literature as well.

American Puritanism

The term "Puritan" has been applied to those who criticized or wished to "purify" the rituals, the religious practice of the Church of England. The word is often applied loosely. "Puritan" refers to two distinct groups: "Separating" Puritans, such as the Plymouth colonists, who believed that the Church of England was corrupt and that true Christians must separate them from it; and non-separating Puritans, such as the colonists who settled the Massachusetts Bay Colony, who believed in reform but not separation.

To Puritans, religion had the highest priority and man should live, think, and act in a way which tended to the glory of God. So, they were aiming at reforms in its doctrines and greater strictness in religious disciplines, and contending that religion should be a matter of personal faith rather than of ritual, with simpler forms of worship instead of those established by tradition and law within the Church of England. Eventually, these "reformers" were so suppressed that they decided to escape. Puritans left Europe for America in order to prove that they were God's chosen people enjoying His blessings on this earth as in heaven. They felt that they were exiles under the special grace of God to establish a most desirable relation between church and state in the new continent: a theocracy.

The group of serious and religious people advocates highly religious and moral principles. This is the group we usually think about when we talk about the "first Americans." They soon established their own religious and moral principles known as American Puritanism which became a dominant factor in American life and one of the most enduring influences in American thought and literature.

The very severity of the frontier conditions taught the American Puritans to be tougher, to be more practical, and to be ever ready for any misfortune and tragic failures that might lie in wait for them. Over the years the Puritans built a way of life that was in harmony with their religion, one that stressed hard work, thrift, piety and sobriety. Puritanism encouraged people to struggle in their careers. If one's business was booming, it proved that he had gained God's providence. Scholars have long pointed out the link between Puritanism and capitalism: Both rest on ambition, hard work, and an intense striving for success. Although individual Puritans could not know, in strict theological terms, whether they were "saved" and among the elect who would go to heaven, Puritans tended to feel that earthly success was a sign of election. Wealth and status were sought not only for themselves, but as welcome reassurance of spiritual health and promises of eternal life. In addition, the Puritans interpreted all things and events as symbols with deeper spiritual meanings, and felt that in advancing their own profit and their community's well-being, they were also furthering God's plans. All this went, in due time, into the making of American literature. Literature of the New England Settlements is mainly a literary expression of the pious idealism of the American Puritan bequest. The pious and self-disciplined Puritans worked with courage and hope toward building a new Garden of Eden in America. In recording ordinary events to reveal their spiritual meaning, Puritan authors commonly cited the Bible, chapter and verse. History was a symbolic religious panorama leading to the Puritan triumph over the New World and to God's kingdom on Earth. The Puritan values dominated much of the earliest American writing, including the sermons, books, and journals.

The self-made and often self-educated Puritans were notable exceptions. It was the Puritans who wrote most of the literature, and it was Puritanism that was most influential in the intellectual and economic life of the settlers. The first colleges in the colonies, such as Harvard University (1638), gave evidences of a great stimulus that the Puritanism afforded to the intellectual life of the settlers. In 1639, the first printing press in America was set up at Cambridge. The colonists also had their grammar schools which prepared for college.

Different from the French and Spanish colonies, the British colonies had opportunities to erect a representative self-government in which both electors and representatives had real political responsibility. This respect paid to essential civil rights began to take root during the colonial period, and bring about increasing changes in the social structure, while breaking down many sorts of special privileges. The direction of the social development seems to be, a great extent, the result of the impact of American Puritanism, and the distinctly American character of generations of settlers was a product of their ideal melted with their life experiences on the frontier.

Early New England Literature

It is generally believed that the orally transmitted myths, legends, tales, and lyrics of Indian cultures existed in North America before the Europeans came. However, American literature was not based on native Indian culture. It was a descendant of European literature. The literature of this period is characterized by that most of the writers were born in Britain. American writing began with the work of English explorers, immigrants, adventurers and colonists in the New World chiefly for the benefit of readers in the mother country. Within a few decades a considerable number of learned people, such as Puritan clergymen and governors, produced a considerable body of writing of high literary quality, yet they were not literary people in the professional sense. The first of American literature was not written by an American, but by John Smith, a British captain, who thus became the first American writer. *A True Relation of Such Occurrences and Accidents of Note as Hath Happened in Virginia* (1608) was a long report recording what he saw and heard in the New World, which he sent back to England and was printed in 1608 without his knowledge. So, the early American literature was also called early New England Literature or "Colonial Literature." The early New England literature grew out of humble origins. Diaries, letters, histories, journals, sermons, poetry, biographies, autobiographies and prose, in short, personal literature in its various forms, occupy a major position in the literature of the early colonial period. The writing style of this period is fresh, simple and direct; the rhetoric is plain and honest, with a touch of nobility often traceable to the direct influence of the Bible.

Early colonial American writing reveals the beginning of a struggle for definition and meaning. A national character is molded by a certain inheritance, environment, and historical experience. From Europe, the early settlers brought with them certain customs, habits and traditions. In adapting themselves to the rough American environment, they were forced to change. While exploring the wilderness, the European ways of living were slowly modified by American frontier experience, with its large tract of free land and dangers from Indians and nature. All these experiences in varying degrees characterize the American national characters—individualism, self-reliance, independence and an optimistic faith—and gave birth to the Puritan values: hard-work, thrift, piety and sobriety.

The Puritanism has exerted a great influence on American literature, and its impact could find expression in almost all respects concerning literature. Puritan doctrine and literary practice contributed to no small extent to the development of an indigenous symbolism. In addition to being true believers of their religious doctrines, the early Puritans generally had college education with a sound knowledge of the literary classics, and learned much about the basic qualities of literature from the ancient and contemporary authors in the old continent. Such religious and cultural background of the Puritan writers was responsible for the two essential characteristics of the early American literature: Their religious subject and imitation of English literary traditions. To the pious Puritan the physical, phenomenal world was nothing but a symbol of God. The Puritan believed that they should spend all their free time studying the Bible. They thought that because they should be studying the Bible, other forms of enjoyment were unacceptable. The conviction that all religious progress centered in the individual led colonial writers to make records of his spiritual development in writings. Hence all the analyses may lead to the conclusion that it is reasonable to consider early New England literature primarily in terms of Puritanism and Puritan writing, and that without some understanding of the Puritan contribution it would be difficult to understand colonial American literature, let alone the subsequent development of American literature. In early Puritan writers, English literary traditions were faithfully imitated and transplanted. The American poets of the 17th century adapted the style of established European poets. In addition, in the categories of the literary works, there were "travel," "diary," and "poem," etc., among which the poetry and prose gained most achievements in this period. The most noteworthy writers were the first American writer John Smith, the first American woman poet Anne Bradstreet, John Cotton, Roger Williams and Edward Taylor.

John Smith

Captain John Smith (1580–1631) is recognized as the first American writer. He was also one of the first early 17th century British settlers in North America and one of the leaders of the Jamestown colony, Virginia.

Captain John Smith is born in Lincolnshire, England, to a freeman farmer family. He was a true soldier of fortune, venturesome, resolute, self-reliant, and resourceful. John Smith received his first states of adventure at 17 when he fought in the Netherlands against Spain. Soon came more adventures. He had been a soldier in the French army and had served in that of Holland. He had wandered through Italy and Greece into the countries of Eastern Europe, and had lived for a year in Turkey and Tartary. He had been in Russia, Germany, Spain, and Africa, and was familiar with the islands of the Mediterranean and those of the eastern Atlantic. By the time he returned to England in 1605, he became Captain John Smith, and was still eager for travel. He then looked to North America for adventure. Of the 143 men who had sailed from England by *Mayflower* late in 1606, 105 survived the voyage. John Smith was one of them, and was appointed as a member of the Council at the head of affairs in the Jamestown colony for his experience and practical sagacity. In 1614, Smith traveled to the place he named "New England," what is now Maine and Massachusetts. After spending the winter, he returned to England, hoping to encourage others to settle in New England. He died in London in 1631.

His writings about North America became the source of information about the New World for latter settlers. The first of his books—*A True Relation of Such Occurrences and Accidents of Note as Hath Happened in Virginia* (1608), was also the first American literature, which was a long report recording what he saw and heard in the New World and was printed in 1608 without his knowledge. John Smith's description of America was filled with themes, myths, images, scenes, characters, and events that served as a foundation for the nation's literature. It supplies the earliest chronicle of the perils and hardships of the American Pioneers. However, his writing was more like an advertisement than a warning. The thrilling incidents of that distressing struggle with the wilderness which makes a genuine appeal to the reader now, as it undoubtedly did to the kinsmen of the colonists in England for whom the book was originally prepared. His books were read carefully by all who contemplated sailing for the colonies. They found in them vivid glimpses of an unknown land and of forest warfare with the redskins. It was natural enough that such a daring rover should catch the spirit of enthusiasm with which the exploration and settlement of the New World had inflamed Englishmen of his time and type and urge emigration to the new land.

Another thing he wrote about that became historically important is his description of the fertile and vast new continent in his *A Description of New England* (1616). His narrative reveals the early settlers' vision of the new land as something capable of being built into a new Garden of Eden. Later, after his explorations along the coast of New England, he published several other books, including *The General History of Virginia, New England, and the Summer Isles* (1624). The book has become an American legend which wrote about his capture by the Indians and his rescue by the famous Indian Princess, Pocahontas.

His writing is the chief source of what we know about the Virginia Indians before they were conquered and all but destroyed by the white men. His writings helped set the form of the exploration and travel narratives that inspired men to move westward to America and across the continent. As an explorer and leader, he has been known as a national hero.

John Cotton

John Cotton (1584–1652) was a highly regarded principal among the New England Puritan ministers, which also included John Winthrop, Thomas Hooker, Increase Mather (who became his son-in-law), John Davenport, and Thomas Shepard. He was the grandfather of Cotton Mather, who was named after him.

Born in England, he was educated at Derby School, in buildings which are now the Derby Heritage Center, and attended Cambridge University, where he also taught, and became a long-serving minister in the English town of Boston, Lincolnshire for nearly twenty years and was known far and wide for his aggressive spirituality. In 1633, he discovered that he was no longer safe in his native land, because his Puritanism and criticism of hierarchy drew the hostile attention of Church of England authorities. The principal colony on Massachusetts Bay had longed for him. In the same year, Cotton, his family, and a few local followers sailed for the Massachusetts Bay Colony. In compliment to him, its members adopted the name of Boston; and John Cotton became the foremost minister in New England—"a most universal scholar, a living system of the liberal arts, and a walking library," as his grandson, Cotton Mather, described him.

John Cotton wrote many theological treatises, and engaged in bitter controversies. His writings lack the picturesque imagery of Hooker and Shepard. His style is lifeless now, but he carried prodigious weight among his contemporaries and was the foremost champion in the theological battles of his age. Cotton's written legacy includes a body of correspondence, numerous sermons, a catechism, and in 1646 a shorter catechism for children titled *Milk for Babes*, which is considered as the first children's book by an American and was incorporated into *The New England Primer* around 1701 and remained a component of that work for over 150 years. His most famous sermon is probably "Gods Promise to His Plantation" (1630), preached at the departure of John Winthrop's fleet for New England.

Because of his early views on the primacy of congregational government, he was an important role in Puritan aspirations to become the "city on a hill" which might help reform the English church. He is best known for other things like his ritual defense of Anne Hutchinson early in her trials during the Antinomian crisis, during which she mentioned him with respect, though he turned strongly against her during the further course of the trial. He is also remembered for his role in the banishment of Roger Williams. Cotton grew more conservative in his views with the years but always retained the estimation of his community.

Roger Williams

Roger Williams (1603–1683) was one of the greatest Puritan dissenters in the early days of Puritan theocracy in New England. In the early days of colonization, there was a powerful champion of American ideals of liberty of conscience and toleration of racial and religious differences. Roger Williams constitutes one of its most influential representatives.

Born in Wales, a university man and a clergyman in the Church of England, he had turned nonconformist, and appeared in Plymouth colony in the usual way. Upon his graduation at Pembroke College, Cambridge, Williams set sail for Massachusetts in 1630. After his arrival in 1631, he began to preach for civil and religious liberty and against the Puritan oligarchy of Boston. In 1633, Williams went to Salem to be the minister there two years after his arrival at Plymouth. However, he soon found himself as a minister in conflict with the Anglican Church and the new churches in America, and his teachings were altogether too radical to suit his stern and narrow-minded Puritan brethren. He taught that it was unrighteous to rob the land belonged to the American Indians, and maintained that the State's authority did not extend over the individual conscience or opinion. His radical ideas were subversive of the prevailing power and theocracy. His opposition to the eviction of the Indians from their ancestral properties and call for democratic government his incurred the wrath and hatred of such "orthodox" Puritans. Hence, he was banished from Massachusetts in 1635, yet he fled into the wilderness to avoid deportation to England. He lived for a while with the Indians before immigrating to Rhode Island, where he established the "Rhode Island Way" to encourage religious toleration, and protect Indian rights. Williams revisited England several times, and he knew Milton and had the friendship of Cromwell. It was on one of these visits that he wrote *The Bloody Tenet of Persecution for Cause of Conscience* in refutation of the arguments by John Cotton and published it at London in 1644. The work furiously attacked the "soul-killing" requirement of religious conformity and vigorously upholding the spiritual freedom of the individual and was the beginning of a famous literary battle between himself and that belligerent Puritan defender, John Cotton. In the eyes of the orthodox Puritan, he was such a rebel against the divine church order that "The Bloody Tenet" was ordered to be burned. The final rejoinder came from Roger Williams in *The Bloody Tenet Yet More Bloody* (1654), by Mr. Cotton's Endeavor to wash it white in the Blood of the Lamb.

Among his major works in defense of religious freedom and social justice, *The Blood Tenet of Persecution for Cause of Conscience* (1644), and *The Blood Tenet Yet More Bloody* (1654) attacked upon the theology of Massachusetts Bay; *Queries of*

Highest Consideration (1644) appealed for separation of church and state. Due to his active role on behalf of Rhode Island as a new colony, in 1654 he was elected president of the colony, serving three terms. Roger Williams was one of those who proclaim the notion that sound government can only function with the approval of the people so far in advance of John Locke (1632–1704) call for "civil right" over forty years. Roger Williams will go down in American history as a staunch fighter for freedom and democracy.

Anne Bradstreet

Anne Bradstreet (1612–1672) was one of the first poets to write English verse in the American colonies and has been praised as a significant poet of colonial period.

Anne Bradstreet was born Anne Dudley in North Hampton, England, in 1612. Thanks to her father's position as the steward of the Earl of Lincoln estate, she was privileged enough to receive her education from tutors and her father. She also had unlimited access to the serious writings of Puritanism. In 1628 she married Simon Bradstreet, her father's assistant, who had been trained at Cambridge and afterward by her father. In 1930, the entire family sailed with other Puritans to immigrate to Massachusetts Bay, where Simon Bradstreet proved successful as governor of the colony for ten years, and represented as judge of Massachusetts at the court of Charles II. In the hardships of early colonial life, Anne Bradstreet struggled to rear eight children, function as a hostess, and perform other domestic duties. At the same time, she found comfort in writing poets. According to the date of her manuscripts, Anne Bradstreet began to write from 1632.

In 1647, Bradstreet's brother-in-law, John Woodbridge, sailed to England with some of her manuscripts, and published them in London without her knowledge, with the title, *The Tenth Muse Lately Sprung Up in America* (1650), later known as *The Tenth Muse*. Because a woman poet was a rarity in America in the first few decades of the seventeenth century, the public had a harsh reaction to Bradstreet's role as a female writer. *The Tenth Muse*, which was the first book of New World poems published in England, reflects the concerns of women who came to settle in the colonies.

Bradstreet was not very successful with her first publications, but the publication of her first works gave her the confidence and experience to write in her own style, and her own emotions were more clearly expressed in her writings. She became a Puritan poet who wrote "ponderous verses of interminable, inter-locking poems" on the four elements, the constitutions and ages of man, the seasons of the year, and the chief empires of the ancient world. The use of her emotions in her writings is a technique that has won her a place in the history of American literature. On September 16, 1672, Anne Bradstreet passed away, in Andover, Massachusetts, at the age 60.

Bradstreet used the plain style of writing that is typical of many early Puritan writers. Her poems of religious experience and domestic intimacy were unique and genuine, delicate and charming, embodying her profound understanding of religion and humanity. Her love poems about her husband "To My Dear and Loving Husband," which denoted the human side of her being clearly, was found among her papers after death and published posthumously.

One more thing to note about Anne Bradstreet is her description of the early settlers' life in the new world. For example, "As Weary Pilgrim," one devoted to God as much as any of her other poems, offers some hints of the hardships that they suffered in their first days there. Her talent and skill to capture the colonial experience in poetry set her in place as one of America's most outstanding early writers and as an important woman poet in the first two hundred years of American literature.

Most of other verses have fallen into the obscurity of time, but her gentle "Contemplations" are still read today. The lyric and descriptive poem about nature and the wonders of creation offers the reader an insight into the mentality of the early Puritan Pioneering in a new world.

Edward Taylor

Like all of New England's first writers, the intense, brilliant poet and minister, Edward Taylor (1645–1729) was born in England. He has now taken his place as the most gifted of the Puritan poets and his poetic art finds no parallel in American literature before the nineteenth century, although his works was unknown until 1930s.

Born into the family of a dissenter in Coventry, England, Taylor began to suffer from religious persecution when he grew up. In his twenties, he left England and immigrated to Massachusetts, where he entered Harvard College to prepare himself for the ministry. Upon his graduation from Harvard in 1671, he spent the remaining fifty-eight years of his life as pastor of the church in the frontier village of Westfield, Massachusetts. Taylor was the best-educated man in the area, and he put his knowledge to use, serving as the town minister, physician, and civic leader.

Taylor believed that writing poetry was not acceptable for a Puritan pastor and considered writing his poems just as a mental exercise, so he command his heirs not publish them. His grandson, Ezra Stile, president of Yale, inherited and deposited the bulky manuscript of Edward Taylor in the library of the college, where it remained undiscovered during more than two centuries. Thomas Johnson discovered the manuscript and recognized the importance of this manuscript as a great literary masterpiece. Then, the manuscript book was published in *The New England Quarterly* in the late 1930s. His work was the finest examples of 17th century poetry in North America. He has been recognized by critics as the greatest American poet before the nineteenth century.

Taylor's manuscript book consists of two major sections: "God's Determination" and "Sacramental Meditations." The first section deals with, from the viewpoint and experience of Taylor as pastor, the central Puritan doctrines of election, grace, church fellowship, and reprobation, including some of his important poems, such as "The Preface," "The Glory of and Grace in the Church set out," and "The Joy of Church Fellowship rightly attended." The second section is a spiritual autobiography which concerns itself with the rite of Christianity, with "The Relaxation" and "Meditation Six" as its representative poems.

Taylor wrote a variety of verse: funeral elegies, lyrics, a medieval "debate," and a 500-page *Metrical History of Christianity*. His best works, according to modern critics, are the series of short *Preparatory Meditations*. The best edition of Taylor's poetry is Donald E. Stanford's *The Poems of Edward Taylor* (1960). His finest poems, filled with vivid imagery and he produced lines of startling vitality and subtle language with metaphors of taste, color and sound, fusing lofty concept and homely detail in the memorable fashion of great poetry. He was a meditative poet, an orthodox Puritan, concerned about how his images speak for God, and his poems show a loving Christ and a joy in Puritanism. Edward Taylor's poems show us that even the most traditional, very orthodox purest Puritan could paint a picture in the form of poetry. For Edward Taylor this form of writing was pure worship of the Lord. Edward Taylor saw the beauty and mystery of God's hand in all of humankind and all of nature and wrote about it. His devotional poetry burns with an intense love for Christ, which is central not only to Taylor's work but to Puritanism in the colonial period.

Bibliography

http://en.wikibooks.org/wiki/American_Literature/Colonial_Period_(1620s-1776), 2013-02-04.

http://en.wikipedia.org/wiki/American_literature#Post-independence, 2013-02-04.

http://www.uncp.edu/home/canada/work/markport/lit/amauth/spg2002/colonial.htm, 2013-02-04.

http://usa.usembassy.de/etexts/oal/lit1.htm, 2013-02-04.

宋元康．美国文学导读．昆明：云南大学出版社，2007: 1–8，10–14.

王卓，李权文．美国文学史．武汉：华中师范大学出版社，2010: 1-2，7-13, 23-29, 33-34.
吴瑾瑾．美国文学史．北京：经济科学出版社，2008: 15-21.
曹曼．美国文学教程．武汉：武汉大学出版社，2007: 13-15，22-23.
何木英，杜平．美国文学简史与作品选读．成都：四川大学出版社，2004: 1-7.
常耀信．美国文学简史（第二版修订本）．天津：南开大学出版社，2003: 11-21.
胡荫桐，刘树森．美国文学教程．天津：南开大学出版社，2003: 1-16.
胡荫桐．美国文学新编．北京：外语教学与研究出版社，2001: 1-5.

PART

II

AMERICAN LITERATURE IN THE AGE OF REASON AND REVOLUTION

(1700–1800)

Historical Introduction

The eighteenth century American history witnessed two great revolutions: one was American Revolution which led eventually to the independence of the nation and exerted on the subsequent development of American society an influence greater and more enduring than any historical event in the preceding American history; the other was Enlightenment, an intellectual movement whose rationalistic spirit inspired American men of letters and brought them into a new horizon beyond the limitation of prevailing Puritanism. The two revolutions produced a number of outstanding political and literary figures, such as Benjamin Franklin, Thomas Paine, and Thomas Jefferson, whose literary talent enabled them to be political leaders with more dynamic and even made literature become part of the revolutions.

Enlightenment and American Revolution

Following Columbus' discovery of the New World, European countries rushed to occupy the new continent as their colonies and the geographical expansion began. Along with the quick expansion of European colonies in North America, European colonies soon came into the conflicts and struggles in terms of commerce, trade, transportation, and other aspects. The wars between the European colonists in the New World were inevitable. The victories of the British colonies in a series of wars and the growth of their economic and military strength brought them into a totally new position with respect to Great Britain. Around the middle of the eighteenth century a number of proposals for a union of the American colonies were broached. The causes of the Revolution were both political and economic. In addition to levy heavier tax on imported products, the British authorities held that Parliament was an imperial body which could exercise the same authority over the colonies as over the homeland, and pass laws for the colonies without the approval of the colonists' own governments. Such was the situation of American society in the first half of the eighteenth century that led to the revolt against the British government. Finally, in 1775, skirmishes broke out in Lexington and Concord, Massachusetts. In 1776, Thomas Paine rallied colonists with a pamphlet called *Common Sense*, and Thomas Jefferson drafted *The Declaration of Independence*. These pamphlets let American people come into full understanding of the just relationship between government and the people governed, and change their attitude toward authority. More and more people threw themselves into the war to strive for the independence of their nation. Over the next 5 years, General George Washington led the Americans against the British. In 1781, a surrender of British troops at Yorktown led the British to give up the colonies. England officially recognized American independence in the Treaty of Paris in 1783.

The hard-fought American Revolution against Britain (1775–1783) was the first modern war of liberation against a colonial power. The triumph of American independence seemed to many at the time a divine sign that America and her people were destined for greatness. The victory brought vast social changes: Governors were now chosen by the people and not by the king; broaden the suffrage and make representation were more equitable. At the same time, the American colonies in the eighteenth century shared with the rest of the Western world an intellectual revolution, Enlightenment Movement, whose potential power gradually brought the mind of man into a new horizon.

An intellectual revolution, the Enlightenment originated in the European continent, and then its impact found expression in America through the efforts of such radical and patriotic thinkers like Franklin. It covers about a century and a half in Europe, beginning with the publication of Francis Bacon's *Novum Organum* (1620) and ending with Immanuel Kant's *Critique of Pure Reason* (1781). From the perspective of socio-political phenomena, the period is considered to have begun with the close of the Thirty Years' War (1648) and ended with the French Revolution (1789). In Europe as well as in America the works of such rationalists as Herbert and Collins in England, Voltaire, Diderot, and Rousseau in France were equally influential, inspiring the men of letters to reconsider their relationship with Nature and God. The eighteenth century thinkers came to take Reason, whether viewed in the natural law or in man, as the measure of all existences. They held that Nature, Reason, and Ancients represented essentially the same ideals and principles. That's why this period has been called the Age of Reason.

The Enlightenment advocates rationality rather than tradition, scientific inquiry instead of unquestioning religious dogma, and representative government in place of monarchy. Enlightenment thinkers and writers were devoted to the ideals of justice, liberty, and equality as the natural rights of man. The Enlighteners emphasized the belief in the attainment of social progress by man himself, by education and by the development of science and technology. They showed larger concerns for civil rights, a more comprehensive democracy in government, and general toleration rather than earlier religious mysticisms. It is without doubt that the ideas of American Enlightenment led to America's independence and the principles of the Government America have today. With an unshakable belief in the power of reason, the Enlighteners regarded "enlightenment" or "education" as the principal means for the development of a society. The wide availability of knowledge was made possible through the production of encyclopedias, serving the Enlightenment cause of educating the human case. Moreover, there was a large emphasis during the Enlightenment for new scientific developments. The emphasis on scientific development naturally led to the industrial revolution both in the European continent and in the New World. A progressive intellectual movement, the Enlightenment contributed to free the Americans from the limitations of Puritanism which had been prevailing in American society since the seventeenth century, and stimulate them to strive for the establishment of their independent and democratic nation. The victory of the American Revolution and the appearance of the *Declaration of Independence* (1776) found an echo of political sense in the French Revolution of 1789, and all these could be regarded as the results of the Enlightenment.

When rationalism was applied to theology, the Enlightenment resulted in Deism and Atheism. Deism, the belief in natural religion, is a religious and philosophical belief that a supreme being created the universe, and that this can be determined by using reason and observation of the natural world alone, without a need for either faith or organized religion. Atheism, an absence of belief in the existence of gods, is the position that there are no deities. More broadly defined, it is the rejection of belief in the existence of any deities, with or without an assertion that no deities exist.

Neoclassicism

The direct and potential impact of the Enlightenment also found expression in the field of literature, and the literature of the Enlightenment became the main current of eighteenth century American literature. From this moment, American people began to understand the meaning of being a real "American."

Influenced by the Enlightenment, American writers believed that the artistic should be order, logic, restrained emotion and accuracy. Different from the Puritans, who took the Bible as the exclusive ideal model, the letters of the Enlightenment found the best embodiment of their own ideals of a rational world in the order and beauty of classical art, exactly speaking, in the humanistic and rational works of the Greeks and Romans. At the same time, American literature resembled in many aspects the English literature of the same period, yet degrees and tastes ranged widely. The Neoclassicism that was characterized by clarity, order, and rationality was dominant among the English letters of the eighteenth century. Addison, Steele and Pope were the representatives of this school. The neoclassicists emphasized reason rather than emotion, form rather than content, and imitate or reproduce the structures and themes of Greek or Roman originals. Neoclassicists upheld that artistic ideals should be in order and in balance, reasonable and harmonious. The power of such a literary style also found an outlet in America, which led American writers, including many of the outstanding of the period, to imitate the precision and clarity of the Pope's heroic couplets as well as the elegance and decorum of his expression. Therefore, throughout the colonies "Enlightened" individuals, who are called neoclassicists now, focused on classical writings for inspiration.

The Neoclassicism in England literature contributed to establishing in the stream of American literature a recognition of some so-called "classic graces," such as order, good form, clearness, conciseness, and restraint, but on the other hand it frequently led to the stereotypes of literary creation, like the use of a conventional language and imagery, a colorless regularity, and an overemphasized appeals to the intellect. An emphasis on the proportion, harmony, and beauty of design evident in the world of reason over the fantastical, stimulating, and often disordered world of the imagination was another indisputable evidence of aesthetic taste of the age. The rationalistic and neoclassical spirit in American literature is set about to wane in the end of the century.

Benjamin Franklin

As the versatile, practical embodiment of rational man of the 18th century America, Benjamin Franklin (1706–1790) embodied the Enlightenment ideal of humane rationality. A leading American statesman, scientist, philanthropist, writer, revolutionary, and thinker, he was the most famous and respected private figure of his time. He helped write *The Declaration of Independence* (1776), which gave the reasons for the final separation of America and England, and *The Constitution of the United States* (1787–1789), which would help make the laws of America. He could hardly find parallel among his contemporaries, in his role in the 18th century American society as well as in his potential and enduring influence upon generations of Americans in terms of morality, ethics, politics, sociability, and other respects of living. Today, Franklin is honored as one of America's Founding Fathers and as one of her greatest citizens.

Born in 1706 in Boston, Massachusetts, Benjamin Franklin was the tenth son in a poor family of 15 children. His father was a candle maker and owner of a tallow shop who came to Boston in 1683 from Northampton shire, England and his mother was the daughter of a teacher to the Indians. The poverty failed to afford young Franklin an opportunity for regular school education. At the age of 12, Franklin was forced to leave school and work for his father. Then he detested his father's occupation and became an apprentice to his brother, a printer. This pleased Benjamin very much, for he loved books and reading. Franklin taught himself languages, read widely, and practiced writing for the public. At sixteen, he took over the editorship of his brother's newspaper *New England Courant* under the pseudonym, Silence Dogood, commenting on various subjects in Boston ranging from an appeal to the freedom of the press, to the necessity of higher education. At 17 he ran away to Philadelphia to make his own fortune, where he soon rose to prominence as master printer, newspaper publisher, scientist, and public man, as narrated realistically in his *Autobiography* (1771, 1783–1790). His entrance into the city marked the beginning of a long success story of an archetypal kind. In 1724, he attracted the notice of the Governor of Pennsylvania, and it was through his influence that the young boy set out for England, where he stayed as the representative of the New England colonies. In 1732, under the name "Richard Saunders," he began publishing *Poor Richard's Almanac* (1732–1758), a calendar filled with advertisements, weather forecasts, recipes, jokes, and a swarm of proverbs that entered the American mind and stuck. During this time he made a reputation for himself, and became wealthy enough to retire from business in 1748. In Philadelphia, Franklin established American's first circulating library. Later he founded the Pennsylvania Hospital, an academy which led to the University of Pennsylvania, and the American Philosophical Society. From his youth Franklin showed a considerable interest in science, and one of the chief reasons for his anxiety to retire from business was his eagerness to devote himself to scientific studies. He is famous for his research on electricity and experiment with his kite line.

Franklin's public career began in the early 1750s. He became a member of the Pennsylvania Assembly, the Deputy Postmaster-General for the colonies, and for some eighteen years served as representative of the colonies in London, making full use of his talents in defense of the rights and interests of the colonies. During the War of Independence, he was made a delegate to the Continental Congress and a member of the committee to draft *The Declaration of Independence*. During the Revolution, he was instrumental in bringing France into an alliance with America against England, which gave timely support to American people in fighting for their independence. He was the only American to sign the four documents that created the United States: *The Declaration of Independence*, the treaty of alliance with France, the treaty of peace with England, and the constitution. His lasting years were spent in Philadelphia, where he served as a member of the Constitutional Convention until his death came in 1790.

Benjamin Franklin remains today the most widely read and influential of all American writers. His reputation as the greatest literary artists of 18th century Americans rested chiefly upon his two masterpieces: *Autobiography* and *Poor Richard's Almanac* (sometimes *Almanak*).

The *Autobiography* is basically a record of self-improvement with one being industrious, frugal, and prudent. It is also a longing account of his family background writing to advise his son William, then colonial governor of New Jersey. In 1771, at 65 years of age, he began to write the *Autobiography* but was obliged to break off and hindered by a multitude of events, when he just finished the account of his first 24 years. About 20 years later, Franklin continued it on the suggestion of his friends, but still leaving the most spectacular decades of his career and international influence unwritten. Some months before his death, he labored to write a brief, fragmentary fourth part, carrying the story up to his retirement. It was not until 1868 that the first complete edition of the four chapters of the autobiography was printed. His purpose was to make the experiences of his own career, the conduct and habit of life which had led to success in his own case, a source of help and inspiration to others. He therefore told the story of his struggles, his errors, and his experiments with himself, his accomplishment, with wonderful frankness and extreme simplicity. No other autobiography has been more widely read than Benjamin Franklin's. His book is more than just a picture of his life; it is an attempt to present his concept of the ideal citizen of the new nation of America. Franklin lists 13 virtues in the book: temperance, silence, order, resolution, frugality, industry, sincerity, justice, moderation, cleanliness, tranquility, chastity, humility. It is an important American literary work, for it deals with the essential values of life. He helped establish a tradition in American writing of the simple, utilitarian style, and with his *Autobiography* he set the form for autography as a genre. Some critics think it would be hard to call this autography a complete work of literature. However it is significant for using his life story as a shining example and as a classic of its kind in American literature.

Another well-known book is *Poor Richard Almanac*. It was a yearly almanac appeared continually from 1732 to 1758. In *Poor Richard's Almanac* Franklin created a character, Poor Richard, in whose name the work appeared, and whose real existence was debated humorously and seriously. Extremely popular both in the New England colonies and in England for its exquisite expression, *Poor Richard's Almanac* took Franklin 25 years to contrive homely aphorism out of whatever source he could tap and improve most of them with his gift for pungent and imagery. Franklin is willing to give advice in common-sense witticism and maxims. He did not always write the maxims himself. His sources are often easily identifiable. But though he borrowed from such writers as Rabelais, Defoe, Swift, and Pope, he made good use of his own wit and wisdom to simplify and enrich their axioms. It was Franklin's idea to teach lessons of thrift to his countrymen. In this annual book of useful encouragement, advice, and factual information, amusing characters such as old Father Abraham and Poor Richard exhort the reader in pithy, memorable sayings. Many of the sentences have become popular quotations. Even to this day it continues to teach its useful lesson of industry, frugality, and honesty over the world.

By cleverness and hard work he changed himself from the poorly educated son of a candle-maker into a world-renowned scientist, diplomat, philosopher, and writer. His humble origins, dedication to self-improvement, and genius for business set a model of the self-made man, a culture-hero whose life exemplifies the American dream of the poor boy who makes good.

Thomas Paine

Thomas Paine (1737–1809) was the greatest propagandist of the Revolution and the most important American prose writers of 18th century. He urged Franklin accept the idea political independence from Great Britain.

Thomas Paine, son of a nominal Quaker, was born in Thetford, England on January 29, 1737. His formal education lasted only until the age of thirteen, at which point he began working for his father, a poor corset maker. By 1768 he became a tax officer in England, educating himself further in his free time. But he didn't exactly excel at the role. In 1772, Paine was fired for publishing an article *The Case of the Officers of Exercise* (1772) arguing that raising tax-collectors' salaries would reduce corruption. In 1774, by happenstance, he met Benjamin Franklin in London and determined to try life in the colonies. Paine immigrated to America in late 1774, only a few months before the revolutionary war began on April 19, 1775. His career turned to journalism while in Philadelphia, where he edited the *Pennsylvania Magazine* and wrote a variety of articles. Paine so fully accepted the American vision of a continental destiny that immediately involved in American political life. Within the next 2 years he persuaded great numbers of his fellow countrymen, including George Washington, that the time had come for separation from Britain. After the first battle of the war, Paine began to argue that the

American colonists should seek complete independence, rather than merely fighting to free themselves from unfair British taxation.

On January 10, 1776, Paine published *Common Sense*, which was widely read and immediately established his reputation as a revolutionary propagandist. In *Common Sense*, Thomas Paine argues for American independence. His argument begins with more general, theoretical reflections about government and religion, and then progresses onto the specifics of the colonial situation. At the same time, Washington was in command of the American army, which had bottled up the British in Boston. *Common Sense* sold a hundred thousand copies within three months, and reprinted abroad; its power and influence electrified the Americans to see the necessity to have an independent nation of their own. Paine's ideas played a central role in rallying public opinion and were an important precursor to the *Declaration of Independence*, which was written 6 months later. The pamphlet thrust Paine into the national spotlight, earning him a prestigious government appointment later on during the war.

Paine's later writings are also important: *The American Crisis* (1776–1783), a series of essays which appeared irregularly throughout the war; *The Rights of Man* (1791–1792), an answer to Burke's *Reflection on the Revolution in France*; and *The Age of Reason* (1794–1795), expressed his view of religion. The last of these aroused great bitterness among pious Americans and severely damaged Paine's reputation.

The American Crisis (1776–1783) is a collection of articles written by Paine during the American Revolutionary War. The essays collected here constitute Paine's ongoing support for an independent and self-governing America through the many severe crises of the Revolutionary War. General Washington found the first essay so inspiring, and ordered it to be read to the troops at Valley Forge.

Burke's resistance to the French Revolution inspired Pained to write his most influential work, *The Rights of Man* (Part I in 1791, Part II in 1792). Paine urged political rights for all men because of their natural equality in the sight of God and even argued for a whole program of social legislation to deal with the shocking condition of the poor. His popularity sounded the alarm and he was forced to leave Britain in September 1792. He was condemned in his absence and declared an outlaw in England for his anti-monarchist views.

By 1793, he was imprisoned in France for not endorsing the execution of Louis XVI. During his imprisonment, he began to write his most famous work at the time, the anti-church text, *The Age of Reason: Being an Investigation of True and Fabulous Theology* (1794–1795). In the deistic pamphlet, Paine acknowledged his debt to Newton and criticizes institutionalized religion and challenges the legitimacy of the Bible. Paine rejected Christianity, denied that the Bible was the revealed word of God, condemned that many of the Old Testament stories as immoral. The bitterness of his attack on the

Christian churches and his attempt to preach deism to the masses made him more enemies than before. His radical views on religion would destroy his success, and by the end of his life, only a handful of people had attended his funeral.

Although Paine's later writings lost him the regard he had gained during the Revolutionary War, no one can dispute his skill as a master of persuasion. He presented his arguments with brilliance, clarity, and force. He understood the power of language to move men to action, and he used this power with never failing skill.

Thomas Jefferson

Thomas Jefferson (1743–1826), a great liberal leader in politics and the third president of the United States, had been taken as one of the most versatile and enlightened men of his generation. It is said that he wished to be remembered for three achievements in his public life: author of "The Declaration of Independence" and "The Statute of Virginia for Religious Freedom," third president of the United States, and founder of the University of Virginia, although he had served as governor of Virginia, U.S. minister to France, secretary of state under George Washington, vice-president in the administration of John Adams.

Thomas Jefferson was born at Shadwell (now Albemarle County, Virginia) on April 13, 1743. His father Peter Jefferson was a successful planter and surveyor and his mother Jane Randolph was a member of one of Virginia's most distinguished families. He had a succession of tutors throughout his childhood. Having attended the College of William and Mary, Jefferson practiced law and drawn to the legal profession. With an eye on politics, Jefferson soon threw himself into public life, which provides a forum for him to display his genius as political leader. He served in local government as a magistrate, and county lieutenant. In time, Jefferson established himself as a lawyer in Williamsburg, which led to his election to the House of Burgesses in 1769. On New Year Day, 1772, Jefferson was married to Martha Wayles Skelton, a young widow and the daughter of a prominent Virginia landowner. Several successes in the House of Burgesses led to Jefferson's nomination to the Second Continental Congress at Philadelphia, where he was the second youngest delegate in attendance. By virtue of timing as much as skill, Jefferson was selected to draft *The Declaration of Independence* in July 1776, which has been regarded ever since as a charter of American and universal liberties. It proclaims that all men are equal in rights, regardless of birth, wealth, or status, and that the government is the servant, not the master, of the people. In it Jefferson said little or nothing that had not been said before, but his ringing sentences, at once a statement of American principles and a review of the quarrel with Britain, presented the American view to the world with classic dignity. In this document Jefferson also showed himself a skillful propagandist, laying most of the blame for the conflict upon King George III rather than upon Parliament or the English people.

In 1776, he returned to Virginia and served in the legislature. He retired to Monticello in 1781 to care for his ailing wife, who died the following year. In 1784, Jefferson re-entered the world of politics in France, first as trade commissioner and then as Benjamin Franklin's successor as minister. In 1790, he accepted the post of secretary of state under his friend George Washington. In 1796, as the presidential candidate of the Democratic Republicans, he became vice-president after losing to John Adams by three electoral votes. Four years later, he defeated Adams and became president. Thomas Jefferson died at the age of eighty-three on July 4, 1826, exactly the fiftieth anniversary of the signing of "The Declaration of Independence."

Although Jefferson as a writer is chiefly known for *The Declaration of Independence*, he also wrote on practically every subject, from agriculture to architecture. He was so productive that his writings may run to fifty volumes, although he only published 8 titles in his lifetime. *The Papers of Thomas Jefferson* embraces everything Jefferson ever wrote and includes eighteen thousand letters written by him. Jefferson's reputation was established in 1774, when he wrote a political pamphlet, *A Summary View of the Rights of British America*. Arguing on the basis of natural rights theory, Jefferson claimed that colonial allegiance to the king was voluntary. Based upon the same natural rights theory contained in *A Summary View*, to which it beard a strong resemblance. *The Declaration of Independence* made Jefferson internationally famous. The first sentence of the Declaration asserts as a matter of Natural law the ability of a people to assume political independence, and acknowledges that the grounds for such independence must be reasonable, and therefore explicable, and ought to be explained. *Notes on the State of Virginia* (1784), his only work that can be called a book, consisted of 23 sections, dealing with such topics as natural resources, geography, landscape, inhabitants, slavery, government, law, education, religion, and social customs. It was a veritable storehouse of humane ideas and liberal democracy, its inspiring and stimulating power touched both the American and the European.

Thomas Jefferson was a man of many talents: an architect, an inventor, a scientist, and a collector of books and artifacts of American history. His final legacy involved forming the nucleus of the Library of Congress and founding of the University of Virginia.

Philip Freneau

Phillip Freneau (1752–1832) has been called the "Father of American Poetry," whose strongest claim for remembrance lies in his unique transitional role between the neoclassicism and the romanticism. Besides his success in poetry, Freneau was also active in public life, his ideal of establishing an independent and democratic America stimulated him to write a great number of political, satirical verses.

Phillip Freneau was born in New York of Huguenot ancestry in 1752, whose ancestors came to America as Protestant refugees from 17th century France. In 1768, he entered Princeton, where he established close friendships with two of his classmates: James Madison, a future president of the United States; Hugh Henry Brackenridge, a future novelist. Freneau created independently his first important poem "The Power of Fancy" at school. In collaboration with Brackenridge, Freneau wrote the poem "The Rising Glory of America" in 1770, which was read at the commencement ceremonies in 1771 and printed the following year. After his graduation, he earned his living as a teacher. But his interest in literature and public affairs soon made him give up the profession and continue his poetic creation. At the outbreak of the Revolution, he was in New York, where he wrote a number of biting satirical poems against the British, which brought him his first popular success. In 1776, he traveled to the West Indian, where he wrote "The House of Night," a poem lush with images of tropical nature and he saw the horrors of slavery that later attacked in "To Sir Toby." In 1780, he was captured by the British and exchanged as a prisoner of war after 6 weeks of brutal treatment and starvation. His experience during the voyage inspired the poem *The British Prison Ship* (1781), filled to the brim with the horror and rancor of his suffering. After the war, Freneau returned to the sea for his livelihood, serving between 1784 and 1790 as master of a merchant ship. By 1790, with 2 collections of poetry in print and a reputation as a fiery propagandist and skillful sea captain, Freneau decided to get married and worked as an assistant editor in New York. With the support of President Jefferson, Freneau also edited *The Daily Advertiser* and established the *National Gazette* in 1791 in defense of the policy of the government. However, his social and religious liberalism was so radical as to cause violent criticism from his opponents. Freneau died of exposure in 1832, when losing his way in a blizzard.

In spite of the uncertainty and poverty of his life, Freneau never stopped writing. His career as a writer lasted more than half a century. In 1795 he published a volume of *Poems Written Between the Years 1768 and 1794*, then in 1799 he issued a series of essays entitled *Letters on Various Interesting and Important Subjects*. His other major works included *Poems* (1786), the first collection of his poems, and *Miscellaneous Works* (1788). His significance lies in his transitional role between neoclassicism and romanticism. His early poem, "The House of Night" is one of the first distinctly romantic poems in American literature. It is filled with demonic and luxurious images that anticipate the gothic horrors and obsession with death evident in the poetry of Poe and his disciples. Under the influence of prevailing deism, some of his poems reveal his heart-felt love for the order and beauty of nature, with an effect that makes the beauty and perfection of nature stand in striking contrast with the ugliness and imperfection of human society. These kinds of poems include "The Wild Honey Suckle" and "To a Honey Bee." "The Wild Honey Suckle" written in 1786 is one of the most quoted works of Freneau. It is a beautiful lyric which established him as an important American precursor of the Romantics, anticipated the 19th century's romantic use of simple nature imagery. "To a Honeybee" addressed to a wandering rover from the hive resting luxuriously on the rim of the poet's glass, is written with the same charming simplicity of style and with a dainty touch of humor befitting the theme. The best of his politically motivated poems include "To Sir Toby," an early voice in protest against slavery; "On Mr. Paine's Right of Man," a popular poem inspired by Thomas Paine's *The Rights of Man*; and "To the Memory of the Brave Americans," an extremely famous poem celebrating General Nathaniel Greene, which Walter Scott considered to be the best of its kind. Literary historians and critics generally hold that American national poetry began with Freneau's verse, thus he has been entitled the "Father of American Poetry."

Bibliography

http://en.wikipedia.org/wiki/The_Age_of_Reason, 2013-02-04.

http://www.improve.com/Literature-During-the-Age-of-Reason/1922, 2013-02-04.

http://en.wikibooks.org/wiki/American_Literature/Enlightenment_Period_(1760s-1820s), 2013-02-04.

http://en.wikipedia.org/wiki/American_Enlightenment, 2013-02-04.

http://www.wwnorton.com/college/english/naal7/contents/a/overview1.asp, 2013-02-04.

宋元康 . 美国文学导读 . 昆明：云南大学出版社，2007: 18-39.

王卓，李权文 . 美国文学史 . 武汉：华中师范大学出版社，2010: 35-37, 41-54.

吴瑾瑾 . 美国文学史 . 北京：经济科学出版社，2008: 21-24.

曹曼 . 美国文学教程 . 武汉：武汉大学出版社，2007: 25-29, 33-34, 38-39.

何木英，杜平 . 美国文学简史与作品选读 . 成都：四川大学出版社，2004: 9-12.

常耀信 . 美国文学简史（第二版）. 天津：南开大学出版社，2003: 22-37.

胡荫桐，刘树森 . 美国文学教程 . 天津：南开大学出版社， 2003: 18-36, 41-47, 59-62.

胡荫桐 . 美国文学新编 . 北京：外语教学与研究出版社，2001: 5-11, 25-26.

PART III

AMERICAN LITERATURE IN THE ROMANTIC PERIOD

(1800–1865)

Historical Introduction

Romantic Period has always been regarded as one of the most important periods in the history of America. It is generally agreed that American Romantic Movement emerged at the beginning of the 19th century under the influence of its European counterpart. Literary Romanticism flourished in America during the period between the War of 1812 and the Civil War. It started with the publication of Washington Irving's *The Sketch Book* (1819–1820) and ended with Whitman's *Leaves of Grass* (1855–1891). Accurately, it refers to the fifty-year period from 1815 to 1865, which witnessed miraculous achievements in American literature, and this period was also called "the American Renaissance." However, at the beginning of the movement, most critics pointed out that the American Romanticism was just imitating, and some formalists pointed out that the works of the early romanticists were not indigenously American enough. After then, the writers, however, clearly reversed the trend to prove that American Romanticism was shaped uniquely because of its particularly historical, cultural, political and economic elements.

Historically, the War of 1812 with British Empire saved the young nation from the danger of being colonized by Britain once again and produced a sense of euphoria over a "second war of independence" against Britain. The United States also emerged from the war with a heightened sense of national feeling and solidarity. In the following years of 1812, the country lived more self-sufficiently and the contact with Europe became less and less due to the inconvenience of transportation and underdevelopment of communication tools. Meanwhile, the United States also witnessed a fast growth of population because of the large amounts of immigrants pouring into America. In 1800, the United States was a country with only 5,308,483 inhabitants, mainly living around the seacoast, but within only a few decades it grew to an immense area with a population of over 76,000,000. American people started gradually migrating toward the west, looking for a better life, which led to the Westward Movement, one of the key elements that influenced the formation of the American Romanticism. The incredible westward expansion had accelerated the construction of American national identity. The conquest of new territories certainly opened new horizons but it did not come without a price: the new settlers had to contend the land with the Native Americans, immigrants from Asia faced widespread discrimination, the heavy hunting of buffalo brought the animal to the verge of extinction, etc., to name a few of the problems that occurred in those years. However, taking "Manifest Destiny" as their slogan and "civilizing the Indian people" as their task, these European descendants believed that westward expansion was one way to stir up their self-righteous feeling and the key to sustain the health of the nation even though there were the negative elements. To Americans, the young nation was destined to expand across the North American continent even if this meant taking Indians' land, destroying their culture and slaughtering Indians. The concept, born out of "a sense of mission to redeem the Old World," was enabled by "the potentialities of a new earth for building a new heaven," and manifest destiny provided the dogma and tone for the largest acquisition of U.S. territory. Just as President Jefferson pointed out that a republic depended on an independent, virtuous citizenry for its survival, and that independence and virtue went hand in hand with land ownership, especially the ownership of small farms. In order to provide enough land to sustain this ideal population of yeomen, the United States would have to continue to expand. During the westward expansion, the country was also confronted with the risk of internal division: the conflicts between the industrial North and the rural-agricultural South, whose economic pattern was largely based on slave labor, which eventually escalated to the secession of eleven Southern States from the young nation, in spite of the treaties of 1820 and 1850. This event led to the American Civil War of 1861–1865 between the United States and several Southern slave states. The war had its origin in the fractious issue of slavery. After four years of bloody combat (mostly in the South), the Southern part was defeated, slavery was abolished, and the difficult Reconstruction process of restoring unity and guaranteeing rights to the freed slaves began. Hence the evils of capitalistic industrialism—unemployment, starvation wages, and the herding of working people in unspeakable slums—developed more slowly in America than in England. During the romantic period, America was the land of opportunity, the welfare of the industrious citizen was assured, and the temper of the American people was accordingly buoyant and hopeful. In the midst of this environment, American Romanticism could hardly fail to be more optimistic than European, more self-satisfied, less radical and challenging. At that time, the American dream had glowed with greatest intensity and American writers had made a great literary period by capturing on their pages the enthusiasm and the optimism of that dream. Moreover, the attention that was turned to internal exploration and expansion encouraged the impulse towards self-definition.

Economically, the whole nation was experiencing the industrial transformation, which affected the rural and urban life. The impact of industrialization and urbanization ushered the youthful country into the self-sufficient mode. The Industrial Revolution occurred in Great Britain stirred up a series of significant changes in American society. The use of steam power in industry and agriculture, the erection of factories and textile mills, the demand of a large employment, and the technical inventions and innovations, all helped restructure the economic life in America. However, the Industrial Revolution, while helping the nation prosper in many ways, also aroused widespread corruption and contradiction between northern and southern states in America. The sudden influx of immigrant gave a big push to the already booming industry. Before the Civil War, northern states have experienced the prosperity in manufacturing and the big cities of the north employed many people, satisfying the demand for job pressure. In contrast, the southern states had fewer big cities and agriculture was the major source of economic pattern. Cotton was the premier crop and staple of the southern economy. To maximize the potential of this agricultural economy to the greatest extent efficiently and to promote their financial prosperity, slave labor was necessary. This ultimately led to a division between northern and southern economic patterns, and later culminated into the Civil War. After the war, the improvement in manufacturing accelerated economic development and altered the nature of American employment. A lot of sizable businesses and factories emerged in the new-born country, with the result of the advent of mechanized factories which allowed greater production of goods. This coupled with the advancements in transportation technology—namely the railroad and steamboat—helped American goods to be sold nationally and even internationally.

Religiously, far more than in Europe, public opinion in America was under the control of aggressively Protestant religious sects. They were the Congregationalists, the direct descendants of the Puritans, and the evangelical denominations—Presbyterian, Methodist, and Baptist—whose power had been founded during the 18th century, which are more widely dispersed. But overall, American moral ideals were largely Puritan that had a profound effect upon American culture. Apart from the culture, the puritanical strands of religious thought and moral judgment continued to influence, in varying degrees, the social and political thinking in America. As one historian stated, "Without some understanding of Puritanism, it may safely be said, there is no understanding of America." Though by no means in agreement on theological matters, the Romanticists insisted as stoutly as the Puritans upon a rigorous personal morality. Together with the Congregationalists, they frowned on any amusement that smacked the sins of the flesh. Sexual laxity was one of the acts they especially abhorred. They upheld the sanctity of marriage and the permanent solidarity of the home. The Puritans also believed in the innate depravity of man. They believed that some people were "predestined" to experience an afterlife with God. Only the "elect" or "chosen" were in a good relationship with God. Puritanism was the very thing that provided a firm foundation for American democracy, and they were remarkably successful in forming the moral opinions of the nation. Puritanism also exerted great impact on the writers' world view and value system. The force of puritan opinions and the control they exercised over American literature could be judged from the relative importance of the themes of writers, such as Washington Irving, Edgar Allan Poe, Nathaniel Hawthorne, and Herman Melville, to name just a few. In positive ways, too, as well as in merely negative, American romanticism adapted itself to American moralism. Polite literature had long been under suspicion from the devout, as being frivolous if not pernicious. Nevertheless, nineteenth-century literature in America does carry an unusually heavy load of didacticism.

Culturally, even though with the founding of an independent government, the young nation, more evidently, also witnessed its writings were influenced by their cultural immaturity as a nation. At that time, American people were seeking the way to make their culture independent and be more mature to identify themselves. American culture, during the romantic period, was a vigorous, fast-growing, adolescent civilization, though immature quality still existed. As a result, the nation felt an urge to have its own literary expression, to make known its new experience: the early Puritan settlement and the confrontation with the Indian, the frontiersmen's life and the Wild West. In literature, they preferred a stilted, formal, and somewhat florid style. They revealed the "sensibility" in the 18th century, extolled the cultured young female and expressed the tender emotions of the romanticists. With a strong sense of optimism and the mood of "feeling good" of the whole nation, a spectacular outburst of romantic feeling was brought about in the first half of 19th century. The so-called "exceptional" character of American culture and politics in contrast to other "developed" nations has been attributed to the absence of feudalism on American soil and to an attendant absence of class struggle and consciousness. This character of the American culture at that time also could be caused by the cultural diversity of the American immigrant population and challenges to the solidification of class consciousness posed by the extreme cultural diversity of the American working class. Furthermore, the flourish of the publishing industry, the appearance of many magazines and newspapers and the financial support to the writers also promoted the development of Romanticism in America. The publication of *Webster's Dictionary* marked the beginning of the American

English. Increasing wealth and increasingly widespread popular education furnished a steadily enlarging reading public and made publication a large commercial venture, a development which increased the rewards of authorship, but which tended at the same time to enslave the professional author to contemporary standards of taste. Financial support for the profession of letters came perhaps more from periodicals than from separately published books. Newspapers were numerous and widely read, and though often up to the ears in political controversies, they found space for an occasional poem. Magazines were especially numerous between the Revolution and the War of 1812; but they were widely scattered and financially uncertain. After 1812, magazines which wielded more influence and showed more stamina began to appear. *The North American Review*, founded at Boston in 1815 under the editorship of William Tudor, served as a dignified medium for conservative New England opinion. Authors received substantial returns not only from the better-established magazines, but from a kind of periodical now almost extinct—the annual. Originating in Germany, the publication of annual miscellanies of literature had spread to England and thence to America. In the United States, annuals became so popular that more than sixty a year were produced between 1846 and 1852.

Politically, democracy and political equality became the ideals of the new nation. Radical changes came about in the political life of the country. Parties began to squabble and scramble for power, and new system was in the making.

Literary Characteristics

When discussing the literary characteristics of American Romanticism, the outstanding differences and relations between European Romanticism and American Romanticism couldn't be avoided to mention first: The New World environment has shaped the attitude of America's writers, but the influence from its European counterparts cannot be ignored. The European Romantic movement reached America in the early 19th century and exerted great impact on the growth of American Romanticism. The European literary masters, especially the English counterparts exerted a stimulating impact on the writers of the new world and the American Romanticists shared many characteristics with British writers.

Europe in the 18th century was an old and familiar land with rooted traditions and cultures, whereas America was a new land without indigenous traditions and cultures other than those of the Indians, which were at first totally rejected and have only recently been faintly recognized and absorbed into our cultural stream. However, the new-born country could not totally get rid of the influence of the European culture.

Because most of citizens at that time were the descendants of the European, the cultures of Europe were still the dominant and shaping inheritance. The life that they knew and the land that they wished to describe and interpret were alien to the modes of thought and the forms of writing to which they was habituated. Accordingly, American romantic literature was affected by its English counterparts to a great extent at early stage. It was greatly inspired by Wordsworth's poetic encounter with nature and himself in *The Prelude*, Coleridge's literary theories about the reconciliation of opposites, the romantic posturing and irony of Byron, the luxurious imagery of Keats, and the transcendental lyricism of Shelley, and even the Gothicism of Mary Shelley and the Bronte sisters. It should be noted that during the 1820s, American took pride in the literature that they regarded not as distinct but rather in close relation with the English literary traditions. Washington Irving's *The Sketch Book* (1819–1820) was largely based on the essays of Addison and Steele, Bryant's poetry was enlightened by Wordsworth, and Copper's novels were modeled after the works of Walter Scott.

At that time, books, literary quarterlies and magazines from England and Europe were readily available as they were frequently published in the New World, or their distribution was facilitated by the relatively inexpensive shipping fees for printed materials coming from Europe. American literature was usually not taught in American universities, and it was referred to as a sub-current of English literature. Even though American writers' works haven't been as popular as those European counterparts' at the beginning of American Romantic period, they shared some common features with the English Romanticists. Some critics judged that American Romanticism is derivative. Like the Europeans, the American Romantics demonstrated a high level of moral enthusiasm, commitment to individualism and the unfolding of the self, an emphasis on intuitive perception, and the assumption that the natural world was inherently good, while human society was filled with corruption. The American writers believed that personal intuitions have moral authority precisely because individuals contain the divine within themselves. Emerson argued that people should trust themselves, reject external rules, express their inner natures, and become self-reliant. Henry Thoreau, another member of the Transcendental Club, proclaimed the individual conscience, not the law, as the supreme moral arbiter: political obligation depends on the moral judgment of the individual, and the best government is one which does not govern. Similarly, British romantics rejected the formal rules and public codes that had dominated the outlook of the Augustans in favor of a belief in the individual questioning and testing of values and experiences, and their rejection of Augustan limits sometimes spilled over into an opposition to all restrictive codes, as evidenced by the appeal of Godwin's anarchism to Wordsworth and Shelley. In general, the romantics' debt to Rousseau appears in their almost unanimous call for a natural, wholesome existence based on our true instincts.

Yet the American romantics drew heavily on frontier individualism in a way the British did not. British romantics typically looked to the example of the Middle Ages, although they rarely agreed on the details of an ideal community, with, for instance, Coleridge calling for a clerisy and national church to balance the forces of progress with those of stability, and Ruskin trying to revive a moral economy based on craftsmanship and guilds. In contrast, the American romantics succumbed to an idealized picture of American democracy. This gave rise to two important theoretical tendencies. First, the American romantics saw their ideal as something which was being realized through the action of the divine purpose in history. Here Emerson, Thoreau and Whitman drew inspiration from Jeffersonian and Jacksonian democratic theory, which in turn restated the eighteenth-century belief in the perfectibility of mankind, a belief which fitted well with their own Immanentism. Just as the democrats described the American polity as part of God's design, so the romantics could take the American ideal to be the summit of the immanent working-out of the divine will. Just as the Jacksonian, George Bancroft, wrote his famous history of America to show how America expressed the will of God, so William Channing spoke of the dawn of a new age in which people would surmount their political difficulties to realize their inner spirit. Second, the American romantics inherited the ideal of a democratic republic composed of self-sufficient farmers. They believed in the virtue of the rough-and-ready life spent working the land. It was true that some British romantics called for the simplification of life and the rejection of the unnatural wants created by industrial society, as when Ruskin used the example of Gothic architecture to illustrate how mechanism had replaced skill in the work-place. But whilst Ruskin wanted a return to the skilled craftsmanship which he thought produced artistic goods, Thoreau wanted people to minimize their possessions; and whilst Ruskin wanted workers to be able to exercise their creative impulses free from the regime of the machine, Thoreau wanted people to become effectively self-sufficient. Thus, whereas Ruskin established new guilds and revitalized the handmade-linen industry in Langdale, Thoreau lived alone in a hut at Walden Pond where he tried to "simplify, simplify" to obtain spiritual wealth by living close to nature, reducing his material wants, and satisfying any residual needs by his own manual labor.

Even though the literature in American romantic period can't totally get rid of the influence from its European counterparts and was criticized to be an imitator, it also exhibited some unique characteristics which only belonged to this special nation and to this special period. In literature, it still was the first great creative period in American history, which experienced a full flowering of the romantic impulse on American soil. As the romantic writers, Irving, Cooper, Poe, Freneau, and Bryant revolted against the literary forms and ideas of the period of classicism. The American Romanticists emphasize the free expression of emotions and psychic states of the characters, and the emotional and imaginative qualities of literature, which includes a liking for the picturesque, the exotic, the sensuous, the sensational and the superstitious. They exalt the individual and the common man, and show the great interest in the external nature. American romanticism was in essence the expression of a "real new experience" and contained "an alien quality" because of the simple reason that "the spirit of the place" was radically new and alien. For instance, the growth of cultural nationalism urged the American writers to draw upon the American experience of "pioneering into the west" as the rich sources to express themselves. Through their works they exhibited the willingness for an escape from society and a return to nature. The wilderness with its virgin forests, the sound of the axe cutting its way westward, the exotic landscape with its different sights, smells, and sounds, and the quaint, picturesque civilization of a primitive race—all these constituted an incomparably superior source of inspiration for native authors. Therefore, they celebrated America's landscape with its virgin forests, meadows, groves, endless prairies, streams, and vast oceans. The wilderness came to function almost as a dramatic character that symbolized moral law, which became a permanent convention of American literature. American character types speaking local dialects appeared in the poetry and fiction with increasing frequency, and the literature began to celebrate the farmers, the poor, the unlettered, the children, the noble savages untainted by society. For example, in Cooper's Leatherstocking series a rude Natty Bumppo in buckskin, dwelling in a frontier blockhouse, treading a solitary bridle path through virgin forests was, perhaps, matter enough for any romantic genius. And indeed, American authors were quite responsive to the stimulus which American life offered. Henry Wadsworth Longfellow's tentative treatment of the frontier and the Indians in his works such as *Hiawatha* (1855), Washington Irving's portrayal of the scenes from the Hudson valley, William Cullen Bryant's sketches of the wild west prairie where no human being had ever set foot and James Fenimore Cooper's five Leatherstocking tales with "their majestic descriptions of America's limitless forests and broad blue inland lakes"—these are but a few instances whereby the new American sensibility began to make itself felt. And, of course, we should not forget to mention Emerson, Thoreau, Hawthorne, Melville and Whitman, all people who were instrumental, in one way or another, in creating an indigenous American literature. Surviving from the Federalist Age were its three major literary figures: Bryant, Irving, and Cooper. Emerging as new writers of strength and creative power were the novelists Hawthorne, Simms, Melville, and Harriet Beecher Stowe; the poets Poe, Whittier, Holmes, Longfellow, Lowell, Dickinson, and Whitman; the essayists Thoreau, Emerson, and Holmes; the critics Poe, Lowell, and Simms. From their works the distinct characteristics of American Romanticism were illustrated clearly and powerfully.

American Romanticism embraced the individual and rebelled against the confinement of neoclassicism and religious tradition. The Romantic Movement in America created a new literary genre that continues to influence American writers. Novels, short stories, and poems replaced the sermons and manifestos of yore. Romantic literature was personal, intense, and portrayed more emotion than ever seen in neoclassical literature. America's preoccupation with freedom became a great source of motivation for Romantic writers as many were delighted in free expression and emotion without so much fear of ridicule and controversy. They also put more effort into the psychological development of their characters, and the main characters typically displayed extremes of sensitivity and excitement. The works of the Romantic Era also differed from preceding works in that they spoke to a wider audience, partly reflecting the greater distribution of books as costs came down during the period. The Romantic period saw an increase in female authors and also female readers.

Moral qualities were significantly present in the verse of Emerson, Bryant, Longfellow, Whittier, Holmes, Lowell, and Thoreau. The sectional issues were debated in poetry by Whittier and Lowell speaking for abolition, and Timrod, Hayne, and Simms speaking for the South. Poe formulated his theories of poetry and in some fifty lyrics practiced a symbolist verse that was to be, despite the change of triviality by such contemporaries as Emerson, the strongest single poetic influence emerging from pre-Civil War America, particularly in its impact on European poetry. Whitman, beginning with the 1855 edition of *Leaves of Grass*, was the ultimate expression of poetry organic in form and romantic in spirit, united to a concept of democracy that was pervasively egalitarian. In essays and in lectures the New England transcendentalists—Emerson, Thoreau, Margaret Fuller, and Alcott—carried the expression of philosophic and religious ideas to a high level. In the 1850s emerged the powerful symbolic novels of Hawthorne and Melville and the effective propaganda novel of Harriet Beecher Stowe. Poe, Hawthorne, and Simms practiced the writing of short stories through the period, taking up where Irving had left off in the development of the form.

When talking about the elements that formed the unique characteristics of American Romanticism, the Puritan factor could not be ignored. Puritan influence over American Romanticism was conspicuously noticeable. As a cultural heritage, the American Puritanism exerted a great influence over the American value. Because of the immense affect American romantic writers tended more to moralize than their English and European counterparts. The Puritans accepted the Calvinistic doctrine of predestination, total depravity, original sin and salvation of a selected few through a special infusion of grace from God (limited atonement). Being a group of seriously religious people, they had a strong sense of mission and were very idealistic, for they thought they were the "chosen" people by God and sent to the New World to purify the beliefs and practices of the Church of England, from which they had separated themselves, and built in

America a new church. The Puritans in New England practiced theocracy, a form of government in which religion and government are combined into one. On the other hand, the Puritans were very practical, for the survival in the New World had taught them to work hard for profits and material success, which they believed as a sign of God's benevolence. Puritans in America were living a very disciplined and simple style of life, devoid of earthly joy and extravagancy. Their way of life were based on their somber religion and stressed hard work, thrift, piety and sobriety. As a dominant factor in American life, a philosophy of life and a culture heritage, American Puritanism was one of the most enduring shaping influences in American thought and American literature. It has become, to some extent, so much a state of mind, rather than a set of tenets, so much a part of the national cultural atmosphere that the American breathes, that we may state with a degree of safety that, without some understanding of Puritanism, there can be no understanding of America and its culture. Under the influence of Puritanism we could not omit the fact remains that many American romantic writings intended to edify more than they entertained. Sex and love were, for instance, subjects American authors were particularly careful in approaching. A preoccupation with the Calvinistic view of original sin and the mystery of evil marked the works of Hawthorn, Melville and a host of lesser writers. Hawthorne's *The Scarlet Letter* illustrates powerfully the effect of the adultery on the people and their lives and the inner sin itself, and Whitman was for a long time misunderstood by his own countrymen because his *Leaves of Grass* contains lines and passages not at all agreeable to their "genteel" taste. Nonetheless, Edgar Allan Poe fought vehemently against "the heresy of the didactic," and the writers like John Greenleaf Whittier tried to advocate both beauty and goodness.

If Irving, Cooper, and other writers raised the curtain of American Romanticism, it was Transcendentalism that energized the movement into a more vigor and vital stage, and inspired many romanticists to greatness. Romanticism became popular in American politics, philosophy and art. The movement appealed to the revolutionary spirit of America as well as to those longing to break free of the strict religious traditions of early settlement. The Romantic Movement gave rise to New England Transcendentalism which portrayed a less restrictive relationship between God and Universe. As a philosophical and literary movement, Transcendentalism flourished in New England from 1830s to the Civil War. In 1836, an informal group gathered in Concord, Massachusetts, to discuss the theology, philosophy, and literature. The scholars in the group were not quite happy about the materialistic-oriented life of their time and rejected rationalism and religious intellect. Then, they formed themselves into an informal club, the Transcendentalist club, which was named by good-intentioned neighbors, and met to discuss matters of interest to the life of the nation as a whole. They expressed their views, published their journal, *The Dial*, and made their voice heard. In the same year, a little book was published which made a tremendous impact on formation of the intellectual life and the value of America, and regarded as the mark of New England Transcendentalism. The publication of the book also witnessed the summit of American Romanticism. It was entitled *Nature* by Ralph Waldo Emerson. Some 30 men and a couple of women such as Emerson, Thoreau, Bronson Alcott and Margaret Fuller, most of them teachers or clergymen, were radicals against rigid rationalism of Unitarianism. As the climax of American Romanticism, Transcendentalism shares the romantic characteristics: the exaltation of the individual over society, the significance of intuition, the new and thrilling exultation and appreciation of nature, fascination with the Gothic and the "Oriental," and the expectation to build a national literature and culture. Moreover, Transcendentalism, as a type of Romanticism peculiar to New England, assumed a specific moral and philosophical tone. The moral implications came from the environment where Puritan idealism persisted, but the philosophical tone was largely defined by Emerson. The New World was excited and thrilled to get the new voice like the following. "The universe is composed of Nature and the Soul," it says, "Spirit is present everywhere." It was apparent that the world had had enough of Benjamin Franklin, and a wind of change was beginning to blow. A whole new way of thinking began to exert its influence on the consciousness of man. Emerson's *Nature* has been called the "Manifesto of American Transcendentalism." The new philosophy presented the individual with a more personal relationship with God. Transcendentalism and Romanticism appealed to Americans in a similar fashion, for both privileged feeling over reason, individual freedom of expression over the restraints of tradition and custom. It often involved a rapturous response to nature. It encouraged the rejection of harsh, rigid Calvinism, and promised a new blossoming of American culture. Transcendentalism, as a kind of epistemology, it placed emphasis on the Oversoul—another expression of spirit, or the omnipresent, omniscient, omnipotent as the most important thing in the Universe. It also stressed the importance of the individual as the most important element of society, and believed the individuals can intuitively receive higher truths otherwise unavailable trough common method of knowing, thus transcending the limits of rationalism. It offered a fresh perception of nature as symbolic of the Spirit or God. Nature was, to Transcendentalists, alive and filled with God's overwhelming presence. Nature was not purely matter, but the garment of the Oversoul. Translated into literature, this belief became an emphasis on symbolic representation. In its moral tone, it reminds us of the Puritan belief in the "divine and supernatural light" or the Quaker "inner light." As formulated by Emerson, this became a call for action encouraging the young not to be enslaved by customs but to follow the God within, and to live every moment with a strenuousness such as found in the Puritan fathers. However, insofar as nature is believed to be the moral good, proving God's presence everywhere in his creation and that human nature is accordingly all good, Transcendentalism was the reversed form of Calvinism. The kind of mysticism characterizing Transcendentalism had always lurked within Puritanism, not in its main doctrines, but in the rebellious beliefs.

Romanticism

Romanticism is a movement in art and literature (in the last years of 18th century and the early 19th century in England) that subordinates form to content, encourages freedom of treatment, emphasizes imagination, emotion, and introspection and the freedom of the spirit. A new romanticism had appeared in England in the last years of 18th century. It spread to continental Europe and then came to America early in the 19th century. Romanticism was pluralistic; its manifestations were as varied as individualistic, and as conflicting as the cultures and the intellects from which it sprang. Yet romantics frequently shared certain general characteristics: moral enthusiasm, faith in the value of individualism and intuitive perception, and presumption that the natural world was a source of goodness and man's societies a source of corruption. Romantic values were prominent in American politics, art and philosophy until the Civil War. The romantic exaltation of the individual suited the nation's revolutionary heritage and its frontier egalitarianism. The romantic revolt against traditional art forms gratified those cramped by the strict limits of neoclassic literature, painting and architecture. The romantic rejection of rationalism gladdened those who were opposed to cool, intellectual religions encrusted with the remnants of Calvinism. Increasing numbers of Americans turned to the fervid joys of camp meeting revivalism or to the buoyant teachings of New England transcendentalism.

American Romanticism

The Romantic Period covers the first half of the nineteenth century. Arising America with its ideals of democracy and equality, its industrialization, its westward expansion, and a variety of foreign influences, such as Sir Walter Scott, were among the important factors which made literary expansion and expression not only possible but also inevitable in the period immediately following the nation's political independence. Romantics frequently shared certain general characteristics: moral enthusiasm, faith in value of individualism and intuitive perception, and a presumption that the natural world was a source of goodness and man's societies a source of corruption. Romantic values were prominent in American politics, art, and philosophy until the Civil War. The romantic exaltation of the individual suited the nation's revolutionary heritage and its frontier egalitarianism.

Washington Irving deserves credit for the part he played in inspiring the American romantic imagination. His fascinating *The Sketch Book* with top of his most famous stories, "Rip Van Winkle" and "The Legend of Sleepy Hollow" will be placed at the top of any reading list for the course on American literature. The importance of the frontier and the wilderness in American literature is for the first time well-illustrated in James Fenimore Cooper's *Leather-stocking Tales* (1823–1841) and was to remain a major concern for many later authors.

American Romanticism culminated around the 1840s in what has come to be known as "New England Transcendentalism" or "American Renaissance," one of the major literary figures in this period is Ralph Waldo Emerson. Emerson's *Nature* has been called "the manifesto of American Transcendentalism." Henry David Thoreau, the writer of *Walden*, was a faithful follower of Emerson.

Shaping an American poetry out of the native elements of the New World, Walt Whitman and Emily Dickinson were the two major American poets of the 19th century. Whitman tried to write poetry describing the native American experience. And Dickinson wrote about the life of her time in her completely original way.

Nathaniel Hawthorn and Herman Melville belonged to another type of Romanticists. Hawthorne did not feel comfortable with Emerson's buoyant sense of optimism about man and his *Nature*. Melville was critical of Emerson's optimistic view of life, as is shown in his famous work *Moby Dick* (1851). Such romantic writers placed increasing value on the free expression of emotion and displayed increasing attention to the psychic states of their characters. Heroes and heroines exhibited extremes of sensitivity and excitement. The novel of terror became the profitable literary staple. A preoccupation with the demonic and the mystery of evil marked the works of Poe, Hawthorne, Melville, and a host of minor writers.

The New England poets, such as Longfellow and Bryant, formed a different school from Emerson, Thoreau, Whitman, Dickinson and Poe.

American Transcendentalism

American Transcendentalism or "New England Transcendentalism" or "American Renaissance" is more of a tendency, an attitude, than the philosophy of Transcendentalists. To "transcend" something is to rise above it, to pass beyond its limits. Transcendentalists took their ideas from the romantic literature of Europe, from new-Platonism, from German idealistic philosophy, and from the revelations of Oriental-mysticism. They spoke for cultural rejuvenations and against the materialism of American society. The major features of New England Transcendentalism can be summarized as follows.

Firstly, the Transcendentalists placed emphasis on spirit or the Oversoul, as the most important thing in the Universe.

Secondly, they stressed the importance of the individual. To them, the individual was the most important element of society.

Thirdly, they offered a fresh perception of nature as symbolic of the spirit or God. Nature was, to them, alive, filled with God's overwhelming presence. Transcendentalism is based on the belief that the most fundamental truths about life and death can be reached only by going beyond the world of the senses.

As a philosophical and literary movement, Transcendentalism flourished in New England from 1830s to the Civil War. Its doctrines found their greatest literary advocates in Emerson and Thoreau. Emerson's *Nature* has been called the "Manifesto of American Transcendentalism" and his *The American Scholar* has been rightly regarded as America's "Declaration of Intellectual Independence." Thoreau built and went to live in a small cottage on Walden Pond for a little over two years, and then came back to write about his experience there in his famous book *Walden*. To later generations, scarred by the horrors of the Civil War, the transcendentalist persuasion that humanity was godlike and that evil was non-existent appeared to be an optimistic folly. As a philosophy, Transcendentalism was neither logical nor systematical. It exalted feeling over reason, individual expression over the restraints of law and custom. Yet Transcendentalism was a powerful expression of the intellectual mood of the age, and the ideas it represented have remained a strong influence on great American writers from the days of Hawthorne and Whitman to the present.

Bibliography

http://en.wikipedia.org/wiki/Romanticism, 2013-02-04.

http://escholarship.org/uc/item/9kq451tc, 2013-02-04.

http://www.doc88.com/p-698272747243.html, 2013-02-04.

http://www.vcu.edu/engweb/eng372/intro-h4.htm, 2013-02-04.

Cerrito, Joann. *Nineteenth-Century Literary Criticism, Vol. 44*. Farmington Hills: Gale, 1994: 74-138.

Toming. *A History of American Literature*. Nanjing: Yilin Press, 2005: 65-73, 86-88.

常耀信 . 美国文学简史（第二版）. 天津：南开大学出版社，2006: 40-44.

吴伟仁 . 美国文学史及选读（第 1 册）. 北京：外语教学与研究出版社，2011: 52-59.

李翠婷 , 李正栓 . 美国文学学习指南 . 北京：清华大学出版社，1998: 219-222.

Washington Irving

His Life and Writing Career

His Life

Washington Irving (1783–1859) was an American author, essayist, biographer, historian, and diplomat of the early 19th century. He was born in a wealthy New York merchant family, the youngest one of 11 children. His first name was taken from George Washington. Irving was raised in a family that was filled with Federalist sentiments. Through his life, Irving remained a man pleased with upper-class tastes and a Federalist in politics and in culture. As a child, Irving was frail in health and was precocious. His early education was received from various seminaries in New York. In his formative years, Washington experienced intimately the literary and cultural vitality of New York. Little by little, Irving developed a great passion for books and began to read widely, such as the novel *Robinson Crusoe*, *Sinbad the Sailor*, and *The World Displayed*, all about the voyages and travel. Besides reading, he also tried his hand at writing some juvenile plays, essays and poems. Later, he studied law privately in the offices of Henry Masterton (1798), Brockholst Livingston (1801), and John Ogde Hoffman (1802), but practiced only briefly and gave up the occupation as a law clerk, due to the enthusiasm for the writing and preference for cultural affairs and literature. In 1803, after giving up his work as a law clerk, he travelled through the frontier of upper state New York and eastern part of Canada. From 1804 to 1806 he travelled Europe widely. In 1804 he went to Rome where he met the American painter Washington Allston and developed an interest in art. He returned from Europe with a sharpened sensitivity to American provincialism. Then he visited Marseilles and Genoa, saw the famous English naval officer, Nelson, in Sicily, and met Washington Allston, the painter, in Rome. After return to the United States, Irving was admitted to New York bar in 1806. He was a partner with his brothers in the family hardware business, New York and Liverpool, England, and representative of the business in England until it collapsed in 1818. During the war of 1812 Irving served as a military aide to New York Governor Tompkins in the U.S. Army.

Even though he enjoyed the success in social life and literature, Irving could not get rid of the personal tragedy, which has almost changed his course for life. He was engaged to Matilda Hoffman, who died at the age of seventeen, in 1809. Later he wrote in a private letter, addressed to Mrs. Forster, as an answer to her inquiry why he had not been married: "For years I could not talk on the subject of this hopeless regret; I could not even mention her name; but her image was continually before me, and I dreamt of her incessantly." However, it has also been claimed that Irving was a homosexual. After the death of his mother, Irving decided to stay in Europe, where he remained for seventeen years, from 1815 to 1832. He lived in Dresden (1822–1823), London (1824) and Paris (1825). In England, Irving had a romantic liaison with Mary Shelley. Eventually he settled in Spain, working there for financial reasons for the U.S. Embassy in Madrid (1826–1829). In 1829–1832 Irving was a secretary to the American Legation under Martin Van Buren. Between the years 1842–1845 Irving served as U.S. Ambassador in Spain. The appointment was sponsored by Daniel Webster, the Secretary of State. At the age of sixty-two Irving wrote to his friends in America: "My heart yearns for home; and I have now probably turned the last corner in life, and my remaining years are growing scanty in number, I begrudge every one that I am obliged to pass separated from my cottage and my kindred..." Irving spent the last years of his life in Tarrytown. In spite of his success, money remained a constant worry and his family members lost much of his earnings in poor investments. Moreover, Irving suffered from writers block and battled a herpetic condition that periodically laid him up for months. From 1848 to 1859 he was President of Astor Library, later New York Public Library. Just before retiring for the night, the author had said: "Well, I must arrange my pillows for another weary night! If this could only end!" Irving died in Tarrytown on November 28, 1859, and was still not married.

His Writing Career

As a writer, Irving's career started in journals and newspapers. In his brother's newspaper, Irving made his literary debut in 1802, when he was 19-year-old, with a series of observational letters to the *Morning Chronicle* to express his satires of the New York life, these letters were written under the pseudonym Jonathan Old style, and was edited by his brother Peter. In order to reflect the spirit of the group and his involvement with the cultural and literary circles then, Irving published his first major literary work *Salmagundi* (1807–1808), in collaboration with his brother William and James Kirke Paulding. *Salmagundi* instantly became the center of a literary circle known as the Knickerbocker School, which included the writers such as James Fenimore Cooper, William Cullen Brant, etc. From 1812 to 1814 he was an editor of *Analetic* magazine in Philadelphia and New York. In 1815 Irving made his second trip to Europe and lingered there for the next 17 years. When living in Europe, the European cultural heritage urged him to make his mind to recreate this culture in American settings.

The Sketch Book (1819–1820), which was heavily influenced by the German folktales, represented his efforts in this respect. With the publication of *The Sketch Book* in 1819, Irving established his literary fame both in America and in Europe. In 1822 another book named *Bracebridge Hall*, the sequel of *The Sketch Book*, was published. In this book, Irving invites the reader to ramble gently with him at the Hall, stating that "I am not writing a novel, and have nothing of intricate plot, or marvelous adventure, to promise the reader." After then he made his trip to Germany to satisfy his interest in German romanticism, which flavored in the *Tales of a Traveler* (1824) and some other later works. During his working in embassy in Madrid in Spain (1826–1829), he began to study Spanish historical sources, from which Irving got the inspiration and created some important works: *A History of the Life and Voyages of Christopher Columbus* (1828), *The Chronicles of the Conquest of Granada* (1829), a short story "The Devil and Tom Walker" (1830) and *Voyages and Discoveries of the Companions of Columbus* (1831), all based on careful historical research. In 1829 he moved to London and published a collection of essays, verbal sketches, and stories: *Tales of the Alhambra* (1832), concerning the history and the legends of Moorish Spain.

After seventeen years abroad on May 21, 1832, Irving returned to New York and was welcomed by his countrymen enthusiastically as the first American author who has won international reputation. He made a trip to the southern and western parts of United States and created two novels: *The Cayon Miscellany* (1835) and *A Tour on the Prairies* (1835), the latter was a work which related his recent travels on the frontier and regarded as an account of a journey, which extended from Fort Gibson, at that time a frontier post of the Far West, to the Cross Timbers in what is now Oklahoma. The book was another popular success and also the first book written and published by Irving in the United States since *A History of New York* in 1809 and was regarded as his desire to portray his own country once again after 17 years abroad. From 1836 to 1842 Irving lived at Sunnyside manor house, near Tarrytown, which has been described in his works as "Sleepy Hollow." In 1840 he wrote a book named *Life of Oliver Goldsmith.* Irving's later publications include *Mahomet and His Successors* (1850), a careful presentation of the life, beliefs, and character of Mohammed, *Wolfert's Roost* (1855). He continued to publish regularly—and almost always successfully—throughout his life, and completed a five-volume biography of George Washington: *The Life of George Washington* just eight months before his death, at age 76, in Tarrytown, New York, which was published from 1855 to 1859. After his death, Irving's major works were published in 1860–1861 in 21 volumes.

Irving's contribution to American literature is unique in more ways than one. He did a number of things that have been regarded as the first of their kind in America and was regarded as the "father of America literature." Irving, along with James Fenimore

Cooper, was among the first American writers to earn acclaim in Europe, and he was the first belletrist in American literature. During almost six decades of his creation, he churned out books, and reviews, letters, and essays for newspapers. And he was a more prolific author compared with his peers. He wrote numerous short stories, biographies, histories, and tales of his travels. He is best known for his short stories "The Legend of Sleepy Hollow" and "Rip Van Winkle," both of which appear in his book *The Sketch Book of Geoffrey Crayon, Gent* (1819–1820). The book touched the American imagination and foreshadowed the coming of Hawthorne, Melville, and Poe, in whose hands the short story attained a degree of perfection as a literary tradition. His historical works include biographies of George Washington, Oliver Goldsmith and Muhammad, and several histories of 15th-century Spain dealing with subjects such as Christopher Columbus, the Moors, and the Alhambra. His characters, such as Ichabod Crane and Rip van Winkle, are now icons of popular American culture, and many of Irving's works have inspired adaptations to the stage and film. As an essayist Irving was not interested in the exploration of the meaning of nature or self-inspection like other Romanticists, such as Emerson or Montaigne. He was more interested in the observation of the vanishing pasts of old Europe, the riverside Creole villages of Louisiana, the old Pawnee hunting grounds of Oklahoma, and how ladies fashion moves from one extreme to the other. "Geoffrey Crayon" was his most prolific fictional mask. Irving once said: "There rise authors now and then, who seem proof against the mutability of language, because they have rooted themselves in the unchanging principles of human nature." Irving's success has encouraged the following American authors, such as Nathaniel Hawthorne, Herman Melville, Henry Wadsworth Longfellow, and Edgar Allan Poe, to create more marvelous works. Irving was also admired by some European writers, including Sir Walter Scott, Lord Byron, Thomas Campbell, Francis Jeffrey, and Charles Dickens. As America's first genuine internationally best-selling author, Irving advocated for writing as a legitimate profession, and argued for stronger laws to protect American writers from copyright infringement.

Irving's literary career could be divided into two phases generally. The first phase spanned from the publication of Irving's first book to his return to America in 1832; the other one was stretching over the rest years of his life after he returned home. His first period of writing was marked by the "Englishizing" style. At this period, he was more attracted by the cultural heritage and historical interests of Europe, so the subjects of his writing at this time were mostly about England or Europe. Europe has provided Irving with the creation sources. We can't deny that most of his works take European folk tales as the source materials. From the works in this period, we could sense his conservative attitude. The love for the European antique, in some extent, has transformed into a kind of obsession in his early creation. At Irving's age, the American culture has experienced an evolution from immaturity to maturity, whereas the European culture has stepped into adulthood. In the traditions of the old world Irving found some valuable things, which could not be offered by his own young nation. His long sojourn in Europe provided him an opportunity to explore the imagination in his works and the old world enabled his fancy, which found its way into his books with its picturesqueness, "ruins," and objects of antiquity, to work. *The Sketch Book* is the powerful illustrations of this. In "The Author's Account of Himself," the first part of *The Sketch Book*, Irving expressed his fascination about the antiquity of Europe:

> But Europe held forth the charms of storied and poetical association. There were to be seen the masterpieces of art, the refinements of highly-cultivated society, the quaint peculiarities of ancient and local custom. My native country was full of youthful promise: Europe was rich in the accumulated treasures of age.
> Her very ruins told the history of times gone by, and every mouldering stone was a chronicle. I longed to wander over the scenes of renowned achievement—to tread, as it were, in the footsteps of antiquity—to loiter about the ruined castle—to meditate on the falling tower—to escape, in short, from the commonplace realities of the present, and lose myself among the shadowy grandeurs of the past.
> I had, beside all this, an earnest desire to see the great men of the earth. We have, it is true, our great men in America: not a city but has an ample share of them. I have mingled among them in my time, and been almost withered by the shade into which they cast me; for there is nothing so baleful to a small man as the shade of a great one, particularly the great man of a city. But I was anxious to see the great men of Europe; for I had read in the works of various philosophers that all animals degenerated in America, and man among the number. A great man of Europe, thought I, must therefore be as superior to a great man of America, as a peak of the Alps to a highland of the Hudson; and in this idea I was confirmed, by observing the comparative importance and swelling magnitude of many English travelers among us, who, I was assured, were very little people in their own country. I will visit this land of wonders, thought I, and see the gigantic race from which I am degenerated.

The year of 1832 marked Irving's writings have stepped into the second period. When returning to America, he felt a totally new spirit of nationalism in America, which urged Irving to write to eulogize his motherland. He found the vigorousness in the art and literature. At that time, the poets started to write the poems to praise the wildness of the west, the prairie, and adventure spirit of the people; the painters stopped to imitate the European masters, but began to paint the beautiful landscape in America. Irving has witnessed the whole country was inspired to establish an indigenous culture and literature because the people, as well as Irving himself, have awaken to the fact that there was indigenous beauty in this continent. The writers used their works to reflect the American people's efforts to break through the shackles of European literature and lay solid foundations for the development of independent American literature. Irving, in his later years, has created some books to depict the Wild West of America, such as *Astoria* (1836), *Adventures of Captain Bonneville* (1837), and *The Crayon Miscellany* (1835). Though these books describing the American west can be used to prove the change of attitude of author's creation, these "Americanized" works still constitute the "minor phase" of his career, and are of the secondary importance in the Irving's canon.

In spite of having been greatly influenced by European writing, especially the German legends, Irving's style is not assimilated by the European culture totally. His works demonstrate something quite profound in his style. Unlike his predecessors, Irving's creation avoided moralizing and was not didactically stated, he wrote to amuse and entertain. Irving's use of imagery—using words to create a picture in the reader's mind to create long descriptions of the American landscape—set his work apart from those of the European writers. It's through those descriptions that the Hudson Valley really comes to life. In his satire and humor, there is always a kindness, an understanding, which reveals his magnanimous humanity. More importantly, beneath the trivialities of comic materials there is a passion for life; and in the sadness of his romantic melancholy there is the presence of the immutable law of change. It is to the law of change that Irving's style responds.

Irving was also famous for his introduction of the idea of the modern short story to the American literature. Prior to this period, the writers were mostly writing instructional, political documents and lots of religious-based poetry. Irving changed up that genre by writing fictional stories and his unique voice. His short stories "The Legend of Sleepy Hollow" and "Rip Van Winkle" are considered American masterpieces, which as so great that they have been infused into popular culture.

Most modern critics classify Irving as one of the greatest American writers, responsible for establishing an American style of writing, especially in the short story genre. However, there are still critics who point out the author's shortcomings: his works lack intellectual depths. In Irving's books, many events would be involved, but without any sustained wisdom regarding the movement of thoughts behind the events; when concerning the issues of American expansion or the relationship between America and Britain, the author didn't seem to provide penetrating insights to analyze the issues; one of the biggest debates to rage in Irving scholarship is over the issue of anti-feminism in his writing, Irving was blamed to satisfy, in his books, the need to maintain patriarchal power and concerns over the role of women in the new society were paramount.

Analyses of and Comments on His Representative Short Stories

Rip Van Winkle (1819)

Plot Summary

"Rip Van Winkle," contained in the collection *The Sketch Book of Geoffrey Crayon, Gent*, is a short story based on German folk tales that Irving learned about through a lifetime of reading and years of travel in Europe. One of his goals was to give the United States, a new country, some of the same feeling of tradition that older nations had because of their traditional lore. For several of his stories Irving borrowed European plots, but transported them into American settings. In a humorous context, "Rip Van Winkle" deals with issues of politics, as he shows how the American Revolution changed one small village, and gender issues, as he shows the comical relationship between a lazy husband and a bad-tempered wife.

The story of Rip Van Winkle is set in the years before and after the American Revolutionary War. In a pleasant village, at the foot of New York's Catskill Mountains, lives the kindly Rip Van Winkle, a colonial British-American villager of Dutch descent. Rip is an amiable man who enjoys solitary activities in the wilderness, but is also loved by all in town—especially the children to whom he tells stories and give toys. However, a tendency to avoid all gainful labor, for which his nagging wife (Dame Van Winkle) chastises him, allows his home and farm to fall into disarray due to his lazy neglect. One autumn day, he wanders into the Catskill Mountains with his hunting dog, Wolf, in order to escape his wife's nagging. In the valley he meets a man dressed in antiquated Dutch clothing, carrying a keg up the mountain, who requires Rip's help. Arriving at the top of the mountain, Rip finds a group of ornately-dressed men who are playing nine-pins. Although there is no conversation and Rip does not ask the men who they are or how they know his name, he discreetly begins to drink some of their liquor, and soon falls asleep. When he awakens, Rip finds everything has changed. 20 years has passed by and he becomes an old man. When he goes into the town, he discovers that his wife has died and the American Revolution has taken place. The old man entertains the people with tales of the old days and his encounter with the dwarfs.

Themes

As a legendary story, it is amusing and full of romantic color. Nevertheless, looking from another angle, it reflects the social conditions of America before and after the War of Independence through contrasting people's outlook and their way of life in different historical periods. Through Rip's fantastic experience Irving expresses the confused state of mind of the people who witnessed the great changes brought by the American Revolution, and like Rip, they felt 20-year behind. They lost in a psychological difficulty in understanding their own recent national history, which brought a kind of uncertainty and confusion. They suffered the clash between the new and the old world like Rip and led them to wonder about their own identity, just as Rip who "doubted his own identity, and whether he was himself or someone else." This confusion doesn't last very long, just like the protagonist Rip, the new citizens in America found their confidence very quickly so as to adapt the new environment and history very well. Meanwhile, the tale also reveals Irving's criticism of the social phenomena brought by the Revolution and his nostalgic longing for the unrecoverable past. Many critics read Rip's twenty-year sleep as a rejection of the capitalistic values of his society—ferociously personified by the shrewish Dame Van Winkle—and an embracing of the world of the imagination.

Literary Techniques

The narrative system of "Rip Van Winkle" is significant. Rip, as the protagonist of the story, does not want to tell the story personally. There is a third person narrator who is omniscient and humorous as well as an effective storyteller. The narrator is identified with Rip in most cases, but far away with the protagonist occasionally to offer some satirical comments on Rip. The whole story, according to the narrator, might be a tale discovered in the papers of the late Diedrich Knickercocker, one of personas invented by Irving, so Diedrich Knickercocker was supposed to be the author of the tale. These two narrative methods helped Irving's protagonist to gain enough confidence to make the readers connect Rip was not only with a fictional Dutch writer but also with the Dutch history in the Hudson region. As a result, the readers would face the fact that they should not inquire whether the story was stated accurately though from its outset the whole story seems so fantastic.

Through the use of irony, which is sort of saying the opposite of what you really mean, Irving is able to poke fun at his characters and their situations. In "Rip Van Winkle," he describes Dame Van Winkle, saying "a termagant wife may, therefore, in some respects, be considered a tolerable blessing; and if so, Rip Van Winkle was thrice blessed." So using his lofty language, he's literally saying that if an abusive wife is good for a person, then Rip was a lucky man. But of course, no one wants that. What he's really saying is that poor Rip was stuck with this mean, old lady for a life. Through the use of irony and sarcasm, he's able to say the opposite of what he wanted the reader to know.

The Legend of Sleepy Hollow (1819)

Plot Summary

"The Legend of Sleepy Hollow," one of the two best short stories of Washington Irving, is a Halloween-themed short story contained in the collection *The Sketch Book of Geoffrey Crayon, Gent*. The story is set in 1790 in the countryside around the Dutch settlement of Tarry Town, in a secluded glen called Sleepy Hollow. In the story, there is the memorable event of an apparently headless horseman throwing his head at his rival in love, and the unforgettable character of Ichabod Crane, a sycophantic, lean, lanky, and extremely superstitious schoolmaster from Connecticut. He competes with Abraham "Brom Bones" Van Brunt, the town rowdy, for the hand of 18-year-old Katrina Van Tassel, the daughter and sole child of a wealthy farmer, Baltus Van Tassel. As Crane leaves a party he attended at the Van Tassel home on an autumn night, he is pursued by the Headless Horseman, who is supposedly the ghost of a Hessian trooper who had his head shot off by a stray cannonball during "some nameless battle" of the American Revolutionary War, and who "rides forth to the scene of battle in nightly quest of his head." Then Ichabod mysteriously disappears from town, leaving Katrina to marry Brom Bones, who was "to look exceedingly knowing whenever the story of Ichabod was related." Although the nature of the Headless Horseman is left open to interpretation, the story implies that the Horseman was really Brom Bones in disguise.

Themes

On the surface, it is a funny love story between Crane, Brom and Katrina. In a deeper sense, the hero, Crane, is an unexpected visitor from Connecticut. The creation of archetypes is a particularly subtle feat of Irving's consummate craftsmanship. We may see in Ichabod Crane a precocious, effete New Englander, shrewd, commercial, a city-slicker, who is rather an interloper, a somewhat destructive force, in village life, and who comes along to swindle the villagers. His book learning turns on him, and he is driven away from where he does not belong, so that the serene village remains permanently good and happy. Brom Bones, on the other hand, is of the Huck Finn-type of country bumpkin, rough, vigorous, boisterous but inwardly very good, a frontier type put out there to shift for himself. Thus the rivalry in love between Ichabod and Brom, viewed in this way, suddenly assumes the dimensions of two ethical groups locked in a kind of historic contest. The plot of the whole story revolves around the conflict between Crane and Brom Bones, which symbolically represents a nation trying to establish and to secure an identity at home and abroad. Ichabod is a bookworm and has the supposed bookworm trait such as frailty and cowardice. Brom is brute and rustic but not without his cleverness and mischief. The contrast seems to point towards a conflict between pretentious intellectualism and anti-intellectualism, which can extend to the disharmony between city and countryside. However, even though the author tried his best to make his story filled with absorbing elements that attracted the reader at the first glance, such as the Romantic description, Gothic elements, supernatural atmosphere, vivid language and portrayal of characters, Exaggerated humor language, neither character wins the heart of the reader. But Brom does win Katrina.

Literary Techniques

Although much of Irving's fiction is today regarded as little more than petty and derivative, many critics agree that Irving did much to establish the American short story in 1819 with "The Legend of Sleepy Hollow." Commentators concur, moreover, that Irving set the artistic standard and model for subsequent generations of American short story writers with the tale. Among the technical innovations ascribed to "The Legend of Sleepy Hollow" include the integration of folklore, myth, and fable into narrative fiction; setting and landscape as a reflection of theme and mood; and the expression of the supernatural and use of Gothic elements.

Bibliography

http://en.wikipedia.org/wiki/Washington_Irving, 2013-02-04.

http://www.enotes.com/legend-sleepy-hollow-essays/legend-sleepy-hollow-washington-irving, 2013-02-04.

Toming. *A History of American Literature*. Nanjing: Yilin Press, 2005: 73-77, 86-88.

常耀信 . 美国文学简史（第二版）. 天津：南开大学出版社，2006: 44-50.

吴伟仁 . 美国文学史及选读（第 1 册）. 北京：外语教学与研究出版社，2011: 59-66.

James Fenimore Cooper

His Life and Writing Career

His Life

James Fenimore Cooper (1789–1851) was one of the first American novelists to undertake the creation of a distinct national literature, appropriating his country's history as the central theme of his work. He was also best known for the tales of frontier adventure, including *The Last of the Mohicans* (1826), an adventure story set in the Lake Champlain. It has been filmed several times between 1936 and 1992. He was a prolific and popular American writer of the early 19th century and best remembered as a novelist who wrote numerous sea-stories and the historical novels. Through his Leatherstocking series Cooper created the archetype of the 18th-century frontiersman, Natty Bumppo, who lives free, close to nature, while the settlers bring "civilization" that destroys the wilderness. Cooper wrote over thirty novels in his life. These novels established a number of cultural archetypes, including that of the noble Native American, as well as the savage and treacherous counterpart of this figure, and using Nathaniel "Natty" Bumppo he created a fictional paradigm of the American character. His historical romances of frontier and Indian life in the early American days created a unique form of American literature.

Cooper was born in Burlington, New Jersey, the son of Quakers, Judge William Cooper and Elisabeth Fenimore Cooper. And he was raised in Cooperstown, New York, established by his father William, where he spent most of his life. Cooper was a lifelong member of the Episcopal Church and in his later years contributed generously to it. He attended Yale University for three years but was expelled in 1805 for engaging in pranks, which included training a donkey to sit in a professor's chair. Subsequently encouraged by his father, Cooper served on a merchant vessel and then joined the Navy and served on the Sterling from 1806 to 1807. On his return to the United States, he received a warrant as a midshipman. In 1808 he served on the *Vesuvius* and on the *Wasp* in the Atlantic in 1809. These experiences later inspired his sea stories and greatly influenced many of his novels and other writings. Upon his father's death in 1809, Cooper became financially independent. He resigned his commission in 1811 and married Susan

Augusta De Lancey, who was a descendent of the early governors of New York colony. Cooper enjoyed a leisured time for about the following ten years, but fell deeply in debt. He started to write as his career was not because he had to repay the debt, but, ridiculously, he made a bet with his wife. After reading some boring English novels, he said to his wife that he could write a better story than that himself, so at the age 31 his first novel, *Precaution* (1820) appeared.

In 1826 Cooper moved his family to Europe, where he hoped he could seek to gain more income from his books as well as provide better education for his children and he met Scott and Lafayette. While overseas, he continued to write.

In 1833 Cooper returned to the United States. In June 1834, Cooper decided to reopen his ancestral mansion, Otsego Hall, at Cooperstown, from where he had been absent nearly 16 years. The mansion had been closed for a long time and falling into decay. Repairs were begun, and the house was speedily put in order. At first, he wintered in New York City and summered in Cooperstown, but eventually he made Otsego Hall his permanent home.

Cooper joined the Episcopal Church a few months before he died. Cooper died at Otsego Hall, on September 14, 1851. He was buried in the cemetery of Cooperstown. His wife followed him four months later. At the time of his death, Cooper was more successful and respected abroad than at home. Out of step with his countrymen, his work was very influential to European writers like Honore de Balzac and Leo Tolstoy. Yet, the weaknesses of Cooper's fiction are quite well known and wide-spread. Mark Twain tore apart Cooper's romanticism in "Fenimore Coopers Literary Offenses" (1895). Clearly, Cooper's tone was criticized as being reactionary, romantic, and pedagogical. However, Cooper did contribute a great deal to the genre of American fiction. Even today, everyone has read books and seen films that are directly and indirectly affected by Cooper's conception of Natty Bumppo and his creation of the American novel.

His Writing Career

Cooper's first story, *Precaution* (1820), an imitation of Jane Austen's novels, was published in response to a challenge by his wife to write a better novel than one they had been reading. With the publication of this book, Cooper hoped it would be financially successful, but it was not as remunerative as he expected. His second novel, *Spy* (1821), which set in Westchester Country, was based on Sir Walter Scott's *Waverly* series, and told an adventure tale about the American Revolution. It was a story about espionage against the British during the Revolutionary War. The protagonist is Harvey Birch, a supposed loyalist who actually is a spy for George Washington, disguised as "Mr. Harper." The book brought Cooper fame and wealth, and he gave up farming. Under the influence of Scott, Cooper was inspired to draw stereotypes of light and dark, good and evil, and dichotomize the female into the fair and pure and the dark and tainted. With his third novel, *The Pioneers* (1823), Cooper started his preoccupation with a series of frontier adventures and pioneer life, and took the historical romance which was made popular by Sir Walter Scott as his model to tell a story of the American frontier in a form that had traditionally depended on the cultural background of European history. The novels, which started the Leatherstockng series of five novels, depicted the adventures of Natty Bumppo, also called Leatherstocking or Hawkeye, and his Indian companion Chingachgook. The uniquely American characters, settings, and themes of *The Pioneers* engaged the nation's nostalgia for an appealing and historically rich period of the recent past, and Cooper developed the frontier romance and the central character of Leatherstocking further in *The Last of the Mohicans* (1826) and *The Prairie* (1827). In the next year, Cooper also published *The Pilot* (1824), the first of eleven sea novels and a genuine American sea tale about the exploits of John Paul Jones. *The Pilot* was a sea story that featured Long Tom Coffin and other memorable characters. During the spring of 1826 or earlier he met a young Pawnee chief who became the model for Hard-Heart in *The Prairie* (1827). For more than a decade thereafter, Cooper participated in its intellectual life and politics, and espoused republican social and political convictions in fiction and nonfiction which criticized European forms of government and condemned American reliance on foreign culture. However, these works were not well received: the readers and critics who extolled Cooper as America's first historical romancer did not accept him in the role of social and political critic.

From 1826 to 1833 Cooper lived in Europe, where he published romances and unsuccessful books about democracy, politics, and society. He served as the US consul at Lyons and travelled a great deal. In Europe he became friends with Sir Walter Scott and Marquis de Lafayette, who partly inspired his essay "Notions of the America" (1828). He was especially inspired by Italy and lived in Tasso's villa at Sorrento, but literary meetings in London annoyed him and the Thames River did not impress him, to whom it was "a stream of trivial expanse." The British writer D. H. Lawrence called him later "A gentleman in the worst sense." In 1827 he published another two of his sea stories, *The Red Rover* and *The Water Witch*, in Paris. During his time in Paris, the Cooper family was seen as the center of the small American expatriate community. At the same time he developed friendships with the painter Samuel Morse, the French general and American Revolutionary War hero Gilbert du Motier, Marquis de Lafayette.

In 1833 Cooper returned to America, and immediately published *A Letter to My Countrymen*, in which he gave his own version of the controversy he had been engaged in, and passed some sharp censure on his compatriots for their share in it. This attack he followed up with *The Monikins* (1835) and *The American Democrat* (1835); with several sets of notes on his travels and experiences in Europe, among which may be remarked his *England* (1837), in three volumes, a burst of vanity and ill-temper; and with *Homeward Bound*, and *Home as Found* (1838), noticeable as containing a highly idealized portrait of himself. All these books tended to increase the ill-feeling between author and public; the Whig press was virulent and scandalous in its comments, and Cooper plunged into a series of actions for libel.

On May 10, 1839, Cooper published *History of the Navy of the United States of America*. It was a work he had long planned on writing. Before departing for Europe in May, 1826, at a dinner given in his honor, he publicly announced his intentions during a parting speech that he would be authoring this great historical work while abroad:

> Encouraged by your kindness, I will take this opportunity of recording the deeds and sufferings of a class of men to which this nation owes a debt of gratitude—a class of men among whom, I am always ready to declare, not only the earliest, but many of the happiest days of my youth have been passed.

It took Cooper fourteen years to research and gather material for the book. His close association with the U.S. Navy and various naval officers and his familiarity with naval life at sea made him more than qualified to research and write this work. His historical account of the U.S. Navy was first well received but later was harshly criticized in America and abroad. However, Cooper's work is said to have stood the test of time and is largely considered an authoritative account of the U.S. Navy during that time.

In 1844 Cooper's *Proceedings of the Naval Court Martial in the Case of Alexander Slidell Mackenzie, a Commander in the Navy of the United States, &C*, was first published in *Graham's Magazine* of 1843–1844. It was a review of the court martial of Alexander Slidell Mackenzie who while at sea, had hanged three crew members of the brig USS *Sommers* for mutiny. One of the hanged men, nineteen-year-old Philip Spencer, was the son of Secretary of State John C. Spencer. He was executed without court-martial along with two other sailors aboard the *Sommers* for allegedly attempting mutiny. Just prior to this affair Cooper was in the process of giving harsh review to Mackenzie's version of the Battle of Lake Erie. Mackenzie had previously given harsh criticism to Cooper's interpretation of the Battle of Lake Erie contained in Cooper's *History of the Navy of the United States* (1839). However he still felt sympathetic to Mackenzie over his pending court martial at the time. In 1846 Cooper published *Lives of Distinguished American Naval Officers* covering the biographies of Commodores William Bainbridge, Richard Somers, John Shaw, William Shubrick and Edward Preble.

His later works include *The Red Rover*, *The Wing-and-Wing*(1842), *The Two Admirals* (1842), *Afloat and Ashore* (1844), *Satanstoe* (1845), which is a historical novel of manners, *The Chainbearer* (1845), and *The Red-Skins* (1846), which form the trilogy called "The Littlepage Manuscripts," and *The Sea Lions* (1849). The novels deal with the anti-rent controversy and its historical background. Cooper defended in the work the landlords' rights — the tenants of the New York had refused to pay rent and the author saw in the controversy a crisis in American democracy. In *The American Democrat* (1835) Cooper he also expressed his political and social views.

In 1856, five years after Cooper's death his *History of the Navy of the United States of America* was published. The work was an account of the U.S. Navy in the early 19th century. Among naval historians of the period the work has come to be recognized as a general and authoritative account, however, it was criticized for accuracy on some points by other students of that period. For example, Cooper's account of the Battle of Lake Erie was said to be less than accurate by some naval historians. For making such claims Cooper once sued a Park Benjamin, Jr. a poet and also editor of the *Evening Signal* of New York, for libel.

As one of the most popular 19th-century American authors, Cooper and his works were admired greatly throughout the world. His stories have been translated into nearly all the languages of Europe and into some of those of Asia. Balzac admired him greatly, but with discrimination; Victor Hugo pronounced him greater than the great master of modern romance. It is only as a novelist that he deserves consideration. His qualities are not those of the great masters of fiction; but he had an inexhaustible imagination, an ability of simple combination of incident, a homely tragic force which is very genuine and effective, and up to a certain point a fine narrative power.

In sum, Cooper's achievement and influence was large. "The imaginative debt that such minor nineteenth century novelists as Simms and Stowe owed to Cooper is obvious," an analyst notes, "and in general popular fiction remained in the mode that Cooper had shaped for it until after the Civil War. Yet it is equally true to say that Cooper first established many of the themes with which the major authors of the century would deal". His peers, such as Sir Walter Scott and Honore de Balzac, regarded Cooper as one of the finest novelists in the world. Nevertheless, his reputation has suffered considerably so that scholars are inclined to place him beneath Nathaniel Hawthorne, Herman Melville, and others who followed him, which could be caused by a number of reasons, noting that Cooper did not produce a masterpiece on the level of *The Scarlet Letter* (1850) or *Moby-Dick* (1851) and that his work suffers from "contradictions." As Mark Twain pointed out in "Fenimore Cooper's Literary Offenses," Cooper's novels also tend to strain some readers' expectations of realism in areas such as dialogue. In *The Pioneers*, for instance, a character threatened by a forest fire proclaims: "Let us endeavor to retire." Indeed, Cooper's Leather-Stocking Tales are best read as fanciful romances and thus do not fit the strict definition of "novel" as a highly realistic form. As Chase argues in "The American Novel and Its Tradition," however, many of America's greatest "novels"—including *The Scarlet Letter* and *Moby-Dick*—are actually romances.

The chief problem in Cooper's literature may be simply concluded as the lack of polish and originality. His literary training was inadequate; his vocabulary is limited and his style awkward and pretentious; and he had a fondness for moralizing tritely and obviously, which destroys his best passages. All other considerations aside, novels such as *Moby-Dick* and *Adventures of Huckleberry Finn* (1884) shine because of their lyrical, highly crafted prose. Despite notable digressions, these novels also have a quality of tightness about them. Melville used a lot of words, and Mark Twain a lot of scenes, but one rarely has the sense that they have wasted them. Cooper, on the other hand, appears to have written without the deliberation that one might expect of a great novelist. His daughter, Susan Fenimore Cooper, who had worked for him, provides this glimpse into her father's creative process: "On this occasion, as on all others when writing a book, he first adopted some general leading idea, sketched vaguely in his mind a few of the more prominent characters, and then immediately began his work in its final shape, leaving the details to suggest and develop themselves during the progress of the volume. Excepting when writing history, he is not known to have ever drawn up a written plan, and in one or two instances only were a few brief notes thrown on paper, regarding some particular chapter. In all the details he depended in a great measure on the thought and feeling of the moment." Furthermore, Professor Stephen Railton explains that "he regularly sent manuscript to the publisher without waiting until he had finished the tale." Cooper also paid little attention to revision. In a letter quoted by Railton, Cooper admits: "I ought in justice to myself to say, that in opposition to a thousand good resolutions, *The Pioneers*, has been more hastily and carelessly written than any of my books—Not a line has been copied, and it has gone from my desk to the printers—I have not to this moment been able even to read it—." Finally, as Railton notes, Cooper was not one to provide readers with highly original conceptions. "No writer was more committed than Cooper to contemporary literary conventions," Railton writes. "He was, for example, simply unable to conceive a tale without a love story, without a comic character, without a narrow escape... In the nineteenth century literary conventions fulfilled the terms of an unwritten, tacit contract that a popular novelist had agreed upon with his audience: readers demanded novelty and suspense, but they also expected to be entertained in a familiar way, and the writer was pledged to satisfy those expectations."

Analysis of and Comment on His Representative Novel

The Pioneers (1823)

Plot Summary

The Pioneers was the first tale of James Fenimore Cooper's Leatherstocking series, the others are: *The Last of the Mohicans* (1826), *The Prairie* (1827), *The Pathfinder* (1840), and *The Deerslayer* (1841). If sorting them according to the plotline, the sequence should be: *The Deerslayer*, *The Last of the Mohicans*, *The Pathfinder*, *The Pioneers* and *The Prairie.* "Leatherstocking" is the nickname for Natty Bumppo who is used to wearing long deerskin leggings in the American Indian fashion. Natty Bumppo is also nicknamed Deerslayer, Hawkeye, Long Rifle, Pathfinder, or the Trapper. As a type of mythic hero, the character of Natty Bumppo is based on the legend of Daniel Boone (a folk hero), the idea of the natural man in Rousseau's primitivism, the idealized image of American manhood, and Cooper's youthful memory of a real character. Taking the development of the character, Natty Bumppo, a resourceful white American living in the woods, as a clue, *The Pioneer* focuses on the evolution of the wilderness into a civilized community.

It is a romantic story which takes place on the rapidly advancing frontier of New York State ten years after the Revolution. Its historical importance lies in the fact that it was probably the first true romance of the frontier in American literature. The story features an elderly Leatherstocking (Natty Bumpo), Judge Marmaduke Temple of Templeton, whose life parallels that of the author's father Judge William Cooper, and Elizabeth Temple (based on the author's sister, Hannah Cooper), of the fictional Templeton, which is said to be modeled after Cooperstown, New York. The story begins with an argument between the Judge and Leatherstocking, and the basic conflict of the story is, in essence, the one between Leathetherstocking, who insists on man's old forest freedom, and Judge Temple, standing at head of the squirearchy on the frontier, to whom man remains savage without law and order. Judge Temple makes some deer laws forbidding shooting out of season, but Leatherstocking breaks them somehow. He is arrested, tried, and found guilt. His young friend, Oliver Effigham, helps him to escape and, when the right moment comes, and tells the truth about his own identity as the grandson of Major Effingham, with whom Leatherstocking has served in the frontier wars, before Oliver and Elizabeth, Judge Temple's daughter, are duly married. Leatherstocking's faithful friend, old Indian John, dies of exhaustion in a forest fire, exemplifying the vexed figure of the "dying Indian." At the end of the novel, Leathestocking is seen, rifle over shoulder, trudging off toward the woods. His statement, "There's them living who say, that Nathaniel Bumppo's right to shoot on these hills is of older date than Marmaduke Temple's right to forbid him," rings clearly and loudly behind his disappearing figure into the sunset.

Themes

In the nearly 200 years since its publication, many have been able to read *The Pioneers* and have found perhaps a few shortcomings, but also an engaging historical romance, an insightful novel of manners, and an important treatment of both humans' difficult relationship with nature and of the nature of manhood. The novel also demonstrates how author dealt with the issues of the civilizing process and the relationship with Native Americans.

One of those themes—perhaps the one Cooper handled most effectively—is Americans' relationship with nature. Since Christopher Columbus had introduced the vast North American and South American continents to the Europeans in 1492, the "New World" had been a source of fascination. Accustomed to the largely settled and "civilized" cultures of the "Old World," Europeans had variously viewed the Americas as a dangerous place, a new Eden, and a land of plenty. In *The Pioneers*, Cooper joins the discussion of the American wilderness, exposing the conflict that naturally occurs when nature and civilization meet. Describing the settlement that Judge Temple and others have cut out of the forest in New York's frontier, he writes: "In short, the whole district is hourly exhibiting how much can be done, in even a rugged country, and with a severe climate, under the dominion of mild laws, and where every man feels a direct interest in the prosperity of a commonwealth, of which he knows himself to form a part." Temple represents a point of view that believes human can improve on nature, as when he speaks of cultivating maple trees for their sugar.

As Cooper shows, however, the cost of this progress may be large. Richard Jones, Temple's comical cousin, shows how little regard some of the settlers have for nature when he tells him: "We must run our streets by the compass, coz, and disregard trees, hills, ponds, stumps, or, in fact, anything but posterity." Richard even sees nature as a foe to be conquered, bringing a cannon to a pigeon shoot and later boasting of having "driven the enemy from the field." Temple, who has some sense that the natural resources here, while abundant, are not endless, tries to keep a lid on progress. When he learns that his house is burning maple wood for fuel, he says: "Really, it behooves the owner of woods so extensive as mine, to be cautious what example he sets his people, who are already felling the forests, as if no end could be found to their treasures, nor any limits to their extent. If we go on in this way, twenty years hence, we shall want fuel." However, Even Temple, who resembles other characters in the novel in his lack of restraint, exhibits some hubris when it comes to humans' dominion over nature. Richard, for example, accuses him of considering the construction of canals simply because the existing rivers and lakes are not moving in the direction he likes.

In all of this, it is the voice of Natty Bumppo that is the most powerful. Bumppo, a white man who has come to be one with nature, not only deplores the wastefulness of the settlers, but complains that the rise of "civilization" here threatens individual liberty. Early in the novel, in a dispute with Temple over the question that who shot a deer, he says: "…I don't love to give up my lawful dues in a free country. Though for the matter of that, might often makes right here, as well as in the old country, for what I can see." Later in the same dispute, he says: "There's them living who say, that Nathaniel Bumppo's right to shoot on these hills, is of older date than Marmaduke Temple's right to forbid him." In short, Bumppo—who describes himself as "a plain, unlearned man" who has "never so much as looked into a book"—comes across as a sort of idealized natural man who is in conflict with the forces of civilization. As such, he is a prototype for many characters who follow him in American literature, among them Huckleberry Finn and Billy Budd.

Cooper, in *The Pioneers*, provides a model of manhood in Bumppo, who not only values physical prowess, but exemplifies it. An expert marksman, Natty scorns the methods that the settlers use in killing pigeons, pointing out that "none do it, who know how to knock over a single bird." Later, Natty demonstrates extraordinary strength and agility, as well as courage, when he straps Mohegan on his back and carries him, while guiding Elizabeth and Oliver, out of danger of a forest fire. To develop the theme of the interaction of nature and civilization is that of manhood.

Literary Techniques

The Pioneers, like Cooper's other Leatherstocking Tales, belongs to the genre of historical romance. It is "historical" in the sense that it is set in a previous time period, in this case one that precedes the publication date by some 30 years. It is a "romance" because, rather than trying to present a detailed and realistic picture of people and places, it borrows from the realm of fancy. Natty Bumppo, much like King Arthur and other literary figures who may have helped inspire Cooper's creation of him, is an idealized man whose nobility of character and physical prowess make him larger than life.

Despite such departures, Cooper does make some attempts at an authentic recreation of reality. Anticipating a number of later writers, notably Mark Twain, Cooper uses dialect throughout the book to give a realistic feel to the speech of various characters, including the Frenchman Monsieur Le Quoi and the German Major Frederick Hartmann. Even Natty reveals his lack of education when he uses such nonstandard pronunciations as "sartain" for "certain" and "fa'n" for "fawn," as well as the nonstandard grammatical construction "his moccasins were getting old." Cooper also provides some detailed physical descriptions. Indeed, in his introduction, he announces that the book contains "literal facts" concerning the academy and other buildings that he apparently sketched according to his memory of them in Cooperstown. His depiction of the interior of his boyhood home of Otsego Hall, fictionalized in *The Pioneers* as Judge Temple's residence, is apparently especially realistic.

Bibliography

http://www.uncp.edu/home/canada/work/markport/lit/amnovel/fall2002/02cooper.htm, 2013-02-04.

http://en.wikipedia.org/wiki/James_Fenimore_Cooper, 2013-02-04.

http://www.kirjasto.sci.fi/jfcooper.htm, 2013-02-04.

http://www.poets.org/viewmedia.php/prmMID/23098, 2013-02-04.

Mullane, Janet. *Nineteenth-Century Literary Criticism (Vol. 27)*. Farmington Hills: Cengage Gale, 1990: 122-190.

Toming. *A History of American Literature*. Nanjing: Yilin Press, 2005: 77-83.

常耀信．美国文学简史（第二版）．天津：南开大学出版社，2006: 50-55.

吴伟仁．美国文学史及选读（第 1 册）．北京：外语教学与研究出版社，2011: 104-111.

William Cullen Bryant

His Life and Writing Career

His Life

William Cullen Bryant (1794–1878) stood among the most celebrated figures in the frieze of nineteenth-century America, and was considered to be the first American poet to achieve widespread international fame within the literary tradition of Romanticism. The fame he won as a poet while in his youth remained with him as he entered his eighties, only

Longfellow and Emerson were his rivals in popularity over the course of his life.

Bryant, the second son of Peter Bryant, was born on November 3, 1794, in a log cabin near Cummington, a small village in the Berkshire hills carved from the forest scantly a generation before his birth, in Hampshire County, Massachusetts. Bryant and his family moved to a new home when he was two years old. The William Cullen Bryant Homestead, his boyhood home, is now a museum. Bryant attended Williams College in 1810, but never graduated, then turned instead to the study and practice of law. After just two years at Williams College, he started to study law. In mid-1814, he left the Berkshires for Bridgewater, the area of his family's origins, to join the law office of a congressman whose absences while in Washington required hiring someone to run his practice. Bryant profited not only from the legal experience but also from writing reports for his employer on the politics of his district—an exercise that served as a drill for his later newspaper work and forced him to examine the issues of the day independently of his father's Federalist views. He then began practicing law in nearby Plainfield, walking the seven miles from Cummington every day. Writing poetry could not financially sustain a family. From 1816 to 1825, he practiced law in Great Barrington, Massachusetts, and supplemented his income with such work as service as the town's hog reeve. Distaste for pettifoggery and the sometimes absurd judgments pronounced by the courts gradually drove him to break with the legal profession. In 1821 he met Fanny Fairchild and got married and lived a happy life of matrimony. In 1825 he was hired as editor first by the *New-York Review*, then by the *United States Review* and *Literary Gazette*, and gained a foothold in New York City. But the magazines of that day usually enjoyed only an ephemeral life-span. After two years of fatiguing effort to breathe life into periodicals, he became Assistant Editor of the *New-York Evening Post* under William Coleman, a newspaper founded by Alexander Hamilton that was surviving precariously. Within two years, he was Editor-in-Chief and a part owner. He remained the Editor-in-Chief for half a century (1828–1878). Eventually, the Evening-Post became not only the foundation of his fortune but also the means by which he exercised considerable political power in his city, state, and nation. Death came to him on June 12, 1878. At a public funeral, arranged contrary to his wishes, great crowds pressed in upon his bier. Later, a special train took the body to Roslyn, Long Island, his home for thirty-five years, where he was interred beside his wife. At the graveside, the minister recited excerpts from Bryant's poems about death, and schoolchildren tossed flowers on his coffin. At Bryant's death, all New York City went into mourning for its most respected citizen, and eulogies poured forth as they had for no man of letters since Washington Irving, its native son, had died a generation earlier. The similarity was appropriate: Irving brought international legitimacy to American fiction; Bryant alerted the English-speaking world to an American voice in poetry.

His Writing Career

The shaping of Bryant's mind and personality owed much to his family circumstances in Cummington. He was raised under the influence of two kinds of cultures and philosophies in his family, which affected his creation to a great extent. Bryant's physician father, a liberal Unitarian, and his conservative grandfather, a Calvinist deacon, were strongly supportive of his youthful poetic efforts. On the one hand, there was his mother Sarah and her father Ebenezer Snell. Squire Snell, Bryant's maternal grandfather, was a Federalist in politics and an extreme Calvinist in religion. The boy's grandfather pressed a contrasting worldview on him. As the head of the house and a deacon in the Congregationalist church, Snell studied theological writers and was as intractable in his interpretation of scripture and in his rulings as a local magistrate. He was in the position to carry harsh justice. He believed thrift and industry to be the main duties of man. He taught his grandson to plant potatoes and hoe corn. When the young Bryant was not speedy enough in the field, he would beat him. In prayer services he conducted for his family every morning and every evening, he made certain that religious precepts must be informed to the Bryant children's upbringing. Young Cullen first learned meter and poetry through the hymns of Isaac Watts, and he found an outlet for a love of language by constructing a makeshift pulpit of the parlor furniture from which he delivered sermons in imitation of what he heard at church. Worship stressed death and the power of the devil, and perhaps because of the boy's vulnerability to illness and chronic severe headaches, made him ponder mortality, even at his tender age, and see God's image as cast in a mold of fear and gloom.

On the other hand, William's father, Peter Bryant, who was a well-educated physician and surgeon, influenced the young Bryant greatly. In addition to his practice and public service, Peter Bryant also wrote verse in the manner of Alexander Pope. His library included poems of the late 18th century romantic poets. To the young Bryant, the physical world is two worlds in one: the world of harsh elements such as wind, rain and snow, as his mother and grandfather saw it; and the herbal garden of romantic beauty and healing potential as his father saw it. The duality within the family in part explains why Bryan grew up a Federalist and Calvinist but gradually became a Democrat, a Unitarian, and a romanticist. His sense of deity, as evidenced in his poetry, was often that of a Unitarian. Yet he retained a slight tinge of Puritanism all his life, as is suggested in the stoical moral undertone in his poems.

Compared with his grandfather, the more compelling influence on Cullen's mental development, however, came from his father, a man of curtailed ambitions who aspired to being a citizen of a society well beyond Cummington's horizons. Peter Bryant, like his father before him, had chosen a career in medicine, and he became an early exponent of homeopathy; his passionate preference, however, was for the arts—for music and, particularly, poetry. As an erudite American, he had immersed himself in the ancients, a classical nurture reflected in his admiration for Alexander Pope and the other eighteenth-century British paragons of the Augustan style in poetry. Dr. Bryant also wrote verse, and if his derivative efforts fell short of distinction, they were nonetheless well-turned. When his precocious son began stringing couplets, Dr. Bryant took delighted notice. Although he held the boy to a high standard and was quick to derogate his exercises as doggerel, Cullen accepted his father as an expert mentor and took satisfaction in being treated as an equal. By the age of thirteen, he was seen as a prodigy. The Northampton *Hampshire Gazette* had published several of his poems, including a fifty-four line exhortation to his schoolmates he had drafted three years earlier. Beginning with patriotic invocation of the Revolution and concluding with a charge to "Keep bright mansions ever in our eyes, / Press tow'rds the mark and seize the glorious prize," it rapidly became a standard selection for school recitations in the region. Given his age, if the pose he struck in a poem composed in 1807 was patently absurd—"Ah me! Neglected on the list of fame! / My works unnotic'd, and unknown my name!"—it nonetheless indicated his grand ambitions.

As mentioned above, Bryant developed an interest in poetry early in life. Under his father's tutelage, he emulated Alexander Pope and other Neo-Classic British poets. "The Embargo; or, Sketches of the Times, A Satire," a savage attack on President Thomas Jefferson published in the spring of 1808, reflected Dr. Bryant's Federalist political views. The first edition of this pamphlet quickly sold out—partly because of the publicity earned by the poet's young age—and a second, expanded edition, in which the 244 lines of the first swelled to 420, and, with the addition of other poems and Bryant's translation of Classical verse, its pages tripled, was printed at the start of 1809. This precocious exhibition remained the talk of Boston, not only as a political weapon but also, a reviewer for *The Monthly Anthology* noted, as the earnest of a talent sure "to gain a respectable station on the Parnassus mount, and to reflect credit on the literature of his country." The youth wrote little poetry while preparing to enter Williams College as a sophomore, but upon leaving Williams after a single year and then beginning to read law, he regenerated his passion for poetry through encounter with the English pre-Romantics and, particularly, William Wordsworth.

The prodigy who had written "The Embargo" and imitated the Classical writers was a skillful mimic of a mechanical concept of verse. Beginning in 1810–1811, however, a surge of wholly new influences changed Bryant's understanding of poetry. Chief among these was *Lyrical Ballads*. His father had brought a copy home from Boston, perhaps because, as a devoted student of poetry, he felt obliged to acquaint himself with this boldly different address to its art and subject matter. Peter Bryant was not much impressed, but to his son, it was a revelation. Remembering the encounter many years later, he claimed he heard Nature for the first time speak with a dynamic authenticity: Wordsworth's language suddenly gushed like "a thousand springs." Quite probably, though, Wordsworth's full effect did not hit until some time after Bryant had begun studying law in Worthington. His mentor there, catching him scrutinizing *Lyrical Ballads*, warned against repetition of the offense, and Bryant, fearful of being sent away, steeled himself to obedience for a year. A vow of abstinence for the sake of the law, however, only stoked his desire to test his powers within the new possibilities Wordsworth had shown.

During the same period, Bryant also fell under the sway of the so-called Graveyard Poets. Henry Kirke White, an English poet, virtually forgotten today, had a brief moment of great renown, though less for the merit of his lugubrious verse than for the controversy sparked by an attack on it in *The Monthly Review* and its defense by Robert Southey; White presently achieved martyrdom by dying, at the age of twenty, in 1809. Bryant no doubt felt an affinity with the ill-starred young Scotsman who had eluded his doom as a lawyer only to perish. Another Scotsman, Robert Blair, had an even stronger influence; his enormously popular 1743 poem, "The Grave," had marked a shift in taste and practice from the crisp wit and erudition of the Neoclassic Age to the brooding emotional indulgence that would fuse with subsequent elements of romanticism. The direct language Blair marshals into blank verse pointed the way of Bryant's development; still more attractive was Blair's emphasis on acceptance of death's inevitability and overcoming the fear of extinction.

Mortality crowded Bryant's mind in 1813. Typhus, or a typhus-like illness, besieged the Worthington area that year. Several friends were stricken, but the suffering and death of a particular young woman plunged Bryant into melancholy. In April, his best childhood friend had coaxed Bryant into supplying a poem for his wedding, even though it meant breaking his pledge to abstain from writing verse while studying law. Weeks later, the bride lay dying, and the groom again asked that "your lyre not be silent." When she died in July, Bryant composed the first of his cluster of funereal poetry. The next month, his grandfather Snell, still vigorous despite his advanced years, was found cold in his bed. As the stern Calvinist had based his relationship with his grandson on obedience and respect rather than on love, the old man's death caused no emotional upheaval, but the sudden absence of such a commanding figure seemed to undermine life's earthly justification. The thought that all his youthful ambition for fame was destined to wither in the dismal light of small town litigation and deed registration resonated in this encounter with emptiness.

In December 1815, Bryant noticed a single bird flying on the horizon; the sight moved him enough to write "To a Waterfowl," in which Bryant commemorated the immanent and benevolent presence of God, one of the finest short poems of the English language. In 1817, "Thanatopsis" was published, laying the foundation for his enduring poetic fame.

Starting with "Thanatopsis," he began to concentrate upon his favorite theme: the fragility of human life contrasted against the permanency of nature. The poem deals with the speaker's transition toward an understanding and acceptance of his own impending demise through the intervention of God's agent, the natural world. It is this world that offers comfort to man and influences him for the good. Eight years later, Bryant abandoned the law profession for the position of co-editor of the *New York Review* and *Atheneum Magazine*. This led to a position with the *New York Evening Post* the following year. From 1829 to the end of his life, Bryant maintained full editorship of the paper. The prose writing he engaged in resulted in a diminishing volume and quality of poetry, so that his early poetic achievements, particularly "Thanatopsis," were regarded as his best.

In January 1821 he married Francis Fairchild, the girl for whom he had written "Oh Fairest of the Rural Maids," lifted his sorrow, and a year later, almost to the day, his wife presented him with a daughter, who was given her mother's name. Bryant's literary prospects also brightened. When a rift over succession to the editorship at the *North American Review* led Richard Henry Dana to resign, this dedicated advocate for the "new" Romantic poetry started his own publication, *The Idle Man*; even though the two had not yet met, Dana assigned a high priority to Bryant's participation in the endeavor. (Their correspondence regarding this matter initiated a close friendship that would last for the rest of their lives). "Green River," as yet unpublished though written the previous year, stands well above the rest.

In the spring of 1821, "The Ages" came out. It is a poem of epic scope. A preamble of sorts raises Bryant's familiar questions about the meaning of mortality and obliquely alludes to his father's death—the echoes of "Hymn to Death" are quite distinct—but then, after a transition recognizing change as the way of all nature, the poem chronicles the march of civilization, age by age, to the discovery of the New World and America's realization of history's purpose.

During 1832 to 1878 Bryant published six volumes, *The Fountain* (1842), *The White-Footed Deer* (1844), *The Flood of Years* (1878), *A Forest Hymn* (1860). Another treasure that Bryant left was his poetic translations of Homer's *Iliad* (1870) and *Odyssey* (1871).

Bryant edited the very successful *Picturesque America,* which was published between 1872 and 1874. This two-volume set was lavishly illustrated and described scenic places in the United States and Canada. His "Library of Poetry and Song" (1871–1872), the first great critical anthology, was his last literary effort.

Even though Bryant has achieved the unique position in American literature, it is believed that he has been influenced by the nature poetry of William Wordsworth. The thoroughly Wordsworthian "Winter Scenes" (later re-titled "A Winter Piece") suffers from comparison to its model in tilting much more toward recollection than emotion; that notwithstanding, it is good enough to be mistaken for portions of *The Prelude*, which would not appear in print for another three decades. "A Walk at Sunset," though it fails to realize at the end the extended meaning it has implicitly promised, reveals Bryant's evolving interest in the cycles of civilization, and particularly in the bearing of the Indian past on white American identity. That interest would soon become compelling.

Bryant nevertheless attained a unique American form that explores recognizably native ideas and subjects. Apart from originality of theme, Bryant's poetry is characterized by morality of poetry. In his most famous work, "Thanatopsis," he wrestled with the issue of man's mortality in contrast to the immutability of the natural world. It was a topic to which Bryant would often return, though never with the same mastery exhibited in this early poem. Bryant celebrated the natural scenery of America in his poetry, utilizing it as tangible evidence of the power and beauty of God. In such works as "Inscription for the Entrance to a Wood" and "The Yellow Violet," Bryant portrayed nature as a vital force form which lessons regarding not only man's spirituality, but man's history itself may be learned. "The Poet" reflects Bryant's desire to enlighten the imagination and to enhance the emotions of his audience through an evocation of the beauty of the American landscape. His devotion to the depiction of God through nature was lifelong. With "The Flood of Years," published in 1878, he returned once again to the theme that garnered him poetic fame: man's mortality. Nearing the end of his own life, Bryant counseled his fellow man on how to approach death, resting secure with faith in God's encompassing goodness and hopefulness for the future of all men.

Analysis of and Comment on His Representative Poem

Thanatopsis (1817, 1821)

Contents Summary

"Thanatopsis," if not the best-known American poem abroad before the mid-nineteenth century, certainly ranked near the top of the list, and at home school children were commonly required to recite it from memory. "Thanatopsis" is a meditative poem of eighty-two lines, granting consolation for human mortality through mankind's unity with nature. The poem was started in 1811. It was frequently revised before its first appearance in North American Review in September, 1817, and was enlarged so as to include a new Wordsworthian opening (lines 1–17) and an extended, vaguely religious conclusion (lines 66–81) for its publication in *Poems*, 1821. In the version of 1821, the speaker in the poem changed from Bryant's own "better genius" to "nature."

Themes

The title of the poem means "view of death" or "meditation on death" in Greek. Death is so connecting to the word Thanatopsis that the word itself came from the combination of two Greek words that are "Thanatos," which means "demise or death", and "opsis" that means "vision" or point of view. Therefore, the new word could be defined as "a way of looking at and thinking about death." The poem should be read in the light of both literary tradition and Bryant's own religious background and taken as a bridge over which the young poet moved towards his father's religious liberalism (Deism and Unitarian Church) and towards Wordsworth's nature. Ignoring Christ and Calvinism, in "Thanatopsis" Bryant stoically announced that every man shall go to the grave with his faith (as to what faith the poem does not specify). In the mediation on death, the poet turned from mankind to nature. Thus, Bryant broke with the more rigorous part of his grandfather's, Snells', religion. It is worth emphasizing that in the eyes of Snells and most New Englanders at the time, Unitarians or deists were a Christ-less lot, nothing short of pagans. For that reason, Bryant hid the poem away from his mother while he revised its lines as his father had taught him.

The poem is a wonderful literary work which explores the often controversial questions of death. Within his well-written lines Bryant attempts to show the relationship between the eternal questions of death and the ongoing cycle of nature and life. "Thanatopsis" shows the deep Romantic spirit of Bryant in his youth. In this famous blank verse masterpiece, nature and death are described with a gentle sadness. The image of death is definitely not horrifying, because you will be melted into nature. At first, this "view of death" might seem a cold and terrifying thought. But, as he explains in later poems, the life of man is part of the wonderful life of nature as a whole. The individual soul is not alone but, as he says in *A Forest Hymn*, part of "the soul of this wide universe." Almost all of his poetry expresses his excitement at the idea of being part of something so vast.

Therefore, Bryant used his famous "Thanatopsis" to show his supportive ideas of looking at the positive side of death and the significance of nature in human beings. In the "Thanatopsis," a sixteen-year-old boy had been supporting and expanding his ideas to express his positive sight on death during his introverted walks on the woods. In this poem, Bryant viewed death from a different perspective than anybody else ever did; he was the poem writer who pointed out on the good points of death. He tells the reader "When thoughts / Of the last bitter hour come like a blight… Go forth, under the open sky, and list / To Nature's teachings…" He believes that nature will guide its listener to a better understanding of life cycle, death and rebirth. He told us to closely paying attention to nature as it is all around us. Because of the facts he told, many people were attracted by his poem as it helped each individual to gain a better understanding of life and death. This poem is about death as it offers a peaceful view of death and comfort for the living. William Cullen Bryant shows his views of death in this poem, however, not directly. Bryant views death as part of the return to nature, like death is just another phase of life itself. "Earth, that nourished thee, shall claim / Thy growth, to be resolved to earth again." Bryant is saying that as a person has lived upon the Earth, the Earth will now live upon that person. The person will live on, but in another way. "Surrendering up / Thine individual being, shalt thou go / To mix forever with the elements." What Bryant is trying to say is that the person goes on living in Nature although each part of the person as an individual is gone.

The writer involved nature deeply in this writing as an explanation that after life is done, we return to the earth as we came from it. He says this with,

> Earth, that nourished thee, shall claim / Thy growth, to be resolved to earth again, / And, lost each human trace, surrendering up / Thine individual being, shalt thou go / To mix forever with the elements, / To be a brother to the insensible rock / And to the sluggish clod, which the rude swain / Turns with his share, and treads upon. The oak / Shall send his roots abroad, and pierce thy mold.

"Thanatopsis" also tells the reader that he or she will not go to death alone. Everyone who has ever died will already be there. Everyone who hasn't gone yet will be there eventually. Social class or age does not matter; we all share one thing, and that one thing is death. In that way, we are all equal and death becomes the great equalizer. "Thanatopsis" also provides comfort for the living: "and what if thou withdraw/In silence from the living, and no friend / Take note of thy departure? All that breathe / Will share thy destiny." For those who seemingly have no one in life, they will not be alone in death. No person ever wants a friend or family member to suffer or to be alone, and Bryant tells us that no person will ever be alone. It is much easier to let someone go in this case.

The real beauty of the poem is that it provides comfort to a person no matter what his or her religious beliefs are. If the reader is an agnostic or atheist, the poem views death as just all part of the cycle of Nature—we return to nature. If the reader is Christian, the poem becomes a split between body and soul. The body returns to Nature, and there is no mention of the soul or spirit. The spirit can be seen as going anywhere because there is no mention of it. So this poem is absolutely able to be translated into Christianity. In fact, Bryant purposely rejected Puritanism in this poem in favor of a more open and accepting Unitarianism. If the reader is Buddhist, the return to Nature can be seen as reincarnation. Therefore the poem is in sync with many different religions.

Literary Techniques

The poetic form that Bryant uses for "Thanatopsis" is blank verse (unrhymed iambic pentameter lines). In the poem, Bryant also uses personification and metaphor quite a bit when referring to some things in nature, and he borrowed some biblical references well. He often tries to use the inversion, a rearrangement of the usual word order in sentences in the poem.

Bibliography

http://andiabeng-pustakaapa.blogspot.com/2011/12/assignment-connection-between-english.html, 2013-02-04.

http://www.poetryfoundation.org/bio/william-cullen-bryant, 2013-02-04.

http://voices.yahoo.com/discussion-thanatopsis-william-cullen-bryant-703319.html, 2013-02-04.

Person, James. *Nineteenth-Century Literary Criticism Vol. 46.* Farmington Hills: Cengage Gale, 1996: 1-57.

Toming. *A History of American Literature*. Nanjing: Yilin Press, 2005: 83-85.

吴伟仁 . 美国文学史及选读（第 1 册）. 北京：外语教学与研究出版社，2011: 119-126.

Edgar Allan Poe

His Life and Writing Career

His Life

Edgar Allan Poe (1809–1849) is known as an American poet, short story writer, editor and literary critic, but most famous as the earliest American practitioners of the short story, especially tales of the mysterious and macabre. He is also considered the inventor of the detective fiction genre in the world. The literary merits of Poe's writings have been debated since his death, but many major American and European writers have professed their artistic debt to him. Now his works have remained popular, and he has been held among the greatest poets and the most popular of American authors due to his great literary success.

Edgar Allan Poe was born in Boston on January 19, 1809, the second of three children. His parents were itinerant actors who wandered from one place to another along the East Coast. Following the sudden disappearance of his father and the subsequent death of his mother, Poe was orphaned at the age of two. Also orphaned were his older brother William Henry and his half-sister Rosalie. He was taken in as a foster-child by a well-to-do Richmond merchant John Allan in 1812 and spent most of his childhood in Virginia and England. The other children were less lucky. Poe's brother William died young and his sister Rosalie later became insane. Never legally adopted, Poe took Allan's name for his middle name. His foster mother Mrs. Allan loved him very much partly because of her inability to give birth and unfaithfulness of her husband. His foster father Mr. Allan was a wealthy tobacco merchant and Poe had all the advantages of a luxurious upbringing in his early days. Poe received much of his early schooling in England and showed his poetic talent when he was still very young. At the age of 5 he could recite passages of English poetry. In 1820, he came back to America with the Allans and studied in some schools in Richmond, Virginia. In 1826, he attended Virginia University, but the quit after one year because he was in debt from gambling and Mr. Allan withdrew his financial support although he had established obvious academic competence. This led to a violent quarrel with Mr. Allan, who refused to pay the debts. Allan later disowned him. During his stay at the university, Poe composed some tales, but little is known of his apprentice works.

In 1827, after a serious quarrel with Mr. Allan, he ran away from home and went to Baltimore and then to Boston to make his own way in the world. The same year at his own expense, his first collection of poems, *Tamerlane and Other Poems* (1827), was published anonymously in Boston. Shortly afterward Poe enlisted in the U.S. Army under the name of Edgar A. Perry and served a two-year term. He became a regimental sergeant major in the army. Poe was partially reconciled with Mr. Allan in March 1829 shortly after Mrs. Allan's death. The year he brought out second volume of poetry entitled *Aaraaf, Tamerlane, and Minor Poems*. There had been additions to the volume issued at Boston, two years before. *Al Aaraaf*, a vague and mystical poem, the longest of Poe's compositions, was added to the first collection. It reflects the influence of Shelley, as the earlier poem, *Tamerlane*, suggests the influence of Byron. In 1830, Poe was admitted to the U.S. Military Academy in West Point through the influence of his grandfather and Mr. Allan although he was beyond the limit age for admission. However, the discipline at West Point proved to be too harsh for Poe's nature. Poe provoked a dismissal by deliberate neglect of duties eight months later because he found life in the army was not suited to his interests and genius in literature. His foster father disowned him permanently. From then on, Poe determined, without any other choice, to be dependent on his pen for his living. In 1831, Poe published his third book *Poems* in New York, which included some of his best poems: *To Helen*, *Israfel*, *The City in the Sea*, *Lenore*, and *The Valley of Unrest*. Already his verse had acquired its haunting music—already found its note of melancholy. From 1831 to 1835 Poe lived in Baltimore with his aunt and her daughter, Virginia Clemm, who became his wife in 1836 when she was only 13. In 1832 five of Poe's short stories were published in the *Philadelphia Saturday Courier*. They were exclusively comic, satiric tales. One of his best tales, "MS. Found in a Bottle," won first prize in a short story contest run by *Baltimore Saturday Visitor* in 1833. From 1835 to his death in 1849, Poe was editor of a number of prominent periodicals, such as the *Southern Literary Messenger* in Richmond (1835–1837), *Burton's Gentleman's Magazine* in Philadelphia (1839–1840), and *Graham's Magazine* (1842–1843). He began to build a national reputation as a writer and critic, but he was a sarcastic, virulent writer and critic of new novels and poems that had been published by American writers. Meanwhile he never stopped his own literary creation. In 1838 he published his one full-length novel, *The Narrative of Arthur Gordon Pym*. His two volumes *Tales of the Grotesque and Arabesque* appeared in 1840 and 1843, which included the famous "The Fall of the House of Usher." The tale, "The Murders in the Rue Morgue" (1841), an ingenious detective story, became the ancestor of the genre, influencing, among others, Conan Doyle. In 1845, Poe moved to New York again and published his major volume of his poems: *The Raven and other Poems*. This marked the climax of Poe's literary career. His poem, "The Raven" (1845), was an immediate success and has remained one of his most enduring works. His poem "Israfel" and his critical essay "The Philosophy of Composition" were also influential. His *Tales* appeared in New York and London, but did not sell well.

Poe's literary output (some 70 short stories and a dozen poems) is small, but it is immensely interesting and influential as a literary inheritance. Yet his literary success and republication as critic never brought him wealth. He was poor all his life. The death of his wife in 1847 left him inconsolable and bitterer with life than even. Then his erratic temperament, his poverty, and his frustrations caused him to lose control of himself. He drank heavily and became addicted to the use of opium. Poe suffered from bouts of depression and madness, and he attempted suicide in 1848. He spent his last years in hack works, lecturing, in association with feminine "literati" of New York, and with much drunkenness. Two more years of loneliness, poverty, intoxication, and illness spoil his health. On October 6, 1849 he was found delirious condition on the streets of Baltimore and taken to a nearby hospital. There he died the following day at the age of 40.

His Writing Career

Poe's works, which include fiction, legend, Gothic tales, poetry, and critical articles, are directed toward universal human response, thus the passage of time and ages can hardly change their values.

Poe enters a new field of fiction, of which he may be regarded as the discoverer; this is the story in which a mystery is apparently solved by analysis and reason. Their appeal is to the reasoning faculty rather than to the emotions. The modern detective story is our present popular example of the type. The representation of a mystery the solution of which is to follow is always fascinating, and Poe's dominion over his reader is nowhere more complete than in these tales. That the romancer, having first built up his mystery, is obviously only retracing his own steps in the working out of its solution, does not at all affect the interest of his story; for here his art is strong enough to produce the illusion that the reader is watching the first unraveling of the plot. It was in 1841 that Poe's masterpiece in this kind of fiction, *The Murders in the Rue Morgue*, appeared. This was followed by another narrative, *The Mystery of Marie Roget*, in which the author applied his method in the study of an actual murder mystery which occurred in New York. *The Gold Bug*, the third in this group of realistic narratives, was published in 1843. This is the most popular one of all his tales and also brought its writer a second one-hundred-dollar prize.

Many of Poe's tales are distinguished by the author's unique grotesque inventiveness in addition to his superb plot construction. Death, horrible and ghastly pestilence and dissolution, the awakening of the dead, the awakening of those prematurely buried: these are the instruments of horrible suggestiveness which are here employed. It is no wonder that one's flesh creeps as he reads—that was in the design. Such stories include his longest piece of fiction, *The Narrative of Arthur Gordon Pym* (1838). It inspired, perhaps, by the popular success of Cooper's romances of the sea, is as realistic in its employment of commonplace and minute details as any of the narratives of Defoe, the first great master of realism in fiction. Poe's imaginative power is exhibited in vivid pictures of murder, mutiny, shipwreck, and starvation, which are gruesome enough, and sometimes become so morbid as to be offensive to sound taste; but in the conclusion of the tale his poetic imagination asserts itself in wonderful descriptions of an unknown land and of the mysterious white sea of the Antarctic. Here are to be included, also, the horrible story of "The Black Cat," "The Hell-Tale Heart," and "Thou art the Man." But Poe's most effective tales are those which are carefully, elaborately designed to produce a vivid effect on the reader's mind. Foremost among these is the remarkable fantasy "The Fall of the House of Usher," a masterpiece of literary art, wherein every sentence is significant and almost every word a contribution to the dismal effect. Here belongs, also, "The Masque of the Red Death," with its weird use of colors, its atmosphere of revelry invaded by the horror of the plague. "Ligeia," a fantasy of transmigration, "The Cask of Amontillado," a study in revenge, and "Hop-Frog," in which the same theme again appears, grotesquely treated, fall in the same group. *The Pit and the Pendulum* (1842), is a spine-tingling tale of cruelty and torture; *The Tell-Tale Heart* (1843), in which a maniacal murderer is subconsciously haunted into confessing his guilt; "The Cask of Amontillado" (1846), an eerie tale of revenge.

Poe's poetry is very small in proportion to his total work, but truthfully embodies his conviction that the function of poetry is to create a mood in which the soul soars toward supernal beauty. Among Poe's poetic output, about a dozen poems are remarkable for their flawless literary construction and for their haunting themes and meters. In "The Raven" (1845), for example, the narrator is overwhelmed by melancholy and omens of death. Poe's extraordinary manipulation of rhythm and sound is particularly evident in "The Bells" (1849), a poem that seems to echo with the chiming of metallic instruments, and "The Sleeper" (1831), which reproduces the state of drowsiness. "Lenore" (1831) and "Annabel Lee" (1849) are verse lamentations on the death of a beautiful young woman.

Poe had little of the sense of humor. He wrote, however, a number of extravaganzas with intent to make them humorous. In "The Devil in the Belfry" (1839), he succeeded fairly. Another phase of his fancy is discovered in two beautiful landscape pictures, masterpieces of natural description, "The Domain of Arnheim and Landor's Cottage" (1846), pure idealizations of romantic scenery worthy of a poet's dream.

Poe insists that the creation of the work of art requires the utmost concentration and unity, as well as the most scrupulous use of words. Many of Poe's conceptions have become a part of the tradition of American literature and its criticism, moreover, they have been exerting a great and enduring influence upon world literature, especially that of France and European symbolism, in their demand for the intellectual analysis and controlled perception of emotional consciousness.

His contribution to American literature lies mainly in two fields. On short stories, his theories are basically expressed in "Letter to B—," and "Review of Nathaniel Hawthorne's Twice-Told Tales." Poe's theories for the short story are equally simple and clear. Poe is the first person in American literature who defined the genre, and emphasized "brevity" and "unity" of impression. In his definition, he formalized the technique of the short story in pursuit of the totality of effect through compression, immediacy, verisimilitude, and finality. The "unity" is the all-important element, by which Poe meant "totality" or "oneness" of impression. He stressed brevity because he thought that unity of impression would be blurred and lost in the mass of details inevitable in a long story.

According to Poe, in almost all classes of composition, the unity of effect or impression is a point of the greatest importance. And this unity can only be thoroughly preserved in productions that can be read at one sitting. The very initial sentence should tend to the out-bringing of this effect. The tendency of every word written in the whole composition, direct or indirect, is to the one pre-established design. A tale should reveal some logical truth and should end with the last sentence, leaving a sense of finality. The composition written in this way will leave in the mind of readers with a sense of the fullest satisfaction.

He also invented the story of detection, and developed a new fiction of psychological analysis. The typical Poe story is, in terms of its action, an allegory of dream-experience, since the action almost always occurs in imagination, the characters are principles of faculties of Poe's divided nature in stead of traditional distinct personalities, the process of the action correspond to the successive states of a mind moving into sleep, and eventually the end of the action is no other than the end of the dream. A best example may be seen in "The Fall of the House Usher."

In poetry, Poe's theories are best elucidated in his "The Philosophy of Composition" (1846) and "The Poetic Principle" (1850). These two essays alone suffice to give one a full understanding of Poe's critical views on the writing of poetry. He said a poem should reasonably short, readable at one sitting. Poe's poetry, which is very small in proportion to his total work, truthfully embodies his conviction that the function of poetry is not to summarize and interpret earthly experience, but to create a mood in which the soul soars toward supernal beauty. As a result of these views, in much of his poetry, the effect Poe most aimed for was beauty and melancholy. "The Raven" demonstrated Poe's theories well in all these respects.

Poe's great contribution offers a set of formulated principles in relation to the creation of American literature, and the creation of the work of art, moreover, to the criticism of literature. In a sense, Poe is considered to be America's first significant literary critic or, at least, the first major writer in America to write seriously about criticism, about the theory of composition, and about the principles of creative art. Poe emphasis upon the value of art, form, and unity played an active role in the development of the analytical approach, a method typical of modern criticism, different from almost all his contemporary romantic critics, who tended to manifest in their criticism excessive appreciative sympathy, moralism and a narrow provincialism.

Poe is the most controversial and misunderstood literary figure in American history. He was defamed by his literary executor Rufus Griswold. Rufus painted him as a Bohemian, depraved and demonic, a villain with no virtue at all. Because of Rufus' defamation and Poe's own scathing criticism of some important writers, he was placed in a very unfavorable light.

Ironically, it was in Europe that Poe enjoyed respect and welcome. Swinburne, Shaw, Lawrence and Auden all admired and spoke highly of him. Especially in France, where Poe's reputation was first made, he was elevated to the status of a literary deity.

Charles, Stephane Marllarme and Valery all paid their homage to Poe. All this filtered back to America and Poe began to receive his reputation in his motherland. In the 20th century, T. S. Eliot proclaimed Poe a critic of the first rank and since then, Poe has been spoken of in loftier and loftier terms.

Poe's position in the history of American literature seems more secure now than in 19th century, when some of his contemporary leading men of letters held a low estimation of him. The greatest difference between Poe and his contemporaries perhaps lies in that Poe insists on the primary importance of the work of art itself, while others follow the romantic stress on the expression of the personality of the artist. His emphasis upon the rational in art, and upon economy and harmony as essential characteristics of art, along with his inventive formation of the new short story and a new fiction of psychological analysis, as well as his discipline of analytical criticism, enable him to stand as one of the really great creative forces in American literature. On the other hand, Poe's conception of the form of a literary work is classical, or rather somewhat mathematical, as if the work of art must be shaped deliberately by fixed principles outside itself. Likewise, his traditional style sometimes seems excessively rational, and lacks the inventiveness that he displays in his literary conceptions, thus it incidentally fails to manifest Poe's original ideas with appropriate effect.

Analyses of and Comments on His Representative Works

The Raven (1845)

Plot Summary

"The Raven" is Edgar Allan Poe's classic narrative poem, which was first published in January 1845. The poem brought Poe national fame immediately and turned him into a national celebrity. Between 1845 and 1849 several critics called it the best American poem ever written. The success of the poem earns Poe the nickname "The Raven." More than one hundred and sixty years after Poe's death, "The Raven" is alive and well.

The 108-line, 18-verse poem tells of a talking raven's mysterious visit to a distraught lover, the narrator, tracing the man's slow descent into madness. The narrator is, often identified as a young student, lamenting the loss of his love, Lenore. Sitting on a bust of Pallas Athena, goddess of wisdom, the raven seems to further instigate his distress with its constant repetition of the word "Nevermore." The poem ends with the raven still sitting on his spot on the bust. The poem is comprised of a two-part structure. In the first half of the poem, stanzas one through nine. The young lover wrestles with his anguish by immersing himself in studious pursuits. But by stanza ten, and throughout the remainder of the poem, he yields to the emotional trauma of his loss and slips into the abyss of madness. A sense of melancholy over the death of a beloved beautiful young woman pervades the whole poem: the portrayal of a young man grieving for his lost Lenore, his grief being turned to madness under the steady one-word repetition of the talking bird introduced right at the beginning of the poem. After he sees the bird, its response—or its imagined one—"nevermore"—keeps breaking upon the young man's psychic wound ruthlessly and ceaselessly as do the waves on the sea shore until his depression reaches its breaking point.

Themes

Poe wrote the poem as a narrative, without intentionally creating an allegory or falling into didacticism. The narrator experiences a perverse conflict between desire to forget and desire to remember. He seems to get some pleasure from focusing on loss. The narrator assumes that the word "Nevermore" is the raven's "only stock and store," and, yet, he continues to ask it questions, knowing what the answer will be. His questions, then, are purposely self-deprecating and further incite his feelings of loss. Although Poe contends that the process of composition of the poem was ultra-rational, the motive for the poem seems to have been unreasoning sorrow. The impetus for the poem doubtless arose from Poe's loss of his mother and of others whom he had loved: the death of his mother, Eliza Arnold Poe; the death of his brother Henry; the death of surrogate mother Jane Stith Stanard; the termination of his romance with young Elmira Royster; the death of foster mother Frances Allan; the illness of his wife Virginia Clemm. As many of Poe's characters in his poems and stories are associated with some personalities who were involved with his life, the "lost Lenore" is also a central experience in Poe's life. Lenore is often identified as Miss Royster, Poe's youthful sweetheart, or as Virginia Clemm, his wife.

Literary Techniques

In "The Poetic Principle," Poe defined true poetry as "the rhythmical creation of beauty," a definition giving unexampled emphasis upon the importance of the rhythmical or musical element in poetry. Poe repeatedly explains that only in music can man come closest to attaining what he calls "supernal beauty." In his "The Philosophy of Composition," Poe described the planning and revealed some of the techniques he utilized in the writing of his famous poem, "The Raven." Poe's intention was to show the importance of conscious effort, rather than intuitive inspiration, in the creation of a work of art. He focused on the length, the province, and the tone of the intended poem.

The poem is often noted for its musicality, stylized language, and supernatural atmosphere. The raven, an ominous symbol, was used consciously to convey bitterness, distress, and desperation. The poem is characterized by its dramatic variation of tone, which starts from mournfulness, and then progresses to delight, and eventually to madness under the raven's steady repetition of "Nevermore." The theme is the death of a beautiful lady; the tone is melancholy, the atmosphere is horrible. The raven's repetition "nevermore" reflects a basic anapestic rhythm that becomes stronger and pronounced more like a drumbeat as the poem reaches its emotional climax.

The poem is written with remarkable poetic technique. The first line of the poem contains alliteration of w in "while," "weak," and "weary" to produce the effect of unsteadiness. It also sets the poem's rhythmical pattern and provides the first example of the use of internal rhyme in "dreary" and "weary." Then the speaker tells of becoming more tired and beginning to doze but being wakened by a sound that he assumes is a quite knock on the door. Internal rhymes of "napping," "tapping," and "rapping" along with repetition of these last two words, create a musical effect. This effect is also produced by alliteration of n. Those sound devices and the steady rhythm of these lines are almost hypnotic.

"The Raven" was first attributed to Poe in print in the *New York Evening Mirror* on January 29, 1845. Its publication made Poe widely popular in his lifetime, though it did not bring him significant financial success. Soon reprinted, imitated, parodied, and illustrated, critical opinion is divided as to the poem's status, though it remains one of the most famous poems ever written. The reputation of "The Raven" is evident in its frequent translations, including the French, the Czech, the Hungarian, the Romanian, the Polish, the Croatian, the Portuguese, and the Chinese. "The Raven" has influenced many modern works, including Walt Whitman's "Out of the Cradle Endlessly Rocking," Vladimir Nabokov's *Lolita*, Bernard Malamud's "The Jewbird" and Ray Bradbury's "The Parrot Who Knew Papa." The poem is additionally referenced throughout popular culture in films, television, music and more.

The Fall of the House of Usher (1839)

Plot Summary

"The Fall of the House of Usher" is generally regarded as Poe's masterpiece of the short story genre, or to be more specific, the Gothic tale, first published widely in the September 1839 issue of *Burton's Gentleman's Magazine*. It was slightly revised in 1840 for the collection *Tales of the Grotesque and Arabesque*. It contains within it the poem "The Haunted Palace," which had earlier been published separately in the April 1839 issue of the *Baltimore Museum* magazine.

"The Fall of the House of Usher" opens with the unnamed narrator arriving at the crumbling mansion of his friend, Roderick Usher, trying to dispel Roderick's gloom. Although his twin sister, Madeline, has been placed in the family vault dead before being permanently buried, Roderick still holds a firm belief that she lives. Then on a stormy night, the sister breaks out of her coffin and dies in the embrace of her brother, who then also dies. The house itself splits asunder and sinks into the tarn. The tale has inspired several film adaptations.

Themes

"The Fall of the House of Usher" shows Poe's ability to create an emotional tone in his work, specifically feelings of fear, doom, and guilt. Roderick Usher is very much a Poe character. What drives Roderick crazy is not immediately clear. Roderick and his sister Madeline are twins. It seems that they are two halves of one whole person. She represented the mental aspect of their lives, but her body was failing her. He, on the other hand, was the physical aspect; his body was healthy, but he was somewhat "mentally ill." He tries to destroy his twin sister with whom he may have committed incest. Her removal might free him from his emotional and physical stress as well as his life, for he knows that one half cannot live without the other. A person must have both the mental and physical aspects of life to survive. As a result, every word, every image, and every description in the story is chosen with the central idea in mind of creating a sense of abject terror and fear within both the narrator and the reader. The destructive, incestuous joining may be responsible for the tragedy of the mind. The central theme of the tale is terror that arises from the complexity and multiplicity of forces that shape human destiny. Dreadful, horrifying events result not from a single, uncomplicated circumstance but from a collision and intermingling of manifold, complex circumstances. In Poe's story, the reasons for the ruin of the House of Usher can explore such themes as evil, isolation, failure to adapt, madness, mystery, and strange phenomena.

Literary Techniques

"The Fall of the House of Usher" is considered to be the masterpiece of American gothic literature. As in many of his tales, Poe borrows much from the Gothic tradition: a haunted house, dreary landscape, mysterious sickness, and doubled personality. The atmosphere is horror. The ancient decaying castle is eerie and moldy and the surrounding moat seems stagnant. The first five paragraphs of the story are devoted to creating a Gothic mood: outside the castle, a storm is ranging and inside the castle, there are mysterious rooms where windows suddenly whisk open, blowing out candles; one hears creaking and moaning sounds and sees the living corpse of Lady Madeline. These are all basic Gothic effects that can be found in any modern horror film, any ghost movie. For all its easily identifiable Gothic elements, however, part of the terror of this story is its vagueness. The story features numerous allusions to other works of literature, including the poems "The Haunted Palace" and "Mad Trist" by Sir Launcelot Canning. Poe composed them himself and then fictitiously attributed them to other sources. Both poems parallel and thus predict the plot line of "The Fall of the House of Usher." The story begins without complete explanation of the narrator's motives for arriving at the house of Usher, and this ambiguity sets the tone for a plot that continually blurs the real and the fantastic. The House of Usher, itself doubly referring both to the actual structure and the family, plays a significant role in the story. The narrator introduces the house to the reader with a humanized description: its windows are described as "eye-like" twice in the first paragraph. The fissure that develops in its side is symbolic of the decay of the Usher family. This connection was emphasized in Roderick's poem "The Haunted Palace" which seems to be a direct reference to the house that foreshadows doom. The collapse of the house is symbolic of the ultimate annihilation of the Usher.

In fact, the story is also considered the best example of Poe's "totality," where every element and detail is related and relevant. At the very beginning, Poe deliberately uses a long periodic sentence to produce an atmosphere of "melancholy" and his "pre-established" design of the story. At the end of the story, a loaded sentence fits his standard of "finality." What's more, human psychological collapse is combined with the physical collapse of the house. Everything is in a state of decay. The house is mossy and each stone is decaying; the inside is falling apart as well. The twins are dying, and everything has a gloomy atmosphere. It exemplifies perfectly Poe's principle of composition that states that everything in the story must contribute to a single unified effect.

Scholars speculate that Poe, who was an influence on Herman Melville, inspired the character of Ahab in Melville's novel *Moby-Dick*.

Bibliography

http://en.wikipedia.org/wiki/The_Fall_of_the_House_of_Usher, 2013-02-04.

http://www.sparknotes.com/lit/poestories/section3.rhtml, 2013-02-04.

http://answers.yahoo.com/question/index?qid=20081102132903AA3C84T, 2013-02-04.

宋元康．美国文学导读．昆明：云南大学出版社，2007: 75-81, 86-88.

王卓，李权文．美国文学史．武汉：华中师范大学出版社，2010: 105-110.

吴瑾瑾．美国文学史．北京：经济科学出版社，2008: 142-144, 148-150, 155.

曹曼．美国文学教程．武汉：武汉大学出版社，2007: 83-85.

何木英，杜平．美国文学简史与作品选读．成都：四川大学出版社，2004: 71-74, 79.

常耀信 . 美国文学简史（第二版修订本）. 天津：南开大学出版社，2003: 104-108.
胡荫桐，刘树森 . 美国文学教程 . 天津：南开大学出版社，2003: 127-131, 138.
胡荫桐 . 美国文学新编 . 北京：外语教学与研究出版社，2001: 105-106, 115-116.

Ralph Waldo Emerson

His Life and Writing Career

His Life

Ralph Waldo Emerson (1803–1882), American essayist, philosopher, and poet of the mid-19th century, was the founder and leader of the American Transcendental movement. His poems, orations, and especially his essays have become landmarks in the development of American literary and intellectual history.

Born in Boston on May 25, 1803, Emerson was the descendant of a long line of New England clergymen. His paternal grandfather built the Old Manse of Concord and was a minister of Harvard College. His father, William Emerson, was minister of the First Church (Unitarian) of Boston. As most of his ancestors were clergymen, Emerson initially seemed destined to continue the ministerial line of his family. However, his father died when Emerson was only eight years old, leaving his wife to face poverty and to educate their five sons. Then he experienced what some critics have termed "genteel poverty." With the efforts of his mother and the help of his relatives, Emerson never failed to receive formal education, first at Boston Latin School, at the Latin School in Concord, and then at Harvard College. In Harvard, he underwent a spiritual "odyssey." The liberal atmosphere of the college made him reconsider his Calvinist belief with which he was brought up. Rejecting such Calvinist tenets as total depravity, unconditional election, limited atonement, God's irresistible grace, and the perseverance of the saints, he embraced the liberal Christianity of Unitarianism. During his Harvard days, Emerson began keeping journals, a practice he continued throughout his life. Those journals became a source of his later lecturers, essays, poetry and books. Graduated from Harvard College in 1821, Emerson taught in school sporadically from 1821 to 1826. After an interlude of school teaching, he entered the Harvard Divinity School and fulfilled the expectations of family members as minister of the Second Church (Unitarian) of Boston in 1829. The same year he married the 17 years old Ellen Louisa Tucker, whose untimely death less than two years deeply grieved him throughout his life. The personal tragedy of the sudden death of his wife probably disturbed Emerson's religious career. Emerson was ardent at first in his service in religion, but gradually grew skeptical of the beliefs of the church. Finding the rationality of Unitarianism intolerable, he finally left the ministry in 1832. He did not become an atheist, but devoted himself to another sort of religion, if one may say so, that could be described as a personal and non-institutional form of faith, a faith that needed no church and no ministers. It was during the period when he stood in conflict with the Church that his ideas of self-reliance and general divinity of man came into being.

On Christmas Day, 1832, he left the United States for a tour of Europe. He stayed for some time in England, where he met and made friends with Taylor Coleridge, Thomas Carlyle and William Wordsworth, and became familiar with the fashionable European ideas of the time, essentially Romanticism and German idealism. He first landed in Malta in early February and enthusiastically worked his way north through Italy, Switzerland, France, England, and Scotland. Eager to meet great men, he sought out Walter Savage Landor in Florence, saw Lafayette, and Wordsworth at Rydal Mount. His meeting with Carlyle marked the beginning of a lifelong friendship, with whom he kept up a correspondence for half a century. Through his acquaintance with these men he became closely involved with German idealism and Transcendentalism. Emerson benefited a great deal from his European travel, which prepared for and initiated his new career as a lecturer.

Returning to America in the fall of 1833, Emerson settled in Concord, Massachusetts, remarried and began a career of teaching, lecturing and writing. In 1836, with a remarkable circle of writers such as Thoreau, Bronson Alcott, and Margaret Fuller, he formed an informal Transcendental Club, talking about literature, philosophy, and moral matters. He frequently contributed poems and essays to their club's journal, *The Dial*, to explain their ideas. For a while ideas like Emerson's were up in the air and regarded by some people as "crazy." The epithet "Transcendentalist" was rather derogatory when it first came into circulation, meaning one whose feet did not touch ground. Although he left his ministry, Emerson never stopped "preaching," not at the pulpit, of course, but in the lecture-room. He was no longer to be a sometime minister and amateur literatus but a professional lecturer and writer committed to the free expression and dissemination of new ideas. He was enjoying success as a lecturer, with "The Philosophy of History" series in the winter of 1836–1837 followed the next year by "Human Culture" and in 1838–1839 by "Human Life." These speeches were based on material in his journals, a collection of observations and notes that he had begun while a student at Harvard. Though the country fell into deep economic depression in 1837, Emerson had the good fortune to receive the second installment of the Tucker estate in July of that year, bringing his invested capital to around 22,000 US dollars. And the unofficial manifesto for the Club was *Nature* (1836), Emerson's first little book, which epitomized the essence of his philosophy of transcendentalism, his theories of symbolism, correspondence, and idealism as well as his unshakable belief in the progress of man and society. This idealist doctrine opposed the popular materialist and Calvinist views of life and at the same time voiced a plea for freedom of the individual from artificial restrains.

Waldo, the first son of Emerson and his second wife, was born shortly after *Nature* made its appearance. Emerson had a new vocation, a family, and the expectation of about 1,200 US dollars in annual income from the settlement of his first wife's estate. Yet misfortune came again unexpectedly. Emerson lost his brother Edward to tuberculosis in the fall of 1834, and his especially beloved youngest brother, Charles Chauncy, followed the same grim path in May, 1836, leading Emerson to feel that his life entered another "gloomy epoch." And indeed, a year later, his lungs also faced the threat of severe ill-health. He reviewed his eventful years in his lecture "The Protest" on January 16, 1839, and four days later preached his last sermon at Concord. Emerson's first daughter was born at this time. Named Ellen Tucker, after his first wife, she never married and served as her father's guide and support in old age.

In the summer of 1841, Emerson went to Waterville College in Maine to deliver one of his most intense and orphic orations, "The Method of Nature," proclaiming ecstasy and metamorphosis as the ruling principles of the universe. Emerson's second daughter, Edith, was born in November, and one month later, on December 23, he expounded his "new views" to a Boston audience in "The Transcendentalist."

Among his speeches, "The American Scholar" and "Address at Divinity College" made him famous. On August 31, 1837, Emerson delivered his famous speech, "The American Scholar," at the Phi Beta Kappa society of Harvard College, this address having been considered America's declaration of intellectual independence, in which Emerson, though not rejecting the past, raised the need for original thinking and for fresh examination of the past and the present. It is also important and popular in expressing the practical aspects of Transcendentalism. In this speech, Emerson called on American writers to write about America in an American way instead of simply imitating foreign things. He prodded the students to become more confident in their abilities and to take pride in native Americanism. He dealt with the scholar in the essay not as a student, or a researcher, but as a "Man thinking" to acquire manhood. A second address commonly referred to as the "Address at Divinity College," delivered on July 15, 1838 at the graduation ceremony of Harvard Divinity College, which aroused considerable controversy because it attacked formal religion and argued for self-reliance and intuitive spiritual experience. The main theme of the lecture is that truth cannot be presented as doctrines or creeds. Emerson argued that moral intuition is a better guide to the moral sentiment than religious doctrine, and truth is only attained through intuition rather than by second-hand experience. This means denial of any church authority and the legitimacy of its right to interpret the Holy Bible and set up religious doctrines. He was reviled as a heretic and was probably relieved to get out of town about a week later, traveling to Dartmouth to deliver an oration later entitled "Literary Ethics." His own spirits were deeply affected by the storm this incident caused, and there followed a period of intense self-examination and reflection. The consequence of the staunch challenge against traditional Christian religion and church aroused such indignation that he was not invited to Harvard again until 1866, when the college granted him an honorary degree.

During the period from 1836 to 1856 the bulk of his important work were published. From this time onward, although his significance and influence had been internationally recognized, his lofty intellect seemed to decline. Though his last years was marked by a decline in his mental powers, his literary reputation continued to spread. He died in Concord on April 27, 1882.

His Writing Career

The first major work of Emerson, *Nature* was published in 1836, an important event for the development of the intellectual movement which later came to be known as Transcendentalism. Based on Emerson's early lectures, *Nature* expresses the main principles of Transcendentalism. Many of his published works after *Nature* frequently return to and continue to elaborate on the groundwork originally established in *Nature* while also demonstrate the constant evolution of Emerson's view and ideas. Following the appearance of *Nature*, his first *Essays* (1841), his second *Essays* (1844), *Poems* (1847), *Representative Men* (1850), and *English Traits* (1856) were published. With these works and his frequent lectures, Emerson manifested his basic ideas to the public, and clearly defined his intellectual position in the American society of the age. After 1856 Emerson published few works of importance, the only one worthy of mention was *The Conduct of Life* (1860). Emerson lived an active life and continued to write and lecture into his seventies, coming to be regarded as the "Sage of Concord." He made a long trip through the sites of ancient western civilization in Egypt, Greece and Italy. In addition, he traveled far and wide in the United States, and Canada and England, taught and spread his Transcendentalist doctrine. During his lifetime he was considered one of the two or three best writers in America, and certainly the most influential among his contemporaries. Thoreau, Whitman, Emily Dickinson, and many others were indebted to him in varying degrees; Hawthorne and Melville, reacting to his doctrine of optimism, benefited in their ways from Emersonianism. His influence extended beyond his own century. Robert Frost and Wallace Stevens were among the authors of the present century responsive to his philosophy.

Emerson is generally known as an essayist. During all his life he worked steadily at a succession of essays, usually derived from his journals or lectures he had already given, thus the style of his essays is usually casual and provocative. *Nature* did not establish him as an important American writer. His lasting reputation began only with the publication of *Essays* (1841). Many of his famous essays are included in *Essays*, which convey the best of his philosophical discussions and transcendental pursuits, such as "The American Scholar," "History," "Self-Reliance," "Compensation," "Spiritual Laws," "Love," "Friendship," "Prudence," "Heroism," "The Over Soul," "Circles," "Intellect," and "Art." The second collection of Emerson's essays, *Essays: Second Series* (1844), including "The Poet," "Manners," and "Character," demonstrated even more thoroughly than the first that Emerson's intellect had sharpened in the years since *Nature*. In it Emerson tempered the optimism of the first volume of essays, placing less emphasis on the self and acknowledging the limitations of real life. *The Poet* and *Experience* are examples, the former a reflection upon the aesthetic problems in terms of the present state of literature in America and the latter a discussion about the conflict between ideal and ordinary life. From 1845 to 1847 he delivered a series of lectures published as *Representative Men* (1850), which contains essays on such figures as Greek philosopher Plato, Swedish philosopher Emanuel Swedenborg, and French writer Michel Eyquem de Montaigne. After a second trip to England in 1847, he gave another series of lectures later published as *English Traits* (1856), a study of English society. His late lecture tours are contained in *The Conduct of Life* (1860) and *Society and Solitude* (1870). *The Conduct of Life* (1860) was the first of his books to enjoy immediate popularity. Included in this volume of essays are "Power," "Wealth," "Fate," and "Culture."

In spite of his difficulty in writing structurally correct verse, he always regarded himself essentially as a poet. Emerson's verse is typically untraditional and unprecedented in the light of the formal and linguistic sense. His common themes were such as that of nature, and deep meditation, not that of rational reflection popular in the preceding century. Although Emerson's verse is small in number, his limited body of verse is impressive for their freshness, intensity, inventiveness, and prophetic power. Emerson's poetry should serve as a moral purification and a passage toward organic unity and higher reality. It is evident that the Romantic organic principle is the governing factor in Emerson's aesthetics. Emerson places emphasis on ideas, symbols, and imaginative words. He called upon American authors to celebrate America which was to him a long poem in itself, to celebrate the life of today. Emerson's aesthetics brought about a revolution in American literature in general and in American poetry in particular. His verse played a transitional role between the traditional blank verse and the free verse, and exerted a great and enduring influence upon such poets as Whitman, Pound, Eliot, and even Robert Frost. The first collection of Emerson's poems appeared in 1847. They are uneven in quality, but always highly individual. In his day, Emerson's poems were criticized for their lack of form and polish. In recent years, however, his poetry has received high praise, his harsh rhythms and striking images appeal to many modern readers as artful techniques. Emerson's poetry was noted for its concentration on concrete image, the simplicity of symbols and diction. Among his best-known poems are "Threnody," "Brahma," "The Problem," "The Rhodora," and "The Concord Hymn." Emerson's poetry reflected the same optimism, mysticism, and love of nature that his essays expressed. In 1867, he published a collection of poems entitled *May Day and Other Pieces*, which had previously been published in *The Dial* and *The Atlantic Monthly*. After this time Emerson did little writing and his mental powers declined, although his reputation as a writer spread.

As the leading New England Transcendentalist, Emerson affected a most articulate synthesis of the Transcendentalist views. His Transcendentalism is actually a philosophical school which absorbed some ideological concerns of American Puritanism and European Romanticism, with its focus on the intuitive knowledge of human beings to grasp the absolute in the universe and the divinity of man. Throughout his works Emerson frequently referred to the endless, circular connection of man, nature, and the universe, no aspect of which could be isolated or divided from the greater whole. In his essays, Emerson put forward his philosophy of the Over-soul, the importance of the individual, and nature.

One major element of his philosophy is his firm belief in the transcendence of the "Over-soul." Emerson rejected both the formal religion of the churches and the Deistic philosophy; instead he based his religion on an intuitive belief in an ultimate unity, which he called the "over-soul," It is an impersonal force that is eternal, moral, harmonious, and beneficent in tendency. They believed that there should be an emotional communication between an individual soul and the universal "Over-soul," since the over-soul is an all-pervading power from which all things come from and of which all are a part. One of the tendencies of the "Over-soul" is to express itself in form, hence the world of nature as an emanation of the world of spirit. Emerson's remarkable image of "a transparent eyeball" marks a paradoxical state of being, in which one is merged into nature, the Over-soul, while at the same time retaining a unique perception of the experience. In a word, the soul has completely transcended the limits of individuality and become part of the Over-soul. Emerson sees spirit pervading everywhere, not only in the soul of man, but behind nature, throughout nature. The world proceeds, as he observes, from the same source as the body of man. "The Universal Being" is in point of fact that the Over-soul that he never stopped talking about for the rest of his life. This is as much as to say that the spiritual and immanent God is operative in the soul of man, and that man is divine. Over-soul religiosity is essentially a moral philosophy, which proclaims the dignity of the individual, cuts the roots of institutional tyranny and turns the mind to imagination, hope, exploration and self-reliance. This naturally led to another, equally significant, Transcendentalist thesis, that the individual, not the crowd, is the most important of all. If man depends upon himself, cultivates himself, and brings out the divine in himself, he can hope to become better and even perfect. He has tried to convince people that the possibilities for man to develop and improve himself are infinite. Men should and could be self-reliant. Each man should feel the world as his, and the world exists for him alone. He should determine his own existence. Everyone should understand that he makes himself by making his world, and that he makes the world by making himself. Trust your own discretion and the world is yours. Emerson's eyes were on man as he could be or could become; he was in the main optimistic about human perfectibility. The regeneration of the individual leads to the regeneration of society. Emerson's self-reliance was an expression, on a very high level, of the buoyant spirit of his time, the hope that man can become the best person he could hope to be. Emerson's Transcendentalism, with its emphasis on democratic individualism, may have provided an ideal explanation for the conduct and activities of an expanding capitalist society. To Emerson's Transcendentalist eyes, the physical world is vitalistic and evolutionary. He sees the world as phenomenal, and emphasizes the need for idealism, for idealism sees the world in God. He regards nature as the purest, and the most sanctifying moral influence on man, and advocates a direct intuition of a spiritual and immanent God in nature. Nature is, to him as to his Puritan forebears, emblematic of God. It mediates between man and God, and its voice leads to higher truth. Emersonian Transcendentalism inspired a whole generation of famous American authors like Thoreau, Whitman, and Dickinson.

As an essayist, philosopher, poet, and leader of the New England Transcendentalists, Emerson's influence was everlasting. He was not only transcendentalist thinker and essayist, but a giant who exerted a strong influence on later generations in American literary history. He was the seminal intellectual, philosophical voice of the 19th century in America. His ideas of humanity and nature as symbolic expressions of universal spirit inspired and encouraged the symbolist trend in American art and literature. His daring spirit of repudiating established dogmas and institutions helped produce a literary revolution in the American Renaissance. His impact can be felt in such diverse authors such as Walt Whitman, Emily Dickinson, Nathaniel Hawthorn, Herman Melville and even modern poets.

Analyses of and Comments on His Representative Works

Nature (1836)

Contents Summary

The essay provided a summary of Emerson's leading ideas that he developed in various later essays and poems. Almost all his fundamental ideas can be found in his famous work *Nature*. Early in 1833 Emerson had mentioned this book in a diary entry, and in 1834 he had finished the first 5 chapters. Its publication in 1836 soon drew critical attention, and began to make a great immediate impact on the intellectual life of New England. It has an introduction and 8 chapters: Nature, Commodity, Beauty, Language, Discipline, Idealism, Spirit, Prospects. It was the publication of *Nature* that helped initiate Transcendentalism and stated Emerson's ideas as a transcendentalist. "Nature," though the first important essay by Emerson, has received high critical acclaim for a long time. The book includes his essay "Nature," which is the first comprehensive expression of American Transcendentalism. The essay "Nature" discusses the love of nature, the use of nature, the idealist philosophy in relation to nature, evidences of spirit in the material universe, and the potential expansion of human souls and works that will result from a general return to direct, immediate contact with the natural environment.

Themes

The major thesis of the essay, in Emerson's words, is that we should now "enjoy an original relation to the universe" and not become dependent on past experiences of others and on holy books, creeks and dogma. "Nature" was the fundamental document of his Transcendentalist pursuit and his constant, deeply-felt love for nature. The essay was called "the Manifesto of American Transcendentalism."

Emerson held the belief that nature is the connecting link between God and man, permitting no separation in between so long as the two can meet in its beautiful world, and that man is a part of the beautiful natural world, every particle of which is animated by the divine spirit, and reflects the mind of God. God exists everywhere in nature, or, more exactly, that nature is an expression of the great omnipresent spirit. Nature is thus sacred; it is a source of nourishment, of beauty and inspiration. In such a world thus conceived of man and nature, God inter-wines and all bathes in divine goodness and peace. Thus, to live the good life man needs only to live close to nature and God, and optimism is his only possible workaday philosophy. Man, therefore, must turns to

Nature in order to discover what Emerson called his true "self," a key-word in this work, and in all his work. Emerson therefore, firmly repudiated his former Unitarian Church, in spite of the influence that Unitarianism first had on his thought, and chose Nature as his new religion.

In this monumental work, Emerson first depicts how he evokes his experience of "perfect exhilaration" in an apparently inconsequential moment, and then reflects his sense of being at one with nature and with God, which makes all "mean egotism" vanish as soon as he feels "the currents of the Universal Being" circulate through him. Then emphasis falls on the significance of nature in serving man by ministering to his material needs, to the needs of his soul, to his moral, intellectual, and spiritual needs by offering him the ability of expressing himself in language, and to all these by teaching him practical and ethical lessons. Therefore, when man lives in the spirit, he can recognize himself in the world of nature and find all nature expressive of his inner being; when he is conscious of the self as separate from nature, what he can do is only to aspire to discover the meaning of the natural world and find his distant connections with such a world. At the end of the work Emerson compares the spirit in the ideal world to the sun in the material world, a metaphor which assumes its light-giving function.

Literary Techniques

Unlike many of Emerson's essays, "Nature" is extremely long and is divided into an introduction and eight chapters, or sections.

Emerson's nature is emblematic of the spiritual world, alive with God's overwhelming presence. It mediates between man and God, and its voice leads to higher truth; hence, it experiences a healthy and restorative influence on human mind. By employing nature as a big symbol of the Spirit, or God, or the Over-soul, Emerson has brought the Puritan legacy of symbolism to its perfection. By describing nature as nothing but expressive of the Spirit, or God or the Over-soul, Emerson has perfected the Puritan legacy of symbolism: Nature is the garment of the over-soul, symbolic and morally bound; nature is not something purely of the matter but alive with God's overwhelming presence; nature exercises a healthy and restorative influence on human beings. In expressing his belief in the mystical "unity of nature," Emerson develops his concept of the "Over-Soul" or "Universal Mind." Emerson's famous metaphor of "a transparent eyeball" is employed to illustrate his philosophical discussion. *Nature* advocates the necessity of a new way of looking at the world: man must learn to open his eyes, as if for the first time in his life, and must learn to look at the world differently, getting rid of his preconceptions and of his moral or educational influences.

Self-Reliance (1837)

Contents Summary

This essay is finished according to a series of speech materials between 1836 and 1837. "Believe in yourself" is the core point of "Self-Reliance." Emerson showed many of his opinions about life in the work. The most important ideas include "The Confidence," "The Independence," "The Personality," and "Showing no Sympathy to the Poor." These ideas are practicable and meaningful for the reader's lives. He criticized all forms of imitation and opposed all self-abased people. The real man should learn how to reject to drift with the stream. The ideas which Emerson expressed in his prose are largely different. They agreed with the American people's optimistic spirit at that time. Above all, he believed in individualism, independence and self-reliance. His works is not easy to be understood. He reconstructed the common literature images in writing skill and endowed the works with new ideas.

Themes

Emerson's variety of individualism grows from the self's intuitive connection with the Over-Soul and is not simply a matter of self-centered assertion or immature narcissism. The essay "Self-Reliance" is the clearest, most memorable example of Emerson's philosophy of individualism, an idea that has been deeply embedded in American culture. For Emerson, individualism was fundamentally grounded in the American experiences. He drew on the colonial experiences in the New World wilderness to advocate the virtues of self-reliance, independence, representative government, and the ubiquitous presence of God in nature. "Self-reliance" is generally regarded as being indispensable for a clear understanding of Emerson's matured philosophy of individualism or the idea that each man must rely on himself, that by heeding the voice of intuition, man can become an independent self-sustained individual. In this essay, Emerson rejects conformism and once again advocates individuality. Every individual possesses a unique genius, Emerson argued, that could only be revealed when that individual had the courage to trust his or her own thoughts, attitudes, and inclinations against all public disapproval. Be yourself. Trust your own inner voice. Emerson repeats that theme throughout the essay in different ways. The ideal individual should be a self-reliant man. He celebrated the "self," the individual, and he urged every American to discover their true "self," to become self-reliant, to free themselves from too rigid traditions and taboos. Indeed, Emerson described an ideal society in the essay, which must be built on distinct individuals and not on a crowd of similar people. He advocated people to retain the outspokenness of a small child and avoid envying or imitating others viewed as models of perfection. Everyone should take pride in his own individuality and never be afraid to express his own original ideas, should refuse to conform to the ways of the popular culture and its shallow ideals. A self-reliant man, therefore, is someone who can define his own needs, rules and beliefs, someone who no longer needs external influences embodied either in educational institutional or churches, someone who had found himself in a harmonious relationship with Nature.

Literary Techniques

Emerson's essays are characterized by a series of fragmentary, short, and declarative sentences to illustrative statements of truth and thoughts. On the other hand, the transition from one sentence, or even one paragraph, to another is not always explicitly made, and this weakness produces an effect of apparent discontinuity. Emerson's language is also characterized by frequent use of metaphor that is full of freshness, imaginativeness, and experience, but less dependent on literature. Generally speaking, Emerson was showing to the world a distinctive American style. "Self-reliance" is compact and cogent in its logic, presenting complex and difficult thoughts in a few words. What's more, its style is a perfect instrument for its emotional intensity and its wit. Therefore, it is regarded by many as the high tide of Emerson's prose.

As the spokesman for the American Transcendentalists, he inspired a group of New England romantic writers, who believed that intuition was the means to truth and celebrated the independent individual and strongly supported democracy. He also urged Americans to avoid mimicking art and ideas from abroad. Emerson played an important part in the development of American cultural independence and American intellectual history.

Bibliography

http://www.cliffsnotes.com/study_guide/literature/emerson-essays/summary-analysis-of-self-reliance/about-self-reliance.html, 2013-02-04.

宋元康 . 美国文学导读 . 昆明：云南大学出版社，2007: 91-98.

王卓，李权文 . 美国文学史 . 武汉：华中师范大学出版社，2010: 91-96.

吴瑾瑾 . 美国文学史 . 北京：经济科学出版社，2008: 69-73，76-78.

曹曼 . 美国文学教程 . 武汉：武汉大学出版社，2007: 98-99.

何木英，杜平 . 美国文学简史与作品选读 . 成都：四川大学出版社，2004: 38-39.

常耀信 . 美国文学简史（第二版修订本）. 天津：南开大学出版社，2003: 59-64.

胡荫桐，刘树森 . 美国文学教程 . 天津：南开大学出版社，2003: 139-143, 153-154.

胡荫桐 . 美国文学新编 . 北京：外语教学与研究出版社，2001: 64-66.

Henry David Thoreau

His Life and Writing Career

His Life

Henry David Thoreau (1817–1862), an American writer, poet, essayist, philosopher, naturalist and transcendentalist, is considered one of the most read and most influential figures in American thought and literature, with a readership and a following around the world. As a supreme individualist, he championed the human spirit against materialism and social conformity. His writings have been reprinted countless times, both in English and in translation into many foreign languages.

Henry David Thoreau was born to a French descent family in Concord, Massachusetts on July 12, 1817, spending most of his life in the town and die there. His father was an unsuccessful storekeeper and a maker of lead pencils, while his mother was an aspiring woman, who determined to send her son to college. After completing grammar school with distinction at Concord Academy, he was admitted to Harvard College in 1833. However, he did not like the curriculum and teaching method at Harvard. One thing that Thoreau benefited most was his reading of *Nature*, a small book by Ralph Waldo Emerson, who later became his chief mentor and friend. After graduation, Thoreau began keeping a journal in 1837 and had probably started writing poetry earlier than that; he also wrote and published essays and reviews. For a steady income, he made his living briefly as a teacher and pencil-maker and mostly as a land surveyor, leading a simple and relatively quiet life. At the same time, he met Concord residents Ralph Waldo Emerson, and became a follower of Transcendentalism. Emerson introduced Thoreau to a circle of local writers and thinkers, including Margaret Fuller, William Ellery Channing and Nathaniel Hawthorne, and urged him to contribute essays and poems to the transcendentalist magazine *The Dial*.

At the age of 28 in 1845, wanting to write his first book, Thoreau built a small cabin on a piece of Emerson's property by Walden Pond on the outskirts of town, and moved to live there in a very simple manner for a little over two years, which gave birth to his masterpiece *Walden, or Life in the Woods* (1854). *Walden* is an eloquent account of his experiment in near-solitary living in close harmony with nature, and it is also an expression of his transcendentalist philosophy. Thoreau did an incredible amount of reading and writing, yet he also spent much time strolling in nature. The book not only fully demonstrates Emersonian ideas of self-reliance but also develops and tests Thoreau's own transcendental philosophy. He is so specific and precise that many readers have approached *Walden* as a manifesto of particular social, economic, and political points of view, while overlooking Thoreau's larger purpose in describing his life at the pond. Unfortunately, few people were interested in purchasing his book, so he spent the next nine years, surveying and making pencils at times but primarily writing and rewriting (creating seven full drafts) *Walden* before trying to publish it. He supported himself by surveying and making a few lectures, often on his experience at Walden Pond. He lectured several times a year at lyceums and private homes from Maine to New Jersey. These lectures were important in his process of composition—most of the ideas and themes in his essays and books were first presented to the public in lectures—but they were not lucrative. One of Thoreau's most important works, the essay "Civil Disobedience" (1849), grew out of an overnight stay in jail for refusing to pay a poll-tax that supported the Mexican War he thought unjust. For Thoreau, the Mexican War represented an effort to extend slavery. Thoreau asserted that governments couldn't be justified because they were typically more harmful than helpful, and democracy was no cure. As a means for the individual to protest these unjust actions of his government, the essay advocates passive resistance to unjust laws of society, which had an impact on the British Labor Movement, the passive resistance independence movement led by Gandhi in Indian, and the nonviolent civil-rights movement led by Martin Luther King in the United States. At the same time, he wrote a book as a memorial to a river trip he had taken with his brother in 1839 on the Concord and Merrimack rivers, *A Week on the Concord and Merrimack Rivers* (1849). The idea was to move away from the rush and bustle of American social life which was, to him, getting more and more sadly materialistic-oriented. This work proved to be the only one in addition to *Walden* and his short piece "Civil Disobedience" that was published during Thoreau's lifetime.

Throughout the 1850's, Thoreau also wrote and presented a number of anti-slavery lectures, directed not so much at the South for practicing slavery, but at the North for allowing it to remain. He did not like the way a materialistic America was developing and was vehemently outspoken on the point. He hated the human injustice as represented by the slavery system and was known to have helped at least one African American slave to get free. He lectured against slavery in an abolitionist lecture, *Slavery in Massachusetts*. He even supported John Brown's efforts to end slavery after meeting him in Concord, as in *A Plea for Captain John Brown*. It is based on a speech Thoreau first delivered at Concord on October 30, 1859, two weeks after John Brown's raid on Harper's Ferry. Thoreau's essay espoused John Brown and his fight for abolition.

Although Brown the radical abolitionist was hanged on December 2, 1859, the raid and his execution impelled the American Civil War.

Many readers mistake Thoreau's tone in *Walden* and his other works, thinking he was a cranky hermit. That was far from the case. He used to collect specimens for Louis Agassiz, a Harvard professor of natural history, without much compensation for his work. From 1851, Thoreau became increasingly fascinated with natural history and expedition narratives. He traveled often, to the Maine woods and to Cape Cod several times, and was particularly interested in the frontier and Indians. He read avidly on botany, became a land surveyor and wrote detailed natural history observations in his huge journal. These observations became the source for Thoreau's later natural history writings. Thoreau actually found greater joy in his daily life than most people ever would. He died of tuberculosis at 44 in 1862. Not only did he leave his two books and numerous essays, but he also left a two-million-word *Journal*, published later in 20 volumes, which may have been his major work-in-progress.

His Writing Career

Although Thoreau is held today in great esteem, he was considered an eccentric and a loafer in his own time. He struggled throughout his life to gain acceptance and understanding, but his work received far less attention during his lifetime and was little known outside Concord at the time of his death. Thoreau's books, articles, essays, journals, and poetry are over 20 volumes. Among them, he got only two books, *A Week on the Concord and Merrimack Rivers* and *Walden*, along with some essays that were first delivered as lectures published in his life time, which won him neither fame nor financial success. It was only years after his death that his work was recognized for his brilliance and forward-thinking ideas. The 20th century found him charming and great. He became one of the three great American authors of the 19th century who had no contemporary readers and yet became great in the 20th century, the other two being Herman Melville and Emily Dickinson. His statue was placed in the Hall of Fame in New York in 1969 alongside those of other great Americans. His major works included *Journals* (1838–1859), "Civil Disobedience" (1849), *A Week on the Concord and Marrimack Rivers* (1849), *Walden* (1854), "A Plea for Captain John Brown"(1859), "Walking" (1862), "Life Without Principle" (1863), and *The Maine Woods* (1864), etc. Thoreau's appeal to modern generations not only lies in his power with words, but his thought and ideas. Thoreau had been regarded as a prophet of individualism in American literature. Thoreau's extraordinary impact on American culture was felt enormously in the counterculture upsurge during the Vietnam War and the Civil Rights period. *Walden* and "Civil Disobedience" inspired many young Americans to express their disapproval of the policies of the government and declare ideological independence. His love of nature, his call to simplicity and his awareness of ecology and environmentalism have stirred countless modern readers. He is now more widely read and more vastly influential than any other transcendentalist, including Emerson. Thoreau was received as an American writer, a champion of democracy and a critic of American capitalist civilization. From 1980s' the study on Thoreau has focused on the issues like Thoreau's notion of civilization, his views of nature, his political thought and ecological awareness, both textually and theoretically.

Thoreau's quiet, one-man revolution in living at Walden has become a symbol of the willed integrity of human beings, their inner freedom, and their ability to build their own lives. He identified himself as a Transcendentalist, a radical religious and political group that incorporated many eastern ideas, like reincarnation, into their philosophy. Thoreau strongly believed in self-culture and was eager to identify himself with the transcendental image of the self-reliant man. To achieve personal spiritual perfection, he thinks, the most important thing for men to do with their lives is to be self-sufficient, so he sought to reduce his physical needs and material comforts to a minimum to get spiritual richness. His positiveness about the importance of individual conscience was such that he even considered the society fetters of the freedom of individuals. At the same time, Thoreau is significantly influenced by ancient Chinese thoughts. He once selected 64 quotations from *The Works of Confucius* and *Four Books* and published them in *The Dial* in 1843. In his works, especially in *Walden*, he cited *The Analects of Confucius* and *The Works of Mencius* many times. There were profound similarities between *Walden* and *Tao Te Ching* in their nature mysticism, love of the simple and distaste for governmental interference.

Thoreau was so curious about the world around him that he never stopped looking into nature for ultimate Truth. Thoreau saw an intimate and specific familiarity with the reality of nature as vital to understanding higher truth. In Thoreau's transcendental sense, the ultimate connectedness of God, man, and nature is in the great oneness of the Over-soul, and the absolutes and the workings of the universe can be grasped by the human mind. Intuitive understanding rather than reason provides the means to such cosmic comprehension. Thoreau expressed a clear vision of the unity of man, nature, and heaven. The leap from the particular to the universal, from the mundane to the divine, is found throughout Thoreau's work. In his Transcendentalist philosophy, nature is of extraordinary significance. To him, nature is a concrete existence, is the integration of all the details in universe. In the eyes of Thoreau, man and nature, man and animal are in an integral and harmonious existence. Thoreau dedicated his whole being to his love of nature. For Thoreau, nature is not merely symbolic, but divine in itself and human beings can receive precise communication from the natural world by way of pure senses. So he was often alone in the woods or by the pond, lost in spiritual communication with nature. He mentioned in "Walking" (1863) that a four-hour walk is his everyday routine, which he considered as a benefit for his physical constitution and an inspiration for his literary creation. Not just a keen observer and lover of nature, Thoreau emphasized the dynamic ecology of the natural world and anticipated modern day environmentalism. He read widely in the scientific literature of his day, showed great interest in and admiration for the latest work of Humboldt and Darwin and discussed his own scientific findings with leading naturalists of the day. His late essay, "The Succession of Forest Trees" is the first scholarly discussions on this subject. In fact, some historians rate Thoreau as one of the founders of the modern science of ecology.

Thoreau was an exacting practitioner of the art of writing. Although he exulted in the intuitive, creative genius that he felt within himself, Thoreau put millions of words on paper throughout his life and worked hard to revise and refine his materials. As a writer, he drew strength from an understanding of the inseparability of his life and his art. He vacillated in the way he viewed and presented some of his themes in this massive body of his work. Thoreau intended his writing to be a fit expression of a life lived according to high ideals and aspirations, guided by integrity and morality, spent in pursuit of spiritual development, of the universal truth that lay behind the particular and the personal. Thoreau saw his writing as a confluence of all his powers—physical, intellectual, and spiritual. He constantly revised his work not out of a fussy sense of perfectionism but because of the tremendous value that he placed his writing as an embodiment of all that he was. Thoreau was a versatile writer, capable of expressing stark reality in strong language and of conveying subtle details. His work is characterized both by directness of style and by the suggestion of far more than appears on the surface. For him, the importance of content far outweighed that of style. He avoided overemphasis on form at the expense of content. Thoreau admired direct, vigorous, succinct and economical prose. He wanted every word to be useful, to convey meaning, and he had no interest in the purely decorative. Romantic writer that he was, he cared little for observing the formalities of established literary genre. He applied himself to translating what he observed of nature and humanity into words. The reader of Thoreau must simply accept some degree of intellectual contradiction as evidence that the author was a complex man, constantly thinking and weighing ideas, open to a variety of interpretations, capable of accepting inconsistency. If Thoreau's thoughts on a subject did not always remain constant, at least there is coherence in his repeated exploration of certain basic themes throughout his writings.

Nature with its meaning and value is one of the most pervasive themes in Thoreau's writings. In Thoreau's philosophy, nature symbolizes this higher truth operating in the universe and the divine is most sublimely expressed in nature. He draws upon various Christian conceptions of the divine, as well as those from Eastern religious with which he is familiar, and re-contextualizes them to create new meaning. For him, the role of God as creator of all of nature is most inspirational, and through this understanding, he expresses the Transcendentalist belief in existence of a spark of divinity in all men. Thoreau's transcendental quest toward the universal drew him to immerse himself in nature at Walden Pond from 1845 to 1847. Thoreau's attraction to nature went far beyond emotional appreciation of its beauty; he embraces its harshness as well. Approached with a sense of wonder and of high purpose, nature provided Thoreau with a means of transcending the distractions of everyday life and of focusing on what was important. Thoreau's excursions in Concord and beyond were made through nature, toward loftier revelations. Nature, he felt, was a particular tonic to the human spirit in an age devoted to commerce, to politics, to the spread of dehumanizing industrialization and urbanization, to unfulfilling social interactions, and to the perpetuation of human institutions at best in need of change, at worst immoral. Thoreau's writing presents a synthesis of optimistic idealism and earthy enjoyment of the here and now. He focused on ultimate meaning, but at the same time revealed in the sensuous details of nature and life as he lived it.

The importance of simplicity is another of Thoreau's recurrent themes. *Walden* is a book about living without luxuries, which were distractions to Thoreau. He went into the woods in order to cut life to the bone and suck out the marrow, to get down the bare essentials, and to make sure that he was living as life was. Thoreau emphasizes the crushing, numbing effect of materialism and commercialism on the individual's life. Property ownership and technological progress consume men before they have a chance to consider how they might live. In his opinion, modern civilized life has dehumanized man and placed him in a spiritual quandary. He felt that man should seek truth directly by himself and not through imitation of others. And the best way to find truth is by leaving the life of hurry and bustle to get ahead in worldly affairs and sinking oneself in the wholesome atmosphere of nature. In "Economy," the first chapter of *Walden*, he presents the details of his simple, efficient and self-reliant life at Walden Pond, calculating the costs of shelter, food, clothing, and other necessities to the half penny. By keeping his needs and wants few, the individual may realize spiritual aims instead of devoting his energies to the material. Thoreau encourages his contemporaries to be content with less materially and self-reliance, the stripping away of luxuries and comforts down to the bare essentials. By doing for himself, the individual maintains his freedom to live deliberately, to cultivate himself, and to explore nature and divinity. Just as Thoreau understood that living simply in nature allowed a man to live fully, he also recognized that society impeded both simplicity and the inner life. Through simplicity and self-reliance, we may get beyond the conventional and come face-to-face with the universal.

Analysis of and Comment on His Representative Work

Walden, or Life in the Woods (1854)

Contents Summary

Between 1845 and 1847, Thoreau lived alone in a cabin he built himself on Emerson's property at Walden Pond. Thoreau's masterpiece, *Walden, or Life in the Woods* is a great Transcendentalist work that came out of the period. *Walden* includes 18 chapters: "Economy," "Where I Lived, and What I Lived For," "Reading," "Sounds," "Solitude," "Visitors," "The Bean-Field," "The Village," "The Ponds," "Baker Farm," "Higher Laws," "Brute Neighbors," "House-Warming," "Former Inhabitants; and Winter Visitors," "Winter Animals," "The Pond in Winter," "Spring," and "Conclusion."

Thoreau didn't live the life of a hermit in the traditional sense at Walden Pond. Rather, he hoped to isolate himself from society to gain a more objective understanding of it. Thoreau was impatient with his fellowmen who took an enormous amount of interest in the developments of the outside world, and yet did not want to spend so little as a single moment on the improvement of his own person. He went to the woods not to gratify his whims as was alleged, but to experiment with a new way of life for himself and for his fellowmen. And he felt that he came out of it a better man, reborn and reinvigorated. He spoke ahead of his time and, like some people of his kind, suffered, while alive, slight, misunderstanding, and even mockery. Only history and time eventually restored him to the place to which he had an inalienable claim. As a young man Thoreau took a more than usual interest in the natural world. He saw nature as a genuine restorative, healthy influence on man's spiritual well-being, and regarded it as a symbol of the spirit. He tried to seek a way to unlock the secrets of the spirit. Thoreau was never tired of staying alone in nature; he was ever seen lost in contemplation of the world around. *Walden* is far from a simple account of his physical life at the pond. Indeed, *Walden* is a faithful record of his reflections when he was in solitary communion with nature, an eloquent indication that he not only embraced Emerson's Transcendentalist philosophy but went even further to illustrate the pantheistic quality of nature. He can sit by a woodchuck for half an hour, talking to it. To him, moose and pine trees are as immortal as he is. Thoreau's idea came very close to being heathenish and nature-worship, a pantheism which tended to destroy the "transcendence" of God. Compressing the two-year period into a single calendar year and using the passage of four seasons to symbolize human development, *Walden* artistically recreated real-life experience and became a symbolic model or paradigm for an embodied spiritual quest.

Themes

Walden is an autobiography, but not a traditional one. As a collection of nature essays, the most common way in which the text has been read, *Walden* provides few solid contributions to the world of natural science since the focus is not so much on nature itself as on the individual's relationship to it. Thoreau stresses nature's power to renew and restore the human spirit rather than a strictly scientific appreciation of nature on its own terms. It is a combination of autobiography with social critique, an attack on a consumerist and materialist western culture and its distance from and destruction of nature. The book is not simply a criticism of society, but an attempt to optimize the good aspects of civilization, suggested both by Thoreau's proximity to Concord community and by his admiration for classical literature. It is a book about self-culture and human perfectibility, a faithful record of his reflection when Thoreau was in solitary communion with nature, an eloquent proof that he not only embraced Emerson's Transcendentalist philosophy but surpassed him to illustrate the pantheistic quality of nature. Thoreau regarded his purpose of Walden experiment in three aspects. First, he was escaping from the dehumanization of the Industrial revolution by returning to a simpler, more natural life-style. Second, he was simplifying his life and work on his writings to find out how one's life should be lived. Third, he was putting into practice the Transcendentalist belief that one can best "transcend" normality and experiences the Ideal, or the Divine, through nature. Thoreau has faith in the inner virtue and inward, spiritual grace of man. He holds that the most important thing for men to do with their lives is to be self-sufficient and strive to achieve personal spiritual perfection. The fact that he moved into his little shabby cabin on July 4, Independence Day, illustrates his desire to be independent and find truth for himself. It is a book about man, what he is and what he should be and must be. *Walden* emphasizes the importance of self-reliance, solitude, contemplation, and closeness to nature in transcending the "desperate" existence of most people.

"Economy" is the first and the longest chapter, in which he discusses the physical necessities of life—food, shelter, clothing, and fuel. Until these needs are met, a person cannot rise above them. As to Thoreau, true economy is what simply provides the flesh with what belongs to it so that the spirit may go about its own business. For him, the problem is that people don't seem to know this but seem to believe that the "gross necessaries of life" represent all their humanity. This is a social fiction which people take to be a God-given truth. All men have both animal instincts and higher capacities. Thoreau underscores this coexistence of animal and higher qualities in "Solitude," in which he describes man as simultaneously a physical entity and as an intellectual spectator within his own body. Thoreau emphasizes the individual's need to maintain independence. Independence of thought requires self-reliance and some degree of separation from others. In solitude, there is a sufficiency of companionship in self and nature, and the possibility of spiritual understanding. Physical and intellectual independence from narrowing influences protect the individual's ability to make the spiritual journey. Some men show intelligence, perception, and a relation to nature. A few actually embark upon the spiritual quest. Those who are comfortable in nature—even if they do not actively seek to understand natural laws—and who are willing to think for themselves may progress from living in reality to a more spiritual life.

It is as a document of American Transcendentalism that Walden truly flourishes. It is a plea for the higher life, and its central chapter is entitled "Higher Laws." *Walden* is a book about spiritual rebirth. It is based upon the cycle of the year, coming to a climax with the rebirth of nature in the spring. Thoreau is convinced that if we only tired, we could reach a higher life here on Earth than we ever dreamed of. It is truly a work that encompasses the essence of Thoreau and of Transcendentalism while at the same time conveying a love of nature and the earth and the simple life.

Thoreau's strategy in *Walden* is to expose this social fiction for what it really is, namely, a false fiction that represents the triumph of the flesh over the spirit. Thoreau wanted to get the most from his life by determining what was really important, and he made it by removing himself somewhat from the normal life of Concord. One side of this was economic: he simplified his material needs so that he would not have to spend much time supporting a life-style that he did not need or care about. The other side was spiritual, which was not unlike the spiritual retreats of eastern and western religions. This final chapter "Conclusion" is more passionate and urgent than its predecessors. In the chapter, Thoreau gave us the main message of the book: if you advance in the direction of how you imagine your life, not how convention dictates that it should be, then you will find success on a scale undreamed through reasonable expectations. In it, Thoreau criticizes Americans' constant rush to succeed, to acquire superfluous wealth that does nothing to augment their happiness. He urges us to change our lives for the better, not by acquiring more wealth and material possessions. Thoreau's quiet, one-man revolution in living at Walden has become a symbol of the willed integrity of human beings, their inner freedom, and their ability to build their own lives. At the same time, the book is full of ideas expressed to jostle his neighbors out of their smug complacency. He records how he tries to minimize his own needs on Walden Pond. Spiritual richness is real wealth. It is worth trying to live a life in which one needs to work only for six weeks to be free for the rest of the year. One's soul might not help one to get up in the world, but it will help make real "progress" in self-improvement

Literary Techniques

Walden is often considered to be the earliest example of modern American prose. But the early reception of *Walden* was less than spectacular: the first edition of 2,000 copies did not sell out for five years. Contemporary critics were divided, some praising its originality, others worrying about the consequences for civilization if everyone were to retreat to the forest in imitation of Thoreau. Despite the slow start, however, *Walden* is now considered one of the best-selling books in the history of American literature, and its critical reputation continues to grow as much as its popular acceptance. The author's unconventional way of life, his quest for spiritual renewal and perfection, and his rejection of material possessions continue to appeal to readers and critics.

Walden is, on the surface, a record of Thoreau's simplified and self-sufficient two years' living alone at Walden Pond. But it contains much deeper and broader implications. In it, beautifully integrated with the actual narration, is a wealth of thoughts, comments on life in the United States and in ancient times. All told with his characteristic ironical humor, startling paradox and poetic imagination. *Walden* at first won few admirers, but today, critics regard it as a classic American work that explores natural simplicity, harmony and beauty as models for social and cultural conditions. There are signs of ambiguity, or an attempt to see an alternative side of something common. Although *Walden* has long been a staple of the American literature curriculum at universities around the country, its most recent use is as a rhetoric text. Appreciated for its tight construction, impressive vocabulary, and the richness of its many allusions, *Walden* is finding new life as an example of good writing.

Bibliography

http://en.wikipedia.org/wiki/Walden, 2013-02-15.

http://www.enotes.com/life-woods-henry-david-thoreau-walden-essays/walden-life-woods-henry-david-thoreau, 2013-02-15.

宋元康 . 美国文学导读 . 昆明：云南大学出版社，2007: 98-106.

王卓，李权文 . 美国文学史 . 武汉：华中师范大学出版社，2010: 97-102.

吴瑾瑾 . 美国文学史 . 北京：经济科学出版社，2008: 80-91.

曹曼 . 美国文学教程 . 武汉：武汉大学出版社，2007: 107-109.

常耀信 . 美国文学简史（第二版修订本）. 天津：南开大学出版社，2003: 64-67.

Nathaniel Hawthorne

His Life and Writing Career

His Life

Nathaniel Hawthorne (1804–1864) is generally considered by critics as one of the most important writers in American literary history. Many of his works center on New England, combining moral allegories with a Puritan inspiration. He sought to explore a distinctly American background and interpret the spiritual history of a nation in his writing. His novel *The Scarlet Letter* (1850) is one of the most representative works, which ranks as masterpieces of the American literature. It is worth noting that the ways he took in portraying the protagonists in this novel set the standard for psychological realism for generations of writers. Besides, he plays an influential role in the development of the modern short story, especially Gothic American fiction. His horrifying tales often contain moral messages and deep psychological complexity. His later writings also reflect his negative view of the Transcendentalism movement.

Nathaniel Hawthorne was born on July 4, 1804, in Salem, Massachusetts to Nathaniel Hawthorne, Sr., and the former Elizabeth Clarke Manning. His father was a sea captain who died of yellow fever in Suriname in 1808. Hawthorne's ancestors were closely related with the history of the Puritan theocracy of that time. William Hawthorne is Hawthorne's great-great-great-grandfather. As the first of the family, he emigrated from England to new continent, first settling in Dorchester, Massachusetts before moving to Salem. There he became an important member of the Massachusetts Bay Colony and held many political positions including magistrate and judge, becoming infamous for his harsh sentencing. William's son and the author's great-great-grandfather, John Hawthorne, was one of the judges who oversaw the Salem Witch Trials and never repented of his actions. After his father's death, young Nathaniel moved to Salem with his family and lived together with maternal relatives. He spent ten years over there, from which he drew inspiration for his later writing. On November 10, 1813, young Hawthorne was hit on the leg while playing "bat and ball" and became lame for the rest of life. In the summer of 1816, the family lived as boarders with farmers for a short time, and then moved to a new house near Sebago Lake in Raymond, Maine. Years later, Hawthorne often looked back at his delightful days in Maine fondly. In 1819, he returned back to Salem for school alone. He suffered from homesickness because of being too far from his mother and sisters. In order to kill boring time and add fun into life, he distributed to his family a homemade newspaper in August and September 1820. This paper provides an opportunity for him to develop literary skills and adolescent humor by writing essays, poems, and news.

In 1821, he began his college life in Bowdoin College of Brunswick, Maine with the financial support of his uncle Robert Manning, where he made many friends including future president Franklin Pierce, the future poet Henry Wadsworth Longfellow, future congressman Jonathan Cilley, and future naval reformer Horatio Bridge. He was an idle student, negligent of college rules and the Procrustean details of academic life, rather choosing to nurse my own fancies than to dig into Greek roots and be numbered among the learned Thebans. Upon graduation from college in 1825, he added a "w" to make his name "Hawthorne" in his early twenties, in order to cut off the relationship with his notorious forebears. Hawthorne anonymously published his first work, a novel-length romance titled *Fanshawe*, in 1828. Eight years later, Hawthorne served as the editor of the American Magazine of Useful and Entertaining Knowledge. During this time he boarded with the poet Thomas Green Fessenden on Hancock Street in Beacon Hill in Boston and published several short stories in various magazines and annuals. His friend Horatio Bridge offered to cover the risk of collecting those stories in 1837 as *Twice-Told Tales*, in which "The Minister's Black Veil" and "Wakefield" are among the best short stories. This publication made Hawthorne known locally, though none drew major attention to the author.

From 1839 to 1840, Hawthorne worked at Boston Custom House, Custom House Street, earning a salary of $1,500 a year. During his time there, he rented a room from George Stillman Hillard, business partner of Charles Sumner. Hawthorne wrote in the comparative obscurity of what he called his "owl's nest" in the family home. Seeking a possible home for himself and Sophia, he moved to Brook Farm to join the transcendentalist Utopian community in 1841 not because he agreed with the experiment but because it helped him save money to marry Sophia. He paid a $1,000 deposit and was put in charge of shoveling the hill of manure referred to as "the Gold Mine." He left later that year, though his Brook Farm adventure would prove an inspiration for his novel *The Blithedale Romance* (1852). Hawthorne married Sophia Peabody on July 9, 1842, and enjoyed a long and happy marriage. After marriage, the couple moved to the Old Manse in Concord, Massachusetts, where they lived for three years. In the Old Manse, his neighbor, Ralph Waldo Emerson, invited him into his social circle, but Hawthorne was almost pathologically shy and stayed silent when at gatherings. There, Hawthorne wrote most of the tales collected in *Mosses from an Old Manse* (1846), including "Young Goodman Brown" and "My Kinsman, Major Molineux." In April 1846, Hawthorne was officially appointed as the "Surveyor for the District of

Salem and Beverly and Inspector of the Revenue for the Port of Salem" at an annual salary of $1,200. This job allowed him to have sufficient time to write, but he found it difficult to concentrate on himself. Like his earlier appointment to the custom house in Boston, this employment was vulnerable to the politics of the spoils system. As a Democrat, Hawthorne lost this job due to the change of administration in Washington after the presidential election of 1848. Hawthorne wrote a letter of protest to the *Boston Daily Advertiser*, a pro-Democrat newspaper, making Hawthorne's dismissal a much-talked about event in New England. Moreover, the death of his mother made Hawthorne deeply affected shortly thereafter in late July. In 1848, he was appointed the corresponding secretary of the Salem Lyceum. Many celebrities were invited to speak during this period, including Emerson, Thoreau, Louis Agassiz and Theodore Parker.

The decade of novel writing between 1850 and 1860 had been his most productive, resulting in the writing and publication of four major romances, including *The Scarlet Letter* (1850), *The House of the Seven Gables* (1851), *The Blithedale Romance* (1852) and *The Marble Faun* (1860). *The Scarlet Letter* was published in mid-March 1850, followed by a succession of other novels. Hawthorne and his family moved to a small red farmhouse near Lenox, Massachusetts at the end of March 1850. Coincidentally, Oliver Wendell Holmes, Sr. and Herman Melville also lived nearby and they became good friends soon after attending a party. Word came that Melville was shocked by Hawthorne's talent when he finished reading *Mosses from an Old Manse* (1846). He wrote an unsigned review titled "Hawthorne and His Mosses" in *The Literary World* on August 17 and August 24, which read that these stories revealed a dark side to Hawthorne. When the masterpiece *Moby-Dick* was printed in 1851, Melville dedicated this book to Hawthorne in token of their friendship. *The House of the Seven Gables* was completed in early 1851 and published in the same year. It was well received upon publication and later had a strong influence on the work of H. P. Lovecraft. The poet and critic, James Russell Lowell, praised it as the most valuable contribution to New England history. *The Blithedale Romance*, his only work written in the first person, was written in 1852. He also published in 1851 a collection of short stories retelling myths, *A Wonder-Book for Girls and Boys*, a book he had been thinking about writing since 1846. Nevertheless, Hawthorne suffered much living in this place, while he was addicted to constructing his literary world. The family couldn't withstand the cold winter in the small red house, though they enjoyed the natural scenery of The Berkshires. Hawthorne left this place on November 21, 1851 and returned to Concord in 1852, where he bought "The Hillside" and renamed it "The Wayside." Ralph Waldo Emerson and Henry David Thoreau were his neighbors there. That year witnessed the birth of *The Life of Franklin Pierce*, the campaign biography of Franklin Pierce, in which Hawthorne depicted Pierce as a great statesman and brave soldier who had accomplished no great feats but peaceful pursuits. With Pierce's election as President, Hawthorne was appointed in 1853 as United States consul in Liverpool shortly after the publication of *Tanglewood Tales*. At that time, the role was considered the most lucrative foreign service and second in dignity to the Embassy in London. His appointment ended at the close of the Pierce administration in 1857, and another political appointment took Hawthorne and family to France and Italy before their return to The Wayside in 1860. That year also saw the publication of *The Marble Faun*, his first new book in seven years.

At the outset of the American Civil War, Hawthorne traveled with William D. Ticknor to Washington, D. C. There, he met Abraham Lincoln and other notable figures. He wrote about his experiences in the essay "Chiefly about War Matters" in 1862. Failing health prevented him from completing several more romances. Suffering from pain in his stomach, Hawthorne insisted on a recuperative trip with his friend Franklin Pierce, though his neighbor Bronson Alcott was concerned Hawthorne was too ill. While on a tour of the White Mountains, Hawthorne died in his sleep on May 19, 1864, in Plymouth, New Hampshire, and was survived by his wife and their three children. Hawthorne was buried on what is now known as "Authors' Ridge" in Sleepy Hollow Cemetery, Concord, Massachusetts.

His Writing Career

In his early career, Hawthorne was predominantly a short story writer, although he began with a novel-romance *Fanshawe* anonymously published in 1828. His most famous short story collections include *Twice-Told Tales* (1837), *Mosses from an Old Manse* (1846) and *The Snow-Image, and Other Twice-Told Tales* (1852). *Twice-Told Tales* became popular after publication and earned him literary fame for the first time, which encouraged him to continue his writing. Some reviews regard *Twice-Told Tales* as the most influential book of 1837. *Mosses from an Old Manse* was named in honor of The Old Manse where Hawthorne and his wife lived for the first three years of their marriage. The first edition was published in 1846, which included some of his best, like "Young Good Man Brown," "The Celestial Rail-road," "Rappaccini's Daughter," and "The Old Manse." These allegories focus on the negative side of human nature. *The Snow-Image, and Other Twice-Told Tales*, appeared in 1852, was the final collection of short stories published by Hawthorne in his lifetime.

The Scarlet Letter, *The House of the Seven Gables*, *The Blithedale Romance* and *The Marble Faun* are his four major romances published between 1850 and 1860. In his opinion, romance is radically different from a novel by not being concerned with the possible or probable course of ordinary experience. He published *The Scarlet Letter* in 1850, which immediately brought great fame, as well as fortune. The manuscript was finished at the Peter Edgerley House in Salem, Massachusetts, still standing as a private residence at 14 Mall Street. It was said that Hawthorne originally planned *The*

Scarlet Letter to be a shorter novelette which was part of a collection to be named *Old Time Legends*. William Ticknor and James Thomas Fields, his publishers and friends, persuaded Hawthorne to turn *The Scarlet Letter* into a full-length novel rather than a short story. The appearance of *The Scarlet Letter* marks the maturity as a novelist and also represents the height of Hawthorne's literary genius.

The House of the Seven Gables was published in 1851. Set in the mid-19th century, this Gothic novel explores themes of guilt, retribution, and atonement in a Puritan New England with suggestions of the supernatural and witchcraft. The story includes fantastical occurrences, improbabilities, and attempts to connect the past with the present, sacrificing literal authenticity for more abstract truths. The connection between the past and the present is the most pressing of Hawthorne's concerns in *The House of the Seven Gables*, which begins with the checkered history of the eponymous house. The house reflects the unfortunate circumstances under which it was built some 160 years before by Colonel Pyncheon, one of the early Puritan settlers on the bleak New England coast.

The Blithedale Romance, the third major romance, appeared in 1852. The novel takes place in the utopian community of Blithedale, presumably in the mid-1800s. It is a novel of intrigue and mystery, set in post-colonial Massachusetts. The story tells of Miles Coverdale's quest for betterment of the world through the agrarian lifestyle and community of the Blithedale Farm. The novel reveals the secrets that exist, even within a very small society. According to critics, the novel can be seen as a reflection of the religious conflict Hawthorne faced throughout his life. In a broader sense, critics have long argued that the majority of the people, places, and events of *The Blithedale Romance* can be traced back to Hawthorne's observations and experiences over his lifetime.

The Marble Faun: Or, the Romance of Monte Beni, also known as *Transformation* was published simultaneously in America and England in 1860. The entire story takes place in Italy-much of it in Rome. The four main characters are pictured in art galleries of one sort or another, and three of them are either artists or have some connection with art. The romance mixes elements of a fable, pastoral, gothic novel, and travel guide. Reviews were generally favorable, though many were confused by the ending. What's worse, Hawthorne intentionally failed to answer many questions about the characters and the plot. Complaints about this led Hawthorne to add a Postscript to the second edition.

Hawthorne is actually considered by critics at large to be a romantic, more specifically, a dark romantic and his works belong to part of American romanticism. He has a strong interest in the Puritan period and his novels and short stories mainly deal with the themes central to this historical period of America. Rather than being caught up with skylarks and the beauty of nature, he chooses to focus on the dark side of humanity. He used Gothicism as a vehicle to present the mental processes of his characters and dissect the inner workings of his characters' minds. Certainly, his cautionary tales explore not only the themes and ideas behind the Puritan period, but also the true spirit of the tradition of Romanticism that he was writing.

Analysis of and Comment on His Representative Novel

The Scarlet Letter (1850)

Plot Summary

The novel takes place in 17th-century Boston, Massachusetts during the summer, in a then Puritan village. A young woman named Hester Prynne has been led from the town prison with her infant daughter in her arms and on the breast of her gown "a rag of scarlet cloth" that "assumed the shape of a letter." It was the uppercase letter "A." The Scarlet Letter "A" represents the act of adultery that she has committed and it is to be a symbol of her sin—a badge of shame—for all to see. A man in the crowd tells an elderly onlooker that Hester is being punished for adultery. Hester's husband, who is much older than she, and whose real name is unknown, has sent her ahead to America whilst settling affairs in Europe. However, her husband does not arrive in Boston, and the consensus is that he has been lost at sea. It is apparent that, while waiting for her husband, Hester has had an affair, leading to the birth of her daughter. She will not reveal her lover's identity, however, and the scarlet letter, along with her subsequent public shaming, is the punishment for her sin and her secrecy. On this day Hester is led to the town scaffold and harangued by the town fathers, but she again refuses to identify her child's father.

The elderly onlooker is Hester's missing husband, who is now practicing medicine and calling himself Roger Chillingworth. He settles in Boston, intent on revenge. He reveals his true identity to no one but Hester, whom he has sworn to secrecy. Several years pass. Hester supports herself by working as a seamstress, and her daughter Pearl grows into a willful, impish child, who is more of a symbol than an actual character, said to be the scarlet letter come to life as both Hester's love and her punishment. Shunned by the community, they live in a small cottage on the outskirts of Boston. Community officials attempt to take Pearl away from Hester, but with the help of Arthur Dimmesdale, an eloquent minister, the mother and daughter manage to stay together. Dimmesdale, however, appears to be wasting away and suffers from mysterious heart trouble, seemingly caused by psychological distress. Chillingworth attaches himself to the ailing minister and eventually moves in with him so that he can provide his patient with round-the-clock care. Chillingworth also suspects that there may be a connection between the minister's torments and Hester's secret, and he begins to test Dimmesdale to see what he can learn. One afternoon, while the minister sleeps, Chillingworth discovers something undescribed to the reader, supposedly an "A" burned into Dimmesdale's chest, which convinces him that his suspicions are correct.

Dimmesdale's psychological anguish deepens, and he invents new tortures for himself. In the meantime, Hester's charitable deeds and quiet humility have earned her a reprieve from the scorn of the community. One night, when Pearl is about seven years old, she and her mother are returning home from a visit to the deathbed of John Winthrop when they encounter Dimmesdale atop the town scaffold, trying to punish himself for his sins. Hester and Pearl join him, and the three link hands. Dimmesdale refuses Pearl's request that he acknowledge her publicly the next day, and a meteor marks a dull red "A" in the night sky. It is interpreted by the townsfolk to mean *Angel*, as a prominent figure in the community had died that night, but Dimmesdale sees it as meaning *adultery*. Hester can see that the minister's condition is worsening, and she resolves to intervene. She goes to Chillingworth and asks him to stop adding to Dimmesdale's self-torment. Chillingworth refuses. She suggests that she may reveal his true identity to Dimmesdale.

Hester arranges an encounter with Dimmesdale in the forest because she is aware that Chillingworth knows that she plans to reveal his identity to Dimmesdale, and she wishes to protect him. While walking through the forest, the sun will not shine on Hester, though Pearl can bask in it. They then wait for Dimmesdale, and he arrives. Hester informs Dimmesdale of the true identity of Chillingworth and the former lovers decide to flee to Europe, where they can live with Pearl as a family. They will take a ship sailing from Boston in four days. Both feel a sense of release, and Hester removes her scarlet letter and lets down her hair. The sun immediately breaks through the clouds and trees to illuminate her release and joy. Pearl, playing nearby, does not recognize her mother without the letter. She is unnerved and expels a shriek until her mother points out the letter on the ground. Hester beckons Pearl to come to her, but Pearl will not go to her mother until Hester buttons the letter back onto her dress. Pearl then goes to her mother. Dimmesdale gives Pearl a kiss on the forehead, which Pearl immediately tries to wash off in the brook, because he again refuses to make known publicly their relationship. However, he too clearly feels a release from the pretense of his former life, and the laws and sins he has lived with.

The day before the ship is to sail, the townspeople gather for a holiday put on in honor of an election and Dimmesdale preaches his most eloquent sermon ever. Meanwhile, Hester has learned that Chillingworth knows of their plan and has booked passage on the same ship. Dimmesdale, leaving the church after his sermon, sees Hester and Pearl standing before the town scaffold. He impulsively mounts the scaffold with his lover and his daughter, and confesses publicly, exposing the mark supposedly seared into the flesh of his chest. He falls dead just after Pearl kisses him.

Frustrated in his revenge, Chillingworth dies a year later. Hester and Pearl leave Boston, and no one knows what has happened to them. Many years later, Hester returns alone, still wearing the scarlet letter, to live in her old cottage and resume her charitable work. She receives occasional letters from Pearl, who was rumored to have married a European aristocrat and established a family of her own. Pearl also inherits all of Chillingworth's money even though he knows she is not his daughter. There is a sense of liberation in her and the townspeople, especially the women, who had finally begun to forgive Hester of her tragic indiscretion. When Hester dies, she is buried in "a new grave near an old and sunken one, in that burial ground beside which King's Chapel has since been built. It was near that old and sunken grave, yet with a space between, as if the dust of the two sleepers had no right to mingle. Yet one tombstone served for both. The tombstone was decorated with a letter "A," for Hester and Dimmesdale.

Themes

Hawthorne's writing is inspired by his personal background and Puritan environment, combining historical romance loaded with symbolism and deep psychological themes, bordering on surrealism. Contemporary response to Hawthorne's work praised his sentimentality and moral purity while more modern evaluations focus on the dark psychological complexity. Beginning in the 1950s, critics have focused on symbolism and didacticism. After all, the book's immediate and lasting success is due to the way it addresses spiritual and moral issues from a uniquely American standpoint. It remains relevant for its philosophical and psychological depth, and continues to be read as a classic tale on a universal theme.

In this novel, Hawthorne mainly refers to two major themes: sin and Puritan legalism. As for sin, the experience of Hester and Dimmesdale recalls the story of Adam and Eve because, in both cases, sin results in expulsion and suffering. The first thing built in the town was the prison. Sin and crime was the major emphasis of the town. Hester and Dimmesdale contemplate their own sinfulness on a daily basis and try to reconcile it with their lived experiences. However, the Puritan elders insist on seeing earthly experience as merely an obstacle on the path to heaven. Therefore, they view sin as a threat to the community that should be punished and suppressed. Their answer to Hester's sin is to ostracize her. Nature was the only thing kind to the condemned. This theme was very important later in the book when Dimmesdale, Hester and Pearl met in the forest. The rose bush, its beauty a striking contrast to all that surrounds it may look more kind on the errant Hester and her child than her Puritan neighbors do.

Throughout the work, the nature images contrast with the stark darkness of the Puritans and their systems.

Another theme is the extreme legalism of the Puritans and how Hester chooses not to conform to their rules and beliefs. Hester was rejected by the villagers even though she spent her life doing what she could to help the sick and the poor. Her thoughts begin to stretch and go beyond what would be considered by the Puritans as safe or even Christian. She begins to believe that a person's earthly sins don't necessarily condemn them. She even goes so far as to tell Dimmesdale that their sin has been paid for by their daily penance and that their sin won't keep them from getting to heaven, however, the Puritans believed that such a sin surely condemns. But Hester had been alienated from the Puritan society, both in her physical life and spiritual life. When Dimmesdale dies, she knows she has to move on because she can no longer conform to the Puritans' strictness. Her thinking is free from religious bounds and she has established her own different moral standards and beliefs. Puritan society is stagnant, while Hester and Dimmesdale's experience shows that a state of sinfulness can lead to personal growth, sympathy, and understanding of others. Paradoxically, these qualities are shown to be incompatible with a state of purity.

Literary Techniques

Hawthorne was outstanding in handling the application of symbolism, and a study of his symbols is necessary to understanding his novels. *The Scarlet Letter* is Hawthorne's most important symbolic novel.

In *The Scarlet Letter*, the letter "A," the spirit of novel, builds up the framework and launches a close link between the human relationships. In the novel, the letter appears on Hester's gown, on Arthur's heart, in Pearl's hands as well as in the evening sky. The letter "A" begins as a symbol of sin, but its symbolic significance changes with the development of the novel. It then becomes a symbol of alone and alienation, and finally it becomes a symbol of able, angel and admirable.

Hawthorne also uses characters as symbols in the novel. The characters of Hester Prynne, Arthur Dimmesdale, Pearl, and Roger Chillingworth are all associated with sin. However, these four characters symbolize different aspects of sin. Hester Prynne represents how sin can make one stronger and Arthur Dimmesdale symbolizes how hidden sins can cause harm. Pearl, a reminder of the scarlet letter to her mother, is a complicated symbol of an act of love and passion, an act which was also adultery. Pearl is also the imagination of the artist, an idea so powerful that the Puritans could not even conceive of it, let alone understand it, except in terms of transgression. Therefore, Hawthorne fully deserves the title "the prophet of symbolism."

The twenty-four chapters of *The Scarlet Letter* are closely knitted together by means of the scaffold scenes which appear three times, almost symmetrically, in the beginning, the middle, and the end of the book, each time bringing the four major characters (Hester, Dimmesdale, Chillingworth, and Pearl) together. Chapters I and II, XII and XXIII serve as the props holding up the frame of the novel. All the major figures have complex psychologies; there is a semblance of interior monologues which reveal their states of mind. One salient feature of Hawthorne's art is his ambiguity, of which the technique of multiple view employed in the last part of the book offers a good illustration. Here in the "Conclusion" people are heard to offer different views concerning the sign of the letter A on the dead minister's chest.

Bibliography

http://en.wikipedia.org/wiki/Nathaniel_Hawthorne, 2013-02-16.
http://www.sparknotes.com/lit/scarlet/summary.html, 2013-02-16.
http://www.gradesaver.com/the-house-of-the-seven-gables/study-guide/short-summary/, 2013-02-16.
http://www.bookrags.com/studyguide-the-blithedale-romance/, 2013-02-16.
http://www.enotes.com/nathaniel-hawthorne-essays/hawthorne-nathaniel-1804-1864, 2013-02-16.
http://en.wikipedia.org/wiki/The_Scarlet_Letter, 2013-02-16.
http://en.wikipedia.org/wiki/The_House_of_the_Seven_Gables, 2013-02-16.
http://en.wikipedia.org/wiki/The_Blithedale_Romance, 2013-02-16.
http://en.wikipedia.org/wiki/The_Marble_Faun, 2013-02-16.
宋元康．美国文学导读．昆明：云南大学出版社，2007: 106-122.
王卓，李权文．美国文学史．武汉：华中师范大学出版社，2010: 77-82.
吴瑾瑾．美国文学史．北京：经济科学出版社，2008: 93-106.
曹曼．美国文学教程．武汉：武汉大学出版社，2007: 129-154.
何木英，杜平．美国文学简史与作品选读．成都：四川大学出版社，2004: 87-98.
常耀信．美国文学简史（第二版修订本）．天津：南开大学出版社，2003: 71-79.
胡荫桐．美国文学新编．北京：外语教学与研究出版社，2001: 83-99.

Herman Melville

His Life and Writing Career

His Life

Herman Melville (1819–1891) was an American novelist, short story writer, essayist, and poet. Born to Allan and Maria Gansevoort Melvill in New York City on August 1, 1819, he was the third of eight children. His father was from a well-established and colorful Boston family. He achieved wealth as a commission merchant and an importer of French dry goods. He could not take after of his children because he spent a good deal of time abroad. Allan was the son of Major Thomas Melvill, who was an honored participant of the Boston Tea Party and a major in General Washington's army. Thomas Melvill was later appointed Commissioner of Boston and Charlestown Harbor. His mother was from an old, socially prominent Hudson Valley Dutch family. Maria was the daughter of General Peter Gansevoort, who was reputed as the "Hero of Fort Stanwix" due to his role in defense of that fort in 1777, during the Revolutionary War. The Gansevoorts had come to the new world in the 1600s and established themselves as one of the first families of Dutch Albany. Like the titular character in *Pierre* (1852), Melville found satisfaction in his double prominent descents that had the revolutionary pedigree.

Herman's parents settled in a historic Dutch community of New York City after their marriage in 1814. The parents had all their children baptized in the Dutch Reformed Church. Melville apparently lived a well-off life with his brothers in this city. He enrolled in the prestigious New York Male High School from 1825 to 1829, and to the Grammar School of Columbia College from 1829 to 1830. Overextended financially and emotionally unstable, his father went bankrupt when Herman was only 11. His family was forced to move to Albany, New York, to flee the creditors in 1830. Allan tried to recover from his setbacks by going into the fur business, but the new venture failed again, because the War of 1812 had ruined businesses that tried to sell overseas. Just two years later, his father died after suffering a financial and mental breakdown, leaving his widow with eight children penniless. Melville's family had to depend on well-off kin for financial support. Herman's older brother, Gansevoort, assumed responsibility for the family and took over his father's fur and cap business.

Melville attended the Albany Academy from October 1830 to October 1831, and again from October 1836 to March 1837, where he studied the classics. He was pulled out of school again and again in order to ease the economic pressures. Inexperienced and now poor, he tried a variety of jobs when he stayed out of school during the 1830s. He clerked in a bank, worked on his uncle's farm, joined his old brother's business in Albany, and did some school teaching near Pittsfield, Massachusetts. He also studied at Landingsburgh Academy to work as a surveyor on the Erie Canal. His efforts, however, failed to obtain a position there. About this time, seemingly at the behest of Melville's brother Gansevoort, Maria added an "e" to alter the spelling of the family name. Herman's younger brother, Thomas Melville, eventually became a governor of Sailors Snug Harbor. In 1839, he made a temporary voyage to Liverpool as a cabin boy on a merchant ship. From 1838 to 1847, he resided at what is now known as the Herman Melville House in Lansingburgh, New York.

On August 4, 1847, Melville married Elizabeth Shaw, daughter of Lemuel Shaw, who served as Chief Justice of the Massachusetts Supreme Judicial Court from 1830 to 1860. They had four children: two sons and two daughters. In 1850 they moved to Arrowhead in Pittsfield, Berkshire County, Massachusetts. Here Melville lived 13 years in a farm house, occupied with his writing and managing his farm. While living at Arrowhead, he became friends with fellow New Englander, Nathaniel Hawthorne. Hawthorne and his family moved to a small red farmhouse near Lenox, Massachusetts, at the end of March 1850. Melville's marriage became unhappy and unstable as his professional fortunes waned. To repair his faltering finances, Melville made lectures to the audience at home and abroad. From 1857 to 1860, he spoke at lyceums when he was on sightseeing in Rome. In 1863, he and his wife gave up country life and resettled, with their four children, in New York City. In 1866, Melville obtained a humble position with the Port of New York, which certainly ensured Melville's adequate paying appointment. Due to his wife and relatives' influence, he remained as deputy inspector of customs for the next twenty years. Melville also became the only honest employee of the customs house, although the institution won the reputation of being notoriously corrupt.

In final years, personal tragedies and failure haunted Melville. None of the books could be well received by critics, although he insisted on writing a few more. First published in England, *Typee* (1846) and *Omoo* (1847) are based on Melville's sea-faring adventures and stays in Polynesia and Tahiti. His next novel *Mardi: and A Voyage Thither* (two volumes, 1849) is "a romance of Polynesian adventure," again reflecting much of Melville's own life on ships and the South Seas. Another semi-autobiographical novel *Redburn: His First Voyage* was published in 1849. *Moby Dick* (1851) appeared to be his last successful book. His first three books gained much contemporary attention and after a fast-blooming literary success in the late 1840s, his popularity declined precipitously in the mid-1850s and never recovered during his lifetime. He suffered greater pains when his two sons died within a year of each other. This recurring depression drove him to the brink of alcoholism and insanity and physical abuse on his wife. Elizabeth's relatives repeatedly urged her to leave him, but she refused. After a while he did recover, with the help of his wife, he however supposedly never wrote again. Melville retired in 1886, after several of his wife's relatives died and left the couple legacies which could support them live comfortably for the rest of life. On September 28, 1891, he died at home in New York City, age 72. When he died, he was almost forgotten by his readers. The doctor listed "cardiac dilation" on the death certificate. He was buried at the Woodlawn Cemetery in The Bronx, New York.

His Writing Career

Melville's roving disposition and a desire drove him out of school at eighteen after a few more years of formal education in the Albany Academy. He tried several jobs to support himself independently of family assistance, but this effort failed. His brother helped him with a job as a merchant sailor, on a New York ship bound for Liverpool, England. Melville made his first sea voyage at nineteen, and returned on the same ship. ***Redburn: His First Voyage*** (1849) is partly based on his experiences of this journey. Melville once again decided to travel at sea at the end of 1840. On January 3, 1841, he signed articles on the whaler Acushnet and sailed from Fairhaven, Massachusetts to the Pacific Ocean. His experiences of this journey ushered in his new life. The events of this 18-month cruise were probably described a lot in his whaling romance, ***Moby-Dick; or, The Whale*** (1851). When the vessel sailed around Cape Horn and traveled to the South Pacific, Melville deserted the Acushnet in the Marquesas Islands in July 1842. He lived as a captive among the Typee natives on the island Nuku Hiva for three weeks. His novel ***Typee*** (1846) was created based on this actual experience.

Melville seemed to enjoy this voyage and left danger aside quickly. He continued his voyage abroad an Australian whaling vessel, the Lucy Ann, bound for Tahiti, after which he was involved in a mutiny and briefly imprisoned in the native "Calabooza Beretanee (the English Jail)." After a few days in jail, he spent several months working as beachcomber and island rover (Omoo in Tahitian). He and a new friend then roamed the beautiful and unspoiled islands and eventually crossed over to Moorea. From November 1842 to April 1843, Melville served on a third whaler six months, and then landed at Honolulu. While in Hawaii, he made a living by doing odd jobs and got involved in a controversial event for his vehement opposition to the activities of Christian missionaries seeking to convert the native population. On Aug. 17, 1843, he enlisted as a common seaman on the frigate USS "United States," and arrived in Boston in October 1844. His long voyage was later woven into the plots of such novels as ***Typee*** (1846), ***Omoo*** (1847), and ***White-Jacket*** (1850), but few readers believed their veracity.

Melville completed *Typee* in the summer of 1845, and eventually published it in 1846 in London. As Melville's first adventure novel, it is a story about a brief love affair with a beautiful native girl, Fayaway, on the island Nukuheva. Upon its publication, it became an instant bestseller and also most popular work during his lifetime. The Boston publisher easily accepted its sequel *Omoo* sight unseen, though it was not as attractive as *Typee*. It as such is also autobiographical, published in London and New York in the spring of 1847. After leaving Nuku Hiva, the narrator sails to Tahiti with other crew on a whaling vessel. He encounters various types of life on the journey in the vast sea. *Typee* and *Omoo* made Melville notorious as a writer and adventurer who lived among the cannibals, but they could not make enough in royalties for him to live on. *Mardi* (1849) experienced a critical failure. For readers, it is highly philosophical and not as humorous and exotic as the first two. This widespread disappointment hurt Melville and his writing career seemed to decline afterward. *Redburn* and *White-Jacket* were published in 1849 and 1850, which made some social criticism. Melville admitted that they were two books produced quickly and mainly under financial duress.

Melville befriended Nathaniel Hawthorne and Oliver Wendell Holmes, Sr. beginning on August 5, 1950, when they meet at a picnic hosted by a mutual friend. He had just read Hawthorne's short story collection *Mosses from an Old Manse*, and his unsigned review of the collection, titled "Hawthorne and His Mosses," was printed in the *The Literary World* on August 17 and 24. Melville was tremendously inspired and encouraged by Hawthorne during the period that he was writing *Moby-Dick*. *Moby-Dick* is classified as American Romanticism, an adventure novel by Herman Melville, first published by Richard Bentley in London on October 18, 1851, in a three-volume edition titled *The Whale*, and weeks later as a single volume, by New York City publisher Harper & Brothers as *Moby-Dick; or, The Whale* on November 14, 1851 respectively. This book was inscribed to Hawthorne, though their friendship was on the wane only a short time later. This novel also saw the publication of Nathaniel Hawthorne, *The Scarlet Letter* (1850) and Harriet Beecher Stowe, *Uncle Tom's Cabin* (1852) as well as Henry David Thoreau, *Walden* (1854), and the first edition of Walt Whitman, *Leaves of Grass* (1855). Now, it has become Melville's most famous work and is often considered to be one of the greatest American literary works and a treasure of world literature of all time. It did not, however, sell its initial printing of 3,000 copies, and make Melville rich in his lifetime. It is reported that the American edition brought him total earnings amounted to just $556.37. The book initially received mixed reviews, but now it is considered the canon of American novels.

However, these works did not achieve the popular and critical success of his earlier books. When he followed *Moby-Dick* with *Pierre* in 1852, his reader began to desert him. Obviously, the public preferred unusual and exciting adventures to pessimistic and tragic stories. On September 8, 1852, The New York Day Book even made an astonishing and venomous attack on Melville with the headline HERMAN MELVILLE CRAZY. This remark indicates that Melville should throw away his pen and ink and accept treatment as a madman. Following this and other scathing reviews of *Pierre* by critics, publishers became wary of Melville's work. His publisher, Harper & Brothers, rejected his next manuscript, *Isle of the Cross*, which has been lost. In order to secure some sort of income, Melville published *Israel Potter* in March 1855. It's a novel of about 60,000 words set during the Revolutionary War in America, which originated from a 108-page pamphlet autobiography, *Life and Remarkable Adventures of Israel R. Potter* that Melville acquired in the 1840s.

Melville turned to writing short stories. Two of them, "*Bartleby the Scrivener*" and "*Benito Cereno*," collected in *The Piazza Tales* in 1856, are considered as classics. *The Piazza Tales*, either ignored or misunderstood by readers, followed the universal excoriation of his previous novel, *Pierre: or, The Ambiguities* (1852). Still, the exploration of the haunting and disturbing question of the meaning of life displeased the public. On April 1, 1857, Melville published his last full-length novel, *The Confidence-Man*, subtitled *His Masquerade*, a complex and mysterious exploration of issues of fraud and honesty, identity and masquerade. Perhaps this is his most difficult prose work in all writing. It has won general acclaim because of a bitter satire on humanity in modern times, although it received negative reviews when it was published. After his novel, he gave up writing.

Above all, Melville was not a successful writer during his lifetime. His writing brought him just over $10,000 financially. His popularity declined dramatically from about age 35, because he tended to write some philosophical, political and experimental novels instead of adventure stories as before. By 1876, all of his books ceased to be printed. In the later years of his life and during the years after his death he was quickly forgotten by the broad audience and placed among minor literary figures by the critics. It was not until the "Melville Revival" in the early 20th century that his work won recognition, especially *Moby-Dick*, which was hailed as one of the literary masterpieces of both American and world literature. The 1920s marked the start of a Melville revival among critics and readers. The literary circles began to re-recognize his importance as a novelist and poet in American literature. By the 1940s, Americans at last recognized his genius. His reputation has since spread throughout the world.

Analysis of and Comment on His Representative Novel

Moby-Dick or The Whale (1851)

Plot Summary

"Call me Ishmael," *Moby-Dick* begins, in one of the most recognizable opening lines in American, or indeed English-language, literature. The narrator, an observant young man setting out from Manhattan, has experience in the merchant marine but has recently decided his next voyage will be on a whaling ship. On a cold, gloomy night in December, he arrives at the Spouter-Inn in New Bedford, Massachusetts, and agrees to share a bed with a then-absent stranger. When his bunkmate, a heavily tattooed Polynesian harpooner named Queequeg, returns very late and discovers Ishmael beneath his covers, both men are alarmed, but the two quickly become close friends and decide to sail together from Nantucket, Massachusetts on a whaling voyage.

In Nantucket, the pair signs on with the *Pequod*, a whaling ship that is soon to leave port. The ship's captain, Ahab, is nowhere to be seen; nevertheless, they are told of him—a "grand, ungodly, godlike man," according to one of the owners, who has "been in colleges as well as 'mong the cannibals." The two friends encounter a mysterious man named Elijah on the dock after they sign their papers and he hints at troubles to come with Ahab. The mystery grows on Christmas morning when Ishmael spots dark figures in the mist, apparently boarding the *Pequod* shortly before it sets sail that day.

The ship's officers direct the early voyage while Ahab stays in his cabin. The chief mate is Starbuck, a serious, sincere Quaker and fine leader; second mate is Stubb, happy-go-lucky and cheerful and always smoking his pipe; the third mate is Flask, short and stout but thoroughly reliable. Each mate is responsible for a whaling boat, and each whaling boat of the *Pequod* has its own pagan harpooner assigned it. Sometime after sailing, Ahab finally appears on the quarter-deck one morning, an imposing, frightening figure whose haunted visage sends shivers over the narrator. (A white scar, reportedly from a thunderbolt, runs down his face and it is hinted that it continues the length of his body.) One of his legs is missing from the knee down and has been replaced by a prosthesis fashioned from a sperm whale's jawbone.

Soon gathering the crewmen together, with a rousing speech Ahab secures their support for his single, secret purpose for this voyage: hunting down and killing Moby Dick, an old, very large sperm whale, with a snow-white hump and mottled skin, that crippled Ahab on his last whaling voyage. Only Starbuck shows any sign of resistance to the charismatic but monomaniacal captain. The first mate argues repeatedly that the ship's purpose should be to hunt whales for their oil, with luck returning home profitably, safely, and quickly, but not to seek out and kill Moby Dick in particular—and especially not for revenge. Eventually even Starbuck acquiesces to Ahab's will, though harboring misgivings.

The mystery of the dark figures seen before the *Pequod* set sail is explained during the voyage's first lowering for whales. Ahab has secretly brought along his own boat crew, including a mysterious harpooner named Fedallah, an inscrutable figure with a sinister influence over Ahab. Later, while watching one night over a captured whale carcass, Fedallah darkly prophecies to Ahab hints regarding their twin deaths.

The novel describes numerous "gams," social meetings of two ships on the open sea. Crews normally visit each other during a gam, captains on one vessel and chief mates on the other. Mail may be exchanged and the men talk of whale sightings or other news. For Ahab, however, there is but one relevant question to ask of another ship: "Hast seen the White Whale?" After meeting several other whaling ships, which have their own peculiar stories, the *Pequod* enters the Pacific Ocean. Queequeg becomes deathly ill and requests that a coffin be built for him by the ship's carpenter. Just as everyone has given up hope, Queequeg changes his mind, deciding to live after all, and recovers quickly. His coffin becomes his sea chest, and is later caulked and pitched to replace the *Pequod*'s life buoy.

Soon word is heard from other whalers of Moby Dick. The jolly Captain Boomer of the *Samuel Enderby* has lost an arm to the whale, and is stunned at Ahab's burning need for revenge. Next they meet the *Rachel*, which has seen Moby Dick very recently. As a result of the encounter, one of its boats is missing; the captain's youngest son had been aboard. The *Rachel*'s captain begs Ahab to aid in the search for the missing boat, but Ahab is resolute. The *Pequod*'s captain is very near the White Whale now and will not stop to help. Finally the *Delight* is met, even as its captain buries a sailor who had been killed by Moby Dick. Starbuck begs Ahab one final time to reconsider his thirst for vengeance, but to no avail.

The next day, the *Pequod* meets Moby Dick. For two days, the *Pequod*'s crew pursues the whale, which wreaks widespread destruction, including the disappearance of Fedallah. On the third day, Moby Dick kills Ahab and sinks the *Pequod*, dragging almost all the crew to their watery deaths. Only Ishmael survives, clinging to Queequeg's coffin-turned-life buoy for an entire day and night before the *Rachel* rescues him.

Themes

Moby-Dick was published in 1851 during the so-called American Renaissance, which explored numerous fundamental and often universal themes. Nathaniel Hawthorne inspired him to radically revise the whaling documentary into a novel of both universal significance and literary complexity. As one of the great novels in literature, Melville's reputation rests largely on this book. Like many of his other works, this novel is also literary creation of a high order—blending fact, fiction, adventure, and symbolism. Melville's vast personal experience in faraway places was remarkable even in the footloose and exploring world of the 1800s. Melville brought to his extraordinary adventures a vivid imagination and a philosophical skepticism, as well as a remarkable skill in handling the new American language. Through the journey of the main characters, the concepts of class and social status, good and evil, the existence of God, the problem of human knowledge, the strength of fate, and the exploitation and oppression are all examined, as the main characters speculate upon their personal beliefs and their places in the universe.

After Ahab lost a leg to the whale, he decided to seek vengeance against the creature. He leaves home and family and even renounces his humanity to achieve this goal. He generally keeps to himself aboard ship, and occasionally comes out for the latest news about Moby Dick. Over the course of the novel, Ishmael offers a simple collection of literary excerpts mentioning whales and attempts to make the essential nature of the whale known. The different symbolic experiences throughout history, however, fail to give an adequate account of the multiplicity of meanings. Human observation seems to be always limited and knowledge insufficient, although Ishmael makes use of nearly every discipline known to man, including art, taxonomy, and phrenology. When it comes to Moby Dick himself, readers discover that this limitation of human takes on allegorical significance. One the one hand, the crew battles the sea and its largest and most fearsome creature, which embodies the uncompromising ambition of men to conquer nature and recreate the world. One the other hand, like the Christian God, Moby Dick is unknowable to man. It is inevitably futile and often fatal to try to interpret him, as Ahab does in his lifetime. The narrator describes many portentous or foreshadowing events, which presents many references to fate. Moreover, many of the sailors believe in prophecies, and some even claim the ability to foretell the future. All of these things suggest that the *Pequod*'s doom is inevitable. It is clear that Ahab exploits the sailors' belief in fate and lures them into a dead end. Most of them think that the quest for Moby Dick is their common destiny. As Ahab's enemy, Moby Dick represents an inscrutable, mysterious power. Starbuck apparently understands what the whale stands for and tries to persuade Ahab not to take revenge on a dumb brute. Actually, Ahab cannot challenge the primal force like Satan who cannot defeat God. In others words, Ahab and other seamen may harpoon the whale, but they cannot harvest it.

Some critics, particularly those interested in social equality studies, have explored the existence of different class, race and social status in Melville's fiction, especially the exploitation and oppression in the whaling. At first glance, the *Pequod* seems like an island of equality and fellowship in the midst of a racist, hierarchically structured world. The ship's crew generally accepts one another and gets along harmoniously even though they come from all corners of the globe with sharply contrasting cultural and religious backgrounds. Ishmael is a Christian and Queequeg is a pagan. Ishmael is initially uneasy upon meeting barbaric Queequeg, but he quickly realizes that it is better to have a sober cannibal than a drunken Christian for a shipmate. This shows how Ishmael's thoughts turn around when he realizes that Queequeg is actually a very kind person. They tolerate each other's beliefs and become good friends. When they work aboard the *Pequod* with other seamen, a certain kind of egalitarianism seems to exist, since all are promoted and paid according to their ability. However, the whaling parallels such other exploitative activities as buffalo hunting, gold mining and unfair trade with indigenous peoples, which characterize American and European territorial expansion and colonization. That's the reason why Ahab even refuses to help the fellow captain of the Rachel search for his son in the pursuit of the whale. Obviously, there is the existence of unequal social structures, especially the white male-dominant model. Moreover, each of the *Pequod*'s mates, who are white, is entirely dependent on a nonwhite harpooner, and nonwhites perform most of the dirty or dangerous jobs aboard the ship. Although the narrator gives voice to the oppressed mates during the hunt of the white whale, the mates are never fully able to come to terms with the oppressor in the end. In fact, not the divine power, but the oppressor controls the world and appears to manipulate the destinies of its inhabitants.

Literary Techniques

Moby-Dick contains large sections—most of them narrated by Ishmael—that seemingly have nothing to do with the plot. The narrator's reflections, along with his descriptions of a sailor's life aboard a whaling ship, are woven into the narrative along with numerous literary techniques such as stylized language, allusion, symbolism, imagery, metaphor, as well as stage directions, extended soliloquies, and asides in Shakespearean plays.

Obviously, the ships sail on as though they were in a play or like they planned to be filmed. They are ordered and seem to have a path already set up for them, like a script for a play. The book employs those literary devices to present destructive obsession and monomania, as well as the assumption of anthropomorphism—projecting human instincts, characteristics and motivations onto animals. All the reader can know is that Moby-Dick, on one level, is the story of the hunt for Moby Dick, a fierce white whale supposedly known to sailors of Melville's time. It brilliantly describes aspects of the whaling business, and presents the dangerous and often violent life on board and a discussion of the nature of whales. On another level Moby-Dick is a deeply symbolic story. The whale symbolizes the mysterious and complex force of the universe, and Captain Ahab represents the heroic struggle against the limiting and crippling constrictions that confront an intelligent person. In fact, the white whale symbolizes many things to various characters in the novel. It is their personal interpretations of Moby-Dick, in addition to their individual ruminations on the gold doubloon Ahab has nailed to the mast to motivate his crew, that serve as a further clue to their own inner makeup. The whale is ruthless in attacking the sailors who attempt to hunt and kill him, but it is Ahab who views Moby Dick as a monster of the sea and invests his natural instincts and strength of revenge with malignant and evil intentions. In fact, it is not the whale but the crippled Ahab who alone possesses this characteristic and caused all sailors' death.

Bibliography

http://www.pbs.org/wnet/americannovel/timeline/melville.html, 2013-02-16.
http://en.wikipedia.org/wiki/Moby-Dick, 2013-02-16.
http://www.melville.org/, 2013-02-16.
http://www.sparknotes.com/lit/mobydick/context.html, 2013-02-16.
http://www.newnetherlandinstitute.org/history-and-heritage/dutch_americans/herman-melville/, 2013-02-16.
http://www.online-literature.com/melville/, 2013-02-16.
宋元康 . 美国文学导读 . 昆明：云南大学出版社，2007: 122-136.
王卓，李权文 . 美国文学史 . 武汉：华中师范大学出版社，2010: 82-88.
吴瑾瑾 . 美国文学史 . 北京：经济科学出版社，2008: 106-114.
何木英，杜平 . 美国文学简史与作品选读 . 成都：四川大学出版社，2004: 99-107.
常耀信 . 美国文学简史（第二版修订本）. 天津：南开大学出版社，2003: 79-87.

Henry Wadsworth Longfellow

His Life and Writing Career

His Life

Henry Wadsworth Longfellow (1807–1882), a poet, a traveler, a linguist, a romantic and an educator, was considered to be a most influential national literary figure in the cultural life of nineteenth-century America. As the most popular American poet of his day and a person who had success overseas, he was not only identified with the great traditions of European literature and thought, but also rooted in American life and history, which charged his imagination with untried themes and made him ambitious for success. He became a national literary figure by the 1850s and a world-famous personality by the time of his death in 1882. Longfellow predominantly wrote lyric poems which are known for their musicality and which often presented stories of mythology and legend. However, he has been criticized for imitating European styles and writing specifically for the masses.

Born in Portland, Maine, then part of Massachusetts, on February 27, 1807, Longfellow was the second son in a big family of eight children and grew up in what is now known as the Wadsworth-Longfellow House. His father, Stephen Longfellow, was a prominent local lawyer and later elected as an Adams-Clay Federalist to the Eighteenth Congress. His mother, Zilpah (Wadsworth) Longfellow, was the daughter of Peleg Wadsworth, a general in the American Revolutionary War and a Member of Congress. He was named after his mother's brother Henry Wadsworth, a Navy lieutenant who died only three years earlier at the Battle of Tripoli. When he was a child, his mother began to encourage his enthusiasm for reading and learning. He loved to read funny stories, especially Robinson Crusoe and Don Quixote's works. He entered a dame school at the age of three and by age six was enrolled at the private Portland Academy. In his years there, he was reputed as being very studious and became fluent in Latin. At the age of 13, he printed his first poem "The Battle of Lovell's Pond" in the *Portland Gazette* on November 17, 1820. He stayed at the Portland Academy until the age of fourteen. He spent much of his summers as a child at his maternal grandfather's farm in the western Maine town of Hiram.

In the fall of 1822, Longfellow and his brother Stephen moved to Brunswick, Maine, and started a new life at Bowdoin College, where Longfellow became acquainted with his classmate, Nathaniel Hawthorne. This college was not strange to him, since his grandfather was a founder and his father was a trustee. During his college life, his passion for writing kept growing, though his father advised Longfellow to take up the law. To achieve his aspiration, he sought to submit poetry and prose to various newspapers and magazines. A professor named Thomas Cogswell Upham also encouraged him to pursue a literary goal. He published nearly 40 minor poems at school, about 24 of which appeared in the short-lived Boston periodical *The United States Literary Gazette*. When Longfellow graduated from Bowdoin, he was ranked fourth in the class, and had been elected to Phi Beta Kappa. He gave the student commencement address. After graduating in 1825, he continued to stay at his alma mater to teach modern languages. His father possibly played an important part in securing for him a professorship at the college in modern European languages under the condition that Longfellow travel and study abroad.

In May 1826, he began his three-year tour of Europe aboard the ship Cadmus to study modern languages, and then returned to Bowdoin to teach them. His time abroad would last three years and cost his father $2,604.24. He traveled to France, Spain, Italy, Germany, back to France, then England before returning to the United States in mid-August 1829. While overseas, he spent time with Washington Irving in Madrid, and was particularly impressed by the author's work ethic. Irving encouraged the young Longfellow to pursue writing. On August 27, 1829, he wrote to the president of Bowdoin that he was turning down the professorship because he considered the $600 salary "disproportionate to the duties required." The trustees raised his salary to $800 with an additional $100 to serve as the college's librarian, a post which required one hour of work per day. On September 14, 1831, Longfellow married his first wife Mary Storer Potter, a childhood friend from Portland. The couple settled in Brunswick, though they were not happy there. During his years teaching at the college, he published several nonfiction and fiction prose pieces inspired by Irving, including "The Indian Summer" and "The Bald Eagle" in 1833. He also translated textbooks in French, Italian, and Spanish, of which the poetry of medieval Spanish poet Jorge Manrique was his first published book in 1833. The first trip to Europe also resulted in his first youthful book, a meditative travelogue called *Outre-Mer* ("Overseas")*: A Pilgrimage Beyond the Sea*. This work was released in 1835 and indicated Longfellow's literary temperament.

In December 1834, he was offering the Smith Professorship of Modern Languages position by Josiah Quincy III, president of Harvard College, but under the conditions that he should spend a year or so studying abroad. There, he further studied German as well as Dutch, Danish, Swedish, Finnish, and Icelandic. But in November 1835, during a second trip to Europe, Longfellow's life was shaken when his wife died after a miscarriage. The young teacher spent a grief-stricken year in Germany and Switzerland. Three years later, he was inspired to write the poem "Footsteps of Angels" about her. Several years later, he wrote the poem "Mezzo Cammin" which expressed his personal struggles in his middle years. He began his teaching career at Harvard when he returned back in 1836. In the spring of 1837, he rented rooms at the Craigie House, now preserved as the Longfellow House–Washington's Headquarters National Historic Site. Three years later, at the age of 32, Longfellow began publishing his poetry, including the collection *Voices of the Night* in 1839. The bulk of *Voices of the Night* was translations, though it included nine original poems and seven poems he had written as a teenager. *Ballads and Other Poems* was published shortly thereafter in 1841 and included "The Village Blacksmith" and "The Wreck of the Hesperus," which were instantly popular. As a professor, Longfellow was highly esteemed by students. He also became part of the local social scene, and created a group of friends called the Five of Clubs. Members included Cornelius Conway Felton, George Stillman Hillard, and Charles Sumner.

Eight months after Mary's death, Longfellow met Frances "Fanny" Appleton, the daughter of a wealthy Boston merchant, Nathan Appleton and sister of Thomas Gold Appleton, during his travels through Germany and Switzerland. He began courting Fanny when he again met Fanny seven years after he returned to Cambridge. During his courtship, Longfellow continued writing and published *Hyperion* in 1839. This prose romance was inspired by his trips to Europe as well as his unsuccessful courtship of Fanny. In the next three years, he was occupied by his duties as a professor and had little time to write more. The year of 1842 saw his new book, a play named *The Spanish Student*, which was about his memories from his time in Spain in the 1820s. In the same year, he also released a small collection, *Poems on Slavery*, which was regarded as his first public support of abolitionism. His concerns about slavery were appreciated by the New England Anti-Slavery Association, who decided to reprint the collection for further distribution.

After a seven-year courtship, he married Frances Appleton as his second wife on July 13, 1843. His father-in-law bought the Craigie House to him as a wedding present, where Longfellow lived for the rest of his life. To express his love for Fanny, Longfellow wrote the sonnet "The Evening Star" in October 1845, which was his only love poem. Their 18 years of happy marriage brought the couple six children. His daughter, also named Fanny, died in 1848, which saddened Longfellow very much. Longfellow sometimes sought for inspiration from his children. The poem "The Children's Hour" describes the poet's idyllic family life with his daughters, which first appeared in the September 1860 edition of *The Atlantic Monthly*. In 1858, Longfellow published *The Courtship of Miles Standish*, which sold over 15,000 copies during the first week of publication. On July 9, 1861, tragedy again tormented Longfellow when his wife died at age 44 after sustaining burns from her dress catching fire. Fanny and her two youngest daughters aged five and seven, were in the library. While melting wax to seal envelopes containing cuttings of her children's hair, she dropped a match onto her dress. Longfellow, in trying to save her by smothering the flames with a rug, had burned himself badly enough for him to be unable to attend her funeral. Since facial injuries caused him to stop shaving due to scars from the fire, Longfellow thereafter grew the beard which has become his trademark. Devastated by her death, Longfellow immersed himself in translating Dante into English and returned to Europe. He expressed his grief in the sonnet "The Cross of Snow" (1879), which he wrote eighteen years later to commemorate her death.

When the Civil War broke out in the same year of Fanny's death, Longfellow supported abolitionism and especially hoped for reconciliation between the northern and southern states. In 1863, his son Charles left home to join the war without father's disapproval. During the 1860s, Longfellow continued to write poetry, and his fame kept growing. His poems became popular throughout the English-speaking world and were widely translated into other languages, which made him the most famous American of his day. He had many admirers, including Lincoln, Dickens, and Baudelaire. From 1866 to 1880, Longfellow published seven more books of poetry. When he was at the age of 75 in 1882, his birthday was celebrated across the country. He had to face his impending death because of severe illness, though honors of every kind were bestowed on him in Europe and America. He died at home in Cambridge on 24 March 1882. When Walt Whitman heard of the poet's death, he praised Longfellow as the national bard most needed in a materialistic age. He was buried with his wives at Mount Auburn Cemetery in Cambridge, Middlesex County, Massachusetts. Two years later, he became the first citizen of the United States whose marble bust was placed in Poets' Corner of Westminster Abbey in London, England.

His Writing Career

Longfellow was the most popular poet in the cultural life of his day and is generally regarded as the most distinguished poet the country has produced, whose work are still learned and cited. His chief achievement rests on the adaptation of various ballads to American materials to establish an American mythology. His writing refers to Native American oral history, the Diaspora of Acadians, the first battle of the Revolutionary War and so on. He tries to combine historical events and materials with an enlightened understanding of the common people, and describes the lives and ideals of humbler Americans.

He published his first collection of poems, *Voices of the Night* (1839), followed in 1841 by *Ballads and Other Poems*. When the first collection came out in 1839, Poe predicted that Longfellow would win an enduring reputation for himself with artistic power. The point was evidenced in the fact that *Voices of the Night* was well received upon publication. Certainly, Longfellow also received wide public recognition with his initial volume of this verse. Many of these poems ("A Psalm of Life", for example) showed people triumphing over adversity, and in a struggling young nation that theme was inspiring. In this volume, "Hymn to the Night" conveys the poet's debt to Novalis and his romantic kinship with the "calm, majestic presence of the Night." Longfellow was fascinated by the night and while grieving for his wife took comfort in the darkness of night. The poem expresses his dark, lonely days of grief by paying homage to the night. The imagery of the hymn is very rich and diverse. Longfellow uses a lot of personifications, similes, metaphors, and other literary figures to create the aesthetic atmosphere of the poem. However, "A Psalm of Life," one of the best-known poems from this first collection, reflects the influence of the famed German poet Johann Wolfgang von Goethe (1749–1832).

Longfellow's next volume, *Ballads and Other Poems* (1842), contained two strong narrative poems, "The Wreck of the Hesperus" and "The Skeleton in Armor," as well as the sentimental verses "Maidenhood" and "The Rainy Day" and the moralizing (explaining in the sense of right and wrong) poem "The Village Blacksmith." His most well-known works include *Evangeline* (1847), *The Song of Hiawatha* (1855), *The Courtship of Miles Standish* (1858) and *Paul Rever's Ride* (1861), the first three of which are three notable long narrative poems on American theme. The last one is in commemoration of American patriot Paul Revere, who alerted Colonial militia of approaching British forces before the battles of Lexington and Concord in the American Revolution. It was first published in the January 1861 and later renamed "The Landlord's Tale" in the collection *Tales of a Wayside Inn*.

On November 1, 1847, he published the unimaginative romantic novel *Evangeline* for the first time, a book-length poem about what would now be called "ethnic cleansing." He wrote *Evangeline* in dactylic hexameters. Dactyls are poetic feet of three syllables, with the first syllable long or accented and the others short or unaccented. Hexameters are verses having six poetic feet. The book was enthusiastically received. The highly sentimental narrative poem takes place as the British drive the French from Nova Scotia, and two lovers are parted, only to find each other years later when the man is about to die. He achieved a national reputation with the publication of *Evangeline* (1847). His literary income was increasing considerably: in 1840, he had made $219 from his work but the year 1850 brought him $1,900. On June 14, 1853, Longfellow held a farewell dinner party at his Cambridge home for his friend Nathaniel Hawthorne, who was preparing to move overseas.

In 1854, Longfellow decided to quit teaching to devote all his time to poetry. He published *The Song of Hiawatha* (1855), a long poem about Native American life. From this work Longfellow drew on Henry Schoolcraft's books on Native Americans. He wrote in trochees or poetic feet of two syllables, the first long or accented and the second short or unaccented. Three years later, he released *The Courtship of Miles Standish* (1858). Both books were immensely successful, but Longfellow was now preoccupied with national events. With the country moving towards civil war, he wrote *Paul Revere's Ride*, a call for courage in the coming conflict. He was awarded an honorary doctorate of Laws from Harvard in 1859. A few months after the war began in 1861, Frances Longfellow was sealing an envelope with wax when her dress caught fire. Despite her husband's desperate attempts to save her, she died the next day. Profoundly saddened, Longfellow had difficulty writing original poems for the next two years and turned his creative energy into the translation of Dante Alighieri's *The Divine Comedy*. He was the first American to translate this world-famous work. To perfect the translation, he even invited good friends to aid him, regularly including William Dean Howells, James Russell Lowell, Charles Eliot Norton, who formed the "Dante Club" later on. *Tales of a Wayside Inn*, largely written before his wife's death, was published in 1863, followed by *Household Poems* (1865), *Flower-de-Luce* (1867) and *The New England Tragedies* (1868). After his last trip to Europe in 1868, he released several books one after another, including *Three Books of Song* (1872), *Kéramos and Other Poems* (1878), *Ultima Thule* (1880) and *In the Harbor* (1882). He spent his last few years translating the poetry of *Michael Angelo*, which was collected posthumously in 1883.

Longfellow was one of the five Fireside Poets, whose popularity rivaled that of British poets, both at home and abroad. Though much of his work is categorized as lyric poetry, Longfellow experimented with many forms, including hexameter and free verse. Much of his work is recognized for its melody-like musicality. To the modern readers, Longfellow's sentimental and optimistic poetry seems to sound old-fashioned. He used his wide knowledge of the literature of other countries as a source for both the form and content of many of his poems. The poet's primary subjects were the domestic life, mythology, and politics of the United States. Several of his poems are set in other countries including Italy, Spain, France, and Norway. It should be remembered that Longfellow did not write for the sake of other poets, but wrote for the common people. Generally speaking, his poems adhere to poetic convention, such as standard forms, regular meter, and rhymed stanzas, which made his poems particularly suitable for memorization and recitation. He greatly influenced artistic and popular culture. His poems were read and recited not only in parlors and schoolrooms, but also at civic ceremonies. For the common people, it was a source of entertainment. In his elegant and clear style he presented popular American values, such as the family circle and heroism.

Analyses of and Comments on His Representative Poems

A Psalm of Life (1838)

Contents Summary

The poem first came out in the literary magazine *The Knickerbocker*, October, 1838. Later on, "A Psalm of Life" and other early poems by Longfellow, including "The Village Blacksmith" and "The Wreck of the Hesperus," were collected and published as *Voices of the Night* in 1839. This volume sold for 75 cents. Longfellow wrote the poem shortly after completing lectures on German writer Johann Wolfgang von Goethe and was heavily inspired by him. He was also inspired to write it by a heartfelt conversation he had with friend and fellow professor at Harvard University Cornelius Conway Felton; the two had spent an evening "talking of matters, which lie near one's soul: —and how to bear one's self doughtily in Life's battle: and make the best of things." The next day, he wrote "A Psalm of Life." In the summer of 1838, Longfellow wrote "The Light of Stars," a poem which he called "A Second Psalm of Life."

Themes

"A Psalm of Life" consists of 28 lines which relates to the topic, "Life." It has a bitter, cold, despairing, detached, dramatic, somber, and sullen tone, set in a minor scheme. Depressing vocabulary usage of the poet is extensive, and such examples include "mournful," "empty," "dead," "grave," "sorrow," "end," "fleeting," "funeral," "battle," "bivouac," "dumb," "sublime," "departing," "leave behind," "solemn," and "fate." The point of view is in "the heart of the young man," of whom is probably a sailor. The poem expresses both the confusion of his feelings in that time of discouragement and his resolve not to succumb to mournful passivity. In this poem, the young man is giving the psalmist advice on how to live their life by dismissing the notion that human life is a meaningless illusion.

Literary Techniques

Mr. Longfellow has ways of bringing out his ideas. He does this by incorporating poetic devices to emphasize his ideas. For example, he asserts that the soul will not die in an allusion to the Genesis, where God says to the fallen Adam, "dust thou *art,* and unto dust shalt thou return." In line 15, he compares the human heartbeat to"muffled drums," which implies that reminds us of the transient nature of life and each beat of our hearts carries us closer to death. He suggests the idea of a record of greatness by using a metaphor "footprints on the sands of time." Additionally, the rhythm of this poem is a-b-a-b, which makes sound quick, quiet and rhythmic. If you read the stanza aloud, it sounds as though you were on the scene.

My Lost Youth (1855)

Contents Summary

"My Lost Youth" was first published in *Putnam's Monthly* in 1855, and later collected in *The Courtship of Miles Standish and Other Poems* (1858). It is a lyrical autobiography of the poet's early life, in which Longfellow pays tribute to the home where he lived his youthful years in Maine and to the imaginative boy who climbed its hilly streets and gazed out over its harbor. Born on Fore Street, the family moved to his maternal grandparents' home on Congress Street when Henry was eight months old. Today, the house has been a museum about the life and times of the poet and his family. Before entering Bowdoin College and traveling extensively abroad, he spent his boyhood mostly in this city, walking round Munjoy's hill, listening to the lashing, lulling sound of the sea, and dreaming faraway dreams.

Themes

In the poem, Longfellow describes the beautiful surroundings and quiet, pure life, and expresses his enduring gratitude and appreciation for the inspiration this scenery brought him.

Literary Techniques

The poem contains 1806 words, and rhymes with a pattern of a-b-a-a-b-c-d-d-e throughout. The style appears simple and conversational. It consists of ten nine-line stanzas, the last two lines of each being the famous refrain "A boy's will is the wind's will, / And the thoughts of youth are long, long thoughts." The two-line refrain from the Lapland song, about a boy's will similar to the wind's will, captures both the nostalgia and the idea of errant youth. Recalling his boyhood in Portland, Longfellow is more concerned with the emotions aroused in his mind than with what his town was like. It could be any seaside town, since few details about Portland is vividly specified. These vague details lead to the emotional theme of private boyhood dreams. It is that time in youth when flights of imagination are most prevalent.

The "Hesperides" is a metaphor in the line "And islands that were the Hesperides, / Of all my boyish dreams." It indicates the Garden of the Hesperides. In Greek mythology, it is a Hera's orchard in a far western corner of the world in which a grove of immortality-giving golden apples grew. The earth, Gaia, offered them to Hera when she accepted Zeus. It is used as the subject matter which occupied his "boyish dreams." The speaker, as a boy, longed for adventure and romance such as this mythical place in mythology.

The Song of Hiawatha (1855)

Plot Summary

Longfellow chose to set *The Song of Hiawatha* at the Pictured Rocks, one of the locations along the south shore of Lake Superior favored by narrators of the Manabozho stories. The *Song* presents a legend of Hiawatha and his lover *Minnehaha* in 22 chapters (and an Introduction). Hiawatha is not introduced until Chapter III. In Chapter I, Hiawatha's arrival is prophesied by a "mighty" peace-bringing leader named *Gitche Manito.* Chapter II tells a legend of how the warrior *Mudjekeewis* became Father of the Four Winds by slaying the Great Bear of the mountains, *Mishe-Mokwa.* His son Wabun, the East Wind, falls in love with a maiden whom he turns into the Morning Star, Wabun-Annung. Wabun's brother, Kabibonokka, the North Wind, bringer of autumn and winter, attacks Shingebis, "the diver." Shingebis repels him by burning firewood, and then in a wrestling match. A third brother, Shawondasee, falls in love with a dandelion, mistaking it for a golden-haired maiden. In Chapter III, in "unremembered ages," a woman named Nokomis falls from the moon. Nokomis gives birth to Wenonah, who grows to be a beautiful young woman. Nokomis warns her not to be seduced by the West Wind (Mudjekeewis) but she does not heed her mother, becomes pregnant and bears Hiawatha. In the ensuing chapters, Hiawatha has childhood adventures, falls in love with Minnehaha, slays the evil magician Pearl-Feather, invents written language, discovers corn, and other episodes. The poem closes with the approach of a birch canoe to Hiawatha's village, containing "the Priest of Prayer, the Pale-face." Hiawatha welcomes him joyously; and the "Black-Robe chief" brings word of Jesus Christ. Hiawatha and the chiefs accept the Christian message. Hiawatha bids farewell to Nokomis, the warriors, and the young men, giving them this charge: "But my guests I leave behind me/ Listen to their words of wisdom,/ Listen to the truth they tell you." Having endorsed the Christian missionaries, he launches his canoe for the last time westward toward the sunset, and departs forever.

Themes

Hiawatha was a probable historical figure associated with the founding of the League of the Iroquois, the Five Nations then located in present-day New York and Pennsylvania. Hiawatha's altruistic nature defines Longfellow's political purpose in the poem. His intention was not to "tame" the savages but to integrate native themes and cultural references into the larger system of shared cultural meanings that, for him, was the business of American literature. Because of the poem, however, "Hiawatha" became the namesake for towns, schools and a telephone company in the western Great Lakes region, where no Iroquois nations historically resided.

Literary Techniques

The Song of Hiawatha is an epic poem, in trochaic tetrameter, featuring an Indian hero. It is loosely based on the legends and ethnography of the Ojibwe and other Native American peoples as contained in *Algic Researches* (1839) and additional writings by Henry Rowe Schoolcraft, an ethnographer and United States Indian agent. In sentiment, scope, overall conception, and many particulars, Longfellow's poem is very much a work of American Romantic literature, not a representation of Native American oral tradition.

Henry Wadsworth Longfellow begins this delightful work with a sort of bibliography. He learned these legends from the lips of Navadaha the musician. Navadaha got his information from the wild animals of America: from the lodges of the beaver, from the eyry of the eagle, etc. Longfellow chose to set *The Song of Hiawatha* at the Pictured Rocks, one of the locations along the south shore of Lake Superior favored by narrators of the Manabozho stories. *The Song* presents a legend of Hiawatha and his lover Minnehaha in 22 chapters (and an Introduction). Hiawatha is not introduced until Chapter III. The poem was published on November 10, 1855, and was an immediate success. In 1857, Longfellow calculated that it had sold 50,000 copies.

Bibliography

http://wiki.answers.com/Q/The_summary_of_the_poem_a_psalm_of_life_by_long_fellow, 2013-02-16.

http://en.wikipedia.org/wiki/A_Psalm_of_Life, 2013-02-16.

http://www.hwlongfellow.org/life_overview.shtml, 2013-02-16.

http://en.wikipedia.org/wiki/Henry_Wadsworth_Longfellow, 2013-02-16.

http://www.notablebiographies.com/Lo-Ma/Longfellow-Henry-Wadsworth.html, 2013-02-16.

http://poetryproject2004.tripod.com/analysis-psalm.htm, 2013-02-16.

http://www.online-literature.com/henry_longfellow/, 2013-02-16.

http://www.enotes.com/my-lost-youth-salem/my-lost-youth#channel=f12d854a4794ac5&origin=http%3A%2F%2Fwww.enotes.com&channel_path=%2Fmy-lost-youth-salem%2Fmy-lost-youth%3Ffb_xd_fragment%23xd_sig%3. Df14127e67f83e71%26, 2013-02-16.

http://en.wikipedia.org/wiki/The_Song_of_Hiawatha, 2013-02-16.

http://www.enotes.com/song-hiawatha-reference/song-hiawatha, 2013-02-16.

宋元康 . 美国文学导读 . 昆明：云南大学出版社，2007: 136-142.

吴瑾瑾 . 美国文学史 . 北京：经济科学出版社，2008: 49-92.
曹曼 . 美国文学教程 . 武汉：武汉大学出版社，2007: 123-129.
何木英，杜平 . 美国文学简史与作品选读 . 成都：四川大学出版社，2004: 51-57.
胡荫桐，刘树森 . 美国文学教程 . 天津：南开大学出版社，2003: 200-206.
胡荫桐 . 美国文学新编 . 北京：外语教学与研究出版社，2001: 100-104.
李翠亭，李正栓 . 美国文学学习指南 . 北京：清华大学出版社，1998: 75-77.

PART IV

AMERICAN LITERATURE IN THE REALISTIC PERIOD

(1865–1900)

Historical Introduction

From the late 19th to the early 20th centuries, the United States experienced enormous industrial, economic, social and cultural changes. A continuous wave of European immigration and the rising potential for international trade brought increasing growth and prosperity to America. The American Civil War, which cost US $ 8 billion and claimed 600,000 lives, exerted a great influence on American society, an influence which no one could ignore. In fact, the War marked a tremendous change in American moral values.

After the Civil War, southern agrarianism was defeated by northern industrialism, which resulted in a society based on mass labor and mass consumption. Mechanization spread rapidly, and machine displaced hand work on farms and in factories. Therefore, the conditions of labor changed. Machine seemed far more valuable and more useful than workers. A great number of farmers had to leave their farms to seek jobs in urban factories.

The total population of the United States doubled (from 1870 to 1890). The growth of population brought forth large cities and towns. At the same time, the national income quadrupled. By mid-1890s appeared about 4,000 millionaires that included Rockefeller, Carnegie and Morgan who dominated the American industry in a large extent in the early half of the 20th century. The gulf between the rich and the poor was widened as a result of the growth of industry. Reform movements and labor unions voiced the grievances of debt-ridden farmers and immigrant workers living in city slums and factories. It was the time of radiant prosperity, when ministers preached and ordinary people believed in a gospel of wealth, which suggested that rich were at last in league with virtue and the age of unlimited progress had finally appeared.

Disillusionment and frustration were widely felt. The national spirit changed to admiration for driving ambition, a lust for money and power.

The railroad changed the way Americans worked and lived. It transported products from west to east and from north to south. People became mobile, too. Steel production became the dominant industry in America. This was an age of steam and steel, oil and electricity. The age was still in an optimistic atmosphere. "The tempo of life accelerated as Americans became increasingly mobile. Journeys of weeks or months were reduced to a few days. In the last surge of westward expansion, Americans lured by the promise of free land, settled the last of the first forty-eight states." By 1890 the westward movement had began. The frontier had thus expanded. It shaped the values of the nation and inspired a lot of legend, novels and western movies.

Meanwhile, the great age of big-city blossom began, and the art of political patronage and graft rose to new heights throughout the land. The first conscription laws were passed and the first federal income taxes were levied, and a national currency, controlled by the federal government, was issued. In 1865 the first step toward racial equality was made when the Thirteenth Amendment to the Constitution was adopted, abolishing slavery within the United States. During the Civil War the powers of the federal government rapidly expanded. However, the increasing imbalance between the rich and the poor would profoundly alter the nation's politics and its social ideals. Traditional political alliances had begun to shift. The lower classes sought greater power at the polls. Business growth and exploitation of natural resources created new wealth. Vast riches and economic power were concentrated in the hands of a few people. It was an age of what Mark Twain called "The Gilded Age," an age of widespread economic growth as the United States jumped to the lead in industrialization ahead of Britain.

Such a rapid growth demanded changes in education and culture. There was a fashion that imitated European culture. American millionaires built Gothic and Romanesque mansions, and decorated them with towers, domes, columns, stained-glass windows. They imported art exhibitions from Europe, as symbols of European culture. Rich people adopted European dress style and manners, and even sent their children to Europe for an education. New York replaced Boston as the nation's literary center. Women became a dominating voice in American cultural force. In literary writing, Realism became the dominating trend. Amy Kaplan has called realism a "strategy for imagining and managing the threats of social change."

Realism

The dominant paradigm in novel writing during the second half of the nineteenth century was no longer the Romantic idealism of the earlier part of the century. What took hold among the great novelists in Europe and America was a new approach to character and subject matter, a school of thought which later came to be known as Realism. Broadly defined as "the faithful representation of reality" or "verisimilitude," realism is a literary technique practiced by many schools of writing. Although strictly speaking, realism is a technique, it also denotes a particular kind of subject matter, especially the representation of middle-class life. A reaction against romanticism, realistic writers took great interest in scientific method. The systematizing of the study of documentary history and the influence of rational philosophy all affected the rise of realism. On one level, Realism is precisely what it sounds like. It lays great emphasis on daily details, and makes every effort to replicate the true nature of reality in a way that novelists had never attempted. There is the belief that the novel's function is simply to report what happens, without comment or judgment. Seemingly inconsequential elements gain the attention of the novel functioning in the realist mode.

Realism coincided with Victorianism, yet was a distinct collection of aesthetic principles in its own right. The realist novels were heavily informed by journalistic techniques, such as objectivity and fidelity to the facts of the matter. It was not a coincidence that many of the better known novelists of the time had concurrent occupations in the publishing industry. The idea of novel-writing as a "report" grew out of this marriage between literature and journalism. To some extent, the rise of realism is closely related to the fast development of journalism.

Another fair comparison would be to think of the realist novels as an early form of docudrama, in which fictional persons and events are intended to seamlessly reproduce the real world. The Victorian Period saw growing concern with the plight of the less fortunate in society, and the realistic novel likewise turned its attention to subjects that beforehand would not have warranted notice. The balancing act that the upwardly mobile middle class had to perform in order to retain their position in the world was a typical subject for realistic novels. There arose a subgenre of Realism called Social Realism, which in hindsight could be interpreted as Marxist and socialist ideas set forth in literature.

The overriding concern of all realist fiction is with characters. Specifically, novelists struggled to create intricate and layered characters who, as much as possible, felt as though they could be flesh and blood creatures. Much of this effect was achieved through internal monologues and a keen understanding of human psychology. Not surprisingly, the field of psychology was in the process of evolving from metaphysical quackery into a bona fide scientific pursuit. Students of the human mind were beginning to realize that an individual was composed of a network of motivations, interests, desires, and fears. How these forces interact and sometimes do battle with each other plays a large part in the development of personality. Realism, at its highest level, attempts to lay these internal struggles bare for all to see. In other words, most of the "action" of the realist novel is internalized. Changes in mood, in perceptions, in opinions and ideas constitute turning points or climaxes.

From Henry James, for example, one gets a sense of being there in the moment, as a dense fabric of minute details and observations is constructed. This change in style meant that some of the traditional expectations about the novel's form had to be pushed aside. In contrast to what came before, the realistic novel rested upon the strengths of its characters rather than plot or turn of phrase. The characters that the realistic school of novelists produced were some of the most famous modes in literary history, from Henry James's *Daisy Miller* (1878) to Fyodor Dostoyevsky's *Crime and Punishment* (1866). They are psychologically complicated, multifaceted, and with conflicting impulses and motivations that very nearly replicate the daily tribulations of being human.

Realist novelists eschewed many of the novel's established traditions, most notably in the form of plot structure. Typically, novels follow a definite arc of events, with an identifiable climax and resolution. They are self-contained and satisfying in their symmetry. Successful careers have been built on the scaffolding of a single story arc. The school of Realism observed that life did not follow such patterns, so for them, neither should the novel. Instead of grand happenings, tragedies, and epic turns of events, the realist novel plodded steadily over a track not greatly disturbed by external circumstances, as is in Henry James's *The Portrait of a Lady* (1881). The same can be said of Dostoyevsky—He composed lengthy and weighty fiction where most, if not all of the action happened in the minds of the characters.

Narrative style also changed with realistic fiction. Instead of an omniscient narrator calmly describing the persons and events, readers often confront unreliable narrators who do not have all the information. Often, the narrator's perceptions are colored by their own prejudices and beliefs. A popular device for many realistic novelists was the frame narrative, or the story inside a story. This device compounds the unreliable narrator by placing the reader at a further remove from the events of the novel. The purpose of all of these innovations, as with the whole of Realism, was to more accurately simulate the nature of reality—unknowable, uncertain, and ever-shifting reality.

Realism encompasses the period of time from the Civil War to the turn of the century during which William Dean Howells, Rebecca Harding Davis, Henry James, Mark Twain, and others wrote fiction devoted to accurate representation and an exploration of American lives in various contexts. Realism was a movement that encompassed the entire country, or at least the Midwest and South, although many of the writers and critics associated with realism (notably W. D. Howells) were based in New England. Among the Midwestern writers considered realists would be Joseph Kirkland, E. W. Howe, and Hamlin Garland; the Southern writer John W. DeForest's *Miss Ravenal's*

Conversion from Secession to Loyalty (1867) is often considered a realist novel.

The beginnings of the realist narrative style can be attributed to French novelist and playwright Honoré de Balzac. His portraits of ordinary French life were remarkable in their careful attention to details. Balzac reportedly consulted with associates in order to learn more about specific subjects, so as to portray them in their fullness. He expressed the idea that characters come to life through the painstaking accumulation of environmental details. His methodology was a departure from the Romantic tradition which was near its zenith when he was crafting his stories. Balzac also put enormous emphasis on the settings of his stories. Whether urban or provincial, the locale almost becomes a character of its own. His most famous work, which was left unfinished, was *The Human Comedy* (1869–1876), an assortment of interwoven tales and novels which depict life in early nineteenth century France. The effect of the narrative buildup in *The Human Comedy* is the realization of an epic that is more than the sum of its parts. Like the realists who would follow in his footsteps, Balzac did not rely on profound or spectacular events to move his stories along. Instead, he paid attention to the small things, the nuances that made up the experience of typical French life.

Samuel Clemens was the early pioneer of Realism. Writing under the pen name Mark Twain, he was noteworthy for his faithful reproduction of vernacular speech patterns and vocabulary. He more or less gave birth to "local color," a sub-genre of the novel that still enjoys wide appeal today. Replicating natural speech required not just great listening skills, but a sense of how the written version sounds to the imagination. In addition to the use of vernacular, Twain was an innovator in focusing on middle and lower class characters. Previously, novels had concentrated on the experiences of the elite. Presumably, the upper crust enjoyed seeing their lives of privilege reflected back to them in art, while salt of the earth readers had something to aspire to and fantasize about. It was a revolutionary concept to incorporate unremarkable characters into an art form as serious as the novel. In a development that continues to bewilder, *The Adventures of Huckleberry Finn* (1884) is one of the most frequently banned books in the public school system. One imagines that certain language is indeed offensive; however Twain was doing nothing other than representing honest speech. Huck Finn was in all reality an astonishing leap forward in racial awareness—Jim, the freed slave, is as fully realized a character as Tom or Huck.

A great friend of Mark Twain, and an eminent American realist in his own right, was the magazine editor William Dean Howells. In charge of the *Atlantic Monthly* for several years, Howells exercised a lot of authority over the currents of taste on his side of the ocean. In his role as editor, he was instrumental in promoting the fame of literary rising stars, such as Frank Norris, Stephen Crane, and Sarah Orne Jewett. Howells wrote copious volumes of fiction of his own, and was an unqualified success in that regard.

For a time, he was widely considered the most accomplished of all American Realists. That reputation faded somewhat and today Howells's work as an editor is held up as his most important contribution. That being said, several of his novels are in the first rank of American Realism. Published in 1885, the ironically titled *The Rise of Silas Lapham* tells the story of an ambitious businessman who tumbles out of fortune through his own mistakes and poor judgment. It is an anti-success story, and illustrates one of the central ideas of Realism, that of crafting honest narratives rather than feel-good sentimental fantasies. In short, there is a kind of grimness to Realism that many readers have found unappealing. *A Modern Instance* (1882) highlights this same principle in detailing the steady disintegration of a seemingly happy marriage.

Realism came under attack largely because it represented such a bold departure from what readers had come to expect from the novel. The fascination with things falling apart was unpleasant to many, and critics sometimes accused the practitioners of Realism of focusing only on the negative aspects of social life. Additionally, the intense focus on the minutiae of character was seen as unwillingness to actually tell a story. Readers complained that very little happened in realistic fiction, that they were all talk and little payoff. Henry James in particular was criticized for his verbosity, especially in his later years. By the end of the nineteenth century, Realism in the pure sense had given way to another form called Naturalism. With Naturalism, authors looked to heredity and history to define character. Ironically, many of the qualities that people found distasteful in realism — the obsession with character, the superficially mundane plots — were all intensified in Naturalism.

Naturalism

Naturalism was a literary movement taking place from the 1880s to 1940s that used detailed realism to suggest that social conditions, heredity, and environment had inescapable force in shaping human character. It was an extension of realism, a reaction against the restrictions inherent in the realistic emphasis on the ordinary, as naturalists insisted that the extraordinary is real, too. Naturalism yielded great influence on the twentieth century. It was depicted as a literary movement that seeks to replicate a believable everyday reality, as opposed to such movements as Romanticism or Surrealism, in which subjects may receive highly symbolic, idealistic, or even supernatural treatment.

Naturalism is the outgrowth of literary realism, a prominent literary movement in mid-19th-century France and elsewhere. Naturalistic writers were influenced by Charles Darwin's theory of evolution. Naturalism came largely from scientific Determinism.

Darwinism was especially important to the genre, as the naturalists perceived a person's fate as the product of blind external or biological forces (chiefly heredity and environment). But in the typical naturalistic novel, change played a large part as well.

Naturalistic writers believed that one's heredity and social environment largely determine one's character and fate. Whereas Realism seeks only to describe subjects as they really are, Naturalism also attempts to determine "scientifically" the underlying forces influencing the actions of its subjects, including the environment and heredity. Naturalistic works often include uncouth or sordid subject matter, for example, Émile Zola's works had frankness about sexuality along with a pervasive pessimism. Naturalistic works exposed the dark harshness of life, including poverty, racism, violence, prejudice, disease, corruption, prostitution, and filth. As a result, naturalistic writers were frequently criticized for focusing too much on human vice and misery.

Naturalistic writers attempt to apply strict scientific principles of objectivity and detachment to its study of human beings. Unlike realism, which focuses on literary technique, naturalism implies a philosophical position: for naturalistic writers, since human beings are, in Emile Zola's phrase, "human beasts," characters can be studied through their relationships to their surroundings. Zola's 1880 description of this method in *Le roman experimental* (*The Experimental Novel*, 1880) follows Claude Bernard's medical model and the historian Hippolyte Taine's observation that "virtue and vice are products like vitriol and sugar." In other words, human beings as "products" should be studied impartially, without moralizing about their natures. Other influences on American naturalists include Herbert Spencer and Joseph LeConte.

Through the objective study of human beings, naturalistic writers believed that the laws behind the forces that govern human lives might be studied and understood. Naturalistic writers thus used a version of the scientific method to write their novels; they studied human beings governed by their instincts and passions as well as the ways in which the characters' lives were governed by forces of heredity and environment. Although they used the techniques of accumulating detail pioneered by the realists, the naturalists thus had a specific object in mind when they chose the segment of reality that they wished to convey.

In naturalistic novels, frequently but not invariably ill-educated or lower-class characters whose lives are governed by the forces of heredity, instinct, and passions are often heroes. Their attempts at exercising free will or choice are hampered by forces beyond their control; social Darwinism and other theories help to explain their fates to the reader.

Themes of naturalistic novels often identify survival, determinism, violence, and taboo, etc. The compassions within each person are composed of strong and often warring emotions: passions, such as lust, greed, or the desire for dominance or pleasure; and the fight for survival in an amoral, indifferent universe. The conflict in naturalistic novels is often "man against nature" or "man against himself" as characters struggle to retain a "veneer of civilization" despite external pressures that threaten to release the "brute within."

As an indifferent force, nature often acts on the lives of human beings. Therefore, the forces of heredity and environment affect and afflict individual lives. An indifferent, deterministic universe is often the setting. Naturalistic texts often describe the futile attempts of human beings to exercise free will, often ironically presented, in this universe that reveals free will as an illusion. Frank Norris, Theodore Dreiser, Jack London, Stephen Crane, Edith Wharton, Ellen Glasgow are the main practitioners.

There are some defining characteristics of literary naturalism. One of these is pessimism. Very often, one or more characters will continue to repeat one phrase that tends to have a pessimistic connotation, sometimes emphasizing the inevitability of death. Characters in naturalistic novels seldom have happy endings and their lives are full of ups and downs.

Another characteristic of literary naturalism is detachment from the story. The author often tries to maintain a tone that will be experienced as "objective." Also, some authors will sometimes achieve detachment by creating nameless characters, which puts the focus on the plot and what happens to the character, rather than the characters themselves. In other words, their fates are doomed no matter who they are and how hard they have struggled.

The third characteristic of naturalism is determinism, the opposite of free will, essentially. For determinism, the idea that individual characters have a direct influence on the course of their lives is supplanted by a focus on nature or fate. Often, a naturalist writer will lead the reader to believe a character's fate has been predetermined, usually by environmental factors, and that he or she can do nothing about it.

Psychological Realism

Psychological Realism is another subgenre of realism. As a kind of ideological trend of literature which appears in the traditional literature in the course from realism to modernism, Psychological Realism gives up the previous realistic works of moral, social, and political criticism. It places more than the usual amount of emphasis on interior characterization and the inner motives. The psychological novelists are not content to state what happens but goes on to explain why this takes place. In this type of writing, character and characterization are more important than usual. Psychological realistic writers often delve deeper into the mind of a character than novels of other genres. In some cases, the stream of consciousness technique, as well as interior monologues, may be employed to better illustrate the inner workings of the human mind at work.

Flashbacks may also be featured. While these three textual techniques are also prevalent in "modernism," there is no deliberate effort to fragment the prose or compel the reader to interpret the text.

As a literary skill, Psychological Realism makes its first appearance in the drama field. The psychological realistic drama, which is in the deep influence of Chekhov, broke away from the tradition of the western drama of external dramatic. Its remarkable feature is the internalization of mind, namely to search people's deep psychological. The acquisition of these artistic characteristics is the result of the artistic creation laws and under the direct impact of modernistic literature. In America theatre, Tennessee Williams paid more attention to the "psychological realism," focusing his attention on the marginal and psychological trauma of personal, putting it onto the dramatic stage with the poetic language and lyrical style with their inner animal characteristics.

When it comes to the American fiction, Henry James is the representative of Psychological Realism. He is the most skilled and accomplished practitioner of Psychological Realism in fiction. He was fascinated by encounters between representatives of the New World, America, with members of the Old World, or Europe. He observed a distinct set of traits that permeated each of these groups. With Americans, he witnessed vigor, innocence, and strict moral righteousness. Europeans, on the other hand, represented decadence, lax morality, and deviousness. With such seeming prejudices built into his aesthetics, one is surprised to learn that James renounced his American citizenship and became a British subject. Nevertheless, James made a cottage industry out of examining what happened when these two worlds collided. Arguably his most famous work was the novella *Daisy Miller*, which relates how a young and rich American girl touring Europe is victimized by sophisticated schemers, with no compunctions about right or wrong.

At the height of his powers, Henry James crafted intricate novels that featured completely realized characters. He was remarkable for his ability to dispense with commentary or subjectivity within his narratives. The reader sees the events through the eyes of the characters; James the author makes himself as invisible as possible. In terms of prose style, he was admired for the simplicity and directness of his language, a quality not generally noted during the Victorian Period. His most successful novel was *The Portrait of a Lady*, published as one volume in 1881. With *Portrait* he expands upon many of the themes one finds in *Daisy Miller*—greed, power, and the exploitation of the New World by the Old. Revealingly, film adaptations of the novel have generally not made good impressions. As with the bulk of fiction that earns the title of Realist, the narrative simply does not lend itself to visual reproduction.

Advances in the field of human psychology also fed into the preoccupation with representing the inner workings of the mind, and the delicate play of emotions. William

James, brother of novelist Henry James, was a gargantuan figure in the early history of human psychology. One can imagine that their conversations proved highly influential in Henry's creative development. Psychologists were just beginning to understand that human consciousness was far more complicated and various than had previously been considered. Debates about nature versus nurture were as popular then as they are today. More than anything, the understanding that in the human mind there are very few absolutes was critical for the realist sensibility. To put it another way, Realism embraced the concept that people were neither completely good or completely bad, but somewhere on a spectrum.

On an outward level, this realism typically involves reacting to external characters and situations in a manner consistent with the expectations of readers (verisimilitude). On an internal level, it may involve the revelation of characters' thoughts and internal meditations about themselves and others. Such internal machinations are a standard part of Elizabethan drama in the form of the soliloquy. However, psychological realism is associated most closely with the movement toward "realism" and "naturalism" in the 19th- and 20th-centuries. After psychoanalysis appeared, Freudian ideas influenced many writers who sought to incorporate his theories into their own depictions of characters.

In the literature of the United States, apart from Henry James, Arthur Miller and Edith Wharton are considered major contributors to the practice of psychological realism.

Bibliography

Wu, Weiren. *History and Anthology of American Literature, Vol 2*. Beijing: Foreign Language Teaching and Research Press, 2012: 1-3.

http://www.online-literature.com/periods/realism.php, 2012-07-04.

http://en.wikipedia.org/wiki/Naturalism_(literature), 2012-07-04.

Walt Whitman

His Life and Writing Career

His Life

Walt Whitman (1819–1892) was born in Long Island, New York, to parents with interests in Quaker thought, Walter and Louisa Van Velsor Whitman, and brought up partly in Brooklyn. The second of nine children, he was immediately nicknamed "Walt" to distinguish him from his father.

He had little formal education, and started work as an office boy; he subsequently worked as printer, wandering school teacher and contributor to and editor of various magazines and newspapers, entering politics as a Democrat, and traveling in 1848 to New Orleans, where he wrote for the *Crescent*.

At age four, Whitman moved with his family from West Hills to Brooklyn, living in a series of homes, in part due to bad investments. Whitman looked back on his childhood as generally restless and unhappy, given his family's difficult economic status.

At age eleven Whitman concluded formal schooling. He then sought employment for further income for his family; he was an office boy for two lawyers and later was an apprentice and printer's devil for the weekly Long Island newspaper the *Patriot*, edited by Samuel E. Clements. There, Whitman learned about the printing press and typesetting.

Whitman worked as a journalist, a teacher, a government clerk, and—in addition to publishing his poetry—was a volunteer nurse during the American Civil War. After a stroke towards the end of his life, he moved to Camden, New Jersey, where his health further declined. He died at age 72 and his funeral became a public spectacle.

His Writing Career

All of Whitman's previous experiences—on newspapers; in teaching; in a somewhat dysfunctional family; in contact with people of ideas and moral values, especially people like Emerson and Thoreau; with writing nearly 3,000 articles and editorials; even with writing a novel and 24 short stories, which were, by today's standards, pretty bad—all of this experience led to his thinking about, making notes for, and finally writing the first poems that would make their way into, and sometimes out from, *Leaves of Grass*.

There was so little in the short stories that prepared Whitman followers for *Leaves of Grass* (1855–1892) that his contemporaries must have wondered if the same person wrote both. The stories are primarily moralistic, perhaps like the stories he told to his public school classes when someone had misbehaved. They are superficial and often poorly written. The poetry of *Leaves of Grass,* on the other hand, is philosophical, often with multiple layers of meaning. And though Whitman did not invent the free verse poetic style he used in *Leaves of Grass* (it is the verse form of much of the Old Testament), he developed it as the perfect form with which to merge his own rich and optimistic belief in the American spirit: free individual, and democratic.

The slim volume did not sell well, and the first reviews were a disappointment to Whitman. It was criticized both for its free-flowing style and for what reviewers saw as an exaltation of the human body in general and sexual love in particular. American readers favored rhyme and standard rhythm patterns, which were still the preference of poets in England and New England. And it was the free style and exaltation that Emerson liked, praising Whitman for his difference. "I find it the most extraordinary piece of wit and wisdom that America has yet contributed," Emerson wrote to him. "I am very happy in reading it, as great power makes us happy... I rubbed my eyes a little to see if this sunbeam were no illusion; but the solid sense of the book is a sober certainty." Whitman managed to have Emerson's letter published in the *New York Tribune* without his permission and later in the second edition of *Leaves of Grass*. Whitman was wrong to take advantage of Emerson's kindness, but Emerson's praise of Whitman turned a number of heads, critics and readers alike, and no doubt made the second edition, published the next year, more popular and probably better read. Emerson met Whitman later on December 11, 1855, at Whitman's home on Ryerson Street in Brooklyn. Bronson Alcott and Henry David Thoreau visited Whitman twice during the fall of 1856, the second time with Sarah Tyndale, an abolitionist and women's rights advocate from Philadelphia, who no doubt noted Whitman's equal treatment of women in his poems.

His work was very controversial in its time, particularly his poetry collection *Leaves of Grass*, which was described as obscene for its overt sexuality. Early in his career, he also produced a temperance novel, *Franklin Evans* (1842). Whitman's major work, *Leaves of Grass*, was first published in 1855 with his own money. The work was an attempt at reaching out to the common person with an American epic. He continued expanding and revising it until his death in 1892.

In fact, the experience of the frontier merged with his admiration for Emerson to produce the first edition of *Leaves of Grass,* 12 poems saturated, as he describes it, "with the vehemence of pride and audacity of freedom necessary to loosen the mind of still-to-be-form'd America from the folds, the superstitions, and all the long, tenacious and stifling anti-democratic authorities of Asiatic and European past." When Emerson was sent a copy he replied hailing the work, with good reason, as "the most extraordinary piece of wit and wisdom that America has yet contributed." The second edition (1856) added 21 poems, and the third edition (1860) 122, including the group entitled "Calamus," which has been taken as a reflection of the poet's homosexuality, although in his own words they celebrate the "beautiful and sane affection of man for man." The six further editions that appeared in Whitman's lifetime were revised or added to, the work enlarging as the poet developed. During the Civil War Whitman worked as a clerk in Washington, but his real business was as a volunteer hospital visitor among the wounded, an experience which affected him deeply, as can be seen in his prose *Memoranda during the War* (1875) and in the poems published under the title of *Drum-Taps* in 1865. In the *Sequel* to these poems (1865-6) appeared the great elegy on

Abraham Lincoln, "When Lilacs Last in the Dooryard Bloomed."

Whitman's sexuality is often discussed alongside his poetry. Though biographers continue to debate his sexuality, he is usually described as either homosexual or bisexual in his feelings and attractions. However, there is disagreement among biographers as to whether Whitman had actual sexual experiences with men.

Whitman was concerned with politics throughout his life. He supported the Wilmot Proviso and opposed the extension of slavery generally. His poetry presented an egalitarian view of the races, and at one point he called for the abolition of slavery, but later he saw the abolitionist movement as a threat to democracy.

Whitman published a series of ten editorials, called "Sun-Down Papers—From the Desk of a Schoolmaster", in three newspapers between the winter of 1840 and July 1841. In these essays, he adopted a constructed persona, a technique he would employ throughout his career.

Whitman claimed that after years of competing for "the usual rewards", he determined to become a poet. He first experimented with a variety of popular literary genres which appealed to the cultural tastes of the period. As early as 1850, he began writing what would become *Leaves of Grass*, a collection of poetry which he would continue editing and revising until his death. Whitman intended to write a distinctly American epic and used free verse with a cadence based on the Bible. At the end of June 1855, Whitman surprised his brothers with the already-printed first edition of *Leaves of Grass*. George "didn't think it worth reading."

Whitman paid for the publication of the first edition of *Leaves of Grass* himself and had it printed at a local print shop during their breaks from commercial jobs. A total of 795 copies were printed. No name is given as author; instead, facing the title page was an engraved portrait done by Samuel Hollyer, but 500 lines into the body of the text he calls himself "Walt Whitman, an American, one of the roughs, a kosmos, disorderly, fleshly, and sensual, no sentimentalist, no stander above men or women or apart from them, no more modest than immodest." The inaugural volume of poetry was preceded by a prose preface of 827 lines. The succeeding untitled twelve poems totaled 2315 lines—1336 lines belonging to the first untitled poem, later called "Song of Myself." The book received its strongest praise from Ralph Waldo Emerson, who wrote a flattering five page letter to Whitman and spoke highly of the book to friends. The first edition of *Leaves of Grass* was widely distributed and stirred up significant interest, in part due to Emerson's approval, but was occasionally criticized for the seemingly "obscene" nature of the poetry. Geologist John Peter Lesley wrote to Emerson, calling the book "trashy, profane & obscene" and the author "a pretentious ass." On July 11, 1855, a few days after *Leaves of Grass* was published, Whitman's father died at the age of 65.

In the months following the first edition of *Leaves of Grass*, critical responses began focusing more on the potentially offensive sexual themes. Though the second edition was already printed and bound, the publisher almost did not release it. In the end, the edition went to retail, with 20 additional poems, in August 1856. *Leaves of Grass* was revised and re-released in 1860 again in 1867, and several more times throughout the remainder of Whitman's life. Several well-known writers admired the work enough to visit Whitman, including Bronson Alcott and Henry David Thoreau.

As the end of 1891 approached, he prepared a final edition of *Leaves of Grass*, an edition which has been nicknamed the "Deathbed Edition." He wrote, "*L. of G.* at last complete—after 33 y'rs of hackling at it, all times & moods of my life, fair weather & foul, all parts of the land, and peace & war, young & old."

Walt Whitman's works include *Franklin Evans* (1842), *Leaves of Grass* (1855), *Drum-Taps* (1865), *Democratic Vistas* (1871), etc.

Analyses of and Comments on His Representative Poems

Walt Whitman's Poems

Whitman's work breaks the boundaries of poetic form and is generally prose-like. He also used unusual images and symbols in his poetry, including rotting leaves, tufts of straw, and debris. He also openly wrote about death and sexuality, including prostitution. He is often labeled as the father of free verse, though he did not invent it.

Whitman wrote in the preface to the 1855 edition of *Leaves of Grass*, "The proof of a poet is that his country absorbs him as affectionately as he has absorbed it." He believed there was a vital, symbiotic relationship between the poet and society. This connection was emphasized especially in "Song of Myself" by using an all-powerful first-person narration. As an American epic, it deviated from the historic use of an elevated hero and instead assumed the identity of the common people.

Owing to the historical causes, the styles of his democratic poems illustrate his democratic ideas as well. First, the ranges of his subjects are remarkable and intentional, for what he wrote includes and celebrates everything, That is, the picture he described is a manifesto. His subjects rang from leaves to mountains, from heaven to hell, from the living to the dead. He wrote everything he touched. He said "A great poet is for ages and ages in common and for degrees and complexions and all departments, and for a woman as much as a man and a man as much as a woman."

Second, he used simple words and avoided a new assess of speech. He appreciated the force of humble speech, and praised such speech as growing out of human life. He bravely broke with convention and tradition of English verse. He disliked the ornaments in his poems. He sworn to his art, "I will not be meddlesome, I will not it is." He did just as what he said in his poem to show the freedom of idea.

Third, it is great for Whitman that he created his own type of free-verse for his own expression. This is an aspect of his democracy. He rebelled against regular meters, other standard poetic devices of sound—alliteration, assonance, balance, and so on. To him, the poet did not show his idea until he used free-verse type. New free form does not only fit for him, but for other fields of science, such as music, art, physics, and so on. When we read his poems, they are just like a person telling us stories freely and frequently. They are not the sonnets with rhyme and solemnity. He organized the words as he liked to show his ideas freely.

Themes of His Poems

Democracy as a Way of Life Whitman envisioned democracy not just as a political system but as a way of experiencing the world. In the early nineteenth century, people still harbored many doubts about whether the United States could survive as a country and about whether democracy could thrive as a political system. To allay those fears and to praise democracy, Whitman tried to be democratic in both life and poetry. He imagined democracy as a way of interpersonal interaction and as a way for individuals to integrate their beliefs into their everyday lives. "Song of Myself" notes that democracy must include all individuals equally, or else it will fail.

In his poetry, Whitman widened the possibilities of poetic diction by including slang, colloquialisms, and regional dialects, rather than employing the stiff, erudite language so often found in nineteenth-century verse. Similarly, he broadened the possibilities of subject matter by describing myriad people and places. Like William Wordsworth, Whitman believed that everyday life and everyday people were fit subjects for poetry. Although much of Whitman's work does not explicitly discuss politics, most of it implicitly deals with democracy: it describes communities of people coming together, and it imagines many voices pouring into a unified whole. For Whitman, democracy was an idea that could and should permeate the world beyond politics, making itself felt in the ways we think, speak, work, fight, and even make art.

The Cycle of Growth and Death Whitman's poetry reflects the vitality and growth of the early United States. During the nineteenth century, America expanded at a tremendous rate, and its growth and potential seemed limitless. But sectionalism and the violence of the Civil War threatened to break apart and destroy the boundless possibilities of the United States. As a way of dealing with both the population growth and the massive deaths during the Civil War, Whitman focused on the life cycles of individuals: people are born, they age and reproduce, and they die. Such poems as "When Lilacs Last in the Dooryard Bloomed" imagine death as an integral part of life. The speaker of "When Lilacs Last in the Dooryard Bloomed" realizes that flowers die in the winter, but they rebloom in the springtime, and he vows to mourn his fallen friends every year just as new buds are appearing. Describing the life cycle of nature helped Whitman contextualize the severe injuries and trauma he witnessed during the Civil War—linking death to life helped give the deaths of so many soldiers meaning.

The Beauty of the Individual Throughout his poetry, Whitman praised the individual. He imagined a democratic nation as a unified whole composed of unique but equal individuals. "Song of Myself" opens in a triumphant paean to the individual: "I celebrate myself, and sing myself." Elsewhere the speaker of that exuberant poem identifies himself as Walt Whitman and claims that, through him, the voices of many will speak. In this way, many individuals make up the individual democracy, a single entity composed of myriad parts. Every voice and every part will carry the same weight within the single democracy—and thus every voice and every individual is equally beautiful. Despite this pluralist view, Whitman still singled out specific individuals for praise in his poetry, particularly Abraham Lincoln. In 1865, Lincoln was assassinated, and Whitman began composing several elegies, including "O Captain! My Captain!" These poems express that although all individuals are beautiful and worthy of praise, some individuals merit their own poems because of their contributions to society and democracy.

Song of Myself (1855)

Contents Summary

"Song of Myself" is a poem by Walt Whitman that is included in his work *Leaves of Grass*. It has been credited as "representing the core of Whitman's poetic vision."

This poem did not take on the title "Song of Myself" until the 1881 edition. Previous to that it had been titled "Poem of Walt Whitman, an American" and, in the 1860, 1867, and 1871 editions, simply "Walt Whitman." The poem's shifting title suggests something of what Whitman was about in this piece. As Walt Whitman, the specific individual, melts away into the abstract "Myself," the poem explores the possibilities for communion between individuals. Starting from the premise that "what I assume you shall assume," Whitman tries to prove that he both encompasses and he is indistinguishable from the universe.

This most famous of Whitman's works was one of the original twelve pieces in the 1855 first edition of *Leaves of Grass*. Like most of the other poems, it too was revised extensively, reaching its final permutation in 1881. "Song of Myself" is a sprawling combination of biography, sermon, and poetic meditation. It is not nearly as heavy-handed in its pronouncements as "Starting at Paumanok"; rather, Whitman uses symbols and sly commentary to get at important issues. "Song of Myself" is composed more of vignettes than lists: Whitman uses small, precisely drawn scenes to do his work here.

While "Song of Myself" is crammed with significant detail, there are three key episodes that must be examined. The first of these is found in the sixth section of the poem. A child asks the narrator "What is the grass?" and the narrator is forced to explore his own use of symbolism and his inability to break things down to essential principles. The bunches of grass in the child's hands become a symbol of the regeneration in nature. But they also signify a common material that links disparate people all over the United States together: grass, the ultimate symbol of democracy, grows everywhere. In the wake of the Civil War the grass reminds Whitman of graves: grass feeds on the bodies of the dead. Everyone must die eventually, and so the natural roots of democracy are therefore in mortality, whether due to natural causes or to the bloodshed of internecine warfare. While Whitman normally revels in this kind of symbolic indeterminacy, here it troubles him a bit. "I wish I could translate the hints," he says, suggesting that the boundary between encompassing everything and saying nothing is easily crossed.

The second episode is more optimistic. The famous "twenty-ninth bather" can be found in the eleventh section of the poem. In this section a woman watches twenty-eight young men bathing in the ocean. She fantasizes about joining them unseen, and describes their semi-nude bodies in some detail. The invisible twenty-ninth bather offers a model of being much like that of Emerson's "transparent eyeball": to truly experience the world one must be fully in it and of it, yet distinct enough from it to have some perspective, and invisible so as not to interfere with it unduly. This paradoxical set of conditions describes perfectly the poetic stance Whitman tries to assume. The lavish eroticism of this section reinforces this idea: sexual contact allows two people to become one yet not one—it offers a moment of transcendence. As the female spectator introduced in the beginning of the section fades away, and Whitman's voice takes over, the eroticism becomes homoeroticism. Again this is not so much the expression of a sexual preference as it is the longing for communion with every living being and a connection that makes use of both the body and the soul (although Whitman is certainly using the homoerotic sincerely, and in other ways too, particularly for shock value).

Having worked through some of the conditions of perception and creation, Whitman arrives, in the third key episode, at a moment where speech becomes necessary. In the twenty-fifth section he notes that "Speech is the twin of my vision, it is unequal to measure itself, / It provokes me forever, it says sarcastically, / Walt you contain enough, why don't you let it out then?" Having already established that he can have a sympathetic experience when he encounters others ("I do not ask the wounded person how he feels, I myself become the wounded person"), he must find a way to retransmit that experience without falsifying or diminishing it. Resisting easy answers, he later vows he "will never translate himself at all." Instead he takes a philosophically more rigorous stance: "What is known I strip away." Again Whitman's position is similar to that of Emerson, who says of himself, "I am the unsettler." Whitman, however, is a poet, and he must reassemble after unsettling: he must "let it out then." Having catalogued a continent and encompassed its multitudes, he finally decides: "I too am not a bit tamed, I too am untranslatable, / I sound my barbaric yawp over the roofs of the world." "Song of Myself" thus ends with a sound—a yawp—that could be described as either pre- or post-linguistic. Lacking any of the normal communicative properties of language, Whitman's yawp is the release of the "kosmos" ("cosmos") within him, a sound at the borderline between saying everything and saying nothing. More than anything, the yawp is an invitation to the next Walt Whitman, to read into the yawp, to have a sympathetic experience, to absorb it as part of a new multitude.

Following its 1855 publication, "Song of Myself" was immediately singled out by critics and readers for particular attention, and today, remains among the most acclaimed and influential poems written by an American.

In 1855, the *Christian Spiritualist* gave a long, glowing review of "Song of Myself," praising Whitman for representing "a new poetic mediumship," which through active imagination sensed the "influx of spirit and the divine breath." Ralph Waldo Emerson also wrote a letter to Whitman, praising his work for its "wit and wisdom."

Public acceptance was slow in coming, however. Social conservatives denounced the poem as flouting accepted norms of morality due to its blatant depictions of human sexuality. In 1882, Boston district attorney threatened action against *Leaves of Grass* for violating the state's obscenity laws and demanded that changes be made to several passages from "Song of Myself."

Theme of Self

In the poem, Whitman emphasizes an all-powerful "I" which serves as narrator, who should not be limited to or confused with the person of the historical Walt Whitman. The persona described has transcended the conventional boundaries of self: "I pass death with the dying, and birth with the new-washed babe...and am not contained between my hat and boots" (section 7).

There are several other quotes from the poem that makes it apparent that Whitman does not consider the narrator to represent a single individual. Rather, he seems to be narrating for all:

"For every atom belonging to me as good belongs to you." (Section 1)

"In all people I see myself, none more and not one a barleycorn less/and the good or bad I say of myself I say of them" (Section 20)

"It is you talking just as much as myself... I act as the tongue of you" (Section 47)

"I am large, I contain multitudes." (Section 51)

Literary critics Alice L. Cook and John B. Mason give interpretations as to the meaning of the "self" as well as its importance in the poem. Cook writes that the key to understanding the poem lies in the "concept of self" (typified by Whitman) as "both individual and universal," while Mason discusses "the reader's involvement in the poet's movement from the singular to the cosmic." The "self" serves as an ideal, yet, in contrast to traditional epic poetry, this identity is one of the common people rather than a hero.

Literary historian Betsy Erkkilä writes that "the drama of identity" in the poem is "rooted in the political drama of a nation in crisis," referring to tensions over slavery, women's rights, religious revival and free love that were sweeping across America when Whitman wrote "A Song of Myself."

Literary Techniques

The poem is written in Whitman's signature free verse style. Whitman, who praises words "as simple as grass" (section 39) forgoes standard verse and stanza patterns in favor of a simple, legible style that can appeal to a mass audience.

Critics have noted a strong Transcendentalist influence on the poem. In section 32, for instance, Whitman expresses a desire to "live amongst the animals" and to find divinity in the insects. In addition to this romanticism, the poem seems to anticipate a kind of realism that would only become important in United States literature after the American Civil War.

Beat! Beat! Drums! (1861)

Contents Summary

As the American Civil War was beginning, Whitman published his poem "Beat! Beat! Drums!" as a patriotic rally call for the North.

Drastic measures need to be taken at times. The choice between what is right and what is wrong is never simple, and the difficulties that must be faced are often beyond the scope of the imagination. "Beat! beat! drums!- Blow! bugles! blow!" by Walt Whitman is a poem that endorses action, and is a call to arms in the face of a cold bitter truth: there is a war, and it affects everyone. Whitman uses symbols throughout this piece to illustrate clearly that there is a need for all those who are able to do so, cease all other less important actions and take up the cause at hand.

Themes

It is the writer's contention that everyone should know of the war, and all who are able have an obligation to respond. In the last stanza he points out the obstacles that someone must avoid when answering the call to arms. Specifically he points out weaknesses, fear, and personal feelings. He urges the reader to "mind not the timid" or the "weeper or prayer" because their inability to act is a flaw and should not delay others to action. "The old man beseeching the young man" is a symbol for fear of loneliness and death. Personal relationships and the sadness of loved ones is another hurdle that must be overcome as seen in "the child's voice" and "mother's entreaties." The final symbol of the poem is death.

Whitman saves all mention of death for the end of the poem and it makes a powerful impact. Death may be both a reason for going to war and the sacrifice for taking up the cause; either way, the presence adds to the demands of the writer on both levels. It bolsters the need for action, as well as comes to the final statement: the ideals of this war are worth dying for.

The piece as a whole is a response to inaction. It is unsympathetic to the apathetic nature of society and attempts to inspire passion through beautiful language. Each of its symbols paint a picture of society and asks for each member of society to act and make the sacrifices necessary.

Literary Techniques

It is clear that the poem is referring to a war because of the two main symbols, the drums and bugles. Traditionally drums and bugles are used in the procession into battle. Both symbolize the common cause and solidify the group in that goal. In the poem, the writer is encouraging the bugles and drums to interrupt the lives of everyone who has ignored them. "Would the talkers be talking? Would the singers attempt to sing?" "Would the lawyer rise in the court to state his case before the judge?" "Then rattle quicker, heavier drums-you bugles wilder blow." The writer is specifically pointing out the various parts of normal life in society and insinuating that it is absurd to continue in that normalcy while there are clearly darker problems that need to be resolved and require everyone's attention.

To this end, Whitman is empowering his instruments to do all that is necessary to get word out by "scattering the congregation" and flowing "over the traffic of cities." While the war rages there can be "no happiness" or "any peace" because of the urgency of the cause. The poem presumes that the importance of the cause even outweighs the possibilities of death as referenced near the end. "Make even the trestles to shake the dead where they lie awaiting the hearses," It seems that death is also another reason for the general public to become more aware of the war, because there are already people dying and the importance of the cause is dire.

The piece calls into the picture many aspects of normal life through multiple symbols. The first groups that Whitman singles out, "the congregation" and "the scholar," are idealistic in nature and as such should be exuberant at the idea of helping a just cause. The intellectual and spiritual leaders embodied in these symbols have an obligation to the ideals they preach and to the peoples they lead.

Then he goes on to single out a few able bodies, specifically "the bridegroom" and "the peaceful farmer." Each symbolizes the young male population because it would be a great asset to an army. The young and able have an obligation to the cause because they are the most capable. They have the duty to protect those who are weaker, and to protect the way of life that they enjoy.

After bringing the war cry to the idealists and the able bodied, Whitman chooses to send his message to a broader population, and his symbols become broader as well. When he talks about "sleepers" he is embodying a very large, general public. The idea of sleep is consistent with the fact that they are not paying proper attention to the war, because sleep is a symbol for willful ignorance. Next, he refers to "bargainers" which is a way of pointing out the shame of materialistic pursuits over the moral demands of a war. Similarly he embodies the idea of merriment and festivities through his symbol, "the singer." Each is a symbol for itself, and collectively they symbolize the whole of society that is attempting to continue performing business as usual. Whitman then continues to press his call to arms with his chosen instruments.

Bibliography

Drabble, Margaret. *The Oxford Companion to English Literature, 6th Edition.* New York: Oxford University Press, 2000.

Killingsworth, M. J. *The Cambridge Introduction to Walt Whitman.* London: Cambridge University Press, 2007.

Kummings, D. D. *The Companion to Walt Whitman.* Oxford: Blackwell Publishing, 2006.

Wikipedia, the free encyclopedia. http://en.wikipedia.org/wiki/Walt_Whitman, 2013-01-20.

Wikipedia, the free encyclopedia. http://en.wikipedia.org/wiki/Leaves_of_Grass, 2013-01-20.

Emily Dickinson

Her Life and Writing Career

Her Life

Emily Elizabeth Dickinson (1830–1886) was born on December 10, 1830 in the quiet community of Amherst, Massachusetts, the second daughter of Edward and Emily Norcross Dickinson. Emily, Austin (her older brother) and her younger sister Lavinia were nurtured in a quiet, reserved family headed by their authoritative father Edward. Throughout Emily's life, her mother was not "emotionally accessible," the absence of which might have caused some of Emily's eccentricity. Being rooted in the puritanical Massachusetts of the 1800's, the Dickinson children were raised in the Christian tradition, and they were expected to take up their father's religious beliefs and values without argument. Later in life, Emily would come to challenge these conventional religious viewpoints of her father and the church, and the challenges she met with would later contribute to the strength of her poetry.

The Dickinson family was prominent in Amherst. In fact, Emily's grandfather, Samuel Fowler Dickinson, was one of the founders of Amherst College, and her father served as lawyer and treasurer for the institution. Emily's father also served in powerful positions on the General Court of Massachusetts, the Massachusetts State Senate, and the United States House of Representatives. Unlike her father, Emily did not enjoy the popularity and excitement of public life in Amherst, and she began to withdraw. Emily did not fit in with her father's religion in Amherst, and her father began to censor the books she read because of their potential to draw her away from the faith.

Being the daughter of a prominent politician, Emily had the benefit of good education and attended the Amherst Academy. After her time at the academy, Emily left for the South Hadley Female Seminary where she started to blossom into a delicate young woman—"her eyes lovely auburn, soft and warm, her hair lay in rings of the same color all over her head with her delicate teeth and skin." She had a demure manner that was almost fun with her close friends, but Emily could be shy, silent, or even depreciating in the presence of strangers. Although she was successful at college, Emily returned after only one year at the seminary in 1848 to Amherst where she began her life of seclusion.

Although Emily never married, she had several significant relationships with a select few. It was during this period following her return from school that Emily began to dress all in white and choose those precious few that would be her own private society. In Emily's entire life, she took one trip to Philadelphia (due to eye problems), one to Washington, and a few trips to Boston. Other than those occasional ventures, Emily had no extended exposure to the world outside her home town. During this time, her early twenties, Emily began to write poetry seriously. Fortunately, during those rare journeys Emily met two very influential men that would be sources of inspiration and guidance: Charles Wadsworth and Thomas Wentworth Higginson. There were other less influential individuals that affected Emily, such as Samuel Bowles and J. G. Holland, but the impact that Wadsworth and Higginson had on Dickinson was monumental.

A romantic figure, Wadsworth was an outlet for Emily, because his orthodox Calvinism acted as a beneficial catalyst to her theoretical inferences. Wadsworth, like Dickinson, was a solitary, romantic person that Emily could confide in when writing her poetry. He had the same poise in the pulpit that Emily had in her poetry. Wadsworth's religious beliefs and presumptions also gave Emily a sharp, and often welcome, contrast to the transcendentalist writings and easy assumptions of Emerson. Most importantly, it is widely believed that Emily had a great love for this Reverend from Philadelphia even though he was married. Many of Dickinson's critics believe that Wadsworth was the focal point of Emily's love poems.

Her Writing Career

When Emily had a sizable backlog of poems, she sought out somebody for advice about anonymous publication, and on April 15, 1862 she found Thomas Wentworth Higginson, an eminent literary man. She wrote a letter to Higginson and enclosed four poems to inquire his appraisal and advice.

Although Higginson advised Dickinson against publishing her poetry, he did see the creative originality in her poetry, and he remained Emily's "preceptor" for the remainder of her life. It was after that correspondence in 1862 that Emily decided against publishing her poems, and, as a result, only seven of her poems were published in her lifetime—five of them in the Springfield Republican. The remainder of the works would wait until after Dickinson's death.

Emily continued to write poetry, but when the United States Civil War broke out a lot of emotional turmoil came through in Dickinson's work. Some changes in her poetry came directly as a result of the war, but there were other events that distracted Emily and these things came through in the most productive period of her lifetime—about 800 poems.

The year of greatest stress was 1862, when distance and danger threatened Emily's friends—Samuel Bowles in Europe for his health, Charles Wadsworth who had moved to a new pastorate at the Calvary Church in San Francisco, and T. W. Higginson serving as an officer in the Union Army. The later years of Dickinson's life were primarily spent in mourning because of several deaths within the time frame of a few years. Emily's father died in 1874, and both Charles Wadsworth and Emily's mother died in 1882. Over those few years, many of the most influential and precious friendships of Emily passed away, and that gave way to the more concentrated obsession with death in her poetry. Throughout the year of 1885, Emily was confined to bed in her family's house where she had lived her entire life, and on May 15, 1886 Emily took her last breath at the age of 55. At that moment the world lost one of its most talented and insightful poets. Emily left behind nearly 2,000 poems.

As a result of Emily Dickinson's life of solitude, she was able to focus on her world more sharply than other authors of her time—contemporary authors who had no effect on her writing. Emily was original and innovative in her poetry, most often drawing on the Bible, classical mythology, and Shakespeare for allusions and references. Eventually when her poetry was published, editors took it upon themselves to group them into classes—Friends, Nature, Love, and Death. These same editors arranged her works with titles, rearranged the syntax, and standardized Dickinson's grammar. Fortunately in 1955, Thomas Johnson published Dickinson's poems in their original formats, thus displaying the creative genius and peculiarity of her poetry.

Analyses of and Comments on Her Representative Poems

Themes of Her Poems in General

Dickinson differs from Whitman in a variety of ways. For one thing, Whitman seems to keep his eye on society at large; Dickinson explores the inner life of the individual. Whereas Whitman is "national" in his outlook, Dickinson is "regional." In formal terms the two poets are vastly different. In her poetry, we can strongly sense the doubts about the existence of God and the realization of after-life. She was so obsessed with this religious uncertainty that about one third of her poems are about death and immortality, themes that lie at the center of her poetic world.

Love is another subject Dickinson showed great interest in. She herself had lived a lonely life of a spinster. She had once or twice fallen in love with someone. But each time she was frustrated. Some of her love poems reflect the unhappy experiences of hers, such as "I never lost as much but twice." There are also poems about the longing of physical love, the union of the bodies. But these poems are mostly written in an allegorical way, with rich images and symbols to imply the sexual desire. Poems like "Wild Nights" express an impressive, passionate desire of returning to the peaceful union in Eden.

Literary Techniques

Her ideas were deeply embedded in her character arousing from her isolated but a deeper and more intense world of imagination. Her style was simple, yet passionate and marked by economy of words and concentration. Instead of following traditional poetic forms, she used rhyme, rhythm and sentence pattern according to the demands of her ideas. She discovered that the sharp, intense image was the poet's best instrument. Dickinson's poems usually had no titles. Later editors at compiling gave them numbers based largely on the internal evidence of differences in the handwriting. Often the first sentence of a poem is taken as its title.

I felt a Funeral in my brain

Contents Summary

The speaker imagines that a funeral is taking place inside her brain, and she can feel the mourners pacing back and forth. The mourners sit down, and the funeral service begins. Unfortunately, this service seems more like a performance of "Stomp" than a religious gathering. The drum-like beating of the service makes her think her mind is going numb. The mourners lift the casket and walk across her "Soul." For some reason, they are wearing heavy lead boots, which is not very thoughtful of them.

At the end of the service, she feels as though a church bell were ringing inside her head. She imagines her mind as the entire universe. She feels like she is "Wrecked" and alone except for "Silence," her only companion. The wooden floor of her mind, now called "Reason"—suddenly breaks, and she falls a long way down. She keeps hitting "worlds" on the way down, and we're not sure what this means. The poem ends on an ominous note.

I felt a Funeral, in my Brain, (line 1)

The most curious word in this line is "felt." We might expect "imagined" or "dreamt" instead. The poem certainly reads a lot like a visual dream, with its frequent and sudden shifts in perspective. But the funeral could also be a metaphor for some conscious feeling or emotion. Whatever kind of reality we're talking about, this poem takes us deep, deep into the mind.

What exactly does a funeral feel like? Is it painful? The person is already dead, so it can't be that painful, right? The first line of the poem raises a distinction between two types of feeling that will return later in the poem. These two types are sensation and numbness. Sensation is the sensitivity to feeling, and numbness is the opposite. The funeral suggests pain or trauma but also quiet and rest.

> That Sense was breaking through— (line 4)

What is her sense "breaking through"? Are these her natural resistances to feeling? Are they mental resistances to some memory she has avoided thinking about? Dickinson is famous for leaving out important words or information. Her poems are incredibly condensed. We think she wants us to fill in the gaps with whatever comes into our imaginations.

> Kept beating–beating–till I thought
> My Mind was going numb— (lines 7-8)

The repeated words in the poem like "beating" and "treading" reinforce a sense of unpleasantness. The sound has invaded her space, and she is not happy about it. In the first stanza, the treading of the mourners causes her to feel more, but now the continued beating of the service makes her mind go numb or lose feeling. This idea is consistent with the principle that the mind can only take so much of anything, whether it be noise, pain, whatever. Does the numbness mean that she won't suffer anymore?

> And creak across my Soul
> With those same Boots of Lead, again,
> Then Space—began to toll, (lines 10-12)

Dickinson's poems often feature some dreamlike space. She spent a lot of her life writing inside her room, and rooms and other closed spaces could seem like an entire universe to her. The sudden shift between the place where the funeral takes place and all of "Space" suggests a dream.

This seems to us to be the most painful line in the poem. "Boots of Lead?" This woman can't catch a break here. The suffering in this poem mostly comes on two fronts: noise and weight. If we imagine her as the floor or as beneath the floor, these heavy boots are pressing down from above. What does "again" mean here? Has she gone through this whole experience some time before in her life, or is she only referring back to the "treading" of the first stanza?

As all the Heavens were a Bell,
And Being, but an Ear, (lines 13-14)

This poem contrasts the incredibly huge with the incredibly small. The largeness of the "Heavens" is placed beside the smallness of a human ear. We're just a tiny speck in a massive, reverberating universe. Makes you feel a bit humble, doesn't it? Throughout the poem, the speaker has been in a passive position, with people literally walking all over her. Now, she reworks this passivity on a cosmic scale. She is just an ear inside a giant, universal bell. If you have ever put your ear next to a gong or the opening of a large bell as it rings, you will know that this is not a pleasant position to be in.

And then a Plank in Reason, broke,
And I dropped down, and down—
And hit a World, at every plunge,
And Finished knowing–then— (lines 17-20)

We thought things could not possibly get bigger than the "Heavens," but now she brings in multiple "Worlds." Sounds a bit like the idea of parallel universes. She could mean something like other states of consciousness that we can not even imagine. This is a very trippy poem.

Themes

Mortality Like many of the Dickinson's poems, "I felt a Funeral, in my Brain" deals with the subject of death. In particular, she likes to deal with the subject of the moment of death and burial. For example, check out her poems "I died for Beauty—but was scarce" or "I heard a Fly buzz—when I died—" It seems that Dickinson was either afraid of death, or really curious about it, or maybe a mix of both. She seemed to believe that people went through death-like experiences throughout their lives. One of the central questions in this poem is whether death is a metaphor for some other experiences.

Versions of Reality "I felt a Funeral, in my Brain" comes about as close to a dream as possible without the poet announcing, "This is a dream I had." The setting shifts with no warning, and the story of the funeral hangs together very loosely. The whole scene takes place inside the speaker's brain, mind, or soul—we're not sure which, or whether these are all the same thing. Her mind is a huge, cavernous place that contains entire worlds. The end of the poem reads like someone waking up from a dream. On top of all that, we're not sure whether the speaker is living or dead. She might be narrating the poem from inside a coffin.

I died for Beauty—but was scarce

Contents Summary

The speaker says that she died for "Beauty", but she was hardly adjusted to her tomb before a man who died for "Truth" was laid in a tomb next to her. When the two softly told each other why they died, the man declared that "Truth" and "Beauty" are the same, so that he and the speaker were "Brethren." The speaker says that they met at night, "as Kinsmen," and talked between their tombs until the moss reached their lips and covered up the names on their tombstones.

Theme of Death

Its manner of presentation belongs uniquely to Dickinson. In this short lyric, Dickinson manages to include a sense of the macabre physicality of death ("Until the Moss had reached our lips—"), the high idealism of martyrdom ("I died for Beauty... One who died for Truth"), a certain kind of romantic yearning combined with longing for Platonic companionship ("And so, as Kinsmen, met a Night—"), and an optimism about the afterlife (it would be nice to have a like-minded friend) with barely sublimated terror about the fact of death (it would be horrible to lie in the cemetery having a conversation through the walls of a tomb). As the poem progresses, the high idealism and yearning for companionship gradually give way to mute, cold death, as the moss creeps up the speaker's corpse and her headstone, obliterating both her capacity to speak (covering her lips) and her identity (covering her name).

The ultimate effect of this poem is to show that every aspect of human life—ideals, human feelings, identity itself—is erased by death. But by making the erasure gradual—something to be "adjusted" to in the tomb—and by portraying a speaker who is untroubled by her own grim state, Dickinson creates a scene that is, by turns, grotesque and compelling, frightening and comforting. It is one of her most singular statements about death, and like so many of Dickinson's poems, it has no parallels in the work of any other writer.

I heard a Fly buzz—when I died—

Contents Summary

The poem describes the scene and the atmosphere at the moment when someone dies, with a weird surprise thrown in. The speaker starts by mentioning the sound of a fly, which cuts across the heavy, silent air around her deathbed. Then the speaker leaves that image behind, and begins to talk about the room where she is dying. She tells us about the people standing around her, who are calmly preparing themselves for her final moment. She even tells us about giving away the last of her possessions, to show us that everything is truly ready. Then, just when everything is in place and as it should be, here comes that fly. It's an intruder, a weird, unnecessary, kind of gross little bug. This was not exactly a happy poem to start with, but it was sort of peaceful. When that fly shows up, everything changes, and things get stranger and a lot less quiet and comfortable.

The Fly Line 1 "I heard a Fly buzz—when I died—": The first image we get in this poem is of that pesky fly. But we don't see it yet. We just hear it "buzz." That's a great word to put in here, because it describes the noise a fly makes, but the sound of the word also imitates the sound of the fly. That's what English teachers call onomatopoeia. That buzzing sound cuts across the quiet in the room. We get a whole landscape of sounds before we even see the fly or what's in the room.

Line 12 "There interposed a Fly—": The fly actually goes away for most of the poem, but then it comes back in a big way here. Check out how she uses the word "interposed" here. The fly interrupts the poem, disrupts this scene, and generally gets in the way. The image of that little buzzing creature cuts across the peaceful deathbed scene. It's dirty and uncontrollable and noisy, while everything else is quiet and calm and carefully prepared.

Line 13 "With Blue–uncertain stumbling Buzz—": Here she gives us a little more detail about the fly. She describes his buzz as "Blue—uncertain–stumbling." This gives us an even stronger image of the colors and the movements that go along with that annoying little sound. Dickinson doesn't have to say, "there was this little blue fly that kept landing everywhere." She just drops a few words into these lines, and we begin to build a picture of this fly in our minds.

Line 14 "Between the light—and me—": Now the fly gets between the speaker and "the light." Literally, this might mean that the fly's shadow blocks out the light of the room. But we think this line has to bring up the idea of the fly as a symbol. Even though it's not really their fault, flies are definitely associated with death, decomposition, maggots, and all that fun stuff. So this fly could be a symbol of death, and then his getting in the way of the light could start to seem kind of evil. He's interrupting the speaker's progress toward the comforting beauty of the light. In this poem, then, the appearance of the fly could be balancing out the arrival of the "King" everyone is waiting for. You can get as spiritual as you want about this, but it's good to remember that traditionally our associations with flies have been pretty negative.

The Storm Dickinson works hard and fast to give us a sense of what the atmosphere is like in this room. She wants to build up a sense of how quiet, calm, and maybe stifling it is around this deathbed. Maybe we haven't all experienced death, so she compares the situation to another one that we might be more familiar with.

Line 4 "Between the Heaves of Storm—": Dickinson uses a simile to compare the air in the room with the feeling of the air during a lull in a storm. It's a pretty great image, actually. Have you ever felt that moment during a storm when suddenly things get weirdly quiet? Maybe the air is wet and heavy, but the rain is gone for a moment. Here the storm is emotional and personal, and we know more is coming. When we arrive on the scene in this poem, though, we are at a point of spooky quiet, when everything stands still for a moment.

The Eyes We don't actually get to see who else is in the room with the dying speaker, but she does help us out by telling us that there are "Eyes around." This helps us to fill in the blanks of the scene. At first we just had a dying person and a fly, but now we can start to imagine the room where this is taking place, complete with crying onlookers.

Line 5 "The Eyes around–had wrung them dry—": There must be whole people here, but all we hear about are "The Eyes." When a part of something is made to stand in for the whole thing like this, we call that synecdoche. It's a neat way for her to give a little detail that our imaginations can turn into an entire story. When she says that "The Eyes around–had wrung them dry—" we know a number of things immediately. There are other people here. They love this dying person enough to cry. They are also beyond crying—maybe exhausted, maybe finally at peace with what is happening. One line, and we get a whole scene, a whole emotional and physical landscape. That's why Emily Dickinson is awesome.

The King This one is pretty mysterious. Someone or something is coming, and the speaker is waiting for him, or it, along with everyone around her. It has something to do with death, with the moment of crossing over, but the poem is pretty careful not to say exactly what.

Line 8 "When the King Be witnessed—in the Room—": There are a few ways to think about this image of "the King." On the one hand, she might be referring to death itself, which does sort of run the show, when you think about it. If that were the case, we'd call that technique personification, since she is giving human qualities to an abstract idea. On the other hand, this could have a more specifically religious meaning. Maybe it's a reference to God or Jesus. Certainly readers in Dickinson's time wouldn't have been surprised to find that kind of reference in a poem about death.

The Windows On a simple level, we think "Windows" is probably just a fancy way of saying "eyes." But it comes at a pretty important moment, and if she picked this specific image, we're willing to bet she wanted us to spend some time with it.

Line 15 "And then the Windows failed—": This is the only spot in this poem where Dickinson uses the word "Windows." This seems to be a metaphor for the speaker's eyes. Once they fail, she can no longer "see to see" (line 16). Also, have you ever heard someone say that "the eyes are the windows of the soul?" That's actually a really old expression, and versions of it go all the way back to the Bible. So the reference to windows makes us think of the spiritual aspects of this poem, and we're willing to bet people in Dickinson's time would have thought of the same thing.

Themes

Mortality Mortality is definitely the big theme in "I Heard a Fly Buzz When I Died," its whole reason for existing. Dickinson uses the poem to explore all kinds of things about death. She thinks about how it might feel, how it tends to happen, what we expect from it, etc. She looks at the idea from a bunch of different angles—before, during, and after the moment of death—and maybe tries to get us to think about it in new ways.

Family The theme of Family is interesting because we don't hear about it directly, but we know it has to be there. Family is hopefully a big part of a deathbed scene in "I Heard a Fly Buzz When I Died." When Dickinson talks about the "Eyes" around the dying speaker, we have to imagine that these are her loved ones. Also, she gives away her "Keepsakes." That ritual of leaving a will is all about family and friends. We can't assume too much about who these people are, but the idea of the bonds of family is a big part of what holds this poem together.

Man and the Natural World "I Heard a Fly Buzz When I Died" isn't a normal nature poem in any way. But Dickinson does spend a lot of time on that fly. In a lot of ways, it's the main symbol and one of the main characters in the poem. So in that sense, this is a poem about how humans relate to the natural world.

Spirituality Spirituality is another theme that's lurking around the edges. "I Heard a Fly Buzz—When I Died—" deals with death and what comes after, and the speaker herself is dead. Because of that, we pretty much need some spiritual framework to deal with what's going on here. Dickinson doesn't come out and say what happens after death, but with all this talk about the King, and the final Onset, and so forth, it definitely has to be on our minds.

Because I could not stop for Death

Contents Summary

Death, in the form of a gentleman suitor, stopped to pick up the speaker and took her on a ride in his horse-drawn carriage. They moved along at a pretty relaxed pace and the speaker seemed completely at ease with the gentleman. As they passed through the town, she saw children at play, fields of grain, and the setting sun. As dusk sets in our speaker gets a little chilly, as she is completely under-dressed—only wearing a thin silk shawl for a coat. She was unprepared for her impromptu date with Death when she got dressed that morning. They stopped at what will be her burial ground, marked with a small headstone. In the final stanza, we found out the speaker's rode with Death took place centuries ago (so she's been dead for a long time). But it seemed like just yesterday when she first got the feeling that horse heads pointed toward "Eternity"; or, in other words, signaled the passage from life to death to an afterlife.

Themes

In the first stanza, the Death is personalized as a gentleman without any vestige of being ugly and horrifying and the poetic usage of the word "stop" is eyeball-catching. Since the poetess has no time for thinking about and waiting for Death, Death patiently waits for her in the carriage of amiable atmosphere, where Immortality also accompanies them as an imaginary passenger. By the personification of Immortality, we can sense that the destination of this carriage is Eternity, which complies with the concept of death in the west that is "when we are born, we begin to die."

In the second stanza, the poetess's realization of the essence of Death is not, as generally supposed, to be imposed on her abruptly at the beginning of the journey because the journey is slow and the driver "Death" knows "no haste." Such being the case, Death appears to be so easy-going and affectionate that the poetess is beginning to embrace his "Civility" and banish her wild mind of the worldly "labor" and "leisure," which are the staple elements to the living creatures.

The third stanza is rich in figurative implications. The three scenes passed by the carriage resemble one's life journey from the childhood to the golden age. Matched with the theme of this poem, one would simultaneously associate the three scenes with childhood, maturity and old age since the children are evident symbols of the beginning of things, the grain ripe of the adulthood, and the sun setting of the rest the days. However, it is also not illogical and irrational to come to such a conclusion that the three things are the symbols of man's recycle after Death—man, nature and universe. In this picturesque frame all things smell the taste of being silent. There presents a cycle by the word "Ring," which indicates a circle from the birth to death, children' s growing into adult, seeds' ripening into grain, the sun's rising and setting.

As the late afternoon crawls to dusk, the evening dew appears. The "Dew" pulls the poetess from fantasy to the reality because of its quivering and chill. Contrasted with the chill air, the poetess is dressed in the light silk gown, similar to a bridal gown or the shroud.

By this deliberate suspense, where she is bound to remain a mystery unveiled in the fifth stanza. They "paused" at the "House" with invisible roof and cornice. From the word "pause," one would deduce that it is not the destination that the carriage is destined to. And with such a suspense that destination appears unveiled, that is where the horses' heads are pointed—the Eternity.

In this final stanza, the poet uses an extravagant hyperbole by yoking "Centuries" to "Day." Even though it seems that centuries have passed since the awareness of Death, these centuries "feel" shorter than the "Day."

After the final stanza, the theme of this poem becomes more concrete despite the topic is abstract—Death is a necessary agent for the completion of the order of things; Death serves Immortality.

Bibliography

Drabble, Margaret. *The Oxford Companion to English Literature (6th edition).* New York: Oxford University Press, 2000.

Wikipedia, the free encyclopedia. http://en.wikipedia.org/wiki/Emily_Dickinson, 2013-02-14.

http://www.shmoop.com/i-heard-a-fly-buzz-when-i-died/, 2013-02-14.

http://www.americanpoems.com/poets/emilydickinson, 2013-02-14.

Harriet Beecher Stowe

Her Life and Writing Career

Her Life

Harriet Elizabeth Beecher Stowe (1811–1896) was born in Connecticut on June 14, 1811, and she was born to outspoken religious leader Lyman Beecher and Roxana Foote, a deeply religious woman who died when Stowe was only five years old. She was the seventh of 13 children, and her sister Henry Ward Beecher (1813–1887) was a divine, religious author and journalist. She was a schoolteacher in Cincinnati before marrying in 1836 C. E. Stowe, a professor at her father's theological seminary.

Harriet enrolled in the seminary (girls' school) run by her sister Catharine, where she received a traditionally "male" education in the classics, including study of languages and mathematics. Among her classmates there was Sarah P. Willis, who later wrote under the pseudonym Fanny Fern. At the age of 21, she moved to Cincinnati, Ohio to join her father, who had become the president of Lane Theological Seminary. There, she also joined the Semi-Colon Club, a literary salon and social club whose members included the Beecher sisters, Caroline Lee Hentz, Salmon P. Chase, Emily Blackwell, and others.

It was in that group that she met Calvin Ellis Stowe, a widower and professor at the seminary. The two married on January 6, 1836. He was an ardent critic of slavery, and the Stowes supported the Underground Railroad, temporarily housing several fugitive slaves in their home. They had seven children together, including twin daughters.

Having lived eighteen years in a town next to a slave state, Mrs. Stowe saw all kinds of savage acts made by the slave owners. She always offered her help to the slaves to escape, or made her house a refuge for them, Stood firmly at the side of the abolition, Mrs. Stowe promised, "If I am alive, I must let the world know the truth of the south." In order to reveal the theme that a society resting on slavery could not long survive, she even went to the slave state to get more evidence. The power of the novel unquestionably comes from the investment of the author's sense of black slave's suffering and oppression. In a nutshell, Mrs. Stowe wrote the novel *Uncle Tom's Cabin* to answer the urgent call of the contemporary era with the advanced thought of the North. It is the contemporary social atmosphere facilitates that allows Mrs. Stowe to produce such an outstanding novel.

In the 1870s, Stowe's brother Henry Ward Beecher was accused of adultery, and became the subject of a national scandal. Stowe, unable to bear the public attacks on her brother, fled to Florida but asked family members to send her newspaper reports. Through the affair, however, she remained loyal to her brother and believed he was innocent.

Mrs. Stowe was among the founders of the Hartford Art School, which later became part of the University of Hartford.

Stowe died on July 1, 1896, at age eighty-five in Hartford, Connecticut. She is buried in the historic cemetery at Phillips Academy in Andover, Massachusetts.

Her Writing Career

Harriet Beecher Stowe has written more than 20 books, including novels, three travel memoirs, and collections of articles and letters. She was influential both for her writings and her public stands on social issues of the day.

In 1850, Congress passed the Fugitive Slave Law, prohibiting assistance to fugitives. At the time, Harriet had moved with her family into a home near the campus of Bowdoin College in Brunswick, Maine, where her husband was now teaching. On March 9, 1850, Stowe wrote to Gamaliel Bailey, editor of the weekly antislavery journal *National Era*, that she planned to write a story about the problem of slavery: "I feel now that the time is coming when even a woman or a child who can speak a word for freedom and humanity is bound to speak...I hope every woman who can write will not be silent." Shortly after, In June 1851, when she was 40, the first installment of her *Uncle Tom's Cabin* was published in the *National Era*. She originally used the subtitle "The Man That Was a Thing," but it was soon changed to "Life among the Lowly." Installments were published weekly from June 5, 1851, to April 1, 1852. *Uncle Tom's Cabin* was published in book form on March 20, 1852, by John P. Jewett with an initial print run of 5,000 copies. Each of its two volumes included three illustrations and a title-page designed by Hammatt Billings. In less than a year, the book sold an unprecedented three hundred thousand copies.

After the start of the Civil War, Stowe traveled to Washington, D. C. and there she met President Abraham Lincoln on November 25, 1862. Legend has it that, upon meeting her, he greeted her by saying, "So you are the little woman who wrote the book that started this great war." In reality, little is known about the meeting. Stowe's daughter Hattie reported, "It was a very droll time that we had at the White house. I assure you... I will only say now that it was all very funny—and we were ready to explode with laughter all the while." Stowe's own letter to her husband is equally vague: "I had a real funny interview with the President."

The novel *Uncle Tom's Cabin*'s success brought Mrs. Stowe to England in 1853, 1856, and 1859, where she was rapturously received, and honored by Queen Victoria, although she later alienated British opinion by her *Lady Byron Vindicated* (1870), in which she charged Byron with incestuous relations with his half-sister. Her other works include *Dred: A Tale of the Dismal Swamp* (1856), which also deals with slavery; *The Minister's Wooing* (1859), a protest against the doctrines of Calvinism; *Old Town Folks* (1869), set in New England; and *Poganuc People* (1878), another tale of New England family life with "solidly remembered scenes—of candle makings, quilting's and apple bees, chestnut tings and huckle-berryings" praised by E. Wilson in *Patriotic Gore* (1962).

Analysis of and Comment on Her Representative Novel

Uncle Tom's Cabin (1852)

Plot Summary

Stowe's anti-slavery novel *Uncle Tom's Cabin,* which was serialized in the *National Era* in 1851-2 and published in book form in 1852, had a sensational success and stirred up great public feeling.

A powerful if melodramatic tale, it describes the sufferings caused by slavery; pious old Uncle Tom, sold by his well-intentioned Kentucky owner Mr. Shelby to meet his debts, is bought first by the handsome, idealistic, sensitive Augustine St. Clair, in whose New Orleans household he becomes the favorite of the daughter, the saintly little Eva. But both Eva and St. Clair die, and Tom is sold again, this time to a brutal cotton plantation owner, Simon Legree, who finally beats the unprotesting Tom to death just before Shelby's son arrives to redeem him.

The wretched situations in which the slaves were tortured and exploited have been exposed objectively to the world as well as depicted vividly in the novel *Uncle Tom's Cabin*. Uncle Tom, one of the leading characters in the novel, is considered the classical image ever described in the literary world. Mrs. Stowe created the image of Uncle Tom based on thousands of slaves living in the slave states. Tom was not alone. He is only the symbol of a large black population. In southern slave states, slaves lived in crowded, one-room huts, usually without beds and sometimes even without enough covering to keep warm. They were supplied a bare minimum of food and clothing, just enough to survive. What is more disgusting is that slaves were encouraged to multiply, for surplus offspring could be sold out for profit. Children born to slaves did not belong to them, but became the property of the master. Slaves were sold at will, a situation that often causes family members to be separated forever. Slave owners ruled the slaves with whips and other instruments of torture. Of course there were also some exceptions, but the evil exist on the very roots of the slavery system. The living conditions of the slave would never change without the abolishment of the vicious system.

Uncle Tom's Cabin opens with a Kentucky farmer named Arthur Shelby facing the loss of his farm because of debts. Even though he and his wife Emily Shelby believe that they have a benevolent relationship with their slaves, Shelby decides to raise the needed funds by selling two of them—Uncle Tom, a middle-aged man with a wife and children, and Harry, the son of Emily Shelby's maid Eliza—to a slave trader Mr. Haley. Emily Shelby is averse to this idea because she had promised her maid that her child would never be sold; Emily's son, George Shelby, hates to see Tom go because he sees the man as his friend and mentor.

When Eliza overhears Mr. and Mrs. Shelby discussing plans to sell Tom and Harry, Eliza determines to run away with her son. The novel states that Eliza made this decision because she fears losing her only surviving child (she had already miscarried two children). Eliza departs that night, leaving a note of apology to her mistress.

Tom and Mr. Haley leave for the South. Tom is placed on a riverboat which sets sail down the Mississippi River. While on board, Tom saves a young white girl named Eva from drowning. Eva's father Augustine St. Clare decides to buy Tom from the slave trader Haley to be his daughter's personal servant and takes him with the family to their home in New Orleans. The little girl, Eva, is also a sweet child, devoted to her servants and family. Tom and Eva begin to relate to one another because of the deep Christian faith they both share.

Unfortunately, the mother, Marie St. Clare, is a more typical slave owner and runs her slaves ragged as they try to satisfy her endless demands. Tom grows fond of little Eva. They discuss their mutual Christian faith on a daily basis. When it is clear that Eva is ill and going to die, she calls all the slaves together to give them a speech about God's love for them. Then she dies of consumption. Meanwhile, Eliza and her husband George are reunited in a Quaker camp. Augustine St. Clare is heartbroken at his daughter Eva's death, as are all the slaves. St. Clare promises Tom his freedom. Before St. Clare can follow through on his pledge, however, he dies after being stabbed outside of a tavern. His wife reneges on her late husband's vow and sells Tom at auction to a vicious plantation owner named Simon Legree.

Simon Legree is an evil and violent man who works his slaves until they die. Despite Legree's treatment, Tom maintains his honesty, kindness. Legree does his worst to "harden" Tom so that he can use Tom as an overseer on the plantation, but Tom refuses to change no matter how hard or how often Legree beats him. When Tom encourages two female slaves, whom Legree uses as prostitutes, to escape, Legree beats Tom to death. At the meantime, his old master's son, George Shelby, arrives to emancipate Tom, but it was too late. The two female slaves who escaped Legree's house, Cassy and Emmeline, end up on the same ship with George Shelby. Although Tom's life ended in tragedy, there is much happiness among those slaves who survived and escaped the trials and tribulations of slavery.

A parallel plot describes the escape to freedom in Canada of Shelby's slave, the beautiful (and almost white) quadroon Eliza, her child, and her husband George. During Eliza's escape, she meets up with her husband George Harris, who had run away previously. They decide to attempt to reach Canada. However, they are tracked by a slave hunter named Tom Loker. Eventually Loker and his men trap Eliza and her family, causing George to push Loker down a cliff. Worried that Loker may die, Eliza convinces George to bring the slave hunter to a nearby Quaker settlement for medical treatment.

Mrs. Stowe's stress on the anguish of parted families was extremely telling, and her contrast between Southern, New England, and Kentucky ways is well observed, but the sensational religiosity of the story and its dubious conclusion (in which most of the survivors, including the once irrepressible little slave Topsy, disappear back to Africa to become missionaries) contributed to a shift of attitude which came to use the phrase "Uncle Tom" pejoratively, to indicate a supine collaboration with the oppressor.

Uncle Tom

Before we can even think about the character of Uncle Tom in this novel, we've got to discuss what "Uncle Tom" has come to mean as a catchphrase in America today. Calling a black American an "Uncle Tom" is a serious insult, usually meaning that the person is subservient to whites or has betrayed other blacks. It sometimes means that the person is complicit in his own suffering and subjection. It also becomes a general term for anyone who is submissive toward their enemies and a traitor to their friends.

In literary circles, there's major debate about whether or not the character of Uncle Tom in *Uncle Tom's Cabin* deserves this reputation. In 1949, critic James Baldwin wrote a famous essay that rejected Stowe's novel, pointing out its use of racist stereotypes especially in relation to Uncle Tom as a character. For decades, literary scholars followed his lead. In recent years, however, several major critics, including Jane Tompkins and Henry Louis Gates, Jr., have sought to put *Uncle Tom's Cabin* and Uncle Tom himself back into the American literary canon.

Uncle Tom is notable for his superhuman religious faith, his gentle nature, and his unfailing honesty. But he's also notable for being a stereotype—a childlike "noble savage," an idealized figure in sentimental fiction, whose finer emotions have not been destroyed by the negative influences of civilization. Bear in mind that one tenet of sentimentalism is that we are all born good, and human society makes us evil. While it may seem like a compliment that Uncle Tom is worthier than the free people around him, it can also be seen as incredibly patronizing to claim that the reason that he's so great is that he is somehow "closer to nature," almost animal-like in his simple loyalty and innocence.

Tom is the Christ figure with black skin. His experience is quite similar to that of Jesus Christ. When Tom's first master, Mr. Shelby sells Tom to the coarse slave-dealer in financial straits, he betrays the loyalty of his most loyal slave since boyhood. His apostle Judas who is prompted by his avarice for money sells Jesus. So they are all betrayed and sold by the ones who are close to them. While he struggles with his faith, as Jesus does in the last hours of his life when he says, "My God, why have you forsaken me?" and he never loses his simple faith. Tom's death scene also has striking likeness with that of Jesus Christ. Tom is flogged near to death, so is Jesus before his crucifixion. When Jesus dies, there are two criminals crucified together with him, one of who believes Jesus is Messiah and is saved at the very moment and spot. Sambo and Qimbo, Degree's two cruel overseers who in every sense are equal to criminals, are moved by Tom' s Christian fortitude and patience and are converted at the very moment and spot. Jesus is crucified to redeem sinners while Tom dies for the two runaway slaves, Cassy and Emmeline. They are all innocent, but all die for others. In essence, they all die for their faith and religious devotion. In fact, Tom dies as a "martyr," which is revealed by the title of chapter forty. Tom is not only similar in his experiences to Jesus Christ. More important, his temperament is like that of Jesus Christ. He is loving, faithful, forgiving and obedient.

Tom is full of love for his neighbors, blacks and whites. While he is at St. Clare's home, he meets that pitiful, wretched old slave Prue whose only left child is starved to death because she devotes all her time to tend her mistress and loses her milk, yet her mistress refuses to buy milk for her baby. Tom offers to carry her basket for her and sends the Gospel to her. Just as when Jesus sees sinners, he pities them, helps them, cures them and tells them "the good news."

Tom not only loves his fellow slaves, but white people. When he sees his second young handsome flighty master St. Clare go to those wining parties, Tom goes down on his knees and pleads with him not to attend those revelries again by quoting from the Bible, "It biteth like a serpent and stingeth like an adder." His love comes to full display when he says on his deathbed to his first young master George Shelby: "...Give my love to mas'r, and dear good missis-and everybody in the place! Ye don't know.' Pears like I loves' em all! I loves every creature,' every what!—It's nothing but love..." Here, Tom is the incarnation of love, just like Jesus is identified with love.

Christ's character has ever been perfect. The perfection here must refer to the knowledge of the inhabitants of the universe. They had known His power, holiness, wisdom, righteousness and love, but now on the cross for the first time they saw that God is most capable of suffering. Not only is it true that "in all their affliction He was afflicted," but also that "the chastisement for our peace was upon Him..." The universe saw the truth that in this ruthless warfare with Satan, God is the greatest victim and makes the greatest sacrifice. His image is rounded out in its perfection and glory on the cross of Christ.

Themes

Uncle Tom's Cabin is dominated by this major theme: the evil and immorality of slavery. While Stowe weaves other subthemes throughout her text, such as the moral authority of motherhood and the redeeming possibilities offered by Christianity, she emphasizes the connections between these and the horrors of slavery. Stowe sometimes changed the story's voice, so that she could give a "homily" on the destructive nature of slavery (such as when a white woman on the steamboat carrying Tom further south states, "The most dreadful part of slavery, to my mind, is its outrages of feelings and affections—the separating of families, for example."). One way Stowe showed the evil of slavery was how this "peculiar institution" forcibly separated families from each other.

Because Stowe saw motherhood as the "ethical and structural model for all of American life" and also believed that only women had the moral authority to save the United States from the demon of slavery, another major theme of *Uncle Tom's Cabin* is the moral power and sanctity of women. Through characters like Eliza, who escapes from slavery to save her young son (and eventually reunites her entire family), or Eva, who is seen as the "ideal Christian." Stowe shows how she believed women could save those around them from even the worst injustices. While later critics have noted that

Stowe's female characters are often domestic clichés instead of realistic women, Stowe's novel "reaffirmed the importance of women's influence" and helped pave the way for the women's rights movement in the following decades.

Stowe's puritanical religious beliefs show up in the novel's final, overarching theme—the exploration of the nature of Christianity and how she feels that Christian theology is fundamentally incompatible with slavery. This theme is most evident when Tom urges St. Clare to "look away to Jesus" after the death of St. Clare's beloved daughter Eva. After Tom dies, George Shelby eulogizes Tom by saying, "What a thing it is to be a Christian." Because Christian themes play such a large role in *Uncle Tom's Cabin*—and because of Stowe's frequent use of direct authorial interjections on religion and faith—the novel often takes the "form of a sermon."

Literary Techniques

Symbolism It's important to remember that the novel is not just titled Uncle Tom—it is titled *Uncle Tom's Cabin*, which makes the cabin the most important symbol around. Tom's cabin, however, is not in the novel for very long. In Chapter Four, with the rather obvious title "An Evening in Uncle Tom's Cabin", we get a sense of the domestic tranquility and religious piety that exist in the cabin. When circumstances permit—when their master is kind enough, or if they could be freed—slaves like Tom and Chloe can create a perfect 19th century household, faithful, hardworking, and principled. At the end of the novel, young George Shelby turns the cabin into an even more obvious symbol when he tells his freed slaves to look at it and remember the sacrifice Uncle Tom made, which indirectly brought about their freedom.

Imagery After Tom leaves the Shelby's, the cabin exists in the mind of the reader as a point of contrast for other places he lives and other households that we see. The cabin's humble piety contrasts with the lavish indulgence of the Shelby's big house or the St. Clare mansion. It also contrasts with the rude wooden shack that Tom occupies on Legree's plantation and the cotton gin shed where Tom lies dying. When he has a cabin, Tom, though a slave, exists as a human being with a home of his own; when he's reduced to the gin shed, he's being treated like just another piece of rusting machinery. The final point of contrast is the cottage where George, Eliza, and their family are reunited in Canada. Uncle Tom may not get back to his cabin, but freed slaves like him can create loving, harmonious households similar to it.

Bibliography

Drabble, Margaret. *The Oxford Companion to English Literature* (6th edition). New York: Oxford University Press, 2000.

Bloom, H. *Bloom's Guides: Harriet Beecher Stowe's Uncle Tom's Cabin*. New York: Bloom's Literary Criticism Publishing, 2008.

Wikipedia, the free encyclopedia. http://en.wikipedia.org/wiki/Harriet_Beecher_Stowe, 2013-02-26.

Wikipedia, the free encyclopedia. http://en.wikipedia.org/wiki/Uncle_Tom%27s_Cabin, 2013-02-26.

Mark Twain

His Life and Writing Career

His Life

Samuel Langhorne Clemens, later known as Mark Twain (1835–1910), was born on November 30, 1835, in the tiny village of Florida, Missouri, the sixth child of John and Jane Clemens. When he was four years old, the Clemens clan moved to nearby Hannibal, a bustling town of 1,000 people. John Clemens worked as a storekeeper, lawyer, judge, and land speculator, dreaming of wealth but never achieving it, sometimes finding it hard to feed his family. He was an unsmiling fellow; according to one legend, young Sam never saw him laugh. His mother by contrast, was a fun-loving, tenderhearted homemaker. She became head of the household in 1847 when John died unexpectedly. The Clemens family "now became almost destitute," writes biographer Everett Emerson, and was forced into years of economic struggle—a fact that would shape the career of Mark Twain.

Sam Clemens lived in Hannibal from age four to age seventeen. The town, situated on the Mississippi River, was in many ways a splendid place to grow up. Steamboats arrived there three times a day, tooting their whistles; circuses, minstrel shows, and revivalists paid visits; a decent library was available; and tradesmen such as blacksmiths and tanners practiced their entertaining crafts for all to see. However, violence was commonplace, young Sam witnessed much death. When he was 9 years old he saw a local man murder a cattle rancher, and at 10 he watched a slave die after a white overseer struck him with a piece of iron.

The small town Hannibal inspired several of Mark Twain's fictional locales, including "St. Petersburg" in *Tom Sawyer* and *Huckleberry Finn*. These imaginary river towns are complex places: sunlit and exuberant on the one hand, but also vipers' nests of cruelty, poverty, drunkenness, loneliness, and life-crushing boredom. All of that had been a part of Sam Clemens' boyhood experience.

Sam kept up his schooling until he was around twelve, when, with his father's dead and needing to earn his keep, he found employment as an apprentice printer at the Hannibal Courier, which paid him with a meager ration of food. In 1851, at fifteen, he got a job as a printer and occasional writer and editor at the *Hannibal Western Union*, a little newspaper owned by his brother Orion.

Then, in 1857, Clemens fulfilled a dream: He began learning the art of piloting a steamboat on the Mississippi. A licensed pilot by 1859, he soon found regular employment plying the shoals and channels of the great river. He loved his career—it was exciting, well-paying, and high-status, roughly akin to flying a jetliner today. However, his service was cut short in 1861 by the outbreak of the Civil War, which halted most civilian traffic on the river.

As the war began, the people of Missouri angrily split between support for the Union and the Confederacy. Clemens opted for the latter, joining the Confederate Army in June, 1861, but serving for only a couple of weeks until his volunteer unit disbanded.

In July Twain climbed onboard a stagecoach and headed for Nevada and California, where he would live for the next five years. At first, he prospected for silver and gold, convinced that he would become the savior of his struggling family and the sharpest-dressed man in Virginia City and San Francisco. But nothing panned out, literally. By the middle of 1862 he was flat broke and in need of a regular job.

He knew his way around a newspaper office, so that September he went to work as a reporter for the Virginia City Territorial Enterprise. He churned out news stories, editorials, and sketches, and along the way adopted the pen name "Mark Twain"—steamboat slang for twelve feet of water.

Mark Twain became one the best known storytellers in the West. He honed a distinctive narrative style—friendly, funny, irreverent, often satirical, always eager to deflate the pretentious. At 34, this Westerner—handsome, red-haired, affable, canny, egocentric, and ambitious—had become one of the most popular and famous writers in America.

Mark Twain's last fifteen years were filled with public honors, including degrees from Oxford and Yale. Probably the most famous American of the late 19th century, he was much photographed and applauded wherever he went. Indeed, he was one of the most prominent celebrities in the world, traveling widely overseas, including a successful round-the-world lecture tour in 1895–1896, undertaken to pay off his debts.

But while those years were gilded with awards, they also brought him much anguish. Early in their marriage he and Livy had lost their toddler son, Langdon to diphtheria; now in 1896 his favorite daughter died at the age of 24 of spinal meningitis. The loss broke his heart. In June 1904, Livy died after a long illness. Her husband had often traveled while she was sick. But absent or not, throughout 34 years of marriage, Twain had indeed loved his wife. "Wheresoever she was, there was Eden," he wrote in tribute to her.

Twain became a bitter old man, even while projecting an amiable persona to his public. Samuel Clemens died at age 74 on April 21, 1910, at his country home in Redding Connecticut and was buried in Elmira, New York.

His Writing Career

Mark Twain was an American writer, journalist and humorist, who won a worldwide audience for his stories of the youthful adventures of Tom Sawyer and Huckleberry Finn.

In 1864 Twain worked in San Francisco as a reporter. He set out on a world tour, traveling in France and Italy. His experiences were recorded in 1869 in *The Innocents Abroad*, which gained him wide popularity, and poked fun at both American and European prejudices and manners.

Between 1876 and 1884 he published several masterpieces, *The Adventures of Tom Sawyer* (1881) and *The Prince and the Pauper* (1881), *Life on the Mississippi* appeared in 1883 and *The Adventures of Huckleberry Finn* in 1884.

In the 1890s Twain toured New Zealand, Australia, India, and South Africa. He wrote such books as *The Tragedy of Pudd'head Wilson* (1884), *Personal Recollections of Joan of Arc* (1885), *A Connecticut Yankee in King Arthur's Court* (1889) and the travel book *Following the Equator* (1897).

During his long writing career, Twain also produced a considerable number of essays, which appeared in various newspapers and in magazines, including the *Galaxy*, *Harper's*, the *Atlantic Monthly*, and *North American Review*. In his "Sandwich Islands" letters (1873) Twain described how the missionaries and American government have corrupted the Hawaiians. "Queen Victoria's Jubilee" (1897) presented the pomp and pageantry of an English royal procession, and "King Leopold's Soliloquy" (1905) revealed in a dramatic monologue the political evils caused by despotism. Twain's finest satire of imperialism was perhaps "To the Person Sitting in Darkness" (1901), in which the author wrote that the people in darkness are beginning to see "more light than...was profitable for us."

Analysis of and Comment on His Representative Novel

The Adventures of Huckleberry Finn (1885)

Plot Summary

The Widow Douglas and her sister, Miss Watson, have taken Huck into their home in order to try and teach him religion and proper manners. Instead of obeying his guardians, however, Huck sneaks out of the house at night to join Tom Sawyer's gang and pretend that they are robbers and pirates.

One day Huck discovers that his father, Pap Finn, has returned to town. Huck is worried about Pap's intentions, especially toward his invested money. When Pap confronts Huck and warns him to quit school but, Huck continues to attend school just to spite Pap. Huck's fears are soon realized when Pap kidnaps him.

Although Huck becomes somewhat comfortable with his life free from religion and school, Pap's beatings become too severe, and Huck fakes his own murder and escapes down the Mississippi. Huck lands a few miles down at Jackson's Island, and there he stumbles across Miss Watson's slave, Jim, who has run away for fear he will be sold down the river. Huck and Jim soon escape down the river on a raft. Jim's plan is to reach the Illinois town of Cairo, and take the Ohio River up to the free states. The plan troubles Huck and his conscience. However, Huck continues to stay with Jim, despite his belief that he is breaking all of society and religion's tenets. Huck's struggle with the concept of slavery and Jim's freedom continues throughout the novel.

The only time that Huck and Jim feel that they are truly free is when they are aboard the raft. This freedom and tranquility are shattered by the arrival of the duke and the king, who commandeer the raft and force Huck and Jim to stop at various river towns in order to perform confidence scams on the inhabitants. Huck and Jim escape and are soon joined by the duke and the king.

Disappointed at their lack of income, the duke and the king betray Huck and Jim, and sell Jim back into slavery. When Huck goes to find Jim, he discovers that Jim is being held captive. The Phelps think Huck is their visiting nephew Tom Sawyer; and Huck easily falls into the role of Tom. Tom Sawyer soon arrives and, after Huck explains Jim's captivity, Tom takes on the guise of his own brother, Sid. After dismissing Huck's practical method of escape, Tom suggests they concoct an elaborate plan to free Jim. Tom's plan is haphazardly based on several of the prison and adventure novels he has read, and the simple act of freeing Jim becomes a complicated farce with rope ladders, snakes, and mysterious messages.

When the escape finally takes place, a pursuing farmer shoots Tom in the calf. Because Jim will not leave the injured Tom, Jim is again recaptured and taken back to the Phelps farm. At the farm, Tom reveals the entire scheme to Aunt Sally and Uncle Silas. Readers learn that Miss Watson has passed away and freed Jim in her will, and Tom has been aware of Jim's freedom the entire time. At the end of the novel, Jim is finally set free and Huck ponders his next adventure away from civilization.

Themes

In *The Adventures of Huckleberry Finn*, Mark Twain deals with several themes. First of all, this novel embodies the search for freedom. Both Huck and Jim are seeking freedom although their shin colors and their background are different: one is a white child living in poverty and the other a black slave. Actually their freedom is closely related. Only when Huck throws away his prejudice towards the black can he acquire the true freedom. If he cannot overcome his prejudice towards Jim, he will never achieve freedom.

In addition, the novel also touches upon notions of race and identity. An obvious complexity exists concerning Jim's character. While some scholars point out that Jim is good-hearted, moral, and not unintelligent, others have criticized the novel as racist, citing the use of the word "nigger" and emphasizing the stereotypically "comic" treatment of Jim's superstition and ignorance. Mark Twain wrote during the post-Civil War period when there was an intense white reaction against blacks. Twain took aim squarely against racial prejudice, rising segregation, and the generally accepted belief that blacks were sub-human. Others have criticized the novel as racist, citing the use of the word "nigger" and Jim's Sambo-like character.

Huck struggles not only with the challenges of his strenuous journey, but also with the 19th century social climate and the role it forces on him regarding Jim. Throughout the story, Huck is in moral conflict with the received values of the society in which he lives, and while he is unable to consciously refute those values even in his thoughts, he makes a moral choice based on his own valuation of Jim's friendship and human worth, a decision in direct opposition to the things he has been taught. Mark Twain in his lecture notes proposes that "a sound heart is a surer guide than an ill-trained conscience," and goes on to describe the novel as "...a book of mine where a sound heart and a deformed conscience come into collision and conscience suffers defeat."

To highlight the hypocrisy required to condone slavery within an ostensibly moral system, Twain has Huck's father enslave him, isolate him, and beat him. When Huck escapes—which anyone would agree was the right thing to do—he then immediately encounters Jim "illegally" doing the same thing.

Finally, by focusing on Huck's education, the novel fits into the tradition of the bildungsroman: a novel depicting an individual's maturation and development. As a poor, uneducated boy, for all intents and purposes an orphan, Huck distrusts the morals and precepts of the society that treats him as an outcast and fails to protect him from abuse. This apprehension about society and his growing relationship with Jim, lead Huck to question many of the teachings that he has received, especially regarding race and slavery. More than once, we see Huck choose to "go to hell" rather than go along with the rules and follow what he has been taught. Huck bases these decisions on his experiences, his own sense of logic, and what his developing conscience tells him. On the raft, away from civilization, Huck is especially free from society's rules, able to make his own decisions without restriction. Through deep introspection, he comes to his own conclusions, unaffected by the accepted—and often hypocritical—rules and values of Southern culture. By the novel's end, Huck has learned to "read" the world around him, to distinguish good, bad, right, wrong, menace, friend, and so on. His moral development is sharply contrasted to the character of Tom Sawyer, who is influenced by a bizarre mix of adventure novels and Sunday-school teachings, which he combines to justify his outrageous and potentially harmful escapades.

Literary Techniques

Mark Twain was the first important writer to consistently use the American speech rather than England's English. His honor, whether it was aimed at pure entertainment or at social satire, was irresistible. His realism and details influenced many later American novelists. And it became Twain's masterpiece. Mark Twain's three years' life on that returned to the Mississippi left such a fond memory with him that returned to the theme more than once in his writing career.

The Adventures of Huckleberry Finn is a veritable recreation of living models. The two major characters, Huck and Jim, represent the two sides of the dilemma: Huck strikes out for an absolute freedom, while Jim requires, in order to gain his own freedom, that Huck qualify his freedom by entering into the pursuit of Jim's. It starts out as a comedy with a hero drawn from the bottom of society rather than the top. The portrayal of individual incidents and characters achieved intense verisimilitude of detail. Serious problems are being discussed through the narration of a little illiterate boy. The fact is that the wilderness is juxtaposed with civilization, the people are half wild and half civilized, many of whom are worse, vulgar, and brutal. As for the style of the book, the form is based on the simplest of all novel-forms, the so-called picaresque novel which strings its incidents on the line of the hero's travels. But, in this novel, rivers are roads that move, and the movement of the road in its own mysterious life transmutes the primitive simplicity of the form: the road itself is the greatest character in this novel of the road, and the hero's departures from the river and his returns to it compose a subtle and significant pattern. *The Adventures of Huckleberry Finn* shows the major achievements of his art: the masterful use of dialects; humor and pathos, innocence and evil. This novel demonstrates his ability to capture the enduring, archetypal, mythic images of America and to create the most memorable characters in all of American fiction.

Colloquial Language The book is written in a colloquial style, in the general standard speech of uneducated Americans. Moreover, the prose of *Huckleberry Finn* established the prose virtues of American colloquial speech. It has something to do with ease and freedom in the use of language. Most of all, it has to do with the structure of the sentence, which is simple, direct, and fluent, maintaining the rhythm of the word's group of speech and the intonations of the speaking voice. *The Adventures of Huckleberry Finn* displays the major achievements of his art: the carefully controlled point of view, with its implicit ironies expressed through the voice of a semiliterate boy: the masterful use of dialects: the felicitous balancing of nostalgic humorist and realism, humor and pathos, innocence and evil, all united for a journey down the Mississippi that serves as the mythic center of the novel.

Vernacular Language Mark Twain wrote in his unpretentious, colloquial, and poetic style. He used vernacular language, dialect with spelling representing pronunciation. Part of this comes from his interest in humor. The directness of the language is a very influential point in Twain's style. Ernest Hemingway in the 20th century said that he had learnt his craft from Mark Twain because of the direct speech and the direct narration that Twain was able to achieve. The hoax and tall tale are also part of twain's style. Hoax is writing something fantastic and pretending that it were true. It tolls as if it were true, and so the reader would laugh that anybody could believe such preposterous things, the burlesque making fun of establishes ways of writing.

Mark Twain wanted his writing to have the sound of easy-going speech. In *Huckleberry Finn* the fountainhead of the American colloquial prose, he wrote seven different dialects and each can be distinguished. If the reader is a linguist, he can examine the different pronunciations that Twain has shown. In his own time, dialect writing was considered humorous. People got a big laugh out of reading these misspell words. Another feature of the book, which helps to make it famous, is its language. The book is written in the colloquial style in the general standard speech of uneducated Americans. Mark Twain's introductory note on accents is an indication of his conscious attempt to achieve accurate detail. The novel, "Painstaking" and "not haphazard," though they possess a humorous ring, denotes the conscientious effort on the part of the author, and trustworthiness and familiarity and the author's awareness of dialects in using which reveal his attempt to reproduce actual daily speech with a degree of accuracy.

Local Color Local color as a trend first made its presence in the late 1860s and early seventies. The vogue of local color fiction was the logical combination of a long, progressive development. It was the outgrowth of historical and aesthetic forces that been gathering energy since early nineteenth century. Twain refers to the elements, which characterize a local culture, elements such as speech, customs, and also a particular place. Local colorists concerned themselves with presenting and interpreting the local character of their regions. They tended to identify and glorify, but they never forgot to keep an eye on the truthful color of local life.

Twain depicted social life through descriptions of local places and people he knew best and believed that "the most valuable capital, or culture, or education usable in the building of novels is personal experience." Twain often played trick on the reader. He often said things when he meant just the opposite. This is the irony that he got the humor from the Far West. He would do things that he did just to make fun, but the reader might think that he really meant it. Then the reader was the tender-foot who was taken in.

Mark twain preferred to respect social life through portraits of local places which he knew best and drew heavily from his own rich fund of knowledge of people and places. *The Adventures of huckleberry Finn* is one such example. Finn is living breathing personality. It is through his use of language and his activities that Twain creates character and sets down objective truth: Finn is uneducated; he dislikes civilized ways because they are restrictive and hypocritical.

Meanwhile, local color mixed romantic plots with realistic descriptions of things which were readily observed, with the customs, dialects, sights, smell and sounds of regional America. After the Civil war, local color had further developed. In this book, this kind of literature mainly describes the local life, the keynote was optimistic, and the language was narrative humorous. The characters he created were humorous and full of wittiness. Mark Twin's work was regarded the witness of America's pure local life.

Pun There are five forms of pun: homophonic pun（同音双关）, paronomasia（近音双关）, antalaclasis（同音异义双关）, sylleptic pun（一词多义双关）, and asteismus（歧解双关）. In a certain context, pun has several pragmatic functions. Throughout all of Twain's writing, the conflict between the ideals of Americans and their desire for money is evident. But Twain never tried to solve the conflict. He is like a newspaperman who reports what he sees. In this situation, his humor was often rather childish.

In *The Adventures of Huckleberry Finn*, find many words and phrases were used vividly to describe the things that happened, such as "I went along slow then, and I wasn't right down certain whether I was glad I started or whether I wasn't." This sentence is very interesting; pun is used to express the author's mood at that moment.

Satire Satire is a way of criticizing people or ideas in a humorous way to show that they have faults or are wrong, or a piece of writing or play, which uses this style. In *The Adventures of Huckleberry Finn*, Twain shows satire on southern culture before the civil war, when the Mississippi valley was still being settled. Twain blended two different subjects, the experience of westward expansion and the experience of southern slavery. And he wrote about both regains of the country. His attitudes toward the south were much less pleasant than his attitudes toward the west, because he confronted the south problem of slave of mistreatment of humans by humans. Through the change of the white boy Huck's attitude toward Jim, a runaway black slave, Twain condemned racial discrimination. Twain made fun of typical American values, yet underneath he felt a brooding pessimism not only about American valuable but also about life itself.

It was a dreadful thing to see human beings be awful cruel to one another. Due to Twain's own experience, satire is successfully used in this novel. There's one significant scene which should be remembered, Huck Finn witnesses many instances of cruelty, brutality and hypocrisy in the township along the river.

Fundamentally, Twain is a great American writer. *The Adventures of Huckleberry Finn* is an outstanding novel; one of the most successful writing styles is a combination of colloquial language and satire. In fact, most of Twain's works are the combination of both colloquial language and satire, but *The Adventures of Huckleberry Finn* was a case in point. On the other hand, it is his masterpiece as a humorist while the novel also can be eyed as a satire on sentimentality and Romanticism on the other. It displays American culture out of the ordinary and the attitude toward the entire society. In this book, the author use the first character to narrate, meanwhile colloquial language as the main writing language has come into the stage, in order to have the effect on vivid writing, satire is come out. In this situation, *The Adventures of Huckleberry Finn* displays the major achievements of his art: writing in a rich and intricate style that supported his intense scrutiny of complex human experience.

Parody *The Adventures of Huckleberry Finn* parodies the popular romance novels. The novel is full of people who base their lives on romantic literary models and stereotypes of various kinds. Tom Sawyer, the most obvious example, bases his life and actions on adventure novels. The deceased Emmeline Grangerford painted weepy maidens and wrote poems about dead children in the romantic style. The Shepherdson and Grangerford families kill one another out of a bizarre, overexcited conception of family honor. These characters' proclivities toward the romantic allow Twain a few opportunities to indulge in some fun, and indeed, the episodes that deal with this subject are among the funniest in the novel. However, there is a more substantive message beneath: that popular literature is highly stylized and therefore rarely reflects the reality of a society. Twain shows how a strict adherence to these romantic ideals is ultimately dangerous: Tom is shot, Emmeline dies, and the Shepherdsons and

Grangerfords end up in a deadly clash.

Symbols Symbols are objects, characters, figures, and colors used to represent abstract ideas or concepts. In *The Adventures of Huckleberry Finn*, one of the most important symbols is the Mississippi River. For Huck and Jim, the Mississippi River is the ultimate symbol of freedom. Alone on their raft, they do not have to answer to anyone. The river carries them toward freedom: for Jim, toward the free states; for Huck, away from his abusive father and the restrictive "civilizing" of St. Petersburg. Much like the river itself, Huck and Jim are in flux, willing to change their attitudes about each other with little prompting. Despite their freedom, however, they soon find that they are not completely free from the evils and influences of the towns on the river's banks. Even early on, the real world intrudes on the paradise of the raft: the river floods, bringing Huck and Jim into contact with criminals, wrecks, and stolen goods. Then, a thick fog causes them to miss the mouth of the Ohio River, which was to be their route to freedom.

As the novel progresses, then, the river becomes something other than the inherently benevolent place Huck originally thought it was. As Huck and Jim move further south, the duke and the dauphin invade the raft, and Huck and Jim must spend more time ashore. Though the river continues to offer a refuge from trouble, it often merely effects the exchange of one bad situation for another. Each escape exists in the larger context of a continual drift southward, toward the Deep South and entrenched slavery. In this transition from idyllic retreat to source of peril, the river mirrors the complicated state of the South. As Huck and Jim's journey progresses, the river, which once seemed a paradise and a source of freedom, becomes merely a short-term means of escape that nonetheless pushes Huck and Jim ever further toward danger and destruction.

Bibliography

http://www.biography.com/people/mark-twain-9512564?page=1, 2012-06-04.
http://en.wikipedia.org/wiki/Adventures_of_Huckleberry_Finn, 2012-06-09.
http://www.sparknotes.com/lit/huckfinn/themes.html, 2012-06-11.
http://blog.sina.com.cn/s/blog_4b8762020100f7qb.html, 2013-02-27.
http://hanlizhizi.blog.163.com/blog/static/1161631022009102633037957/, 2013-02-27.

Henry James

His Life and Writing Career

His Life

Henry James (1843–1916) was born in New York City into a wealthy family. His father, Henry James Sr., was one of the best-known intellectuals in mid-nineteenth-century America, whose friends included Thoreau, Emerson and Hawthorne.

In his youth James traveled back and forth between Europe and America. He studied with tutors in Geneva, London, Paris, Bologna and Bonn. At the age of nineteen he briefly attended Harvard Law School, but was more interested in literature than studying law. From an early age James had read the classics of English, American, French and German literature, and Russian classics in translation. James wrote his first novel while he was traveling through Venice and Paris.

After living in Paris, where James was contributor to *New York Tribune*, he moved to England, living first in London and then in Rye, Sussex. During his first years in Europe James wrote novels that portrayed Americans living abroad.

Between 1906 and 1910 James revised many of his tales and novels for the so-called New York Edition of his complete works. The outbreak of World War I was a shock for James and in 1915 he became a British citizen as a loyalty to his adopted country and in protest against the US's refusal to enter the war.

James suffered a stroke on December 2, 1915. He expected to die and exclaimed: "So this is it at last, the distinguished thing!" However, James died three months later in Rye on February 28, 1916.

His Writing Career

James's literary career can be divided into three main stages of development. In his early period, Henry James developed the international novel, which brings together persons of various nationalities who represent certain characteristics of their respective countries. Although James wrote a novel with an international setting, he was concerned about how Americans behave in an international setting. Europeans were more cultured, more concerned with art, and more aware of the subtleties of social situations. Americans were innocent, and more concerned about moral issues. The author seems to value both the sophistication of Europe and the idealism of America. One example is *Daisy Miller* published in 1878. This book established his reputation at home and abroad and helped to make of the American girl a celebrated cultural type.

The international theme of the traditionless Americans confronting the complexity of European life is one that is typical for James's fiction and it is also typical for realist writers to examine the interplay between innocence and experience. James used the image of America as the youthful innocent land. Now his view is somewhat more complicated. Experience is not necessarily positive. Innocence is not necessarily negative. James himself had also lived in Europe and he knew the rigidity of European culture that the rules under which it lived did not allow any change, and vitality. He saw the decadence of the European culture at this time. But at the same time James admired the rich heritage of the European artistic culture, something that America lacked. So his theme in the international novel is innocence versus experience. Other examples are *The American* (1877) and *The Portrait of a Lady* (1881).

In the second stage, he experimented with various subjects and forms: first, between 1886 and 1890, three novels in the naturalistic mode: *The Bostonians* (1886), *The Princess Casamassima* (1886), *The Tragic Muse* (1890); second, between 1895 and 1900, he turned to three dominant subjects, troubled writers and artists, ghosts and apparitions, doomed or threatened children and adolescents. *The Turn of the Screw* (1898) and *The Beast in the Jungle* (1903) are good examples of the period. Between 1890 and 1895, he wrote seven plays and two of them were staged but without success.

In the third stage, he returned to his international themes and produced the complex and profound novels such as *The Wings of the Dove* (1902), *The Ambassadors* (1903), and *The Golden Bowl* (1904). He wrote, late in his life, three autobiographical reminiscences *A Small Boy and Others* (1913), *Notes of a Son and Brother* (1914), and *The Middle Years*. (1917) *The American Scene* (1907) is about his extensive travel in America. His last novel is *The Outcry* (1911) and *The Ivory Tower* and *The Sense of the Past* were left unfinished.

Analysis of and Comment on His Representative Novel

The Portrait of a Lady (1881)

Plot Summary

Isabel Archer is a woman in her early twenties who comes from a genteel family in Albany, New York, in the late 1860s. Her mother died when she was a young girl, and her father raised her in a haphazard manner, allowing her to educate herself and encouraging her independence. As a result, the adult Isabel is widely read, imaginative, confident in her own mind, and slightly narcissistic; she has the reputation in Albany for being a formidable intellect, and as a result she often seems intimidating to men. She has had few suitors, but one of them is Caspar Goodwood, the powerful, charismatic son of a wealthy Boston mill owner. Isabel is drawn to Caspar, but her commitment to her independence makes her fear him as well, for she feels that to marry him would be to sacrifice her freedom.

Shortly after Isabel's father dies, she receives a visit from her indomitable aunt, Mrs. Touchett, an American who lives in Europe. Mrs. Touchett offers to take Isabel on a trip to Europe, and Isabel eagerly agrees, telling Caspar that she cannot tell him whether she wishes to marry him until she has had at least a year to travel in Europe with her aunt. Isabel and Mrs. Touchett leave for England, where Mrs. Touchett's estranged husband is a powerful banker. Isabel makes a strong impression on everyone at Mr. Touchett's county manor of Gardencourt: her cousin Ralph, slowly dying of a lung disorder, becomes deeply devoted to her, and the Touchetts' aristocratic neighbor Lord Warburton falls in love with her. Warburton proposes, but Isabel declines; though she fears that she is passing up a great social opportunity by not marrying Warburton. She still believes that marriage would damage her treasured independence. As a result, she pledges to accomplish something wonderful with her life, something that will justify her decision to reject Warburton.

Isabel's friend Henrietta Stackpole, an American journalist, believes that Europe is changing Isabel, slowly eroding her American values and replacing them with romantic idealism. Henrietta comes to Gardencourt and secretly arranges for Caspar Goodwood to meet Isabel in London. Goodwood again presses Isabel to marry him; this time, she tells him she needs at least two years before she can answer him, and she promises him nothing. She is thrilled to have exercised her independence so forcefully. Mr. Touchett's health declines and Ralph convinces him that when he dies, he should leave half his wealth to Isabel: this will protect her independence and ensure that she will never have to marry for money. Mr. Touchett agrees shortly before he dies. Isabel is left with a large fortune for the first time in her life. Her inheritance piques the interest of Madame Merle, Mrs. Touchett's polished, elegant friend; Madame Merle begins to lavish attention on Isabel, and the two women become close friends.

Isabel travels to Florence with Mrs. Touchett and Madame Merle; Merle introduces Isabel to a man named Gilbert Osmond, a man of no social standing or wealth, but whom Merle describes as one of the finest gentlemen in Europe, wholly devoted to art and aesthetics. Osmond's daughter Pansy is being brought up in a convent; his wife is dead. In secret, Osmond and Merle have a mysterious relationship; Merle is attempting to manipulate Isabel into marrying Osmond so that he will have access to her fortune.

Osmond is pleased to marry Isabel, not only for her money, but also because she makes a fine addition to his collection of art objects.

Everyone in Isabel's world disapproves of Osmond, especially Ralph, but Isabel chooses to marry him anyway. She has a child the year after they are married, but the boy dies six months after he is born. Three years into their marriage, Isabel and Osmond have come to despise one another; they live with Pansy in a palazzo in Rome, where Osmond treats Isabel as barely a member of the family: to him, she is a social hostess and a source of wealth, and he is annoyed by her independence and her insistence on having her own opinions. Isabel chafes against Osmond's arrogance, his selfishness, and his sinister desire to crush her individuality, but she does not consider leaving him. For all her commitment to her independence, Isabel is also committed to her social duty, and when she married Osmond, she did so with the intention of transforming herself into a good wife.

A young American art collector who lives in Paris, Edward Rosier, comes to Rome and falls in love with Pansy; Pansy returns his feelings. But Osmond is insistent that Pansy should marry a nobleman, and he says that Rosier is neither rich nor highborn enough. Matters grow complicated when Lord Warburton arrives on the scene and begins to court Pansy. Warburton is still in love with Isabel and wants to marry Pansy solely to get closer to her. But Osmond desperately wants to see Pansy married to Warburton. Isabel is torn about whether to fulfill her duty to her husband and help him arrange the match between Warburton and Pansy, or to fulfill the impulse of her conscience and discourage Warburton, while helping Pansy find a way to marry Rosier.

At a ball one night, Isabel shows Warburton the dejected-looking Rosier and explains that this is the man who is in love with Pansy. Guiltily, Warburton admits that he is not in love with Pansy; he quietly arranges to leave Rome. Osmond is furious with Isabel, convinced that she is plotting intentionally to humiliate him. Madame Merle is also furious with her, confronting her with shocking impropriety and demanding brazenly to know what she did to Warburton. Isabel has realized that there is something mysterious about Madame Merle's relationship with her husband; now, she suddenly realizes that Merle is his lover.

At this time, Ralph is rapidly deteriorating, and Isabel receives word that he is dying. She longs to travel to England to be with him, but Osmond forbids it. Now Isabel must struggle to decide whether to obey his command and remain true to her marriage vows or to disregard him and hurry to her cousin's bedside. Encouraging her to go, Osmond's sister, the Countess Gemini, tells her that there is still more to Merle and Osmond's relationship. Merle is Pansy's mother; Pansy was born out of wedlock. Osmond's wife died at about the same time, so Merle and Osmond spread the story that she died in childbirth. Pansy was placed in a convent to be raised, and she does not know that

Merle is her real mother. Isabel is shocked and disgusted by her husband's atrocious behavior—she even feels sorry for Merle for falling under his spell—so she decides to follow her heart and travel to England.

After Ralph's death, Isabel struggles to decide whether to return to her husband or not. She promised Pansy that she would return to Rome, and her commitment to social propriety impels her to go back and honor her marriage. But her independent spirit urges her to flee from Osmond and find happiness elsewhere. Caspar Goodwood appears at the funeral, and afterwards, he asks Isabel to run away with him and forget about her husband. The next day, unable to find her, Goodwood asks Henrietta where she has gone. Henrietta quietly tells him that Isabel has returned to Rome, unable to break away from her marriage to Gilbert Osmond.

Themes

James' first idea for *The Portrait of a Lady* was simple: a young American woman confronting her destiny, whatever it might be. Only then did he begin to form a plot to bring out the character of his central figure. This was the uncompromising story of the free-spirited Isabel losing her freedom—despite suddenly coming into a great deal of money—and getting "ground in the very mill of the conventional."

The novel exhibits a huge panorama of trans-Atlantic life, a far larger canvas than any James had previously painted. This moneyed world appears charming and leisurely but proves to be plagued with treachery, deceit, and suffering, which symbolizes the prototype of the Old or the Europe.

Several themes are predominant in Henry James' novel *The Portrait of a Lady*, such as the main themes of Romance, freedom, and vagueness, and the minor theme of defiance of the traditional female role in the nineteenth century. Throughout the novel Isabel seeks to assert her independence through denying marriages to eligible suitors and instead seeking adventure; through her "Romantic" and vivid imagination James creates a character ripe with pragmatic ideals.

Isabel claims on several occasions that she desires to be placed in a difficult situation so that she can have the chance to be "as heroic as the occasion demanded." Through this quote it is made obvious that Isabel serves to embody the theme of Romance by daring to embrace the unknown and give up a life of predictable stability in order to assert her independence. In this sense Isabel addresses the philosophical problem of her freedom by breaking away from sheltered married life and instead exploring the life of a financially independent single woman.

The theme of independence in the novel comes full circle when we see Isabel's naïve and unreflective embodiment of American ideals. We see her express her independence only to be ironically imprisoned in her marriage because she was naive enough to marry strictly for love in a society where women married for security and political reasons.

The vagueness of twentieth century Romance is another evident theme in the novel on account of the fact that Isabel refuses to divulge her plans for the future to her suitors and says instead that she wishes to travel and experience adventure. Everything about Isabel's motives, from her emancipation to her eventual decision to marry and then leave Osmond is not directly revealed to the reader, and instead must be inferred based on the qualities of her character that are revealed. Even the ending of the novel in which the reader is uncertain as to whether Isabel returns to her horrific marriage is an embodiment of the vagueness theme because it leaves the reader to create a conclusion based upon their interpretation of Romance in the novel as a piece of American modernist literature. The theme of vagueness is articulated perfectly in the quote because the reader is indeed left wondering what exactly Isabel has gained from the attainment and loss of her freedom, and from her unhappy marriage.

The Portrait of a Lady also explores the conflict between the individual and society by examining the life of Isabel Archer, a young American woman who must choose between her independent spirit and the demands of social convention. After professing and longing to be an independent woman, autonomous and answerable only to herself, Isabel falls in love with and marries the sinister Gilbert Osmond, who wants her only for her money and who treats her as an object, almost as part of his art collection. Isabel must then decide whether to honor her marriage vows and preserve social propriety or to leave her miserable marriage and escape to a happier, more independent life, possibly with her American suitor Caspar Goodwood. In the end, after the death of her cousin Ralph, the staunchest advocate of her independence, Isabel chooses to return to Osmond and maintain her marriage. She is motivated partly by a sense of social duty, partly by a sense of pride, and partly by the love of her stepdaughter, Pansy, the daughter of Osmond and his manipulative lover Madame Merle.

As the title of the novel indicates, Isabel is the principal character of the book, and the main focus of the novel is on presenting, explaining, and developing her character. James is one of America's great psychological realists, and he uses all his creative powers to ensure that Isabel's conflict is the natural product of a believable mind, and not merely an abstract philosophical consideration. In brief, Isabel's independence of spirit is largely a result of her childhood, when she was generally neglected by her father and allowed to read any book in her grandmother's library; in this way, she supervised her own haphazard education and allowed her mind to develop without discipline or order. Her natural intelligence has always ensured that she is at least as quick as anyone around her, and in Albany, New York, she has the reputation of being a formidable intellect.

After she travels to England with her aunt, Mrs. Touchett, however, it becomes clear that Isabel has a woefully unstructured imagination, as well as a romantic streak that suits her position as an optimistic, innocent American. (For James, throughout *The Portrait of a Lady*, America is a place of individualism and naïveté, while Europe is a place of sophistication, convention, and decadence.) Isabel often considers her life as though it were a novel. She also has a tendency to think about herself obsessively and has a vast faith in her own moral strength—in fact, recognizing that she has never faced hardship, Isabel actually wishes that she might be made to suffer, so that she could prove her ability to overcome suffering without betraying her principles.

When Isabel moves to England, her cousin Ralph is so taken with her spirit of independence that he convinces his dying father to leave half his fortune to Isabel. This is intended to prevent her from ever having to marry for money, but ironically it attracts the treachery of the novel's villains, Madame Merle and Gilbert Osmond. They conspire to convince Isabel to marry Osmond in order to gain access to her wealth. Her marriage to Osmond effectively stifles Isabel's independent spirit, as her husband treats her as an object and tries to force her to share his opinions and abandon her own.

James skillfully intertwines the novel's psychological and thematic elements. Isabel's downfall with Osmond, for instance, enables the book's most trenchant exploration of the conflict between her desire to conform to social convention and her fiercely independent mind. It is also perfectly explained by the elements of Isabel's character: her haphazard upbringing has led her to long for stability and safety, even if they mean a loss of independence, and her active imagination enables her to create an illusory picture of Osmond, which she believes in more than the real thing, at least until she is married to him. Once she marries Osmond, Isabel's pride in her moral strength makes it impossible for her to consider leaving him: she once longed for hardship, and now that she has found it, it would be hypocritical for her to surrender to it by violating social custom and abandoning her husband.

Literary Techniques

Generally regarded as the masterpiece of Henry James' early phase, *The Portrait of a Lady* is described as a psychological novel, exploring the minds of his characters, and almost a work of social science, exploring the differences between Europeans and Americans, the old and the new worlds.

In the same way that James unites his psychological and thematic subjects, he also intertwines the novel's settings with its themes. Set almost entirely among a group of American expatriates living in Europe in the 1860s and 70s, the book relies on a kind of moral geography, in which America represents innocence, individualism, and capability; Europe represents decadence, sophistication, and social convention; and England represents the best mix of the two. Isabel moves from America to England to continental

Europe, and at each stage she comes to mirror her surroundings, gradually losing a bit of independence with each move. Eventually she lives in Rome, the historic heart of continental Europe, and it is here that she endures her greatest hardship with Gilbert Osmond.

Narratively, James uses many of his most characteristic techniques in *The Portrait of a Lady*. In addition to his polished, elegant prose and his sedate, slow pacing, he utilizes a favorite technique of skipping over some of the novel's main events in telling the story. Instead of narrating moments such as Isabel's wedding with Osmond, James skips over them, relating that they have happened only after the fact, in peripheral conversations. This literary technique is known as ellipses. In the novel, James most often uses his elliptical technique in scenes when Isabel chooses to value social custom over her independence—her acceptance of Gilbert's proposal, their wedding, her decision to return to Rome after briefly leaving for Ralph's funeral at the end of the novel. James uses this method to create the sense that, in these moments, Isabel is no longer accessible to the reader; in a sense, by choosing to be with Gilbert Osmond, Isabel is lost.

The use of contrast is another technique. James is one of the major figures of trans-Atlantic literature. His works frequently juxtapose characters from the Old World (Europe), embodying a feudal civilization that is beautiful, often corrupt, and alluring, and from the New World (United States), where people are often brash, open, and assertive and embody the virtues—freedom and a more highly evolved moral character—of the new American society. James explores this clash of personalities and cultures, in stories of personal relationships in which power is exercised well or badly. His protagonists were often young American women facing oppression or abuse.

James used the consciousness stream skills and tried to avoid omniscient point of view. Critics have jokingly described three phases in the development of James's prose: "James the First, James the Second, and The Old Pretender" and observers do often group his works of fiction into three periods. In his apprentice years, culminating with the masterwork *The Portrait of a Lady*, his style was simple and direct and he experimented widely with forms and methods, generally narrating from a conventionally omniscient point of view. Plots generally concern romance, except for the three big novels of social commentary that conclude this period. In the second period, from 1890 to about 1897, he wrote short stories and plays. Finally, in his third and last period he returned to the long, serialized novel. Beginning in the second period, but most noticeably in the third, he increasingly abandoned direct statement in favor of frequent double negatives, and complex descriptive imagery. Single paragraphs began to run for page after page, in which an initial noun would be succeeded by pronouns surrounded by clouds of adjectives and prepositional clauses, far from their original referents, and verbs would be deferred and then preceded by a series of adverbs. The overall effect could be a vivid evocation of a scene as perceived by a sensitive observer. In its intense focus on the consciousness of his major characters, James's later work foreshadows extensive developments in 20th century fiction.

Indeed, he might have influenced stream-of-consciousness writers such as Virginia Woolf, who not only read some of his novels but also wrote essays about them. Then and later many readers find the late style difficult and unnecessary; his friend Edith Wharton, who admired him greatly, said that there were passages in his work that were all but incomprehensible. H.G. Wells harshly portrayed James as a hippopotamus laboriously attempting to pick up a pea that has got into a corner of its cage. Some critics have claimed that the more elaborate manner was a result of James taking up the practice of dictating to a secretary. He was afflicted with a stutter and compensated by speaking slowly and deliberately. The late style does become more difficult in the years when he dictates, but James also was able to revise typewritten drafts more extensively, and his few surviving drafts show that the later works are more heavily revised and redrafted. In some cases this leads critics to prefer the earlier, unrevised versions of some works because the older style is thought to be closer to the original conception and spirit of the work, *Daisy Miller* being a case in point: most of the current reprints of this novel contain the unrevised text. On the other hand, the late revision of the early novel *The Portrait of a Lady* is generally much preferred to the first edition, even by those who dislike the late style, because of the power of the imagery and the depth of characterization, while his shorter late fiction, such as *The Turn of the Screw*, is considered highly accessible and remains popular with readers.

More important for his work overall may have been his position as an expatriate, and in other ways an outsider, living in Europe. While he came from middle-class and provincial belongings he worked very hard to gain access to all levels of society, and the settings of his fiction range from working class to aristocratic, and often describe the efforts of middle-class Americans to make their way in European capitals. He confessed he got some of his best story ideas from gossip at the dinner table or at country house weekends. He worked for a living, however, and lacked the experiences of select schools, university, and army service, the common bonds of masculine society. He was furthermore a man whose tastes and interests were, according to the prevailing standards of Victorian era Anglo-American culture, rather feminine, and who was shadowed by the cloud of prejudice that then and later accompanied suspicions of his homosexuality.

It is also possible to see many of James's stories as psychological thought-experiments. *The Portrait of a Lady* may be an experiment to see what happens when an idealistic young woman suddenly becomes very rich. In many of his tales, characters seem to exemplify alternate futures and possibilities, as most markedly in *The Jolly Corner*, in which the protagonist and a ghost-doppelganger live alternate American and European lives; and in others, like *The Ambassadors*, an older James seems fondly to regard his own younger self facing a crucial moment.

In 1968 the BBC produced a television miniseries of *The Portrait of a Lady*, starring Suzanne Neve as Isabel and Richard Chamberlain as Ralph Touchett. This novel was turned into a film in 1996 by New Zealand director Jane Campion, starring Nicole Kidman as Isabel, John Malkovich as Osmond, and Barbara Hershey as Madame Merle. The movie gained lukewarm reviews; the author thought the book too elusive for dramatic presentation. When the actor Lawrence Barrett wanted James to turn the novel into a play, he replied that he did not think it could be done. In James' opinion, given in the preface to the New York Edition, the best "scene" in the book consists of Isabel sitting motionless in a chair.

Bibliography

http://en.wikipedia.org/wiki/The_Portrait_of_a_Lady, 2012-07-10.
http://www.docin.com/p-453648690. html, 2013-02-27.
http://weiyanlei2003.blog.163.com/blog/static/6608832006327327360/, 2013-02-27.

Edith Wharton

Her Life and Writing Career

Her Life

Edith Wharton (1862–1937), born Edith Newbold Jones, was a Pulitzer Prize-winning American novelist, short story writer, and designer.

Edith Wharton was born into the wealthy family of George Frederic Jones and Lucretia Rhinelander on 24 January 1862 in New York City. She had two brothers, Frederic and Henry "Harry" Edward. To escape the bustling city, the family spent summers at Rhode Island. When Edith was four years old they moved to Europe, spending the next five years traveling throughout Italy, Spain, Germany and France. Back in New York, young Edith continued her education under private tutors. She studied literature, philosophy, science, and art. She also started to write short stories and poetry.

In 1885, at 23 years of age, she married Edward (Teddy) Robbins Wharton, who was 12 years older. From a well-established Boston family, he was a sportsman and gentleman of the same social class and shared her love of travel, although they had little in common intellectually. From the late 1880s until 1902, he suffered acute depression, and the couple ceased their extensive travel. At that time his depression manifested as a more serious disorder, after which they lived almost exclusively at The Mount, their estate designed by Edith Wharton. In 1908 her husband's mental state was determined to be incurable. She divorced him in 1913. Around the same time, Edith was troubled with the harsh criticisms leveled by the naturalist writers. Later in 1908 she began an affair with Morton Fullerton, a journalist for *The Times*, in whom she found an intellectual partner.

Wharton built The Mount, her estate in Lenox, Massachusetts in 1902, in which she entertained the cream of American literary society, including her close friend, the novelist Henry James. Although she spent many months traveling in Europe nearly every year, The Mount was her primary residence until 1911. When living there and when traveling abroad, Wharton was usually driven to appointments by her longtime chauffeur and friend Charles Cook, a native of Massachusetts. When her marriage deteriorated, she decided to move permanently to France.

Helped by her influential connections to the French government, primarily through Walter Berry (then president of the American Chamber of Commerce in Paris), she was one of the few foreigners in France allowed to travel to the front lines during World War I. Wharton described those trips in the series of articles *Fighting France: from Dunkerque to Belfort*.

Throughout the war she worked tirelessly in charitable efforts for refugees and, in 1916 was named a Chevalier of the Legion of Honor in recognition of her commitment to the displaced. The scope of her relief work included setting up workrooms for unemployed Frenchwomen, organizing concerts to provide work for musicians, opening tuberculosis hospitals and founding the American Hostels for Belgian refugees. In 1916 Wharton edited *The Book of the Homeless*, composed of writings, art and musical scores by almost every major contemporary European artist. When World War I ended in 1918, she abandoned her fashionable urban address and moved to countryside.

In 1927 she purchased a villa, Castel Sainte-Claire, on the site of a 17th-century convent, in the hills above Hyères in Provence, where she lived during the winters and springs. She called the villa "Sainte-Claire du Chateau" and filled the garden with cacti and subtropical plants. She returned to the U.S. only once after the war, to receive an honorary doctorate degree from Yale University in 1923.

Wharton was a friend and confidante to many gifted intellectuals of her time. Henry James, Sinclair Lewis, Jean Cocteau and André Gide were all guests of hers at one time or another. Theodore Roosevelt, Bernard Berenson, and Kenneth Clark were valued friends as well. But her meeting with F. Scott Fitzgerald was described by the editors of her letters as "one of the better known failed encounters in the American literary annals."

Edith Wharton died of a stroke in 1937 at the domaine Le Pavillon Colombe, her 18th-century house on Rue de Montmorency in Saint-Brice-sous-Forêt. The street is today called rue Edith Wharton. She is buried in the American Cemetery in Versailles, France.

Her Writing Career

Wharton's first novel *Fast and Loose* was published in 1877, and *Verses*, a collection of poems was published next year. These early works were appreciated by Henry Wadsworth Longfellow and William Dean Howells, the editor of *Atlantic Monthly*.

In addition to novels, Wharton wrote at least 85 short stories. She was also a garden designer, interior designer, and taste-maker of her time. She wrote several design books, including her first published work, *The Decoration of Houses of 1897*, co-authored by Ogden Codman. Another is the generously illustrated *Italian Villas and Their Gardens of 1904*.

In 1902 she built The Mount, her estate in Lenox, Massachusetts, which survives today as an example of her design principles. There, Edith Wharton wrote several of her novels, including *The House of Mirth* (1905), the first of many chronicles of the nature of old New York.

Wharton was a committed supporter of French imperialism, describing herself as a "rabid imperialist", and the war solidified her political conservatism. After World War I, she travelled to Morocco as the guest of the resident general, Gen. Hubert Lyautey and wrote a book about her experiences. After the war she divided her time between Paris and Hyères, Provence, where she finished *The Age of Innocence* in 1920. This novel won the 1921 Pulitzer Prize for literature, making Wharton the first woman to win the award.

In 1934 Wharton's autobiography *A Backward Glance* was published. In the view of Judith E. Funston, writing on Edith Wharton in American National Biography, "What is most notable about *A Backward Glance*, however, is what it does not tell: her criticism of Lucretia Jones [her mother], her difficulties with Teddy, and her affair with Morton Fullerton, which did not come to light until her papers, deposited in Yale's Beinecke Rare Book Room and Manuscript Library, were opened in 1968."

Many of Wharton's novels are characterized by a subtle use of dramatic irony. Having grown up in upper-class pre-World War I society, Wharton became one of its most astute critics, in such works as *The House of Mirth* and *The Age of Innocence*. In all she published 22 novels: *The Touchstone* (1900), *The Valley of Decision* (1902), *Sanctuary* (1903), *The House of Mirth* (1905), *Madame de Treymes* (1907), *The Fruit of the Tree* (1907), *Ethan Frome* (1911), *The Reef* (1912), *The Custom of the Country* (1913), *Summer* (1917), *The Marne* (1918), *The Age of Innocence* (1920), *The Glimpses of the Moon* (1922), *A Son at the Front* (1923), *Old New York* (1924), *The Mother's Recompense* (1925), *Twilight Sleep* (1927), *The Children* (1928), *Hudson River Bracketed* (1929), *The Gods Arrive* (1932), *The Buccaneers* (1938), *Fast and Loose* (1938) (first novel, written in 1876–1877).

Wharton was one of the most prolific writers in her time. Apart from novels, Wharton also produced a series of short stories and is particularly well regarded for her ghost stories. She published 16 short story collections: *The Greater Inclination* (1899), *Souls Belated* (1899), *Crucial Instances* (1901), *The Reckoning* (1902), *The Descent of Man and Other Stories* (1903), *The Other Two* (1904), *The Hermit and the Wild Woman and Other Stories* (1908), *Tales of Men and Ghosts* (1910), *Xingu and Other Stories* (1916), *Old New York* (1924), *Here and Beyond* (1926), *Certain People* (1930), *Human Nature* (1933), *The World Over* (1936), *Ghosts* (1937), *Roman Fever* (1934).

Analysis of and Comment on Her Representative Novel

The Age of Innocence (1920)

Plot Summary

The Age of Innocence is Edith Wharton's 12th novel, which won Pulitzer Prize in 1921. The story is set in upper-class New York City in the 1870s. *The Age of Innocence* was firstly serialized in four parts in the *Pictorial Review* magazine in 1920, and later released by D. Appleton and Company as a book in New York and in London.

The novel centers on an upper-class couple's impending marriage, and the introduction of a woman plagued by scandal whose presence threatens their happiness. Newland Archer, gentleman lawyer and heir to one of New York City's best families, is happily anticipating a highly desirable marriage to the sheltered and beautiful May Welland. Yet he finds reason to doubt his choice of bride after the appearance of Countess Ellen Olenska, May's exotic, beautiful thirty-year-old cousin, who has been living in Europe. Ellen has returned to New York after scandalously separating herself from a bad marriage to a Polish count. At first, Ellen's arrival and its potential taint to his bride-to-be's family disturbs him, but he becomes intrigued by the worldly Ellen who ridicules New York society's hypocritical rules. As Newland's admiration for the countess grows, so does his doubt about marrying May, a perfect product of Old New York society; his match with May no longer seems the ideal fate he has imagined.

Ellen's decision to divorce Count Olenski is a social crisis for the other members of her family, who are terrified of scandal and disgrace. Living apart can be tolerated, but divorce is unacceptable. To save the Welland family's reputation, a law partner of Newland asks him to dissuade Countess Olenska from divorcing the count. He succeeds, but in the process comes to care for her; afraid of falling in love with Ellen, Newland begs May to accelerate their wedding date, but May refuses.

Newland tells Ellen he loves her. Ellen corresponds, but is horrified that their love will aggrieve May. She agrees to remain in America, separated but still married, only if they do not sexually consummate their love. Newland receives May's telegram agreeing to wed sooner.

Newland and May marry. He tries forgetting Ellen but fails. His marriage is loveless, and the social life he once found absorbing has become empty and joyless. Though Ellen lives in Washington and has remained distant, he is unable to cease loving her. Their paths cross while he and May are in Newport, Rhode Island. Newland discovers that Count Olenski wishes Ellen to return to him, but she has refused, despite her family pushing her to reconcile with her husband and return to Europe. Frustrated by her independence, the family cuts off her money as the count has already done.

Newland desperately seeks a way to leave May and be with Ellen, obsessed with how to finally possess her. Despairing of ever making Ellen his wife, he attempts to have her agree to be his mistress. Then Ellen is recalled to New York City to care for her sick grandmother, who accepts her decision to remain separated and agrees to reinstate her allowance.

Back in New York and under renewed pressure from Newland, Ellen relents and agrees to consummate their relationship. However, Newland then discovers that Ellen has decided to return to Europe. Newland makes up his mind to abandon May and follow Ellen to Europe when May announces that she and Newland are throwing a farewell party for Ellen. That night, after the party, Newland resolves to tell May he is leaving her for Ellen. She interrupts him to tell him that she learned that morning that she is pregnant; she reveals that she has told Ellen of her pregnancy two weeks earlier, despite not being sure of it at the time. The implication is that she did it because she suspected the affair. Newland guesses that this is Ellen's reason for returning to Europe. Hopelessly trapped, Newland decides not to follow Ellen, surrendering his love for the sake of his children, remaining in a loveless marriage to May.

Twenty-six years later, after May's death, Newland and his son are in Paris. The son, learning that his mother's cousin lives there, has arranged to visit Ellen in her

Paris apartment. Newland is stunned at the prospect of seeing Ellen again. On arriving outside the apartment building, Newland sends up his son alone to meet Ellen, while he waits outside, watching the balcony of her apartment. Newland considers going up, but in the end decides not to; he walks back to his hotel without seeing her.

In the novel, Newland Archer is a young, popular, successful lawyer living with his mother and sister in an elegant New York City house. Since childhood, his life has been shaped by the customs and expectations of upper-class New York City society. His engagement to May Welland is a perfect accomplishment. At the story's start, he is proud and content to dream about a traditional marriage in which he will be the husband-teacher and she the wife-student. His life changes when he meets Countess Ellen Olenska. Through his relationship with her—first friendship, then love—he begins questioning the values on which he was raised. He sees the sexual inequality of New York society and the shallowness of its customs, and struggles to balance his commitment to May with love for Ellen. He cannot find a place for their love in the New York society. After many ups and downs, Newland Archer finds that the only place for their love is in his memories.

Newland Archer's fiancée May Welland is a traditional New York lady. Raised to be a perfect wife and mother, she follows and obeys all of society's customs perfectly. Mostly, she is the shallow, uninterested and uninteresting young woman that New York society requires. After marriage, however, she suspects Newland is Ellen's lover. Nonetheless, May pretends happiness before society, maintaining the illusion that she and he have the perfect marriage expected of them. Her unhappiness activates her manipulative nature, and Newland does not see it until too late. To drive Ellen away from him, May tells Ellen of her pregnancy before she is certain of it. Yet, there still is compassion in May, even in their loveless marriage's long years after Ellen's leaving. After May's death, Newland Archer learns she has always known of his continued love for Ellen; as May lies dying, she tells their son Dallas that the child can always trust their father Newland, because he surrenders the thing most meaningful to him out of loyalty to their marriage.

Newland Archer's lover Ellen Olenska is May's cousin and Mrs. Manson Mingott's granddaughter. She becomes a countess by marrying a European nobleman. Her husband is allegedly cruel and abusive, steals Ellen's fortune and has affairs with other women and possibly even with men. When the story begins, Ellen has fled her unhappy marriage, lived in Venice with her husband's secretary, and has returned to her family in New York City, America. She is a free spirit who helps Newland Archer see beyond narrow New York society. She treats her maid, Nastasia, as an equal. She attends parties with disreputable people such as Julius Beaufort and Mrs. Lemuel Struthers, and she invites Newland, the fiancé of her cousin May to visit her. Ellen suffers as much as Newland from their impossible love, but she is willing to live in a distant place as long as they can love each other. Ellen's love for Newland makes her to decide to divorce from Count Olenski and to remain in America. But when she learns of May's pregnancy, Ellen immediately decides to leave America, refusing Newland's attempt to follow her to Europe, and so allow cousin May to start her family with her husband Newland.

Themes

By the time Edith Wharton wrote *The Age of Innocence*, she had seen World War I destroy much of the world as she knew it. She looked back on her early years in New York as a time of social continuity, and felt that the passing of values from parent to child had a civilizing influence. However, she also saw the hypocrisy and cruelty practiced by individuals who wore the veneer of respectability. Both of these ideas are seen throughout *The Age of Innocence*, making it a timeless novel of both the Gilded Age and of social change. In a 1920 New York Times Book Review, William Lyon Phelps applauded the novel, noting, "I do not remember when I have read a work of fiction that gives the reader so vivid an idea of the furnishing and illuminating of rooms in fashionable houses as one will find in *The Age of Innocence*." He added, "New York society and customs in the seventies are described with an accuracy that is almost uncanny."

Wharton's reputation rests on "her ability to memorialize old New York culture with its peculiar manners and mores, and to expose the hypocrisies of the wealthy." Set in 1870's New York City, Wharton examines upper-class values and morals in all their conventionality and tradition, rigidity and hypocrisy, at times with her subtle irony and wit. As Newland Archer is living the life of the just and doing all the right things to establish his respectability in society, his naivety comes to the fore when his affections are torn between two women. The central struggle, between Newland Archer and his conscience, is resolved and unresolved in subtle, understated ways. Wharton gently poked fun at the world of Old New York society in which she lived, such as when Newland was asked how he would spend the afternoon and he replied that he would "save it."

In *The Age of Innocence*, the setting is so dominant and predominant that it almost becomes a character. It also plays a key role in the story. Society in the novel is a powerful force that demands that individuals sacrifice themselves to its forms and conventions. Through detail and lush description, Wharton brings to life the social world of the wealthy in 1870s New York. Wharton describes the New York City society vividly, which is composed of powerful, wealthy families. These people follow and impose a strict, rigid code of social custom and behavior, and judge the people who do not follow their rules as unacceptable and disreputable. A case in point is Ellen, who has difficulty adapting to the behavior that such a society thinks appropriate for a woman separated from her husband. New York society's judgment is clear. Almost everyone refuses to attend the dinner party honoring Ellen's return, and turns his or her back to Ellen.

As a realistic novel, *The Age of Innocence* is a detailed portrayal of social conventions and respectability in late nineteenth-century high society. Newland has grown up in this environment and has internalized all the manners that dictate behavior in old New York. Even intimate matters are subject to rules of etiquette, as May tells Newland that she cares for him, which is the only declaration of love allowed a young unmarried woman. Gossiping is completely acceptable, yet members of society strive to uphold, above all things, their own reputations. Every event in old New York is subject to ritual. When May and Newland are engaged, they must make a series of social calls.

Though the novel questions the customs and morals of 1870s New York society, it never condemns the hypocritical institution directly and fiercely. In fact, Wharton considered this novel an "apology" for her earlier, more brutal and critical novel *The House of Mirth*. Not to be overlooked is Wharton's attention to detailing the charms and customs of the upper caste. The novel is lauded for its accurate portrayal of how the 19th-century East Coast American upper class lived, and this, combined with the social tragedy, earned Wharton a Pulitzer Prize—the first Pulitzer awarded to a woman. Edith Wharton was 58 years old at publication; she lived in that world, and saw it change dramatically by the end of World War I. The title is an ironic comment on the polished outward manners of New York society, when compared to its inward machinations.

Her Literary Techniques

Irony Actually, *The Age of Innocence* is filled with irony about innocence—true innocence, feigned innocence, ironic innocence, and unhappy innocence. Wharton's life, the Gilded Age of the novel, and the characters all contribute to the irony of the novel's title. By the time she wrote this book, Edith Wharton had survived an unhappy 25-year marriage, ignoring her husband's affairs and business improprieties. She had divorced and moved to a more congenial atmosphere for divorcees: Paris. Looking back at her childhood, she was critical of a society that kept girls innocent, sheltered, and away from obstacles they might have to solve.

May Welland is the perfect embodiment of the feigned innocence. She has been taught to remain innocent and avoid life's difficulties. Throughout her marriage she pretends not to know about Newland's passion for Ellen. Even on her honeymoon, her attitude toward all things European is to ignore, be critical, or avoid them. "Her incapacity to recognize change made her children conceal their views from her...a kind of innocent family hypocrisy." Her photo on Newland's desk following her death reflects the carefully groomed ignorance criticized by Wharton: "And she had died thinking the world a good place, full of loving and harmonious households like her own."

Newland, while seemingly in charge of his world as well as the narrative, is actually one of the more naive characters in the story. He never realizes until the end that his wife has known about his sacrifice all along; even after her death he has cultivated the viewpoint that she is ignorant of real life from beginning to end. Until Ellen's farewell dinner, he does not even know that his entire family has plotted and planned without him, leaving him intentionally ignorant of their machinations.

Ellen begins the novel naively, thinking that New Yorkers will welcome her and seeing them as the harmless, innocent youngsters of her childhood. Quickly, because she has lived in a less dissembling culture, she learns that beneath the surface are cruelty, judgment, and hypocrisy. Not having been taught the rules of the game, she stretches the tolerance of New Yorkers, eventually forcing her exit. Of all the characters in the novel, she is perhaps the least naive, forcing the reader to wonder how much of her knowledge is based on Wharton's life as an adult living in Paris.

Even New York City in the 1870s is a society of innocence. It worries about its social code—wedding details, the season, rituals, and rules. The supreme example of this is the farewell dinner for the Countess, a dinner that seems innocently gracious and honorable on the surface but which hides rigid assertiveness in enforcing the social order. This is an age of innocence for a society that cannot conceive of the devastating war that will change all life and history, and sweep away this innocence forever.

Contradiction Order, loyalty, morals, and duty are all values upheld and also criticized in *The Age of Innocence*. Order is epitomized by the repetition of certain rituals. Newland Archer's wife must be sexually innocent and pretend not to know about affairs or passions. When May Welland appears for the first time in the novel, she is in white with white lilies of the valley, oblivious to the sexual gossips of the play she is watching. Later, she knows all along of Newland's passion for Ellen, but she follows the accepted code of ignorance. The wedding at Grace Church is a perfect replication of the order in which things must be done; even Newland has a deep love for Ellen.

Loyalty is also a virtue, not only among families and marriages, but also among men. Newland must go to the Mingott box to show his family loyalty when the notorious Ellen arrives. Ellen's "last supper" is presided over by the family showing its loyalty to May and ousting the interloper. At that same dinner, Lawrence Lefferts asks Newland to "cover" for him and lie to give him an alibi so that he can carry on an affair. Newland will lie and tell no one. Loyalty must be maintained at any cost.

Morals also is a "virtue" all social members must observe at any cost, including personal freedom and happiness. Ellen wants to divorce her husband and be free, but Archer persuades her that she will hurt her family and be censured by society. Her family even wants her to go back to the husband who mistreats her in order to uphold society's values, and they cut off her allowance when she refuses. After a heroic attempt to change herself and fit into New York society, she gives up and returns to Europe, though not to her husband. Her defeat is completed by May's announcement to her that she is pregnant: society upholds a man who sticks by his wife and baby, and abhors one who abandons them. Archer is instrumental in teaching Ellen to deny her own wish to be with him for others' sake, though ironically, he does not wholly believe that this is the right thing to do—it is simply what the family and society wants.

Duty is the idea that one must abide by in the gilded age. Newland's commitment to May after she tells him she is pregnant is a duty understood. When he decides to follow Ellen to Europe, May reveals that she is pregnant, and he knows that this turn of events seals his fate. Finally, he cannot muster the determination to go against the mores of his world. He believes that he will stay with her in a boring and desperate marriage. At every turn of his passion, Newland sees the door closed by May and duty. Archer wants desperately to be with Ellen, but society would not approve such a choice.

The Age of Innocence is one of the most important novels of Edith Wharton. It has been moved to screens several times. In 1924, a silent film adaptation was released by Warner Brothers, directed by Wesley Ruggles, and starring Beverly Bayne as Countess Olenska and Elliott Dexter as Newland Archer. In 1928, Margaret Ayer Barnes adapted the novel into a play, first produced on Broadway, starring Katharine Cornell as Countess Ellen Olenska. In 1934, an eponymous film adaptation directed for RKO Studios by Philip Moeller (based upon the 1920 novel and 1928 play), starring Irene Dunne as Countess Ellen Olenska and John Boles as Newland Archer. In 1993, an eponymous film adaptation, *The Age of Innocence,* was directed by Martin Scorsese, starring Michelle Pfeiffer as Countess Ellen Olenska, Daniel Day-Lewis as Newland Archer, Winona Ryder as May Welland Archer, Richard E. Grant, and Miriam Margolyes. Ryder won a Golden Globe Award for her portrayal of May Welland Archer, and the film won an Oscar for costume design.

Bibliography

Elliott, Emory. *Columbia Literary History of the United States.* New York: Columbia University Press, 1988: 605.

Funston, Judith E. "Edith Wharton." *American National Biography. Vol. 23.* New York: Oxford University Press, 1999: 111–112.

Wegener, Fredrick. "Rabid Imperialist: Edith Wharton and the Obligations of Empire in Modern American Fiction." *American Literature*, 2000 (4): 783–812.

Jack London

His Life and Writing Career

His Life

John Griffith London (1876–1916) was born in San Francisco of an unmarried mother of wealthy background, Flora Wellman. His father may have been William Chaney, a journalist, lawyer, and major figure in the development of American astrology. Because Flora was ill, Jack was raised through infancy by an ex-slave, Virginia Prentiss, who would remain a major maternal figure while the boy grew up. Late in 1876, Flora married John London, a partially disabled Civil War veteran. The family moved around the Bay area before settling in Oakland, where Jack completed grade school.

As an adolescent, the boy adopted the name of Jack. He worked at various hard labor jobs, pirated for oysters on San Francisco Bay, served on a fish patrol to capture poachers, sailed the Pacific on a sealing ship, joined Kelly's Army of unemployed working men, hoboed around the country, and returned to attend high school at age 19. In the process, he became acquainted with socialism and was known as the Boy Socialist of Oakland for his street corner oratory. He would run unsuccessfully several times on the socialist ticket as mayor. Always a prolific reader, he consciously chose to become a writer to escape from the horrific prospects of life as a factory worker. He studied other writers and began to submit stories, jokes, and poems to various publications, mostly without success.

Spending the winter of 1897 in the Yukon provided the metaphorical gold for his first stories, which he began publishing in the Overland Monthly in 1899. From that point he was a highly disciplined writer, who would produce over fifty volumes of stories, novels, and political essays. London's long voyage (1907–1909) across the Pacific in a small boat provided material for books and stories about Polynesian and Melanesian cultures. He was instrumental in breaking the taboo over leprosy and popularizing Hawaii as a tourist spot.

London was among the most publicized figures of his day, and he used this pulpit to endorse his support of socialism, women's suffrage, and eventually, prohibition. He was among the first writers to work with the movie industry, and saw a number of his novels made into films. His novel *The Sea-Wolf* became the basis for the first full-length American movie. He was also one of the first celebrities to use his endorsement for commercial products in advertising, including dress suits and grape juice.

Because he was an autodidact, London's ideas lacked consistency and precision. For example, he clearly accepted the Social Darwinism and scientific racism prevalent during his time, yet he seems troubled that the "inevitable white man," as he called him, would destroy the rich cultures of various native groups he had encountered over the years. Although he supported women's suffrage and created some of the most independent and strong female characters in American fiction, he was patriarchal toward his two wives and two daughters. His socialism was fervent, but countered by his strong drive toward individualism and capitalist success. These contradictory themes in his life and writing make him a difficult figure to reduce to simple terms.

London's great love became agriculture, and he often stated he wrote to support his Beauty Ranch in Glen Ellen. He brought to California techniques observed in Japan, such as terracing and manure spreading, and was accomplished in animal husbandry. He was far ahead of his time in conceiving of the ranch as self-sufficient and self-regenerating. His Wolf House, for example, was built of rock and lumber from his property.

London's first marriage (1900) was to Bess Maddern, with whom he had two daughters, Joan and Bess. In choosing her, he followed the precept in a book he co-wrote with Anna Strunsky, The Kempton-Wace Letters, that mates should be selected for good breeding, not love. (Bess agreed.) Following an affair with "New Woman" Charmian Kittredge, five years his senior, he divorced Bess. In 1905 he married his "Mate Woman," who became the persona for many of his female characters and who avidly joined him on his many travel ventures. He encouraged her own writing career, and she wrote three books concerning their life (*The Log of the Snark*, *Our Hawaii*, and *The Book of Jack London*).

Often troubled by physical ailments, during his thirties London developed kidney disease of unknown origin. He died of renal failure on November 22, 1916 on the ranch. Because his writings were translated in several dozen languages, he remains more widely read in some countries outside of the United States than in his home country. Study of his life and writings provides a case through which to examine the contradictions in the American character, along with key movements and ideas prominent during the Progressive era.

Following London's death, for a number of reasons a biographical myth developed in which he has been portrayed as an alcoholic womanizer who committed suicide. Recent scholarship based upon firsthand documents challenges this caricature. But its persistence has resulted in neglect of his full literary oeuvre and his significance as a seminal figure in turn-of-the-century social history.

His Writing Career

Without having much formal education, London spent much time in public libraries reading fiction, philosophy, poetry, political science, and at the age of 19 gained admittance to the University of California in Berkeley. During this period he had already started to write.

In 1894 London was arrested in Niagara Falls and jailed for vagrancy. These years gave later material for such works as *The Sea-Wolf* (1904), which was partly based on his horrific experiences as a sailor in the Pacific Ocean.

His early stories appeared in the *Overland Monthly* and *Atlantic Monthly*. In 1901 he started to steadily produce novels, nonfiction, and short stories, becoming in his lifetime one of the most popular authors. London had early built his system of producing a daily quota of thousand words. He did not give up even during his travels and drinking periods. London's first novel, *The Son of the Wolf*, appeared in 1900. By 1904 Jack London was the author of 10 books. *The Son of the Wolf* gained a wide audience as did his other Alaska stories, *The Call of the Wild* (1903), *White Fang* (1906), and *Burning Daylight* (1910).

In 1902 London went to England. *The People of the Abyss* (1903), was a surprise success in the U.S. but criticized in England. London produced this classic of investigative reporting in seven weeks. In the middle of a bitter separation in 1904, London traveled to Korea as a correspondent for Hearst's newspapers to cover the war between Russia and Japan (1904–1905). Next year he published his first collection of non-fiction pieces, *The War of the Classes* (1904), which included his lectures on socialism. In 1907 London and his second wife Charmian started aboard the *Snark*, the author's self-designed ketch, on a sailing trip around the world. On the voyage he began to write *Martin Eden* (1909), which brought him worldwide fame. But later, London's financial affairs were in chaos, and he began to buy plots from a struggling writer, such as Sinclair Lewis, to produce more articles and stories for sale.

Analyses of and Comments on His Representative Novels

The Sea Wolf (1904)

Plot Summary

Like *The Call of the Wild*, *The Sea Wolf* tells the story of a soft, domesticated protagonist, in this novel's case an intellectual man named Humphrey van Weyden, forced to become tough and self-reliant by exposure to cruelty and brutality. The story starts with him aboard a San Francisco ferry, called *Martinez*, which collides with another ship in the fog and sinks. He is set adrift in the sea, eventually being picked up by Wolf Larsen. Larsen is the captain of a seal-hunting schooner, the *Ghost*. Brutal and cynical, yet also highly intelligent and intellectual (though highly biased in his opinions, as he was self-taught), he rules over his ship and terrorizes the crew with the aid of his exceptionally great physical strength. Van Weyden adequately describes him as an individualist, hedonist, and materialist. Larsen does not believe in the immortality of the soul, he finds no meaning in his life save for survival and pleasure and has come to despise all human life and deny its value. Being interested in someone capable of intellectual disputes, he somewhat takes care of Van Weyden, whom he calls "Hump," while forcing him to become a cabin boy, do menial work, and learn to fight to protect himself from a brutal crew.

A key event in the story is an attempted mutiny against Wolf Larsen by several members of the crew. The organizers of the mutiny are Leach and Johnson. Johnson had previously been beaten severely by Larsen, and Leach had been punched earlier while being forced to become a boat-puller, motivating the two. The first attempt is by sending Larsen overboard; however, he manages to climb back onto the ship. Searching for his assailant, he ventures into the sleeping quarters, located beneath the main deck, the only exit being a ladder. Several, at least seven men, take part in the mutiny and attack Larsen. Larsen however, demonstrating his inhuman endurance, strength, and conviction, manages to fight his way through the crew, climb the ladder with several men hanging off him, and escape relatively unharmed. Van Weyden is promoted as mate, for the original mate had been murdered. Larsen later gets his vengeance by torturing his crew, and constantly claiming that he is going to murder Leach and Johnson at his earliest convenience, being after the hunting season is done, as he can't afford to lose any crew. He later allows them to be lost to the sea when they attempt to flee on a hunting boat.

During this section, the *Ghost* picks up another set of castaways, including a female poet named Maud Brewster. Miss Brewster and van Weyden had known each other previously—but only as writers. Both Wolf Larsen and Van Weyden immediately feel attraction to her, due to her intelligence and "female delicacy." Van Weyden sees her as his first true love. He strives to protect her from the crew, the horrors of the sea, and Wolf Larsen. As this happens, Wolf Larsen meets his brother Death Larsen, a bitter opponent of his. Wolf kidnapped several of Death's crew and forced them into servitude to fill his own rank, lost previously during a storm. During one of Wolf Larsen's intense headaches, which render him near immobile, van Weyden steals a boat and flees with

Miss Brewster.

The two eventually land on an uninhabited island, heavily populated with seals. They hunt, build shelter and a fire, and survive for several days, utilizing the strength they gained while on the *Ghost*. The *Ghost* eventually crashes on the island, with Wolf Larsen the only crew member. As revenge, Death Larsen had tracked his brother, bribed his crew, destroyed his sails, and set Larsen adrift at sea. It is purely by chance that van Weyden and Miss Brewster meet Larsen again.

Van Weyden obtains all of the firearms left on the ship, but he cannot bear to murder Larsen, who does not threaten him. Van Weyden and Miss Brewster decide they can repair the ship, but Larsen, who intends to die on the island and take them with him. After a headache, Larsen is rendered blind. He feigns paralysis and attempts to murder van Weyden when he draws within arm's reach but just then is hit with a stroke that leaves him blind and the right side of his body paralyzed. His condition only worsens; he loses usage of his remaining arm, leg, and voice. Miss Brewster and van Weyden, unable to bring themselves to leave him to rot, care for him. Despite this kindness, he continues his resistance, setting fire to the above bunk's mattress.

Van Weyden finishes repairing the *Ghost*, and he and Miss Brewster set sail. During a violent storm, Wolf Larsen passes away. They give Larsen a burial at sea, an act mirroring an incident van Weyden witnessed when he was first rescued. The story ends with them being rescued by an American revenue cutter.

Themes

The Sea Wolf is a story of how man has to overcome man, and in the face of brutality one must stand strong and not be afraid of the outcome. It shows how it is possible to overcome adversity even when it seems impossible. Jack London shows how not even man can control a free will. For every man has a purpose on this earth, God put us all in the world to make a difference and not be afraid to stand up for beliefs.

Jack London's belief in God is not entirely evident in the novel, *The Sea Wolf* as London seems to have ideas but no exact truth. Hump, the main character seems to have been a Christian, but this self taught captain has one theory that he believes throughout the course of the novel. Several long philosophical conversations between Hump and Captain Larsen lead only to more questions that seem to go un-answered. Darwinism is brought up but pushed aside and the Bible is the one book Larsen cannot get his fingers around. London expresses the idea of believing in God but does not seem like he wants to. Captain Larsen however, shows stubbornness in not changing his ways of un-Godliness.

London looks at man with the superman type of way, only the strongest, fittest, and toughest should have the right to survive. Captain Larsen talks of how a man will do anything to sustain his own life, and often will betray even his own beliefs to survive. Larsen does not hesitate in taking someone else's life, for it is their fault for putting their life in jeopardy. London displays a caring for only the life of his own, willing to allow any act just to survive.

Barbarianism and savagery are repeated acts of the morality held on the vessel Ghost. Instead of having fisherman, it is almost as if Larsen recruited murders and fighters. Living a life of peace on the *Ghost* almost seems that it might be an impossible task that no one wants to try.

London showed the readers that he knew of God and that there is a higher being than himself and how God must have created this world but does not express a personal belief. He shows how to him a man can be useless depending on his values and what he has accomplished. He suggests that even if things may not seem fair or just, and men need to quarrel—then quarrel and solve the problem with brutality. *The Sea Wolf* tells how it is possible to overcome adversity even when it seems impossible. Being Human makes capable of sinning, there is no such thing as a perfect anything.

Last but not the least, the novel also touches upon Social Darwinism. The term Social Darwinism was not coined until 1944 and thus does not appear within the novel. The term, however, is an appellation given to the philosophy espoused by Wolf Larsen as justification for his tyrannical domination of others. Larsen's library is noted to contain works by Darwin, Malthus and Spencer, all of whom are seminal theorists of the concept. Darwin himself rejected the concepts of Social Darwinism even though his biological theories were generally used to support and inform the sociological concept that social inequality is the inexorable result of meritocratic division of available resources. The same basic premises have been used to justify laissez-faire capitalism and racism—concepts that Wolf Larsen would almost certainly espouse. Larsen summarizes the concepts of Social Darwinism in his extended analogy of a yeasty ferment of existence. For Larsen, all of life can be viewed as a boiling ferment full of yeasty particles.

Literary Techniques

The novel is narrated in the first person limited point of view by Humphrey "Hump" Van Weyden. Hump is a reliable and insightful narrator who is cognizant and forthright about his own shortcomings. Additionally, Hump begins the narrative as a mature and very educated—perhaps over-educated—individual, and he concludes the narrative as a fully experienced and capable individual. In this sense, the novel is an atypical Entwicklungsroman, or Apprenticeship Novel. Hump, at thirty-five, is notably aged for such a protagonist, but by his own admission, he has no worldly experience. Thus thrust from the "realm of mind and idea" into the "world of the real", Hump begins his painful but exceptionally successful maturation into a capable individual who finds self-assurance, competence and love. Hump's personal development is later mirrored by a similar developmental track enjoyed by Brewster.

The Sea Wolf is also an example of symbolic naturalism, a novel that is simultaneously a study of environmental conditioning and a symbolic tale of initiation, a ritual of death and rebirth. Saved from drowning by Wolf Larsen, Humphrey van Weyden is shanghaied and set to work as a cabin boy. Conditioned by the violent "world of the real" aboard the *Ghost*, van Weyden is transformed from an elitist aesthete into a man of courageous action. In contrast, Wolf Larsen, the bullying materialist, is gradually incapacitated by raging headaches. The conflict between van Weyden and Larsen is as much a war of ideas as it is a physical battle. Van Weyden is an idealist for whom "life had always seemed a peculiarly sacred thing," but he discovers that on the *Ghost* "it counted for nothing." In contrast, Larsen is a complete materialist.

In general, naturalism is the literary movement that provides the best context for Jack London. Naturalism has been understood as dialectic between free will and determinism, but it is probably most intelligible through social history. The appeal of naturalistic tales is often escape. The urban problems of unemployment, labor wars, and poverty are left behind for a spare scenario in which an individual can be tested. A stock naturalistic device involves taking an "over-civilized" man from the upper classes into a primitive environment where he must live by muscle and wit.

In another common naturalistic pattern, the hero who stays in the city either becomes an ineffectual dandy or degenerates into a lower-class brute. London treats these materials more realistically, yet employs the same pattern whereby the city is associated with degeneration and the open country with rebirth. The novel contrasts the vitality of the heroes in the country to the dissipation and bad luck they encounter in the city.

Martin Eden (1909)

Plot Summary

Semi-autobiographical novel by Jack London, *Martin Eden* was published in 1909. The title character Martin Eden becomes a writer, hoping to acquire the respectability sought by his society-girl sweetheart. She spurns him, however, when his writing is rejected by several magazines and when he is falsely accused of being a socialist. She tries to win him back after he achieves fame, but Eden realizes her love is false. Financially successful and robbed of connection to his own class, aware that his quest for bourgeois respectability was hollow, Eden travels to the South Seas.

Martin Eden is an intelligent and self-educated young man who wants nothing more than to be accepted by and to be like the young, educated rich he sees as a struggling writer in turn-of-the 20th century Northern California. Martin is certain that once in the ranks of these beautiful people who speak in casual conversation of Greek myth and French poetry, he will finally be happy. He uncomfortably accepts the rude comments from these rich snobs, resolves to rise to their level and falls in love with a woman he feels as a goddess walking the Earth. Martin Eden struggles to rise far above his destitute proletarian circumstances through an intense and passionate pursuit of self-education in order to achieve a coveted place among the literary elite. The main driving force behind Martin Eden's efforts is his love for Ruth Morse. Because Eden is a rough, uneducated sailor from a working class background, and the Morses are a bourgeois family, a union between them would be impossible until he reaches their level of wealth and perceived cultural, intellectual refinement.

Just before the literary establishment discovers Eden's talents as a writer and lavishes him with the fame and fortune that he had incessantly promised Ruth (for the last two years) would come, she loses her patience and rejects him in a wistful letter: "if only you had settled down…and attempted to make something of yourself." When the publishers and the bourgeois—the very ones who shunned him—are finally at his feet, Martin has already begrudged them and become jaded by unrequited toil and love. Instead of enjoying his success, Eden retreats into a quiet indifference, only interrupted to mentally rail against the genteelness of bourgeois society or to donate his new wealth to working class friends and family. The novel ends with Martin Eden committing suicide by drowning himself.

Themes

Social Class Social class—and Eden's perceptions of it—is a very important theme in the novel. Eden is a sailor from a working class background, who feels uncomfortable but inspired when he first meets the bourgeois Morse family. Spurred on by his love for Ruth Morse, he embarks on a program of self-education, with the aim of becoming a renowned writer and winning Ruth's hand in marriage. As his education a progress, Eden finds himself increasingly distanced from his working class background and surroundings. Notably, he is repelled by the hands of Lizzie Connolly, who works in a cannery. Eventually, when Eden finds that his education has far surpassed that of the bourgeoisie he looked up to, he finds himself more isolated than ever.

Machinery Aside from the machines that toughened Lizzie Connolly's hands, Jack London conjures-up a series of allusions to the workings of machinery in the novel. Machinery eats up people, vitality and creativity. To Eden, the magazine editors operated a machine which sent out seemingly endless rejection slips. When Eden works in a laundry with Joe, he works with machines but feels himself to be a cog in a larger machine. Similarly, Eden's Blickensdorfer typewriter gradually becomes an extension of his body. When he finally achieves literary success, Eden sets up his friends with machinery of their own, and

Lizzie tells him "Something's wrong with your think-machine."

Individualism versus Socialism Although Jack London was a socialist, he invested the semi-autobiographical character of Martin Eden with a strong dose of individualism. Eden comes from a working class background, but he seeks self-improvement, rather than an improvement for his class as a whole. However, London was keen to stress that it was this individualism that eventually led to Eden's suicide. He described the novel as a parable of a man who had to die "not because of his lack of faith in God, but because of his lack of faith in men."

Love At first Martin thought that his love for Ruth is a fairy tale love because he idealized Ruth and everything what was related with her. He tried to fight for their love — he did everything to get better education and manners. He wanted to prove to her and himself that he is worth to be with her but he didn't understand their relationship like it can't be real because Ruth and her world were superficial. This novel showed that real love can't be based on material things like wealth or recognition. People can't be happy together if there aren't real feelings. Jack London also showed that it is difficult for two people from different social classes to be happily in love with each other because their values and understanding of world or life are not similar.

Literary Techniques

Jack London's *Martin Eden* falls under two genres: novel and Bildungsroman (a story in which education/self-growth is the focus). *Martin Eden* is a novel in that it is both connected to history—in London's portrayal of the proletariat class in the beginnings of the twentieth century—and in that it contains romantic qualities of a heroic, knight errant. This literary work also falls under the Bildungsroman genre because the progression of the novel follows *Martin Eden*'s psychological and moral growth as he attempts to educate himself to become a literate writer and to overcome unrequited love.

The genre of this novel also draws upon naturalism. Naturalism is a philosophy that only natural laws and forces operate in the world and that nothing exists beyond the natural world. Followers of naturalism believe that natural laws are the rules that govern the structure and behavior of the natural world. *Martin Eden* presents this genre in the form of class structure. Martin's vain attempts to push through the boundaries of natural social structure seem to just confirm the philosophy in the novel that it is unnatural to move outside one's social standing. In fact, Martin's character proves this genre true because he breaks the laws of naturalism and finds him self outside of all natural society.

Jack London's style in Martin Eden is commonly referred to as a semi-autobiographical novel. He seems to incorporate his own opinions that he developed through his own class struggle and career as a writer through the fictional characters in the novel.

Martin Eden is semi-autobiographical, thus, a very interesting narrative style can be seen. The narrator is in the mode of omniscient third person. Martin could not be privy to this information but the narrator tells us anyway. This distance from the main characters does not happen often but it is there. However the narrator goes into the heads of the characters, even so far as to use free indirect discourse. It happens throughout the novel at many points with mainly Ruth and Martin. The narration keeps the characters at many distances. Sometimes keeping them far away, and sometimes being so close as to being in their minds.

London also seems to choose certain words and use them repeatedly in a paragraph to emphasize his points. This technique allows one to consider the many avenues and aspects of a certain idea, much as the characters would do. An example of this type of meditation is in Chapter Fifteen during the fight with Cheese-Face. Throughout the chapter blood is used many times as are allusions to greater nature and animals. Using these words in conjunction with each other and repeatedly is how London can set up his tone and, through that, his greater themes.

Another interesting facet of the style of *Martin Eden* is as Martin Eden's education grows, the vocabulary of the book grows as well. For example, after the heated fight over Lizzie Connolly, Martin uses professional literary language when reflected on the argument. It seems as the novel and Martin's literary knowledge progresses his inner thoughts are crafted in a way that he is writing about his life in one of his novels. For example, he refers to a scrappy fight as a "zest of combat." He over dramatizes his language that makes him sound like he thinks in prose. London makes it apparent in his later style of writing that Martin's vocabulary has increased and he has become more educated throughout the novel.

Bibliography

http://london.sonoma.edu/jackbio.html, 2012-06-06.
http://en.wikipedia.org/wiki/Martin_Eden, 2012-07-03.
http://london.thefreelibrary.com/, 2013-02-27.

Theodore Dreiser

His Life and Writing Career

His Life

Theodore Herman Albert Dreiser (1841–1945) was an American novelist and journalist of the naturalist school. He was born in Terre Haute, Indiana, to Sarah and John Paul Dreiser, a strict Catholic family. John Paul Dreiser was a German immigrant from Mayen in the Eifel region, and Sarah was from the Mennonite farming community near Dayton, Ohio. She was disowned for marrying John and converting to Roman Catholicism. Theodore was the twelfth of thirteen children (the ninth of the ten surviving). The popular songwriter Paul Dresser (1857–1906) was his elder brother.

After graduating from high school in Warsaw, Theodore attended Indiana University in the years 1889–1890 before dropping out. Within several years, he was writing for the Chicago newspaper *Globe* and then the *St. Louis Globe-Democrat*. He wrote several articles on writers such as Nathaniel Hawthorne, William Dean Howells, Israel Zangwill, John Burroughs, and interviewed public figures such as Andrew Carnegie, Marshall Field, Thomas Edison, and Theodore Thomas. After proposing in 1893, he married Sara White on December 28, 1898. They ultimately separated in 1909, partly as a result of Dreiser's infatuation with Thelma Cudlipp, the teenage daughter of a work colleague, but were never formally divorced. In 1919 Dreiser met his cousin Helen Richardson with whom he began an affair. They eventually married on June 13, 1944.

Politically, Dreiser was involved in several campaigns against social injustice. This included the lynching of Frank Little, one of the leaders of the Industrial Workers of the World, the Sacco and Vanzetti case, the deportation of Emma Goldman, and the conviction of the trade union leader Tom Mooney. In November 1931, Dreiser led the National Committee for the Defense of Political Prisoners (NCDPP) to the coalfields of southeastern Kentucky, where they took testimony from coal miners in Pineville and Harlan on the pattern of violence against the miners and their unions by the coal operators known as the Harlan County War.

Dreiser died on December 28, 1945 in Hollywood at the age of 74. Dreiser had an enormous influence on the generation that followed. Alfred Kazin characterized Dreiser as "stronger than all the others of his time, and at the same time more poignant; greater than the world he has described, but as significant as the people in it," while Larzer Ziff remarked that Dreiser "succeeded beyond any of his predecessors or successors in producing a great American business novel." Irving Howe, a renowned mid-century literary critic, spoke of Dreiser as "among the American giants, one of the very few American giants we have had." One of Dreiser's strongest champions during his lifetime, H.L. Mencken, declared "that he is a great artist, and that no other American of his generation left so wide and handsome a mark upon the national letters. American writing, before and after his time, differed almost as much as biology before and after Darwin. He was a man of large originality, of profound feeling, and of unshakable courage. All of us who write are better off because he lived, worked, and hoped."

His Writing Career

Dreiser's first novel *Sister Carrie* (1900) tells the story of a woman who flees her country life for the city (Chicago) and there lives a life far from a Victorian ideal. It sold poorly and was not widely promoted largely because of moral objections to the depiction of a country girl who pursued her dreams of fame and fortune through relationships to men. The novel was made into a 1952 film by William Wyler, which starred Laurence Olivier and Jennifer Jones. The book has since acquired a considerable reputation. It has been called the "greatest of all American urban novels."

Dreiser's second novel, *Jennie Gerhardt*, was published in 1911, which failed to attract public attention. His first commercial success was *An American Tragedy*, published in 1925, which was made into a film in 1931 and again in 1951 (as *A Place in the Sun*). Already in 1892, when Dreiser began work as a newspaperman he had begun to observe a certain type of crime in the United States that proved very common. It seemed to spring from the fact that almost every young person was possessed of an ingrown ambition to be somebody financially and socially. Fortune hunting became a disease with the frequent result of a peculiarly American kind of crime, a form of murder for money. When the young ambitious lover of some poorer girl found a more attractive girl with money or position but could not get rid of the first girl, usually because of pregnancy, he often resorted to violence. Dreiser claimed to have collected such stories every year between 1895 and 1935. The 1906 murder of Grace Brown by Chester Gillette eventually became the basis for *An American Tragedy*.

Though primarily known as a novelist, Dreiser published his first collection of short stories, *Free and Other Stories* in 1918. The collection contained 11 stories. Another story, "My Brother Paul," was a brief biography of his elder brother, Paul Dresser, who was a famous songwriter in the 1890s. This story was the basis for the 1942 romantic movie, "My Gal Sal."

Dreiser also wrote poetry. His poem, "The Aspirant," continues his theme of poverty and ambition, as a young man in a shabby furnished room describes his own and the other tenants' dreams, and asks "Why? Why?" The poem appeared in *The Poetry Quartos*, collected and printed by Paul Johnston, and published by Random House in 1929.

Dreiser's other works include *Trilogy of Desire*, which was based on the life of the Chicago streetcar tycoon Charles Tyson Yerkes and composed of *The Financier* (1912), *The Titan* (1914), and *The Stoic*. The last was published posthumously in 1947. Dreiser was often forced to battle against censorship because his depiction of some aspects of life, such as sexual promiscuity, offended authorities and challenged popular opinion. Dreiser's great theme was the tremendous tensions that can arise among ambition, desire, and social mores.

Dreiser was a committed socialist, and wrote several non-fiction books on political issues. These included *Dreiser Looks at Russia* (1928), the result of his 1927 trip to the Soviet Union, and two books presenting a critical perspective on capitalist America, *Tragic America* (1931) and *America Is Worthy Saving* (1941). His vision of capitalism and a future world order with a strong American military dictate combined with the harsh criticism of the latter made him unpopular within the official circles.

He was a prolific writer, published 13 fictions, 2 dramas and 10 nonfictional works. These fictions are *Sister Carrie* (1900), *Old Rogaum and His Theresa* (1901), *Jennie Gerhardt* (1911), *The Financier* (1912), *The Titan* (1914), *The "Genius"* (1915), *Free and Other Stories* (1918), *Twelve Men* (1919), *An American Tragedy* (1925), *Chains: Lesser Novels and Stories* (1927), *A Gallery of Women* (1929), *The Bulwark* (1946), *The Stoic* (1947). The two dramas are *Plays of the Natural and Supernatural* (1916) and *The Hand of the Potter* (1921). These nonfictional works are *A Traveler at Forty* (1913), *A Hoosier Holiday* (1916), *Hey Rub-a-Dub-Dub: A Book of the Mystery and Wonder and Terror of Life* (1920), *A Book About Myself* (1922), *The Color of a Great City* (1923), *Dreiser Looks at Russia* (1928), *My City* (1929), *Tragic America* (1931), *Dawn* (1931), *America Is Worth Saving* (1941). Dreiser's best known novels include *Sister Carrie* (1900) and *An American Tragedy* (1925).

Analyses of and Comments on His Representative Novels

Sister Carrie (1900)

Plot Summary

Sister Carrie is about a young country girl who moves to the big city where she starts realizing her own American Dream by first becoming a mistress to men that she perceives as superior and later as a famous actress. It has been called the "greatest of all American urban novels." Dissatisfied with life in her rural Wisconsin home, 18-year-old Sister Carrie takes the train to Chicago. On the train, Carrie meets Charles Drouet, a traveling salesman, who is attracted to her because of her simple beauty and unspoiled manner. In Chicago, Carrie soon takes a job running a machine in a shoe factory. Before long, however, she is shocked by the hard work and harsh factory conditions. One day she encounters Drouet on a downtown street. Once again taken by her beauty, he encourages her to dine with him, where he persuades her to leave her sister and move in with him. The next day, he takes her shopping at a Chicago department store and securing a jacket she covets and some shoes. That night, she moves in with Drouet.

Drouet installs her in a much larger apartment. She gets a sophisticated wardrobe and, begins to improve her clothes and provincial mannerisms, even as she struggles with the moral implications of being a kept woman. By the time Drouet introduces Carrie to George Hurstwood, the manager of Fitzgerald and Moy's, her material appearance has improved considerably. Hurstwood instantly becomes infatuated with Carrie's youth and beauty, and before long they start an affair, communicating and meeting secretly.

One night, Drouet casually agrees to find an actress to play a key role in an amateur theatrical presentation. Upon returning home to Carrie, he encourages her to take the part of the heroine, Laura. Unknown to Drouet, Carrie long has harbored theatrical ambitions and has a natural aptitude for imitation and expressing pathos. Both Drouet and Hurstwood are moved by Carrie's stunning performance.

The next day, Drouet discovers he has been cheated by Carrie. Carrie learns that Hurstwood is married, and Hurstwood's wife learns that Hurstwood has an affair with another woman. After a night of drinking, Hurstwood stumbles upon a large amount of cash in the unlocked safe in Fitzgerald and Moy's offices. He succumbs to the temptation to embezzle a large sum of money. Under the pretext of Drouet's sudden illness, he lures Carrie onto a train and escapes with her to Canada. Once they arrive in Montreal, Hurstwood's guilty conscience induces him to return most of the stolen funds, but he realizes that he cannot return to Chicago. Hurstwood mollifies Carrie by agreeing to marry her, and the couple move to New York City.

In New York, Hurstwood buys a minority interest in a saloon and, at first, is able to provide Carrie with a satisfactory standard of living. The couple grows distant, however, as Hurstwood abandons any pretense of fine manners toward Carrie, and she realizes that Hurstwood no longer is the polite, powerful manager of his Chicago days. As Hurstwood gambles away most of his savings, Carrie turns to New York's theatres and becomes a chorus girl. Once again, her aptitude for theatre serves her well, and, as the rapidly aging Hurstwood declines into obscurity, Carrie begins to rise from chorus girl to small speaking roles. Hurstwood ultimately joins the homeless of New York, taking odd jobs, falling ill with pneumonia, and finally becoming a beggar. Reduced to standing in line for bread and charity, he commits suicide in a flophouse. Meanwhile, Carrie achieves stardom, but finds that money and fame do not satisfy her longings or bring her happiness and that nothing will.

Themes

Dreiser touches upon a wide range of themes and experiences in *Sister Carrie*, from grinding poverty to upper-middle class comfort, from American Dream to class divisions. In the process of economic development, thousands of rural Americans rushed to the cities to find jobs and to build themselves new lives and identities. However, most of these new comers live a poor and hard life in big cities, without enough food and clothes. They are threatened by unexpected unemployment, crime and violence from time to time. For them, American Dream is actually a nightmare. A case in point is Carrie's sister and brother-in-law.

Different from these losers, Carrie seems to be fortunate and her American Dream appears to come true. Imagining the elegant clothes she will wear, the exciting places to which she will go, and the fashionable people with whom she will associate, Carrie comes to Chicago. After many ups and downs, she acquires great fortune and fame. But all these things fail to bring her happiness and satisfaction. To some extent, her American Dream fails in another way.

Carrie's fear of poverty and desire for material possessions are the only two factors which disturb her from her passivity. Consumerism often dominates her decisions as she is mainly characterized by her love of new clothes and need for comfort. Interestingly, the narrative does not condemn her for this predilection. She and Drouet represent polar opposites of the puritan work ethic as they prefer finery and living for the moment. Although she is not punished by the author for her extravagant tastes, and is a likeable figure at times, she is never given a great amount of depth. Her encounters with Ames teach her that desire for wealth will lead to dissatisfaction, and she considers him as wise for holding such views, but it is not until the end that she appears to ponder these thoughts more closely. For this reason, it is possible to see that through Carrie Dreiser is attempting to convey a convincing human rather than a good or evil main protagonist. Carrie's desires are recognizable, as is her sense of melancholy when the desires are fulfilled.

It is suggested in the narrative that Hurstwood's fall from grace into eventual suicide has partially come about because of his loss of social standing. In a society that overvalues appearance and the appearance of money, he gradually becomes ousted from his position of respectability. Through necessity and apathy he begins to wear his old clothes when living with Carrie and this symbolizes his decline into being a poor.

As his position weakens, Carrie's is seen to strengthen as she acquires independence and a level of wealth and is metaphorically accepted back into the fold when Mrs. Vance visits her in her dressing room. It is of interest that Carrie is allowed to succeed and achieve such acceptance, as a so-called fallen woman, because such women are traditionally punished in literature (remembering Eve, Madame Bovary and Anna Karenina). This novel may be regarded, therefore, as challenging the moral codes of the late nineteenth century because she is depicted as rising, rather than declining, in perceived value. By contrasting Carrie and Hurstwood's change in fortune, their separate lives become all the more pronounced. Her newly acquired fame is emphasized in relation to his eventual suicide. The novel's use of contrasts depends on the relativity of meaning, and so employs the same technique of defining by comparison as the city dwellers under observation.

During the late 1800s and early 1900s, industrial growth brought the United States a period of prosperity. With factories flourishing, job opportunities were abundant. People made good money in factory management positions and other white-collar jobs. Factory workers, however, not only earned low incomes, but also worked long hours. Consequently, a wide division existed between the wealthy and the poor. Throughout *Sister Carrie*, the distinction between social classes is obvious. The clothes people wear, the homes in which they live, and the activities in which they are involved distinguish the rich from the poor. The wealthy wear stylish clothes and attend elaborate performances of the arts. The poor buy factory-made clothes and jeans and are lucky to go to the penny arcade or the local dance pavilion. In the final chapter, the description of Hurstwood's last days offers a vivid picture of the ultimate plight of the poorest.

In the early 1900s, the morals and virtues of the Victorian era still guided people's actions. People with proper upbringing did not speak of sex. The public was shocked that Dreiser's characters so openly participated in explicit relationships and that Dreiser seemed to condone it. Carrie uses sex to gain status for herself. She sees nothing wrong in living with Drouet to get the clothes she wants and to have opportunities to move in Chicago's affluent circles. Later, Carrie sees that Hurstwood can offer her an even higher standard of living. She ignores the fact that he is already married and the two of them will be committing adultery. With no regard for Drouet's emotions, she breaks off their relationship and pursues one with Hurstwood. After living with Hurstwood for some time, she realizes she can no longer benefit from the arrangement and leaves him, too.

Literary Techniques

Point of View Dreiser uses a third person omniscient point of view to tell the story of his heroine, Carrie. Through this point of view, Dreiser provides readers with insight into not only Carrie's thoughts but also those of all his characters. One example of this is found in chapter 27, when Hurstwood discovers a note from Carrie and later steals money from his employer's safe. Dreiser portrays Hurstwood's distorted thinking as well as Carrie's confusion over Hurstwood's actions vividly.

Naturalism *Sister Carrie* impresses reader with its realistic depiction of the human condition. A 1901 review in the Academy said that *Sister Carrie* was "absolutely free from the slightest trace of sentimentality or pettiness, and dominated everywhere by a serious and strenuous desire for truth." The *London Express* claimed that this realism is what makes the book appealing: "It is a cruel, merciless story, intensely clever in its realism, and one that will remain impressed in the memory of the reader for many a long day." The novel has also been praised for its accurate depiction of the protests in New York and the city life in Chicago.

Dreiser portrays New York and Chicago of that time in great details. This kind of writing style has encountered both criticism and praise of his unique literary. In 1930 Arnold Bennett said, "Dreiser simply does not know how to write, never did know, never wanted to know." Other critics called his style "vulgar," "uneven," "clumsy," "awkward," and "careless." His plotlines were also decried as unimaginative, critics citing his lack of education and claiming that he lacked intellectualism. However, Michael Lydon claims that his patience and powers of observation created accurate depictions of the urban world and the desires and ambitions of the people of the time. Lydon said that Dreiser's intent was to focus on the message of *Sister Carrie*, not on its writing style. H. L. Mencken, an avid supporter and friend of Dreiser believed that Dreiser's raw, honest portrayal of Carrie's life should be seen as a courageous attempt to give the reader a realistic view of the life of women in the nineteenth century.

An American Tragedy (1925)

Plot Summary

The novel opens on a summer evening in Kansas City, Missouri, in the early years of the twentieth century. Dreiser introduces twelve-year-old Clyde Griffiths along with his family: his father Asa, and mother Elvira, poor evangelists who run a mission in a shabby part of the city; and his two sisters and one brother. From the beginning, Clyde is antagonistic toward his parents' beliefs and activities. He is entranced by the material world that his parents shun. As a teenager, Clyde gets a series of jobs in increasingly glamorous settings—from street corner (as a newsboy) to department store basement to drugstore to upscale hotel—that take him farther and farther from his parents' dingy life. All the while, Clyde daydreams about his rich Uncle Samuel who owns a factory in Lycurgus, New York.

The ambitious but immature Clyde Griffiths, raised by poor and devoutly religious parents who force him to participate in their street missionary work, is anxious to achieve better things. His troubles begin when he takes a job as a bellboy at a local hotel. The boys he meets are much more sophisticated than he, and they introduce Clyde to the world of alcohol and prostitution. Clyde enjoys his new lifestyle and does everything in his power to win the affections of the flirtatious Hortense Briggs. But Clyde's life is forever changed when a stolen car in which he's traveling kills a young child. Clyde flees Kansas City, and after a brief stay in Chicago, he reestablishes himself as a foreman at the shirt-collar factory of his wealthy long-lost uncle in Lycurgus, New York. While remaining aloof from him as a kinsman and doing nothing to embrace him personally or advance him socially, the uncle does give Clyde a job and ultimately advances him to a position of relative importance within the factory.

Although Clyde vows not to consort with women in the way that caused his Kansas City downfall, he is swiftly attracted to Roberta Alden, a poor and innocent farm girl working under his supervision at the factory. Roberta falls in love with him. Clyde initially enjoys the secretive relationship (forbidden by factory rules) and ultimately persuades Roberta to have sex with him, but Clyde's ambition precludes marriage to the penniless Roberta. He dreams instead of the elegant Sondra Finchley, the daughter of a wealthy Lycurgus man and a family friend of his uncle's.

Having unsuccessfully attempted to procure an abortion for Roberta, who expects him to marry her, Clyde cannot give her a promise while his relationship with Sondra continues to mature. When he realizes that he has a genuine chance to marry Sondra, and after Roberta threatens to reveal their relationship unless he marries her, Clyde hatches a plan to murder Roberta in a way that will seem accidental.

Clyde takes Roberta on a row boat on Big Bittern Lake in upstate New York and rows to a remote area. As he speaks to her regarding the end of their relationship, Roberta moves towards him, and he strikes her in the face with his camera, stunning her and capsizing the boat. Unable to swim, Roberta drowns while Clyde, who is unwilling to save her, swims to shore. The narrative is deliberately unclear as to whether he acted with malice and intent to murder, or if he struck her merely instinctively. However, the trail of circumstantial evidence points to murder, and the local authorities are only too eager to convict Clyde, to the point of manufacturing additional evidence against him. Following a sensational trial before an unsympathetic audience, and despite a vigorous defense mounted by two lawyers hired by his uncle, Clyde is convicted, sentenced to death, and executed. The jailhouse scenes and the correspondence between Clyde and his mother stand out as exemplars of pathos in modern literature.

Themes

An American Tragedy is a complex novel which touches upon many themes. Firstly, Dreiser reveals the illusion of American Dream, which means that all Americans have the opportunity to improve themselves economically and socially. In America, it is said, a person's circumstances at birth place no limit on his or her potential; people can make of themselves whatever they choose and rise as high as they are willing to climb. If Dreiser's message in *An American Tragedy* can be summed up in a sentence, it is: the American Dream is a lie.

Dreiser sees life as determined solely by forces beyond the control of the individual, mainly heredity and environment, but also chance and the mysterious, unknowable workings of fate. Individuals do not have free will; they are merely small creatures struggling against whatever fate the inscrutable forces of life have conjured up for them. This is the key theme of the novel. Clyde is born into poverty, and the qualities he inherits from his parents do not equip him for success. Clyde is an outsider in a 1920s American society that is becoming increasingly complex and industrialized—a society that grinds its wheels indifferent to the fates of individuals who fail to find their place in it. In Clyde's favor is the strength of his desire and his will to achieve what he wants. These qualities enable him to climb a few rungs up on the ladder that leads to the attainment of the American Dream, but he will never climb higher. He will never get to the top because he is a participant in an unequal struggle. There are too many forces ranged against him.

An American Tragedy is therefore a long repudiation of the American idealization of the individual and of the falsity of the American Dream, the idea that anyone can rise to the top through hard work and application. Clyde does all he can, and he fails. He is like a man pushing a boulder uphill. One false move and the boulder will crush him. This feeling that he is a man facing insuperable obstacles makes Clyde at times a sympathetic figure, as Dreiser intended him to be. Dreiser presents him as an individual who has no freedom to change his life; his belief that he does is merely an illusion.

The society that is presented in *An American Tragedy* is relentlessly materialistic. The only qualities that are admired are material wealth, prosperity, and social status as measured by power and possessions. The pursuit and the enjoyment of wealth is everything. This is the society into which Clyde Griffiths is born. Since he rejects the religious values of his parents, the only thing that interests him is the acquisition of money and the social status he thinks this will bring him. This is how he defines success.

His materialistic value system is obvious from the moment he steps into the luxury of the Green-Davidson Hotel in Kansas City. He thinks of the hotel as possessing a "glorious atmosphere," and he is in awe of it, thrilled to be admitted to this "grand world." Because he grows up in poverty and has had little education, he does not question the idea that life is all about acquiring money and spending it. He thinks that if he can acquire money life will become one long holiday.

Dreiser's writing style is not the most compelling aspect of his work. Even admirers of his novels admit that Dreiser's style is clumsy, overworked, lacking in subtlety, and even dully ungrammatical at times. However, there is also a critical consensus that *An American Tragedy* is a great work of literature, provoking the question: what makes it so great if it's often a chore to read?

Literary Techniques

The main feature of *An American Tragedy* is the details Dreiser brings to each setting, a dense reportage that comes from his background as a journalist. Indeed, Dreiser is known to integrate his journalistic work with his fiction, the former being a basis for large sections of the latter.

Due to this density of detail applied to various aspects of the story, Dreiser is able to create a sense of inevitability in his writing. Plots aren't a simple A to B progression but a complex weave of events that are outside of any one individual's control. Dreiser often explores the psychological background of characters to help explain their behavior, no matter how irrational or immoral it may seem. And as narrator, Dreiser often takes the time to expose cultural assumptions and biases (some of which he himself holds) which also contribute to the outcome of events. As a result, the moments of odd coincidence in the novel often feel as natural as the events which seem more circumscribed. Readers may feel that it's odd for Clyde and Roberta to first meet outside of the workplace at a small lake, and yet Dreiser goes out of his way to provide a common-sense rationale for this occurrence: a romantic longing in each, mutual limitations on their travel plans.

An American Tragedy is considered as the defining work of American naturalism, and it does incorporate all the hallmarks of the naturalist movement. Naturalism emerged in France in the 1870s and 1880s in response to new philosophical and scientific ideas, especially Charles Darwin's theory of evolution. Emile Zola defined the movement in France. It flowered in the United States from the final years of the nineteenth century through World War I and into the 1920s. *An American Tragedy* portrays the social conditions in great details and stresses the importance of heredity and environment, which are the final forces that decide characters' fates. Because of *An American Tragedy* and *Sister Carrie,* Dreiser became "the greatest chronicler of America's cities."

Bibliography

http://www.library.upenn.edu/collections/rbm/dreiser/tdbio.html, 2012-12-10.

Miller, Donald L. *City of the Century*. New York: Simon & Schuster, 1996: 263-264.

Rodden, John. *Irving Howe and the Critics: Celebrations and Attacks*. Lincoln, Nebraska: University of Nebraska Press, 2005: 64.

Salzman, Jack. *Theodore Dreiser: The Critical Reception*. New York: Davis Lewis, 1972: 125.

Michael, Lydon. "Justice to Theodore Dreiser." *The Atlantic*. Aug. 24, 1993.

Henningfeld, Diane Andrews. "Overview of 'Sister Carrie.'" *Novels for Students, Vol. 8*. Eds. Marie Rose & Deborah A. Stanley. Detroit: Gale, 2000: 437.

Elliott, Emory. *Columbia Literary History of the United States*. New York: Columbia University Press, 1988: 543.

Willa Cather

Her Life and Writing Career

Her Life

Willa Cather (1873–1947), American author and teacher, is considered to be one of the best chroniclers of pioneering life in the 20th century. She is one of the most influential American writers of the first half of the twentieth century, establishing her reputation with both novels and short stories. Willa Cather was born on December 7, 1873 in Back Creek Valley, Virginia. Her father was Charles Fectigue Cather, a farmer, and her mother was Mary Virginia Boak, a former school teacher. Within a year of Cather's birth, the family moved to Willow Shade, a Greek Revival-style home on 130 acres given to them by her paternal grandparents.

The early years of young Willa's life left a memorable impression on her and formed the basis for many of her stories and characters. Cather enjoyed travelling west very much and had been to six states. In 1883 she lived at her grandfather's farm in Nebraska, Webster county. At this time many Swedish, French and Bohemian immigrant pioneers had moved to the area with dreams. Willa became acquaintance and friend to many of the new Americans. This experience had a great effect on her later writing, most of which centered on the frontier life on the Great Plains. Cather's time in the western state, still on the frontier, was a deeply formative experience for her. She was intensely moved by the dramatic environment and weather, and the various cultures of the European-American, immigrant and Native American families in the area. Her town was named for the renowned Oglala Lakota chief.

Cather entered the University of Nebraska at Lincoln in 1891. She had planned to major in science, for she hoped to become a medical doctor. After her essay on Thomas Carlyle was published in the *Nebraska State Journal* during her freshman year, she became a regular contributor to the Journal, changed her major, and graduated in 1894 with a B.A. in English. As a student at the University of Nebraska in the early 1890s, Cather sometimes used the masculine nickname "William" and wore masculine clothing. A photograph in the University of Nebraska archives depicted Cather dressed like a young man.

In 1896, Cather moved to Pittsburgh after being hired to write for the *Home Monthly*, a women's magazine patterned after the successful *Ladies Home Journal*. A year later, she became a telegraph editor and drama critic for the *Pittsburgh Leader* and frequently contributed poetry and short fiction to *The Library*, another local publication. In Pittsburgh, she taught Latin, algebra, and English composition at Central High School for one year. She also taught English and Latin at Allegheny High School, where she became the head of the English department.

In 1906 Cather moved to New York City upon receiving a job offer on the editorial staff from *McClure's Magazine*. During her first year at McClure's, she wrote a critical biography of Christian Science founder, Mary Baker Eddy. Cather was the principal writer of the biography. *Mary Baker Eddy: The Story of Her Life and the History of Christian Science* was published in McClure's in fourteen installments over the next eighteen months and later in book form.

Although she was born into a Baptist family, Cather joined the Episcopal Church in 1922. She had been attending Episcopal services since 1906. Beginning in 1922, Cather spent summers on Grand Manan Island, in New Brunswick, Canada. She bought a cottage in Whale Cove, on the Bay of Fundy. It was the only house she ever owned. She stopped coming to Grand Manan Island when Canada entered WWII, since travel was more difficult and the island doctor had died, making her cancer more uncomfortable. She valued the seclusion of the island, and may have even preferred that she and her companions be the only inhabitants.

Cather died on April 24, 1947 in New York City of a cerebral hemorrhage and was buried in the Old Burying Ground in Jaffrey, New Hampshire. Her tombstone reads:

THE TRUTH AND CHARITY OF HER GREAT

SPIRIT WILL LIVE ON IN THE WORK
WHICH IS HER ENDURING GIFT TO HER
COUNTRY AND ALL ITS PEOPLE.

Throughout Cather's adult life, her most significant friendships were with women. These included her college friend Louise Pound; the Pittsburgh socialite Isabelle McClung, with whom Cather traveled to Europe; opera singer Olive Fremstad; pianist Yaltah Menuhin; and most notably, the editor Edith Lewis, with whom Cather lived the last 39 years of her life. Cather's sexual identity remains a point of contention among scholars.

A resolutely private person, Cather destroyed many old drafts, personal papers, and letters. Her will restricted the ability of scholars to quote from those personal papers that remained. Since the 1980s, feminist and other academic writers have explored Cather's sexual orientation and the influence of her female friendships on her work.

Cather admired Henry James as a "mighty master of language and keen student of human actions and motives." She generally preferred past literary masters to contemporary writers. Some particular favorites were Dickens, Thackeray, Emerson, Hawthorne, Balzac, Flaubert, and Tolstoy. While Cather enjoyed the novels of George Eliot, the Brontës, and Jane Austen, she regarded most women writers with disdain, judging them overly sentimental and mawkish. Cather's biographer James Woodress notes that Cather "so completely...embraced masculine values that when she wrote about women writers, she sounded like a patronizing man." One contemporary exception was Sarah Orne Jewett, who became Cather's friend and mentor. Jewett advised Cather to use female narrators in her fiction, but Cather preferred to write from a male point of view.

Her Writing Career

In 1907 Cather wrote a short story, "The Namesake," which contains autobiographical significance. McClure's serialized Cather's first novel, *Alexander's Bridge* (1912). Most reviews were favorable. *The New York Times* praised "the dramatic situations and the clever conversations," and the *Atlantic* called the writing "deft and skillful."

Cather followed *Alexander's Bridge* with her Prairie Trilogy—*O Pioneers!* (1913), *The Song of the Lark* (1915), and *My Ántonia* (1918). These deeply felt works became both popular and critical successes. Cather was celebrated by national critics such as H.L. Mencken for writing in plainspoken language about ordinary people. Sinclair Lewis praised her work for making the outside world know Nebraska as no one else had done.

Through the 1910s and 1920s, Cather was firmly established as a major American writer, receiving the Pulitzer Prize in 1922 for her novel *One of Ours*. By the 1930s, critics began to dismiss her as a romantic, nostalgic writer who could not cope with the present. Critics such as Granville Hicks charged Cather with failing to confront contemporary life as it was and escaping into an idealized past. Cather's own conservative politics and the same subject matter that appealed to H. L. Mencken, Randolph Bourne, and Carl Van Doren soured Cather's reputation with younger, often left-leaning, critics such as Granville Hicks and Edmund Wilson. Discouraged by the negative criticism of her work, Cather became reclusive. She burned letters and forbade anyone from publishing her letters. Willa is a prolific writer, whose writings cover nonfiction, novels, poetry and short stories. Her Nonfiction works are: *The Life of Mary Baker G. Eddy and the History of Christian Science* (1909, reprinted by University of Nebraska Press, 1993), *Not Under Forty* (1936, essays), *Willa Cather: On Writing* (1949, reprinted by University of Nebraska Press, 1988).

She published 12 novels in all: *Alexander's Bridge* (1912), *O Pioneers!* (1913), *The Song of the Lark* (1915), *My Ántonia* (1918), *One of Ours* (1922), *A Lost Lady* (1923), *The Professor's House* (1925), *My Mortal Enemy* (1926), *Death Comes for the Archbishop* (1927), *Shadows on the Rock* (1931), *Lucy Gayheart* (1935), *Sapphira and the Slave Girl* (1940).

Cather had a long illustrious career writing essays, poems, short stories. Her collections include: *April Twilights* (1903, poetry), *The Troll Garden* (1905, short stories), *Youth and the Bright Medusa* (1920, short stories), *Obscure Destinies* (1932, three stories), *Not Under Forty* (1936, essays), *The Old Beauty and Others* (1948, three stories), *Willa Cather: On Writing* (1949, essays), *Five Stories* (1956, published by the Estate of Willa Cather).

Analysis of and Comment on Her Representative Novel

One of Ours (1922)

Plot Summary

One of Ours is a novel by Willa Cather that won the 1923 Pulitzer Prize. This novel had been inspired by reading her cousin G. P. Cather's wartime letters home to his mother. He was the first officer from Nebraska killed in World War I. *One of Ours* is a complex, slow-moving, but beautiful character study set before and during World War I. It tells the story of the life of Claude Wheeler, a Nebraska native around the turn of the

20th century. The hero is the son of a successful Midwestern farmer and an intensely pious mother, who is guaranteed a comfortable livelihood. Nevertheless, Wheeler views himself as a victim of his father's success and his own inexplicable malaise. Claude is troubled by his apparent inability to find purpose with his life. Everything he does seems to turn out wrong, at least in his own mind. Although he is a skilled farmer, Claude believes his destiny lies elsewhere.

While attending Temple College, Claude tries to convince his parents that attending the State University would give him a better education. His parents ignore his pleas and Claude continues at the Christian college. After a football game, Claude meets and befriends the Erlich family, quickly adapting his own world perception to the Erlichs' love of music, free-thinking, and debate. The Ehrlichs' also opens his eyes to other possibilities in life. His career at university and his friendship with the Erlichs are dramatically interrupted, however, when his father expands the family farm and Claude is obligated to leave university and operate part of the family farm.

Once settled on the farm, Claude marries Enid Royce, a childhood friend. His notions of love and marriage are quickly devastated when it becomes apparent that Enid is more interested in political activism and Christian missionary work than she is in loving and caring for Claude. This marriage turns out to be a marriage of convenience rather than love. Enid tries to convert her new husband to her many other causes such as Prohibition in Nebraska. When Enid departs for China to care for her missionary sister, who has suddenly fallen ill, Claude is somewhat relieved to see her go and moves back to his family's farm. As World War I begins in Europe, the family is fixated on every development from overseas. When the United States decides to enter the war, Claude enlists in the US Army. All of a sudden, as if it's a revelation, Claude feels a sense of duty, a sense of belonging, a sense of existing purpose.

Finally believing he has found a purpose in life—beyond the drudgery of farming and marriage—Claude revels in his freedom and new responsibilities. Despite an influenza epidemic and the continuing hardships of the battlefield, Claude Wheeler nonetheless has never felt as though he has mattered more. His pursuit of vague notions of purpose and principle culminates in a ruthless front-line encounter with an overwhelming German onslaught. The patriotism of Claude and his fellow soldiers, as well as their innocent (and at times ignorant) desire to do good deeds, makes the war effort seem like a noble cause. However, it ends—as real war always does—with death, leaving Claude Wheeler and the novel as a whole suspended in a state of emotional incompleteness and pain.

One of Ours is made up of five books. Book I, "On Lovely Creek," introduces the young Claude Wheeler in small-town Nebraska. Claude visits a traveling circus with friends and then goes back to school at Temple, the religious college he is attending in Lincoln. While there, he adds special classes in European history at the nearby state college and plays football for Temple. This allows him to make friends with new boys, and he begins to explore new intellectual worlds. Two girls show interest in Claude while he is at school, but he does not get involved with either of them. College is going well, but then his father buys a new ranch in Colorado. While Mr. Wheeler runs the ranch, Claude is left in charge of the family's Nebraska farm. Even though it means giving up his studies, Claude pours his energy into his new position.

Book II, "Enid," follows the next change in Claude's life, which culminates in his marriage to Enid Royce. It begins when his father sends him to Colorado to see the new ranch. The distance makes Claude feel exceptionally lonely, and once he is back in Nebraska, he begins to visit the mill to see Enid. Their courtship is fairly slow until they get caught in the rain while driving and Enid drives them closer to home. Soon after that, Claude gets stuck by a barbwire fence and falls ill. Enid tends to him, and Claude falls in love with her.

In Book III, "Sunrise on the Prairie," Claude proposes, and Enid agrees. They get married, hoping a happy and bright future. Claude thinks that he can find inner peace in marriage, but things turn out to be different. Shortly after marriage, Claude finds that Enid is not his ideal wife, who often annoys and offends him. Soon, World War I breaks out, and Claude enlists.

Book IV, "The Voyage of the Anchises" and Book V, "Bidding the Eagles of the West Fly On" depicts Claude's service in the American Expeditionary Forces. The war brings the chance of redemption: Claude begins to experience feelings of challenge and purpose as he becomes an officer in the army. Once in France, he forms a friendship with a fellow officer, David Erhardt, a former concert violinist who has lived in France and speaks the language fluently. Through David, Claude is exposed to French art and culture. In one poignant scene, Claude listens to David playing the violin in the home of a cultured French family and becomes fully aware of what has been missing in his life.

Claude's admiration and envy of David and his camaraderie with the men under his command heighten his commitment to the justice of the war: "I never knew there was anything worth living for, till the war came on. Before that, the world seemed like a business proposition." His newly discovered vitality and confidence produce a psychological transformation, as the hesitant young farmer becomes a skilled and courageous leader of men.

In September 1918, Claude and David's battalion is transferred to the Meuse Argonne front, in preparation for the offensive. When the fighting begins, Claude, now a company commander, is ordered to occupy a critical position where the Germans are expected to counterattack. The designated spot is a former German trench, which the Germans had mined before retreating. Just prior to their counterattack, the enemy detonates the mine, wiping out the American machine guns placed there. With only rifles to defend his position, Claude exposes himself to danger by directing his men's fire, and he successfully holds the line until reinforcements arrive. In the process, however, both Claude and David are killed.

Themes

As with most of the early Pulitzers, *One of Ours* is a book about a very specific time in American life. This novel reflects the rural and urban American life around World War I. The Wheeler farm on Lovely Creek represents the rural life at that time. Cather describes the change of seasons, scenes and animals vividly. Under Cather's pen, the picturesque Wheeler farm is so tranquil and beautiful that it leaves a deep impression on readers. From Cather's description, readers can find immense traces of her great nostalgia. However, World War I broke this picturesque old farming life style forever. Actually Cather herself never fully recovered from the "shock" of World War I, with its ten million casualties and host of industrialized horrors, and that her sense of living in a world forever broken by war colored virtually everything she wrote after *One of Ours.*

Cather is an outstanding example of a writer whose work is deeply rooted in a sense of place and at the same time universal in its treatment of theme and character. The corner of earth that she is best known for depicting is Nebraska, where she lived as an adolescent and young woman and where she was educated. This dominant subject is the setting for all or significant parts of six of her twelve novels and many of her short stories. She is typically preoccupied with her Nebraska material. She evokes indelibly the shaggy virgin prairie around Red Cloud, Nebraska, where the Scandinavian, Bohemian, German, and many other early immigrants lived during the late decades of the nineteenth century.

One of Ours is also a Bildungsroman novel, which records the growing process of Claude. Claude Wheeler is a Nebraska farm boy, but he always wants more. He tries to be a good son and he tries to do what his parents want him to do. He does everything that's expected of him: he works on the farm and he marries a girl from town, but she turns out to be a person he doesn't know. At each new stage of life he continues to be unsatisfied. He has a constant, underlying feeling that there should be more to life. He battles with his demons every day. When America finally enters World War I, he signs up right away. As he travels farther and farther from home, he feels more and more alive. During World War I, Claude finally becomes the man he wants to be. He sees suffering and terrible things, but he can't help feeling happy to be there. Cather certainly doesn't portray the war as a good thing, but she does show how some of the men who go may have made something good from it. She gives us scenes of death and battle, but everything is very quiet and understated. What is important here is Claude's growth, not the war itself. It's an intimate portrait of one man's experience of war. And, more importantly, of one man's experience of life.

Identity is another theme of *One of Ours*. Claude is a young man when the story opens, and he puts a great deal of energy into trying to figure out who he is. Claude and his brothers all attempt to distinguish themselves from others. They push against one another and push against their parents even as they pull close to them. When he goes to college, Claude tries to make himself something and someone new. He is moderately successful, but as happens often in the novel, he and other men can't find their true identities. They seek to find or establish their identities through many ways. When their values are realized in war front, they do not despair and feel discouraged any longer.

One of Ours also touches upon the unavoidable modernity and the new femininity, which is represented by Claude Wheeler's wife, Enid Royce. On the one hand, Cather expresses her nostalgia for natural pre-industrial frontier life implicitly from Claude's standpoint. Faced with the newly-emerged industry, Claude is excited and considers this as a scientific progress. But he is also homesick, missing his birth farm very much. On the other hand, Cather exhibits the threatening new femininity and modernity, which is embodied by Enid Royce. In the novel, Enid is completely different from the Victorian women who are angels in rooms. Instead, she is a dangerous New Woman, whose defiance of traditional gender roles brings her inevitably into conflict with her husband. Enid represents the unavoidable modernity in World War I. Enid's scientific domestic economy, for example, reflects the discourse used to mobilize women on the home front, in their kitchens, parlors, and gardens.

Likewise, Enid's accomplished handling of an automobile evokes the entry of American women into the Motor Corps, one of many wartime expediencies that destabilize conventional notions of gender. Actually, World War I is a crucial time that hatches and yields the new femininity. During World War I, most men went to the war front, leaving their mothers, sisters and wives behind. It is these women who support the whole family. Apart from sewing, washing, cooking and other house chores, they also need to plant on their farms and work in factories. Women become the supporting force in American families. This gives rise to the new femininity. Cather finds this, and records this new phenomenon in *One of Ours*.

Literary Techniques

Published in 1922, *One of Ours* proved to be pivotal in Willa Cather's career. Although she had already penned four novels and gained increasing critical acclaim, *One of Ours* elevated her to the highest rank of twentieth-century American authors. *One of Ours* is sometimes referred to as a "war story," but Cather's intent was to portray a young man from the Plains who came to France in World War I and found himself. Cather's narrative voice, her evocation of youthful energy and aspirations and frustrations, her memoriam to the young soldiers who died in World War I—these qualities add up to a classic American novel.

Although *One of Ours* was a commercial success, and Cather received the Pulitzer Prize for it in 1923, many influential writers were disappointed with the novel when it first appeared. H. L. Mencken and Earnest Hemingway, who admired Cather's earlier novels, both wrote unfavorable reviews of *One of Ours*. However, *One of Ours* has some unusual artistic features. In this novel, Cather encompassed the entire package: great storytelling, exquisite writing and memorable characters, as well as visually clear and exciting imagery.

Unbalanced Structure Although Cather failed to provide readers with vivid and authentic war scenes in *One of Ours*, she did bring readers some literary aesthetic aspects. *One of Ours* is a slow novel, in the sense that there is a lot of character development and, although there is action, much of it isn't in the form of a "plot." The majority of the action and plot begins when Claude leaves for World War I, and that doesn't happen until the last third of the book. But the buildup and character development are essential to understanding the action and to feeling satisfied with how the book ultimately ends. The slow moving pace of the early part of the book reflects Claude's attitude with how slow and meaningless his life has been so far. He has little enthusiasm for farm work, merely tolerates his family and feels a constant sense of agitation. Cather makes use of this beginning section of the book to expertly develop his character as well as the long list of supporting characters.

Imagery In the first part of the book, Cather interjects some beautiful and pleasant imagery. When Claude and his friend visit the farm together during Christmas break from college: "...they scrambled down the bank to admire the red clusters on the woody, smoke-colored vine, and its pale gold leaves, ready to fall at a touch. The vine and the little tree it honored, hidden away in the cleft of a ravine, had escaped the stripping winds and the eyes of schoolchildren who sometimes took a short cut home through the pasture. At its roots, the creek trickled thinly along, black between two jagged crusts of melting ice."

During the latter part of the novel, when Claude experiences war, Cather's imagery was also very impressive: "The stench was the worst they had yet encountered, but it was less disgusting than the flies: when they inadvertently touched a dead body, clouds of wet, buzzing flies flew up into their faces, into their eyes and nostrils. Under their feet, the earth worked and moved as if boa constrictors were wriggling down there, soft bodies, lightly covered..."

Characterization Cather is skilled at characters portray. In *One of Ours*, the protagonist Claude is portrayed impressively. At first, Claude considered himself

Christian, "wanted little to do with theology or theologians," and, in many respects, found himself leaning toward liberal ideology. However, in the climax of the book, he surprises himself (and the reader) by asking God in the face of tragedy and asking for nothing short of a miracle. In exchange, Claude makes his own promise with God.

Along with Claude are a series of characters who are real, engaging and diverse. His mother, a Protestant Christian, carries an underlying bias against Catholics, but truly loves her sons and her husband in the only way she knows. Claude's father has little tolerance or acceptance of his son's frustrations with life. Claude's wife Enid, who, under the guise of a self-deluded belief that she is doing God's will, leaves Claude to serve as a missionary in China.

One of Ours pays tribute to the World War I generation in a coming-of-age story, a nuanced character study, and is not—as some of her contemporaries said—a pro-war novel. Cather has not an aggressive bone in her body, and she takes care to remind readers of the cynicism of some soldiers who fought and returned home, also mentioning the men who could not adjust to their post-war civilian environment. The novel celebrates the lives of all the young American men, including Cather's cousin, who died in France during World War I. With over four million U.S. soldiers having served in the costly war, it is no wonder American readers of literary fiction respond to the book about a young man who dies for what he believes in. Cather uses dialogue to good effect throughout the book, but it is her representation of the young man's inner life that drives the novel. Cather is a hard author to categorize, and her style is hard to sum up. The most distinctive thing about her is her plain style. She does not elaborate ornate phrases or communicate in sly subtleties. She isn't a blunt force like Hemingway, but she is much closer to that end of the style spectrum than she is to Wharton and Fitzgerald.

Bibliography

http://en.wikipedia.org/wiki/Willa_Cather, 2013-03-12.

http://cather.unl.edu/life.woodress.html, 2013-03-15.

http://www.online-literature.com/willa-cather/, 2013-03-03.

Elliott, Emory. *Columbia Literary History of the United States*. New York: Columbia University Press, 1988: 619.

PART V

AMERICAN LITERATURE IN THE MODERN PERIOD

(1900–1945)

Historical Introduction

The modern period in American literature refers to the period between the two World Wars, WWI (1914–1918) and WWII (1939–1945). It was a period that witnessed economical boom and recession and a period that underwent great social changes. It was a period of spiritual crisis, a time of turmoil and a time characterized by artistic experimentation and a time of literary prosperity. It was a period when America established its leadership in world politics, military as well as literature. In short, it was a period of great importance, with lasting influence.

The First World War (1914–1918) The first World War, also called the "Great War," broke out in 1914. It was fought between the *Entente* countries/Allies: Britain, France, Italy and tsarist Russia, and the Allied Nations: Germany and Austro-Hungary. America did not enter the war until the day when the U.S. Congress formally declared war on Germany. It was April, 6, 1917. While the war thrust the Europe into a world of killing, blood, death and chaos, it served as an important stimulating factor to American economic development. Between 1914 and 1916, the American industrial production increased gradually. By the end of the war, the United States had emerged as a new world leader with an expanding economy and the unmatched prosperity. In spite of that, with the ending of the war there was a prevailing new disillusionment, especially among writers. Americans were confident and optimistic when they initially participated in the war. But that cheerful mood was soon taken over by the brutality, savagery, cruelty and horror of the war. Many Americans took to the battle field for the sake of patriotism, heroism and the devotion to a great cause, "saving" civilization. To their disappointment, the war didn't change the world for the better. It caused heavy toll/loss of lives, and Europe was still plagued by turmoil and economic crisis which made the sacrifices meaningless. The victors, while made great sacrifices, also committed killing. The ending of the war brought with it a sense of failure and disillusionment. In America, the shift from patriotism to disillusionment was also intensified by the fact that the social problems existent before the war, such as racial discrimination, inequality between men and women, and so on, remained the same.

The Roaring Twenties (1919–1929) American economy suffered from an acute recession in 1920–1921, which is known as the post–World War I recession. But it soon recovered as soldiers returning from the battlefields re-entered the labor force and factories shifted back to produce consumer goods. The economy of the country successfully transitioned from a wartime economy to a peacetime economy. Mass production made it possible for the middle class to gain access to technological products like radios and cars. As the first mass broadcasting medium, radio enjoyed a "golden age," together with movies and advertising, it played a very important role in giving rise to the mass culture. With the expansion of the automobile industry, cars, no longer a luxury as they used to be before the war, now mass-produced, became a commonplace throughout the country. Its popularity not only led to the development of such industries as highway building, motels, service stations, and so on, but also enhanced mobility, which in a way contributed to urbanization. 1923 to 1929 was the "thriving" stage of American economy marked by the enormous economic growth, such as the rapid rise of auto, electric, architectural, and iron and steel industries, and widespread prosperity. Now the U.S.A became one of the richest countries in the world, with its culture becoming consumer-orientated.

The 1920s was an age of affluence. It was also an age of swift social changes and a decade of deep cultural conflicts, a time full of disturbing noises. Industrialization and urbanization generated excitement but also shock and chaos. The rise of a consumer-oriented economy and of mass entertainment became impetus of and helped to bring about a "revolution in morals and manners." The decade witnessed a huge conflict between the old and the new. Immigration, race, alcohol, evolution, gender politics, and sexual morality, etc. all became major cultural issues.

Prohibition Among the events that dramatically affected the American society was the issuing of Prohibition. On January 16, 1919, Prohibition was instituted with ratification of the Eighteenth Amendment to the United States Constitution. It was actually a major reform movement from the 1840s into the 1920s. The law prohibited the "...manufacture, sale, or transportation of intoxicating liquors within, the importation thereof into, or the exportation thereof from the United States..." On October 28, 1919, the American Congress passed the "Volstead Act" to enforce the law.

But the law was not strictly implemented in most large cities. As a result, it led to an increase in organized crime, although alcohol consumption declined. Many became millionaires by bootlegging. During the "thriving" years of the 1920s, people were parting everywhere and indulging in a life of dissipation.

After years of endeavor, women finally won the struggle for suffrage. "The Nineteenth Amendment to the United States Constitution" passed in 1920 granted women the right to vote. The passage of the law was the major victory of the movement to be known as the First-wave feminism movement. The passage of the law also marked the end of this movement. The 1920s saw significant change in the lives of women. The old mentality about the role of women were challenged and replaced by the new ideas that women could pursue both a career and a family successfully. Women began to receive higher education. Women, especially, young women, took part in a sexual liberation of their generation. Ideas like equality and free sexuality were very popular. These young, rebellious, middle-class women, labeled "flappers" by older generations, did a breaking-off from the rigid Victorian way of life. Unlike the older generation, these "new women" were less interested in politics but they were more concerned about personal fulfillment. They wore short dresses, raccoon coats, had short hair, a chin-length bob. They smoked and drank in public, celebrated the sexual revolution, and embraced consumer culture. Opposing to these new ideas and changes, the notion of the "feminine mystique" was produced, which re-stressed the women's role as housewives, causing frustration and dissatisfaction among many well-educated women.

In the 1920s, the American government tightened its law on immigration. Racial discrimination still existed. The Ku Klux Klan executed persecution on the blacks. The "Red Hunt" after the war, the Prohibition led to the contempt on and the widespread violation of law. Despite the soaring of economy, there was a prevailing mood of discontentment with the society. The justice of the war was questioned. The war did nothing to the world's problems. Serious social problems such as racial and gender discrimination existent before the war remained unsolved. Disillusion with the war prevailed. Darwin's theory of evolution and Nietzsche's statement that "God is dead" broke the myth of God. God was no longer the center of the universe. Men were left alone helplessly at the mercy of natural forces, obsessed by the loss of faith and the sense of dislocation. The development of modern science on the one hand enriched and facilitated human life, but on the other hand, it impelled men to be skeptical about everything, generating a strong sense that life was fragmented and chaotic and hence meaningless and futile. Industrialization and mass production intensified this feeling. The sense of spiritual disorientation and nihilism became the mood of the time. In summary, the 1920s was a period in which the economic boom was accompanied by the pursuit of pleasure and material comfort and simultaneously the prevailing pessimism.

The Jazz Age The 1920s is also nicknamed the Jazz Age. Jazz was introduced into the mainstream of American culture and became the most popular form of music for young people, but to older generations, it was immoral and threatening to old cultural values. Jazz played a significant part in promoting cultural changes during the period, and had a lasting influence on pop culture. Jazz was originally played by black Americans. It has a strong beat, with the characteristic of improvising, full of changes, free of control and spontaneous. It expresses an open, free, casual and even bold and wild mood. It was seen to well represent the rebellious spirit of the time. The desire to break with the old tradition, to welcome changes, to follow the vogue of the day found its expression in the music. Hence the name, it was called the Jazz Age.

The Great Depression of the 1930s The "frenetic," "glittering" and "feverish" time was brought to an end by the sudden collapse of stock prices on Wall Street. The Wall Street crash occurred on October 29, 1929, also known as Black Tuesday, throwing America into what is later called the Great Depression, which also added to a worldwide depression throughout the 1930s. During this time, the American economy was stuck in severe recession. By the winter of 1932–1933, the country was caught in the deepest crisis since the Civil War, with women, the urban poor and all people of color suffering the most. People began to doubt and question the social system and the nation's way of life. President Franklin Delano Roosevelt issued the New Deal as anti-crises measures. The New Deal took effect and helped the country out of crisis.

The economic crisis between 1929 and 1933 intensified the contradictions already existent in the capitalist system and led to wars in the imperialist countries, which finally triggered the outbreak of the Second World War on a full scale. In America, after the economic crisis, the American monopoly capital was further concentrated. In 1941, the U.S. entered the war. The Second World War greatly stimulated the American industrial production. By the time the War ended in 1945, the whole productive forces of the country had increased by 40 per cent compared with 1939.

The Development of Literature

The Influence of New Theories and New Ideas From the mid-19th to the early 20th centuries, the developments in natural sciences and the social sciences, and innovations in industry as well as in the field of art in Europe functioned as impetus for the rise of modernism in the United States. Darwinism and Marxism still influenced the writers, artists and intellectuals of this period. Besides, German philosopher Arthur Schopenhauer (1788–1860), French philosopher of positivism Hippolyte Adolphe Taine (1828–1893) and German philosopher Friedrich Nietzsche (1844–1900) also exerted influence on the writers, artists and intellectuals of this time. But more direct and more important influence came from French philosopher Henri Bergson (1859–1941) and French Existentialism. Bergson put forward the theories of intuitionism and psychological time, viewing the interior "duration" and "*élan* vital" as the real existence, which could be perceived through intuition rather than experience. Existentialism held a negative view on life, believing that man's life is full of suffering, loneliness and pain. These philosophies became the sources of the post-war pessimism, skepticism, nihilism and anarchism. The keynote of literary writing in this period is "tragic sense of life." The development of psychology also contributed to the birth of modernism. Austrian neurologist Sigmund Freud (1856–1939) developed what was known as psychoanalysis, which put great importance on the unconscious or the irrational in the human psyche. Freud's interpretation of dreams was another influence on the development of modernism. In addition, American psychologist, William James' theory of "stream of consciousness," and Swiss psychiatrist, Carl Jung's theory "collective unconscious" and "archetypal symbol" were also contributing factors. Their theories, plus that of Freud, prompted the modernist writers to shift their attention from the external world to the inner world and to probe into the inner world of human reality.

The Historical and Socio-Cultural Background The first World War (1914–1918) serves as a dividing line between the 19th-century American literature and the modern American literature. The war and its aftermath had enormous impact on the postwar America. The war consumed countless property, took millions of lives and traumatized the survivals. War means violence, devastation, blood and death, helpless in solving the existent problems, instead, leaving the world fragmented and chaotic. Traditional ideas and values and the "American dream" collapsed. After a short-time economic boom, a severe economic crisis broke out. The whole country was stuck in the ten-year depression. The world was disintegrated and turbulent, with a sense of unease and restlessness underneath, and spiritual and moral decline, which resulted in the feelings of fear, loss, disorientation and disillusionment. New ideas and new approaches and techniques were needed to define and present the postwar life and the society. It was under these circumstances that modernism emerged.

The Impact of European Avant-Garde Art Prior to WWI, the modernist movement, labeled as the avant-garde movement, in painting, photography, sculpture, music, and so on exerted a great impact on American literature, catalytic to its reform and innovation. This influence was evident in the works of American modernist writers. For example, in 1909, Gertrude Stein (1874–1946), by then an expatriate in Paris, published her innovative fiction *Three Lives* (1909), which was a result of the influence of cubism, jazz, and other contemporary movements in art and music. In painting, both the French Impressionist and the German Expressionist artists tended to represent the human reality from subjective perspective, offering a highly personal vision of the world. This approach was employed in literature as a revolt against realism and naturalism, with the attempt to depict psychological or spiritual reality instead of reflecting external reality. The employment of Impressionism and Expressionism was apparent in the works of F. Scott Fitzgerald, William Faulkner, Eugene O'Neill, etc. Eugene O'Neill's plays like *Emperor Jones* (1920), *The Hairy Ape* (1922), etc. are typical plays written in the mode of Expressionism. In America, Cubism, a popular school of modern painting in the early 20th century also found its way into the works of American writers of the modern period. It emphasized the formal structure of a work of art and the multiple-perspective viewpoints, which gave the American writers the idea to depict the reality from multiple perspectives.

The Lost Generation The catastrophes of the war and traumatic experience it brought to people shattered people's belief in the former ideas and values and gave them a strong feeling of uncertainty and disillusionment. There was a prevailing new disillusionment, especially among writers. They rebelled against former ideals and values, but replaced them only by despair or a cynical hedonism. Disillusioned and disgusted by the frivolous, greedy, and heedless way of life in America, many writers and poets left America for European countries, esp. Paris France. They formed a community of writers and artists there experimenting with new modes of writing with other European counterparts. These "expatriates" who lived in Paris in the 1920s and 1930s were called the "Lost Generation," a label given by Gertrude Stein. Included in this group were distinguished artists such as T. S. Eliot (1888–1965), F. Scott Fitzgerald (1896–1940), Ernest Hemingway (1899–1961), John Dos Passos (1896–1970). Writers of this group were disillusioned with former ideals and values and even with the so-called civilization of the capitalist society. In literary creation, they sought to break with the traditional and the obsolete and experiment with new approaches and techniques to capture the essence of the postwar life. In addition, many of them had war experiences and they used them as the basis for their writings.

The Waste Land Image American literature of the 1920s was characterized by a prevailing disillusionment, pessimism and nihilism. T. S. Eliot's poem *The Waste Land* (1922) presents a picture of the sterility and chaos of the postwar western world, the decline of Western culture and expresses the despair and depression of the postwar era. This waste land image is recurrent in the works of Eliot's contemporaries. F. Scott Fitzgerald, the representative of the Jazz Age, portrays a spiritual wasteland of the age in his books. The theme of disillusionment and spiritual decadence is expressed poignantly in his novel *The Great Gatsby* (1925). Beneath the restlessness, pleasure seeking, there was only meaninglessness and emptiness, a kind of spiritual and moral deterioration and the collapse of ideals. As the spokesman of the Lost Generation, Ernest Hemingway gives a portrait of the expatriate group, the Lost Generation with his novel *The Sun Also Rises* (1926). His novels convey the sense of loss and despair among the postwar generation both physically and psychologically important. William Faulkner illustrates the modern society as a wasteland through his own fictional world, the Yoknapatawpha County, which is not only the mirror of the decline of the Southern society but also the spiritual decadence of the modern American society devoid of essential human values.

Literary Achievements in the 1920s The decade of the 1920s witnessed a "flowering" of literature so that it "can be termed the second renaissance in the history of American literature." (P216) Heavyweight writers in great number emerged, many of whom gained international recognition and helped to promote the popularity of American literature in the world. In 1920, Sinclair Lewis published *Main Street* and in 1922, *Babbitt*. The year 1922 saw the appearance of a monumental modernist innovative work of art, T. S. Eliot's *The Waste Land*. In 1925, Theodore Dreiser's masterpiece of naturalism, *An American Tragedy* came out. In 1926, F. Scott Fitzgerald novel *The Great Gatsby* caught the attention of the public. In 1926, Ernest Hemingway brought out his novel *The Sun Also Rises*. The 1929 was signalized by two important modern novels, *A Farewell to Arms* by Hemingway and *The Sound and the Fury* by William Faulkner. American playwright, Eugene O'Neill, published three important plays successively in 1920, 1921 and 1922. These plays, *The Emperor Jones* (1920), *Anna Christie* (1921) and *The Hairy Ape* (1922), established him as an international playwright. Of the writers of this decade, Sinclair Lewis, T. S. Eliot, Ernest Hemingway, William Faulkner and Eugene O'Neill were winners of the Nobel Prize in literature.

The literary thrive of this decade was also indebted to some other important writers who wrote and published their works then. Sherwood Anderson (1876–1941) published *Poor White* (1920) and *The Triumph of the Egg* (1921). Willa Cather (1873–1947), who continued to write in the realistic tradition, published *Professor's House* (1925) and *Death Comes for the Archbishop* (1927). Thomas Wolfe (1900–1938) published his first book *Looking Homeward, Angel* (1929).

Literary Development in the 1930s America of the Depression era was shrouded in a prevailing despair and panic. The economic crisis and the rise of fascism in Europe set the keynote for American literature during this period. Writers were greatly concerned with social problems and the living conditions of the lower class. Literature at this time was characterized by its blunt and direct social criticism. The "social conscience" novels became prosperous again. The then proletarian writers, Marxists and their fellow travelers, exposed and criticized the capitalist system, the cause of the Depression, and also spread their revolutionary ideas by means of fiction. Among them were John Dos Passos and John Steinbeck (1902–1968). John Dos Passos was best known for his *U.S.A.* trilogy composed of *The 42nd Parallel* (1930), *1919* (1932), and *The Big Money* (1936). The trilogy is a record of the history of America beginning with the Gilded Age through the First World War to the booming twenties. It shows how America as an industrial giant dominates and depersonalizes the individuals. John Steinbeck was preoccupied with the poor, working-class people and wrote about their struggle for a decent and honest life. His masterpiece *The Grapes of Wrath*, a "Social conscience" novel tells the story of the Joads, a poor family from Oklahoma. In search of a better life, the family embarked on a journey to California, which turned out to be a journey accompanied by pain, suffering and death. With their journey, the author presents a landscape of decay and desolation. The author also expresses his sympathy with the poor and wretched and more importantly his belief in humanity and the future, and that's where he is different from other writers of his time. Another popular novel of his published in the same decade was *Of Mice and Men* (1937). He was awarded the Nobel Prize in Literature in 1962.

The Second American Literary Renaissance The 1920s and the 1930s were considered as the second American literary renaissance due to the emergence of the large number of great writers and the enormous quantities of books they created and the huge influence both national and international they produced, which enhanced American literature to a new height.

The Southern Renaissance The 1920s and 1930s also witnessed the revival of American Southern culture and literature known as the Southern Renaissance. It is considered as the most striking literary development of the thirties. Important writers in this period included William Faulkner, Caroline Gordon, Elizabeth Madox Roberts, Katherine Anne Porter, Allen Tate, Tennessee Williams, and Robert Penn Warren, and others, among whom William Faulkner was the most influential and famous. Different from the writers before the Southern Renaissance, writers in this period tended to deal with such major themes as the burden of history, the Southern history being a history burden with slavery and military defeat, the existence of individuals in the conservative culture of the South where one's personal value was not important as compared to those of family, religion, and community, and racial issues. Writers also experimented with modernistic techniques, such as stream of consciousness and complex narrative techniques in their artistic activity. The Southern literature shares some distinctive features of modern literature. For example, it also expressed the sense of dislocation and alienation. It was central to the Southern writing in the 1930s, which stemmed partly from the South's ambivalence about America's advance toward secularism, progress, prosperity and power. The predicament, the desire to honor its past and the desire to desert it, led to a tension involved in the Southern fiction of the 1930s. It dealt with the issues of class, caste, race and gender, and produced "stories about being other." Faulkner gave voices to the poor, female and the black. His fiction bears features of modern fiction, pessimistic, violent, brutal and despairing. Eudora Welty wrote in the formalist tradition common with world modernism. Other Southern writers of this time include Thomas Wolfe and Anne Porter.

The Harlem Renaissance In addition, the 1920s and the 1930s saw the thrive of Afro-American literature—The Harlem Renaissance. The Harlem Renaissance was a cultural movement between the 1920s and 1930s. At the time, it was known as the "New Negro Movement." The concept of "New Negro" was first introduced in the 19th century and became popular during the Harlem Renaissance. The term stressed African American assertiveness and self-confidence during the years following World War I and the Great Migration, achieving a new image of pride and dignity, a striving after "spiritual emancipation," as a contrast to the "Old Negro." Its headquarter was in northern Manhattan, Harlem, where gathered African American writers, mostly newcomers from the South. The publication of Countee Cullen's "I Have a Rendezvous With Life (with apologies to Alan Seeger)" and Langston Hughes' poem "The Negro Speaks of Rivers" in 1921 marked the beginning of the movement. The peak of this "flowering of Negro literature" was between 1924 and 1929. The movement dated back to the late 1910s. The Harlem Renaissance was a burst of creative activity by African American writers and artists. African-American literature and art developed rapidly during this period. There emerged many important African American writers including Langston Hughes, Countee Cullen, Claude McKay, and Zora Neale Hurston, and others, most of whom moved to Harlem during the renaissance. Through literature and art, they expressed their racial pride, challenged the pervading racism and stereotypes against the blacks and promoted progressive politics, and racial and social integration and equality. The art that emerged in this period involved a wide variety of cultural elements and styles. The Renaissance was more than a literary or artistic movement and it did a lot in promoting social development through proclaiming a new racial consciousness and advocating racial integration. It made it clear that the Black experience was part of American cultural history in terms of culture and sociology. It redefined how America, and the world, viewed the African-American population. It encouraged the new appreciation of folk roots and culture. It contributed a lot to the rise of jazz. But in its attempt to create a new culture and art, the Harlem Renaissance could not sufficiently be immune to White, European culture. African American writers and artists were consciously or unconsciously drawn to the social norms and values created by the whites. The Harlem Renaissance continued throughout the 1920s and into the 1930s. It ended abruptly due to the Great Depression.

High Modernism American literary modernist movement experienced three phases: early modernism, high modernism and late modernism. The modernist movement between the end of the First World War and the beginning of the Second is referred to as high modernism. The term is specially used to describe literary modernism of this time. American modernist writers of this time include Ezra Pound, T.S. Eliot, William Faulkner, Ernest Hemingway and others. The American modernist movement reflected American life in the 20th century. The prevailing sense of disillusionment found its way into American literary works, which were becoming more and more cynical and more tended to explore the darker aspects of human nature. Artistically, American Modernists abandoned traditional literary modes, doubting if they were adequate in depicting the harsh realities of the time. They experimented with all kinds of new approaches and techniques to capture the essence of modern life. They broke up the narrative continuity and coherence by omitting the transitions, expositions, explanations and resolutions common in traditional literature so that their works were full of fragments which were well suited for presenting a picture of the modern world, a world that was fragmented. Instead of directly stating their themes, they endeavored to have them implied so as to create a sense of uncertainty, the kind of sense the modern world evoked. The works of American modernist writers covered a wide variety of themes concerning race relations, gender roles, sexuality, and so on. Affected by the trauma of the First World War or disillusioned with their war experience, many American modernist writers explored the psychological and spiritual wounds caused by the war. The economic crisis in America at the beginning of the 1930s was also the theme of their works. Another theme is the loss of self and need for self-definition.

Modernism

Modernism is a general term used to describe the widespread movement or a trend of thought concerning art, literature, architecture, music, and so on, which took place around 1850 and lasted for about a century. In a narrow sense, this term is specially used to refer to the modernist movement in literature and the other arts in the early decades of the twentieth century, especially after World War I (1914–1918). Modernism is characterized by its revolt against some of the traditional bases constituting the Western society, culture, religion and art. Modernists deliberately and radically sought to break with conventional notions and the established norms and experimented with new and even “shocking” modes and means of expression to reflect the reality of their time. The spiritual sources of modernism are from the thinkers who had questioned the plausibility of the traditional social systems, religion, morality as well as the traditional conception about the human self. The catalytic factors of modernism include the development of natural sciences and social sciences, industrialization and urbanization, rapid social changes and the outbreak of WWI and its aftermaths, as well.

The origins of this movement can be traced back to the early 19th century. Two ideas originating in France had particular impact on modernist movement. The first was Impressionism, a school of painting. The second was Symbolism, whose beginning was marked by *Les Fleur du Mal* (1857), a poem by the French poet Charles Baudelaire (1861–1867). There were two thinkers who exerted major influences on the development of modernism in this period. They were biologist Charles Darwin (1809–1882), author of *On Origin of Species by Means of Natural Selection* (1859), and political scientist Karl Marx (1818–1883). From the late 19th to the early 20th centuries, the influential intellectuals and thinkers were Sigmund Freud (1856–1939), Carl Jung (1875–1961), Friedrich Nietzsche, Henri Bergson (1859–1941). Important literary precursors of Modernism at this time included Fyodor Dostoevsky (1821–1881), Walt Whitman (1819–1892), and others. From 1910–1930, the development of modernism entered a new phase. Pablo Picasso shocked the world with his radical painting practice. In 1907, the first Expressionist play came out. In 1909, Futurism came into being. The year 1911 saw the first abstract painting. In 1913, Ezra Pound founded imagism. Modernism in this period assumed new characteristics. It preferred discontinuity to smooth change. It favored disruption, rejecting simple realism. All this showed that modernists were more radical, seeking to overthrow traditional norms and traditional social structure, as they were hindering progress. Two events, the First World War (1914–1918) and the Russian Revolution of 1917, further pushed modernism forward. Modernism which used to be a minority pursuit before the war came to permeate into the public life. It appeared in various forms and in various fields. For example, in painting, it appeared as Dada and in literature, it appeared as surrealism. Each of them sought to break with the traditional and the obsolete and experiment with new approaches and techniques, just as the poet Ezra Pound appealed to "Make it new " in 1934. The modernist movement between the end of the First World War and the beginning of the Second is referred to as high modernism. The term is specially used to describe literary modernism of this time. Modernist writers of this time include Ezra Pound, T. S. Eliot, Virginia Woolf, Yeats, Joyce, and others. By 1930, modernism had become part of the mainstream, either politically and artistically and had entered popular culture.

The core of modernism is its self-conscious break with tradition and desire for innovation. Many modernists believed that tradition should be abandoned so that new modes of artistic creation could be found. They stressed the freedom of expression, experimentation, the use of radically new and even primitive means. In literature this often meant the rejection of plots or characterization easy to understand in novels, or the defying of clear interpretation in composing poetry. Literary modernists were keen on disjunctive narratives, surreal images, and incoherence.

American literary modernist movement experienced three phases: early modernism, high modernism and late modernism. In America, modernism as a literary movement reached its peak in the 1920s and ended by 1939. The American modernist movement reflected American life in the 20th century. In a quickly industrializing world, the pace of life was hastened, social norms, boundaries and structure were all being challenged and were dissolving and the individual was left alone, wandering, purposeless, with no identity. Loss of identity led to a feeling of isolation and alienation. In addition, the catastrophe of the First World War shook faith in Western civilization and idealism about the country. The world was falling apart and violence, vagueness and spiritual emptiness were all what were left. The Great Depression at the end of the 1920s and during the 1930s intensified the sense of disillusionment and crashed the optimism about the economic prosperity and stability of the country.

This prevailing sense of disillusionment found its way into American literary works, which were becoming more and more cynical and more tended to explore the darker aspects of human nature. Artistically, American Modernists abandoned traditional literary modes, doubting if they were adequate in depicting the harsh realities of the time. They experimented with all kinds of new approaches and techniques to capture the essence of modern life. They broke up the narrative continuity and coherence by omitting the transitions, expositions, explanations and resolutions common in traditional literature so that their works were full of fragments which well suited/ reflected/ vividly presented a picture of the modern world, a world that was fragmented. Instead of directly stating their themes, they endeavored to have them implied so as to create a sense of uncertainty, the kind of sense the modern world evoked. In this aspect, two American modernist writers are worth special mentioning. They are T. S. Eliot (1888–1965) and Gertrude Stein. T. S. Eliot's *The Waste Land* (1922) is considered to be a "monument of modernist innovation." It is composed with a fragmented structure without an obvious central, unifying narrative, a reflection of the Western Culture, decayed and fragmented, a spiritual waste land. Gertrude Stein, a trail-blazing modernist, experimented with automatic writing and other modes of sentence structure as a means of rebellion. Her abstract writings have been compared to her friend Pablo Picasso's Cubist paintings, fragmentary and multi-perspective. William Faulkner's *The Sound and the Fury* (1929) is another good example of modernist novel.

The works of American modernist writers covered a wide variety of themes concerning race relations, gender roles, sexuality, and so on. Affected by the trauma of the First World War or disillusioned with their war experience, many American modernist writers explored the psychological and spiritual wounds caused by the war. The economic crisis in America at the beginning of the 1930s was also the theme of their works. Another theme was the loss of self and need for self-definition.

Other important American modernist writers include Ezra Pound (1885–1972),

Eugene O'Neill (1888–1953), William Carlos Williams (1883–1963), Wallace Stevens (1879–1955), F. Scott Fitzgerald (1896–1940), Ernest Hemingway (1899–1961) and William Faulkner (1897–1962). Though largely a romantic poet, Walt Whitman is sometimes regarded as a pioneer of American modernist movement. Black writers also made a breakthrough in literature in American modernist movement.

Terms of Modernist Literature

Imagism Imagism was a poetic movement launched in England and America in the early 20th-century, lasting from 1909 to 1917. It was the first organized Modernist English language literary movement and the prelude to the American literary modernist movement. It was a revolt against the sentimentality and discursiveness typical of much Romantic and Victorian poetry. Short-lived as it was, it marked, in T. S. Eliot's words, "the starting-point of modern poetry."

The founder of the theory of imagism was T. E. Hulme (1883–1917), an English critic and poet. The most important influences on his thought were Bergson and, later, Wilhelm Worringer (1881–1965), German art historian and critic. Hulme founded the Poets' Club in London and had his two poems published in 1909 by the Club. They were known as the first Imagist poems. Hulme advocated the use of free verse with an attempt to reform the contemporary poetry through it. In 1908, Hulme delivered his paper *A Lecture on Modern Poetry* to the club, in which he stated his ideas about modern poetry. In 1909, Hulme left the Poets' Club and started meeting with other poets in a new group. One prominent member of this Imagist group was F. S. Flint (1885–1960), an English poet and critic, and a champion of free verse and modern French poetry. In April 1909, the American poet Ezra Pound was introduced to the group. Later, Flint became a leading spokesman for Imagism. Theoretically, he contributed a lot to the later Imagist movement.

The March 1913 issue of *Poetry* carried an essay entitled *Imagism* written by Pound but attributed to Flint. This essay contained the statement about the poetic principles of the Imagist group. And Imagism as a movement was launched.

The principles are:

1. Direct treatment of the "thing", whether subjective or objective.

2. To use absolutely no word that does not contribute to the presentation.

3. As regarding rhythm: to compose in sequence of the musical phrase, not in sequence of the metronome.

The first principle indicates that the expression should be made as concrete as the "object" and abstractions should be avoided. Poets should resort to an image "which presents an intellectual and emotional complex in an instant of time." "Direct treatment" means avoiding the use of unnecessary words, particularly adjectives. This is a revolt against the over use of rhetoric, like, the inversion of word order, and over-use of adjectives. The second emphasizes brevity, the economy of words. That is, in Hulme's words, "absolutely accurate presentation and no verbiage." This can be seen as a reaction to the sentimentality and discursiveness typical of much Romantic and Victorian poetry. The third suggests the rejection of conventional versification, pointing out the similarity between music and poetry.

To promote the work of the Imagists, in 1914, Pound published an anthology with the title *Des Imagistes*. The book contained thirty-seven poems, including those by Richard Aldington, H.D. (Hilda Doolittle), Ezra Pound, F. S. Flint, Amy Lowell, William Carlos Williams, and James Joyce. It became one of the most important and influential English-language collections of modernist poetry.

Later, Pound left the group and went on to co-found the Vorticists with his friend, the name of which was given by him in 1913. Around this time, the American Imagist Amy Lawrence Lowell (1874–1925) moved to London. She replaced Pound as the leading figure of the movement. The Imagist movement gradually declined after Pound abandoned it. During her leadership of the movement, Amy Lowell and other Imagists expanded Imagist principles into six:

1. Direct treatment of the "thing," whether subjective or objective.
2. To use absolutely no word that does not contribute to the presentation.
3. As regarding rhythm: to compose in sequence of the musical phrase, not in sequence of the metronome.
4. Complete freedom of subject matter.
5. Free verse was encouraged along with other new rhythms.
6. Common speech language was used, and the exact word was always to be used, as opposed to the almost exact word.

The additional three principles put emphasis on the freedom in subject matter, versification and language.

Three anthologies edited by Amy Lowell, with the title *Some Imagist Poets,* were published respectively in 1915, 1916, and 1917. The 1917 anthology marked the end of Imagism as a movement.

Although the movement didn't last for a long time, it played an important role in the history of 20th-century poetry. It was to have a lasting influence on later poets and poetic movements to come, such as the Objectivist poets, the Beat generation, the Black Mountain poets, etc.

Symbolism The term "symbolism" refers to the use of symbols as means of representation or the practice of endowing a symbolic meaning or character to something. A symbol is what that represents something that is often of a more abstract nature.

One distinctive literary feature of Romanticism is the employment of symbols as an effective mode of representation. Many writers and poets in this Period favored the technique of symbolism, such as the England poets Percy Bysshe Shelley and William Blake, American novelists Nathaniel Hawthorne and Herman Melville, and American Transcendentalist writers Emerson and Henry David Thoreau, and American novelist, poet and literary theorist Edgar Allan Poe, to name only a few. As the key figures of the Romantic movement, they either used recurrent or dominating symbols, or invested symbolic meanings to objects, or systematically made use of symbolic elements in their works. This artistic practice was rooted in the Puritan tradition of typology and the theory of "correspondences" of Emanuel Swedenborg (1688–1772), a Swedish theologian. American Puritan's mode of perception was chiefly responsible for the development of American literary symbolism.

In historical criticism, symbolism denotes a loosely organized literary and artistic movement in the late 19th century. It was initiated by a group of French poets, later, it spread to other areas like painting and the theatre. In literature, the beginning of symbolism was marked by the publication of *Les Fleurs du mal* (*The Flowers of Evil*, 1857) by Charles Baudelaire (1821–1867), a French poet, essayist and art critic. Baudelaire was a follower of the American poet Edgar Allan Poe. He saw in him a precursor. His translation of Poe's works provided an initial impetus for the Symbolist movement. Another important influence Baudelaire received came from the ancient theory of correspondences holding that the human mind is correspondent with the outer world, so is the material world with the spiritual world. Other three influential French poets are Stéphane Mallarmé (1842–1898), Paul Verlaine (1844–1896), and Arthur Rimbaud (1854–1891). They contributed a lot to the development of French Symbolism in terms of its aesthetics, its goal, and so on.

Symbolism was largely a reaction against naturalism and realism, which were anti-idealistic styles seeking to represent reality with particularity, and to celebrate the humble and the ordinary instead of the ideal. In contrast, symbolism was in favor of spirituality and the ideal. The symbolist poets upheld the doctrine of "art for art's sake" inherited from Parnassianism, a French literary style between romanticism and symbolism. They believed in the supremacy of art over all other means of expression or knowledge. They held that art should represent absolute truths and the best way to do that was through indirect, suggestive and metaphorical means, endowing particular images or objects with symbolic meaning. They also believed that there was another reality underlying the physical world. The best way to have a glimpse of the essence of this reality was through the subjective emotional responses. Thus, symbolists sought to represent individual emotional experience or describe the fleeting, immediate sensations of man's inner life and experience by using private metaphors or symbols, uniquely identifiable with the individual poet, so as to convey the state of the poet's mind and give some hint to the reality.

In technique, the symbolist poets were inclined to the use of free verse as a resort to escape rigid metrical patterns governing the traditional poetry. Another important technique is the use of symbolic imagery. Unlike the Romantic poets whose symbols were unique and privileged objects, the symbolist poets were more extreme, investing all things with symbolic meanings. Besides, symbolist symbols were intended to evoke particular states of mind rather than primarily to describe. In terms of thematic matter, symbolists favored the themes of mysticism, mortality, and sexuality, as a revolt against the conventional poetic themes.

The French symbolist movement in poetry reached its peak around 1890 and began to decline rapidly in popularity about 1900.

As a vital part of the development of literary modernism, symbolism exerted a significant influence on European, England and American literatures in the twentieth century. This influence was specially noticeable in the Modern Period, the decades after World War I. Many of the major writers of the period had strong affinities with symbolism, including T. S. Eliot, Wallace Stevens, W. B. Yeats, Hart Crane, James Joyce, Virginia Woolf, Gertrude Stein and William Faulkner. Symbols or patterns of images, an integral component, often play a preeminent role in their works. For example, the persistent use of symbols is evident in such works as T. S. Eliot's poem *The Waste Land*, James Joyce's novel *Finnegans Wake* (1939) and William Faulkner's novel *The Sound and the Fury* (1929).

Psychological Analysis Psychological Analysis refers to literary criticism or literary theory based on the theory of psychoanalysis developed by Austrian neurologist Sigmund Freud (1856–1939) in the late 19th and early 20th centuries.

In the early decades of the nineteenth century, there emerged a literary critical approach which stressed the correlation between a work of literature and the psychology of its author. The theoretical basis of this psychological criticism was the assumption that a work of literature, including its details and form, was inextricable with its author's personality. So during the Romantic Period, literary criticism was conducted to explain and interpret a literary work by referring to the author' personality, to establish the personality of the author by referring to literary works, or to experience the subjectivity or consciousness of the author through reading his/her literary work.

Since the 1920s, a form of psychological literary criticism known as psychoanalytic criticism has been widely employed in literary criticism. The basis of this literary critical approach is the theory of psychoanalysis developed by Austrian neurologist Sigmund

Freud (1856–1939) in the late 19th and early 20th centuries. Freud used the theory for the treatment of neuroses but soon he applied it to many others fields including literature.

The core of Freud's theory is the unconsciousness. In his view, the unconscious is where the socially unacceptable ideas, wishes or desires, traumatic memories, and painful emotions are repressed. The unconscious is a force that can only be recognized through the symptom with which it expresses itself. Freud proposes that the mind is made up of the conscious mind, the ego and the unconscious mind composing the id and the superego. The id involves the instinct, libidinal and other desires, the superego means the conscience, the internalization of social norms and moral standards, and the ego functions to negotiate the conflicts between the id and the superego. Another important concept of Freud's theory is Oedipus complex. It denotes a boy's desire to sexually possess his mother, and kill his father, which is repressed in the adult's unconscious.

Freud compares artistic creation to dreams and neurotic symptoms. In his view, the creation of literature and the other arts is the vehicle of the fulfillment of wishes in the manner of imagination and fantasy because they are either denied or prohibited in reality by social norms or moral standards. The forbidden wishes are mainly sexual, that is "libidinal." They are repressed into the unconsciousness of the artist's mind by the "censor," the "internalized representative" of moral standards and social norms within each individual. They can only be fulfilled through fantasy in distorted forms which help to disguise their real motives. According to Freud, the Oedipus complex is the foundational source of all art, myth, religion, philosophy, therapy—indeed of all human culture and civilization.

Influenced by Freud, early psychoanalytic literary criticism would often treat the text as if it were a kind of dream, that is, the real or latent content of the text is repressed behind its obvious or manifest content. Critics analyze the language and symbolism, etc. of the text so as to arrive at the underlying latent content. The criticism of the author is very similar to psychoanalysis itself. Critics would treat the fictional characters as a psychological case study by referring to such Freudian concepts as Id, ego and superego, Oedipus complex, penis envy, etc. Psychoanalytic criticism provides a new perspective for reading and analyzing a literary work of art and can throw light on the sometime baffling symbols, actions, and settings in it. However, it is not without limits. A great literary work is rich in significance and it also provides aesthetic experience. It should not be primarily treated as a psychological case study.

Stream of Consciousness The term was first used by the American philosopher and psychologist William James (1842–1910) in his book *The Principles of Psychology* (1890) to describe the continuous flow of conscious and sub-conscious thoughts, feelings and impressions in the mind. It was later applied to the world of literature. With the rise of modernism in the 20th century, it became an important literary technique. Besides William James, other theoretical precursors for the birth of it were Sigmund Freud and Henri Bergson. Freud laid emphasis on the play of basic drives and instincts, which was the basis of all subjective reality and through which the outside world was perceived. Bergson's idea on psychological time and consciousness had special influence on modernist novelists who adopted the stream of consciousness technique.

As a literary technique, stream of consciousness was the product of the time. It was innovated and used as a revolt against the traditional norms regarding artistic creativity, esp. realism. The stream-of-consciousness writers, Virginia Woolf in particular, attacked the realistic writers for their over emphasis on the external world, calling them materialists. To capture the essence of the time and to present the inner state and chaos, the inner reality of the modern people, they turned to explore and expose the complex and chaotic psychic of the modern people.

Stream of consciousness is primarily a technique used in fiction. As a mode of narration, it undertakes to present the natural flow of the character's thoughts, memories, feelings, sense impressions and random associations. Stream-of-consciousness writing is usually considered as a special form of interior monologue. As a matter of fact, interior monologue and the term stream of consciousness are used interchangeably by some critics. The stream-of-consciousness novel commonly uses the narrative technique of interior monologue to present a character's thoughts directly, precisely as it occurs in his/ her mind. The author does not intervene as describer, guide, or commentator, and does not put the mental process into grammatical sentences or into a logical or coherent order. In form, a stream-of-consciousness passage appears without punctuation so that the flowing thoughts continue without being interrupted. To represent the richness, speed, and subtlety of the mind working, the writer incorporates fragments of incoherent thought, ungrammatical constructions, and free association of ideas, images, and so on.

Probably the most famous example is James Joyce's *Ulysses* (1922), a complex representation of the inner states of the characters. William Faulkner's *The Sound and the Fury* (1929), a record of the characters' fragmentary and impressionistic mental responses to events; and Virginia Woolf's *The Waves* (1931), a complex novel presenting the psychological development of the six characters and their common conscious.

Bibliography

Abrams, M. H. *A Glossary of Literary Terms, 9th Edition*. Beijing: Foreign Languages

Teaching and Research Press, 2010.

Levenson, Michael. *The Cambridge Companion to Modernism.* Shanghai: Shanghai Foreign Languages Education Press, 2000.

Bercovitch, Sacvan. *The Cambridge History of American Literature, Volume 6.* Cambridge U.K. and New York: Cambridge University Press, 2002.

Wikipedia, the free encyclopedia. http://en.wikipedia.org/wiki/Slaughterhouse-Five, 2012-08-14.

http://www.britannica.com/EBchecked/topic/290310/interior-monologue, 2012-08-12.

虞建华 . 美国文学的第二次繁荣 . 上海：上海外语教育出版社，2007.

李维屏 . 英美现代主义文学概观 . 上海：上海外语教育出版社，1998.

常耀信 . 美国文学简史 . 天津：南开大学出版社，1995.

胡荫桐 . 美国文学教程 . 天津：南开大学出版社，1995.

Ezra Pound

His Life and Writing Career

His Life

Ezra Pound (1885–1972) was born in Harley, Idaho Territory, the only child of Homer Loomis Pound (1858–1942) and Isabel Weston (1860–1948). Both parents' ancestors emigrated from England in the 17th century. From 1898 until 1900 he attended the Cheltenham Military Academy, where the boys wore uniforms and taught to submit to authority. Pound thought independently and wanted to be a poet. Later he entered Hamilton College and the University of Pennsylvania, in which he studied Romance languages and literature. He received a master degree for arts in the University of Pennsylvania in 1905. In the following year, he won a fellowship for travel to Spain and Italy to prepare for his doctoral dissertation. He returned soon from Europe.

In the fall of 1907 he took a job as a teacher of Romance languages at Wabash College in Crawfordsville, Indiana. But his unconservative actions were unaccepted there. After teaching at Wabash College for two years, he was dismissed and arrived in London in august 1908 where he stayed almost continuously for 12 years. He met W. B. Yeats whom he thought was the greatest living poet. They became close friends though Yeats was senior to Pound by 28 years. Their friendship is often treated as an example of friendship between generations.

Pound was convinced that London was to be the centre of a new Renaissance. But his hopes were damaged in the waste of the First World War, and the consequent disappointment was to color the rest of his life's work. Pound married Dorothy Shakespeare in April 1914 who was introduced to him in February 1909. In 1924, he moved to Italy, during this period of voluntary exile, Pound became involved in Fascist politics, and did not return to the United States until 1945. Pound came to believe that the cause of the First World War was finance capitalism, "usury" in his word. Usury usually refers to the taking of unnecessarily high interest in loans. Anti-Semitism often used this word for the economic illness of modern society. Pound's interest in anti-Semitism was based on this monetary theory. He gave a series of lectures on economics, and made contact with politicians in the United States about education, interstate commerce and international affairs. It seemed that he was more interested in social reform than literature. Although Hemingway advised against it, on 30 January, 1933 Pound met Mussolini, the notorious figure in Fascism. During the meeting he tried to present Mussolini with a digest of his economic ideas and the Cantos. Mussolini looked through the Cantos and said it was entertaining. Later Pound told his friend that he had never met anyone who seemed to get his ideas so quickly. He broadcasted Fascist propaganda by radio and recorded hundreds of broadcasts criticizing the United States, Roosevelt, and Roosevelt's family, and sometimes he talked about his idea about literature, economics and Chinese philosophy.

In 1945, the death of Mussolini and Adolf Hitler marked the collapse of fascist world. Pound was interrogated by FBI and arrested on charges of treason. On 24 May he was transferred to the United States and was put in a steel cage without bed or communication. After several weeks, he began to break down under the strain. Medical staff moved him out of the cage and one of the psychiatrists examined him and declared Pound had symptoms of a mental breakdown. He was transferred to another place, being allowed to read. His imprisonment brought about an artistic recovery. He began to write *The Pisan Cantos*. In 1946, he was acquitted, but declared mentally ill which saved him from life imprisonment. He was moved to St. Elizabeths Hospital in Washington, D. C., where he spent the next 12 years. During his confinement, his friends, some literary figures tried to get him released. The jury of the Bollingen Prize-Library of Congress Award decided to recognize his poetic achievements rather than focus on his political interest. He was awarded the prize for *Cantos* 74–84 under the title *The Pisan Cantos* in 1948. But the award aroused a heated discussion in America and as a result it was the last time the prize was administered by the Library of Congress. After continuous appeals from his friends, such as Robert Frost and Ernest Hemingway, Pound finally won his release. Pound returned to Italy and settled in Venice, where he died, a semi-recluse, in 1972.

His Writing Career

Later in 1911, Pound, Doolittle and Aldington lived in Church Walk and worked daily in British Museum Reading Room, where he was introduced to the East Asian artistic and literary concepts that would become so essential to the imagism. Under the influence of the scholar Ernest Fenollosa's unpublished notes, Pound became interested in Japanese and Chinese poetry. Beginning in 1912, Pound was exploring a new way of making poetry in an effort to break free from the mimetic. He named this new form imagism, which derived its technique from classical Chinese poems and Japanese Haiku. The movement got rid of poetry of excessive rhetoric, overly stated images or inessential details through the direct treatment of the "thing."

On the eve of the First World War Pound found the limitation of Imagist Movement, which in his understanding was sentimentalized by Amy Lowell. Pound extended the definition of imagism to art, which began another modernist movement named Vorticism. It was an intensive art in an attempt to seek the most intense means of expression. The Vorticists published two issues of the literary magazine *BLAST*, in June 1914 and July 1915. Ezra Pound and T. S. Eliot published their works in it, but it was even shorter lived and vanished soon.

In addition to the two literature movements, Pound was also famous for his translation of ancient Chinese poems. In 1915 Pound published *Cathay*, which was an alternative name for China in English. In Pound's own words, the book for the most part was from the notes of the late Ernest Fenollosa, and the Decipherings of the professors Mori and Ariga, who make research on the Chinese Rihaku. *Cathy* consists of 19 Chinese poems, and the words are largely indebted to Chinese verses.

Pound assured that West could meet East as long as human beings shared the common ground. He introduced Chinese literature and culture to western world by translating poems from ancient poets such as Li Bai's, but his poem is said to have mistakes and distorted meanings since his translation is not based on original versions. On the other hand, Pound's translation of Chinese poems is highly praised by a lot of people, because it brings freshness to western language and literature as well. The poems themselves are good translation practices of poems between two different cultures which were originally thought untranslatable.

All his life Pound had made a lot of contributions. He was a pioneer in launching famous movement of Imagism and Vorticism. He was famous for *Cathy* which shows brilliant literary value as well as thought inspiration. Although he did not make a bestseller as *The Waste Land* (1922), *Ulysses* or *The Old Man and the Sea* (1952), works that appeal to both common people and criticism, he did help the young poets and novelists to reach their summit.

As an editor of several American literary magazines, Pound helped to discover and shape the work of contemporaries such as T. S. Eliot, James Joyce, Robert Frost, and Ernest Hemingway. Pound had blue-penciled a few of Hemingway's adjectives, and eliminated a great deal of Eliot's superfluous words in *The Waste Land*, thus T. S. Eliot dedicated his poem to Pound and called him "a better craftsman." Pound even cut a large of W. B. Yeat's vague general terms and influenced the prestigious old poet's process of modernity. Because of his help, he was jokingly called the mid-wife for new literary talent.

Analyses of and Comments on His Representative Poems

Ezra Pound's Poems

Ezra Pound was the initiator of the two literature movements: imagism and vorticism. His masterpiece *In a Station of Metro* embodies his example about creating an ideal poem and is held as a milestone in the history of American literature. In 14 words instead of 14 lines of a sonnet, the poem conveys a condensed impression once he came across in the subway station.

The Cantos (1917–1959) is a long, incomplete poem in 120 sections, each of which is a canto. The first draft of the first three Cantos was published in 1917. It occupied Pound's attention and energy in the next sixty years. Among them *The Pisan Cantos* was awarded the first Bollingen Prize in 1948. *The Cantos* is somewhat an encyclopedic epic poem and is generally considered one of the most significant works of modernist poetry in the 20th century. It is a book-length work and presents formidable difficulties to readers. It explores western civilization from the classical past through the medieval period and the Renaissance to the modern age, and prescribes remedies for its cultural ills. It has been called Ezra Pound's intellectual diary. Pound's Cantos addresses the profound human issues in history and in our time, and it is an encyclopedic masterpiece concerning themes of economics, governance, and culture and so on. *The Cantos* (1917–1959) has always been a controversial work because of the experimental nature of the writing and his idea of anti-Semitism and Confucian ideals of government. However, there is no argument that *The Cantos* is Ezra Pound's most significant contribution to world literature, in which his enduring concerns and artistic innovations are presented.

During the long period creation of *The Cantos,* Pound composed *Homage to Sextus Propertius* (1919) and *Hugh Selwyn Mauberley* (1920). *Homage to Sextus Propertius* is widely considered to be the finest Latin elegiac poet, because he wrote in a formulated couplet. A large number of readers apparently thought that the work was intended to be a literal translation of classical Roman poetry. In fact, the free-verse Homage, an ironic persona poem based on this Roman poet, is a defense against the imperialism promoted by war. *Hugh Selwyn Mauberley* is a long poem by Ezra Pound. It has been regarded as a turning point in Pound's career and after its completion Pound left from England for Italy. *Hugh Selwyn Mauberley* comprises eighteen short poems which are grouped into two sections. The first section is a biography of Ezra Pound himself. The second introduces the struggling minor poet Mauberley. Mauberley expresses Pound's self-claimed failure as a poet. Speaking of himself in the third person, Pound criticized his earlier works to pursue aesthetic goals of art for art's sake and his disillusionment on his own career. It can also be read as a wider attack upon the attitudes of society in the post-war period. The name and personality of the subject is also the reminiscent of T. S. Eliot's main character in "The Love Song of J. Alfred Prufrock" (1915).

Ezra Pound's Imagist Poetry

The fragmentation and dislocation in new age demanded new expressions in poems. Instead of traditional iambic pentameter, Ezra Pound found a new way to convey his idea of the momentary impression in the ever-changing world. As an American expatriate and critic, he made use of his knee observation and became an important figure in the early modernist movement in poetry. His life as well as his career was very controversial as some people said he was a genius in poetry and an honest man in heart but some people argued his works deserved nothing at all and he was a nation betrayal. Anyway, he was central to the development of modernist poetry in the twentieth century. Pound is the mountain there, whom you can dislike but cannot ignore.

Pound and his followers made principles for imagism in an effort to make it clearer and easier to follow:

1. Direct treatment of the "thing" whether subjective or objective.
2. To use absolutely no word that does not contribute to the presentation.
3. As regarding rhythm: to compose in the sequence of the musical phrase, not in sequence of a metronome.

The point of imagism is that it does not use images as ornaments; the image itself is the speech. In Pound's mind, the image presents an intellectual and emotional complex in an instant of time, conveying these momentary impressions. As for language, he proposed using no superfluous words, no adjectives which do not reveal something. But at the same time, he also warned people of abstractions.

The boundary of imagism and symbolism can be easily blurred, in fact, they have different points. Symbolism deals with association and allusion, while image is immediate and direct. Symbols have a fixed value but imagists' images have a variable significance. As a literary movement, imagism lasted only a few years (1909–1917). A single dominate image is hardly capable of sustaining long poems. The coverage area is narrow, which is not suitable for representing the significant society and the life subject. But imagism is widely discussed and influences the poems to come.

In a Station of the Metro (1913)

Contents Summary

This short poem consists of only two lines:

The apparition of these faces in the crowd;
Petals on a wet, black bough.

The poem can be paraphrased like this: "Several beautiful faces showing up in the crowd; / Petals on a wet, black branch." Pound's masterpiece of "In a Station of the Metro" is the embodiment of the imagism method. The process began in 1911 when he emerged from a Metro in Paris and saw suddenly a beautiful face, and then another, and then a beautiful child's face, and then another beautiful woman, which build a sharp contrast to the dark subway. The sudden emotion came out not in words but in colors. He tried all the day to find words for what this had meant to him. That evening, almost unconsciously, the single-image poem was his way out. He originally wrote a thirty-two-line Metro poem but six months later, he shortened the poem half that length, a year later he made it in two lines. Such a poem, he explained, was an attempt to record the precise instant when a thing outward and objective transformed itself into something inward and subjective in imagination.

Themes

As a typical imagist poem, it is written in free verse and approaches the things as precisely and tersely as possible without any comment or generalization. The scene is rather ideographic and pictographic with the characteristics of Chinese characters. The scene of the metro viewed at that moment by Pound juxtaposes with the natural scene with beautiful petals and black, wet bough. Though short and alone, it presents every keen feeling of the poet and enables readers to experience the same feeling many years later. He only felt that someone else would understand what he understood. Poetry transcends time and place.

One word stands out: APPARITION. The word "apparition" alone means a ghostly figure, something strange or unusual that suddenly comes into view. Pound may have seen different faces in a Paris subway in the dark and noisy surroundings, but a few faces with pure and flawless beauty suddenly catch his eyes. With the word apparition, it enables Pound to convey the expression of shock and awe once he steps into the metro station. More importantly, he might have not seen the faces clearly but only a blur. He imagined more than saw the real vision.

In the second line of the poem, one word overshadows all the rest: PETALS. Petals are one part of the blossomed flowers, which are various in shape, size, color and so on. Pound identified petals with the "faces in the crowd" which are diverse and beautiful. The humid and dark subway station is vividly described through the comparison to a wet, black bough. The realistic view changes into an envisioned imagination, but the portrayal of nature is more impressive and colorful. Readers can have a colorful picture, and feel the beauty of music through its repetition of different vowels and consonants, such as /au/ and /p/.

The apparition of these faces in the crowd;
Petals on a wet, black bough.

Literary Techniques

Imagism Obviously, it is a typical masterpiece that embodies Pound's way of interpreting on how to make a poem. The boiled down language and the intensive information reveal Pound's talent. Pound also compared his experience in Paris to a painting. The scene came into his consciousness just like an artist presented his memory or imagination into a picture in mind and marked it on a piece of paper to let it last forever.

The poem is incredibly short but meaningful. It is worth noting that the number of words in the poem (fourteen) is the same as the number of lines in a sonnet. Eight words in the first and six words in the second may as well suggest an Italian sonnet. Fourteen words expressed one dominant image of petals in a wet and black bough, which brings out the impression Pound experienced at that time and place. In this sense, the poem gives the equation of the same feeling. In Pound's words, image is not an ornament but a speech.

Metaphor Pound connected the man-made subway station with the images of petals and boughs in a natural scene. The two scenes are harmoniously connected because they share something in common. Attractive faces and dark subway station form a contrast, while beautiful petals and dark boughs form a contrast. The two contrasts give people the same impact. Second, both of them are constantly moving, changing and growing. People in the subway are diversifying; similarly, no two petals will ever look exactly the same. In the comparison of the two scenes, Pound added a sense of natural beauty to the modern metropolitan, and simultaneously, he added humanity to flowers and trees.

A Pact (1913)

Contents Summary

The following is the paraphrase of the original:

I make an agreement with Walt Whitman
I dislike you for a long time
I am a child growing up
Who has a stubborn father
I am old enough to be independent
You are the person that get the new wood
Now it is time to make it a fine piece of art
We are one tree sharing the same sap and root
Let us make a deal.

A pact is "something agreed upon." In this poem, the ambivalence of Pound's response to Walt Whitman reflects his complicated feeling towards his American literary heritage. On the one hand, Pound recognized the authentic Whitman's "barbaric yawp." The self-conscious craftsmanship in him reminded him that he disliked Whitman for his crudeness and exaggeration. In his 1909 essay *What I Feel about Walt Whitman*, he expressed his distaste for Whitman's expansive self-singing struggles. He distrusted Whitman's nakedness and crudity. He considered Whitman something of an artistic barbarian, which was somewhat not in accordance with his subtle and elaborate way. On the other hand, Pound expressed his respect to Whitman, the American poetry forefather. Pound's confrontation with Walt Whitman allowed him to come to terms with a debt to his forebear Whitman, the father of free verse expressionism and the advocator of democratic spirit. Pound was aware that he also used Whitman's open and spontaneous style and he decided to make a pact with Whitman to continue his American way.

Theme of Ambivalence

The result of this mixed feeling: repelling and accepting is a curious hybrid formed in the poem "A Pact." On the whole, it registers Pound's reconciliation with Whitman in 1913. Whitman is to America "what Dante is to Italy." Whitman's democracy spirit is paralleled with Daniel's aristocracy of craftsmanship. Although he disliked Whitman, he admitted that Whitman was the forefather of American literature who broke the traditional rules and made the new way. He acknowledged the development of modernism from its foundations. However, "A grown child" who is "old enough to make friends" declares his own craftsmanship in making poems. He is mature enough to make his own way of writing. Pound declares independence and gives freer rein to his own imagination. "Now is a time for carving." Pound demanded for greater conscious techniques implied by "carving." Whitman broke the "new wood" of free verse, but the works were crude and Pound sought to refine the style, carving a finer product. At the end of the poem, Pound intended to continue Whitman's new way of expression, and carve the future of poetry in a more precise and concrete way, thus achieving a contract between himself and his predecessor.

Literary Techniques

Metaphor Pound composed this poem through a series of metaphors: "a father breaks the new wood," "a grown child carves the tree" and "two branches share one sap and one root." Pound's ambivalent attitude towards Whitman is indirectly conveyed through the metaphors. Whitman's breaking "the new wood" refers to his contribution of making free verse and singing for American democratic spirit. A grown child who now needs to carve the wood implies Pound's determination of making a piece of finer poetic art better than the forefather. "One sap and one root" suggests their common culture and literature heritage.

Contrast Contrast is also applied in this poem. The wood broken by the father is crude. In 1909, Pound in his essay "What I Feel About Walt Whitman" denounced "the older poet" in terms of his "crudity" and "barbaric yawp." So in this poem, Pound turns to be a grown child who is determined to continue the works that the father doesn't finish—to refine the wood and make it a fine piece of art. The contrast is formed through the different ways of the father and the son in composing poems.

The River-Merchant's Wife: A Letter (1917)

Contents Summary

The speaker is a young wife about sixteen years old who married at fourteen. And about their relationship we know only that they were childhood playmates in a small Chinese village. The speaker communicates indirectly to her absent husband. First, she remembers their friendly play as children "without dislike or suspicion." From the beginning of her monologue we detect nostalgia feeling not only for the time when she first met her husband, but for innocence once when her hair was still cut straight across her forehead. Their marriage originally was not a matter of personal choice. Though married, she is unhappy about the marriage for the first year. "At fifteen," she begins to love him. Through various images, she expresses her loneliness and isolation she feels when separated from her husband, who went out for a five-month business trip.

Stanza One Lines 1–6 This opening stanza of 6 lines is organized around a central image of two children. The image goes like this: the picture of a little girl with her hair cut before her forehead plays games with a boy playmate. According to the ancient Chinese culture, the mark of an unmarried woman still cut hair straight across the forehead. By saying the two children are on bamboo stilts playing with blue plums, it means that the man and the woman grow up together from childhood to adulthood. Each line contributes to a clearer understanding of the central image of a girl and a boy growing up without thinking of love. The repetition in three separate lines of the verb "playing" is to describe the happy time they spent together. The two images emphasize the natural, contented, innocent activity of children. This stanza introduces the two characters: the "I" and the "you" in the world of the poem.

Stanza Two Lines 7–10 The central image of this stanza is the newly marriage between the young husband and wife. "Never laughed, being bashful." In ancient China, the marriage is usually not a personal choice but a deal made by a matchmaker. Being young, the wife knows nothing about love and she is only timid to meet her man. She follows the role of being an obedient wife, lowering her head and looking at the wall.

Stanza Three Lines 11–14 The central image of this stanza is the growth of love between the young husband and wife. One year after their marriage, she starts to love her husband and be deeply involved in this relationship. The vows of the marriage ceremony, "till death do us apart," are seen in lines 12 and 13: "desired my dust to be mingled with yours" are strengthened by the triple repetition of "forever" in line 13.

Stanza Four Lines 15–18 An image of separation is expressed in these lines as the husband takes on his role as a river-merchant who travels the waters, doing his business on a distant island. The 16-year-old wife's statement of the length of his absence for already five months is expressed in line 18. Thinking of it in terms of its perilous "river of swirling eddies", she worries about the dangers of the far-away place where her husband is, and she is eager to be reunited with him. She feels worried as well as lonely. The effect of this long absence is affected by the use of the natural image of the sounds of the monkeys. Nobody answers her call of her husband but only the monkeys respond with sorrowful yells.

Stanza Five Lines 19–29 Line 20 the phrase "by the gate" maybe is the same gate they played about as children, and in her memory she sees him reluctantly leaving months ago. For her it is the scene of the beginning of his absence. How moss has grown up over the unused gate; she has been counting the days, the slow passage of time and also she is afraid her husband may leave her for another woman. She has her own fugitive feelings of betrayal. And she knows this scene well: not only is there moss growing there, but she is aware that there are different kinds of mosses, which she has not cleared away since his departure. The mosses and the worries are now too deep to clear away.

In lines 22–23 the sadness of the river-merchant's wife is again reflected back to her by the natural world, by the falling leaves and wind of autumn. The leaves, full of greenness and energy, are now falling, which conveys the feeling of loneliness and depression. The leaves are becoming "yellow" changing with the season. She grows older as the winter is coming and another year is not far away. The image of autumn leaves becomes more defined with her observation of the butterflies in the garden, for they are "paired" but she now is single. The yellow leaves and paired butterflies "hurt" her because they emphasize the pain of her realization that she is growing older, but alone, not with her husband.

Theme of Love

The whole poem portrays a girl's progressing love towards her husband and also conveys the loneliness as well as worries after his leaving home for several months. In these closing lines of the "letter" the river-merchant's wife composes, she gets out of her lonely world of sorrow to address her husband in a direct request: please let me know when and by what route you are returning, so that I can come to meet you. Her village is a suburb of Nanking and she is willing to walk to a beach several hundred miles upstream to meet her husband, so deep is the love that she is willing to close the distance between them.

Unlike western women who directly express love for their husbands, the River-Merchant's wife, an ancient Chinese woman conveys her love in a very subtle and repressed way. Only one direct statement about her love is her statement that she desires her dust be mingled with his "forever and forever and forever." Between lines, one can sense her sincere and deep love. The exotic Chinese setting of the River-Merchant's Wife calls the modern English reader's attention to the patriarchal obedience structure which has shaped and constrained the wife's voice. Some critics argue Pound's exploitation of the Western projection of sexual oppression onto the "orient."

Literary Techniques

Allusion This is one of the most delicate poems in *Cathay*. For the most part of the book, it is from the Chinese book *Rihaku*. The poem "The River-Merchant's Wife: A Letter" was originally composed by ancient Chinese poet Li Bai. Pound got the notes from the Late Ernest Fenollosa, who studied Chinese poems. Even when he was given only the barest details, he was able to get into the central consciousness of the original author. But obviously some translators including Arthur Waley were apparently very unhappy with Pound's translation. They argued Pound did not translate for the literal meaning. For the very first line Waley translated as: "Soon after I wore my hair covering my forehead." Pound's translation is as this: "While my hair was still cut straight across my forehead." But Pound's piece is a masterpiece for those who hold dynamic translation. They think Pound's is the very example that exemplified the translation of exerting the same feeling in both the original readers and the target language readers, for the same effect has been achieved. Pound's translation creates exactly this picture in the mind of a Chinese reader. Pound crossed the border of textual translation into cultural translation rather than being close to the original. Pound developed a method and a style in free verse, coupling with the Whitmanic principle of the syntactic and rhythmic integrity.

Imagism The translation of Pound's version of ancient Chinese poem serves also as an example of Pound's idea about imagism. The poem resorts to a series of images to convey the heroine's feeling towards a long leaving husband. The effect of an intense, repressed emotion is conveyed through carefully selected images: the games playing with bamboo, the plums, the mosses, the yellow leaves, the paired butterflies etc. Rather than directly say love towards the husband, she memorizes in pictures of their play at young and their marriage later as well as the days he is gone. Accidentally, the emotion of the woman coincidences with the aim of imagists: a precise, objective rendering.

Pound got his inspiration from Fenollosa's notes, the "ideogrammic method." It is the Chinese principle of poetic and metaphysical parallelism at work. The exotic way of composing poems inspires the practitioners in the modern and contemporary periods and imports a tender, melancholic tone into English.

Bibliography

http://www.english.illinois.edu/maps/poets/m_r/pound/pound.htm, 2012-03-20.

http://en.wikipedia.org/wiki/Ezra_Pound, 2012-01-10.

Chang, Yaoxin. *A Survey of American Literature*. Tianjin: Nankai University Press, 1990.

Erkkila, Betsy. *Ezra Pound: the Contemporary Reviews*. England: Cambridge University Press, 2011.

Nadel, Ira Bruce. *The Cambridge Introduction to Ezra Pound*. Shanghai: Shanghai Foreign Language Education Press, 2008.

Wilson, Peter. *A Preface to Ezra Pound*. Beijing: Peking University Press, 2005.

Robert Frost

His Life and Writing Career

His Life

Robert Frost (1874–1963) was born in San Francisco, California. His mother was of Scottish descent, and his father descended from England. Although known for his later association with rural life, Frost grew up in the city, and published his first poem in his high school's magazine. He attended Dartmouth College for two months. Frost returned home to teach and to work at various jobs—including helping his mother teach her class of unruly boys, delivering newspapers. He did not enjoy these jobs, feeling his true calling was poetry. In 1894 he proposed marriage to Elinor Miriam White, but she wanted to finish college before they married. Frost then went on an excursion and asked for her hand again upon his return. Having graduated, she agreed, and they were married at Harvard University, where he attended liberal arts studies for two years. He did well at Harvard, but left to support his growing family. Robert's grandfather purchased a farm for Robert in Derry, New Hampshire. Robert worked the farm for nine years, writing early in the mornings and producing many of the poems that would later become famous. However, his farming proved unsuccessful and he returned to the field of education as an English teacher at New Hampshire's Pinkerton Academy from 1906 to 1911, then at the New Hampshire Normal School in Plymouth, New Hampshire. In 1912 Frost sailed with his family to Great Britain. In England he made some important acquaintances, including T. E. Hulme, and Ezra Pound. Surrounded by his peers, Frost wrote some of his best work while in England. WWI brought Frost's work to the general public's notice.

As World War I began, Frost returned to America in 1915 and returned to New Hampshire, where he launched a career of writing, teaching, and lecturing. During the years 1916–1938, Frost taught English at Amherst College, Massachusetts. His works were generally praised, but his short of concerning about social and economic problems of the 1930s depression, and his hostility toward the policies of the New Deal, annoyed some more socially orientated critics. In 1940 he bought a 5-acre plot in South Miami, Florida, naming it Pencil Pines. He spent his winters there for the rest of his life. In the five decades following the publication of *North of Boston*, Frost reaped every possible reward and honor an American poet can get. Although Frost enjoyed a great honor in his public life, his private life was shrouded with gloomy atmosphere. His wife Elinor and Robert Frost had six children but only Lesley and Irma outlived their father. Frost's wife who had heart problems throughout her life developed breast cancer in 1937 and died of heart failure in 1938. Frost was 86 when he spoke and performed a reading of his poetry at the inauguration of President John F. Kennedy on January 20, 1961. He died in Boston two years later, on January 29, 1963, of complications from prostate surgery. At the time of his death, Frost was considered a kind of unofficial poet laureate of the US. He was buried at the Old Bennington Cemetery in Bennington, Vermont. His epitaph quotes a line from one of his poems: "I had a lover's quarrel with the world."

His Writing Career

In 1894, Frost sold his first poem,"My Butterfly: An Elegy" for $15. Later, he published nine books of poems. *A Boy's Will* (1913) was his first poetry book and *North of Boston* (1914) the second volume was published a year later. When he was forty, he marked his talent in poetry. His masterful poems include "The Witch of Coös," "Home Burial," "A Servant to Servants," "Directive," "Neither Out Too Far Nor In Too Deep," "Acquainted with the Night," "After Apple Picking," "Mending Wall," "The Most of It," "An Old Man's Winter Night," "Departmental," "A Considerable Speck," "Stopping by the Woods on a Snowy Evening" and "The Road Not Taken."

A popular and often-quoted poet, Frost received more than forty honorary degrees from different colleges and universities including Harvard, Oxford and Cambridge. He also was a recipient of four Pulitzer Prizes for Poetry and a poet that read his poem at the Presidential Inauguration Ceremony. He was the unofficial poet laureate of America. Robert Frost was generally regarded as the poet of the countryside with philosophic understanding of life and the surroundings. He was more like an old gentleman farmer concerned about folksy rural settings. Warmly received during his lifetime, Robert Frost still enchanted readers today.

Analyses of and Comments on His Representative Poems

Robert Frost's Poems

Frost's poems can be sorted into four kinds. The first is dramatic poetry, such as

"A Servant to Servants," "The Death of a Hired Man," "Home Burial." The poetry that simply expresses emotions is actually lyric poetry. Dramatic poetry also involves emotion but it is more of a narrative poem telling a story of a person in a specific situation. Frost's dramatic poetry is based on the background of New England farms, fields and forests; the language is everyday spoken language, the poem's characters are the people around normal life. The second class of poetry is meditative poetry. He had such poems as "The Road Not Taken," "Mending Wall," "Birches," "Stopping by Woods on a Snowy Evening." They describe a scene of nature or an event in people's lives at the beginning, and then the scene of nature or event in the life become symbols, which draw out the philosophic thinking about the significance of life. The third type is satirical poetry such as "Departmental," "A Considerable Speck." He borrowed some nature scenes, especially certain animals or insects which he made comments on, and ultimately pointed out problems in human life. His criticism of some of the shortcomings in the social life and people's behavior is not direct, but hidden between the lines with ironically spicy sense of humor. His forth type of poetry is philosophical poems such as "Design," "Fire and Ice," "Nothing Gold Can Stay" and "Once by the Pacific." There are many similarities between his philosophical poetry and his meditative poems. They describe the scene or event, and then deduce from the scene to further thinking. But there exist differences. Philosophical poems generally are shorter and they involve more abstract concepts. The tone of philosophical poems is both caustic and pessimistic.

Frost's Natural and Pastoral Poetry

Robert Frost was highly regarded for his realistic depictions of rural life in New England in the early twentieth century. His images are often woods, stars, houses, brooks which are usually taken from everyday life. It seemed he was very positively predisposed toward his surroundings—particularly toward nature. By using seemingly simple direct and natural symbols, he actually suggested complicated social and philosophical themes. His poems resist easy interpretation, as if they were to fool the innocent readers. In fact, he was likely to choose traditional forms for his poem, but the themes of his poems are mostly modern. He didn't try to create anything new to reform poetic forms, but he combined new content with old forms of expression in his own ways. His fluency and creative thinking on the everyday things or phenomena leave readers with great impression.

His poetry concerns New England's nature. He saw nature as a collection of analogy and symbols, so his concern with nature reflected deep moral uncertainties. His choice at normal life may reveal a deep philosophical thinking. However, there is a difference between the way a European perceives nature and the way Frost did. Europeans think of the civilization of nature by human's working. The poems are tinged with history and allusions and the poets are only the witnesses, whereas Frost treated nature as his equal, free from references, neither past nor future, neither hostile nor hospitable.

The Road Not Taken (1916)

Contents Summary

"The Road Not Taken" was published in 1916 in the collection *Mountain Interval*. The following is the paraphrase of the original:

One road split into two in a yellow wood.
I'm sorry I could not travel both at the same time
As a travel, I stood there for a long time
And looked down as far as I could
But I just saw the road bent in the bush

It seemed the second choice was as good as the first one
Maybe it had better scene
Because it was grassy and it invited people to walk on
Even though both tracks seemed to have had about the same number of people
Passing there and had been worn about the same.

Both of the roads had not been used in the morning
Because no steps had trodden in the leaves.
I might keep the first one another day
But I know one road may lead to another road
I doubt whether I could ever come back to where I started

Recalls the road taken and not taken, I signed.
Many, many years later
One road split into two and I took the one less travelled by
And that has made all the difference to my life, to make the person I am today.

The poem begins when the poet is walking in a wood in late autumn at a fork in the road. And he stands looking as far down each one as he can see. He would like to try out both, but doubts he can do that; therefore he continues to look down the roads for a long time trying to make his decision about which road to take. Actually, it is concerned with the important decisions people must make in life. He must give up one desirable thing in order to possess the other. Stanza Two: After the judgment and hesitation, the traveler makes up his mind to take the road which looks grassy and wants wear. This is often believed to be the symbol of the poet's choice of a solitary life—taking poetry writing as his life profession. But then he goes on to say that they actually are very similarly worn. The second one that he takes seems less traveled, but as he thinks about it, he realizes that they are "really about the same." Not exactly that same but only "about the same." This stanza reveals the poem's meditation upon choices. Stanza Three: The third stanza continues with the cogitation about the possible differences between the two roads. The two roads are equally pretty. For the less travelled road, he has noticed that the leaves have freshly fallen on it and has not been walked on. But the poet feels painful for abandoning the other. Then again he claims that maybe he would come back and also walk the first one sometime, but he doubts he would be able to. He is quite aware that his intention of "next choice" will be nothing than an empty promise. Because in life one thing leads to another and time is short. Stanza Four: the poet is imagining many years later when he will be recalling the choice he has made today, he would respond with nothing else but a sigh, for it would be too hard for anyone, after many more experiences in life, to make any comment on the choice made early in life.

Themes

It is the first poem in the volume and is printed in italics. The title is often mistakenly given as "The Road Less Traveled" from the line: "I took the one less traveled by." It has been one of the most analyzed, quoted, anthologized poems in American poetry. The poem has two recognized interpretations; one is a more traditional interpretation, while the other is more ironic. Frost himself warned readers to be careful of the tricky poem.

Dilemma in Choices As a more traditional interpretation, it goes like this. In a situation of nature, the poet actually reveals a significant and philosophic contemplation of dilemma in making choices. It somewhat embodies the existentialism proposed by Paul Sartre (1905–1980). One has the choices in life and he is free to choose, but he has to be responsible for what he has chosen. He has options, but when he takes one, he will have to give up others. The result will be different. Life is one-way journey; thus, you cannot go back.

The commonly suggested theme will be: the poem put forwards the tough choices people need to make when traveling the road of life. It shows the difficulty of making choices in life and calls for courage to make the untraditional choice. To some extent, it is an ode of individualism and nonconformism.

Equality in Different Choices The second interpretation will be a little bit satirical. Frost intended the poem as a gentle jab at his great friend and fellow poet Edward Thomas. Frost used to take walks with him through the forest while Thomas always complained at the end that they should have taken a different path and seemed amused at this certain interpretation of the poem as inspirational. The lines "I took the one less traveled by / And that has made all the difference" are ironic: the choice made little or no difference at all, which is on the contrary with the interpretation we previously view. The speaker admits in the second and third stanzas that both paths may be equally worn and equally leaf-covered, and it is only in his future recollection that he will call one road "less traveled by." It is the chosen road that makes him the man who he is. The road that will be chosen leads to the unknown, because in the poem as much he may extend his eyes to see as far the road stretches, eventually it surpasses his vision and he can never see where it is going to lead. It is the way he chooses that sets him off on his journey and decides where he is going. It may be a kind of regret or self-satisfaction. In either case, the irony lies in the distance between what the speaker has just told us about the roads' similarity and what his later claims will be.

A close reading of the poem does not moralize about choices. It simply says that choice is inevitable, and you never know what your choices will mean until you have lived it.

Literary Techniques

Traditional Form As one of Frost's most popular works, this is a narrative poem consisting of four stanzas of iambic tetrameter with four stress syllables each line. It is written in classic five-line stanzas, with the rhyme scheme of a-b-a-a-b. The rhyme is strict and masculine.

Metaphor Frost compares one thing to another when the two have similarities. A fork in the road refers to choices we have in life; which road to take refers to making decisions in life; the well-trodden road refers to common life. The grassy and wanted-wear road refers to rare and different life; a traveler, a living person.

Symbolism Frost uses concrete image to represent abstract meanings. The "yellow" color of the woods represents the light, hope, and harvest; "woods" are quiet, deserted places with no signs or people to stop and ask for directions. Similarly, people are left alone in making choices in life. "Road" is the symbol of life we choose; "morning" represents a new beginning and the endless possibilities the day ahead has to offer.

Stopping by Woods on a Snowy Evening (1922)

Contents Summary

It is a poem written in 1922 by Robert Frost, and published in 1923 in his *New Hampshire* volume. The following is the paraphrase of the original:

Whose are these woods?
I think they belong to a man in the village,
But he won't see me stop here to watch
The snow fall in the woods.

The horse that I am with must be thinking
It is odd to stop where there is no stable.
I stopped in-between the woods and the frozen lake,
On the night with no moon.

The horse shakes the bells,
As if he were to ask if I had made a mistake.
There is no other sound in the woods
Except the eerie whistle of the wind.

The woods are beautiful and dark,
But I have a commitment to keep,
And I have to travel a long time,
A long way before I have time to rest.

Stanza One: The speaker stops by woods which are far from the village. In other words, the woods are removed from the village—a world of human order. The poet is alone except for his horse. He stops by the woods of a neighbor, a man who lives in the village. The woods are filling with snow, and he simply wants to watch the scene. Stanza Two: The introduction of the foil—the little horse. Unlike the speaker, the horse, an animal that cannot reason or think, does not know why they stop here. "Queer" leads to an even lonelier scene, a kind of northern nowhere connected with the strangeness of the winter. In this second stanza the pattern is catching on to the reader, pulling him into its drowsy current. Stanza Three is heightened by the "shake" of bells, and "to ask," humorously taking the horse's point of view, tells us that the driver is awake and sane. In the second and third stanzas the poet conjectures that his horse must think him crazy to stop in a deserted spot on such a cold night. Stanza Four: The speaker's wish to go on the journey before he finally ceases to be. The last stanza is the closing lines with the repetitions. It contains the poet's statement on the beauty of the scene, but he does not linger any longer—he has a long way to go home, and things to do when he gets there. The settling down on one sleepy rhyme running against what is being said, and with the speaker's echoing his sensible self in "I have promises" and "miles to go," he almost seems to be nodding off.

Apparently, the poem is descriptive. It is dark and cold. The poet stops his sleigh by the lovely, dark woods and lingers on to watch the snow filling up the wood. He, however, realizes that he can't stay there for long because he has miles to go before he sleeps. He acknowledges the pull of obligations and the considerable distance yet to be traveled before he can rest for the night.

Some critic suggests the poem is about the temptation of death, even suicide, symbolized by the woods that are filling up with snow on the darkest evening of the year. The speaker is powerfully drawn to these woods, which are "lovely, dark and deep," and they are much more seductive to speaker than a field. He wants to lie down and let the snow cover and bury him. The third stanza, the line "Of easy wind and downy flake" is drowsy, dream-like. The recognition of the power of nature, especially of snow, obliterates the limits and boundaries of things and of himself in the real world. It is a furtive impulse toward extinction. The horse's instinctive urge for home opposes to the man's subconscious desire for death in the dark, snowy woods. The speaker says, "The woods are lovely, dark and deep," but he resists the attraction at the end in order to return to the mundane duties of daily life. Life in the sophisticated world is full of duties and tasks. Pressed by living pressure and challenged by the ambition, people are living so intensely and tiredly that the thought of rest—death is somewhat a resort from the demanding journey. Death is an attraction to many poets.

Another interpretation is that Robert Frost was writing about Santa Claus. The evidence supporting this is as follows: 1) In the second stanza, the first two lines say, "My little horse must think it queer/ To stop without a farmhouse near." It means that the horse is accustomed to stopping beside houses, so Santa could deliver his presents. 2) In the last stanza, the second and third lines say, "But I have promises to keep/ And miles to go before I sleep." The speaker says that because he knows all the little children are waiting for him and he can't disappoint them by being late.

Themes

The poem is a figurative and metaphorical summary of life. The horseman is every man of the world; the horse stands for the resources of life. Woods are sometimes a symbol for wildness, madness, the looming irrationality. The village stands for society and civilization, responsibility and sensibility. The end of the journey is the end of life; the owner of the forest is God who is never completely known to man though man thinks that he is unknown to his God. Every man is tired but he is to continue his voyage. The important aspect to his journey is that there is no end to it. After one milestone or station of rest or activity another milestone appears and thus even at the time of death, one cannot cover the whole part of this journey.

Literary Techniques

Traditional Form The poem is written in iambic tetrameter, each verse (save the last) follows a rhyming scheme of a-a-b-a with the following verse's a's rhyming with that verse's b, which is a chain rhyme. Overall, the rhyme scheme is a-a-b-a, b-b-c-b, c-c-d-c, d-d-d-d. The poet employs the drawing back rhyme, i.e. in the first stanza the third line is b, while in the second stanza the poem draws back to continue the rhyme b, it gives the poem a tone of hesitation, which shows the poet's deliberate consideration.

Personification Like Frost's other poems, this poem is also associated with the scene of nature. Nature here is full of mystery, darkness and irrationality while man is put in the bleak and chaotic landscapes of an indifferent universe. Horse is compared to a person who is more rational than the poet. In the drowsy state of the owner, he intelligently gives "a shake" to remind the owner of the danger by lingering in the woods in winter.

Contrasts Contrasts are formed in several ways. 1) The impractical poet and the practical owner of the woods. 2) The poet and his horse. The horse cannot imagine why his driver should want to stop in this inhospitable place. 3) The present natural world and the future world the speaker is heading for. 4) Life's responsibilities and the "lovely, dark, and deep" attraction that death offers.

Mending Wall (1914)

Contents Summary

The poem was published in 1914, setting in the countryside. This is Frost's typical poem: what begins in folksy straightforwardness ends in complex ambiguity. A traditional form tinges with modern theme. The poem is telling a story about the speaker and his neighbor repairing the wall that collapses in parts due to interference of nature annually. The speaker starts to question why he and his neighbor must rebuild the stone wall dividing their farms each spring. As a matter of fact, the speaker just wants to communicate with his neighbor by spending time with him and repairing the wall. They work together to repair the wall, but they don't talk to each other as they do so. The speaker tries to convince his neighbor that there is no need for the wall. The neighbor rebuilds the wall without question, quoting "Good fences make good neighbors." But Frost's narrator questions the proverb, observing that neither his apple trees nor his neighbor's pine trees are likely to disturb each other.

Themes

Barriers Between People The poem is a description of an ordinary and simple thing—repairing wall. However, behind this wall repairing, it contains the profound philosophy of life: communication between people. These implications inspire numerous interpretations and make definitive readings suspect. The first interpretation is a political one: throughout the poem, it tells us that the United States in the twentieth century is abundance in industrial prosperity, and material, but people feel the loneliness, longing for free and relaxed life. Frost thinks that the stone wall is the barrier between countries because of tradition, culture and conservative thinking. The wall doesn't need to exist. The stone wall in real life might be just an excuse not to communicate with other people, to hide the embarrassment and estrangement between people. It is the one and only way to ignore other people in a "polite way."

Protecting Privacy Some argue walls are necessary. The neighbors have different interests, different background, and different opinions about life. They wouldn't be interested in each other's topic. While coming out to walk, they save themselves from the embarrassing silence. They just pretend they don't see each other, because of the wall. This wall doesn't only exist in reality; it exists in people's minds. The collapse of the wall is not going to solve the problem. The barrier can not be removed; there is an invisible wall between the neighbors. What's more, the wall serves as a shield to protect privacy. Some sort of mystery and space sometimes is not that bad. Too much intimacy is not as good as we think. The saying "A hedge between keeps friendship green" coincides with the saying "Good fences make good neighbors."

Meaningless Modern Life The poem is the old form of Frost, that is, the description of nature in this poem. "Something there is that doesn't love a wall that sends the frozen-ground-swell under it, and spills the upper boulders in the sun." "Something" is hunters, sprites, frost and thaw of nature's invisible or supernatural power that spill the upper boulders in the sun. Still, the neighbors persist. Every spring they are going to make it out of habit or tradition. The whole task reminds us of Sisyphus, who is a figure in Greek mythology. He is condemned perpetually to push a boulder up a hill, only to have the boulder roll down again. It may lead to the understanding of Sartre's Existentialism. The individual's starting point is characterized by what has been called "the existential attitude" or a sense of disorientation and confusion in the face of an apparently meaningless or absurd world. These men push boulders back on top of the wall; just as inevitably Sisyphus pushes a boulder up a hill again and again. Hence, it may tell us the condition of modern human in the modern world. Seemingly endless choices actually give you no space to choose and the result may end as the same.

Literary Techniques

Metaphor "Mending Wall" is a metaphorical poem written in blank verse, with little rhythm from line to line. The wall is a metaphor that refers to barrier between people. The wall could be any other walls in the world: the Berlin Wall, the forbidding array of defenses between North and South Korea, which cause the originally united countries to separate. The borders or walls segregate rather than unify. In today's modern world, there is still a hidden wall between all of us. We have little tolerance because of social and religious differences. We use walls to keep enemies out, mostly for political, economic, or social reasons. Walls are used to claim power, suppress people, perhaps just to mask insecurities, flaws or weakness.

Irony Some people suggest that the title "Mending Wall" is an ironic one. From the beginning to the end, the speaker tries to confirm that fences aren't necessary. The Fence can be used for some reasons, and might be needed for some conditions, but in this poem, Frost asks and answers, "Where there are cows? But here there are no cows," stating that although fences may be necessary, there is no use of mending wall.

Bibliography

http://www.english.illinois.edu/maps/poets/a_f/frost/frost.htm, 2012-01-10.

http://en.wikipedia.org/wiki/Robert_Frost, 2012-01-23.

Frost, Robert. *The Poetry of Robert Frost: the Collected Poems, Complete and Unabridged.* New York: Henry Holt and Company, 1975.

Huang, Zongying. *A Road Less Traveled By: On the Deceptive Simplicity in the Poetry of Robert Frost.* Beijing: Peking University Press, 2000.

Poirier, Richard. *Robert Frost: the Work of Knowing.* Oxford: Oxford University Press, 1977.

Wallace Stevens

His Life and Writing Career

His Life

Wallace Stevens (1879–1955) was an American Modernist poet. He was born in Reading, Pennsylvania, October 2, 1879, and died at the age of seventy-six in Hartford, Connecticut on August 2, 1955. He was writing the poetry of modernism and recognized as a father figure in contemporary literature. At the same time he was a successful businessman, even reaching the position of vice-position of an insurance company. The seemingly two incompatible fields both witnessed his success.

Stevens' father was a prosperous lawyer who contributed a lot to the son's early education by providing their home with an extensive library and by encouraging reading. At the age of twelve Stevens began studying classics in Greek and Latin. He showed some early talents as a man of letters by reporting for the school's newspaper. Stevens attended Harvard as a special student from 1897 to 1900 but did not graduate, while he had received all of the school's honors for writing and published his poems at both the magazines of Harvard: *The Harvard Advocate* and *The Harvard Monthly*. He moved to New York City and briefly worked as a journalist. He then attended New York Law School, graduated in 1903 and was admitted to the New York bar in 1904. In the same year he met Elsie Kachel, a young woman from Reading, whom he married in 1909 over the objections of his parents. They considered her lower-class. After working for several New York law firms from 1904 to 1907, he was hired on January 13, 1908, as a lawyer for the American Bonding Company. By 1914 he had become the vice-president of the New York office of the Equitable Surety Company of St. Louis, Missouri. In 1914, under the pseudonym "Peter Parasol," he sent a group of poems under the title "Phases" to Harriet Monroe for a war poem competition for *Poetry* magazine. Stevens did not win the prize, but the poems were published by Monroe in November of that year. In 1916, his job as the vice-president was abolished as a result of mergers, he left New York City to live in Hartford to join the home office of the Hartford Accident and Indemnity, of which he became vice-president in 1934. Amazingly, Stevens managed to maintain his career in an insurance company and at the same time he presented his special talent in his poems for over twenty years. He spent his last days suffering from stomach cancer and died on August 2, 1955, at the age of 76. He was buried in Hartford's Cedar Hill Cemetery.

His Writing Career

As young, Stevens had begun to establish an identity for himself outside the world of law and business, however, his first book of poems, *Harmonium*, published in 1923 by the distinguished firm of Alfred A. Knopf when he was already forty-four. Stevens felt that the reviews of this book were not as good as he expected, and was discouraged. He wrote nothing through the 1920s, but his business career achieved steadily during 1920s. Like Frost, Stevens was relatively late in reaching his poetic maturity. His works exhibited the influence of both the English Romantics and the French symbolists, infused with the light and color of an Impressionist painting. For the next several years, Stevens focused on his business life. However, he began to publish new poems in 1930, and in the following year, Knopf published a second edition of *Harmonium*, which included fourteen new poems and left out three of the decidedly weaker ones. His major works include *Ideas of Order* (1935), *The Man with the Blue Guitar* (1937). In 1939, Stevens was sixty—an age when most poets are ready to retrospect on what they have achieved. But Stevens' best writing still lay before him. The loosely connected sequences are *Parts of a World* (1942), *Notes toward a Supreme Fiction* (1943), *Transport to Summer* (1947) and *The Auroras of Autumn* (1950). At the same time, he began to grow interested in putting his thoughts on aesthetics together in prose sentences, and his collection of essays on poetry was published as *The Necessary Angel* in 1951. *Collected Poems* (1954) and *Opus Posthumous* (1957) include his uncollected works. His reputation grew slowly, and his work was less generally known than that of Frost, or Pound. Steven's status as a major American modernist was not clearly established until near the end of his life. After he won the Pulitzer Prize in 1955, he was offered a faculty position at Harvard but he refused.

Although he made great achievement in poetry, he considered himself an outsider of the literary world, even the encounters with Robert Frost and Hemingway remained unhappy.

Analyses of and Comments on His Representative Poems

Wallace Stevens' Poems

Stevens' poems are quite often packed with special images, especially musical ones. Figurative statements are brought into play to convey subtle ideas. What's more, his poems also emphasize meaning and emotion supported by variations in rhythm and sound. Thus, his poems are considered as willfully difficult and are not easy to comprehend or paraphrase. But he was also regarded as an eminent abstractionist and a provocative thinker. In his ideas, reality was the product of the imagination as it shapes the world. Stevens considered the world and our perception of the world to be separate. To make sense of the world is to construct a worldview through an active exercise of the imagination.

Among his poems "Anecdote of the Jar" published in his collection of poems *Harmonium* was considered as his masterpiece, in which he talked about human arts or creation's superiority over wilderness in nature. He perceived in a different way when most of his peers thought ill of the modern technology and creation, which broke the harmony of nature. The same thing happened when people regarded physical beauty was inferior to spiritual beauty, he wrote the poems "Peter Quince at the Clavier" in 1915 about the sensual beauty and desire. Physical beauty trigged art and it was the permanent. Stevens' idea about beauty was different from Plato's who emphasized the spiritual love rather than the physical love. He highlighted the significance on the enjoyment of sensual emotions, delighting in depicting the world as revealed to the senses. In Stevens' poems, he talked of hedonism. In "The Emperor of Ice-Cream" written in 1922, it tells a story about people thought of sensuality when a woman is going to be buried. In this way he wanted to tell us life and appetite went on when death occurred.

Wallace Stevens' Modernist Poetry

Most of Wallace Stevens' topics were concerning the relationship between reality, poetry and imagination. Stevens considered there were two kinds of realities. One was the objective reality: the perceptions by the five senses. The other was the subjective reality: mental world dominated by imagination. He explored the notion of poetry as the supreme fusion of the creative imagination and objective reality. His theory of poetry is the theory of life. Stevens considered poetry as a mode of thinking.

What he enjoyed most was the climate, nature, the sky, the natural aspect. However, he did hold the perspective of a Romanist, but he viewed it in a different angel. He thought nature was submissive to human's creation. The world was fantastic because of human's interference.

Wallace Stevens was opposed to T.S. Eliot's pessimistic attitude. He took the initials of a new poetic lyricism. If T.S. Eliot created waste land to present the modern barren world, then Steven tried to reconstruct the meaningless world through the use of arts and imagination. In the society, art was a thread that collects everything in the world. Any society without art was unimaginable. Although the faith to God was fading, he held faith in poetry. He assumed that when people doubted about God, it was necessary to believe in something else, such as poetry, a thing created by imagination. It was the important role of the poets to point out the order and faith through arts and poems.

Stevens was very much an atheist, and his poetry has a strong atheistic undercurrent, as in "The Man with the Blue Guitar": "Poetry // Exceeding music must take the place / Of empty heaven and its hymns."

Anecdote of the Jar (1919)

Contents Summary

The following is the paraphrase of the original:

I placed a jar on the hill of Tennessee,
It was round
It made the untidy wilderness orderly
The hill became the center.

The wilderness was submissive to the jar
The jar tamed the wilderness.
The round jar was put on the ground
It was tall and like a harbor in the air

It was in charge of everywhere
Although it was gray without decoration.
It did not give life like a bird or bush
But it was unique in Tennessee.

"Anecdote of the Jar" is a poem from Wallace Stevens' first book of poetry:

Harmonium. It was first published in 1919. The poem is mainly about the relationship between nature, art and human beings. A plain and round jar is put on the top of a hill in a wild environment. According to Stevens, the basis of art comes from creative consciousness of human beings, thus the jar may serve as a controller of the slovenly wilderness. In this poem, Stevens forced the readers to feel the confusion and chaos presented between the jar and its surroundings, two of which form an analogy with a sculpture at that moment. It invites different interpretations from different perspectives ever since, ranging from a New Critical angle to a poststructuralist perspective concerning with linguistic disjunction. A feminist perspective reveals the poem concerns with male dominance over a traditionally feminized landscape. A cultural critic might find a sense of industrial imperialism.

Themes

Human Creativity Manipulates Nature The poet thinks that nature is a disordered world and only ideas can make it united as a whole. In fact, "the slovenly wilderness" is the symbol of crudity and ignorance, which indicates that the world is in a state of chaos. "Wilderness in Tennessee" is the symbol of nature. The jar is the design of a created object embodying a human, cultural purpose. Being put on the top of a hill, it gives a sense of human purpose through nature. "The wilderness rose up to it, / And sprawled around." The jar is controlling the outside, the wilderness, and compels a "surrounding."

The jar does not have life as animals or has the power as a king, but it has its unique specialty, which overshadows other ordinary creature in nature; it tames the wilderness. "It took dominion everywhere." While as a piece of beautiful and irreplaceable art work, it also represents imaginative creativity and makes the slovenly wilderness orderly. Here, Steven is less interested in describing the objects presented than the imaginative ideas played out between them. What's more, a poet should find beauty and pleasure and meaning in the chaotic world and sordidness of reality.

Some compare the poem with its famous Romantic precursor—Keats, who wrote *Ode to a Grecian Urn*. Keats viewed the Grecian urn as "a friend to man" in the final stanza of the poem. He reinforced his belief that classical Greek art was idealistic and captured Greek virtues, which forms the basis of the poem. There is paradoxical relationship between the poem's world and reality. While this poem of Wallace Stevens concerns the relationship with man's creation and nature in a different way, the jar is placed in a strange environment and divorced from its practical function. The jar becomes the object of imaginative creation of man which surpasses nature. More is emphasized on the object itself. The sense of an object as an event rather than a thing of sense characterizes as a modern poem.

Human Creativity and Nature Work upon Each Other Some scholars notice something peculiar in this poem. Generally speaking, a jar contains what is inside it. However, the jar "contains" what is outside of it, because civilization, or art created by man, is composed within the jar. In the opening stanza, Stevens mentions that the jar was round, and then he repeats that in the second stanza: it was "round upon the ground." The jar's roundness exerts a centripetal force on the "slovenly wilderness." The shape is a symbolic artifact that expresses its desire to dominate all that is senseless or shapeless or wild. The geometric feature of the jar does "contain" what is outside of it. But ironically, at the end of the poem, the jar "was gray and bare." It implies that art without the support of reality is not with life. "It did not give of bird or bush." It will not be of use to a bird or bush and it does not have real life as plants and birds. Emptily, it "contains" the wilderness. It becomes part of what surrounds it. The poet may suggest art also depends on reality, the physical world. We need to accept the real world as it is. The last two lines enforce this statement with two negatives. This sudden shift proves more thinking about the relationship between art and nature. Although it is higher than others, it does not mean that the jar can replace the position of the wilderness. The jar and the wilderness together knit the whole picture, and they are closely related to each other. Nature and human beings are depending on each other. Human beings as well as nature are indispensable. It, in some sense, reconsiders man's manipulation over the natural elements.

Responsibility of Artists The "I" of the poem places a tall, round jar on the top of a hill. In this sense, it may suggest the poet should shoulder the responsibility to recreate an aesthetic order in the disordered world. In T. S. Eliot's eyes, modernization and creations of human beings, altogether with the desire of man destroy the harmony of the world. The two World Wars greatly damaged the world as well as the spiritual world of man. However, Wallace Stevens placed the jar higher than other things in nature, which suggests that he holds a positive attitude upon human's creation and imagination. Civilization is originated from wildness, but it is superior to the original wildness. And equal emphasis is placed upon the gifted perceiver rather than the craftsman who made the jar. Poems are the instruments to make people see the scattered life whole again and it is artists' responsibility to reconstruct a meaningful world for the readers.

Literary Techniques

Imagism Stevens' poems are obviously marked with imagism, because the imagists hold that the most effective means is through the use of one dominant image. In this poem, Stevens made use of one dominant image—the jar, but compared with the imagists who often catch the momentary expression of the real world, Stevens' poem is pure imagination rather than the impression of momentary feeling from the real world. As the leader of imagist movement, Pound's image was often concerned with history, mythology and cultural traditions. While according to Stevens, imagism was split into two, the world of the reality and the world of imagination. What's more, Stevens' imagism is movable and dynamic.

Metaphor The poem "Anecdote of the Jar" is a metaphor for Humans' Existence in Nature. Industry and the urbanization of the early twentieth century largely changed the landscape of nature. By the 1950s and 1960s, technology formed the American way of life, because human beings stamp their sign everywhere in the world. The poem contains a modern pastoral theme to create an existence of "harmony" surrounding where man attempts to order wilderness against nature's inert state. The jar made the wilderness "no longer wild" and therefore inhabitable for humankind's pastoral vision.

Surrealism The poem also is tinged with surrealism, which is best known for its visual artworks and writings. It has the element of surprise, unexpected juxtapositions. The poet purposely puts the relatively discordant two objects together so as to create a feeling of surreal. It is strange, not like reality, like a dream. In this poem, the jar and the slovenly wilderness are placed together to produce the effect of being surreal.

The Emperor of Ice-Cream (1922)

Contents Summary

This poem was published in 1922 alluring pleasures of the senses. The story in the poem can be divided into two equal stanzas: one for the kitchen where the ice cream is being made, one for the bedroom where the corpse waits for decent covering. Faced with slovenly and sensual life in the kitchen and cold death on the bed, one must recognize the true face of life. The poem goes like this: it happened in a poor residential place in the United States. People of Latin-American ancestry live in the neighborhood and roll cigars to earn money. A muscular cigar maker was asked to make ice cream to serve the visitors who help "lay out" (arrange for decent viewing) the corpse in the bedroom. Both the symbolic kitchen stanza and the symbolic bedroom stanza end with the same line echoed by the title: "The only emperor is the emperor of ice-cream." In earlier times, the wake took place in the home of the deceased. Besides paying their last respects to the dead person, visitors often ate, drank, and told stories. In *The Emperor of Ice Cream*, the narrator tells what will happen before and during the wake. There will be the ice cream, and men from the neighborhood will bring flowers. The dresser for the dead woman lacks three glass knobs that is a symbol of luxury. The dead woman will lie in her bedroom under a bedsheet. Her bedding may be too short to cover both head and feet. Feet are the earthen root, but the sheet cannot mask them, which may suggest poverty in lifetime and finally in death. Her prone body, mocking how the wench lived, lies flat in the indignity of death. "If her horny feet protrude", those limbs protruding tell us "how cold she is, and dumb." She made beautiful embroidery the day she was alive. But now the embroidery covers her face and body but exposes her callused feet. Art is exposed as too inert in its powers to cover up death.

So a wench is dead, stretched out cold at the ice cream party. The visitors will socialize and have fun, not with mourning for the loss of a neighbor. The woman's death presents an opportunity for her acquaintances to hold a party. The pleasure they will derive from the occasion apparently matters more than the memory of the deceased woman they are supposed to be mourning. The "muscular" one is called for before "dawdling wenches." The Cigar has phallic connotations and "concupiscent curds" evokes gender issues. No doubt, the women will pay more attention to the muscular man who makes the "concupiscent curds." Appetizer is symbolized as sensuality in the ice cream. The muscular man and the ice cream represent sensual or physical pleasure. In turn, the "boys" will no doubt want to live it up with the "wenches," even if they are attending a funeral. Everyone wants to seize the day, the temporary pleasure.

Themes

The poet appears to speak from a godlike, distant, perspective even though he uses imperative mood and second-person point of view in almost all the sentences. He is the person to help "lay out" (arrange for decent viewing) the corpse in the bedroom. Stevens seems to suggest in this poem what people perceive are the concupiscent pleasures and what people should embrace is reality, namely, Death. But the verses "Let the lamp affix its beam" implies to say that let light show itself. As a seeing eye celebrates an inner light in mortal darkness, a comeback optics of imagining sunrise is reborn at sunset. Whether the narrator approves of the partying about to take place is unknown. He (or she) leaves it up to the reader to pass judgment on its propriety. It may also signify that life will continue to attach importance to the festive moods despite gruesome realities like poverty and death.

There is a peculiar phenomenon presenting in this poem. A series of commands from an unknown master of ceremonies, directing the neighbors in their funeral duties: "Call the roller of big cigars, / The muscular one, and bid him whip / In kitchen cups concupiscent curds. /. . . / / Take from the dresser ... / ... that sheet /... / And spread it so as to cover her face." The orders have echoed by the title as well as the last sentence: "The only emperor is the emperor of ice-cream." The coldness of the ice-cream may refer to the fact that life goes on although the reality is harsh. The only god of this world is the cold god of persistent life and appetite.

Literary Techniques

Symbolism The poem is full of metaphysics or exoticism. It resisted explication for some decades, perhaps because no one took the trouble to deduce its implicit meaning. Some suggest it derives from Stevens' mother's death ten years earlier. Symbolically, it may represent the bitter moment of choosing life over death, at a time when life seems particularly lonely, lustful, and sordid. It may also serve as an indictment on the superficiality and absolute materialism of Americans.

Contrast A muscular cigar maker who is making appetite in the kitchen is contrasted with the dead body of an old woman in the bedroom waiting to be buried. Life goes on along with death and misfortune. The Flowers are juxtaposed with last month's newspapers—something fresh is contrasted with something stale.

Peter Quince at the Clavier (1915)

Contents Summary

"Peter Quince at the Clavier" is a poem from Wallace Stevens' first book of poetry, *Harmonium.* The poem was first published in 1915 in the "little magazine" *Others: A Magazine of the New Verse.*

Peter Quince in the title is the director of the naive troupe of tradesmen-players in Shakespeare's *Midsummer Night's Dream* (1595). He is a comic figure. The title gives us the ironic image of Peter Quince at the delicate instrument, his rough hands attempting to play. The somewhat awkward man at his instrument wishes to find some adequate chords to communicate his desire. Later he is compared to the lust of the elders in the story of Susanna, which is told in the book of Daniel of the biblical Apocrypha. Peter Quince suggests that desire is the origin of art; beauty plays on the spirit of the perceiver just as the perceiver plays on the keys of his instrument. There is a correspondence between the dynamic of arousal and that of artistry.

The two events of the poem—Quince at the clavier and Susanna and the elders in the garden—seem to occur simultaneously. A fair Hebrew wife named Susanna was falsely accused by lecherous voyeurs. As she bathes in her garden, having sent her attendants away, the red-eyed elders are bewitched into yearning for the sight of Susanna bathing. When she makes her way back to her house, they accost her, threatening to claim that she was meeting a young man in the garden unless she agrees to have sex with them. She refuses to be blackmailed and is arrested and about to be put to death for promiscuity when a young man named Daniel interrupts the proceedings, shouting that the elders should be questioned to prevent the death of an innocent. After being separated, the two men are questioned about details (cross-examination) of what they have seen but disagree about the tree under which Susanna supposedly met her lover. The first says they were under a mastic. The second says they were under an evergreen oak tree. The great difference in size between mastic and an oak makes the elders' lie plain to all the observers. The false accusers are put to death and virtue triumphs.

Themes

The poem gives direct expression of sexual desire. But "Peter Quince" has dimensions beyond Susanna's ablutions and the elders' desire.

In this poem, a beautiful woman's humiliating encounter with lustful elders gives further meditation on the nature of beauty. And it suggests the woman's physical beauty exist forever in memory and through death in the union of body and nature: "The body dies; the body's beauty lives. / So evenings die, in their green going, / A wave, interminably flowing." The poem's Part IV contains a stunning inversion of Platonism beauty. Instead of saying that beauty is an abstract unchanging Platonic Form existing perfectly in a world separate from the five senses, or an abstract unchanging concept in the mind, the poem says that, paradoxically, "Beauty is momentary in the mind": only transient beauty in the flesh is immortal. The poem may suggest that desire is the origin of art.

Literary Techniques

Allusions Peter Quince in the title reminds us of a comic figure in Shakespeare's *Midsummer Night's Dream* who plays the instrument with his rough hands to communicate his desire. The second episode suggests the story of Susanna and two old men who attempt to rape the former when they see her bath according to the Bible. The allusions imply the poem is succinct in form but profound in meaning. It enables the content richer and more connotative, making the communication more valid.

Musical Effect Musical elements are prominent in this poem. According to Stevens, poetry is music into words, and words into music. The poem develops the theme that "music is feeling" by combining the poetic devices of alliteration, assonance, and consonance with puns on musical terms to suggest the sounds of the musical instruments mentioned, as in this passage describing the feelings of the lascivious elders:

The basses of their beings throb
In witching chords, and their thin blood
Pulse pizzicati of Hosanna.

Stevens created an excellent example of his musical imagism. There are three imagist poetic principles. 1. Direct treatment of poetic subjects. 2. Elimination of ornamental words. 3. Rhythmical composition in the sequence of the musical phrase rather than in the sequence of a "metronome." Stevens' *Peter Quince at the Clavier* is a case in point to bring music and poetry closer together. At the beginning of the first section there is tenderly reflective music. In contrast to this, there is the sudden intrusion of the bass music at the end. The throbbing and pulsing are made acute through the repetition of the b and p sounds. "Pulse pizzicati of Hosanna" is mimicking the plucking of strings to suggest sexual itch. The woman's situation is emphasized by descriptions of sounds from nature and musical instruments. In section II of the poem, Susanna's thinking is subtly expressed through a few rhymes, but it is interrupted by the crash of the cymbal and the roaring horns. In section III, the nervous rhythms and the couplets create a mincing, simpering music. "And as they whispered, the refrain / Was like a willow swept by rain..." The music of Section IV is stately and sweeping. This section also evokes a sense of the continuity underlying change, partially by the use of the series of four rhymes ending in "-ing," which creates a long delaying effect.

Color Effect In the poem, colors are also used to present the feelings. Stevens made use of color images, such as "blue-shadowed silk," "green evening," "in the green water," even the "red-eyed elders." This is a reminder that he insisted also on the analogy between poetry and painting.

In sum, certain literary techniques are used in the poem: 1) Allusions of the Bible and Shakespeare's work; 2) Musical effects in its plot and its rhetoric to build up tension; 3) Color elements naturally interwoven within the poem.

Bibliography

http://www.english.illinois.edu/maps/poets/s_z/stevens/stevens.htm, 2012-04-30.

http://en.wikipedia.org/wiki/Wallace_Stevens, 2012-05-03.

http://wenku.baidu.com/view/d560b565783e0912a2162a4f.html, 2012-05-04.

http://wenku.baidu.com/view/8cb7d56db84ae45c3b358ca7.html, 2013-03-09.

Doggett, Frank A. *Wallace Stevens: a Celebration.* Princeton: Princeton University Press, 1980.

Rehder, Robert. *The Poetry of Wallace Stevens*. London: Macmillan Press, 1988.

T. S. Eliot

His Life and Writing Career

His Life

T. S. Eliot is a shortened name for Thomas Stearns Eliot (1888–1965). Eliot was born into a middle class family from New England on September 26, 1888. His father was a successful businessman and his mother wrote poetry. His four sisters were between eleven and nineteen years older; his brother was eight years older. He was the youngest of seven children and his parents were both 44 years old when he was born. Known to family and friends as Tom, he was named after his grandfather on his mother's side Thomas Stearns. Several elements contribute to his way on literature. First, when he was a child Eliot had to overcome physical limitations and thus he had little interaction with other children; hence, he was a little bit timid and deep in thinking. Secondly, his mother Charlotte Champe Stearns, a former teacher, was an amateur poet with a taste for Emerson. Thirdly, Eliot's talent also was credited to his hometown which filled his imagination with literary vision. From 1898 to 1905, Eliot attended Smith Academy, where he studied languages included Latin, Ancient Greek, French, and German. He began to write poetry when he was 14. His first published poem *A Fable For Feasters* was written as a school exercise and was published in the *Smith Academy Record* in February 1905 and later in *The Harvard Advocate*, Harvard University's student magazine. After graduation, Eliot attended Milton Academy in Massachusetts for a preparatory year and he studied philosophy at Harvard from 1906 to 1909. He earned his bachelor's degree within three years instead of four. Eliot moved to Paris one year later and studied philosophy there. He was back at Harvard studying Indian philosophy in 1911–1914, and was awarded a scholarship to Merton College, Oxford in 1914.

In London he met his wife Vivienne Haigh-Wood, a Cambridge governess, who married him in 1915, but the marriage was not supposed to be a happy one. For her, it was to save the poet by keeping him in England, and to him, it brought the state of mind out of which came *The Waste Land.* By 1916, he had completed a PhD dissertation for Harvard on Knowledge and Experience. On June 29, 1927 Eliot converted to Anglicanism and in November he took British citizenship. He specifically identified himself as classicist in literature, royalist in politics, and Anglo-catholic in religion. By 1932 Harvard offered him a Professorship, Eliot left Vivienne in England and thought about the separation. His work *Four Quartets* led to his being awarded the Nobel Prize in Literature in 1948. On January 10, 1957, Eliot at the age of 68 married Esmé Valerie Fletcher, who was 32. Eliot died of emphysema in London on January 4, 1965 due to his heavy smoking. In accordance with Eliot's wishes, his ashes were taken to St. Michael's Church in East Coker, the village from which his ancestors had immigrated to America.

His Writing Career

T. S. Eliot settled in England for many years. There he became a schoolmaster and a bank clerk, but eventually he became the literary editor for the publishing house Faber & Faber. It paved the way later for him to become a director. He founded and edited the influential literary journal *The Criterion*, which published from October 1922 to January 1939. Eliot's goal was to make it a literary review. The first issue of the magazine included Eliot's *The Waste Land*. It received contributions from Virginia Woolf, Ezra Pound, E. M. Forster, and W. B. Yeats.

T. S. Eliot was a poet, playwright, and literary critic, and one of the most important English-language poet of his time. He had been one of the most daring innovators of twentieth-century poetry. He never compromised either with the public or indeed with language itself. Followed his belief that poetry should aim at a representation of the complexities of modern civilization in language, he was famous for his description and concern for the spiritual barrenness of the modern people in his masterpieces. *The Love Song of J. Alfred Prufrock* (1915) was followed by some of the best-known poems in the English language, including *Gerontion* (1920), *The Waste Land* (1922), *The Hollow Men* (1925), *Ash Wednesday* (1930), and *Four Quartets* (1945). Those poems were notoriously obscure in understanding for their various languages and allusions from afar. His works as well as his nationality invited a lot of arguments. He was born an American, but on June 29, 1927 Eliot converted to Anglicanism from Unitarianism, and in November that year he took British citizenship. This is the reason why both American Literature and British Literature claim T. S. Eliot as their writer.

T. S. Eliot was a spokesman of modernity. He portrayed the modern world as the waste land and the modern people as hollow men. In addition to his poetry he also wrote dramas such as *Murder in the Cathedral* (1935), *The Family Reunion* (1939), *The Cocktail Party* (1949), *The Confidential Clerk* (1954), *The Elder Statesman* (1959). Eliot also made significant contributions to literary criticism. He wrote such critic books as *The Sacred Wood* (1920), *Essays on Style and Order* (1929), *Elizabethan Essays* (1934), and *After Strange Gods* (1934). He dominated criticism in the period between two World Wars and shaped the tastes and the critical vocabulary of a generation. He insisted that poetry should be impersonal and the poet's private life and the world he lived in have nothing to do with a true understanding of his work, which strongly influenced the school of New Criticism at that time. His perspective of viewing the world and his genius and talents in conveying his idea exerted a great influence on modern literature and poets to come.

Analyses of and Comments on His Representative Poems

T. S. Eliot's Poems

The Love Song of J. Alfred Prufrock, begun in February 1910 and published in Chicago in June 1915, is the poem that made his name and also is seen as a masterpiece of the Modernist movement. He successfully portrayed a modern everyman with the method of using interior monologue. It somewhat established his fame in the literature world. *The Waste Land*, a 434-line poem published in 1922 was regarded as the representative of the modernist movement and the disillusionment of the post-war generation. It is of obscure nature with satire, prophecy and changes of speaker, location, and time. "The Waste Land" is another name for the modern world at that time. Eliot wrote that he produced the title "The Hollow Men" by combining the titles of the romance "The Hollow Land" with the poem "The Broken Men", but the title derives more from the character Kurtz in Joseph Conrad's *Heart of Darkness* who is referred to as "hollow at the core". *The Hollow Men* contains some of Eliot's most famous lines, notably its conclusion: This is the way the world ends/ Not with a bang but a whimper. *The Hollow Men* in 1925 together with *The Waste Land* in 1922 constructed his main work in the 1920s. It is concerned most with post-World War I Europe, in which the poet expressed the difficulty of hope and religious conversion.

Ash Wednesday (1930) is the first long poem written by Eliot after his 1927 conversion to Anglicanism. The poem itself is a transition in style. It deals with the aspiration to move from spiritual barrenness to hope for human salvation. But personally, Eliot regarded *Four Quartets* as his masterpiece, and it is the work that led to his being awarded the Nobel Prize in Literature in 1948 "for his outstanding, pioneer contribution to present-day poetry." *Four Quartets* is a set of four poems that were published individually over a six-year period. It consists of four long poems, each first published separately: "Burnt Norton" (1936), "East Coker" (1940), "The Dry Salvages" (1941), and "Little Gidding" (1942). They represent the meditations on man's relationship with time, the universe, and the divine. Eliot combines his Anglo-Catholicism with Eastern and Western religious and cultural traditions. Both *Ash Wednesday* and *Four Quartets* are regarded as confessional poems.

T. S. Eliot's Modernist Poetry

There is no exaggeration to say that T. S. Eliot shaped the taste and the form of the modern poems. As a talent in language, he mastered a variety of languages and knew many myths, fables and stories. Allusions are seen everywhere, which prevent people from understanding. That may partly explains the reason why his poems are notoriously difficult to comprehend. His poems are for the elites rather than the common people. In addition to the allusions, the scenes in his poems shift quickly from one to another: past to present, home to abroad. They juxtapose together to make the poem appear in the reader's mind like montage the film technique. In his poems even the dead people or the people from myth are to tell their stories and talk to the living people. It seems the poems are not organized by logic but with random thoughts. And at the same time, by using the fragmentary pieces in the poems, T. S. Eliot intended to present the mental state of modern people. In the wake of WWI, buildings as well as civilization were broken into pieces. The waste land appeared in physical world as well as mental world. People witnessed the tragedy of wars and they never knew whether they would be still living tomorrow, thus they refused to think of tomorrow and lingered in the street thinking of the past. T. S. Eliot's poetry presented the spiritual state at that time and his disillusioned view largely influenced the poets to come. They saw the world with their sorrowful eyes, thought with an empty mind and felt with sentimental heart.

The Love Song of J. Alfred Prufrock (1915)

Contents Summary

The poem is commonly known as "Prufrock." It started in 1910 and published in Chicago in 1915, describing a middle aged man Prufrock's journey one evening in an attempt to seek women. Prufrock, a modern everyman, is a kind of tragic figure caught in a sense of defeated idealism and tortured by unsatisfied desires. The poem represents his inability to live a meaningful existence in the modern world.

The title "a love song" usually reminds us of the romantic language the man uses in the courtship for a woman and more often the boy will think highly of the beauty of the girl and simultaneously boast of his strength and power. But Profrock presents his negative sides. He is neither a prophet (Lazarus) nor a tragic hero (Hamlet). He is eager for women while his cowardliness and timidity prevent him from moving forward.

He is somewhat an anti-hero of modern time who is lacking in the heroic qualities of a traditional hero such as courage, honesty, heroism and idealism.

As the poem goes like this: "Let us go then, you and I", the readers may wonder about the meaning of the pronouns "I" "us" and "you", which altogether produce a sense of uncertainty. "I" should be the speaker, of course, but "J. Alfred Prufrock" suggests no certain identity. Compared with Robert Browning's dramatic monologue, which is to explore the inner feeling of the historical characters, J. Alfred Prufrock is nobody but an invented person. To think that who are "you" in the poem and what is the relationship between "you" and "I" eventually forms the sense of "us." Some critics suggest that "you" is the implied reader whoever reads this poem, some suggest that "you" is the imagined person that Prufrock keeps in mind in order to accompany him to overcome his timidity, but others with Freudian ideas in mind argue that "you" is another aspect of the same person: their relationship is the ego and superego.

Through the random thoughts going through a person's head, the poem is psychological rather than logical. Similarly, critics dispute whether Prufrock is going somewhere during the course of the poem. Prufrock uses various outdoor images: the sky, streets, cheap restaurants and hotels and fog, which enable people to think that Prufrock is on his way to an afternoon tea. Others, however, believe that Prufrock is not physically going anywhere, but rather, is playing through it in his mind.

They will say: "How his hair is growing thin!" "But how his arms and legs are thin!" Prufrock is concerned about his hair and limbs. Collar mounting firmly to the chin and the simple pin show his concern over aging. Prufrock thinks that he has passed his prime of life and he is no more attractive and handsome, which causes his indecisiveness, but "Do I dare/ Disturb the universe?" enormously exaggerates the crippling fear. How can an ordinary court generate such a huge power to disturb the universe? It is a typical modern cultured man who is good at empty thinking while lacking in a step forward. And "there will be time, there will be time," the repetitions endlessly delay his action.

The women are no better portrayed. Women in sawdust restaurants with oyster-shells are no upper class ladies, but they are "Talking of Michelangelo", an Italian Renaissance painter, sculptor, architect, poet, and engineer who exerted an unparalleled influence on the development of Western art. Michelangelo was considered the greatest living artist in his lifetime, and ever since then he has been held to be one of the greatest artists of all time. How can the women come and go in a cheap restaurant talking of Michelangelo? It is just a way to show a pretentious artistic style or a false or exaggerated interest in art.

Themes

Indecisions and Delays Significance of the poem: the story of J. Alfred Prufrock is the one that many people can relate to their own personal feelings and desires. He is the image of an ineffectual sorrowful, tragic 20th century Western man, possibly the modern intellectual who is divided between passion and timidity, between desire and impotence. He is hesitating whether he should go to the party to meet the lady and constantly ask the question, "Do I dare." He just proposes the excuses for his delay and indecision. He even compares himself to prince Hamlet but he says he is not Hamlet, because he is not even courageous to carry out some meaningful actions.

Lack of Confidence The whole poem is presented through the interior monologue. He in fact doesn't talk about anything to an actual person in reality. He is afraid of the judgment about his appearance by other people. He continually worries that he would make a fool of himself for his bold spot, his clothes and his limbs. Because of lacking of confidence, he only sees the negative side of himself, and finally misses the possible loves and companionship.

Loneliness and Alienation Prufrock is a pitiful person whose anxiety and obsession have isolated him with the outer world. He has nobody to turn to talk about his feeling. The form of interior monologue is the suitable one for the lonely soul like him.

Literary Techniques

Metaphor The evening is compared to a patient who is etherized. Modern people are so inert that they are paralyzed bodily as well as mentally. The image of the evening is in fact the projection of Prufrock's mind. "The yellow fog" and "yellow smoke" appear in the poem. The color of yellow represents weakness and morbidity. The images of "fog" and "smoke" are characterized by passiveness and listlessness which are typical of Prufrock's existence.

Different Languages It may suggest the poet's ability in mastering different languages and simultaneously expressing his ideas more thoroughly. Or it is conveying the idea that the phenomenon is a universal one at present time.

Allusions "I know the voices dying with a dying fall" echoes Orsino's first lines in Shakespeare's *Twelfth Night*. Phrases such as, "there will be time" and "there is time" are also reminiscent of the opening line of English metaphysical poet Andrew Marvell's (1621–1678) poem. In the final section of the poem, Prufrock rejects the idea that he is Prince Hamlet.

Irony The very title of the poem can serve as a good example of irony. It is not a love song but a story of a love failure. The name is a combination of two contradictory words "prude and frock." In fact, Alfred was a great emperor in the British history, but the character here is a nobody, which adds more to the ironic effect. The images of sawdust restaurants with oyster-shells make readers feel languor and decay rather than the warmth of love. This is the first poem of importance by Eliot, one of the most memorable pieces because of its unflinching undisguised satire on the genteel society, showing the emptiness, the listlessness and the boredom of these men and women in a superb, effectively ironic style.

The Waste Land (1922)

Contents Summary

T. S. Eliot composed *The Waste Land* in the autumn of 1921, while taking a vacation in Switzerland. Before returning to London, he visited Ezra Pound at Paris and left the draft with him. Pound blue-penciled it and reduced its length which was nearly twice as long as its present form. So T. S. Eliot dedicated the poem to him. In October 1922, Eliot published the poem in *The Criterion*. The first appearance of the poem in the US was in the November 1922 issue of *The Dial* magazine.

This poem concerns the spiritual crisis of postwar Europe of the 1920s and is frequently quoted for "April is the cruelest month" and "I will show you fear in a handful of dust." The poem established T. S. Eliot's position as the leader of a whole generation of writers who were called as "Waste Land Painters" like Hemingway and Faulkner.

This 434-line modernist poem consists of 5 parts: 1) The Burial of the Dead; 2) A Game of Chess; 3) The Fire Sermon; 4) Death by Water; 5) What the Thunder Said.

In the first section, the poem begins with a description of the seasons. The paradox is there at the very beginning of the poem: April is the cruelest month. Shouldn't it be the kindest? The lovely image of lilacs in the spring is here associated with "the dead land". In spring, "memory and desire" mix. The poet becomes acutely aware of what he is missing, of what he has lost, of what has passed him by. The narrator clings to memories that would seem to suggest life in all its vibrancy and wonder: summer rain in Munich, coffee in a German park, sledding with a cousin in the days of childhood. The second stanza returns to the tone of the opening lines, describing a land of "stony rubbish"—dead tree, dry stone quite simply the "waste land" of the poem's title. Eliot used biblical language to construct a sort of dialogue between the narrator—the "son of man"—and a higher power. The former is desperately searching for some sign of life, but all he can find are dry stones, dead trees, and "a heap of broken images." There is no relief from the beating sun, and no trace of water. Suddenly Eliot switches to German, quoting directly from German composer Richard Wagner's Tristan and Isolde. In Wagner's opera, Isolde, on her way to Ireland, overhears a sailor singing this song, which brings with it ruminations of love promised and of a future of possibilities. After this digression, Eliot offers the reader "hyacinth girl". Looking upon the beloved girl, he "knew nothing"; that is to say, faced with love, beauty, and "the heart of light," he saw only "silence." From here Eliot switches abruptly to a more prosaic mode, introducing Madame Sosostris. This fortune-teller is known across Europe for her skills with Tarot cards. The narrator remembers meeting her when she had "a bad cold". Her meeting with the narrator concludes with a hasty bit of business. The final stanza of this first section of *The Waste Land* begins with the image of an "Unreal City" echoing Baudelaire's "fourmillante cite," in which a crowd of people flows over London Bridge while a "brown fog" hangs like a wintry cloud over the proceedings. The narrator sees a man he recognizes named Stetson. He cries out to him, and it appears that the two men fought together in a war. He then asks Stetson whether the corpse he planted last year in his garden has begun to sprout.

The next section, "A Game of Chess" shifts the narrator from the streets of London to a gilded drawing room, in which sits a rich lady who complains about her nerves and wonders what to do. The poem drifts again to a pub where two Cockney women gossip. Within a few stanzas, the poem has moved from the upper class to London's lower class.

The third section, "The Fire Sermon" opens with an image of a river. The narrator sits on the banks where he sees maidens sing a song of lament, one of them crying over her loss of innocence to a similarly lustful man.

"Death by Water" the fourth section of the poem describes a dead Phoenician lying in the water, perhaps the same drowned sailor of whom Madame Sosostris spoke.

The fifth section, "What the Thunder Said" is the ending, which shifts from the sea to rocks and mountains. The narrator cries for rain, and it finally comes. The thunder generates three-pronged dictum sprung from the Brihadaranyaka Upanishad: "Datta, dayadhvam, damyata": to give, to sympathize, to control. It seems to suggest the collapse of civilization, corresponding with the scene that "London bridge is falling down falling down falling down."

Themes

Death and Rebirth The epigraph in the beginning of the poem talks about the Sibyl from the Greek mythology. Sibyl was a famous prophetess. She was given the power of prophesy and a thousand year life by Apollo. She forgot to ask for eternal youth and she shrank into withered old age. At last, she preserved herself within a jar. When the boys asked her, "Sibyl, what do you want?" She answered, "I want to die." Death alone offers escape; death alone promises the end, and therefore a new beginning. Here, death and life are easily blurred. Death can spring life, and life in turn necessitates death.

The Link Between the Present and the Past While introducing the present situation, the poem puts forwards both a mythic and historical past. The past and present are juxtaposed to make the poem more squalid and lifeless. In this disjointed structure, Eliot jumped from the past and the present without clearly stating these shifts for the readers. The poem seems to suggest that modern life is chaotic and fragmented, so such kind of writing just reflects and projects this fragmentary nature of life.

The Emptiness and Sterility of Modern Life The natural scene described in the poem is dry, rocky, polluted and unfruitful. Spiritually, people no longer believe in religious values and regard Christ as the spiritual savior. In real life, people find it difficult to communicate with each other and unable to love. In fact, the First World War initiated this modern spiritual barrenness and the despair and depression of the people. The sterility and turbulence of the modern world may suggest decline of Western culture and impotence of the governments.

Literary Techniques

Dramatic Monologue and Dialogue Just like *The Love Song of J. Alfred Prufrock,* Eliot resumed to explore the possibilities of dramatic monologue. But differently, *The Waste Land* is not a single monologue like the previous one; it is made up of a wide variety of voices: monologue, dialogue or conversation between the two characters.

Various Times, Places and Languages The poem is known for its obscure nature with satire and prophecy. There are abrupt and unannounced changes of speakers, locations and times. Its elegiac but intimidating summoning up of a vast and dissonant range of places and times makes the poem obscure in understanding. But it may simultaneously suggest Eliot intended to project modernity and internationality. The poem has become a touchstone of modern literature, a poetic counterpart to James Joyce's *Ulysses*.

Allusions and Quotations The title of the poem draws its significance from the Fisher King story, which is a part of the Grail legend. As the story goes, the Fisher King sins against God, who then punishes him by making him sexually impotent. The disability of the King is reflected on his land, so that his kingdom becomes a waste land. Hence is the title. To restore the King and his land to fertility, a quest (search) is undertaken to search for the Holy Grail, the cup which is said to have been used by Jesus Christ at the Last Supper. Thus the story of the Fisher King and the quest of the Holy Grail serve as the governing myth of *The Waste Land.* Eliot used a variety of other allusions, ranging from Shakespeare to Dante, from Baudelaire to Wagner and so on. He also cited the Buddhist, folk songs and works of many anthropologists.

Bibliography

http://www.english.illinois.edu/maps/poets/a_f/eliot/eliot.htm, 2011-12-10.
http://en.wikipedia.org/wiki/T._S._Eliot, 2012-01-10.
http://www.gradesaver.com/the-waste-land/study-guide/short-summary/, 2013-02-19.
http://en.wikipedia.org/wiki/The_Hollow_Men, 2013-03-17.
http://www.nobelprize.org/nobel_prizes/literature/laureates/1948/eliot-bio.html, 2013-03-17.
https://wenku.baidu.com/view/a5a1811e6bd97f192279e9ab.html?from=search, 2018-01-14.
Chinitz, David. *A Companion to T. S. Eliot*. New Jersey: Wiley-Blackwell, 2009.
Moody, Anthony David. *The Cambridge Companion to T. S. Eliot*. Shanghai: Shanghai Foreign Language Education Press, 2000.
Tamplin, Ronald. *A Preface to T. S. Eliot*. Beijing: Peking University Press, 2005.

F. Scott Fitzgerald

His Life and Writing Career

His Life

Francis Scott Key Fitzgerald (1896–1940) is usually viewed as the spokesman of the "Jazz Age" and the "Roaring Twenties" in the American history, an epoch characterized by booming wealth, exuberance, excessive consumption as well as decadence and carelessness. Of all American writers concerned with the inventions of Modernism, F. Scott Fitzgerald was the most autobiographical. "Sometimes," Fitzgerald once said, "I don't know whether I'm real or whether I'm a character in one of my own novels." It is, in a sense, true in that many of Fitzgerald's works are vivid portraits of his and his wife's lavish lifestyle and eventual downfall as Fitzgerald descended into alcoholism and his wife, Zelda, into madness.

Fitzgerald was born in Saint Paul, Minnesota—the Mid-West, "the provinces" of America. He was the namesake and second cousin three times removed of Francis Scott Key, the author of the U.S. national anthem. His father Edward Fitzgerald (1853–1931) was an unsuccessful manufacturer of wicker furniture in Saint Paul and later dismissed from his job as a salesman in upstate New York. After that, the family went back to

Saint Paul and lived a comfortable and respectable life on his mother Mary or "Mollie" McQuillan (1860–1936)'s inheritance. Fitzgerald attended the St. Paul Academy and at the age of 13, got his first piece of writing—a detective story published in the school newspaper. At the age of 15, he was sent to the Newman School, a prestigious Catholic preparatory school in New Jersey, where he met Father Sigourney Fay, who noticed his incipient talent with the written word and encouraged him to pursue his literary ambitions. After graduating from the Newman School in 1913, Fitzgerald decided to stay in New Jersey to continue his artistic development at Princeton University. Although talented in writing, he was a failure in terms of academic performances and finally dropped out of school in 1917 to join the army. The war ended just before Fitzgerald saw combat—he actually never left the country. While stationed in Alabama, he met the most important woman in his life, Zelda Sayre, an outshining eighteen-year-old southern belle, and fell in love with her immediately. The two were engaged, but Zelda was not willing to marry him until the publication of his first novel *This Side of Paradise* (1920) was a spectacular success. The two got married eventually and a year later, their daughter (only child) Frances Scott "Scottie" Fitzgerald was born.

Young, seemingly wealthy and beautiful, the Fitzgeralds soon became literary celebrities in New York and embarked on an extravagant and reckless lifestyle that earned him a reputation as a playboy. Throughout the rest of his career, Fitzgerald supported his family financially by writing great numbers of short stories for popular publications such as *The Saturday Evening Post* and *Esquire*. In 1922, Fitzgerald published his second novel, *The Beautiful and the Damned*, which helped to cement his status as one of the great chroniclers and satirists of the culture of wealth, extravagance and ambition that emerged during the affluent 1920s—which Fitzgerald Christened "the Jazz Age." "It was an age of miracles," Fitzgerald wrote, "it was an age of art, it was an age of excess, and it was an age of satire." The public attention helped to sell Fitzgerald's stories and to make him the most highly paid magazine fiction writer of the twenties, but gradually he could hardly make ends meet because of the couple's opulent lifestyle.

In 1924, the Fitzgeralds moved to France and remained there until the end of 1926, alternating between Paris and the Riviera. In France, Fitzgerald befriended Gertrude Stein and Ernest Hemingway, whom he admired greatly. And he wrote, revised and published his masterpiece *The Great Gatsby* (1925). However, contrary to Fitzgerald's expectations, *Gatsby* was not as financially successful as his previous novels, although critics thought highly of it. From the late 1920s until his death, Fitzgerald suffered one misfortune after another—Zelda's affair with a French aviator and her mental illness, his own unsuccessful stint of screenwriting in Hollywood back in the United States and his drinking and financial problems. The Fitzgeralds returned to France in 1929, where Zelda suffered her first breakdown and Fitzgerald had to work on short stories to pay for his wife's psychiatric treatment. They returned to America and rented a house in Montgomery, Alabama. Zelda remained in and out of mental hospitals, but while she was hospitalized, she wrote *Save Me the Waltz*, an autobiographical novel, which Fitzgerald regarded as pre-empting the material that he was using in his novel-in-progress, *Tender Is the Night* (1934). Although it was his most ambitious novel, it was a commercial failure and its merits were matters of critical dispute. For several years Fitzgerald lived near Baltimore and made several failed efforts to write.

Drunk, ill, in debt, and unable to write commercial stories, Fitzgerald went to Hollywood alone in the summer of 1937 to write screen scripts. Although he managed to earn a considerable amount of money to pay off most of his debts, he was unable to save. His trips east to visit Zelda were disastrous. In California, Fitzgerald fell in love with a movie columnist, Sheilah Graham. In 1939, he began his Hollywood novel, *The Love of the Last Tycoon* (which was published posthumously and incomplete as *The Last Tycoon* in 1941) and had written more than half of a working draft when he died of a heart attack in Graham's apartment on December 21, 1940 at the age of 44. Zelda Fitzgerald perished in a fire at Highland Hospital in 1948.

F. Scott Fitzgerald died believing himself a failure. None of his works received anything more than modest commercial or critical success during his lifetime. However, since his death Fitzgerald has gained a reputation as one of the preeminent authors in the history of American literature due almost entirely to the enormous posthumous success of *The Great Gatsby*. As perhaps the quintessential American novel, as well as a definitive social history of the "Jazz Age," *The Great Gatsby* has become required reading for virtually every American high school student for the past half century, and had a transportive effect on generation after generation of readers.

His Writing Career

Literary opinion makers used to be reluctant to accord Fitzgerald full marks as a serious craftsman. His reputation as a drinker inspired the myth that he was an irresponsible writer; yet he was a painstaking reviser whose fiction went through layers of drafts. Fitzgerald's clear, lyrical, colorful, witty style evoked the emotions associated with time and place. When critics objected to Fitzgerald's concern with love and success, his response was: "But, my God! It was my material, and it was all I had to deal with." His manuscripts corroborate his conscientious craftsmanship. Even in his commercial stories, "there was one little drop of something not blood, not a tear, not my seed, but me more intimately than these, in every story, it was the extra I had."

Like most writers, Fitzgerald's thematic interests ran deeper than wider. Whether exploring the inevitability of loss and the thin line that separates failure from success, the quest for self-determination, the effects of class and money on morality, the attenuating values of the 1920s, or the dangers of dissolution and the struggle to maintain self-discipline, he rarely sought to reinvent himself to patent his imprimatur. As he insists in "One Hundred False Starts," a good writer must repeat himself: "Otherwise, one would have to confess to having no individuality at all." The chief theme of Fitzgerald's work was aspiration—the idealism he regarded as defining American character. Another major theme was mutability or loss.

Fitzgerald wrote altogether five novels in his life, including an unfinished one. As one of the earliest examples of a novel about college life, his first novel *This Side of Paradise* (1920) was accepted as the voice of the younger generation in a society increasingly oriented toward youth. He combined the traditional narrative and rhetorical gifts of a good fiction writer, it appeared, with a thoroughly modern sensibility. Perhaps the definitive novel of the "Lost Generation," it tells the story of Amory Blaine, a handsome, wealthy Princeton student who halfhearted involves himself in literary cults, "liberal" student activities and a series of empty flirtations with young women. When he finally does fall truly in love, however, the young woman rejects him for another. After serving in France during the war, Blaine returns to embark on a career in advertising. Still young, but already cynical and world-weary, he exemplifies the young men and women of the 20s, described by Fitzgerald as "a new generation grown up to find all Gods dead, all wars fought, all faiths in man shaken."

His second novel *The Beautiful and Damned* (1922) provides a portrait of the Eastern elite during the Jazz Age, exploring New York Café Society. It tells the story of Anthony Patch (a 1920s socialite and presumptive heir to a tycoon's fortune), his relationship with his wife Gloria, his service in the army, and alcoholism. As with his other novels, Fitzgerald's characters are complex, especially in their marriage and intimacy, much like how he treats intimacy in *Tender Is the Night*. The book is believed to be largely based on Fitzgerald's relationship and marriage with Zelda Fitzgerald.

With his third novel *The Great Gatsby*, Fitzgerald made a conscious departure from the writing process of his previous novels. Fitzgerald set out, as he put it, to "make something new—something extraordinary and beautiful and simple and intricately patterned." And, to achieve this, the first and most important choice he made was to drop the third-person narrator of his two previous novels. Instead of an omniscient viewpoint, there is a fictional narrator, Nick Carraway, a man who is only slightly involved in the action but who is profoundly affected by it. The structure of The Great Gatsby is compact; the style dazzling; and its images of automobiles, parties, and garbage heaps seem to capture the contradictions of a consumer society. It is *The Great Gatsby* that establishes Fitzgerald's status as one of the most important American writers.

His fourth novel *Tender Is the Night* (1934) follows the decline of a young American psychiatrist whose personal energies are sapped, and his career corroded equally by his marriage to a beautiful and wealthy patient and his own weakness of character ("character" was one of Fitzgerald's favorite concepts). As in *The Great Gatsby,* the character begins as a disciple of the work ethic and turns into a pursuer of wealth, and the American Dream accordingly turns into a nightmare. Although the novel was not sold well when it was published, it is considered now as another Fitzgerald's masterpiece, aside from *Gatsby*.

According to *Publishers Weekly*'s 1993 review of the edition reconstructed by Fitzgerald scholar Matthew J. Bruccoli, Fitzgerald's last and unfinished novel *The Love of the Last Tycoon* is "[g]enerally considered a roman a clef," inspired by the life of film producer Irving Thalberg, on whom protagonist Monroe Stahr is based. The story follows Stahr's rise to power in Hollywood, and his conflicts with rival Pat Brady, a character based on studio head Louis B. Mayer. Fitzgerald wrote the novel in a blend of first person and third-person omniscient narrative. While the story is ostensibly told by Cecelia, many scenes are narrated in which she is not present. Occasionally a scene will be presented twice, once through Cecelia and once through a third party. The revised edition of *The Love of the Last Tycoon* won the Choice Outstanding Academic Books award of 1995.

At the peak of his fame, Fitzgerald so flaunted the connection between his life and his writing that the resulting facade of self-absorption became a defining facet of his literary persona. Yet interpreting Fitzgerald's protagonists as versions of himself underestimates the amount of imaginative transformation that went into his fiction. While the autobiographical impetus behind a certain plot or motif is often easily identified, his works usually deviate from authorial actualities to serve a literary purpose. Fitzgerald was certainly the poet laureate of the Jazz Age and his way of writing about that age, and its aftermath, laid bare fundamental issues—about American and modern society and how "we" define ourselves as human beings. He was no doubt a romantic, but a romantic with a firm grip on reality, a cold, knowing eye. For Fitzgerald, the personal was the political; he saw the quality of private experience as gauge of society, a way of understanding history. That is why his fiction is an intimate disclosure of its author and his times and of ourselves, the "we" of his audience, as well.

In addition to his novels, Fitzgerald wrote many short stories that treat themes of youth and promise along with despair and age. Four collections were published in his lifetime—*Flappers and Philosophers* (1921), *Tales of the Jazz Age* (1922), *All the Sad Young Men* (1926) and *Taps at Reveille* (1935), and six after his death—*Afternoon of an Author* (1957), *Babylon Revisited and Other Stories* (1960), *The Pat Hobby Stories* (1962), *The Basil and Josephine Stories* (1973), *The Price Was High: Fifty Uncollected Stories* (1979) and *The Short Stories of F. Scott Fitzgerald* (1989). Some of his most notable stories include "The Diamond as Big as the Ritz," "The Curious Case of

Benjamin Button," "The Camel's Back," and "The Last of the Belles."

Analysis of and Comment on His Representative Novel

The Great Gatsby (1925)

Plot Summary

The Great Gatsby is a story told by Nick Carraway, a young man who has moved from the Midwest to West Egg, Long Island, seeking his fortune as a bond salesman in the summer of 1922. He rents a house in the West Egg district of Long Island, a wealthy but unfashionable area populated by the new rich, a group who have made their fortunes too recently to have established social connections and who are prone to garish displays of wealth. Nick's next-door neighbor in West Egg is a mysterious man named Jay Gatsby, who lives in a gigantic Gothic mansion and throws extravagant parties every Saturday night.

Nick is unlike the other inhabitants of West Egg—he was educated at Yale and has social connections in East Egg, a fashionable area of Long Island home to the established upper class. Nick drives out to East Egg one evening for dinner with his cousin, Daisy Buchanan, and her husband, Tom, an erstwhile classmate of Nick's at Yale. Daisy and Tom introduce Nick to Jordan Baker, a beautiful, cynical young woman with whom Nick begins a romantic relationship. Nick also learns a bit about Daisy and Tom's marriage: Jordan tells him that Tom has a lover, Myrtle Wilson, who lives in the Valley of Ashes, a gray industrial dumping ground between West Egg and New York City. Not long after this revelation, Nick travels to New York City with Tom and Myrtle. At a vulgar, gaudy party in the apartment that Tom keeps for the affair, Myrtle begins to taunt Tom about Daisy, and Tom responds by breaking her nose.

As the summer progresses, Nick eventually garners an invitation to one of Gatsby's legendary parties. He encounters Jordan Baker at the party, and they meet Gatsby himself, a surprisingly young man who affects an English accent, has a remarkable smile, and calls everyone "old sport." Gatsby asks to speak to Jordan alone, and, through Jordan, Nick later learns more about his mysterious neighbor. Gatsby tells Jordan that he knew Daisy in Louisville in 1917 and is deeply in love with her. He spends many nights staring at the green light at the end of her dock, across the bay from his mansion. Gatsby's extravagant lifestyle and wild parties are simply an attempt to impress Daisy. Gatsby now wants Nick to arrange a reunion between himself and Daisy, but he is afraid that Daisy will refuse to see him if she knows that he still loves her. Nick invites Daisy to have tea at his house, without telling her that Gatsby will also be there. After an initially awkward reunion, Gatsby and Daisy reestablish their connection. Their love rekindled, they begin an affair.

After a short time, Tom grows increasingly suspicious of his wife's relationship with Gatsby. At a luncheon at the Buchanans' house, Gatsby stares at Daisy with such undisguised passion that Tom realizes Gatsby is in love with her. Though Tom is himself involved in an extramarital affair, he is deeply outraged by the thought that his wife could be unfaithful to him. He forces the group to drive into New York City, where he confronts Gatsby in a suite at the Plaza Hotel. Tom asserts that he and Daisy have a history that Gatsby could never understand, and he announces to his wife that Gatsby is a criminal—his fortune comes from bootlegging alcohol and other illegal activities. Daisy realizes that her allegiance is to Tom, and Tom contemptuously sends her back to East Egg with Gatsby, attempting to prove that Gatsby cannot hurt him.

When Nick, Jordan, and Tom drive through the Valley of Ashes, however, they discover that Gatsby's car has struck and killed Myrtle, Tom's lover. They rush back to Long Island, where Nick learns from Gatsby that Daisy was driving the car when it struck Myrtle, but that Gatsby intends to take the blame. The action then switches back to Wilson who, distraught over his wife's death, sneaks out and goes looking for the driver who killed Myrtle. Nick retraces Wilson's journey, which placed him, by early afternoon, at Gatsby's house. Wilson murders Gatsby and then turns the gun on himself.

After Gatsby's death, Nick is left to help make arrangements for his burial. What is most perplexing, though, is that no one seems overly concerned with Gatsby's death. Daisy and Tom mysteriously leave on a trip and all the people who so eagerly attended his parties, drinking his liquor and eating his food, refuse to become involved. Even Meyer Wolfshiem, Gatsby's business partner, refuses to publicly mourn his friend's death. Only a few people attend Gatsby's funeral—Gatsby's father Henry Gatz, a few servants, the postman, and the minister at the graveside. Despite all his popularity during his lifetime, in his death, Gatsby is completely forgotten.

Nick, completely disillusioned with what he has experienced in the East, prepares to head back to the Midwest. Before leaving, he sees Tom Buchannan one last time. Their discussion reveals that Tom was the impetus behind Gatsby's death. When Wilson came to his house, he told Wilson that Gatsby owned the car that killed Myrtle. In Tom's mind, he had helped justice along. Nick, disgusted by the carelessness and cruel nature of Tom, Daisy, and those like them, leaves Tom, proud of his own integrity.

On the last night before leaving, Nick goes to Gatsby's mansion, then to the shore where Gatsby once stood, arms outstretched toward the green light. The novel ends prophetically, with Nick noting how we are all a little like Gatsby, boats moving up a river, going forward but continually feeling the pull of the past.

Themes

The Decline of the American Dream in the 1920s On the surface, *The Great Gatsby* is a story of the thwarted love between a man and a woman. The main theme of the novel, however, encompasses a much larger, less romantic scope. Though all of its action takes place over a mere few months during the summer of 1922 and is set in a circumscribed geographical area in the vicinity of Long Island, New York, *The Great Gatsby* is a highly symbolic meditation on 1920s America as a whole, in particular the disintegration of the American dream in an era of unprecedented prosperity and material excess.

Fitzgerald portrays the 1920s as an era of decayed social and moral values, evidenced in its overarching cynicism, greed, and empty pursuit of pleasure. The reckless jubilance that led to decadent parties and wild jazz music—epitomized in *The Great Gatsby* by the opulent parties that Gatsby throws every Saturday night—resulted ultimately in the corruption of the American dream, as the unrestrained desire for money and pleasure surpassed more noble goals. When World War I ended in 1918, the generation of young Americans who had fought the war became intensely disillusioned, as the brutal carnage that they had just faced made the Victorian social morality of early-twentieth-century America seem like stuffy, empty hypocrisy. The dizzying rise of the stock market in the aftermath of the war led to a sudden, sustained increase in the national wealth and a newfound materialism, as people began to spend and consume at unprecedented levels. A person from any social background could, potentially, make a fortune, but the American aristocracy—families with old wealth—scorned the newly rich industrialists and speculators. Additionally, the passage of the Eighteenth Amendment in 1919, which banned the sale of alcohol, created a thriving underworld designed to satisfy the massive demand for bootleg liquor among rich and poor alike.

Fitzgerald positions the characters of *The Great Gatsby* as emblems of these social trends. Nick and Gatsby, both of whom fought in World War I, exhibit the newfound cosmopolitanism and cynicism that resulted from the war. The various social climbers and ambitious speculators who attend Gatsby's parties evidence the greedy scramble for wealth. The clash between "old money" and "new money" manifests itself in the novel's symbolic geography: East Egg represents the established aristocracy, West Egg the self-made rich. Meyer Wolfshiem and Gatsby's fortune symbolize the rise of organized crime and bootlegging.

As Fitzgerald saw it (and as Nick explains in Chapter 9), the American dream was originally about discovery, individualism, and the pursuit of happiness. In the 1920s depicted in the novel, however, easy money and relaxed social values have corrupted this dream, especially on the East Coast. The main plotline of the novel reflects this assessment, as Gatsby's dream of loving Daisy is ruined by the difference in their respective social statuses, his resorting to crime to make enough money to impress her, and the rampant materialism that characterizes her lifestyle. Additionally, places and objects in *The Great Gatsby* have meaning only because characters instill them with meaning: the eyes of Doctor T. J. Eckleburg best exemplify this idea. In Nick's mind, the ability to create meaningful symbols constitutes a central component of the American dream, as early Americans invested their new nation with their own ideals and values.

Nick compares the green bulk of America rising from the ocean to the green light at the end of Daisy's dock. Just as Americans have given America meaning through their dreams for their own lives, Gatsby instills Daisy with a kind of idealized perfection that she neither deserves nor possesses. Gatsby's dream is ruined by the unworthiness of its object, just as the American dream in the 1920s is ruined by the unworthiness of its object—money and pleasure. Like 1920s Americans in general, fruitlessly seeking a bygone era in which their dreams had value, Gatsby longs to re-create a vanished past—his time in Louisville with Daisy—but is incapable of doing so. When his dream crumbles, all that is left for Gatsby to do is die; all Nick can do is move back to Minnesota, where American values have not decayed.

The Hollowness of the Upper Class One of the major topics explored in *The Great Gatsby* is the sociology of wealth, specifically, how the newly minted millionaires of the 1920s differ from and relate to the old aristocracy of the country's richest families. In the novel, West Egg and its denizens represent the newly rich, while East Egg and its denizens, especially Daisy and Tom, represent the old aristocracy. Fitzgerald portrays the newly rich as being vulgar, gaudy, ostentatious, and lacking in social graces and taste. Gatsby, for example, lives in a monstrously ornate mansion, wears a pink suit, drives a Rolls-Royce, and does not pick up on subtle social signals, such as the insincerity of the Sloanes' invitation to lunch. In contrast, the old aristocracy possesses grace, taste, subtlety, and elegance, epitomized by the Buchanans' tasteful home and the flowing white dresses of Daisy and Jordan Baker.

What the old aristocracy possesses is in taste, however, it seems to lack in heart, as the East Eggers prove themselves careless, inconsiderate bullies who are so used to money's ability to ease their minds that they never worry about hurting others. The Buchanans exemplify this stereotype when, at the end of the novel, they simply move to a new house far away rather than condescend to attend Gatsby's funeral. Gatsby, on the other hand, whose recent wealth derives from criminal activity, has a sincere and loyal heart, remaining outside Daisy's window until four in the morning in Chapter 7 simply to make sure that Tom does not hurt her. Ironically, Gatsby's good qualities (loyalty and love) lead to his death, as he takes the blame for killing Myrtle rather than letting Daisy be punished, and the Buchanans' bad qualities (fickleness and selfishness) allow them to remove themselves from the tragedy not only physically but psychologically.

Literary Techniques

Fitzgerald relies heavily on images to function as symbols to serve a thematic purpose. For example, the green light, which is situated at the end of Daisy's East Egg dock and barely visible from Gatsby's West Egg lawn, represents Gatsby's hopes and dreams for the future. Gatsby associates it with Daisy, and in Chapter 1 he reaches toward it in the darkness as a guiding light to lead him to his goal. Because Gatsby's quest for Daisy is broadly associated with the American dream, the green light also symbolizes that more generalized ideal. In Chapter 9, Nick compares the green light to how America, rising out of the ocean, must have looked to early settlers of the new nation.

Another symbol is the Valley of Ashes between West Egg and New York City consisting of a long stretch of desolate land created by the dumping of industrial ashes. It represents the moral and social decay that results from the uninhibited pursuit of wealth, as the rich indulge themselves with regard for nothing but their own pleasure. The Valley of Ashes also symbolizes the plight of the poor, like George Wilson, who live among the dirty ashes and lose their vitality as a result.

Instead of an omniscient viewpoint, Fitzgerald adopted a dual narrative system with a first-person narrator—Nick. Partly influenced by Joseph Conrad, this technique is able to filter action and meaning through Nick, who is at once involved with the action and profoundly affected by it. To some extent, Nick is quite like the protagonist Jay Gatsby. Both are young people from the Midwest trying to prove themselves in the East. The East, and in particular its cities, have become for them a new frontier, a neutral space in which their dreams of wealth, measureless power and mobility may perhaps be realized. And both of them have a love affair with charismatic woman that ends in disillusion: Gatsby with Daisy and Nick with Jordan. This creates a bond of sympathy between the two men. Nick is looking back on an action already completed that, as we know from the beginning, ended in disaster, some "foul dust" that "floated in the wake" of Gatsby's dreams; he is also recording how he grew to sympathize with, like and admire Gatsby. Like, however, does not mean approval, and it does not inhibit criticism. Nick has had "advantages" that Gatsby, born to poverty as James Gatz, has not had. He has a reserve, a common sense and even an incurable honesty that make him quite different from the subject of his meditations. That helps to create distance, enables him to criticize Gatsby and the high romanticism he embodies, and it makes his commentary vividly plural; Nick is, as he himself puts it, "within and without, simultaneously enchanted and repelled" by the hero he describes. The use of Nick as a narrator, in effect, enables

Fitzgerald to maintain a balance for the first time in his career between the two sides of his character. The idealist, the romantic who believed in possibility and perfectibility, and the pragmatist, the realist, convinced that life is circumscribed, nasty, brutish and short: these opposing tendencies are both allowed their full play, the drama of the narration is the tension between them. "The test of a first-rate intelligence," Fitzgerald was later to say in his autobiographical essay *The Crack-Up* "is the ability to hold two opposed ideas in the mind at the same time, and still retain the ability to function." That is precisely what he does in *The Great Gatsby*, thanks to the use of Nick Carraway as a narrator: by his own stringent standards, the book is the product not only of refined sensibility and a strenuous act of imaginative sympathy but also of "a first-rate intelligence."

As many critics have pointed out, the method Fitzgerald adopts in *The Great Gatsby* is a brilliant one. He starts the novel in the present, giving us, in the first three chapters, a glimpse of the four main locales of the novel: Daisy's house in East Egg (Chapter 1); the Valley of Ashes and New York (Chapter 2); and Gatsby's house in West Egg (Chapter 3). Having established the characters and setting in the first three chapters, he then narrates the main events of the story in Chapters 4 to 9, using Chapters 4, 6, and 7 to gradually reveal the story of Gatsby's past. The past and present come together at the end of the novel in Chapter 9.

Fitzgerald gives us the information as Nick gets it, just as we might find out information about a friend or acquaintance in real life, in bits and pieces over a period of time. Since we don't want or can't absorb much information about a character until we truly become interested in him, Fitzgerald waits to take us into the past until close to the middle of the novel. As the story moves toward its climax, we find out more and more about the central figure from Nick until we, too, are in a privileged position and can understand why Gatsby behaves as he does.

Thus the key to the structure of the novel is the combination of the first person narrative and the gradual revelation of the past as the narrator finds out more and more. The two devices work extremely effectively together, but neither would work very well alone.

Bibliography

Baym, Nina, ed. *The Norton Anthology of American Literature, Shorter Fifth Edition*. New York & London: W. W. Norton & Company, 1999: 2124-2125.

Curnutt, Kirk. *The Cambridge Introduction to F. Scott Fitzgerald*. Shanghai: Shanghai Foreign Language Education Press, 2008: 13-27, 41, 44, 53.

Fitzgerald, F. Scott. *This Side of Paradise*. New York: Dover Publications, Inc., 1996.

Gray, Richard. *A History of American Literature*. Cornwall: Blackwell Publishing Ltd., 2004: 435-440.

Gross, Dalton & Mary Jean Gross. *Understanding The Great Gatsby*. Beijing: Renmin University of China Press, 2008: 2-5, 17-25.

Oakes, Elizabeth H. *American Writers.* New York: Facts on File, Inc., 2004: 126-128.

Prigozy, Ruth, ed. *F. Scott Fitzgerald*. Cambridge: Cambridge University Press, 2002: 1-27.

http://www.biography.com/people/f-scott-fitzgerald-9296261?page=1, 2013-02-05.

http://en.wikipedia.org/wiki/F._Scott_Fitzgerald, 2013-02-05.

http://en.wikipedia.org/wiki/The_Beautiful_and_Damned, 2013-02-06.

http://en.wikipedia.org/wiki/The_Great_Gatsby, 2013-02-06.

http://en.wikipedia.org/wiki/The_Love_of_the_Last_Tycoon, 2013-02-06.

http://www.cliffsnotes.com/study_guide/literature/great-gatsby/book-summary.html, 2013-02-07.

http://www.studyworld.com/studyworld_studynotes/great_gatsby/themes.htm, 2013-02-07.

Ernest Hemingway

His Life and Writing Career

His Life

Ernest Miller Hemingway (1899–1961) was an American author and journalist. The prime of his artistic creation was between the mid-1920s and the mid-1950s, during which he produced most of his works. As a prolific writer, he published seven novels, six short story collections, and two non-fiction works in his life time, while three novels, four collections of short stories, and three non-fiction works were published posthumously, many of which are ranked among the classics of American literature. Being the spokesman for the Lost Generation, Hemingway, in his books, well captured and reflected the mood of his generation and his time. His philosophy and beliefs were embodied in the characters he portrayed known as the "Hemingway hero." He experimented with new and effective techniques and developed his unique style, influential in the 20th century and beyond. His ideas about literary creation were well summarized in his "iceberg theory." Hemingway was awarded the Pulitzer Prize for Fiction in 1953 and the Nobel Prize in Literature in 1954.

Hemingway was born on July 21, 1899, in Oak Park, Illinois. His father was a physician and his mother was a musician. His father loved outdoor sports like hunting and fishing. When he was a child, his father taught him to hunt, fish and camp in the woods and lakes, which cultivated his love for outdoor adventure. He took part in a number of sports, such as boxing, track and field, water polo, and football when he was at high school. Throughout his life, he remained a sports lover, fascinated by bullfighting, deep-sea fishing and big game hunting. This fondness had a great influence on his writing. His writing practice began as early as when he was a teenager. When he was a school boy, he took a journalism class and contributed to the school newspaper. This laid the foundation for his writing. Hemingway worked as a journalist before becoming a novelist.

After graduating from high school, he went to work for *The Kansas City Star* as a reporter. The six-month working experience as a reporter laid the foundation for his later writing style. In 1918, Hemingway was recruited as a voluntary ambulance driver working with the Red Cross. While serving in the Italian front, he was seriously wounded. This war experience was to be the basis for his novel *A Farewell to Arms* (1928) and it had a lasting effect on his life and writing as well.

Back to the United States, he worked with a commercial journal for some time and then on Sherwood Anderson's advice, he went to Paris, where he worked as a foreign correspondent for the Canadian *Toronto Star*. Paris was then the centre where many modernist writers and artists lived. In Paris, Hemingway got acquainted with such modernist writers as Gertrude Stein, James Joyce and Ezra Pound, who, among other modernist writers and artists of the 1920s, exerted an immense influence on him. Stein, the leading figure of modernism in Paris, became Hemingway's mentor. The term "Lost Generation" she used to refer to the expatriate artists and writers became popular with the publication of his first novel *The Sun Also Rises* (1926). The novel portrays the post-war expatriate generation, the so called Lost Generation. It was well received and established his reputation as an important writer and the spokesman for the post–World War I generation. Hemingway visited Spain in 1923, where for the first time, he watched/participated the fiesta and became fascinated by bullfighting. It was shortly after the fiesta when he began to write the draft of what would become *The Sun Also Rises*, which involved the fiesta as its background. Also in Spain, during the summer of 1929, Hemingway worked on his next work, *Death in the Afternoon* (1932), a non-fiction book about the ceremony and traditions of Spanish bullfighting, covering the theme of fear, death and courage. In 1933 Hemingway embarked on a 10-week journey to East Africa. This experience provided material for Hemingway's second work of nonfiction *Green Hills of Africa* (1935) as well as for the short stories "The Snows of Kilimanjaro" and "The Short Happy Life of Francis Macomber." On his return from abroad, in early

1934, he began to work on *Green Hills of Africa*, which was published in 1935.

In 1936, the Spanish Civil War broke out. It was fought from 1936 to 1939 between the Republicans and the Nationalists. In 1937 Hemingway went to Spain to work as a correspondent for the North American Newspaper Alliance (NANA). What he observed while reporting on the war provided material for his novel *For Whom the Bell Tolls* (1940). The novel tells a story about a young American, Robert Jordan, in the International Brigades attached to a republican guerrilla unit, fighting heroically for the Republicans in the Spanish Civil War. It was an immediate success. It was sold half a million copies within months and was nominated for a Pulitzer Prize. As an important novel in ten years, it successfully re-established Hemingway's literary reputation. It is regarded as one of Hemingway's best works. Also in 1937 while he was in Spain, his novel *To Have and Have Not* was published. Like *The Torrents of Spring* (1926), it is also set in the United States. It is a social commentary on the 1930s.

In 1946, Hemingway began working on *The Garden of Eden* (1986), his second posthumously published novel. He worked on it for 15 years. In this novel, Hemingway explores the male-female relationships and the reversal of gender roles. In 1950, *Across the River and into the Trees* came out. It was inspired by his platonic love affair with the then 19-year-old girl he fell in love with while travelling in Europe in 1948. The book met with negative reviews. Critics began to doubt his literary talent. To answer their doubt, the following year, Hemingway wrote the draft of *The Old Man and the Sea* (1952) in eight weeks. Published in 1952, it turned out to be his last major novel. It was well received both by the reading public and the critics. It reached five and a half million people when published in *Life* magazine, which sold 5,318,650 copies within 48 hours. The novel not only restored his reputation but also made him internationally famous. It was awarded the Pulitzer Prize for Fiction in 1953 and contributed to the awarding of the Nobel Prize in Literature to Hemingway in 1954. In 1957, Hemingway began to work on *A Moveable Feast* and finished it in 1959. It is a set of memoirs about his years in Europe, especially in Paris, when he was a young writer in the American expatriate circle of writers in the 1920s. The book was published posthumously in 1964. On July 2, 1961, Hemingway committed suicide.

His Writing Career

Hemingway was a very productive writer with distinguishing mastery of modern art. His major works include *The Sun Also Rises* (1926), *A Farewell to Arms* (1929), *For Whom the Bell Tolls* (1940) and *The Old Man and the Sea* (1951). When he was an apprentice in literature, he took such established writers as Anderson as his mentors. *Three Stories and Ten Poems* (1923), his first published work and also his first short story collection, is a good example of Anderson's influence both in theme and style. His first novel. *The Torrents of Spring* (1926) is a parody of Anderson's style.

In Our Time (1925), Hemingway's first collection of short stories, is of great importance in his writing career. Its publication earned him a place among the most promising American writers of the period. And it is in this book that Hemingway invented a recurrent semi-autobiographical character Nick Adams, established the primary themes resonant in his later stories and novels and almost formed a distinctive style of his own. The book was first published in Paris in 1924 with the title *In Our Time*. The 1925 volume contains several well-known stories, including the Nick Adams stories, stories with Nick Adams as the protagonist mainly about his initiation and adolescence. They are "Indian Camp," "The Doctor and the Doctor's Wife," "The End of Something," "The Three-Day Blow," "The Battler," and "Big Two-Hearted River." and so on. Nick Adams was Hemingway's semi-autobiographical character who appeared repeatedly in his later stories and novels. The first story with Nick Adams as the protagonist was *Indian Camp*, one of Hemingway's greatest short stories, first published in 1924 in a literary magazine in Paris and republished in *In Our Time*. Nick Adams was the initial prototype/ a character type of Hemingway hero. In "Indian Camp," an initiation story, Nick Adams is exposed to childbirth and to violent death—an experience that causes young Nick to face the grisly reality and learn to live in grace under pressure. In the last story of the collection, "The Big-Two Hearted River," Nick Adams is once more confronted with the issues of life and death and endeavors to cope with them. The world in which Nick Adams grows up is one of violence, disorder and death. His physical wound in the war results in his psychological and emotional wound, he turns to nature for solace and learns to cope with them with grace and dignity. Starting with Nick Adams, this type of Hemingway hero dominates almost all of Hemingway's later stories and novels. It appears not only in such collections as *Men without Women* (1927) and *Winner Take Nothing* (1933) but also in such novels as *The Sun Also Rises* (1926), *A Farewell to Arms* (1928), *For Whom the Bell Tolls* (1940) and *The Old Man and the Sea* (1952). Jake Barnes, the protagonist of *The Sun Also Rises* suffers from the physical impotence caused by the war. Caught in a world of violence, disorder and meaninglessness, he can do nothing but rely on himself and combat against fate with heroism. Likewise, the protagonist of *A Farewell to Arms,* Frederic Henry, thrusts into a world of killing, death and chaos, fights on his own against odds with grace under pressure. Both Jake Barnes and Frederic Henry have war experiences and both are disillusioned at the war and the world. The horrible reality alienates them from the society and makes them turn inwardly for strength and fight a solitary fight against a hostile force. Robert Jordan in *For Whom the Bell Tolls* (1940), too, fights fiercely a battle with the slim chance of winning it. Unlike Jake Barnes and Frederic Henry, he is not fighting single-handedly but he is fighting for a cause—democracy. Hemingway hero is presented at its fullest in *The Old Man and the Sea.* Santiago, an old Cuban fisherman, fights a battle with a great marlin. Though he is fully aware of the futility of his effort, yet he keeps on fighting because this is the way to display his unbeatable spirit. Santiago is the epitomized of Hemingway hero. Nick Adams, Jake Barnes, Frederic Henry, and Santiago all adhere to the same principle or the code of honor.

In *The Old Man and the Sea* the Hemingway hero, or the "code hero," is shown to be one who complies with the "code of honor" that "...a man is not made for defeat... A man can be destroyed but not defeated." This "code of honor" is summed up as "grace under pressure." The Hemingway hero lives out this code while confronting adversity and death. Hemingway holds a very negative and pessimistic world view. The world to him is one that is "all a nothing" and "all nada" ("A Clean Well-Lighted Place"). This nihilistic world view is well illustrated by the fictional world he creates. His world is one full of chaos, killing, violence and death, without meaning and hope. The true Hemingway code hero is fully aware that the universe without God is indifferent, horrific, chaotic and meaningless. He learns that he is the one to create meaning and order through his personal values, such as integrity, dignity, courage, and so on. He knows that life is full of tension and pain and that there is no possibility of winning the struggle with it. A true Hemingway hero endures the pains of life without complaint and keeps on fighting with "despairing courage" because what matters is his heroism exercised during his fighting and by so doing he succeeds in living out his code of honor that is "grace under pressure."

Besides "grace under pressure," death is another common theme of Hemingway's work, which is established in stories as early as "Indian Camp." In this story, Nick Adams is made to witness the death of the father who commits suicide, an event that shapes his personality. The theme of death is central in Hemingway's writings.

Another primary theme permeating much of Hemingway's subsequent work is war, the destructive quality of war. This is evident in *The Sun Also Rises*. Jake Barnes gets wounded in the war, leaving him physically impotent. The destructive effect of war is even more notably exemplified in *A Farewell to Arms*, where war and death go hand in hand. Death is the most horrific reality. It is a mysterious power, unpredictable and inescapable. The war, a futile struggle of man against man, is an example of the indifference of the universe, the death it causes being an extending consequence of the cruel world. Death is prevailing. Catherine's death is such an example. The theme of war and death is also uttered through Henry: "But they killed you in the end. You could count on that. Stay around and they would kill you" (the final chapter).

Obviously Hemingway's world view is the result of the influence of nihilism and existentialism. As his books demonstrate, life is suffering, resulting from purposeless, meaningless, and valueless of living, and from the loneliness and uselessness of man's effort, as well as from the indifference of the universe and the society. This suffering is intensified by the sense of emptiness and meaninglessness it generates. Another distinctive characteristic of modern life is absurdity, a product of the so-called development of civilization, modernization and material-orientedness of the modern society, in which man gets lost, alienated as order-taking machines and killing machines as in purposeless wars. Hemingway hero is meant to seek and create meaning out of the meaningless world. This is where the meaning of his books lies and where the power of his books comes from. And this is one reason why his books endure.

Hemingway is indebted to his literary precursors such as Sherwood Anderson, Gertrude Stein and others, when it comes to writing style. In his literary apprenticeship, Hemingway learned from them, but over the years he had developed a unique style. Hemingway called his style the iceberg theory, which he explained in *Death in the Afternoon* (1932), "The dignity of movement of an iceberg is due to only one-eighth of it being above water." This style is also referred to as the "theory of omission," that is to "get the most from the least." Below the seemingly simple surface of factual description or narration lies the real meaning of the work.

Right from his first volume of short stories *In Our Time* (1925), Hemingway began to employ his iceberg theory of writing. A good example is "Big Two-Hearted River," the last story of the collection. In this story, the author describes in great detail the activities carried out by Nick, underneath these activities is hidden the emotional turmoil. Nick's physical wound and internal war are hinted at instead of being made explicit. Meaning is established through his action.

Hemingway is well-known for his simple style of writing or the economical style of writing, characterized by a spare, reportorial prose based on simple sentence structure and use of simple diction. This is in part due to the fact that Hemingway was a journalist before becoming a novelist. He learned the economical writing techniques from writing for newspapers. Hence, the journalistic style of omission. His distinctive style gained the recognition even with the publication of *In Our Time* (1925). Its author was praised for his use of spare language—about 70 percent of the sentences are simple sentences. Linguistically, Hemingway's prose style is simple, clear, direct, and precise. His diction is simple, concrete, and fundamental. His sentences are short, simple, declarative and sometimes ungrammatical. He favored the repetition of words, phrases, and sentence structures and habitually used the word "and" to replace commas. Sometimes this simplicity is even to the point of monotony. Yet, much is conveyed through this simplicity. In fact, the minimum use of words can achieve the strongest effect. The short simple sentences are laden with implications as well as strong emotions. This is the way Hemingway applied his principle to "get the most from the least."

Hemingway's style can also be seen as an achievement of the revolution he accomplished along with Ezra Pound, T. S. Eliot and James Joyce in literary style and language, a reaction against the elaborate style of 19th century writers. His influence in style as a modern writer is so immense that it is beyond time and space. In 1954, when Hemingway was awarded the Nobel Prize for Literature, his citation by the Nobel Prize Committee spoke highly of "his powerful style-forming mastery of the art" of creating modern fiction.

His major published books are: *In Our Time* (1925), *The Sun Also Rises* (1926), *Death in the Afternoon* (1929), *A Farewell to Arms* (1929), *To Have and Have Not* (1937), *For Whom the Bell Tolls* (1940), *Across the River and Into the Trees* (1950), *The Old Man and the Sea* (1951), *A Moveable Feast* (1964, posthumous).

Analyses of and Comments on His Representative Novels

The Sun Also Rises (1926)

Plot Summary

Jake Barnes is the protagonist. He is an expatriate American journalist living in Paris. He gets wounded in a war, leaving him physically impotent. Brett Ashley, an Englishwoman, is his lover. She is a new woman, twice-divorced, with numerous love affairs.

The story opens with Jake playing tennis with his college friend Robert Cohn. He picks up a prostitute (Georgette), and accidentally meets Brett and Count Mippipopolous in a nightclub. Brett and Jake leave together by taxi. On the way, she tells him that she loves him, but they know their love can not last long.

Bill Gorton from New York and Brett's fiancé Mike Campbell from Scotland have just arrived and join Jake. Jake and Bill travel to Spain with the intention to meet Robert Cohn north of Pamplona for a fishing trip. Cohn, however, leaves for Pamplona to wait for Brett and Mike. Cohn used to be Brett's lover. Although she is engaged to Mike, he still wants to keep the relationship with her. With their absence, Jake and Bill spend five days peacefully, fishing the streams near Burguete. After that they rejoin Cohn and Brett in Pamplona, where they indulge in drinking.

Cohn is becoming less and less welcome in the group who insult him with anti-semitic remarks. Now comes the fiesta, during which the group enjoy themselves by drinking, eating, watching the running of the bulls, attending bullfights, and they quarrel with each other, too. At Montoya's hotel, Jake introduces Brett to Romero, a 19-year-old matador. Brett is so attracted by him that she seduces him, resulting in jealousy as well as fistfights among the men. Jake, Campbell, Cohn, and Romero each love Brett. After the fiesta, sober again, they leave Pamplona for different places. Brett had left with Romero, but later she decided to go back to Mike. In a cheap hotel, without money, she sends Jake a telegram for help when he is about to return to Paris. The novel ends with Jake and Brett in a taxi.

Themes

The themes of *The Sun Also Rises* are implied in its two epigraphs. The first refers to the post-war generation, the Lost Generation, including the young English and American expatriates and those involved in the war. They were disillusioned with the old ideals and values as well as western civilization in general and at the same time they could find no trustworthy spiritual guides. The war left them with a psychic trauma, frustrations and a sense of emptiness, to which they reacted with cynical hedonism. Jake's wound is a metaphor for the disability of the entire generation. The other epigraph is a long quotation from Ecclesiastes. Hemingway used it to convey his world view, that is, the universe is indifferent to human sufferings. It has its own law, its own purpose and value. It is immortal. What one can do in the face of adversity is to face up to it, accept the grim reality and bear with it with grace and courage.

Jake Barnes is the representative of the Lost Generation and an example of Hemingway hero. The novel vividly presents his spiritual growth, from one indulging in seeking sensory pleasure to escape the painful reality to one learning to confront it with courage and live with dignity. Three places and events are vital to his spiritual journey. They are Paris—the symbol of the Waste Land, the trout streams of the Irati River symbolizing the restorative power of nature and the bullfight—metaphor for courage and the power of dominance.

Jake is the representative of those "battered" by the war both physically and mentally or either physically or mentally. His wound is the symbol of the devastation done by the war on the whole post-war generation physically, mentally and morally. His sexual impotence implies the spiritual inadequacy and decadence of the entire generation, the signal of the decline in morality and the values of the period. Jake and his company, Brett, Cohn, Mike and Bill are shown wandering in Paris seeking momentary solace by drinking, eating and playing. By so doing, they try to forget pain and escape from reality. Paris is like the Waste Land devoid of vitality, and above all, morality, with its dwellers living pointlessly without thought and feeling. Different from others, Jake struggles to learn how to live with purpose and dignity in the world of emptiness and meaninglessness, despite all the odds.

Jake's fishing with Bill Gorton on their way from Paris to Pamplona prepares him for his spiritual enhancement in Spain. The tranquility of nature makes him settle down and feel life with a fresh feeling. Fishing is obviously a symbolic activity separating him from his old dispirited life in Paris. The trout streams of the Irati River at Burguete signals a sort of spiritual rebirth, a recovery of health after the emotional crisis.

Jake's return to health is achieved through his watching the bullfight in Spain. Bullfight is a central metaphor in the novel. It serves as a paradigm for the game of life and death. Jake discovers in the primitive game of Spain about the Spaniard's tragic sense of life and death. He comes to accept suffering and death as they are because they are inescapable realities. This realization helps to heal his psychological wounds in a way. Another lesson Jake draws from bullfight is given by Romero. Romero is a code hero. As a torero, he must learn to live with fear and death. In the bullring, he confronts violence and death with skill and courage so that he attains honor and dignity. The ultimate act of domination over the death of the bull is demonstrated in the last moments of the bullfight, in the act of the final sword thrust. The way Romero conducts bullfighting exemplifies a kind of disciplined and courageous life. His ability to dominate the bull symbolizes his ability to control and dominate his fate. Jake sees the similarity between the torero and himself. From the bullfight, he acquires a model of masculine conduct displayed by Romero when he performs bullfight with courage and grace. He becomes mature, his psychological wounds healed, his confidence restored. Now he is a man with integrity, discipline, and control.

Other themes including love, death, and the nature of masculinity are also explored.

Literary Techniques

The Iceberg Theory Hemingway's writing style is characterized by his application of his Iceberg Theory, also known as the "theory of omission." This is a sort of minimalistic style with a focus on the surface descriptions of the landscapes or activities of the characters while the themes lurking underneath. Hemingway believes the true meaning of a piece of writing lies below the surface just like the movement of an iceberg with only one-eighth of it being above water. Hemingway applied his iceberg theory excellently in *The Sun Also Rises*. Much of the book is devoted to the description of the activities of the characters, their excessive drinking, partying, and seeking sensory pleasure. Underneath this frenzy and absurd behavior are the disillusion, the frustrations, and helplessness. The spiritual crisis the post-war generation suffers from is not presented but implied. The description of the bullfighting scene is another good example illustrating Hemingway's use of his iceberg theory. Hemingway's description focuses on the bullfighter. It is detached, reportive, with short and simple sentences typical of his writing style. What's happening in the bullring is the one-eighth above water while the implications it carries is the seven-eighth under the water. Obviously the bullfighting scene is essential in conveying the meaning or the theme of the novel. However, it is concealed under the surface story. It invites the reader to detect and savor.

Symbolism A concrete application of his iceberg theory is the use of symbolism. Jake Barnes' "wound" is an important symbol symbolizing the physical and spiritual sufferings the First world War imposed on "the Lost Generation" as well as those involved in the war. And Jake Barnes' sexual impotence caused by the "wound" stands for the spiritual impotence, that is, the spiritual decay, the disillusion, and the frustrations of "the Lost Generation" in particular and that of the post-war westerners in general. In the novel, Jake Barnes' sexual impotence is only hinted at by means of understatement, and its symbolic meaning is implied. In the middle section of the novel, the author elaborates the fishing trip Jake Barnes takes with his friends. Obviously the hard facts convey something else, a different message about the action. Here the trip stands for self-examination, self-rediscovery and above all, rebirth. Likewise, the underlying truth the scene of bullfighting bears is also presented via symbolism. Bullfighting functions as a symbol for the real world, a world of life and death. The matadors dancing in the bullring are heroes who are confident and courageous enough to face up to death and skillfully triumph over death and end up as the one to dominate rather than being dominated. The bullring epitomizes the real world. Another dominant symbol in the novel is the symbol of taxi. The story begins with Jake Barnes taking taxi and ends with Jake Barnes meeting Brett in a taxi, and throughout the story, now and then, Jake Barnes and his friends are shown wandering around aimlessly by taxi. Their physical action is used to provide an interpretation of the nature of man's existence. Here, taxi symbolizes the taxi takers' aimless, purposeless, and meaningless state of existence and their endless quest for meaning as well. But this symbolic meaning is what under the water. What is above the water is the author's factual representation of the characters' actions.

Hemingway's concrete application of his iceberg theory is also exemplified by his use of understatement, presenting images and scenes without explanations to convey meanings and themes, and his restrained use of description to depict characters and actions.

The Sun Also Rises was regarded as one of the first American modernist novels, which marked the real rise of American modern novels. It emerged with brand-new themes, characters and features both in form and style. After World War I, Hemingway and other modernists "lost faith in the central institutions of Western civilization." As a revolt against the elaborate style of 19th century writers, they created a style in which meaning is established through dialogue, through action, and so on, and in which little is stated explicitly. Hemingway's novel, *The Sun Also Rises,* written on "the iceberg theory" is a good case in point.

The Old Man and the Sea (1952)

Plot Summary

The Old Man and the Sea is Hemingway's final work published during his lifetime. It was awarded the Pulitzer Prize for Fiction in 1953 and was specifically cited by the Nobel Committee as contributing to the awarding of the Nobel Prize in Literature to Hemingway in 1954. The success of the book won Hemingway an international recognition.

The novella's overall structure can be divided into three parts based on the three phases of Santiago's journey, a cycle from the land to the sea and then back to the land again.

84 days have passed and Santiago, an old, experienced Cuban fisherman, has not caught a fish in the familiar waters of the Gulf of Mexico north of his seacoast village in Cuba. He is considered to be the most unlucky person. It is for that reason that Manolin, his young apprentice, was forced to leave him by his parents. Santiago began to teach him to fish when he was just five. Manolin still visits him each night when he comes back from fishing. He offers to help him and gets him food. The two usually talk about American baseball, especially the player Joe DiMaggio.

On the eighty-fifth day, Santiago sets out alone in his skiff. He sails far out onto the Gulf. By noon of the first day, a big fish takes his bait. It must be a marlin. It is so big that Santiago is unable to pull it in but instead it is pulling his skiff. Two days and two nights pass in this manner, though wounded by the struggle with it, Santiago refers to him as a brother out of compassion and appreciation for him.

On the third day of the ordeal, both the old man and the fish are worn out. The old man puts an end to the long battle between them by stabbing the marlin with a harpoon with all the strength left in him. Santiago straps the marlin to the side of his skiff and heads home.

The trail of blood left by the marlin in the water attracts sharks. Santiago fights a heroic battle with them, killing five of them and driving the others away, but they keep coming. By nightfall the sharks have almost devoured the entire marlin, leaving only a skeleton with its backbone, its tail and its head. Finally reaching the shore before dawn on the next day, Santiago struggles on his way home. Reaching home, he throws himself onto his bed and falls into a deep sleep.

Santiago is still asleep the next morning when Manolin comes to check on him. Manolin cries at the sight of the old man's injured hands and quietly goes out to get him some coffee. A group of fishermen gather around the boat where the fish's skeleton is still attached. One of them measures it to be 18 feet (5.5 m) from nose to tail.

Manolin brings the old man newspapers and coffee. When the old man wakes, Manolin tells the old man that he wants to come back to fish with him for he still has much to learn from him. Santiago asks what his family will say, the young man replies that he doesn't care and so they promise to fish together once again. Manolin tells the old man to get well, for there is much he can teach him, and then asks how much the old man suffered. Santiago replies that he suffered a lot. Manolin says he'll get him some medicine for his hands.

That afternoon, some tourists at the Terrace see the remains of the marlin. They mistaken it for a shark and remark to one another that they didn't know sharks had such beautiful tails. Back in his shack, with the boy beside him, Santiago sleeps again and dreams of his youth—of lions on an African beach.

Themes

Grace under Pressure One central theme of the novella is the recurrent theme in Hemingway's novels, that is, living with "grace under pressure," which is demonstrated by his "code hero" Santiago, an old fishing man. Santiago possesses many of Hemingway code heroes' characteristics, a man of action, who never shies away from adversity and lives by his own beliefs or codes. Santiago describes himself as "a strange old man." He is strange in the sense that he is unconventional in his community. And what makes him unconventional is his philosophy and internal code of behavior. He remains dedicated to them and to his passion for his profession above concerns for material gain or survival. He sees his profession as a more spiritual way of life and a part of nature's order in the eternal cycle in which all creatures are brothers sharing the common condition of being both predator and prey. It is his dedication to his craft that separates him from the pragmatic fishermen motivated by money. Santiago is a man of action, who faces up to his odds, 84 days without catching a fish and begins his solitary quest for the big fish. Far out at the sea, he fights single-handed a gallant battle against the repeated attacks of the vicious sharks. Exhausted and helpless as he is, he never gives up. Now and then he draws his inspiration and confidence from religion, baseball, memories of his own youth, his love for Manolin, and so on. He is a man who is able to keep alive in himself the hope and dreams to withstand suffering. He lives up to his conviction that "A man can be destroyed but not defeated." For Santiago, what matters most in life is to live with great fervor and nobility following his beliefs, to do his best to use his skills and nature's gifts, and to accept inevitable destruction with dignity. What ennobles and makes him a success is his perseverance against overwhelming odds. He accepts the formidable challenge and sees it through to the end. Whether he wins or loses his battle with the great fish is less important than fighting a good and honorable fight in which he exercises his heroism. Despite a lifetime of hardships he suffers from, he is still a man in charge. His eyes remain young, cheerful, and undefeated. He has successfully reasserted his identity as a great fisherman, proving once again his dedication to his craft and the value of his philosophy, the basis of that dedication. The skeleton of the marlin stands as the testimony of the old man's failure and the symbol of his spiritual triumph, too.

Suffering and Redemption An underlying theme of the novella is religious, the theme of suffering and redemption. The novel is rich in its religious images and allusions, esp. the allusions to the crucifixion. Santiago, the old fisherman, can be interpreted as the incarnation of Jesus Christ. He is compared with Christ in His struggle to redeem fallen man. The early descriptions of him suggest that he has endured many ordeals. He is old, thin and gaunt, with deep wrinkles on the back of his neck and blotches of skin cancer on his face and hands and with scars on his hands from handling heavy fish on cords, all of which is the consequence of a long life of hard work and meager existence. Besides, he never had children and his wife has died. Indeed, he is a poor man whose best days are behind him. Worse still, as a fisherman, he has gone 84 days without catching a fish. Amid the sneer and despise of his fellow fishermen, he embarks on a solitary fishing trip. Far out at sea, he undergoes a three-day ordeal, the worst ordeal of all, suffering piercing injury to the palms of his hands and back, experiencing extreme thirst, struggling with the marlin and the attacking sharks, through which he demonstrates "what a man can do and what a man endures" and proves that he is indeed "a strange old man," who can be "destroyed but not defeated." Returning from the trip, exhausted, staggering and falling, he carries the mast up the hill toward home while keeps looking back at the marlin's skeleton. It is an allusion to Christ carrying the cross to Golgotha. When he reaches home and finally lies down in bed, he sleeps with his arms straight out. Again, it alludes to Christ, the crucified Christ. Christ submits to the crucifixion for the redemption of mankind. Likewise, Santiago must accept his suffering and defeat so as to redeem his individual life. His trip to the sea is a trip of self-redemption and self-reassertion. Its meaning is affirmed by the skeleton of the marlin and Manolin the boy. The skeleton, the evidence of Santiago's epic catch, is already becoming the stuff of legend, which turns out to be a vehicle for the intrinsic values of his existence. Manolin helps Santiago recognize that he has succeeded in reasserting his identity as an incomparable fisherman dedicated to his craft and the value of his belief. As the story goes, the next morning, when Santiago finally awakens and tells Manolin, "They beat me," Manolin replies, "*He* didn't beat you. Not the fish." His redemption is achieved through his suffering and endurance. Here, the Hemingway code hero and the God-like figure merge into one whose greatness lies in their firmness in holding on to their beliefs, their courage to endure ordeals and their unbeatable spirit of never giving up as well as accepting destruction with dignity.

Santiago arises high above those caught between the two World Wars, who were disillusioned with traditional values and ideals, even disenchanted with life, indulging in hedonism, leading an aimless and meaningless life. Santiago's experience of self-redemption and self-reassertion might offer inspiration, courage and hope to them. In this sense, his trip at the sea is beyond its own significance. Just like Christ who sacrifices his life for the redemption of mankind and whose resurrection also gives hope and the promise of eternal life, Santiago endures all the hardships and sufferings so as to save all the men. In this way, the image of the old man and the image of God merge into one. They both have the sense of responsibility, the spirit of self-sacrifice and fraternity, and above all, personal strength which comes within. This might explain Hemingway's intention in identifying the ordinary old man in real life with the biblical figure, the God. Through this image, Hemingway affirms the values and meanings of life.

The Natural Order and Man's Role in It The novella also explores the theme of the natural order and man's role in it. The story revolves around Santiago's journey from the land to the sea and then back to the land again. This cyclical journey forms the basic structure of the novel and more importantly it suggests the condition of human life and the nature of the natural world.

All living creatures are interdependent in the universe. The natural order binds together all creatures in mutual dependency and a common fate. Recognizing his connection to nature, Santiago affectionately refers to the sea as *la mar* (the Spanish feminine), beautiful, temperamental and emotional. He loves her and knows quite well that as part of nature, it can be very cruel occasionally. Rowing alone, he feels he is at one with nature. He hears the flying fish and regards them as friends. He feels sympathy for the delicate sea birds that must cope with an ocean at times beautiful and cruel for survival. Santiago affirms his place in the natural order and his kinship with all other living creatures. This kind of relationship is more intensely dramatized through his interaction with the marlin. From the moment Santiago feels the marlin's first tug at the other end of the line, he feels connected to it. This connection becomes more intimate as they remain locked in the life-and-death battle for three days. He first sympathizes with and admires the fish and then empathizes and identifies with it. Out in the middle of the sea, they are both alone without help. Santiago finds in it the same qualities he possesses and admires: nobility of spirit, endurance, beauty, and dignity. He even wonders if it is sinful to kill it for whatever purposes. He eventually decides that he kills it because he is a fisherman. He is born to be a fisherman just as the fish is born to be a fish. They coexist in a world where "everything kills everything else" and where they are locked in the natural cycle of predator and prey. He has to do what he is destined to do and what his role in the eternal nature demands. Just as he says, "I love you and respect you very much. But I will kill you dead before this day ends." The marlin's death represents his victory. Yet shortly after his victory, he is attacked by the first shark. Victor as he is , he inevitably must fall subject to nature's endless cycle of predator and prey. Like the marlin, he must lose and become victim. The shark, as the predator, only assumes its rightful place in the natural order and does what it is born to do, just as what Santiago does. All creatures are predator and prey, but they also nourish one another, which is symbolized by Santiago's eating the marlin's flesh to sustain himself. By taking part of it, he becomes one with it. The two of them reach a kind of communion. And the marlin's death is not meaningless.

Here the fundamental message is that in the natural world where "everything kills everything else" and also nourishes everything else, all creatures are interdependent, and they all remain subject to nature and the eventual destruction in the natural order. The meaning of individual life in nature's endless cycle is to live with great enthusiasm, making good use of one's skills, and whatever offered by nature, and then accepting the eventual destruction with dignity. Similarly, life is an endless cycle. This natural cycle of life consists of a passage from youth to old age and a passing on of whatever one generation possesses and values to the next generation, just as Santiago's relationship with Manolin suggests. Santiago is mentor, spiritual father, old man, or old age while Manolin is pupil, son, boy, or youth. Santiago is the great fisherman and Manolin his apprentice faithful to him and what he represents. In giving the marlin's spear to the boy, the old man is passing on whatever he possesses and values to him, his successor. In accepting the marlin's spear from the old man, Manolin accepts for all time Santiago's legacy. By dramatizing Santiago's connection with nature and the other creatures and his relationship with the boy, Hemingway affirms on a deeper level the values and meanings of individual life.

Techniques

The Iceberg Theory Hemingway's application of his Iceberg Theory in this novella is to the utmost. One primary way to apply his iceberg principle is the use of religious allusions. From its first paragraphs, the novella is laden with religious images and allusions which are what under the water, expanding and deepening its spectrum in meaning. The central allusion is that to the crucified Christ. On the surface, Santiago is an ordinary old fisherman, yet various inexplicit evidences suggest his association with Jesus Christ in a variety of ways. In fact, he can be interpreted as the incarnation of Jesus Christ. The details concerning Santiago's plight, his fishing trip out at sea and his returning are surface stories, what underlies is the message about man's suffering and redemption. Like Christ who submits to the crucifixion for the redemption of mankind, Santiago must accept his suffering and defeat so as to redeem his individual life. His trip to the sea is suggestive of a trip of self-redemption and self-reassertion. Just like Christ who sacrifices his life for the redemption of mankind, Santiago endures all the hardships and sufferings so as to save himself and all the men.

Hemingway's application of his iceberg theory also lies in the allegorical quality of the old man's story. On the surface, it is a realistic story about an old fisherman and a young man who loves him, and the old man's battle with a giant fish. Yet it is a story with under-the-surface meanings. It is similar to an *allegory*. Likewise, the characters become more than themselves—they become *archetypes*. Santiago becomes an *archetype* representing the human condition. And his story becomes everyone's story. It is truly universal and genuinely uplifting, too. Ultimately, his heroic struggle not only redeems himself but inspires and saves those around him.

Resorting to resonances from historical and factual references is again an effective method Hemingway used to apply his iceberg theory. These references provide background information, establish the story's cultural context, and advance the plot. On top of that, they indirectly reveal the characters, and contribute to the story's integral thematic dimensions. For example, having read yesterday's newspaper, Santiago tells the boy about "the baseball" by referring to Joe DiMaggio. His reference to DiMaggio predicts his upcoming battle at sea and reflects his deep faith in the indomitability of the human spirit Joe DiMaggio stands for. By associating the old fisherman with the great baseball player, Hemingway reveals his endurance and indomitable spirit and strengthens one central theme of the story, as well.

Hemingway prefers to use the detailed description of activities to reveal characters and convey themes. On the surface, these descriptions are realistic, yet they touch on the story's multiple themes and reveal layers of meaning and larger significances embraced in the story. Take the section at the sea for example. In this section, the old man's fishing process is described in great detail. This elaboration demonstrates Santiago's considerable skill as a fisherman, his commitment and devotion to his profession, and his capacity to cultivate and draw upon the inspiration to sustain himself in the face of hardship. Here we see that Santiago, though stuck in plight, is still a man in charge, confronting all the new challenges with calm and ease. The descriptive details resonate with the ever-expanding meanings of the story.

The materialization of Hemingway's Iceberg Theory is also achieved by the use of Symbolism. Among the various symbols scattering in the novella, the sea, baseball and the baseball player Joe DiMaggio, and the lions are the dominant symbols. The sea not only serves as the setting of the story, but also symbolizes the universe. The old man affectionately refers to it as *la mar*, the feminine. Alone at sea, he is at one with it. Yet, as part of the universe, it is also cruel, full of danger and challenges. It stands for the battle field where the old man's battle against nature is unfolded. The more vicious and fierce the sea is, the more heroic, and tragic the old man's combat against it is. The sea is undefeatable. Similarly, the old man is unbeatable in spirit. Against the background of the sea, the old man's courage and strength is highly intensified. Baseball and the great baseball player Joe DiMaggio plays an important role as symbols. Again and again, they are mentioned or appear in the old man's talk with the boy or in his memories. Baseball is a very competitive and demanding game, challenging one's courage and endurance. DiMaggio stands for the indomitability of the human spirit. Hemingway again and again connects Santiago to the great DiMaggio to show that like DiMaggio the old man also possesses such noble spirit. When Santiago is alone far out at the sea, he dreams of young lions on the beach in Africa, where he sailed as a young man. On the one hand, the lions are a source of inspiration for him, and on the other hand, he identifies himself with them. The lions are symbolic of qualities such as courage, strength, grace, dignity—all the qualities of a fighter that Santiago appreciates, admires and cherishes. Back home after accomplishing his heroic feat at the sea, the old man dreams of the lions again when he falls asleep. It seems to suggest that he feels relieved that, though no longer a young man, he still maintains the spirit represented by the lions and that he has exercised and exhibited that spirit to the fullest. That's what matters. The sea, baseball and the baseball player, and the lions are actually interrelated symbols which coordinately and indirectly reveal the protagonist and the central theme of the novella, the theme that is articulated by the old man himself, "...a man is not made for defeat... A man can be destroyed but not defeated."

Stream of Consciousness This technique is employed in the story's middle part when Santiago is alone at sea, with no one to talk to. The narrative increasingly shifts from the omniscient narrator to Santiago's perspective by entering his mind. Sometimes, Santiago is made to talk aloud to himself, sometimes a third-person narration of his thoughts is presented, at other times, the narrative drifts subtly from either of these into a kind of interior monologue. To present this limited *stream of consciousness*, Hemingway lets the seemingly disorganized thoughts leap into the old man's fatigued mind. In fact, they are loosely connected through recurring images, allusions, actions, and themes.

Shift in the Point of View The story begins and ends with a third-person, omniscient narration, which is limited to and concentrates on Santiago and his actions without dipping into his thoughts, while the part at sea, when Santiago is alone, with no one to talk to, is narrated from Santiago's perspective by entering into his mind. The shift in the point of view is conducive to establishing a certain psychic distance. The two parts of the story that take place on land benefit from this psychic distance in that the emotional impact aroused by Santiago's plight at the story's beginning and the tragedy of his defeat at the story's end make itself acutely felt. This detached reporting is typical of Hemingway's writing style.

Bibliography

Wikipedia, the free encyclopedia. http://en.wikipedia.org/wiki/Slaughterhouse-Five, 2012-08-14.

Berman, Ronald. *Translating Modernism: Fitzgerald and Hemingway*. Tuscaloosa, Alabama: The University of Alabama Press, 2009.

Hays, Peter L. *Teaching Hemingway's The Sun Also Rises*. Caldwell: University of Idaho Press, 2003.

Donaldson, Scott. *The Cambridge Companion To Ernest Hemingway*. 上海：上海外语教育出版社，2000.

杨金才 . 新编美国文学史（第三卷）. 上海：上海外语教育出版社，2002.

李维屏 . 英美现代主义文学概观 . 上海：上海外语教育出版社，1998.

常耀信 . 美国文学简史 . 天津：南开大学出版社，1995.

胡荫桐 . 美国文学教程 . 天津：南开大学出版社，1995.

吴伟仁 . 美国文学史及选读 . 北京：外语教学与研究出版社，1993.

William Faulkner

His Life and Writing Career

His Life

William Cuthbert Faulkner (1897–1962) was an American writer primarily known and acclaimed for his novels and short stories though he also wrote poetry, essays and screenplays during his career. He was one of the greatest modern writers of the 20th century and the outstanding representative of the Southern Renaissance and the Southern Literature of the United States. He was awarded Nobel Prize in Literature in 1949. He received the Pulitzer Prize for Fiction respectively in 1955 and 1963.

William Cuthbert Faulkner was born in New Albany, Mississippi. On September 21, 1902, only a few days prior to his fifth birthday, his family moved to Oxford, Mississippi and settled there, where he lived for the rest of his life. Faulkner was the first of four sons in the Falkner family with a long history tracing back to the time of the Civil War. His great-grandfather, after whom he was named, William Clark Falkner, was the pride of the family. He was a successful businessman who built a railroad, a writer with two novels and a play, and a Civil War hero. The Falkner family called him "Old Colonel," and enjoyed telling his stories, which exerted a great influence on Faulkner and which were to be one important source of his later literary creation. His father Murry Cuthbert Falkner (1870–1932) worked on the family railroad, then he ran his own business and ended up as a business manager of the University of Mississippi. Murry enjoyed the outdoors sports and taught his sons such sports as hunting, tracking, and fishing. His mother Maud Butler (1871–1960) and his maternal grandmother Lelia Butler who liked reading, painting and photographing played a crucial role in cultivating Faulkner's artistic imagination. Maud put emphasis on her children's education and taught them to read before sending them to public school and exposed them to the classical works of especially English writers. Another important person who had a great influence on Faulkner in the Falkner family was Caroline Barr, the black woman who raised him from infancy. Her lifelong education Faulkner received was essential to his preoccupation with the politics of sexuality and race as a writer.

Faulkner didn't have much formal schooling. He only attended two years of high school in Oxford. Yet he had his self-education beyond classroom by reading widely in his grandfather's library and listening to stories told to him by his elders, including war stories, stories of the Civil War, slavery, the Ku Klux Klan, and the Falkner family. He was greatly influenced by the history of his family, his home state of Mississippi where he was born and raised and the history and culture of the American South altogether. His sense of humor, his sense of the tragic position of Black and White Americans, his characterization of Southern characters, and his timeless themes all bear the mark of his home state.

Faulkner began writing poetry in adolescence. Among the first to discover his talent and artistic potential was Philip Stone whom he met at the age of seventeen. A literary mentor to him, Stone made it possible for him to read extensively, discussed literature with him and introduced him to the rising writers such as James Joyce, Frost, Pound and Sherwood Anderson. His literary horizons were greatly expanded. His literary influences are deep and wide.

In 1918, Faulkner enlisted in the Royal Air Force in Canada, there he was trained as a pilot. When he was still in training, the First World War came to a close. He returned to Oxford and then spent a year or so studying languages and English literature at the University of Mississippi. In 1925, he moved to New Orleans, Louisiana, then a literary center, where the little magazine, *Double Dealer*, published avant-garde poetry. It was there he came to learn about James Joyce, Joseph Conrad, and Sigmund Freud. And it was there he got acquainted with Sherwood Anderson. Under his influence and help, Faulkner began to attempt fiction writing, the result of which was his first novel, *Soldiers' Pay* (1926). Anderson offered help in the publication of this novel and Faulkner's second novel, *Mosquitoes* (1927). In 1925, Faulkner spent six months travelling in Europe and met his idol James Joyce. Instead of settling in Paris like most intellectuals of his generation did, he decided to return to his hometown to be a "provincial" writer. During the summer of 1927, Faulkner wrote his first novel with his fictional Yoknapatawpha County as its setting. It was *Flags in the Dust*, which was based on the traditions and history of the South, in which Faulkner was brought up. It was first rejected by the publisher. When it finally came out in 1928, it was entitled *Sartoris*. Its publication marked the establishment of his fictional world, the fictional county of Yoknapatawpha County, and the end of his literary apprenticeship. In the fall of 1928, at the age of thirty, Faulkner began working on *The Sound and the Fury* (1929) in a much more experimental style. The novel turned out to be a masterpiece of American modern literature.

In 1929 Faulkner married Estelle Oldham, who brought with her two children from her previous marriage. To support his new family as a writer, Faulkner had to work as a screenwriter in Hollywood. Throughout the 1930s and 1940s, Faulkner continued to find work as a screenwriter. Meanwhile he continued to work on his fictional county, the Yoknapatawpha County. During this period, his major works came out one after another, including *As I Lay Dying* (1930), *Light in August* (1932), *Absalom, Absalom!* (1936) and *Go Down, Moses* (1942).

In both 1957 and 1958, Faulkner served as Writer-in-Residence at the University of Virginia at Charlottesville. He was seriously injured in a horse-riding accident in 1959, and died from a myocardial infarction, at the age of 64, on July 6, 1962.

His Writing Career

Faulkner began his writing career by writing poetry. As a matter of fact, he wrote two volumes of poetry, published in small printings, *The Marble Faun* (1924) and *A Green Bough* (1933). He did not write his first novel until 1925. With the encouragement and help of Sherwood Anderson, he wrote and published his first novel, *Soldiers' Pay* (1926). It is about a wounded soldier returning home, a "waste land." It presented the disillusionment prevailing after the First World War and fell into the category of the works of the "Lost generation." In 1927, again with the help of Sherwood Anderson, he published his second novel *Mosquitoes* (1927). Like his first novel, it was not well received either. The publication of his third novel *Sartoris* (1929) revealed that Faulkner had began to develop his own style. As the first of his Yoknapatawpha series, this novel signaled the beginning of his constructing his famous Yoknapatawpha Saga, which is composed of 14 novels and many short stories. Set in his fictional county, Yoknapatawpha County, these novels and stories give a vivid presentation of the rise and fall of the big old Southern families and the destiny of several generations, a panorama of the Southern society after the Civil War. His Yoknapatawpha County became the most well-known "miniature world" in the 20th century literature. Faulkner's maturity as a writer was marked by his next novel *The Sound and the Fury*. The novel tells the story of the inevitable deterioration of the Compson family, an old aristocratic family in the South. As it is revealed its tragedy is rooted in its lack of love and humanity. In technique it is experimental and innovative. It uses the "stream of consciousness" technique to present the inner realities of the characters so successfully that it is acclaimed as the first American stream of consciousness novel in the real sense, representing the highest achievement of American novels in this genre. With the publication of this novel, the first period of Faulkner's literary career drew to a close and the second period of his literary creation began.

His second period, the main creative period extended from 1930 to 1942. During this period, Faulkner successively published two collections of short stories and nine novels. Most of them are components of the Yoknapatawpha Saga and are ranked among the modern classics. *As I Lay Dying* (1930), another stream of consciousness novel by Faulkner, further established his leading position in American stream of consciousness fiction writing. Composed of 59 monologues, the novel narrates in great detail the unusual journey a poor white family takes to bury their mother, reveals the thoughts and feelings of the family members on the journey and conveys the meanings of life through them. *These 13* (1931), his first short story collection, includes many of his most acclaimed and most frequently anthologized stories, including "A Rose for Emily," "Red Leaves," "That Evening Sun," and "Dry September." *Light in August* (1932), a realistic novel, revolves around racial problems. It exposes the evils of racial discrimination and appeals compassion and understanding. *Absalom, Absalom!* (1936), a fable about the South, focuses on the theme of doom brought about by the denial of humanity. *The Hamlet* (1940), the first volume of a trilogy, tells stories about the Snopes. *Go Down, Moses* (1942), a collection of short stories, is again about moral injustice responsible for the decline of southern civilization.

In the third period of his literary career, Faulkner spent some years writing screenplays in Hollywood. It was between 1942 and 1945. In his later years, he produced five novels, including *Intruder in the Dust* (1948), *A Fable* (1954), the other two volumes of the trilogy concerning the Snopes stories: *The Town* (1957) and *The Mansion* (1959), which wind up his Yoknapatawpha Saga and *The Reivers* (1962).

Although his work was published as early as 1919, and most of his works were published during the 1920s and 1930s, Faulkner remained relatively unknown until he was awarded Nobel Prize in Literature in 1949. Worse still, in the 1940s, his works were treated with indifference and even hostility. They were thought to be pessimistic and full of violence. The experimental technique employed in them was considered as bewildering. The 13 novels including his most celebrated novels such as *The Sound and the Fury* (1929), *As I Lay Dying* (1930), *Light in August* (1932), and *Absalom, Absalom!* (1936) as well as numerous short stories he published from the early 1920s to the outbreak of World War II constituted the basis of his reputation and accounted for his being awarded the Nobel Prize in 1949. What is sad about it is that they were written by an obscure writer out of the need for money.

In spite of that, Faulkner was a serious writer with a strong sense of the South. He was, first of all, a Southern writer, deeply rooted in the history, tradition, and culture of his hometown, Mississippi, devoting all his life working on this "postage stamp of native soil." He not only modeled his fictional Yoknapatawpha County on it but also made people there and even the members of his family the prototypes for his fictional characters. He drew heavily on what his hometown could provide for his literary creation, its tormented history, the civil war tales, local legends and his own family history he was raised on, and painted an extraordinary portrait of a community united by a common heritage with his Yoknapatawpha stories. With the South as the basis for his literature, he reflected the changes the old society went through and the impact of the changes upon its people, the conflicts between the old and new, the past and present. He probed into the root of the decline of a number of southern aristocratic families, presented their inevitable doom brought about by their own evil deeds—driving the native Indians out of their land, establishing the institution of slavery and so on, and further demonstrated the disintegration of the southern society, the decline of southern tradition and the southern civilization as a result of that. He mercilessly exposed the evils of slavery, racism, the lack of love and humanity of the aristocrats. He is the champion of the illiterate poor white, working-class Southerners, the Negro, the Indians who were the original owners of the land. Their kindness is expressed in their relation to nature and their ability to love. It is the proud who are doomed and the humble who endure. Faulkner's vision of the South is complex and even contradictory. He elegizes the agrarian virtues of the Old South, but at the same time he sees clearly the guilt conducted by the institution of slavery. His stories convey a kind of nostalgia for a past golden age. This southern complex makes itself intensely felt and adds a touch of sadness and complexity to his works.

Faulkner was more than a Southern writer. His books explore a wide range of human experience both regional and universal, transcending time and space. He was a modern writer concerned with modern man's plight and dilemma in general. With the cosmos of his own, he portrayed characters and explored the themes to reflect the life of the southerners in particular and the situation of the post-war modern man in general. Both were caught between the old and the new, the past and the present, confronted with a world of swift changes, a world falling apart. Both were disenchanted with life, finding themselves living in an absurd, sterile and meaningless world. Spiritual deterioration and nihilism were shared characteristics of modern life. The post-war world was a spiritual waste land. The root of the spiritual decadence, as his stories reveal, is the loss of love and the denial of humanity.

Faulkner was more than a writer. He was a humanist preoccupied with the general human situation. His works explore the basic human nature and the basic patterns of human behavior, expose the lack of love and humanity of the aristocrats and celebrate the humanistic brilliance of the unprivileged—the poor whites, the blacks and the primitives. He values such virtues as honor, pride, pity, justice, courage, love and compassion which are rare to modern life. In his Nobel Prize acceptance speech, he said "...I decline to accept the end of man... I believe that man will not merely endure, he will prevail. He is immortal, not because he alone among creatures has an inexhaustible voice, but because he has a soul, a spirit capable of compassion, and sacrifice, and endurance..." He once said to the effect that if he belonged to any school then he belonged to the school of humanitarianism.

Faulkner was a modernist ceaselessly experimenting with modern techniques in order to represent precisely the "reality" as he saw it. His experiments in the dislocation of narrative time and his use of stream-of-consciousness technique categorized him as among the avant-garde. He believed that it is the writer's responsibility to truthfully represent the reality and the most important and the most significant reality is the inner reality of man. In his works, he used interior monologue, free association, montage and the dislocation of time to represent the spiritual world and spiritual chaos of his characters. For example, in *The Sound and the Fury*, a masterpiece of "modernism," he used such new techniques as stream-of-consciousness, juxtaposition, counterpoint, flashback, montage, symbolism and so on. His achievement in the use of stream-of-consciousness technique is parallel to that of James Joys and Virginia Woolf. His verbal innovations and labyrinthine organization of his novels, his sense of time: time as a completed whole, seamless are all evidence of his being a modern writer. Faulkner developed his unique style—an integration of modernistic techniques and the southern literary tradition. He was awarded Nobel Prize in Literature in 1949 for "his powerful and artistically unique contribution to the modern American novel."

His major published books are: *Sartoris* (1929), *The Sound and the Fury* (1929), *As I Lay Dying* (1930), *These 13* (1931), *Light in August* (1932), *Absalom, Absalom!* (1936), *Go Down, Moses* (1942).

Analysis of and Comment on His Representative Novel

The Sound and the Fury (1929)

Plot Summary

The Sound and the Fury was Faulkner's first critically-acclaimed novel published in 1929. It is one of the greatest modern novels of the world and may be the greatest Southern novel ever written. Set in the fictional Yoknapatawpha County, the novel revolves around the Compson family, former Southern aristocrats who are struggling to deal with the decline of their family and its reputation. It is composed of four distinct sections. The first section, April 7, 1928, is written from the perspective of Benjamin "Benjy" Compson, a 33-year-old man with severe mental handicaps. The second section, June 2, 1910, centers in Benjy's older brother, Quentin Compson, and the events leading up to his suicide. The third section, April 6, 1928, is narrated from the perspective of Jason, Quentin's cynical younger brother. The fourth section, the final one, set a day after the first, on April 8, 1928, is related from a third person omniscient point of view, which primarily focuses on Dilsey, one of the Compsons' black servants.

Part 1: April 7, 1928

This section of the novel is narrated by Benjamin "Benjy" Compson, covering the period 1898–1928. Benjy's narrative develops in a nonlinear manner. It is a series of non-chronological events presented in stream of consciousness. The opening scene presents Benjy accompanied by Luster, a servant boy, watching golfers on the nearby golf course while waiting to hear them call "caddie"—the name of his favorite sibling. Upon hearing one of them calling for his golf caddie, Benjy's mind recalls the memories of his sister Caddy. His mind focuses on one critical scene in 1898 when their grandmother died. During the funeral, the four Compson children were forbidden to stay inside. Caddy climbed a tree in the yard to see what was going on there, and while looking inside, her brothers—Quentin, Jason and Benjy—looked up and noticed that her underwear was muddy. Other crucial memories presented through Benjy's mind are his change of name (from Maury, after his uncle) in 1900 when he was discovered to be handicapped; the marriage and divorce of Caddy (1910), and his castration, a result of his attack on a girl when he is not under supervision.

Part 2: June 2, 1910

This section focuses on Quentin, a freshman at Harvard. He is presented wandering the streets of Cambridge, thinking about death and his sister Caddy. He is concerned very much about Caddy's virginity and purity. Preoccupied with Southern ideals of chivalry, he is ready to protect women, especially his sister. Quentin is horrified to find that Caddy has lost her virginity and purity. He turns to his father for advice but is only told that virginity is an invention of men and should not be serious about it. Quentin fails to prove his father wrong though he has tried to. Shortly before Quentin leaves for Harvard in the fall of 1909, Caddy becomes pregnant. To protect her, Quentin tells his father that they have committed incest. He feels he should be responsible for her sin. Caddy then marries another man Herbert Head whom Quentin dislikes but Caddy is determined to do so because she must marry before the child is born. But Herbert finds out that he is not the father of the child and the marriage ends up in Caddy's being sent away. Quentin is wandering through Harvard, heartbroken over losing Caddy, thinking sadly of the decline of the South after the American Civil War. Unable to come to terms with the amorality of the world around him, he commits suicide.

Part 3: April 6, 1928

The third section is narrated by Jason, the third child of the Compson family. The narrative takes place the day before Benjy's section, on Good Friday. Jason's narration is straightforward, a reflection of his single-minded pursuit for material wealth. After his father's death, he becomes the financial supporter of the family. Due to the burden of the family, he becomes bitter and cynical. When this section begins, Jason decides to leave work to search for Caddy's daughter Miss Quentin of whom he is the guardian. Miss Quentin has run away again. In both of them there exist two conflicting predominant traits of the Compson family: Miss Quentin's recklessness and passion which is inherited from her grandfather and, ultimately, from the Compson side and Jason's ruthless cynicism which passes down from his mother's side.

Part 4: April 8, 1928

This section focuses on Dilsey, a black servant. April 8, 1928, is Easter Sunday, on which Dilsey takes her family and Benjy to church. Though mistreated and abused by the Compsons, she nevertheless remains loyal. With the help of her grandson Luster, She cares for Benjy. Her strength comes from her faith.

Meanwhile, the family discovers that Miss Quentin has run away with a carnival worker, taking with her the money which her mother Caddy sends to support her but was embezzled by Jason and her uncle Jason's life savings. Therefore, he sets off once again to find her on his own, but ends up in failure.

After church, Dilsey's grandson Luster drives Benjy to the graveyard, but he drives the wrong way around a monument. Benjy begins to cry. His hysterical sobbing and violent outburst can only be stopped by Jason.

Themes

Love *The Sound and the Fury* explores the root of the deterioration of an old aristocratic family in the Old South. A variety of reasons attributes to the downfall of the family, but one main reason appears to be the family's inability to express and share normal love. Disillusioned with life and the society in which he lives, Mr. Compson indulges in alcoholism and nihilism with little attention or love to spare for others, and Mrs. Compson is obsessed with self-pity and excessive concern for the family's "good name" so much so that she is unable to carry out her duty as a loving mother. Of the four children, Caddy takes care of Benjy with love, yet, in her own search for love, she loses her virginity. Quentin puts an end to his own life in disappointment with his dreams of love and old ideals. What Jason loves is nothing but himself and money. Caddy's daughter, Miss Quentin, reenacts her mother's false pursuit of love.

In contrast to the members of the Compson's family, Dilsey Gibson, the Compsons' black cook, possesses just what they don't have: love and compassion though she is at the bottom of the segregated Old South society. She takes care of the Compson's family and the children in stead of Mrs. Compson. She never treats Benjy as an idiot, instead, she loves him just as she loves other children. With her story, the author celebrates such values as love and compassion.

Death The central theme of the novel is death, which is symbolized by the decline of a once noble Southern family whose ancestry traces back to the U.S. Civil War hero General Compson. The Compson family is doomed due to such vices as racism, greed, selfishness, and the psychological inadequacy of individuals to cope with changes which were responsible for the problems in the South. It is deteriorating with its money dwindling, its ancestral home decaying, its land holdings shrinking and, most importantly, its loss of religious faith and Caddy's loss of virginity. There is no promising future for the young generation of the aristocratic Compsons. Benjy is insane and cannot marry, Quentin commits suicide and Jason refuses to marry. Caddy marries, but gets divorced. Caddy's daughter, Miss Quentin rejects the family and runs off with a man. The world these people live in is one of decadence and sterility, a waste land devoid of vitality and humanity. Gone with the decline of the Compson family are the traditional ideals, values and the traditional morality as well as the old system.

Time Each of the four sections of the novel is entitled with a precise time, which is a marker of a particular occurrence and suggestive of the theme of the novel, that is time. Faulkner's idea of time is based on the theory of time of French philosopher, Henri-Louis Bergson (18 October 1859–4 January 1941). Faulkner agrees with him on his concept of psychological time, a continuous, successive and seamless time, which cannot be measured by second, minute or hour, but it is related to one's stream of consciousness flowing from the present to the past in reflection or to the future in imagination. Faulkner probes the characters' interior reality by presenting their psychological time or sense of time with stream of consciousness so as to reveal their relationship to the future, to the world around them, to their concepts of freedom, and to the way they view themselves.

With little or no sense of the passage of time Benjy lives *outside* of time. For him, time exists not as past, present, and future, but rather as a chaotic mix of them. Life to him is a cyclical progress rather than a linear one. He cannot progress in any way. Neither can his family. It can never progress to arrive at an ending, a resolution of past problems. In a way, Benjy is the symbol of his family's doom. In contrast to Benjy who has no knowledge of time, Quentin is obsessed with it so much so that he watches shadows, breaks watches, and divides his day into clear sections. In addition, Quentin is obsessed with what time brings. To him, time is both obsessive and futile. An anachronism, he transcends time by putting an end to his own life. Quentin perceives humanity as one of continual loss with slim hope of recovery. His suicide is one more sign of the growing regression of the family. Mr. Compson holds that "clocks slay time" and that "time is dead as long as it is being clicked off by little wheels; only when the clock stops does time come to life." Jason, the final Compson brother, longs to possess time and makes use of it for his financial gain. Money provides the only value he can place on life and the only means by which he can prove his humanity. In Benjy's world, there are more past remembrances than present-day occurrences. Quentin's world is full of constant recalling of his past, and he longs in vain to change the past in order to embrace the future. Jason does not waste his time longing to change the past, but he is unable to come to terms with the past. Different to them all, Dilsey is capable of living in the present because her sense of time is much larger than that of the Compsons. Her vision of time, family and humanity is larger and more positive than the others.

Literary Techniques

Stream of Consciousness *The Sound and the Fury* is a psychological novel. Faulkner uses the stream-of-consciousness technique in the first three sections of it. These sections are narrated by the three brothers of the Compsons in first-person point of view. Their thought patterns and modes of expression are presented while they try with desperation and hopelessness in their own way to mourn the loss of their sister, Caddy. By tracking their mental movement, the novel traces the decline of the traditional values of the Southern society. Benjy's section is narrated in a nonlinear manner, covering the period 1898–1928. Benjy's narrative consists of a series of non-chronological events presented in a seamless stream of consciousness. It is full of highly disjointed narration, free association, frequent chronological leaps, interior monologues, presenting a picture of the chaotic flow of consciousness, the mental state of an idiot. Faulkner uses italics to indicate significant shifts in the narrative. In the opening scene, Benjy is seen watching golfers on the nearby golf course waiting to hear them call "caddie." The sound of the word "caddie" triggers the flow of his memories of his sister, Caddy, his change of name, the marriage and divorce of Caddy, and his castration. As an idiot, he lives permanently in the present. For him, there is no past or future. The scenes or what is happening before his eyes can immediately take him back to the past or disturb his reflections and cause his thinking to leap into another past event. Therefore, in his narrative, the present and the past, and various kinds of past events at all levels are smashed into fragments and pieced together. Though chronologically incoherent, Benjy's narrative gives objectively a glimpse into the true motivations of many characters. Like Benjy's section, Quentin's narrative is not strictly linear. Quentin is shown wandering the streets of Cambridge, contemplating death, and remembering his sister Caddy. To demonstrate the confusion and chaos generated by Quentin's severe depression and deteriorating state of mind, the chronological events are entangled together. What's more, this section, especially the end of it, is written in a rambling series of words, phrases, and sentences with no separation indicating where one thought ends and another begins, completely disregarding grammar, spelling, or punctuation. This section gives the novel's best example of Faulkner's employment of the stream-of-consciousness technique. The third section is narrated by Jason. The stream-of-consciousness technique is once more used. But here, Jason's narrative is more straightforward.

Multiple Point of View Multiple point of view is another important technique adopted in the novel. Faulkner breaks the limit of the first person point of view by effectively using the multiple first person point of view. The first three sections are related respectively by the three brothers of the Compsons in the first person narrative. The 3 characters, Benjy, Quentin, and Jason, living separately in their own world, observe the world in his own way. Through them, Faulkner presents glimpses of the thoughts and deeds of everyone in the family. Many of the same events are related in the three sections, each from a different point of view. They are overlapping and interwoven. They provide insights into them from different perspectives and put emphasis on different themes. For example, the three brothers tell the story of the central character Caddy, her sexuality, her early pregnancy, and her quick and unhappy marriage, from their own perspectives through interior monologues. Their accounts reveal their different impressions of, views on, attitudes toward and passions for her. The information from any one point of view is subjective, rambling, fragmented and one-sided, but the information from the three narrators when assembled will produce an overall impression of her on the reader, and in return this impression will reflect the narrators' personalities and biases. In the novel, besides the main lines of the story, significant details are embedded in a mass of information, allusion, and conjecture. Put together, all of them come to present a comprehensive and authentic and chronological picture of the Compson family, its history, its problems and their causes, the desires, concerns and worries of the family members, and above all, its inevitable decay.

Other prominent techniques used in the novel are: flashback, juxtaposition, the use of time, and so on. Flashback is used to represent what happened in the past, linking the past and the present. For example, Chapter 1 takes place on Saturday, April 7, 1928, the day before Easter, but flashes back frequently to previous years. Chapter 2 takes place on June 2, 1910. It also flashes back to previous years. Juxtaposition is employed to highlight the presentation of a state of mind or attitude of a character through interior monologues. Time used as negotiation between the past and the present makes Faulkner's novel a brilliant example of modern technique. The playing with time as a technique that Faulkner employs in the novel becomes a hallmark of a new literary form and a fine example of modernist aesthetics.

Bibliography

Wikipedia, the free encyclopedia. http://en.wikipedia.org/wiki/Slaughterhouse-Five, 2012-08-14.

Weinstein, Philip M. *The Cambridge Companion to William Faulkner*. Shanghai: Shanghai Foreign Languages Education Press, 2000.

杨金才 . 新编美国文学史（第三卷）. 上海：上海外语教育出版社，2002.

李维屏 . 英美现代主义文学概观 . 上海：上海外语教育出版社，1998.

肖明翰 . 威廉·福克纳研究 . 北京：外语教学与研究出版社，1997.

常耀信 . 美国文学简史 . 天津：南开大学出版社，1995.

胡荫桐 . 美国文学教程 . 天津：南开大学出版社，1995.

吴伟仁 . 美国文学史及选读 . 北京：外语教学与研究出版社，1993.

Eugene O'Neill

His Life and Writing Career

His Life

Eugene Gladstone O'Neill (1888–1953) is generally acclaimed as one of the greatest American playwrights, who influence American drama extensively and profoundly. He is the first to fully explore serious themes as subject matter for the theater. Some critics hold that O'Neill has been ranked, along with William Shakespeare and George Bernard Shaw, as one of the three greatest playwrights in English language theater. O'Neill has won four Pulitzer Prizes for his plays: *Beyond the Horizon* (1918); *Anna Christie* (1920); *Strange Interlude* (1928); and *Long Day's Journey into Night* (1941). Moreover, he is so far the only American playwright who has won the Nobel Prize for literature (1936) to award "for the power, honesty and deep-felt emotions of his dramatic works, which embody an original concept of tragedy." The power of his drama lies not only in its external action, but also in the depth of his characterization and the deep concerns for human fate. O'Neill is credited with raising American dramatic theater from its narrow origins to an art from respected around the world. He is regarded as America's premier playwright.

The son of a professional actor, O'Neill was brought up on the road and acquires a precocious knowledge of the theater. His mother, Ella Quinlan O'Neill, was the emotionally fragile daughter of a wealthy father who died when she was seventeen. O'Neill's mother never recovered from the death of her second son, Edmund, who had died of measles at the age of two, and she became addicted to morphine as a result of Eugene's difficult birth.

His early years were profoundly affected by the pressures of his mother's recurring mental illness and his father's coldness, which he later vividly portrayed in *A Long Day's Journey into Night* (1941). Although he was a voracious reader, O'Neill was a poor student; he preferred to spend his adolescence in barrooms with his profligate brother James. After expulsion form Princeton University for his frequent drinking, and a brief, unsuccessful marriage, O'Neill attempted suicide, then left his family for a life at sea. O'Neill spent several years as a sailor, during which time he suffered from depression and severe alcoholism. O'Neill lived for six years as a wanderer, working occasionally as a sailor and spending a great deal of time as an unemployed drifter in Buenos Aires, Liverpool, and New York City. O'Neill would later jokingly refer to this time of his life as his "real education."

O'Neill's parents and elder brother Jamie (who drank himself to death at the age of 45) died within three years of one another, not long after he had begun to make his mark in the theater. Despite his depression he had a deep love for the sea, and it became a prominent theme in many of his plays, several of which are set onboard ships like the ones that he worked on. The turning point in his life came in 1912, when he suffered a mild attack of tuberculosis. While convalescing in a dramatist he spent the next several years assiduously studying his craft.

O'Neill briefly found employment during this period as a writer for the New London Telegraph, dabbling in playwriting from time to time. It wasn't, however, until his experience at Gaylord Farms Sanatorium (where he was recovering from tuberculosis) that he experienced an epiphany and devoted his life to writing plays. O'Neill enrolled in the famous playwriting course taught by George Pierce Baker at Harvard University, spending 1914–1915 writing prolifically, though he would later disown all his writings from this period. In 1916, O'Neill had his first big break, when he joined the Provincetown Players, a raggedy band of young writers, artists, and actors who had assembled in the tiny coastal village of Provincetown. Although many other writers wrote plays for the company to perform, O'Neill soon became their biggest attraction. During this period, O'Neill concentrated primarily on writing small, one-act plays that drew heavily from his experiences at sea. *Bound East for Cardiff* (1914) would become the most famous of these, and it would ultimately be O'Neill's first work to be performed in New York City, to rave reviews.

Following the success of *Bound East for Cardiff*, O'Neill moved back to New York and became a regular on the Greenwich Village literary scene. In 1920, O'Neill's first full-length play, *Beyond the Horizon* (1918), was produced on Broadway. O'Neill would win a Pulitzer Prize for the play, and soon after he became a major literary celebrity. His productivity during this period was legendary; he wrote several plays a year, obsessively revising earlier drafts of plays for reproduction. In 1929, O'Neill moved to the Loire Valley of northwest France. Later, he moved to Danville, California, in 1937, living there until 1944.

After suffering from multiple health problems over many years, O'Neill ultimately began to suffer from a severe tremor in his hands which made it impossible for him to write. He attempted to write via dictation, but found it impossible to compose by that method; O'Neill never wrote another play for the remaining ten years of his life.

O'Neill died from the advanced stages of Parkinson's disease in room 401 of the Shelton Hotel in Boston, on November 27, 1953, at the age of 65. He was interred in the Forest Hills Cemetery in Jamaica Plain, Massachusetts.

His Writing Career

O'Neill's writing career can be divided into five somewhat distinct periods. The first, the period of his dramatic apprenticeship, leads nothing of consequence to his reputation. Included in the period is his first collection, *Thirst, and Other One Act Plays*, and the so-called *Lost Plays*, works so poor that O'Neill made no attempt to publish them. O'Neill first gained recognition during his second period which was devoted primarily to one act plays about the sea. According to some critics O'Neill initial production, *Bound East for Cardiff* (1914), marks the first departure for nineteenth-century melodrama and the beginning of serious American theater. All of these plays are slice-of-life dramas dealing with the delusions and obsessions of common people. He is particularly representative of this period with its naturalistic style, its tragic irony and its use of the sea as symbol of malignant fate.

During his third period, from 1920–1924, O'Neill turned to no longer plays. Foremost among these is *Desire under the Elms* (1925), one of O'Neill's few conventional tragedies, which examines the power of repressed sexuality in a staid New England town. Throughout this period O'Neill exploited many experimental dramatic techniques. His most successful experiments were with symbolism in *The Emperor Jones* (1920) and expressionism in *The Hairy Ape* (1922), a grim play in which a brutish laborer is destroyed by industrial civilization.

O'Neill's fourth, sometimes called his "cosmic" period extends to 1935. Throughout this era he was preoccupied with the problems of identity and the nature of fate, and these vast, sprawling plays are often much longer than traditional productions. O'Neill was still experimenting heavily with theatrical techniques and he successfully utilized such effects as masks, split personalities and stream of consciousness monologues. The most important play of this era, *Mourning Becomes Electra* (1931), is a powerful examination of the ways that guilt, jealousy, and sexual passion lead to the downfall of an old New England family. Uncharacteristic of this period, and of O'Neill's career as a whole, is *Ah, Wilderness!* (1933), a nostalgic and idealistic comedy about adolescence that critics find one of his most unpretentious and thus most successful works.

Despite his award of the Nobel Prize in literature in 1936, O'Neill's reputation declined steadily after 1935. It was not until after his death that the plays of his last period gained recognition. Of these, *The Iceman Cometh* (1939), a realistic study of the fragility of illusions, is generally considered his masterpiece, while *Long Day's Journey into Night* (1941), a portrait of a tormented, destructive family, is called one of the most powerful dramas in American theater.

O'Neill's third wife and literary executor, Carlotta Monterey, to whom *Long Day's Journey into Night* is dedicated, recounted that O'Neill's oldest son asked his father that the play should not be published or performed because of the negative light cast on his father's family. O'Neill acquiesced, depositing the play with his publishers with the injunction that it not appear until twenty-five years after his own death. However, according to Monterey, O'Neill believed his son's suicide removed this constraint. After O'Neill's death, she authorized the play's production in 1956 in Sweden—a country O'Neill had always felt was particularly receptive to his drama and it debuted in the United States later that year.

It is generally agreed that O'Neill wrote some of the most important and some of the most lackluster of modern dramas. In his plays he experimented with almost every dramatic innovation of the early twentieth century. Unfortunately, experimentation with theatrical effects sometimes became an end in itself, and techniques could not enhance such puerile, poorly conceived works as *Lazarus Laughed* (1925–1926) and *The Great God Brown* (1926). For this reason O'Neill's most realistic plays are considered his best. Similarly, while O'Neill was a master at sketching character, he also wrote melodramatic, needlessly verbose dialogue. It is such seeming contradictions that make O'Neill's work fascinating to contemporary critics; they often attack several elements of his plays while applauding the ultimate effects. O'Neill is universally acknowledged as an important tragedian who is credited with creating the traditions of twentieth-century American drama and is as integral to modern world literature as Bertolt Brecht and August Strindberg.

Some clear and indisputable summarizes on O'Neill's accomplishments and status are justifiable. Firstly, almost all the critics share a conviction that O'Neill has made American theatre a serious endeavor. Before O'Neill, American theatre is usually an escapist entertainment. It is from O'Neill on that the American drama starts to highlight its political, moral and social significance. His greatest contribution to American drama also lies in his tremendous impact on many dramatists of later generations who are able to aim high and handle serious subjects in a serious manner. O'Neill takes his art seriously and is totally committed to his work. The playwright has made American drama significant and serious, and thus renders it powerfully enough to compete with its European counterparts. In some sense without O'Neill the American drama will have been nothing.

Secondly, O'Neill is acclaimed as the boldest American literary experimenter for his technical inventiveness. During his early writing the application of realism has brought a new slight in sharp contrast with the former entertainment plays. The playwright has applied various techniques during his creation career. Later, O'Neill returns to realism with his serious contemplation on human fate and human history. O'Neill's application of sound, light, gesture, movement and setting is highly emotive and impressing, for he expresses an instinctive understanding of the theatre and what the audience wants. He "was able to make demands on that audience in the face of opposition form produces and directors. He took risks, and usually his audience went along with him, responding to his sincerity of purpose."

Beyond the Horizon (1918) is written by Eugene O'Neill in 1920. It was O'Neill's first full-length work, and he became the winner of the 1920 Pulitzer Prize for Drama. The play focuses on the portrait of a family, and particularly two brothers Andrew and Robert. In the first act of the play, Robert is about to go off to sea with their uncle Dick, a sea captain while Andrew looks forward to marrying his sweetheart Ruth and working on the family farm as he starts a family.

The Emperor Jones (1920) is Eugene O'Neill's most important play written in the technique of expressionism, which tells the tale of Brutus Jones, an African-American man who kills a man, goes to prison, escapes to a Caribbean island, and sets himself up as emperor. The play recounts his story in flashbacks as Brutus makes his way through the forest in an attempt to escape former subjects who have rebelled against him. The play displays an uneasy mix of expressionism and realism, which is also characteristic of several other O'Neill's plays, including *The Hairy Ape* (1922). It was O'Neill's first play to receive great critical acclaim and box-office success, and the one that launched his career.

Strange Interlude (1928) is an expressionist play about a woman who tries to control her father, her husband and her lover by various means to compensate for the dead aviator that she once loved. Her attempts to indulge her mothering instinct are repeatedly frustrated, first when she attempts to take care of her father and then later when she can't have a child by her husband because his family's history in insanity. Finally, she had a child by her lover. The play is widely known for its 5-hour length and its use of expressionist techniques such as masks, asides and an onstage chorus that delivers the internal thoughts of each character.

The Iceman Cometh in 1939 is perhaps the finest of O'Neill's tragedies. The story is set in a dockside bar of the lower west side of New York City. It concerns a group of drunken derelicts who spend their time in the back room of Henry Hope's saloon where they discuss their hopeless lives. One man wants to get back into the police force, another to be re-placed as a politician. Their daily routines are shattered when Hickey, a salesman and the son of a preacher, appears as a messiah, and encourages them to start rehabilitation. They find out that their new hero is himself a madman and murderer, who has killed his wife, and lapse once more into their comfortable world of whiskey.

Long Day's Journey into Night in 1941 is an autobiographical play in four acts. The action takes place during a single day in August in 1912 at the summer home of the

Tyrone family. The members of the family are father, James Tyrone, and actor; the drug-addicted mother, Mary; the elder brother, Jamie; and Edmund, bases on O'Neill himself, who is stricken with tuberculosis. The play explores the tragic nature of family relations, and questions the possibility of forgiveness and redemption.

Eugene O'Neill's outstanding plays include: *Beyond the Horizon* (1918), *Anna Christie* (1920), *The Emperor Jones* (1920), *The Hairy Ape* (1922), *All God's Chillun Got Wings* (1924), *Desire under the Elms* (1925), *Lazarus Laughed* (1925–1926), *The Great God Brown* (1926), *Strange Interlude* (1928), *Mourning Becomes Electra* (1931), *Ah, Wilderness!* (1933), *The Iceman Cometh* (1939), *Long Day's Journey into Night* (1941), *A Moon for the Misbegotten* (1943), *A Touch of the Poet* (1942), *More Stately Mansions* (1967).

Analysis of and Comment on His Representative Play

The Hairy Ape (1922)

Plot Summary

The Hairy Ape is an expressionistic play. In the play man's miserable position in a mechanical world is symbolically presented. Yank, the "hairy" protagonist, is a strong and sordid stoker on modern ocean liner. He feels that he belongs to the powerful world of steam, steel and iron until he encounters Mildred Douglas, the daughter of the owner of the steamship line. Seeing Yank, the delicate, supercilious, neurotic and rich woman becomes horrified. She says, "Oh, the filthy beast" and faints.

The struggle of Yank, a fireman who works aboard a transatlantic liner, is the subject of *The Hairy Ape*. Yank, his real name is Bob Smith, was born in New York City. Yank does not reveal many details of his family history, but, from what he does say, it is clear that it was painful. His mother died of the "tremens" and his father, a shore-worker, was abusive. Yank tells Long that on Saturday nights his parent's fighting was so intense that his parents would break the furniture. Ironically, his parents made him attend church every Sunday morning. After his mother died, Yank ran away from home, tired of lickings and punishment.

Yank, perplexed, goes ashore to find out if he belongs to the modern world. On Fifth Avenue, he finds that the wealthy people are walking idly without seeming to have seen the sailors. Yank, infuriated, insults some of the wealthy people and is arrested and put into prison. In jail, he hears about an organization which would overthrow the capitalist society. But when he wants to work for the organization after his release, he is rejected and tossed out. He stays outside at night, dislocated and lost.

Yank, in the final scene, attempts to find his identity in the zoo. He talks with a gorilla and sets the animal free, hoping to join them and find his sense of belonging, but the animal kills him and throws his body into the cage. Yank belongs nowhere.

This is a symbolic tragedy of modern man who can neither be accepted by his society nor return to his primitive state. The tragedy is a cosmic presentation of modern man's dislocation in an alien world.

The play is divided into 8 scenes. Scene 1 takes place in the firemen's forecastle of a cruise ship, where they sleep. Their racks resemble the bars of a cage. They are sailing from New York, where Yank and the other firemen are talking and singing drunkenly. Yank is shown to be a leader among them. Other featured characters are Long, a socialist, and Paddy, a particularly drunken Irishman.

Scene 2 takes place on the deck, where Mildred Douglas (the rich girl) and her aunt are talking. They are almost constantly arguing.

Scene 3 takes place in the stokehold. Yank and the other firemen take pride in their work. When Mildred comes to visit the stokehold, Mildred hears Yank cursing. When he turns around and she sees him, she is so shocked by him she calls Yank a filthy beast and faints.

Scene 4 also takes place on the ship. Yank is very depressed and the other men try to understand why.

In scene 5, Yank and Long go to 5th Avenue in New York. Yank argues with Long about how best to attack the upper class. Long leaves, fearing arrest, and Yank is arrested after attacking a Gentleman.

Scene 6 takes place at the prison at Blackwell's Island. Yank tells the prisoners his story and one of the prisoners gives him an article about the Industrial Workers of the World. Yank tries to escape.

Scene 7 takes place at the IWW office that Yank goes to after his month in jail. They are happy to have him at first because there are not many ship firemen in the union—but he is thrown out after he says that he wants to blow up things, and they think he is a spy.

Scene 8 takes place at the zoo, when Yank is crushed after trying to talk to an ape and releasing it from its cage.

Themes

In the beginning of *The Hairy Ape*, Yank seems fairly content as, if not proud to be, a fireman. He defends the ship as his home and insists that the work he does is vital—it is the force that makes the ship go twenty-five knots an hour. Yank's continual references to Paddy (an old Irishman on the same ship) as "dead" and "old" and not "belonging" with the other men aboard the Ocean Liner reveals Yank's own rejection of freedom. The acceptance and attachment to the modern-ship machine enslaves men like Yank. The need for belonging, without the knowledge of what else to belong to, is dangerous as exemplified by Yank's encounter with Mildred.

Mildred Douglas's reaction to Yank is the catalyst which makes Yank come to class awareness. His attempt to get revenge on Mildred Douglas widens to revenge on the steel industry and finally the entire Bourgeois. Throughout this struggle Yank defines "belonging" as power. When he thinks he "belongs" to something he gains strength. When Yank is rejected by a group, he is terribly weak. However, Yank is rejected by all facets of society: his fellow firemen, Mildred, the street goers of 5th Avenue, the I.W.W., and finally the ape in the zoo. Yank symbolizes the struggle of modern man within industrial society—he cannot break class or ideological barriers, nor create new ones. Yank is the outsider and eventually just the freak at the zoo for people to cage and point at.

Although Mildred should be considered the antagonist of *The Hairy Ape*, she is equally victimized by class as Yank. Though Mildred has more education and cultural experience than Yank, she still cannot escape her cultural identity. Mildred describes herself as the waste of her father's steel company, as she has felt the benefits, but not the hard work that brought them. She shares with Yank the need to find a sense of usefulness or belonging—the fate of both characters was decided before they were born. Thus, Yank and Mildred desperately search to find an identity that is their own.

The failure of both characters lies in their conscious and unconscious refusal to shed their values and knowledge while searching for a new identity. For example, Mildred will not change out of her white dress and Yank's coal dust is saturated into his skin.

The industrial environment is presented as toxic and dehumanizing; the world of the rich, superficial and dehumanized. Yank has also been interpreted as representative of the human condition, alienated from nature by his isolated consciousness, unable to find belonging in any social group or environment.

The Hairy Ape displays O'Neill's social concern for the oppressed industrial working class. Despite demonstrating in *The Hairy Ape* his clear belief that the capitalist system persecuted the working man, O'Neill is critical of a socialist movement that can't fulfill individual needs or solve unique problems.

O'Neill is a typical representative of American writers though the European tradition can be identified in his plays. O'Neill represents the influence of New England Puritanism in his vivid portrayals of different spectrums in society, but the most striking feature of his creation is the sense of fatality in human lives. The portrayal of the dark side of human existence manifests his inheritances as an American writer. Growing up in a theatre but feeling disgusted with the melodrama of his father's day, the playwright wants to reform this situation with his serious thinking and his emotive creations. O'Neill has exerted himself to pave a serious way of dramatization in reflecting life and expressing human life and social problems. Almost all of his plays concern the problems in human life and human history from the physical, psychological and spiritual dimensions.

Literary Techniques

O'Neill was still experimenting heavily with theatrical techniques and he successfully utilized such effects as masks, split personalities and steam of consciousness monologues. O'Neill uses the device of symbolic expressionism. The ship symbolizes modern society and Yank the man who struggles to make improvement but is defeated. O'Neill presents his own reaction to the modern state through his central character Yank, for Yank is, according to O'Neill, "every human being." In the drama, when Yank realizes that he is viewed as an object, he starts to muse over his existence. Freedom is badly desired. However, does that mean he is growing? No. People are all in want of freedom, but do we really get it? Contrarily, they are chosen by freedom instead of their choosing. The ship is an epitome of capitalist society. Workers like Yank have to endure cruel treatment. If they want to change, they will definitely meet more miserable situation. Actually, a numerous obstacles and frustrations occur in the way of Yank's seeking for his position, which reflects survival crisis of most modern people. The more people think about, the clearer people realize about freedom. His vengeance only wants to prove the sense of his existence, so he gets to know freedom is the root of bitterness. Faced with this kind of freedom, Yank is sad, isolated and unhopeful. Moreover, all the attempts are in vain. Yank has nothing to do but degenerate—death that is inevitable.

Yank, symbolizing human, hasn't been afoot for the tough task of searching for freedom, therefore the tragedy of Yank become a fight between human and self produced with existence of human. In addition, the costume of upper class and the bars that are around the stokehole are also related to expressionism. The former tells that that group of people stick to convention and are nonchalant. The latter shows that people are in a cage. *The Hairy Ape* is well worth studying, for it can be considered the first important play that attacks the materialism of American society. It has a strong and political dimension.

One of the most famous naturalistic playwrights, O'Neill was essentially concerned with the miserable position of modern man. For the sense of the tragic, his plays are unsurpassed and unequaled by other American playwrights. But he was against the old naturalism of surface-reality, for he was interested in the inscrutable forces behinds life. He liked to create extremes of unhappiness. He treated man as an animal at the mercy of basic urges either in the form of passion or violence and caught or trapped in a meaningless universe. His creative capacity renders his characters as living realities. O'Neill was more interested in the inner conflicts of his characters rather than in social problems. In the study of his characters, he frequently uses his knowledge of Freudian and Jungian psychology.

Bibliography

Hall, Sharon K., ed. *Twentieth-Century Literary Criticism, Vol. 6*. Detroit, Michigan: Gale Research Company, 1982: 323-327.

Poupard, Dennis, ed. *Twentieth-Century Literary Criticism, Vol. 27*. Detroit, London: Gale Research Inc., 1988: 156-157.

http://en.wikipedia.org/wiki/Eugene_O'Neill, 2013-02-15.

http://www.newworldencyclopedia.org/entry/Eugene_O'Neill, 2013-02-15.

常耀信 . 美国文学简史（第二版修订本）. 天津：南开大学出版社，2006: 290-295.

王卓，李权文 . 美国文学史 . 武汉：华中师范大学出版社，2010: 335-341.

吴瑾瑾 . 美国文学史 . 北京：经济科学出版社，2008: 403-412.

Arthur Miller

His Life and Writing Career

His Life

Arthur Asher Miller (1915–2005) was an American playwright and essayist. He was a prominent figure in American theatre, writing dramas which are still widely studied and performed worldwide.

Arthur Miller, the son of moderately affluent Jewish-American parents, Isdore and Augusta Miller, was born in Harlem, New York City in 1915. His father owned a coat-manufacturing business, which failed in the Wall Street Crash of 1929, after which, his family moved to humbler quarters in Brooklyn.

Because of the effects of the Great Depression on his family, Miller had no money to attend a university in 1932 after he had graduated from high school. After securing a place at the University of Michigan, Miller worked in a number of menial jobs to pay for his tuition.

At the University of Michigan, Miller first majored in journalism and worked as a reporter and night editor for the student paper, the *Michigan Daily*. It was during this time that he wrote his first play, *No Villain* (1936). Miller switched his major to English, and subsequently won the Avery Hopwood Award for *No Villain*. The award brought him his first recognition and led him to begin to consider that he could have a career as a playwright. Miller enrolled in a playwriting seminar taught by the influential Professor Kenneth Rowe, who instructed him in his early forays into playwriting. Rowe emphasized how a play is built in order to achieve its intended effect, or what Miller called "the dynamics of play construction." Rowe provided realistic feedback along with much-needed encouragement, and became a lifelong friend. Miller retained strong ties to his alma mater throughout the rest of his life, establishing the university's Arthur Miller Award in 1985 and Arthur Miller Award for Dramatic Writing in 1999, and lending his name to the Arthur Miller Theatre in 2000. In 1937, Miller wrote *Honors at Dawn* (1938), which also received the Avery Hopwood Award.

On August 5, 1940, he married his college sweetheart, Mary Slattery, the Catholic daughter of an insurance salesman. The couple had two children, Jane and Robert (a director, writer and producer whose body of work includes producer of the 1996 movie version of *The Crucible*).

Arthur Miller's eminence as a dramatist is based primarily on four plays he wrote early in his career: *All My Sons* (1947), *Death of a Salesman* (1949), *The Crucible* (1953), and *A View from the Bridge* (one-act, 1955; revised two-act, 1956). Although his later works are generally considered inferior to his early masterpieces, Miller remains among the most important and influential dramatists to emerge in the United States since World War II.

In December 2004, the 89-year-old Miller announced that he had been in love with 34-year-old minimalist painter Agnes Barley and had been living with her at his Connecticut farm since 2002, and that they intended to marry. Miller's final play, *Finishing the Picture* (2004), opened at the Goodman Theatre, Chicago, in the fall of 2004. He stated that the work was based on the experience of filming *The Misfits* (1957).

Miller died of heart failure after a battle against cancer, pneumonia and congestive heart disease at his home on the evening of February 10, 2005 at the age of 89.

His Writing Career

In 1940 Miller wrote *The Man Who Had All the Luck* (1940), which was produced in New Jersey in 1940 and won the Theatre Guild's National Award. The play closed after four performances and disastrous reviews. In 1947 Miller's play *All My Sons* (1947), the writing of which had commenced in 1941, was a success on Broadway (earning him his first Tony Award, for Best Author) and his reputation as a playwright was established. With the success of *All My Sons*, he devoted himself entirely to drama.

Miller always acknowledges the strong influence of Henrik Ibsen on his work. He has learned from Ibsen the technique of providing information about the past little by little, and in this way false ideas of reality are gradually replaced by the underlying truth.

In 1948 Miller built a small studio in Roxbury, Connecticut. There, in less than a day, he wrote Act I of *Death of a Salesman* (1949). Within six weeks, he completed the rest of the play, one of the classics of world theater.

Death of a Salesman was hailed as an American myth and a contemporary tragedy. Directed by Elia and Kazan, *Death of a Salesman* was premiered on Broadway on February 10, 1959 by the Morosco Theatre, and the play was commercially successful and critically acclaimed, winning a Tony Award for Best Author, the New York Drama Circle Critics' Award, and the Pulitzer Prize for Drama. It was the first play to win all three of these major awards. The play was performed 742 times. This play not only won six famous awards but also won him reputation as one of the best American dramatists after the War.

Arthur Miller was summoned by the House Un-American Activities Committee on his political views, but he refused to cooperate. This bitter experience of the "McCarthy Era" led him to write *The Crucible* (1953), in which Miller likened the situation with the House Un-American Activities Committee to the witch hunt in Salem in 1692, opened at the Beck Theatre on Broadway on January 22, 1953. Though widely considered only somewhat successful at the time of its initial release, today *The Crucible* is Miller's most frequently produced work throughout the world and was adapted into an opera by Robert Ward which won the Pulitzer Prize for Music in 1962. It was now seen to have a more lasting and universal significance than had earlier been apparent. As Robert Martin later maintained, *The Crucible* "has endured beyond the immediate events of its own time. If it was originally seen as a political allegory, it is presently seen contemporary audiences almost entirely as a distinguished American play by an equally distinguished American playwright."

After *A View from the Bridge* (1955) and *A Memory of Two Mondays* (1955), he abandoned the stage for about eight years. In June 1956, Miller left his first wife Mary Slattery and on June 25 he married Marilyn Monroe. Though Marilyn Monroe was a famous movie star, she was exploited by the film industry. In 1961, Miller began to work on *The Misfits*, starring his wife. Miller later said that the filming was one of the lowest points in his life; shortly before the film's premiere in 1961, the pair divorced. Nineteen months later, Monroe died of a possible drug overdose.

He returned to the theatre in 1964 with two works, *After the Fall* (1964), and, near the end of the year, *Incident at Vichy* (1964). *After the Fall* is considered Miller's most experimental and, perhaps, most pessimistic piece. That same year, Miller was elected the first American president of International PEN, a position which he held for four years. During this period Miller wrote the penetrating family drama, *The Price*, produced in 1968. It was Miller's most successful play since *Death of a Salesman*. The three plays deal with failure in human relationships and the question of guilt and responsibility of people to each other. These realistic plays explore his old subjects: individual responsibility, contrasting brothers, and alienated generations.

His next work, *The Creation of the World and Other Business* (1972), as series of comic sketches based on the Biblical Book of Genesis, met with severe critical disapproval when it was produced on Broadway in 1972, closing after only 20 performances. All of Miller's subsequent works premiered outside of New York. Miller staged the musical *Up from Paradise* (1974), an adaptation of *The Creation of the World* (1972), at his alma mater, the University of Michigan. *The Archbishop's Ceiling* (1977) was presented in 1977 at the Kennedy Center in Washington, D. C.

In the 1980s, Miller produced a number of short pieces. *The American Clock* (1980) is based on Studs Terkel's oral history of the Great Depression, *Hard Times*, and is structured as a series of vignettes that chronicle the hardship and suffering that occurred during that period. *Elegy for a Lady* (1982) and *Some Kind of Love Story* (1982) are two one-act plays that were staged together in 1982. Reviewers have generally regarded these later plays as minor works, inferior to Miller's early masterpiece.

During the early 1990s Miller wrote three new plays, *The Ride Down Mt. Morgan* (1991), *The Last Yankee* (1991), and *Broken Glass* (1994). In 1996, a film of *The Crucible* starring Daniel Day-Lewis and Winona Ryder opened. Miller spent much of 1996 working on the screenplay to the film. *Mr. Peters' Connections* (1998) was staged Off-Broadway in 1998, and *Death of a Salesman* was revived on Broadway in 1999 to celebrate its fiftieth anniversary. The play, once again, was a large critical success, winning a Tony Award for best revival of a play.

In 1993, he was awarded the National Medal of Arts. Miller was honored with the PEN/Laura Pels International Foundation for Theater Award for a Master American Dramatist in 1998. In 2001 the National Endowment for the Humanities (NEH) selected Miller for the Jefferson Lecture, the U.S. federal government's highest honor for achievement in the humanities. Miller's lecture was entitled "On Politics and the Art of Acting." Miller's lecture analyzed political events (including the U.S. presidential election of 2000) in terms of the "arts of performance," and it drew attacks from some conservatives such as Jay Nordlinger, who called it "a disgrace," and George Will, who argued that Miller was not legitimately a "scholar."

In 1999 Miller was awarded The Dorothy and Lillian Gish Prize, one of the richest prizes in the arts, given annually to "a man or woman who has made an outstanding contribution to the beauty of the world and to mankind's enjoyment and understanding of life." On May 1st, 2002, Miller was awarded Spain's Principe de Asturias Prize for Literature as "the undisputed master of modern drama." The following year Miller won the Jerusalem Prize.

Arthur Miller has published many influential plays such as: *No Villain* (1936), *Honors at Dawn* (1938), *The Man Who Had All the Luck* (1940), *All My Sons* (1947), *Death of a Salesman* (1949), *The Crucible* (1953), *A View from the Bridge* (1955), *A Memory of Two Mondays* (1955), *Incident at Vichy* (1964), *After the Fall* (1964) , *The Price* (1968), *The Creation of the World and Other Business* (1972), *Up from Paradise* (1974), *The Archbishop's Ceiling* (1977), *The American Clock* (1980), *Elegy for a Lady* and *Some Kind of Love Story* (1982), *The Ride Down Mt. Morgan* (1991), *The Last Yankee* (1991), *Broken Glass* (1994), *Mr. Peter's Connections* (1998), *Resurrection Blues* (2002), *Finishing the Picture* (2004).

Analysis of and Comment on His Representative Play

Death of a Salesman (1949)

Plot Summary

Death of a Salesman is Miller's masterpiece. The play premiered on Broadway in February 1949, running for 742 performances, and has been revived on Broadway four times winning three Tony Awards for Best Revival. With the production of *Death of a Salesman*, Miller firmly established his reputation as an outstanding American dramatist. This play represents his most powerful dramatization of the clash between the individual and materialistic American society.

Arthur Miller based Willy Loman, the protagonist, on his own uncle, Manny Newman. Miller started writing the play in 1947 after a chance encounter he had with his uncle outside the Colonial Theatre in Boston.

Willy Loman is an aging salesman who returns home one night from a sales trip, unable to concentrate on the road. He needs to keep making sales since there are so many payments to make, and they need the money. His wife, Linda, is worried about him, and is completely devoted to him and encourages him to find a job where he does not have to travel anymore. His two adult sons, Happy and Biff, are back in the house for the first time in years, talking about their future job prospects. Both Biff and Willy are determined to ask for better jobs: Biff from Bill Oliver, a successful man whom he knew long ago, and Willy from Howard Wagner, the son of the man who first hired Willy to the firm. Both are unsuccessful.

As the play unfolds, the observer learns about various incidents in the Loman family in the past which account for their present condition. Biff, having always relied on athletics, fails math and does not graduate high school. Willy, having always encouraged Biff not to concentrate on academics since he had such great athletic potential, does not want to be blamed for Biff's failures. Moreover, one day, Biff catches Willy cheating on Linda with another woman in Boston, and his esteem for Willy completely vanishes. Willy thinks Biff is intentionally spiteful to him and only wants to hurt Willy, but soon Willy realizes that Biff just wants Willy to accept him for who he is. Biff says that he is not the business type and just wants to work on a farm in the open air, and he breaks down crying since Willy keeps forcing him to pursue a job with Bill Oliver. Biff says he does not want to lie anymore.

When Willy sees Biff crying, he finally realizes that Biff loves him and has not been trying to hurt him all these years. He wants to make up for it by giving Biff $20,000 with which to start a new business with, and Willy will get the money by killing himself and collecting the insurance policy. Willy kills himself by crashing the car before Biff can make amends with him. Biff realizes that they have all been living a false dream, but Happy is determined to carry out Willy's dreams. Linda is distraught, especially since she has just paid the last payment on the mortgage but now there is no one to live in the house.

The play doesn't end with Willy's death. The dilemma is projected forward as Biff rejects the dream that hounded his father to his death and Happy dedicates himself to it. The spiritual and the material remain in tension.

Themes

The Disillusionment of the American Dream Willy Loman believes wholeheartedly in what he considers the promise of the American Dream—that a "well-liked" and "personally attractive" man in business will indubitably and deservedly acquire the material comforts offered by modern American life. Oddly, his fixation with the superficial qualities of attractiveness and likeability is at odds with a more gritty, more rewarding understanding of the American Dream that identifies hard work without complaint as the key to success. Willy's interpretation of likeability is superficial—he childishly dislikes Bernard because he considers Bernard a nerd. Willy's blind faith in his stunted version of the American Dream leads to his rapid psychological decline when he is unable to accept the disparity between the Dream and his own life.

Willy's life has fallen apart in his hands. Willy seems childlike and relies on others for support. His first name, Willy, reflects this childlike aspect as well as sounding like the question "Will he?" His last name gives the feel of Willy being a "low man," someone low on the social ladder and unlikely to succeed. Derided by the buyers on whom he depends, alienated form his son, Biff, no longer in touch with his life, he plans a suicide that will redeem him. A believer in the dreams paraded as social realities, he finds himself holding nothing that will give meaning to his life, so he revisits his past, searching for the moment when promise had turned to failure, when the myth that had provided his life with structure and purpose had collapsed.

Biff Loman represents Willy's more realistic and depressed side. Biff is Willy's pride and joy. Willy always talks about Biff, and his visits bring great excitement to Willy. However, Biff has been raised with the wrong values, since Willy encourages Biff to ignore his academics, rely on athletics and personality, and to steal. When Biff finally sees that his father is a fake, he becomes lost, since he had relied so heavily on Willy's values in the past to guide him, yet now those values have led him astray. When Biff is pressured into seeing Bill Oliver to ask for a job, he unfortunately steals a fountain pen from Oliver's office. When Biff realizes what he is doing, he sees for the first time that he is not doing what he wants to do but has always been doing what Willy has wanted him to do. He is no one special and if Willy had not puffed him up so much in the past, maybe Biff would have been someone. When Biff tries to confront Willy and get him to see how false his dreams were, Willy refuses to listen, so Biff has to be turned away, which causes him to cry. Willy sees the tears as a symbol of Biff's love for him, which leads him to commit suicide for Biff's sake, but his action was to no avail. At Willy's funeral, Biff accuses Willy of having false dreams, and Biff is glad that he has finally escaped them. Intent on revealing the simple and humble truth behind Willy's fantasy, Biff longs for the territory obscured by his father's blind faith in a skewed, materialist version of the American Dream. Biff's identity crisis is a function of his and his father's disillusionment, which, in order to reclaim his identity, he must expose.

Happy Loman is the neglected son of the family. Throughout his life, he has always been second string to Biff in Willy's eyes. He is moderately successful with a good job and his own apartment, but he still feels lonely, since he knows that he is missing the love and care that his parents pay to Biff. He is always looking for attention from his parents, but rarely gets any, and he even goes as far as to make things up just for attention, such as telling his parents he is going to get married and his determination to carry out the Loman dreams of being successful in business. He tries to discourage Biff from telling Willy the truth by keeping up the front that Biff is going into business with Bill Oliver and that Biff and Happy will go into business together as the Loman Brothers, which makes Willy proud. In the end, Happy still tries to live Willy's dream, even though

Biff knows they are false. Happy is a doomed, utterly duped figure, destined to be swallowed up by the force of blind ambition that fuels his insatiable sex drive.

Betrayal Willy's primary obsession throughout the play is what he considers to be Biff's betrayal of his ambitions for him. Willy believes that he has every right to expect Biff to fulfill the promise inherent in him. When Biff walks out on Willy's ambitions for him, Willy takes this rejection as a personal affront (he associates it with "insult" and "spite"). Willy, after all, is a salesman, and Biff's ego-crushing rebuff ultimately reflects Willy's inability to sell him on the American Dream—the product in which Willy himself believes most faithfully. Willy assumes that Biff's betrayal stems from Biff's discovery of Willy's affair with the woman—a betrayal of Linda's love. Whereas Willy feels that Biff has betrayed him, Biff feels that Willy, a "phony little fake," has betrayed him with his unending stream of ego-stroking lies.

Literary Techniques

The play is mostly told from the point of view of the protagonist, Willy, and the previous parts of Willy's life are revealed in the flashback, sometimes during a present day scene. It does this by having a scene begin in the present time, and adding characters onto the stage whom only Willy can see and hear, representing characters and conversations from other times and places.

The play's structure resembles a Stream of Consciousness account: Willy drifts between his living room downstage to the apron and flashbacks of an idyllic past, and also to fantasized conversations with Ben. When we are in the present the characters abide by the rules of the set, entering only through the stage door to the left; however, when we visit Willy's "past" these rules are removed, with characters openly moving through walls. Whereas the term "flashback" as a form of cinematography for these scenes is often heard, Miller himself rather speaks of "mobile concurrences." In fact, flashbacks would show an objective image of the past. Miller's mobile concurrences, however, rather show highly subjective memories. Furthermore, as Willy's mental state deteriorates, the boundaries between past and present are destroyed, and the two start to exist in parallel.

The real force of the play (*Death of a Salesman*) lays in its method, in a use of time that opens up process and compacts past and present into the same space. How fantastic, Miller said to himself, "a play would be that did not still the mind's simultaneity, did not allow a man to 'forget' and turned him to see present through past and past through present, a form that in itself, quite apart from its content and meaning, would be inescapable as a psychological process and as a collecting point for all that his life in society has poured into him." There were three categories of time in the play: surreal time, psychological time, and the time created by the play as it is perceived by the audience. *Death of a Salesman* was a wholly original creation.

Symbolism In the play, seeds represent for Willy the opportunity to prove the worth of his labor, both as a salesman and a father. His desperate, nocturnal attempt to grow vegetables signifies his shame about barely being able to put food on the table and having nothing to leave his children when he passes. Willy feels that he has worked hard but fears that he will not be able to help his offspring any more than his own abandoning father helped him. The seeds also symbolize Willy's sense of failure with Biff. Despite the American Dream's formula for success, which Willy considers infallible, Willy's efforts to cultivate and nurture Biff went awry. Realizing that his all-American football star has turned into a lazy bum, Willy takes Biff's failure and lack of ambition as a reflection of his abilities as a father.

Diamonds to Willy represent tangible wealth and, hence, both validation of one's labor (and life) and the ability to pass material goods on to one's offspring, two things that Willy desperately craves. Correlatively, diamonds, the discovery of which made Ben a fortune, symbolize Willy's failure as a salesman. Despite Willy's belief in the American Dream, a belief unwavering to the extent that he passed up the opportunity to go with Ben to Alaska, the Dream's promise of financial security has eluded Willy. At the end of the play, Ben encourages Willy to enter the "jungle" finally and retrieve this elusive diamond—that is, to kill himself for insurance money in order to make his life meaningful.

Willy's strange obsession with the condition of Linda's stockings foreshadows his later flashback to Biff's discovery of him and the woman in their Boston hotel room. The teenage Biff accuses Willy of giving away Linda's stockings to the woman. Stockings assume a metaphorical weight as the symbol of betrayal and sexual infidelity. New stockings are important for both Willy's pride in being financially successful and thus able to provide for his family and for Willy's ability to ease his guilt about, and suppress the memory of, his betrayal of Linda and Biff.

The rubber hose is a stage prop that reminds the audience of Willy's desperate attempts at suicide. He has apparently attempted to kill himself by inhaling gas, which is, ironically, the very substance essential to one of the most basic elements with which he must equip his home for his family's health and comfort—heat. Literal death by inhaling gas parallels the metaphorical death that Willy feels in his struggle to afford such a basic necessity.

Motifs

Mythic Figures Willy's tendency to mythologize people contributes to his deluded understanding of the world. He speaks of Dave Singleman as a legend and imagines that his death must have been beautifully noble. Willy compares Biff and Happy to the mythic

Greek figures Adonis and Hercules because he believes that his sons are pinnacles of "personal attractiveness" and power through "well likedness"; to him, they seem the very incarnation of the American Dream.

Willy's mythologizing proves quite nearsighted, however. Willy fails to realize the hopelessness of Singleman's lonely, on-the-job, on-the-road death. Trying to achieve what he considers to be Singleman's heroic status, Willy commits himself to a pathetic death and meaningless legacy (even if Willy's life insurance policy ends up paying off, Biff wants nothing to do with Willy's ambition for him). Similarly, neither Biff nor Happy ends up leading an ideal, godlike life; while Happy does believe in the American Dream, it seems likely that he will end up no better off than the decidedly ungodlike Willy.

The American West, Alaska, and the African Jungle These regions represent the potential of instinct to Biff and Willy. Willy's father found success in Alaska and his brother, Ben, became rich in Africa; these exotic locales, especially when compared to Willy's banal Brooklyn neighborhood, crystallize how Willy's obsession with the commercial world of the city has trapped him in an unpleasant reality. Whereas Alaska and the African jungle symbolize Willy's failure, the American West, on the other hand, symbolizes Biff's potential. Biff realizes that he has been content only when working on farms, out in the open. His westward escape from both Willy's delusions and the commercial world of the eastern United States suggests a nineteenth-century pioneer mentality—Biff, unlike Willy, recognizes the importance of the individual.

Bibliography

Bercovitch, Sacvan. *The Cambridge History of American Literature (Vol. 7)*. Cambridge U.K. and New York: Cambridge University Press, 1999: 20-43.

Draper, James P. *World Literature Criticism (Vol. 4)*. Detroit: Gale, 1992: 2359-2365.

http://en.wikipedia.org/wiki/Death_of_a_Salesman, 2013-02-15.

http://www.newworldencyclopedia.org/entry/Arthur_Miller, 2013-02-15.

常耀信 . 美国文学简史（第二版修订本）. 天津：南开大学出版社，2006: 305-312.

吴瑾瑾 . 美国文学史 . 北京：经济科学出版社，2008: 424-432.

PART VI

AMERICAN LITERATURE IN THE POSTMODERN PERIOD

(1945–)

Historical Introduction

We are now entering the post-World War Ⅱ period, the postmodern period. So much has occurred since 1945 that recent American literature, prominently American postmodern literature, dealing with the new experience in the postindustrial society, the postmodern society, the information society, or the society of late capitalism in the context of globalization, has acquired an imposing stature. American ended the decade of the 1930s in an inward-looking mood, concerned with economic issues, unemployment, and the need to heal internal ideological divisions. By the close of World War Ⅱ, however, that mood had changed. The United States had become a global superpower, committed to the international arena. In the new era of postwar, postcolonial politics, it had come to stand for the "American" way of capitalism, individualism, and the open market, opposed in every respect to the "Russian" or "communist" way of collectivism and the organized economy. A war machine that had managed to treble munitions production in 1941 continued, if in a slightly lower gear. The cessation of conflict did not mean an end to arms production, now that the United States discovered new treats in international socialism, and the next decade or so saw the rapid expansion of what one president was to term the military-industrial complex: a compact between military interests, eager to acquire ever newer and more powerful armaments, and industrial interests, just as eager to produce them, that was to prove satisfactory and profitable to both. The only nation to emerge from World War II with its manufacturing plant intact and its economy strengthened, America presented itself to the rest of the world—and, in particular, to Europe—as an economic miracle.

The business of America was not only to flourish its economic abundance but also, perhaps, to dictate the terms as modern culture, at least to its Western allies, and to other parts of the globe where it claimed a right of intervention and control. As the 1940s passed into the 1950s, America seemed to set the style in everything, from high art to advanced technology to popular culture. In Eisenhower, the president from 1952 to 1960, Americans also had someone at the head of state whose main aim seemed to be to preserve this economic abundance and cultural hegemony through a strategy of masterly inactivity. Like Ronald Reagan thirty years later, Eisenhower made a dramatic exhibition of not working too hard; as he apparently saw it, his job as president was to leave Americans alone to go about their business, and to discourage the state from any interference in the day-to-day life of the individual. If self-help was to be encouraged, then citizens had to be left to themselves, to work hard and then to enjoy the material comforts thereby earned. Many intellectuals and artists—although by no means all of them—participated in this era of consensus. This was the so-called value-free sociology; much of the literal intelligentsia acted on the assumption that it was possible to exercise the critical function untouched by social or political problems; and many writers withdrew from active involvement in issues of public concern or ideology into formalism, abstraction, or mythmaking.

No consensus, however, is quite as complete as it seems, just as no society is without its areas of dissent. Abundance breeds its own anxieties, not least the fear of losing the comforts one enjoys; in many ways, the calm society is the one most susceptible to sudden, radical fits of panic. In literature, related insecurities in a preoccupation with evil, the possible eruption of weariness, guilt, and remorse, into the rhythms of routine experience. In the political life of the period perhaps the most significant expression of this fear of invasion, subversion, or even destruction by covert agencies was the phenomenon known as McCarthyism. Joseph McCarthy was a young senator from Wisconsin who had a self-appointed mission to wage war on anything he saw as communist subversion. Exploiting his position on the Un-American Activities Committee, playing on popular anxieties about the growing power of Russia and the possible presence of an "enemy within," he embarked on a modern-day witch-hunt, the result of which was that many people were sacked from their jobs and blacklisted on the mere suspicion of belonging to the Communist Party. Guilt was established by smear; loss of job followed on false witness, and a cast of characters that included Hollywood scriptwriters, intellectuals, and academics suddenly found themselves the subject of vicious public abuse.

One crucial fear that McCarthy exploited was the fear of the betrayal of atomic secrets. America had unleashed strange and terrible forces when it dropped atom bombs on Hiroshima and Nagasaki. The bomb cast its shadow over the immediate postwar decades, just as it has done ever since; and the discovery that certain people in the United States, Canada, and Britain had passed atomic secrets to the Russians, who could now explode nuclear weapons of their own, clearly exacerbated public anxieties about hidden enemies and conspiracies, and made it that much easier for McCarthy and his committee flourish. Fear of the potential nuclear capability of the enemy, allied to this suspicion of a powerful enemy within, also increased the tensions of what Winston Churchill christened the Cold War: that policy of brinkmanship between the United States and Russia, their respective satellite states and allies, that was based on the premise that the two superpowers were engaged in a life-or-death struggle for global supremacy. Eisenhower years was more than just a useful weapon in the hands of certain ambitious politicians, helping to generate policies of confrontation and containment.

By the late 1950s this threat—and, more specifically, the bomb that embodied it—had become a potent symbol for the destructive potential of the new society: the dark side of those forces that had created apparently limitless wealth. Everywhere in the culture there were signs of revolt. There was a renewed spirit of rebelliousness, opposition to a social and economic order that had produced the possibility of global death. In music, the emergence of rock and roll, derived mainly from black musical forms, signaled a reluctance to accept the consensual mores, and the blandness, of white middle-class America: which is why, until they were absorbed into the mainstream, performers were perceived by political and religious leaders as such a potent threat, offering a gesture of defiance to "civilized standards." In the movies, similarly, new heroes appeared dramatizing an oppositional stance to the dominant culture. And in literature, too, there were analogous developments. Two key fictional texts of the period were *The Catcher in the Rye* (1951) by J. D. Salinger and *On the Road* (1957) by Jack Kerouac. Radically dissimilar as these two books were, they had in common heroes at odds with modern urban-technological life: outsiders who moved between fragile mysticism and outright disaffiliation in their search for an alternative to the orthodox culture. They were willing, in effect, to say no, in thunder, just as earlier American heroes had been. This was also true of many writers of the period who bore witness to a gradual slipping away from the formalism and abstraction—and, to some extent, the conformism—of the postwar years and toward renewed feelings of freedom, individualism, and commitment. Recovering the impulse toward the personal, sometimes to the point of the confessional, and the urge toward an individual, perhaps even idiosyncratic beat, they gave voice to a growing sense of resistance to the social norms. Reinventing the old American allegiance to the rebellious self, and weaving together personal and historical traumas, they sought in their line and language for a road to liberation: a way of realizing their fundamental estrangement. No cultural development is seamless, and it would be wrong to suggest that the story of the first two decades after World War II is one, simply, of abundance and anxiety merging into revolt and repudiation of fixed forms.

President John F. Kennedy spoke in terms of a general direction or tendency at his Inaugural in January 1961. He brought with him to office the expectation of great change, an optimism and confidence about the character of the United States and its role in the world that many Americans were eager to share. His words were ambitious and struck a responsive chord in the heart of the nation. "We stand today on the edge of a new frontier," Kennedy declared, "a frontier of unknown opportunities and perils... I am asking each of you to be pioneers on that New Frontier." The appeal to the apparently timeless myth of the West, pioneering and conquest captures the confidence, the ambition, the sense of potential, and the arrogance of a "new generation of Americans," and weds all this to the ideology of a long-vanished frontier.

The America to which president spoke was a constellation of many attitudes and forces: a nation of 180 million people, a growing number of whom were white suburbanites living in quiet comfort on the edge of the older, urban areas, buying their goods in out-of-town shopping malls, and working in white-collar service-sector industries. While the income of middle-class Americans of working age continued to improve, that of the bottom 20 percent showed hardly any advance at all. There was conspicuous abundance, but there was equally conspicuous poverty: the rhetoric of the president possibly acknowledged this, but it tended to be forgotten amid the general euphoria, the sense of irresistible expansion and movement forwards toward a "New Frontier." And it was only in the later 1960s that the seeds of discontent and dissension sowed by this conspicuous contrast between haves and have-nots began to be harvested.

In the meantime, in the 1960s, optimism and the promise of adventure were in the air. Responding to the sense of new frontiers to be conquered, many artists of the period, of every kind, were notable for their willingness to experiment, to confront and even challenge cultural and social norms. A decade is an artificial measure and, in this respect as in most others, "the Sixties" had really begun in the middle to late 1950s: when the popular arts were revivified by a new sense of energy and power, and a lively avant-garde embarked on challenging conventional norms and forms. Happenings, festivals, multimedia performances became commonplace events. Readings of poetry and prose, often to jazz accompaniment, attracted dedicated audiences. There was a sense of risk, of venturing beyond the formalism, the preoccupation with craftsmanship of earlier decades. Writing became more open, rawer, alert to the possibility of change and the inclusion of random factors. There was a renewed emphasis on chance, difference, impermanency, a new willingness to see the new artistic object as shifting, discontinuous, part of the flux and variety of things. Modernism was, in effect, shading into postmodernism, with its resistance to finality or closure, to distinctions between "high" and "low" cultures, to grand explanations and master narratives—and to the belief that there is one, major or monolithic truth to be apprehended in art. With its preference for suspended judgments, its disbelief in hierarchies, mistrust of solutions, denouements and completions, the postmodernist impulse was a characteristic product of these times. It encouraged forms of writing that thrived on the edge that denied the authoritative in favor of the arbitrary and posited a random, unstructured world as well as an equally random, unstructured art. This was a different kind of new frontier, perhaps, from the one Kennedy anticipated. But it tapped a similar excitement: "this country might have been a pioneer land, once," declared the black poet Sonia Sanchez, "and it still is."

If one growing tendency of American writing of the 1960s and later was toward postmodernism, another was toward the political. Nowhere was this more notable than among African-American writers like Sanchez. The Black Arts movement, in particular, reacted to calls for "black power" and a new feeling of racial pride captured in the slogan "black is beautiful." Its attempt to define a "black aesthetic," what it meant to be a specifically black writer, encouraged analogous developments among other ethnic minorities and among women of all races. In conferences and workshops like the Second Black Writers' Conference at Fisk University in 1967, critics and writers worked with the issues of how literature might properly express and promote political causes. "The Black Arts and the Black Power concept," Larry Neal (1937–1981) wrote at the beginning of his essay "The Black Arts Movement" (1968), "both relate broadly to the African-American's desire for self determination and nationhood. Both concepts are nationalistic." And, just as African-American writers became intent on explaining and expressing their solidarity with their black brothers and sisters—the urban poor and dispossessed, the people of the newly independent African nations—so women writers, many of them, expressed a commitment to the new forms of feminism. "We can no longer ignore that voice within women that says, 'I want something more than my husband and my children and my home,'" wrote Betty Friedan (1921–2006) in *The Feminine Mystique* (1963). Following on from her, there was an exponential increase in writing about experiences and issues that vitally affected women—women's sexuality, the "feminine" role, childbirth, domestic politics, lesbianism—and a steady development of feminist criticism and theory, social history and aesthetics. Not long after *The Feminine Mystique* was published, in 1965, Luis Valdez (1940–) combined Mexican-American literature with political purpose when he joined with the farm-workers' union led by César Chavez to form El Theatre Campecino. This theater company mixed traditional Spanish and Mexican dramatic forms with agit-prop techniques to create dramatic sketches in support of union issues. The publication of *House Made of Dawn* by N. Scott Momaday in 1968, heralding the emergence of a major movement in Native American writing, coincided with an upsurge in Indian protest: the symbolic seizing of Alcatraz and later armed conflict on reservations that helped generate revisionist histories like *Bury My Heart at Wounded Knee* (1971) by Dee Brown (1908–2002). Asian-Americans, too, gradually asserted their presence, first male writers such as Louis Chu (*Eat a Bowl of Tea*, 1961) and then later female writers like Chuang Hua (*Crossings*, 1968). In these works, a similar confluence of the personal and political was perceptible: the lives of Chinese men, who have left their wives and children for a better existence in America (*Eat a Bowl of Tea*), the lives of women struggling with the racial and cultural constraints imposed on them by an ancient culture (*Crossings*).

Both the impulse toward more openly political forms of writing, and the postmodern inclination toward the absurd, received a push from events that took place not long after President Kennedy took office. Indeed, if his inauguration acted as a catalyst for the optimism of the early 1960s, then his assassination in Dallas in November 1963 served as a focus for energies of another kind. The belief in the radical change persisted, but it was now continued within a harsher, more abrasive and confrontational sense of the social realities. The divisions and discontent that had been always been there—in a society still painfully split between rich and poor, white and colored, suburbanite and ghetto-dweller—now came to the surface; the violence that brought the president's life to an end was echoed in the national life, at home and abroad. The protest became more widespread and exacerbated, and the uneasiness burgeoned into open revolt. The civil rights movement, for example, grew more militant. Instead of merely boycotting segregated businesses and services, black and white activists began to use them, challenging the authorities to enforce iniquitous segregationist laws. Confrontations occurred in several Southern townships between civil rights workers and white authorities. In August 1963 there was a massive demonstration in Washington, DC involving over a quarter of a million people, who heard Martin Luther King, the movement's inspired leader, talk of his dream of a multiracial society. The demonstration was notably and triumphantly peaceful but, in this respect, it marked the end of an era. Within a few years, King himself had been assassinated and the ghettos of Los Angeles, Detroit, New York, Washington, and many other cities were aflame. During the late 1960s it seemed as if rioting in the streets of the cities had become an annual event, as black people expressed their anger with a social and economic order that tended to deprive them of their basic rights. At the same time, the nation's universities were the scene of almost equally violent confrontations, as students expressed their resistance to local university authorities and the power of the state.

For university students, as for many other protest groups of the time, the central issue was the Vietnam War. In the summer of 1964, President Lyndon Johnson persuaded Congress to give him almost unlimited powers to wage war against what was perceived as the communist threat from North Vietnam. American troops were committed to a massive land war against an indigenous guerrilla movement; the American military was involved in saturation bombing and what was euphemistically known as "defoliation"—that is, destruction of the forests, the vegetation, and plant life of a country situated about 12,000 miles from Washington; and American policy was, effectively, to bleed the nation's human and economic resources in support of what was little more than a puppet government in South Vietnam. By 1967, millions of Americans were beginning to feel that the war was not only useless but also obscene, and took to the streets in protest: these included novelists like Norman Mailer, and poets like Robert Lowell and Allen Ginsberg. Simultaneously with this, in response to what looked like the obscenity of the official culture, a vigorous alternative culture developed. Much of this alternative culture was especially political in its direction. Young man buries their draft cards; and, when the Democratic Party met in Chicago in 1968 to nominate their candidate for president, young people upstaged the proceedings by engaging in pitched battles with the police in the streets. But much of it, too, had to do with styles of life and styles of art. Hair was worn unconventionally long, skirts unconventionally short; hallucinogenic drugs, psychedelic art, and hugely amplified rock concerts all became part of an instinctive strategy for challenging standard versions of social reality, accepted notions of behavior and gender. The analytical mode was supplanted by the expressive, the intellectual by the imaginative; artists as a whole went further toward embracing a sense of the provisional, a fluid, unstructured reality; and artistic eclecticism became the norm, as writers in general hit upon unexpected aesthetic mixtures—mingling fantasy and commitment, myth and social protest, high and popular art.

One of the paradoxes of the year 1968 was that it witnessed alternative culture at its zenith and the election of Richard Nixon, self-proclaimed spokesman for the "silent majority" of white, middle-class Americans, to the office of president. To the extent that "the Sixties" have become a convenient label for a particular frame of mind—radical, experimental, subversive, and even confrontational—they did not end in 1970 any more than they began in 1960. Many aspects of the alternative culture survived well into the next decade; and some, like the feminist and ecological movements, effectively became part of the cultural mainstream. Nevertheless, the election of such an un-alternative, un-radical president as Nixon, and his reelection in 1972, did signal a shift in the national mood that was gradually confirmed in the 1970s and beyond. The Vietnam War was brought to an ignominious end, removing one of major sources of confrontation and revolt. Black Americans remained economically dispossessed, but the civil rights movement did increase their electoral power, and so gave them the opportunity of expressing their dissatisfaction through the ballot box rather than taking to the streets. The children of the postwar "baby boom," who had fueled the fires of apparent revolution, began to enter the workforce and take on the responsibilities of jobs, homes, and families. And, while the United States continued to prosper—the gross national product had risen to 974 billion in 1970—there were worrying signs of possible economic crisis. Inflation was worse than in most Western European countries; the balance of payments deficit began to grow to frightening proportions; while the dollar steadily lost its purchasing power. As the economic situation grew harsher, especially after the oil crisis of the early 1970s, more and more Americans narrowed their horizons, devoting their attention and energies to the accumulation and preservation of personal wealth. One commentator christened the 1970s "the me decade"; another referred to the culture of narcissism. And these significant tendencies did not alter with the resignation of Nixon. The rhetoric of Reagan might have sounded similar, at times, to that of Kennedy—when, for instance, he talked about building a shining city upon a hill or declared that the best years of America were yet to come. But this rhetoric occurred within structures of belief and assumptions that were quite different from those of the assassinated president. For Reagan, the crucial appeal was to the past, the mythical American past of stable, familial, and to an extent pastoral values, that, as he saw it, it was the duty of Americans to recover; and to this predominantly backward-looking impulse was added a strong sense of personal responsibility, a feeling that each American should look after himself or herself, which found little room for accommodating the communal vision of an earlier decade.

Reagan might have appealed to the past. Later, in the 1990s, Bill Clinton might have tried to claim some of the spirit of the 1960s for himself, with his talk of being part of a raw, new postwar generation, his declaration of belief in a place called Hope, and, not least, his use of an old movie showing him, as a boy, shaking hands with John Kennedy. The two President George Bushes, father and son, might suggest in turn a warier and more conservative America. What all these presidents have in common, however, is what they have presided over: a dissolution of the old social and cultural markets. Many of the great nation-states have disintegrated: notably, the sinister "other" of Cold War America, the Union of Soviet Socialist Republics. Along with them the great narratives, the meta-narratives used once to explain historical movement, have lost plausibility. The myth of Plymouth Rock, for example, of America as the exclusive domain for Europeans seeking religious and political freedom, has far less resonance in a world characterized by transnational drift and an American nation that is more than ever multicultural. So does the classic iconography of the United States as a melting pot, in which all cultures, all nationalities are resolving into one, which brings in the most significant series of markers that have now disappeared. American popular culture has become internationally dominant. In the global market place it is America that is the biggest item on sale. In a postcolonial world, our imaginations have been colonized by the United

States. At the same time, and crucially, the United States itself has been internationalized. It has become, not a melting pot, but a mosaic of different cultures—what one American writer, Ishmael Reed, has called "the first universal nation."

"The world is here," Reed declared in an essay called, appropriately enough, "America: The Multinational Society" (1988). And the world is here, in the United States, for three seminal reasons. In the first place, particular ethnic groups that have been there for centuries have gained in presence and prominence. The National Census of 1990, for instance, reported 1,959,234 Native Americans living in a total population of over 248 million Americans. The figure was almost fourfold increase on the number of 523,591 Native Americans in the 1960 census, which in turn built upon the population nadir of around 250,000 in 1900. The huge rise in the Native American population was down to a consistently high birth rate and improved medical care, but also due to the increased number of people who claimed Native American ancestry. Whether or not, as some cultural commentators have claimed, ethnicity is a matter of consciousness rather than cultural difference, it is clear that the consciousness of ethnicity has secured the status and significance of certain ethnic groups in the United States. Many more Americans are proud, eager to define themselves as Native American. Many Mexican-Americans, in turn, have lived in a cultural borderland for two centuries, what they call *la frontera*, thanks to Spanish conquest and then American annexation. Along with certain other ethnic groups, notably those from Cuba, Dominica, and Puerto Rico, Mexican-Americans have effected a sea change in American culture and transformed the demographic destiny of the nation.

"American literature, especially in the twentieth century, and notably in the last twenty years," Toni Morrison wrote in 1992, "has been shaped by its encounter with the immigrant," which leads to the second, seminal reason why the United States has become "the first universal nation." Along with immigrants from the Hispanic world, those from the third world generally have been changing the character and destiny of the United States, especially after legislation in the 1960s first abolished national-origin quotas (which tended to favor northern Europeans) and then expanded immigration from countries such as China and India. Almost nine million legal immigrants came to America during the 1980s, along with two million undocumented immigrants. They accounted for 29 percent of the population growth from 226.5 million during the decade. From 1990 to 1997 another 7.5 million foreign-born individuals entered the United States legally, accounting for 29.2 percent of the population. By the middle of the twenty-first century, it has been calculated, "nonwhite" and third world ethnic groups will outnumber whites in the United Sates. Revealing the central dynamic of Western life, and in some sense global life, today, which is marked by the powerful shaping force of shifting, multicultural populations, America has witnessed the disappearance of the boundary between the "center" and the "margins." And with white Americans moving, it seems, inexorably into a minority, it has lost any claim it may have had, or any pretence of one, to a Eurocentric character and an exclusive destiny.

Not that everyone would agree. The attacks by al-Qaeda terrorists on September 11 2001 left almost three thousand people dead, the World Trade Center in New York City destroyed, and Americans rightly feeling that they were seriously threatened. The American government, led by President George W. Bush, responded to this by launching a "war on terror," first invading Afghanistan, which had harbored al-Qaeda terrorists, and then embarking on a lengthy diplomatic campaign to associate Iraq with international terrorism. In particular, it was claimed that Iraq possessed "weapons of mass destruction" that endangered the security of the United Sates and its allies. The diplomatic campaign was followed by a military one, which began on March 20, 2003 with the invasion of Iraq by a multinational force led by troops from the United States and United Kingdom. The military operation was swiftly finished, with the coalition declaring on April 15 that the invasion was effectively over and, later, Bush making what became known as his "mission accomplished" speech. What followed the operation, however, was continued chaos and conflict. Saddam Hussein was certainly removed from power, his totalitarian regime toppled. But the cost was high, with civil war and sustained acts of terrorism leaving five thousand members of the coalition army and up to seven hundred thousand Iraqis dead by the beginning of 2009. A vast majority of Americans and the international community came to believe that the Iraq War was a mistake; most intelligence experts agreed that it had only increased terrorism. The situation was exacerbated by the failure to discover any weapons of mass destruction in Iraq and by a series of human rights abuse in coalition detention centers, including the now notorious ones of Abu Ghraib and Guantanamo Bay. If the mission of the war was to bring peace and prosperity to Iraq, it certainly failed. If it was to demonstrate a continued belief, at least in some quarters, in the special destiny of America, then it succeeded—but at an enormously high cost to the national reputation. The gap between the promise and performance of the mission was measured by two events. On April 9, 2003 a statue of Hussein was torn down by crowds in Baghdad to mark the fall of the city. Exactly six years later, tens of thousands of Iraqis gathering in Baghdad to demand the immediate departure of coalition forces, burned an effigy of George W. Bush.

By the time of the second event, Bush had ceased to in power. The war, an economic crisis that came to be known as the Great Recession, a gathering sense that the nation had lost its way—all contributed to a remarkable event: the election of the first African-American, Barack Obama, to the office of president. Obama was born in Kenya, raised in Indonesia and then in Hawaii; and the "experience of a variety of cultures in a climate of mutual respect," he has said, became "an important part" of his "worldview."

That worldview, after he was elected to the senate, made him one of the few major politicians initially opposed the Iraq War. During and after the presidential campaign, it also prompted him to stress the importance of reducing energy dependence and extending healthcare. Whether Obama will fulfill his stated ambitions as president—a rapid withdrawal of troops from Iraq, a reduction in carbon emissions, a radical increase in energy sources, and the realization of a universal healthcare system—remains to be seen. What is clear, however, is that like Franklin D. Roosevelt in the 1930s, Obama has restored the international reputation of the United States and reignited America's belief in itself. And his agenda, if exceptionalist, is so only in the sense that he embraces the idea of the United States as the first universal nation. What the story of the last ten years has told us is that there is still a deep division of opinion about the place and destiny of America, its position either as a crusade with a special mission, a Manifest Destiny to be realized at home and abroad, or as crossroads of culture, part of an international community of nations. In his inauguration speech, Obama referred to the "patchwork heritage" of America and called it a "strength, not a weakness." "We are shaped by every language and culture," "drawn from every end of this earth," he added. It is this notion of mosaic of cultures that has now reasserted itself, recapturing the center ground from the idea of mission, an exclusive destiny. But both ideas still command loyalty, and will presumably continue to struggle for supremacy, as Americans continue to engage in the task of reinventing themselves—or in what Obama, in his inauguration speech, called "the work of remaking America."

The consequence of all this for literature in America are debatable. Given that writers are responding on some level to their own unique encounters with history, they are in any event not easy, perhaps impossible, to summarize. For some, there has been a notable shift away from public affairs and commitment and toward introspection, the cult of the personal. Writers, quite a few of them, have turned away from immediate history, the pressures of the times, and devoted their imaginations to the vagaries of consciousness, the deeper forms of myth, ritual, and fantasy, the imagery figured and the language articulated by the isolated mind. For others, particularly many women writers and writers from "ethnic" or "nonwhite" cultures, the engagement with history remains pressing, even painful, although the terms in which that engagement is expressed may vary from the literal, the direct, as in the New Journalism and forms of social realism, to the resonantly abstract, the figurative, or the archaic. Writers may devote themselves, say, to the interrogation and alteration of verbal structures, in the belief that what we see and think is shaped by such structures; our social life being grounded in language, in order to change society it is language that must be changed. Or they may respond to what Clifford Geertz has called "the international hodgepodge of postmodern culture" by creating an art of palpable discontinuity: yoking together wildly incongruous elements, mixing voices and genres, pursuing the inconsistent, the divergent and indeterminate. They may be inclined to the use of fabulation, magic, or dreams in the conviction that consciousness shapes history—or the simpler assumption that only a literature of the strange, the fantastic, can begin to recover the strangeness of contemporary America. Or they may turn to the oral or other traditions of one of the ancient cultures that inform American history: not to legitimate that culture (the time for that, if there ever was one, has long gone) but to explore the meaning of those traditions for all American society.

What surely all these, and other, forms of writing in contemporary America share is their condition: their presence in a permeable space where nations and cultures meet. It is a luminal space, the space of postmodernity, post-postmodernity or radicalized modernity, marked by dissolution and dispersal, mobility and fragmentation, the heterogeneous and the hybrid—all on a global scale. Representing different cultures, living between them, and responding to their diverse origins and experiences, all these writers effectively challenge the notion of common heritage and fixed boundaries. Of course, in doing so, they challenge the assumptions so central to the grand narrative of the American state. The country they discover and describe in their work does have the order, absolute contours of the American Eden. It is a place with fluid boundaries, where rival, overlapping, and ultimately interdependent cultural histories meet, conflict, and perhaps converge. American writers are still, as much as ever, concerned with the possibles and variables of American life, the material and mental contours of the American landscape, the imperatives of American history, and the inspiration of the American dream. But the possibles of American life have multiplied; the contours of American landscape have assumed a more elusive, enigmatic character; the imperatives of American history are more plural, more polyglot than ever before; and the American dream now is inspired by what seems a process of accelerated transformation, insistent reinvention. Responding to these changes, American writers have changed. What has happened may be measured in a small but significant shifting of words: American writing is now writing in America. The point is simple but fundamental. Nationality, at the scene of writing, is less determined and determining than it ever was previously, more open to other stories and histories. The scene of writing is one that is now genuinely transnational. In the postmodern period, American literature, with its unique thinking of the world from the perspective of pluralism and globalization and the innovative ever-changing various techniques and hybridization of all sorts of forms in textual structure to represent the uncertain reality and history, has exerted great influence on world literature in the 21st century.

Postmodernism

The postmodernist thought is the product of the postmodern society (or the post-industrial society, the information society, the late capitalism). It was gestated in the womb of its modernist mother in the 1930s, tore itself out of it after World War II and became a cultural specter being praised and blamed at the same time and wandering in the whole field of Western culture. Postmodernism formally appeared in the late 1950s and the early 1960s, engendered into an overwhelming momentum, and shocked the thinking circles in the 1970s and the 1980s.

Postmodernism deems that in the world today the important functions of such various phenomena as instability, indeterminacy, discontinuity, disorder, rupture, sudden changes, etc. have been more and more recognized and paid great attention to. In the circumstances, a new concept to look on the world has begun to go deep into people's consciousness. It opposes the practice of using the single, fixed logic, formula, principle and the universally applicable law to explain and rule the world, advocates changes and innovations, emphasizes openness and pluralism, acknowledges and tolerates differences. The era nowadays has already given up the effort to constitute the unified and universally applicable patterns. Some new categories such as openness, polysemousness, polyphony, indeterminacy, possibility, unpredictableness, etc. have entered postmodern languages. In the postmodern era, thorough pluralism has become a universal basic concept; the postmodern pluralism is the nature of all fields of knowledge and all aspects of social life. The basic experiences in the postmodern times are the inalienable right of the totally different formations of knowledge, the designs of life, and the ways of thinking and behavior; the old pattern that everything revolves round one sun has been no longer effective; even truth, justice, humanity, and reason are all plural. The direct conclusion of the principles of pluralism is that it opposes any attempt at unification; that the postmodern thinking actively maintains the diversity and richness of things; that it firmly argues against any ambition for hegemony to impose one's own choice on others and make the alien things submit to one's own will; that it respects and acknowledges all the choices of social conceptions, ways of life, and cultural forms. The basic postmodernist contents "as the tenets of science and art had already existed in the first half of the twentieth century, most of them merely rested on a kind of proposition, manifesto or design, or they were merely special phenomena in a certain field. But today they have already begun to become the reality of our life roundly and thoroughly" (Welsch 48). In the sense of time, postmodernist thought might be understood as the continuity and development of modernism. But "in some problems, there are fundamental differences between postmodernism and modernism:

postmodernism opposes any dream for oneness, negates all universally applicable and ever-unchanging principles, formulas and laws, and gives up all the patterns for unification. Then, in this sense, postmodernist thought is the criticism and transcending of modernism" (Welsch 48).

Postmodernism is a social thought that is completely different from the movement of modernization since Renaissance. The appearance of postmodernism in the humanities and the social sciences signals the birth of another novel academic paradigm: "Rather, a radically new and different cultural movement is coalescing in a broad-gauged re-conceptualization of how we experience and explain the world around us. In its *extreme* formulations, postmodernism is revolutionary; it goes to the very core of what constitutes social science and radically dismisses it. In its more *moderate* proclamations, postmodernism encourages substantive re-definition and innovation. Postmodernism proposes to set itself up outside the modern paradigm, not to judge modernity by its own criteria but rather to contemplate and deconstruct it" (Rosenau 4-5). Modernity stresses reason, democracy and freedom. It cries up the progress of science and technology, equality and universal fraternity in the modern times. But all that modernity has created makes people doubt its original faiths. Postmodernists conclude that modernity is no longer a force of emancipation; on the contrary, it is the source of enslavement, oppression and repression. Postmodernists take a spurning attitude towards all the theories of modernity. They equally treat various concepts of modernity without discrimination and destroy them all, regarding them as the things of Logos-centrism, foundationalism, and essentialism, as all-embracing things, and as the things narrated by meta-narrative. Having compared the system of modern thoughts with pre-modern things, postmodernists hold that, just as ancient people created myths, magic, alchemy and primitive worship, modern people themselves have created modernity as a new myth. Postmodernism has abandoned all kinds of authorities, centers, foundations and essences about modernity and caused delegitimation of all codes (Hassan 169). The philosophical foundation of modernism is seeking the present metaphysics, a never-changing truth, the noumenon and epistemology of the ultimate value. But postmodernism "opposes not only the discourse considering that man has the natural essence of the mirror type but also the discourse holding that the world has identity, consistency, wholeness and centricity; argues against not only the hierarchical division between different disciplines but also the quest for a certain first discipline" (Zhang 45). Postmodernism has abolished the antitheses and gaps established by modernity between this shore and the other shore, transience and eternity, center and margin, depth and surface, phenomenon and essence, subject and object, etc. It has actually cancelled the dimensions of knowledge such as foundation, center, essence, and noumenon. It wants to break through the whole well-organized and orderly world constructed by modernity and make the whole world go into the dimensions of pluralism, seemingness, transience, disorder, anarchism, ambiguity and indeterminacy.

Postmodernist Fiction

The writing of the fiction as a literary form reached its peak in the period of critical realism in the late 19th century, having established a pattern that everybody could imitate: a work should narrate a vivid and interesting story, portray one character or several characters, with these characters often falling into a kind of psychological or social contradictions and conflicts; along with the development of the plot the contradictions and conflicts would be solved in a certain way (Zhang 6). The writing method of this sort of fiction takes characters as its core and the plot of the story can only unfold round the characters. The characters, especially protagonists, must have their own looks, personalities, behavior and conduct, even their language is different from the common run, and they must live in given circumstances. In its narrative, the realistic fiction takes imitating or reproducing the objective reality as the basic principle; the unfolding of plots and the development of events are arranged according to the time sequence of reality, being shown in linear narrative and causal logic; the circumstances in which the characters are and the descriptions of their activities are confined in the conventional geometrical space. This kind of structure of time and space tightly fetters the reader in the everyday reality and he or she can only see the seeming phenomena of life but is unable to understand the deep meaning of the existence hidden behind them. The realistic fiction has definite intentions and themes of writing. The stories that it narrates aim at showing a certain determinate and concrete concept of value, moral principle or truth of life, trying to lead the reader to draw a specific moral conclusion and to realize the goal of moralization. The semantic meaning of this sort of fiction is onefold and transparent.

Like the other fields of human studies in which new thoughts constantly emerge, literature and art as the products of human society in given historical periods are also continually developing and innovating. From the end of the 19th century, the concepts of values and aesthetics of realistic literature were challenged forcefully by the methods of modernist literature such as symbolism, expressionism, surrealism, stream-of-consciousness, etc. The appearance of modernism brings with it the fundamental changes of the notions of fiction, the techniques of writing, the contents of thought, the forms of expression, artistic artifices, and styles. Modernist fictionists think that the reality does not mean only people and things in the superficial and objective world but also includes man's inner world and that man's subconscious and unconscious activities are a reality which is more important and more essential than that of the outside world. Therefore, the essential task of fiction is to represent man's innermost activities covered by the seeming phenomena of everyday life. Thus, in the modernist fiction, the description of outside circumstances and the things that take place in it is reduced to the minimum limit, and a majority of space is used to represent man's experience, recept and reflection of the outside, disorderly and absurd reality and goes deep into man's subconsciousness and unconsciousness, probing into man's innermost concealed secret and revealing man's despair and the sense of crisis, the absurdity of world and the meaninglessness of life, etc. In consequence, modernist fiction abandons the integrality and dramaticness of story plots and the protagonists and characters in it do not have vivid personalities any more. The characters are observed from different points of view and from different situations in which they are put. They appear to be dim and fragmented. Because in the modernist fiction man's inner world is not restricted by realistic time and space, imaginations, reminiscences, associations, hallucinations and dreams can move about freely and quickly and can go boundlessly to many faraway places, disordering and reversing the sequence of realistic event, making the past, the present and the future intervein with each other arbitrarily. Thus, modernist fiction overthrows the principle of representation (imitating the reality) and the mode of representation (narrating a story) of realistic fiction and makes inside innovations in the structures, techniques, and language of fiction. It, however, does not touch the totality, closeness, and oneness of fiction as a literary form. Instead, it reserves the outside boundary between it and other literary forms and genres, still pays attention to the purity of its genre, and does its utmost to preserve the pureness and elegance of literary language and artistic artifices. Modernist fiction tries hard to express a certain metaphysical meaning or a suggestion that provides this meaning. Once they are extensively imitated and used, the techniques and forms of modernist fiction that are regarded as innovations quickly become new criteria and ossified modes that can no longer play any new designs. Consequently, the assertion claiming that "The fiction has died" is heard: "I believe that the genre of the fiction, if it is not yet irretrievably exhausted, has certainly entered its last phase, the scarcity of possible subjects being such that writers must make up for it by the exquisite quality of the other elements that compose the body of a fiction" (Gasset 56).

Postmodernist fiction restores the vitality of "the literature of exhaustion" (Barth 64) with new forms and techniques. As the art of the postmodern mass society, postmodernist fiction has destroyed the metaphysical conventions of modernist art, broken its close and self-contained aesthetic forms, and advocates thorough pluralism in thinking patterns, writing techniques, artistic genres, and language games (Kitler 13). Postmodernists think that "Reality is brought out by language, that is, a false language brings out a false reality. The narrative manner of traditional fiction (including realistic and modernist fiction) is one of the makers of the false reality: the fact itself that it fabricates a story to 'reflect' is a false reality, thus leading the reader into the double falsehood. The task of fiction is debunking this kind of beguilement and displaying the falsehood of reality and the falsehood of invented stories before the readers, thus urging them to think" (Zhang 16-17). Postmodernist fiction, however, not only subverts the internal formation and structure of traditional fiction but also shows its doubts about the fictional form and narrative itself. Postmodernist metafiction is the reflection, deconstruction and subversion of the fiction as a literary form and narrative itself. Though it reserves the appearance and outline of fiction, metafiction tells the reader how this story is fabricated while "telling" this story. It is a fiction about fiction. It overthrows the concept of pure fiction, destroys the narrative conventions of traditional fiction (e.g. linear narrative, causal logic, etc.), blurs the dividing line between it and other literary genres, adopts a great deal of representational techniques of other literary genres. In metafiction, the time crosses the past, the present and the future and the names and identities of characters are all uncertain. In the postmodernist fiction there is not any objective or transcendental meaning; the so-called meaning is only produced in the differences of man-made language signs, namely, the effect produced by the permutation and combination of signs. Therefore, the writing of invented texts is only a language game. Any text is open and incomplete. It depends on other texts (on its differentiation from and relation with them) and especially on the reader's interpretation. It is the reader's interpretation that gives a certain meaning to the combination and permutation of signs. Postmodernist fiction transcends the dividing lines between belles-lettres and popular literature and between high literature and light literature, thus turning the literature as the privilege of the high-browed intellectuals into the literature of the reading public (Fiedler 19) and showing a tendency towards popularization. In addition, in the postmodernist fiction, the artistic techniques of modernist fiction such as the interior monologue of stream-of-consciousness, symbolism, free association, the disorder of time and space, etc. have already dropped back to the secondary position though they have not yet been completely abandoned; the more frequently-used forms of expression are metafiction, language games, the tendency towards popularization, parody, collage, montage, labyrinth, black humor, etc. Such characteristics as the language subject, fragmented narrative, shifting signifiers, writing zero, etc. have also appeared in the postmodernist fiction.

Metafiction

A postmodernist writer deconstructs the traditional fictional form and narrative itself. First of all, he does this by means of metafiction. In order to explore the relation between fiction and reality, metafiction intentionally and systematically stresses its position as a man-made product. This sort of fiction provides a kind of criticism of its own structure and methods. While narrating stories, metafiction not only examines the basic structure of narrative itself but also explores the possible fictiveness of the world outside of literary work. Postmodernist writers pay close attention to the theoretical problem of the fictional structure. Their works usually have the characteristic of self-reflection and at the same time show their inclination to doubt the fictional form. Every important feature of metafiction is used to inquire into the theory of writing and the practice of fictional production.

Since the 1960s, people have been extremely interested in how to reflect, how to describe, and how to spread the knowledge of their social experiences. Metafiction attempts to find the answers to these questions through its self-exploration of its own form. The writers of metafiction adopt the traditional simile that sees the world as a book, and often use contemporary theories of philosophy, linguistics and literature to reconstruct fiction. These theories consider that we as individuals are not in the position of the selves but play all sorts of roles. Therefore, to study the characters in fiction can provide a useful pattern to understand the subjective structure of the world outside of fiction. Our knowledge of this world is spread through language, and the fiction as a literary genre (a world completely constructed with language) becomes a useful pattern to know the structure of realistic world.

People realize that, to the smallest pieces of material construction, every process of observation will cause a great stir; people also realize that it is impossible to describe a natural world because the observer always changes what he is observing. However, what metafiction is concerned about is more complicated than this because metafiction thinks that man cannot describe anything. The writers of metafiction have been aware of an essential dilemma: if he or she attempts to describe a world, he or she will soon realize that the world cannot be described. They consider that they can only describe the theory and the language about that world in the invented work of literature—fiction.

In the writing of metafiction, these writers use a kind of metalanguage that is not the language to describe the non-language events, situations or objects but the language used to depict another sort of language. Along with the continuous growth of the self-consciousness about society and culture, the knowledge of the independence of language and experience is also continuously growing. The viewpoint that language only passively reflects a coherent and meaningful objective world can no longer hold water. Language is regarded as an independent and self-contained system. It can produce meaning by itself. The relation between language and realistic world is complicated, indeterminate, and controlled by convention. The writers of metafiction probe in their works the relation between this language system and the world outside of fiction. Consequently, they make their works constantly manifest the literary language that they consciously use and the habitual practice of writing fiction, clearly and definitely showing their features of artificial products and revealing the disjointedness between the sense of crisis, the sense of alienation, and the sense of oppression, and the traditional literary form (for instance, realism) which is no longer applicable to the representation of postmodern experience. Thus, metafiction has transformed the passive value of old habitual practice into the basis of the potential and constructive social criticism. In fact, it indicates that, just like using it to directly reflect the supposed human nature existing as an entity outside of the system of expression, using the artistic mirror to reflect its own language or its descriptive structure can achieve the same effect.

Metafiction is also usually based on essential, sustained opposite principles. While constructing the mirages of fiction (like the traditional realistic works), metafiction also reveals the nature of these mirages, making the readers realize that they are not copies of real life but only stories invented by the writer. This is clearly shown by the fact that in metafiction a story can be provided with several endings. If we define metafiction by using common language, metafiction is the fiction that comments on the writing of fiction itself while writing fiction. The two processes are closely combined, thus breaking the obvious dividing line between writing and criticism and merging them into the concepts of interpretation and decomposition.

According to the views of metafiction, both reality and history are transient. In the realistic fiction there are completely invented plots, the coherent narration by time sequence, the omniscient and omnipotent writer or narrator, the reasonable relation between the characters' behavior and their identities, and a kind of causal relation between the detailed description on the surface layer and the scientific laws on the deep layer. The writers of metafiction consider that the realistic fiction is a fictional form that is identical with the orderly social reality but the present world is no longer a permanent reality but a series of constructions, a non-perpetual structure. Consequently, the traditional form of fiction is no longer applicable for representing this reality and a kind of meta-language should be used to construct a fictional form that can be suitable for this reality.

Metafiction attaches importance to the examination of the fictional form itself. Its method of deconstruction not only helps the fictionist and the reader better understand the narrative structure of fiction but also offers an extremely clear pattern to understand the human experience of the contemporary world. For the writers of metafiction, the contemporary world is a composed product, a combination of techniques and a systematic network of signs that depend on each other in existence.

Modernist writers describe the struggle for individual independence as a conflict between the existing social system and the traditional conventions. This conflict or struggle inevitably leads to individual alienation and common spiritual death. The power structure of contemporary society tends to become more complicated, more diverse, more covert, and more mysterious so that postmodernist writers meet with greater difficulties when they recognize and represent rebellious objects. The method that the writers of metafiction use to solve the problem is to move their attention from the description of the outside objective world to the exploration of the techniques of expression of fiction itself. Its purpose is to examine the relation between the fictional form and the reality. In the final analysis, however, metafiction limits its rebellion within the range of the fictional form itself.

In order to analyze another kind of language, namely, the language of the traditional fiction, metafiction pays close attention to the habitual practice of fiction and exposes the process of its formation. For example, John Fowles uses the habitual practice of the omniscient and omnipotent writer in his novel *The French Lieutenant's Woman* (1969). Metafiction also often uses the form of parody that is written through the imitation of another work in order to comment on the mode of fiction. For example, John Gardner's novel *Grendel* (1971) recounts and comments on the ancient story *Beowulf* from the monster's narrative angle. John Hawkes' fiction *The Lime Twig* (1961) forms both a sample of popular thrillers and the criticism of it at the same time.

Among all the types of experimental fictions, metafiction does not appear very radical because metafiction only reveals the habitual practice of traditional fiction, neither ignoring it nor abandoning it. The traditional writing techniques provide a kind of control, a kind of standard or background for metafiction. On this basis, the writers of metafiction put to good use of their experimental techniques. They often use anti-traditional techniques to weaken (not abandon) the omniscient and omnipotent writers or narrators, the complete endings and the definite explanations, and defamiliarize the traditional techniques and structures through the imitation of another language. Though some readers have become estranged from this kind of language as well as from the habitual practice and thought, this estrangement has been done on a basis that the readers are extremely familiar with them. Therefore, metafiction can be understood through the old structure. This sort of work not only makes itself welcome to the readers but also makes the readers participate in the construction of the meaning of works. Metafiction does not abandon the realistic world; its purpose is to look for a fictional form that is closely related with and understandable to the contemporary readers and to reexamine the habitual practice of the traditional fiction through its self-reflection. Metafiction reveals for us how literary works construct their imaginative worlds and by doing this helps us understand that the reality in which we live every day is similarly constructed and similarly written down (Yu 455-456).

Metafiction can be defined as the fiction about fiction and it can also be subdivided into the fiction about how this fiction becomes a fiction, the fiction about a previous fiction and the fiction similar with other texts (Zhao 11-12).

Terms of Postmodernist Literature

There are some important literary terms of postmodernist literature such as black humor, collage, montage, parody, hybridization, carnivalization, labyrinth, language games and the readers' interpretation, anti-genre, indeterminacy, immanence, just name a few frequently mentioned ones.

Black Humor Though very deeply influenced by existentialist philosophy, black humor as a postmodernist technique of expression, regarding the world as absurd and unreasonable and giving a smile after feeling extremely pessimistic, does not advocate the ways to save the world as existentialism does—to participate, to choose or to cry and protest or to struggle to resist or to lament and sigh mournfully because doing like that can only make the absurdity more chaotic and more unendurable. To black humor fictionists, the absurdity of existence can only be accepted because it is an unchangeable part of the world. They indifferently consider that absurdity is a part of the world that is a farce in nature. They no longer make an effort to replace the value with the value of mission and responsibility or bemoan the state of the universe and pity the fate of mankind. But instead, they continue, by using language, to play the game in which existence does not put forth a card with reason. The writing characteristics of black humor generally manifest themselves as the following: comically and even absurdly dealing with intrinsically tragic subjects, representing the single-dimension character and the wasteland background, constructing loose and usually disjointed structures without paying attention to time, confusing facts and invention to reveal the unreliability of reality, stressing techniques and formal designs, coldly looking on the despairing, fantastic, rude and cruel events, telling the story with mockingly questioning-God tone and often with a laughter having no intention to punish the evil and praise the good. The origin of these is the writer's doubt about traditional philosophy and science.

Collage Imitating the method of newsreels adopted by John Dos Passos, some postmodernist fictionists combine together other texts such as fragments of some literary works, common sayings in everyday life, abstracts from newspapers and magazines, news reports, etc. and make these seemingly totally irrelevant fragments form an entity whose elements are related to each other, thus having broken the solidified formal structure of traditional fiction, caused a strong shock upon the reader's aesthetic habit, and produced the effect that the conventional narrative manner could not achieve. In the postmodernist fiction, the scattered and fragmented materials are everything. They will never give a certain combination of meanings or the final solution but can only give the reader a sense of moving combination in the eternal and present reading experience. This thorough pileup of fragmented images opposes the combination in any form. Barthelme thinks, "The principle of collage is the central principle of all the arts in all the media of dissemination in the 20th century" (*SW* Trans. 331-332). Again he explains, "The key point of collage lies in that the unsimilar things are glued together, which can create a reality when it is at best. This new reality, when it is at best, may be or suggest a comment upon the other reality from which it originates, or, not only these" (*SW* Trans. 331-332). *Snow White* is like a continuous gather-together of fragments which are loosely organized round the fairy tale about Snow White by means of collage of fragments.

Parody Parody is one of the important writing techniques used by many postmodernist fictionists. This is the most intentional and analytical literary method. Through its destructive imitation, this method exerts itself to stress the weakness, affectation, and the lack of self-consciousness of the target of its imitation. The so-called target of its imitation can be a work and the common style of some writers as well. Parody imitates the contents or the style of a serious literary work or a literary genre and makes this imitation very funny through the incoordination between the form, style and absurd subjects of the work or the genre. It mocks a given work but its way of mocking is to use a joking and funny method and genre to deal with a lofty subject. The essence of parody is a phenomenon of genre—an exaggerative imitation of a writer or the forms and characteristics of a genre, whose mark is its inconformity in genre, structure, or theme. The obvious function of parody is satire. Its way of satirizing is to indirectly attack its target through the way of genre. Parody cites or indirectly mentions the work that it ridicules and uses the typical method of the latter in a way to abolish or subvert it. Critics have seen that the intentional and distorting imitation of a certain pattern may produce a very original work.

Montage If collage is an unconscious hodgepodge that is accidentally pieced together, montage, another expressive means of postmodernism, is a conscious combination. Like collage, montage also represents discontinuity—a time concept in the postmodern times. The characteristic of the postmodern times is a sort of schizophrenia or a rupture of the chain of signs. Because in the mind of a schizophrenic, the organization of syntax and time has completely disappeared and there are only the pure signifiers left, that is to say, in the minds of postmodern people, the time concepts of the past and the future have completely disappeared and only the eternal present is left. The method of montage links up the pictures and scenes that are not related to each other in contents and forms and on the different levels of time and space or rearranges and reorganizes different genres, the sentences in different styles and characteristics, and contents. It uses the artifices such as pre-narration, flashback, insertion, reiteration, close-up, the contrast between still and moving scenes, etc. to strengthen the stimulation of the reader's sense organs and acquire strong artistic effect.

Labyrinth Fredric Jameson claims, "If modernist architecture tells you how to read and interpret and how to live a life, then postmodernist works are the labyrinths that you can never read and interpret" (Jameson 165). Labyrinth refers to the intricate and dazzling structure without giving a way out that a postmodernist writer builds in his fiction. It is not like a detective fiction that is complicated and confusing but everything in it will certainly become clear and solved at last. What rules labyrinth is chaos or absence. It is like the image with no meaning or the bamboo fish trap with no fish. John Barth, Vladimir Nabokov, and Thomas Pynchon are all adept at building labyrinths. A theme that appears again and again in Pynchon's works is the essential disorder or disintegration of the Western world. Pynchon metaphorically introduces entropy, an important concept in thermodynamics and information theory, into literary writing. In thermodynamics in physics, in a closed thermodynamic system having no material and energy exchange with the outside world, the movements of molecules will become more and more disordered, finally reach the limit of disorder and form the state of heat balance with the same temperature. Entropy is a measure unit of the extent of this disorder. That is to say, in an isolated thermodynamic system, entropy will become bigger and bigger. Entropy is also a measure unit of the extent of disorder in information theory. According to the theory of heat death, the universe is an enormous closed system. Following the second law of thermodynamics, it is going towards disorder, decline, and death. In his works, Pynchon, using this view as a metaphor, regards the world in which he lives as a closed system and points out the inherent disorder, corruption in the Western society and its fate: it will inevitably die in the end. Entropy indicates that all kinds of mechanisms and orders in the human society will finally go towards heat death, that is, towards chaos and disorder. The more orderly a mechanism or an institution or a system is, the greater its tendency towards heat death is, because the existing institutions and organizations in the human society will certainly exert strict controlling function upon it. The tighter the organizations are, the more complicated the information and meanings are and the more easily they will cause heat death and go towards its opposite side: order will change into disorder and civilization will be finally controlled by chaos.

Hybridization Hybridization, or the mutant replication of genres, includes parody, travesty and pastiche. Hassan thinks, "The 'de-definition,' deformation, of cultural genres engenders equivocal modes: 'paracriticism,' 'factual discourse,' 'new journalism,' 'non-fiction fiction,' and a promiscuous category of 'para-literature' or 'threshold literature,' at once young and very old. *Cliche* and plagiarism, parody and pastiche, pop and kitsch enrich *re*-presentation. In this view image or replica may be as valid as its model...may even bring an '*augment d'etre*.' This makes for a different concept of tradition, one in which continuity and discontinuity, high and low culture, mingle, not to imitate but to expand the past in the present. In that plural present, all styles are dialectically available in an interplay between the Now and the Not Now, the Same and the Other. Thus, in postmodernism, Heidegger's concept of 'equitemporality' becomes really a dialectic of equitemporality, an intertemporality, a new relation between historical elements, without any suppression of the past in favor of the present..." (Hassan 170). To put it simpler, hybridization is a sort of variant imitation of genres including the funny and humorous imitations of poems and the mixed stew of various imitated works. Postmodernists have enriched the intention and extension of prototypes and enhanced the vitality of original texts (original works and prototypes) by means of decayed and plagiarized subjects, clumsy imitation and piecing together, the interveining and reversion of time sequence, the displacement of places and spaces, the appearance of the higher language together with the lower language, and the convergence of serious and popular subjects. Hybridization oversteps the dividing line between traditional disciplines and academic rules. It makes readers not know what to turn to, compels them to exist constantly in the specific language contents, refuses all their expectations of the preceding things, and makes them fall into the all-sided disorder of the inner world via the language world as medium from the outside physical world.

Carnivalization Carnivalization, a term borrowed by Hassan from the Russian literary theorist Mikhail Bakhtin, riotously embraces indeterminacy, fragmentation, decanonization, selflessness, irony, and hybridization, all of which were mentioned before. The term also conveys the comic or absurdist ethos of postmodernism, anticipated in the "heteroglossia" of Rabelais and Laurence Sterne, jocose prepostmodernists. Carnivalization further means "polyphony," the sense of fragmentation caused by the centrifugal power of language, the "gay relativity" of things, perspectivism and performance, participation in the wild disorder of life, the immanence of laughter. Indeed, what Bakhtin calls fiction or carnival—that is, antisystem—might stand for postmodernism itself, or at least for its ludic and subversive elements that promise renewal. For in carnival "the true feast of time, the feast of becoming, change, and renewal," human beings, then as now, discover "the peculiar logic of the 'inside out' (*a l'envers*), of the 'turnabout,' ...of numerous parodies and travesties, humiliations, profanations, comic crownings and uncrownings. A second life" (Hassan 171). Carnivalization removes all kinds of differences and dividing lines, makes all participants both actors (or actresses) and audience. Carnivalization makes man have the hallucination that he is the real master or dominator of the world. In the game, in the confusion, in the madness, and in the rebellion against traditional reason, carnivalization swallows everything, reconstructs everything, and acculturates everything.

Language Games and the Readers' Interpretation In the postmodern world, the thinking activities of thinkers and literary critics are all basically on the level of language. Their language statements are a sort of language structures that are purely controlled by the logic of language itself and are not identical with the realistic existence and the objective social reality. To postmodernist writers, everything is indeterminate, there is not any transcendental and objective meaning, and therefore they can only place their feelings on writing itself. Writing is nothing but a process through which a writer's introspection is symbolized (Hawkes 145). In other words, writing is a sort of information that refers to itself, expecting to gradually establish its own meaning in the process of exploring itself. Value originates from invention; meaning is generated in the differences of language symbols, that is, meaning is the effect produced by the permutation and combination of signs. Therefore, writing (especially the writing of invented texts) is only a language game. Jean-Francois Lyotard, French famous philosopher, thinks that in each discourse with a different nature people can design and determine language games by using optional game rules that explain the nature and usage of the discourse. But these game rules themselves cannot provide their own legitimacy for themselves and they can only be the products of the contract type between game players. Rules are the keys that games can be used. Any of their changes will change the nature of games. Like games, the speaking of any discourse has the implications of confrontation and competition and therefore has a characteristic that constantly gets rid of the stale and brings forth the fresh (Wang Yuechuan 181). Roland Barthes, French famous literary critic, thinks that a postmodernist writer is not a person who uses language as a tool to manifest his own ideas, express his own feelings or represent his own imaginations but a person who thinks over language, a thinker-linguist (in other words, a person who is neither a complete thinker nor a complete linguist) (Barthes 87). The contemporary writing has already freed itself out of the dimension of expressing meaning and only refers to itself. Like playing games, writing reveals itself in its continually going beyond its own rules and violating its own limitations.

According to a very important idea in the theory of discourse, the language philosophy of postmodernism, language symbols have increasingly lost their ability to express meaning, that is, they can no longer hit meaning itself, and our written and spoken discourses including writing itself all have been lost in the endless chain of signifiers. This means that any postmodern text does not have a unified core of meaning. The meaning of a text does not come from the writer's creation but from the reader's interpretation of the text. Anybody can give his own interpretation of the text. The postmodern reader, taking a critical and creative attitude and exploring the implications or the overtones of the text through the subjective construction of meaning, has finally rewritten the original text. Barthes thinks that, in the process of writing of a postmodernist writer, firstly, the subject (the writer) experiences the courses of deconstruction and reconstruction. Secondly, on the subconscious level, he thirsts for his reader's understanding and helping, and longs for establishing a kind of mechanism of the dialogue type between him and the reader. Barthes regards a literary work as a process of production and reproduction and changes the reader from a consumer into a producer who participates in the process of production and reproduction. The meaning of a work is not decided by the writer but created by the reader who redisplays the productive process of the text and participates in this process. The reading manner of postmodernist fiction attaches importance to aesthetic delight instead of aesthetic joyfulness, emphasizes digging out infinite plural meaning in the endless movement of signifiers of texts, stresses symbolic thinking, active participation, direct experience, and sudden realization, and dedicates itself to the breakthrough of the subconscious activities in rational and visual thinking (Barthes, *The Noise of Language* 108). In the postmodern times, the reading activity is no longer the activity to grasp the writer's original intentions but has changed into the activity to look for and explain the logic of texts, trace the activities of dismantling and recombining texts for the value of language itself, thus finding out the multiplicity of meaning and the infinitely various interpretations of the meaning of texts.

Anti-genre In the eyes of Charles Newman, American famous literary theorist and critic, postmodernist writers are a generation who bravely subvert the old orders and undertake the play of dispelling as their profession. They dissolve the identity of the propositions such as emancipation and liberty and replace it with a plural, centerless and centrifugal structure. Having separated themselves from the influence of traditional writers of the old generation, they are going along the road that the literary paradigm is thoroughly innovated (Newman 285). Consequently, being opposite with the serious fiction of the old generation, postmodernist writers are forced into a lane that their works are not only different from serious fiction but also different from pastime fiction. On the one hand, they try to break away from the influence of the old generation and on the other, they make an effort to take the differentiation engendered from an ordinary but low-grade common denominator as their strategy for continuous development. In order to satirize the pastime fiction or the classic fiction, they intentionally write the completely contrary works whose characteristics are not established on some remains that they have destroyed but on the success of their opposition to the stylization of the pastime fiction. Anti-genre has become a dominant pattern in our times. Like the refined language in the past, traditional genres are also regarded as the adversaries (Newman 296). The writing of fiction has become a bold risk. Now that the boundaries do not exist any more, any writing can be named fiction. Thus, fiction is bound to invade and occupy the fields of other genres and appears to be hybrid. At the plural present, all the genres have appeared in the interweaving of the present and the non-present, and of identity and difference (Hassan 170). Barthelme's short stories "The Glass Mountain" (1970) (*Snow White*, Trans. 212-218) and "Kierkegaard Unfair to Schlegel" (1970) (*Snow White*, Trans. 202-211) are the products of this anti-genre pattern of writing.

The form of the short story "The Glass Mountain" is very strange. It is constructed with the phrases, sentences, and paragraphs that are arranged in the order of serial numbers from 1 to 100. It is a reversely writing of a Scandinavian story "The Princess on the Glass Mountain." Though the hero in Barthelme's short story also woos the princess and has climbed up the top of the mountain with the help of a hawk, he lifts the princess and throws her down from the mountain to his acquaintances, letting them treat her the way they like with his heart at rest. The short story suddenly ends with the words like codes: "100. Even many hawks seem not to be believable, not a bit, not a second" (*SW* 218). Having rewritten the traditional story with a postmodern city as its background, Barthelme has disturbed the true and false values of the traditional story. He does not use the classic plots to show the existence of some lasting human values and concerns but instead he insults the classic plots to display how unable the traditional narrative is when it deals with the postmodern conditions. On the one hand, Barthelme's hero runs after his objective but on the other, he dismantles it and finally acquires nothing. Here is no honor and dignity. Barthelme has not only weakened the traditional values but also broken the conventions of fictional writing with his fiction appearing to be the gather-together of language fragments from 1 to 100. This sort of anti-genre writing has generated two results. Firstly, what the writer has given prominence to is techniques instead of contents, appearance instead of depth, and artificiality instead of credibility, and thus the writer has debased characterizing, imitation, hallucination and the like that traditional narrative concerns itself about and also broken the usual reading structure. Secondly, these phrases, sentences and paragraphs with serial numbers indicate that traditional genres having become conventions have turned to be so dull, so empty, and so easy to reproduce that they can be written with numerals to some extent. Like a group of codes, the last concluding sentence means to suggest: traditional creeds and structures are unable to deal with postmodern experiences. The hawk's function lies in that it is an absurd mechanical god descending to help the hero detach himself from his real difficult position and realize his ideal. Thus, he has proved the ineffectiveness and incredibility of old narrative forms and contents. Barthelme's "The Glass Mountain" has become an allegory that dismantles the transcendental signified that is symbolized by the princess.

The short story "Kierkegaard Unfair to Schlegel" goes on in the form of questions and answers, appearing in the disordered state, and seems to be pieced with scattered fragments. The short story begins with the answerer's narration about a European girl whom he met in a train. Then, the answerer tells the reader that he participates in politics, criticizes the government, and then turns to discuss the function of irony: to make fun of the special ways that people choose to deal with boredom, with which the writer introduces Kierkegaard's theoretical explanation of the concept of irony. He thinks that an irony aiming at the whole of existence can generate poetry and estrangement. Thus, irony becomes an infinite and absolute negation and the essence of irony is poetry. Therefore, Kierkegaard describes Schlegel's novel *Lucinde* as a book written with poems and thinks that Schlegel has built an esse that is superior to and able to replace the historical esse. The answerer, however, thinks that the relation between Schlegel's novel and the esse is not the one that Kierkegaard has explained. Kierkegaard only fixes his eyes on the prescriptive aspect of Schlegel's novel—a text that tells us how to live but ignores the other aspects, for instance, its different objects to different persons. Therefore, the answerer thinks that Kierkegarrd is unfair to Schlegel. Obviously, the fiction here has entered the field of literary criticism and lost its own field with its strong theoretical coloring.

Indeterminacy Ihab Hassan thinks that indeterminacy is the first essential characteristic of postmodernism. It includes all kinds of ambiguities, ruptures and displacements that affect knowledge and society. Indeterminacy has permeated all the thoughts and actions of the people in the postmodern society and formed the most basal situation of the world that people actually face. Hassan gives a specific explanation of indeterminacy. He thinks that indeterminacy is a category consisting of different concepts that help delineate: ambiguity, discontinuity, heterodoxy, pluralism, randomness, revolt, perversion and deformation. Deformation alone subsumes a dozen current terms of unmaking: disintegration, deconstruction, decenterment, displacement, discontinuity, decomposition, detotalization, delegitimation, etc.—let alone more technical terms referring to the rhetoric of irony, rupture, silence. It is just indeterminacy that reveals the spirit and nature of the postmodern times. Through all these signs a vast will moves to unmake and affect the body politic, the body cognitive, the erotic body, and the individual psyche—the entire realm of discourse in the West (Hassan 92). Only in literature, all of our ideas about writers, readers, reading, writing, texts, schools, critical theories and literature itself are suddenly queried. Barthelme himself asserts like this: "My song of songs is the principle of indeterminacy" (O'Hara, *SW* Trans. 10). His novel *Snow White* embodies this indeterminacy in portraying the images of characters.

Immanence Postmodernism has two most essential features: one is indetermanacy and the other is immanence. Immanence "refers, without religious echo, to the growing capacity of mind to generalize itself through symbols. Everywhere now we witness problematic diffusions, dispersals, dissemination; we experience the extension of our senses...through new media and technologies. Languages, apt or mendacious, reconstitute the universe—from quasars to quarks and back, from the lettered unconscious to black holes in space—reconstitute it an immanent semiotic system. The language animal has emerged, his/her measure the intertextuality of all life. A patina of thought, of signifiers, of 'connections,' now lies on everything the mind touches in its gnostic (noo)sphere, which physicists, biologists, and semioticians...explore. The pervasive irony of their explorations is also the reflexive irony of mind meeting itself at every dark turn. Yet in a consuming society such immanence can become more vacuous than fatidic. They become...pervasively 'obscene,' a collective vertigo of neutralization, a forward escape into the obscenity of pure and empty form" (Hassan 172-173). Immanence indicates the effort of a postmodern individual to realize self-expansion, self-increase and self-multiplication in virtue of all kinds of discourses or signs. Immanence stresses personification, the semiotic respect of nature, the society, the world, and knowledge. Everything in the world is the projection of man's immanence and finally shows itself in the form of signs. Immanence means that postmodernism no longer has transcendental meanings and it is no longer interested in transcendent values such as spirit, value, ultimate concern, truth, the beautiful, the good, and the like. On the contrary, it is an inward shrink to the subject and an inherent adaptation to the circumstances, the reality, and the creation. Postmodernism becomes intoxicated with the pleasure produced by the language signs in trivial circumstances.

As a general artistic, social, cultural and philosophical phenomenon, "postmodrnism has veered towards open, playful, provisional (open in time as well as in structure or space), disjunctive or indeterminate forms, a discourse of ironies and fragments, a 'white ideology' of absences and fractures, a desire of diffractions, an invocation of complex, articulate silences. Postmodernism has veered towards pervasive procedures, ubiquitous interactions, immanent codes, media languages." It is startling that when people are looking for the legitimated basis of a new authority in the postmodern world that has already appeared the authority itself has already self-disintegrated! Everything is all right but everything is meaningless. For postmodernism, philosophy does not exist in explaining or changing the world but in inherently adapting itself in this indeterminate world.

Writing Zero Roland Barthes thinks that in literature the function of writing activity "is not only to transmit or express but also impose a thing outside of language upon the reader" (Barthes 196); a writer's writing "is a way to ponder literature instead of a way to extend literature" (Barthes 203). He adds, "From Flaubert to our times, the whole literature has become a problem of language" (Barthes, *The Principles of Semiotics* 65). Writers no longer pay attention to concepts, ideas, and contents but they pay close attention to media, language, forms, and the aspects of style. Literature shows solicitude for language itself instead of social life. Writing has become an intransitive action: unlike classicism that writes about a specific subject for a given purpose, writing itself becomes a purpose and a passion. People try to develop a neutral and non-emotional writing to realize writing zero, which means to realize a pure writing without considering a writer's social and political missions. Barthes thinks that writing zero is an indicative writing in a straightforward manner, a writing without moods that is not commanding, nor imperative as he says that "This neutral writing lies in the boundless ocean of all kinds of voices and judgments but does not get involved in it... Thus, we can say that this is a completely unexcited writing or a pure writing," literature becomes the problem of language and "the utopia of language," and the writer inevitably becomes "a prisoner of his own myth of forms" (Barthes, *Elements of Semiology* 103). The writer's position as the subject and his consciousness of social participation are confined in the cage of language. The main characteristics of Barthes' concept of writing zero are stressing the forms and disputing the subject.

Bibliography

Barth, John. "The Literature of Exhaustion." *The Friday Book: Essays and Other Nonfiction*. Baltimore: The Johns Hopkins University Press, 1997.

Barthelme, Donald. *Snow White*. Trans. Zhou Rongsheng and Wang Baihua. Harbin: Harbin Publishing House, 1994.

Barthes, Roland. *The Pleasure of the Text*, 1973. *From Modernism to Postmodernism*. Ed. Liu Mingjiu. Beijing: China Social Science Press, 1994.

——. *The Noise of Language*, 1984. *From Modernism to Postmodernism*. Ed. Liu Mingjiu. Beijing: China Social Science Press, 1994.

——. *Elements of Semiology*. Beijing: Sanlian Bookshop, 1988.

Chen, Shidan. *A Study of American Postmodernist Fiction*. Tianjin: Nankai University Press, 2010: 1-13.

Fiedler, Leslie. *Cross the Border—Close the Gap*. New York: Stein and Day, 1972.

Gasset, Jose Ortega Y. *The Dehumanization of Art and Other Writings on Art, and Culture.* New York: Doubleday, 1956.

Gray, Richard. *A History of American Literature*, Second Edition. Malden, MA / Oxford, UK: Wiley-Blackwell, 2012: 519-531.

Hassan, Ihab. *The Postmodern Turn: Essays in Postmodern Theory and Culture*. Columbus: Ohio State University Press, 1987.

Hawkes, Terence. *Structuralism and Semiotics*. Shanghai: Shanghai Translations Press, 1987.

Jameson, Fredric. *The Theory of Postmodernism and Culture*. Tran. Tang Xiaobing. Beijing: Beijing University Press, 1997.

Kitler, Friedrich. "The Being of Postmodern Art." *Texts in March*, 1984.

Newman, Charles. *The Postmodern Aura: The Act of Fiction in an Age of Inflation*. Evanston: Northwestern University Press, 1985.

Rosenau, Pauline Marie. *Post-modernism and the Social Sciences: Insights, Inroads, and Intrusions.* Princeton, N.J.: Princeton University Press, 1992.

Welsch, Wolfgang. "*Our Postmodern* Modernity." Trans. Zhang Guofeng. *Postmodernism*. Trans. Zhao Yifan et al. Beijing: Social Science Documents Press, 1999.

Yu Baofa. "Metafiction." *A Handbook of New Disciplines and New Methods of Literature*. Eds. Lin Xianghua et al. Shanghai: Shanghai Literature Press, 1987.

Zhang, Guofeng. "From 'Modern' to'Postmodern.'" *From Modernism to Postmodernism*. Ed. Liu Mingjiu. Beijing: China Social Science Press, 1994.

Zhao, Yiheng. "The Criteria to Judge Postmodernist Fiction." *A Study of Foreign Literatures*. Beijing: The Book and Newspaper Information Center of Renmin University of China, 1994.

Robert Lowell

His Life and Writing Career

His Life

Robert Trail Spence Lowell IV (1917–1977) was an American poet, one of the founders of the confessional poetry movement. He was appointed the sixth Poet Laureate Consultant in Poetry to the Library of Congress and won many prizes including the Pulitzer Prize, the National Book Award, and the National Book Critics Circle Award.

Lowell was born to Commander Robert Traill Spencer Lowell III and Charlotte (née

Winslow) on March 1, 1917 in Boston, Massachusetts, two distinguished families. His father was a naval officer. His mother was a descendant of William Samuel Johnson, a signer of the United States Constitution.

Many distinguished poets played an important role in Lowell's poetry career. Richard Eberhart influenced Lowell so much that Lowell decided to be a poet in the future. Lowell attended Harvard University for two years. At Harvard College, Lowell asked Robert Frost for feedback on a long poem he'd written on the Crusades. Allen Tate offered Lowell a lot of guidance. At that time, Lowell converted to Catholicism, a religion he shared with Tate. Then, Lowell transferred to Kenyon College to study with poet and critic John Crowe Ransom. Lowell studied with and befriended fellow students Peter Taylor, Robie Macauley and Randall Jarrell. In 1940 Lowell graduated from Kenyon with a degree in Classics, and pursued a Masters degree in English literature at Louisiana State University under critics Cleanth Brooks and Robert Penn Warren. Before finishing graduate school, Lowell moved to New York, where he became an editor for a Catholic publishing house.

Lowell's nickname "Cal" originated from tyrannical Roman emperor Caligula because he had a tendency for violence and bullying other children when he was young. Lowell wrote to President Roosevelt and refused to fight in World War II in 1943. Because of his conscientious objector stance, Lowell served several months at the federal prison in Danbury, Connecticut. Before that he was held in a prison in New York City which he later wrote about in the poem "Memories of West Street and Lepke" from his book *Life Studies*. In 1944, Lowell's first book, *The Land of Unlikeness* was published, followed by *Lord Weary's Castle* two years later. During 1947, Lowell was poetry consultant to the Library of Congress. During 1949 he served on the committee for the first Bollingen Prize. In the 1950s, Lowell travelled in Europe and taught at Kenyon, the University of Iowa, Indiana University, the University of Cincinnati and Boston University, forming great influence on many writers. At the University of Iowa, Lowell taught in the famous Iowa Writers' Workshop and Paul Engle, Robie Macauley, and Anthony Hecht became his fellow colleagues. Among his many students were poets W.D. Snodgrass, Sylvia Plath, and Anne Sexton and critic Helen Vendler. Lowell also published three books of verse, won two prestigious awards, and had his first child, Harriet Winslow. For the whole of the 1960s, Lowell lived in New York City, worked as a poet-librettist for the Metropolitan and New York City operas, published poetry and plays, received more awards and a lifelong appointment at Harvard, and taught at Yale University. Lowell also participated actively in the civil rights movement and opposed the US involvement in Vietnam. His participation in the October 1967 peace march in Washington DC caused his later arrest. In 1967, Lowell was introduced in an article of *Time* magazine and he was well-known as the most public, well-known American poet of his generation. From

1970 to 1976, Lowell lived in England and taught at Essex University for two years. In 1973, Lowell's tenth volume of poetry, *The Dolphin*, won the Pulitzer Prize. Still more awards followed for books and lifetime achievement.

Lowell had three marriages. Lowell married the novelist Jean Stafford in 1940 and their tumultuous marriage ended in 1948. In 1949 Lowell married the writer Elizabeth Hardwick with whom he had a daughter, Harriet. But their marriage still could not escape the fate of failure. In 1972, he was divorced from Elizabeth Hardwick and then married writer Caroline Blackwood, with whom he had already had a child, Sheridan, in 1971. Lowell also became the stepfather to Blackwood's young daughter, Ivana. Elizabeth Bishop and Randall Jarrell had been Lowell's best friends. Lowell had a close friendship with the poet Elizabeth Bishop that lasted from 1947 until Lowell's death in 1977. Both writers influenced one another's work by means of critiques of their poetry respectively. And, the friendship between Lowell and Randall Jarrell began from the time when they met at Kenyon College in 1937 until Jarrell's death in 1965. Lowell continuously sought out Jarrell's input about his poems before he published them and publicly appreciated Jarrell's influence over his writing.

Lowell suffered from manic depression and was hospitalized many times throughout his adult life for this mental illness. However, his manic depression and mental illness produced some of his most important poetry, particularly his book *Life Studies*. Lowell died in 1977, having suffered a heart attack in a taxi in New York City on his way to see his ex-wife, Elizabeth Hardwick. By the time he died at the age of sixty, Lowell was considered one of the most important writers in English in the latter half of the twentieth century. He was buried in Stark Cemetery, Dunbarton, New Hampshire.

His Writing Career

Lowell's first book of poems, *Land of Unlikeness*, appeared in 1944, and his next book, *Lord Weary's Castle*, came out in 1946. It contained thirty-five poems, five among which were slightly revised from *Land of Unlikeness*. *Lord Weary's Castle* received critics' attention and was awarded the Pulitzer Prize in 1947. "Mr. Edwards and the Spider" and "The Quaker Graveyard in Nantucket" are the better known poems in the volume. Lowell adopted formal and ornate style to illustrate the theme of violence and theology, especially in "The Quaker Graveyard."

In 1951, Lowell published *The Mills of the Kavanaughs.* It was an epic poem but failed to receive the high praise from critics and readers. However, Lowell revived his reputation and his most influential book, *Life Studies* (1959), won him the National Book Award for poetry in 1960. *Life Studies* introduces many of the stylistic and thematic elements that would characterize what many called "confessional" poetry. The poems were largely free-verse, colloquial, and autobiographical; among their subjects was the poet's psychological turmoil. Many of the poems in *Life Studies* documented Lowell's family life and personal problems, and Lowell adopted the language much more informal than that he had used in his first three books. *Life Studies* signaled a turning point in Lowell's career, and even in American poetry in general. These poems were labeled "confessional" by M.L. Rosenthal and thereby, Lowell was grouped together with other influential confessional poets like Lowell's former students W. D. Snodgrass, Sylvia Plath, and Anne Sexton.

The poems in *Imitations* (1961) were different from Lowell's previous works. It was a volume of loose translations of poems by Rilke, Montale, Baudelaire, Pasternak, and Rimbaud. The 1962 Bollingen Poetry Translation Prize was awarded to Lowell for his contribution to the translation of these classical and modern European poets. However, critical response to *Imitations* was mixed and sometimes hostile. The poet Michael Hofmann thought *Life Studies* was Lowell's best book, *Imitations* was Lowell's most "pivotal book," because *Imitations* was full of "international style," as Lowell explained in the book's introduction that his translations should be regard as "imitations" rather than strict translations since he translated the originals in comparatively free way and he would rather think of authors of the originals as people in modern and American context.

His next book *For the Union Dead* (1964) was widely praised. *For the Union Dead* began with a description of the decaying South Boston Aquarium, focused on a memorial at the Statehouse for Colonel Robert Gould Shaw and black army regiment in the Civil War. The poems in *For the Union Dead* were not notably "confessional" and more emphasized the interplay of past and present, the social and the political. *Life Studies* focused on Lowell's emotionally personal life and family history, while *For the Union Dead* dealt with the spiritual hollowness of modern society. In the poems, Lowell showed individual's alienation and isolation which technologically advanced society brought them. Lowell's mental illness was obvious in *Life Studies* but rare in *For the Union Dead*. Lowell wrote about a number of world historical figures in poems like "Caligula," "Jonathan Edwards in Western Massachusetts," and "Lady Raleigh's Lament." The subject matter in *For the Union Dead* was much broader than it was in *Life Studies*.

Lowell's *The Old Glory* was produced off-Broadway in New York City in 1964 and was published in 1965 (with a revised edition following in 1968). It was three one-act plays including "Endecott the Red Cross," "My Kinsman, Major Molineux" and "Benito Cereno." Among them the first two were adapted by Nathaniel Hawthorne's short stories, and the third was adapted by Herman Melville's novella. *The Old Glory* won five Obie Awards in 1965, one of which was an award for "Best American Play."

In 1967, Lowell published his next book of poems, *Near the Ocean*. Lowell's writing style changed again. His verse returned more formal and metered. The loose translations (including verse approximations of Dante, Juvenal, and Horace) again appeared in *Near the Ocean*. The contemporary American politics overtly entered into Lowell's work, which was shown in his best known poem "Waking Early Sunday Morning."

Notebook 1967–1968 was published as a verse journal and later was republished in a revised and expanded edition, titled *Notebook*. In *Notebook 1967–1968* Lowell wrote his sonnets in blank verse with a definitive pentameter and a small handful included rhyme. Some poems in *Notebook* were originally published in his previous works. "In The Cage" originated from *Lord Weary's Castle*; "Caligula" and "Night-Sweat" from *For the Union Dead;* "1958" and "To Theodore Roethke: 1908–1963" from *Near the Ocean.* In addition, Lowell's source materials for the poems derived from a number of other writers including Jesse Glenn Gray's "The Warrior," Simone Weil's "Half a Century Gone," Herbert Marcuse, Aijaz Ahmad, R.P. Blackmur, Plutarch, Stonewall Jackson, and Ralph Waldo Emerson.

Lowell liked sonnet form so much that he reworked and revised many of the poems from *Notebook* and used them as the foundation for his next three volumes of verse: *History* (1973), *For Lizzie and Harriet* (1973), and *The Dolphin* (1973). *Notebook 1967–1968* is a combination of polished verse and spontaneous expression. Actually, in his later life Lowell wrote and revised extensively, expressing his strong sense of personal history and literary tradition, uncovering the problems in his private life and the world around him. *History* basically concerned world history from antiquity till the mid-20th century except that some poems dealt with Lowell's friends, peers, and family. *For Lizzie and Harriet* described the breakdown of Lowell's second marriage in the voices of his daughter, Harriet, and his second wife. *The Dolphin* was reputed works and won the 1974 Pulitzer Prize. It addressed such actual events in Lowell's life as an extramarital affair, the birth of a child out of wedlock, divorce, and remarriage, including poems about his daughter, his ex-wife, and his new wife Caroline Blackwood. *The Dolphin* also featured a self-conscious depiction of the poem. It reflected Lowell's emotional candor and the confessional nature of his verse. Derek Walcott and William Meredith praised *Notebook* and *The Dolphin* upon their publication. Meredith thought that Robert Lowell's *Notebook 1967–1968* was a beautiful and major work. Michael Hofmann, William Logan, and Richard Tillinghast praised the sonnets in reviews of Lowell's *Collected Poems*. The negative reviews mainly came from A.O. Scott and Marjorie Perloff, the latter of whom called the sonnet poems "trivial and catty," considering them to be Lowell's least important volumes.

In 1977, Lowell published his last volume of poetry, *Day by Day*. *Day by Day* was awarded that year's National Book Critics Circle Award for poetry. Anthony Hecht praised highly the poetry and thought "it was a very touching, moving, gentle book, tinged with a sense of [Lowell's] own pain and the pain [he'd] given to others." In *Day by Day*,

Lowell reflects on his life, his past relationships, and his own mortality. "Epilogue" is the best-known poem from this collection in which Lowell reflects upon the "confessional" school of poetry. *Day by Day* more focused on personal life and ignored ambitious metaphors and political engagement. Vendler praised some of Lowell's descriptions, particularly his descriptions of impotence, depression, and old age and she wrote, "Now [Lowell] has ended [his career], in *Day by Day*, as a writer of disarming openness, exposing shame and uncertainty, offering almost no purchase to interpretation, and in his journal-keeping, abandoning conventional structure, whether rhetorical or logical. The poems drift from one focus to another; they avoid the histrionic; they sigh more often than they expostulate. They acknowledge exhaustion; they expect death."

Although changes in artistic forms in his poetry were diverse, Lowell had been engaged in demonstrating connected theme, expressing his personal torment and the contemporary and historical struggles of the nation. Obviously, his body of work was unified and related between the past and present periods. Lowell became a distinguished poet in that in his work he combined formal technique and personal concerns, showed completely the conflict between the public and private selves, and reflected his superior talent in crafting work.

He had published 18 major works (poetry, drama and translation) such as *Land of Unlikeness* (1944), *Lord Weary's Castle* (1946), *The Mills of The Kavanaughs* (1951), *Life Studies* (1959), *Phaedra* (translation) (1961), *Imitations* (1961), *For the Union Dead* (1964), *The Old Glory* (1965), *Near the Ocean* (1967), *The Voyage & other Versions of Poems of Baudelaire* (1969), *Prometheus Bound* (translation) (1969), *Notebooks, 1967–1968* (1969), *History* (1973), *For Lizzie and Harriet* (1973), *The Dolphin* (1973), *Selected Poems* (1976) , *Day by Day* (1977).

Analyses of and Comments on His Representative Poems

Robert Lowell and the Confessional Poetry

In 1959, M. L. Rosenthal first used the term "confessional" in a review of Robert Lowell's *Life Studies* entitled "Poetry as Confession." *Life Studies* was the first book in the confessional mode. In the poems, Lowell alludes to his struggles with mental illness and his experiences in a mental hospital. The "Confessional Poetry" was associated with several poets including Robert Lowell, Sylvia Plath, John Berryman, Anne Sexton, Allen Ginsberg, and W. D. Snodgrass. They redefined American poetry in the generation following World War II. Some key texts of the American "confessional" school of poetry include Lowell's *Life Studies*, Plath's *Ariel*, Berryman's *The Dream Songs*, Snodgrass' *Heart's Needle*, and Sexton's *To Bedlam and Part Way Back*.

Confessional poetry is the poetry of the personal or "I." This style of writing appeared in the late 1950s and early 1960s. Lowell's book *Life Studies* was a highly personal account in which his life and familial ties were represented. Lowell's work influenced greatly his students—Plath and Sexton. The confessional poetry dealt with total new subjects such as people's feelings about death, trauma, depression and relationships. Sexton in particular was interested in the psychological aspect of poetry, having started writing at the suggestion of her therapist. The confessional poets recorded their emotions in their poems, in the meanwhile, they used corresponding poetic craft and construction to stress the theme of poems, most of which were often written in an autobiographical manner. The confessional poets maintained a high level of craftsmanship through their careful attention to and use of prosody.

The confessional poets pioneered a type of writing, and it changed the landscape of American poetry forever. The generations of writers absorbed the tradition of confessional poetry, and they started to focus on their personal experience. Marie Howe and Sharon Olds are two contemporary representative poets who were greatly influenced by the confessional poetry. Confessional free verse poetry became the popular approach in the second half of the 20th-century American poetry. One of the most prominent, consciously "confessional" poets to emerge in the 1980s was Sharon Olds whose focus was on taboo sexual subject.

For the Union Dead (1964)

Contents Summary

For the Union Dead is a book of poems by Robert Lowell that was published by Farrar, Straus & Giroux in 1964. It was Lowell's sixth book. Lowell originally wrote the poem "For the Union Dead" for the Boston Arts Festival in 1960.

"For the Union Dead" refers to the 1928 poem "Ode to the Confederate Dead" by Lowell's former teacher and mentor Allen Tate. "For the Union Dead" contemplates the legacy of the Civil War, embodied in the memorial to Colonel Robert Shaw, a white soldier who died while commanding an all-black regiment. To many Northerners, Shaw symbolized Union idealism: one hundred years after his death, Lowell contrasts Shaw's heroism with contemporary forms of self-interest and greed in "For the Union Dead."

In the poem, Lowell's visit to the park leads to a series of associations. Lowell sees construction of the underground parking garage beneath the Common, and he remembers his childhood and the changes of Boston. It reminds him of the Robert

Gould Shaw Memorial, especially the history associated with the memorial including Colonel Robert Gould Shaw and the all-black 54th Massachusetts Volunteer Infantry. Besides, Civil Rights Movement which was controversial and the images of black and white school-children on television came into his mind.

The opening stanza describes the old South Boston Aquarium: "broken" and "boarded" windows; "lost" weathervane's scales; "airy" and "dry" fish tanks. The ruined, broken, and bare scenery emphasizes a sense of loss and dilapidation and evokes melancholy mood.

The next two stanzas suggest that the past was far from ideal. The speaker remembers a childhood visit to the aquarium. "To burst the bubbles" brings him delight and fish in the tanks are trapped and submissive. The kingdom of fish is literally heading "dark downward" as they swim away from the aquarium light. More broadly, like the fish kingdom, the kingdom of humans is getting worse, darker, and nobler. "For the Union Dead" addresses the mood of American society as it regresses from idealism to despair.

Then, the poem describes the "new barbed and galvanized fence on the Boston Common." The Boston Common symbolizes a public area for people to gather usually while the new barbed and galvanized fence is a menacing border between people and preventing people from enjoying together. Lowell portrayed bulldozers as "dinosaur[s]" and "the underground garage" as an "underworld." Thus, modern construction tools evoke a prehistoric, animalistic world, a savage and hellish world.

The poem's central figure is a memorial to Colonel Robert Gould Shaw, who led the 54th Massachusetts Volunteer Regiment on an attack on Fort Wagner, South Carolina during the Civil War. The monument commemorates the honorable moments in that Boston's past. "For the Union Dead" portrays the threat of contemporary existence to the monument. The monument symbolizes the idealism displayed by the soldiers for a just cause while contemporary society struggles for more parking spaces, destroying the idealism.

"For the Union Dead" also contrasts Boston's present with its past. Lowell presents deep appreciation and respect for the soldiers' heroism and sacrifice. However, a few generations later, the city's attitude toward the soldiers changed a lot. The stern images of Colonel Shaw presented in the poem suggest Shaw's discomfort with the public role others claim for him.

Themes

Shaw displayed some particular heroism. Shaw's self-sacrifice seems incomprehensible to the contemporary age. New England is full of "small town New England greens," "white churches," and the monument. New England's present is becoming increasingly different from its past. "For the Union Dead" idealizes Shaw's sacrifice, also points out that Shaw's noble actions are not appreciated by people in modern society.

A series of apocalyptic images of twentieth-century life are shown in "For the Union Dead." The ditch of "The ditch is nearer" is just the place where Shaw and the black soldiers were hastily buried. The television set presents images of civil rights strife: civil rights activists faced various difficulties and African-American schoolchildren encountered great hostility in their life.

"For the Union Dead" reflects paradox in Colonel Shaw's idealism and reality. Shaw thinks that the power that he chooses life and death is "lovely." It is full of love, because he, like Christ, desires to sacrifice himself. In addition, the "peculiar power" is strange to humans in that Colonel Shaw cannot save his life and only die for his idealism. The "peculiar power" is particular to humankind in that Colonel Shaw realizes that he risks his life although he behaves like a hero.

"For the Union Dead" also reflects devolution of humankind. According to "For the Union Dead," technology works to make humans turn into beasts. Technology blurs the boundaries between the kingdom of "fish and reptile" and that of humans. "For the Union Dead" is full of fear that technology devolves humankind. "Dinosaur steam shovels" and "cars nose" are inanimate technological products. Modern technology including atomic bombs, "Space is nearer", and "the blast" puts humankind closer to the point of extinction.

"For the Union Dead" concerns a public subject: the Civil War's tortured legacy. At the beginning, Lowell recalls his visiting the South Boston Aquarium. Then, he gradually addresses various public events and places: a memorial to the Union dead, William James's comments, and a photograph of Hiroshima. In the poem, Lowell introduces personal anecdote which guides readers to reflect on the larger societal, cultural, and historical forces at work.

Literary Techniques

"For the Union Dead" is written in free-verse quatrains. Each stanza consists of four lines whose lengths are different from each other. In the poem Lowell does not adhere to a metrical or rhyming pattern.

Skunk Hour (1958)

Contents Summary

"Skunk Hour" was the final poem in *Life Studies* (1959), but it was the first to be completed. Lowell began work on the poem in August 1957, and the poem was first published in the January 1958 issue of the *Partisan Review*.

"Skunk Hour" is one of Robert Lowell's most frequently anthologized poems. It was published in his groundbreaking book of poems, *Life Studies*, and is regarded as a key early example of Confessional poetry.

In general, the speaker in the poem reflects on a town in Maine. An elderly, wealthy woman seems to have a ton of property, but is alone at that time. Lowell describes the millionaire, the depressed and poor town decorator, and the pretty sad place. Then the speaker shifts the focus to himself. He remembers his driving through the town one night, his sight and feeling at that time. It all seems pretty gloomy, depressed and crazy. As the poem progresses, it gets pretty bleak.

Specifically, first, an heiress in Nautilus Island in Maine doesn't get out much. She still gets by colder weather in her simple cottage. Her sheep graze on her property, her son's occupation is noble, and her farmer holds a seat in local government. She doesn't live a luxurious life and she's old and weak. She wants to be left alone during her prosperous golden years. She buys all the houses that are blocking her sea view and then gets rid of them. The millionaire who lived in Nautilus Island over the summer is gone now. He seems to be from L. L. Bean (a Maine company) and his nice boat is sold to the lobstermen. It is fall of year, and the leaves on Blue Hill turned red. The local shoe-repair shop owner is decorating his store with orange things for fall, and he doesn't make a lot of money but he prefers to settle down.

The speaker is driving his old car (a Ford Tudor) up Blue Hill, looking for parked cars with lovers but finding bleak graveyard. A love song from one of the cars causes him to feel terrible. The speaker realizes that his own agony lies in himself. Nobody's in the private hell or in the hill except that only "skunks" are looking for something to eat. The skunks walk under the night shadows of this big, Gothic-looking church in the main part of the town. A mother skunk with her babies is walking around in a garbage can, get some sour cream, and will not scare.

Themes

The speaker's madness is demonstrated in "Skunk Hour" in some sense. The sentence his "mind's not right" is an evidence of his madness. In the poem, we learn that he's feeling a little down in the dumps and is tired as he's driving around at night. Actually, He becomes more disturbed at night; he's restless, searching for something he never finds.

Isolation is another theme of "Skunk Hour." The speaker of "Skunk Hour" is stuck on an island, so his human interaction is limited to people there. Although he knows a lot of folks from the outside, he doesn't actually know them very well. He is isolated from outside actually. He tried to change the situation, driving around in the town at night to look for signs of human life, and find nothing but skunks. Class issues and envy are the reasons for our speaker's feelings of loneliness and madness.

Home is what Lowell tries to explore in "Skunk Hour." In Nautilus Island the speaker doesn't feel "at home" although he lives there year-round. He tells us others come here only for summer and he doesn't feel more comfortable and easier there. The speaker used to feel at home there, but now that the mystery person has left, he's feeling too lonely to feel homey.

"Skunk Hour" is a play on "witching hour" and the skunks are like "witches." At "witching hour," witches do all their weird stuff actively. The skunks' behavior is strange and disturbing. They accompany the speaker's madness. The skunks can be considered as the eyes of a mentally ill man. They take on a stranger, darker light.

Literary Techniques

This poem is told through the lens of the mentally ill. Therefore, the words and phrases in this poem have shifting, sneaky, and double meanings. For example, "Spartan" describes something simple or severe but it also tracks back to ancient Greece. "A red fox stain" describes red leaves of fall in Blue Hill, but it also makes us think of a bloodstain. The nets containing fish reminds us of the stockings.

The stanzas in the poem are six lines apiece and there's definitely some rhyming. But, all through the poem the rhyme scheme is not perfect harmonious. In some stanzas (the fourth stanza) Lowell sticks to a perfectly predictable pattern: a-b-c-b-c-a. But none of the other stanzas follow that pattern exactly. Most of the time each end word (the last word in a line) has a rhyming match within the stanza, but when and where the match comes varies throughout the poem.

Bibliography

http://en.wikipedia.org/wiki/Confessional_poetry, 2013-02-17.

http://www.shmoop.com/skunk-hour, 2013-02-15.

Ruby, Mary K., ed. *Poetry for Students, Volume 7*. Detroit: Gale, 2000: 65-72.

Charles Olson

His Life and Writing Career

His Life

Charles Olson (1910–1970) was a second generation American modernist poet and was recognized as a major shaper of a postmodern American poetry, the chief successor to Ezra Pound and William Carlos Williams. Critics commonly regarded him as a representative figure of Black Mountain Poets which included Robert Creeley, Robert Duncan, Edward Dorn, and Joel Oppenheimer among others. Many postmodern groups, such as the poets of the language school, regarded Olson as a primary and precedent figure.

Olson was born to Karl Joseph and Mary Hines Olson on December 27, 1910 and grew up in Worcester, Massachusetts. His father was a Swedish letter carrier and his mother was a Catholic Irish-American. At Classical High School in Worcester, Olson was a distinguished orator and took third place in the National Oratorical Contest, winning a tour of Europe as a prize. In Europe he met Irish poet William Butler Yeats. From 1928 to 1933, he attended Wesleyan University in Middletown, Connecticut, earning his bachelor's degree and master's degree in literature and American studies. His thesis for M.A. was "The Growth of Herman Melville, Prose Writer and Poetic Thinker." Then, he began teaching English at Clark University in Worcester as an instructor for two years. In 1936, he went on a swordfishing cruise and the sea drew him to Melville and to the old fishing town of Gloucester, a city that became inseparable from his life and his poetic career ever after. In the same year, Olson attended Harvard University as a doctoral candidate, first in English and American Literature, then in new American Civilization program. He studied with Frederick Merk and F. O. Mattthiessen. However, Olson only completed his coursework for a Ph.D. and failed to earn his degree because he didn't submit his dissertation. In 1939 and 1948 he received two Guggenheim fellowships for his studies of Herman Melville twice.

In 1941, Olson moved to New York and became a publicity director for the American Civil Liberties Union. He lived with Constance Wilcock in a common-law marriage in 1942, having one child, Katherine. In September, Olson and his wife moved to Washington, D. C., where he became assistant chief of the foreign language section of the Office of War Information (OWI), the forerunner of the U.S. Information Agency. Olson was strongly interested in politics and the Franklin D. Roosevelt revolution. He was active in the Franklin D. Roosevelt campaign, "Everyone for Roosevelt." In 1945, Roosevelt died and an era of liberalism in Washington came to an end. Olson left politics and he moved to Key West, Florida, dedicated himself to poetry. In 1946 he defended Ezra Pound against charges of treason, and during the following two years Olson visited Ezra Pound at St. Elizabeths psychiatric hospital in Washington D.C. regularly.

Between 1947 and 1951 Olson lectured at the University of Washington in Seattle, American University in Washington, D.C., and Black Mountain College, in western North Carolina. During these years, he established his intellectual relationships with many people. Especially, in 1951, as a visiting professor, Olson came to Black Mountain College, an innovative arts school. He met thinker Buckminster Fuller, choreographer Merce Cunningham, painters Franz Kline and Josef Albers, and poets Robert Duncan and Robert Creeley. Olson became the rector of Black Mountain College. From 1951 to 1956, he raised a literary movement known as Black Mountain poetry. Many students and fellow poets admired him for his verse experiments, and his theories on history and myth. At Black Mountain College, Olson separated from Connie Wilcock and lived with Betty Kaiser in a common-law marriage. Betty Kaiser was a Black Mountain music student.

Olson left Black Mountain College in 1957. He settled down in Gloucester and lived in poverty with his second wife, Betty Kaise, and their son, Charles Peter Olson. From 1963 to 1965 he taught American poetry and mythology at the State University of New York at Buffalo. But Olson's second wife was killed in a car accident in January 1964. His wife's death haunted him deeply and he resigned from the State University of New York at last. In 1969 he was invited to teach at the University of Connecticut, but after several sessions he was obliged to give up his work due to his liver. Olson's life was marred by alcoholism, which led to his early death from liver cancer. In the last years of his life, he was extremely isolated and worked hard. He died in New York Hospital on 10 January, 1970, two weeks past his fifty-ninth birthday, while in the process of completing *The Maximus Poems*. Although Olson aroused many controversies from critics circle in his life, his reputation as an innovator and thinker was acknowledged widely.

His Writing Career

Olson's literary output was prolific, including his poetry and prose works that expounded his theories about writing. His achievements in literary history includes his epic series, *The Maximus Poems* (1953–1975), the theoretical manifesto "Projective Verse" (1950), essays such as "Human Universe" (1951), his study of Herman Melville, myth and America, *Call Me Ishmael* (1947), his energetic letters, as well as his acknowledged influence on an entire generation of poets.

Olson's first book, *Call Me Ishmael* (1947), a study of Herman Melville's novel *Moby Dick*, was evolved from his master's thesis at Wesleyan. Melville's *Moby-Dick* was perceived as a new myth of the West. Ishmael, the lone survivor of the tale, was the counter to the egocentric and imperial Ahab. Ishmael was full of curiosity and interested in the life around him. Olson tried to show Ishmael's careful scrutiny of life.

In 1950, Olson published his essay "Projective Verse" in Poetry New York, a manifesto for the Post-modernist poetry movement in America. It was first published as a pamphlet, and then was quoted extensively in William Carlos Williams' *Autobiography* (1951). The essay introduces his ideas of "composition by field" through projective or open verse. Actually, Olson continually represented the views of Ezra Pound and William Carlos Williams. Pound asked poets to "compose in the sequence of the musical phrase, not in sequence of a metronome," and William Carlos Williams proposed that a poem should be approached as a "field of action." Composition by field differs from the traditional method of poetic composition, and the latter depends on received form and measure. Olson argues that a received structure including rhyme, meter, and sense is no longer regarded as a propulsive force by a poet and the breath should be a poet's central concern.

Olson argues that simile and description should not play a major role in the construction of a poem, and syntax should be shaped by sound rather than sense, with nuances of breath and motion to be conveyed to the reader through typographical means. As Nicholas Everett pointed out in *Charles Olson's Life and Career,* "Projective Verse" aims to transfer energy from the world to the reader without artificial interference, syntax is shaped by sound, not sense; sense is conveyed by direct movement from one perception to another, not rational argument; and the reader's rendition directed by freely varied spacing between words and lines on the page. Olson argued that poetic language must be spontaneous, expressing what is actually seen and felt, rather than following traditional rules of logic and order. He put forward his projective mode in poem writing. In brief, a poetic meter was based on the poet's breathing and an open construction was based on sound and the linking of perceptions rather than syntax and logic. He favored that meter was not based on syllable, stress, foot or line but using only the unit of the breath. In the projective poem, the flow and mingling of words in the poet's mind were projected onto paper. In "Projective Verse", Olson expounded his "objectivism" (Ishmael's selfless scrutiny of life), meaning that poet was mere object for writing poetry, and human subjects are cast among the flowers and animals of everyday life. Olson argued that human had no privilege as the observer of nature. Surrounding nature was important, regarded as resources and implements of poems.

His first book of poetry, *In Cold Hell, in Thicket* was published in 1953. Olson went to the Yucatan Peninsula, studying Mayan temples and artifacts. Olson's research into Mayan hieroglyphs was recorded in letters to the poet Robert Creeley, collected in *Mayan Letters* (1953). Many short poems followed the publication of "Projective Verse", variously collected in *In Cold Hell* (1953), *The Distances* (1960), *Archaeologist of Morning* (1970), and *The Collected Poems of Charles Olson* (1987). These poems dealt with subjects like war, death, and the nature of history. *The Distances*, his second collection, is less formally innovative but more ambitious in treating personal dreams and universal myths. Olson's shorter verse, poems such as "Only The Red Fox, Only The Crow," "Other Than," "An Ode on Nativity," "Love," and "The Ring Of" manifested a sincere, original, emotionally powerful voice.

Human Universe and Other Essays was published in 1965. It concerns most Olson's reviews and speculations on objectivism and explores animistic roots in non-western thought. In "Human Universe," Olson illustrated in detail Mayan myth and its reflection in contemporary poetry; in "The Gate and the Center," Olson argued that human migration played an important role in human history, and the individual came into being when western alienation from nature appeared.

Olson spent many years in writing *The Maximus Poems. The Maximus Poems* was published gradually with the completion of each part. In 1953 *The Maximus Poems 1-10* was published, *Maximus 11-22* followed in 1956. The first volume of the work appeared in 1960 as *The Maximus Poems*. The second volume, *Maximus IV, V, VI* was issued in 1968, and the final volume, *The Maximus Poems: Volume Three*, appeared posthumously in 1975. Olson's epic remained unfinished at the poet's death. *The Maximus Poems* explored social, historical, and political concerns. The long poem dealt with the origins of America and its long and ancient cultural background, which even dated back to Mesopotamia. Olson explored the present western civilizations by means of ancient myths, cultural morphologies, and the archetypal events.

Maximus explored American history in the broadest sense and reflected also an epic of place, Massachusetts and specifically the city of Gloucester where Olson had settled. Dogtown, the wild, rock-strewn centre of Cape Ann, next to Gloucester is important in *The Maximus Poems*. Maximus, as speaker of *The Maximus Poems*, represented Maximus of Tyre, an itinerant Greek philosopher, and Olson himself. In the first volume, *The Maximus Poems*, Maximus, dismayed by the culture of contemporary Gloucester, examined its origins in the European settlement of America. Olson told the history how Cape Ann became the Plymouth Bay colony and then Massachusetts. Olson demonstrated how British investors controlled a small community of fishermen, and then controlled America. In the second volume, *The Maximus Poems, IV, V, VI* (1968), Olson employed ancient myths and religious texts, and scrutinized certain documentary details of Gloucester's past. Olson used the cascade of words, numbers, and documents to map the phases of Western migration, the origins of Gloucester, and the growth and decay of American culture. *The Maximus Poems, Volume Three* followed the logic of the preceding books, Olson imagined a new Gloucester in which material and commercial values were abandoned and spiritual and communal values were restored. *Maximus* reflected modern Gloucester by means of the rise and fall of civilizations elsewhere. Many myths in everyday life were scattered in the elegiac or contentious, but elegant poems. The minutiae of the town revealed the grand cosmic design. *Maximus* bears a memory, a "history of time."

Olson's papers are deposited in the Olson Archive of the University of Connecticut and the Humanities Research Center at the University of Texas, Austin. Other works by Olson are *Causal Mythology* (1969), *The Fiery Hunt and Other Plays* (1977), and *The Post Office: A Memoir of His Father* (1974). Olson's reading list for poets is in *A Bibliography on America for Ed Dorn* (1964). *Selected Writings* (1966), and *Additional Prose* (1974). *The Special View of History* (1970) and *Muthologos: The Collected Lectures and Interviews* contain his work on history. *Charles Olson and Ezra Pound: An Encounter at St. Elizabeths* (1975) reprints his notes on Pound.

Analyses of and Comments on His Representative Poems

Charles Olson and the Black Mountain Poetry

The Black Mountain Poets were American avant-garde or postmodern poets, and they were loosely associated with Black Mountain College, near Asheville, North Carolina, during the 1950s. Black Mountain College, founded in 1933, became an experiment in community education. Many avant-garde musicians, artists, and writers came to the college and grew up around the poets Robert Creeley, Robert Duncan, and Charles Olson while they were teaching at Black Mountain College. These poets emulated the freer style of William Carlos Williams and refused the poetic tradition espoused by T.S. Eliot. Charles Olson was the core of the Black Mountain Poets.

Charles Olson's essay "Projective Verse" (1950) became The Black Mountain Poets' manifesto, on which these poets based their poems' approach. Olson believed that a poem's essential energy is translated through the poet to the reader. This theory of projective verse called for poets to return to an organic basis for their form, to a poetic line controlled by the physiology of the poet's breathing instead of by preset meter. The essay stressed the reader's share in the creative process and called for the use of colloquial language. Robert Creeley argued that form is never more than the extension of content. Robert Duncan liked to use lyric, magical language in his poems. Much of the group's early work was published in the magazine *Origin*. Dissatisfied with the lack of critical material in that magazine, Creeley and Olson established the *Black Mountain Review*. It featured the work of William Carlos Williams, Paul Blackburn, Denise Levertov, Allen Ginsberg and Gary Snyder.

Olson owed much to Pound. He urged an open form that would allow for poetry to be a process of discovery. Olson's call influenced many writers, who were dedicated to undermining the orthodox insistence on predetermined, closed form. Some of the Black Mountain poets are often considered to have contributed to the San Francisco Renaissance.

The Kingfishers (1949)

Contents Summary

The poem was published in 1949 and then collected in Olson's first book of poetry, *Cold Hell, in Thicket* (1953).

As Olson's first long poem, "The Kingfishers" is so crucial to understanding every aspect of Olson's early life and thought. It provides an insight into Olson's apprenticeship and purposes. The understanding of this poem can remove obstacles in the path of further study of Olson. "The Kingfishers," a lyrical meditation on the ruins of an Aztec burial ground, is one of Olson's finest poems concerning Aztec religion, modern Mexico, archaeology, and world events. In "The Kingfishers," Olson breaks away from his European heritage and believes the Indian cultures of the New World.

Themes

The poem has the shades of thrill and enigma around itself, which provokes a sense of horror, uncertainty and yearning. The poet seems to have a mixed feeling about changes. The year of its composition reflects the strong sense of conflicts in the poet's mind: 1949. It is the same year as Mao's forces triumphed in China; It was just four years after the throwing of the nuclear bombs on Hiroshima and Nagasaki, when the outcomes of the disasters were just appearing. Again, it was just four years after the gates of Auschwitz camp were broken open and the unfathomable lies and the miserable sufferings in this unadulterated hell were disclosed. Obviously, Olson was greatly influenced by these events and ideas. For example, Olson's "La lumiere de l'aurore est devant. Nous nous devant nous lever et agir" is from Mao, which means "The light of dawn is before us. We must arise and act."

The unpredictable and unavoidable changes all over the world give the poem a stirring voice. The opening line "What does not change / is the will to change" reminds the reader of the philosophy of Heraklitus. It seems to be telling the readers "all is change, stasis is Thanatos (a death wish; Death as a personification or as a philosophical notion)", or simply "All is flux, nothing is stationary." In the poem, one phrase follows the other, producing different effects, for example, hectoring and bursting through the dead silence and complacency often associated with this Cold War moment in U. S. history. The poet seems to have resolved to get rid of all the conformity, wiping everything that intends to stay in history, especially in literary history. One thought is overlaid on another, a veritable palimpsest. Everything contributes to the tendency of change. The rhetorical power is echoing and reproducing Ezra Pound's manifesto "Make it new." Hence, a poetics of dynamic movement.

Beyond the strong desire to change, the poem should also be noted for its complicated attidude toward history. The use of references implies the attractions and profoundity of human cultural histories. For example, the lines "the priests rush in among the people," "of green feathers feet, beaks and eyes / of gold" reminds the readers of Prescott's *History of the Conquest of Mexico*. The line "I thought of the E on the stone" goes to Frank O'Hara. Then comes "Si j'ai du goût, ce n'est guère / Que pour la terre et les pierres" ("I only find within my bones / A taste for eating earth and stones"), a couplet from *Rimbaud's Season in Hell* ("Alchemy of the Word"). Thus, Rimbaud, Heraklitus, Prescott, Delphi are not only stones with which a new world might be built, but also the weights of a still not satisfactory world. The dilemma provokes the poet's uncertainty about where to go: "shall you uncover honey / where maggots are?/ I hunt among stones."

Literary Techniques

The poem takes on a radical new mode of poetic expression including the tenets of modernism and objectivism, which Charles Olson explained shortly after in his essay of 1950, "Projective Verse." "The Kingfishers" is a most striking application of his Projective Verse. The poem proceeds through a succession of widely varying stanzaic units instead of the traditional formalities such as rhyme, regular meters, symmetrical stanzas, and the normal pattern of argument. The design of the poem inspires rich imagination. The changing lengths and the layout of the sentences makes the poem a bracing test of nonlinear reading, using a scattered *ideogram* layout to facilitate the display of changes.

Olson is not seeking a place within the "modern movement," but rather, because what does not change "is the will to change," he is creating the ground for a new and different future, a postmodern turn and he is acknowledging the crisis in Western culture in the wake of the war. The poet is calling his doubts about the current world:

"The kingfishers! / who cares / for their feathers / now?"

Maximus to Gloucester, Letter 27 [withheld] (1968)

Contents Summary

The poem was published in *The Maximus Poems* in 1968. At the very beginning, Olson takes his readers into his personal background, sharing childhood experiences that he is reminiscing now. In his memory, readers can sense "the land falling off to the left where my father shot his scabby golf" and "the summer darkness until no flies could be seen." These vivid images are so familiar to common readers that they can immediately create a sense of carefreeness and recall their own happy and easygoing early life as if they were reliving it for the moment. Meanwhile, Olson's analysis of his pastimes is profound and deep, which can naturally suggest that his early experiences must have been of great significance to his later life. The fact that Gloucester wasn't over-crowded with technology when he was growing up in it foreshadows his whole thinking of "changes."

In the second part of his memory, Olson recollects the specific details of his parents' daily life. He remembers that "she laughing, so sure, as round as her face, Hines pink and apple" and he is "a man for kicks." The details help Olson convey his inner feelings of his parents, indicating the value of his parents in his life. Besides, this particular memory has "the geography of it," the geography of Polis. Again, the nostalgic feeling remind the readers of the time when the major technology was not applied in the city.

The first two stanzas in the poem are in two bunches and then the lines begin to scatter around the page. Olson's purpose in spacing out the rest of his poem and scattering his words around the page may have been to reflect the idea of change and how different the new Polis is than the old one. This juxtaposition is important because it relates back to the idea of "breath" that Olson had mentioned in his projective verse. Instead of focusing on punctuation of a poem, Olson preferred to emphasize the significance of breath when reading a poem and how readers should read a poem exactly how the author intended.

Finally Olson ends his poems by "compelling Gloucester to yield to change." This is where Olson contradicts his previous assertions about moving forward. It's as if he wants to move forward but yet doesn't want the change that he sees occurring, which brings us back to the idea that he wants positive change to happen. So in this one poem, Olson combines his lyric, historic, and aesthetic concerns.

Themes

In the poem "Maximus to Gloucester, Letter 27 [withheld]," Charles Olson suggests that the city of Polis is in desperate need of change but not "bad change," rather "good change." It is addressed not to individuals, but to the people of a city.

Literary Techniques

Olson uses different literary techniques throughout his poem such as imagery, simile, and metaphor to create a nostalgic setting for the reader to follow all the way to the end. Thus, the subtext of the poem is quite complex and well-hidden in the several lines of his stanzas.

Bibliography

http://www.anb.org/articles/16/16-02171.html, 2013-02-13.

http://charlesolson.uconn.edu/Personal_and_Professional_Life/biography.htm, 2013-02-12.

http://www.english.illinois.edu/maps/poets/m_r/olson/life.htm, 2013-02-15.

Joseph Heller

His Life and Writing Career

His Life

Joseph Heller (1923–1999) was born in Coney Island in Brooklyn, New York, the son of poor Jewish parents, Lena and Isaac Donald Heller, from Russia. Even as a child, he loved to write; as a teenager, he wrote a story about the Russian invasion of Finland and sent it to *New York Daily News*, which rejected it. At least one scholar suggests that he knew that he wanted to become a writer, after recalling that he received a children's version of the *Iliad* when he was ten. After graduating from Abraham Lincoln High School in 1941, Heller spent the next year working as a blacksmith's apprentice, a messenger boy, and a filing clerk. In 1942, at age 19, he joined the U.S. Army Air Corps.

Two years later he was sent to the Italian Front, where he flew 60 combat missions as a B-25 bombardier. His Unit was the 488th Bombardment Squadron, 340th Bomb Group, the 12th Air Force. Heller later remembered the war as "fun in the beginning... You got the feeling that there was something glorious about it." On his return home he "felt like a hero... People think it quite remarkable that I was in combat in an airplane and I flew sixty missions even though I tell them that the missions were largely milk runs."

After the war, Heller studied English at the University of Southern California and New York University on the G.I. Bill. In 1949, he received his M.A. in English from Columbia University. Following his graduation, he spent a year as a Fulbright scholar at St. Catherine's Society in Oxford University. After returning home, he taught composition at The Pennsylvania State University for two years. He also taught fiction and dramatic writing at Yale. He then briefly worked for Time, Inc., before taking a job as a copywriter at a small advertising agency, where he worked alongside future novelist Mary Higgins Clark. At home, Heller wrote. He was first published in 1948, when *The Atlantic* ran one of his short stories. That first story nearly won the "Atlantic First." Heller did not begin work on a story until he had envisioned both a first and last line. The first sentence usually appeared to him "independent of any conscious preparation." In most cases, the sentence did not inspire a second sentence. At times, he would be able to write several pages before giving up on that hook. Usually, within an hour or so of receiving his inspiration, Heller would have mapped out a basic plot and characters for the story. When he was ready to begin writing, he focused on one paragraph at a time, until he had three or four handwritten pages, which he then spent several hours reworking. Heller maintained that he did not "have a philosophy of life, or a need to organize its progression. My books are not constructed to 'say anything." Only when he was almost one-third finished with the novel would he gain a clear vision of what it should be about. At that point, with the idea solidified, he would rewrite all that he had finished and then continue to the end of the story. The finished version of the novel would often not begin or end with the sentences he had originally envisioned, although he usually tried to include the original opening sentence somewhere in the text.

On Sunday, December 13, 1981, Heller was diagnosed with Guillain-Barré syndrome, a debilitating syndrome that was to leave him temporarily paralyzed. He was admitted to the Intensive Care Unit of Mount Sinai Medical Hospital the same day, and remained there, bedridden, until his condition had improved enough to permit his transfer to the Rusk Institute of Rehabilitation Medicine, which occurred on January 26, 1982. His illness and recovery are recounted at great length in the autobiographical *No Laughing Matter*, which contains alternating chapters by Heller and his good friend Speed Vogel. The book reveals the assistance and companionship Heller received during this period from a number of his prominent friends—Mel Brooks, Mario Puzo,

Dustin Hoffman and George Mandel among them. Heller eventually made a substantial recovery. He later married Valerie Humphries, one of the nurses who helped him get better.

His Writing Career

Joseph Heller is a popular and respected writer whose first and best-known novel, *Catch-22* (1961), is considered a major work of the post-World War II era. He began his writing career as the author of short stories and the novel *Catch-22* in 1961. After he won his acclaim with his first novel, he continued to finish other works, *Something Happened* (1974), *New Haven* (1967), *Good as Gold* (1979), *God Knows* (1984), *Poetics* (1987), *Picture This* (1988) and *Portrait of an Artist* (1999). Heller's works are characterized by a satirical sense of the absurd, speaking out against the military-industrial complex and those organized institutions which seem to manipulate people's lives in the name of reason or morality. Heller's tragicomic vision of modern life, found in all of his novels, focuses on the erosion of humanistic values and highlights the ways in which language obscures and confuses reality. In addition, Heller's use of anachronism reflects the disordered nature of contemporary existence. His protagonists are antiheroes who search for meaning in their lives and struggle to avoid being overwhelmed by such institutions as the military, big business, government, and religion. While Heller's later novels have received mixed reviews, *Catch-22* continues to be highly regarded as a trenchant satire of the big business of modern warfare. Presenting existence as absurd and fragmented, this irreverent, witty novel satirizes capitalism and the military bureaucracy. Heller's tragicomic vision of modern life, found in all of his novels, focuses on the erosion of humanistic values and highlights the ways in which language obscures and confuses reality. In addition, Heller's use of anachronism reflects the disordered nature of contemporary existence. His protagonists are antiheroes who search for meaning in their lives and struggle to avoid being overwhelmed by such institutions as the military, big business, government, and religion. While Heller's later novels have received mixed reviews, *Catch-22* continues to be highly regarded as a trenchant satire of the big business of modern warfare.

Catch-22 is most often interpreted as an antiwar protest novel that foreshadowed the widespread resistance to the Vietnam War that erupted in the late 1960s. Heller's penchant for anachronism, evident in all of his novels, reflects the disordered nature of contemporary existence. His protagonists are antiheroes who search for meaning in their lives and struggle to avoid being overwhelmed by such institutions as the military, big business, government, and religion. *Catch-22* is like no other novel. It has its own rationale, its own extraordinary character. It moves back and forth from hilarity to horror. It is outrageously funny and strangely affecting. It is totally original. This novel is a microcosm of the twentieth-century world as it might look to someone dangerously sane. It is a novel that lives and moves and grows with astonishing power and vitality—a masterpiece of our time. Joseph Heller's manic, bleak, blackly humorous, and brilliant novel has become a classic of American literature. It is a brilliant satirical critique of a number of modern social phenomena. It is generally referred to as an antiwar novel, but Heller's criticisms extend beyond the absurdity of war to capitalism itself and the social relations that arise from it. To be sure, his analysis is at times confused, and is often directed at surface elements while neglecting more fundamental issues. Nonetheless, *Catch-22* stands as a strong protest against the conditions of modern society.

Shortly after *Catch-22* was published, Heller thought of an idea for his next novel, which would become Something Happened, but did not act on it for two years. In the meantime he focused on scripts, completing the final screenplay for the movie adaptation of Helen Gurley Brown's Sex and the Single Girl, as well as a television comedy script that eventually aired as part of "McHale's Navy." He also completed a play in only six weeks, but spent a great deal of time working with the producers as it was brought to the stage. In 1969, Heller wrote a play called *We Bombed in New Haven*. It delivered an anti-war message while discussing the Vietnam War. It was originally produced by the Repertory Company of the Yale Drama School, with Stacey Keach in the starring role. After a slight revision, it was published by Alfred A. Knopf and then debuted on Broadway, starring Jason Robards. Heller's follow-up novel, *Something Happened*, was finally published in 1974. Critics were enthusiastic about the book, and both its hardcover and paperback editions reached number one on the *New York Times* bestseller list. Heller wrote another five novels, each of which took him several years to complete. One of them, *Closing Time*, revisited many of the characters from *Catch-22* as they adjusted to post-war New York. All of the novels sold respectably well, but could not duplicate the success of his debut. Told by an interviewer that he had never produced anything else as good as *Catch-22*, Heller famously responded, "Who has?"

Analysis of and Comment on His Representative Novel

Catch-22 (1961)

Plot Summary

The setting of *Catch-22* is the island of Pianosa, the base of the Twenty-seventh Air Force. *Catch-22* concerns a World War II bombardier named Yossarian who believes his foolish, ambitious, mean-spirited commanding officers are more dangerous than the enemy. In order to avoid flying more missions, Yossarian retreats to a hospital with a mysterious liver complaint, sabotages his plane, and tries to get himself declared insane. Variously defined throughout the novel, Catch-22 refers to the ways in which bureaucracies control the people who work for them. The term first appears when Yossarian asks to be declared insane. In this instance, Catch-22 demands that anyone who is insane must be excused from flying missions. The catch is that one must ask to be excused; anyone who does so is showing rational fear in the face of clear and present danger, is therefore sane, and must continue to fly. In its final, most ominous form, Catch-22 declares they have the right to do anything we can't stop them from doing. Although most critics identify Yossarian as a coward and an antihero, they also sympathize with his urgent need to protect himself from this brutal universal law. Some critics have questioned the moral status of Yossarian's actions, noting in particular that he seems to be motivated merely by self-preservation and that the enemy he refuses to fight is led by Adolf Hitler. Others, however, contend that while *Catch-22* is ostensibly a war novel, World War II and Air Force base where most of the novel's action takes place function primarily as a microcosm that demonstrates the disintegration of language and human value in a bureaucratic state.

The novel follows Captain John Yossarian, a U.S. Army Air Forces B-25 bombardier. Most of the events in the book occur while the fictional 256th squadron is based on the island of Pianosa, in the Mediterranean Sea west of Italy. The novel looks into the experiences of Yossarian and the other airmen in the camp, and their attempts to keep their sanity in order to fulfill their service requirements, so that they can return home. The phrase "Catch-22," "a problematic situation for which the only solution is denied by a circumstance inherent in the problem or by a rule," has entered the English language. *Catch-22* tells many stories, but its central figure is a bombardier named Yossarian. The war has come to seem to Yossarian quite crazy. Men went mad and were rewarded with medals. All over the world, boys on every side of the bomb line were laying down their lives for what they had been told was their country; and no one seemed to mind, least of all the boys who were laying down their young lives. Yossarian minds very much: "He had decided to live forever or die in the attempt, and his only mission each time he went up was to come down alive." Yossarian is a rational man trying not to be killed in a wholly irrational world, forced to resort to even more irrational behavior than that of his superiors in order to survive. He is an expert malingerer; he performs minor acts of sabotage on his own plane; he takes every possible form of evasive action. But he cannot succeed against the appalling Colonel Cathcart, who continually raises the number of missions the men have to fly before they can be sent home, solely to get a reputation as a tough leader of men. Whatever Yossarian does, there is always a catch—Catch-22 that "says they have a right to do anything we can't stop them from doing." It is an unwritten law which is ruthlessly enforced.

Themes

Like many 1960s' novels, *Catch-22* is about the anarchic, individualistic human spirit and also its systematic denaturing, by society, corporate capitalism, and the military machine, as well as by mortal weakness and the threat of danger and death. But it also acquires a metaphorical and indeed metaphysical dimension; war is the general human condition, and Pianosa and the Eternal City are the landscapes in which we live. Since the world denatures us, or renders us inhuman or inanimate, the subject itself requires, in part, a similarly denatured tone: a comic method that, for much of the time, itself renders all things impersonal, inhuman and cruel. Human beings are eccentrics, or nothing more than the sum of their rules. Since the world is absurd, language renders itself to us in the form of absurdities; and logic only in the form of contradiction or paradox.

Heller creates an artistic world which is higher and also is based on the reality with the symbolization of "Catch-22," expressing the westerners' bewilderment towards human's situation. The artistic world created by Heller belongs to a postmodernist art which advocates a thorough pluralism in thinking modes. In this sense, *Catch-22* is one of the postmodernist novels. The postmodernist novel is no longer the novel in the traditional sense, but is a rethinking, deconstruction and subversion of the novel form and narrative itself. Since its appearance, this kind of new novel has rethought, deconstructed, even self-mockingly imitated and analyzed the novel form and narrative and has become more and more popular. The postmodernist novelists claim that reality is made by language, and the false language makes the false reality. So in *Catch-22*, the mad and absurd social reality is made by a chaos and formless language.

Although *Catch-22* deserts the writing techniques of the traditional novel, it neither lacks of the writing methods nor the forms. In fact, its narration and structure are both under the author's control. This novel not only intensifies the mad and absurd theme, but also establishes the mad and absurd measures. *Catch-22* is an antiwar novel. This novel, for obvious and tragic reasons, is one of the dominant and shaping literary forms of the troubled twentieth century. It has not only played its part in defining the historical story of the century, but also shaped the techniques, the flavor, and the artistic essence of the postmodernist novel. War had shattered older notions of art, of form and representation; it had transformed notions of reality, the rules of perception, and the structures of artistic expression. It fragmented, hardened, post modernized the voice of fiction, increased its sense of extremity, of irony, of tragedy, passing its critical lesson on into the history of postmodern fiction, and the whole literary and cultural tradition.

Critical appreciation of *Catch-22* was a bit slow in developing because the character of the novel was misunderstood. The book was presumed to be about World War II in particular and war in general, whereas Heller has said that he was inspired by the civilian situation in this country in the 1950s, and that *Catch-22* certainly has more meaning in regard to the Vietnam War than World War II. Heller has even bluntly insisted that *Catch-22* is not about World War II. Moreover, as critics to the issues of war, they have tended to argue that the theme of *Catch-22* is the absurdity, irrationality, and nightmare of a disordered universe, a universe in which fantasy and the grotesque are indistinguishable. The novel's chaotic surface has been seen as imitative form, a fictional texture expressing Heller's deepest intuition that the universe is absurd, irrational, and nightmarish. Though others have recognized the inadequacy, indeed the inaccuracy of this view, I think that much more needs to be said about what Heller was really trying to do in *Catch-22* and how well he has in fact done it.

Heller goes beyond his liberal predecessors to show that the enemy is not just the corporations and their authorities (in this case the military and its commanding officers). Humanity exists behind the absurdity, and this is what the book gradually discloses. Meantime, as the number of missions demanded of him rises and rises, and the frequency of death and the intensity of pain increases, Ocarina, deciding to live forever or at least die trying, tries to resist the universal victimization. This involves a struggle of identity, a quarrel with the contract, a battle with the language, as he increasingly defines himself in conflict and revolt. Language spawns counter-language, logic counter-logic, giving the narrative its growing order and structure, deepening its distinctive comic linguistic register. By the end of the book much of what has been first stated as absurd farce is recreated as tragedy. The characters that die in battle are no longer unknown. The victims are also the culprits, the culprits also the victims.

Heller's book hardly seems an act of literary propaganda, as so many of these earlier books do, nor is it a dramatic action in the tradition of Crane, Dreiser, and Steinbeck. *Catch-22* continues the tradition of literary protest. Like the books cited above, Heller's novel is informed by a militantly liberal point of view. A close friend once said that Heller is an ultra-liberal, and Heller himself has remarked that *Catch-22* is a liberal book. Asked to name the major American novelists of the early twentieth century, Heller cited Faulkner and Steinbeck—the choice of Steinbeck surely suggesting Heller's sympathies with the social protest tradition. What Heller does in *Catch-22* is to address traditional social problems from the usual point of view but by means of quite modern—even modernist—literary techniques.

Literary Techniques

Black Humor *Catch-22* is considered one of the typical novels of black humor, regarding the world as absurd and unreasonable and giving a smile after feeling extremely pessimistic, comically and even absurdly dealing with intrinsically tragic subjects, representing the single-dimension character and the wasteland background, constructing loose and usually disjointed structures without paying attention to time, confusing facts and invention to reveal the unreliability of reality, stressing techniques and formal designs, coldly looking on the despairing, fantastic, rude and cruel events, telling the story with mockingly questioning-God tone and often with a laughter having no intention to punish the evil and praise the good. *Catch-22* voices the anxious, absurd, outrageous reaction of a generation to a dark conflict that had taken American soldiers and airmen to Europe, and concludes not only in the defeat of totalitarianism, but in a victory on behalf of the world of our glossy, often alienating, and postmodern affluence. And the book is not just a satire on war but a story of that age of burgeoning affluence and all it brings with it—the grim period of arctic hostilities called the Cold War, the affluent society, and finally the postmodern phase of confident, narcissistic, consumptive late capitalism in which we, and Heller's elderly survivors of wartime, have ended up. The book owes much to the tradition of surrealism and grotesquerie, but it is not simply a novel of war as grotesque farce, nor a surreal burst of laughter in the face of chaos, meaninglessness, cruelty, or a journey into the fantastic unconscious. It also possesses a vivid satirical energy and a distinctive rage, and a pained moral aspiration. The plot that starts in festive disorder and misrule, in the realm of the carnivalesque, gradually makes its way toward an individual search for meaning and order. Those characters who see it as a just cause or a defence of American values are themselves absurd innocents, and objects of satire; the ones who do succeed are the ambitious, the cynical, the depraved, the self-seeking, the corrupt, and the mad.

Formlessness, Repetition, and Tonal Structure The plot structure of this fiction enables us to see clearly the plot arrangement of this novel, including formlessness, repetition, and tonal structure. Heller presents his story in such a way that at certain points it is literally impossible to determine the order of events. But Heller was trying to match form and content. At the same time Heller fashions a fictional world in which he introduces numerous repetitions without undue awkwardness. Heller speaks of the novel's recurring and cyclical structure. These three features about the novel's structure are all fit together to advance Heller's radical protest against the modern social order. The structural complexity of *Catch-22* thus embodies the novel's theme more thoroughly.

Bibliography

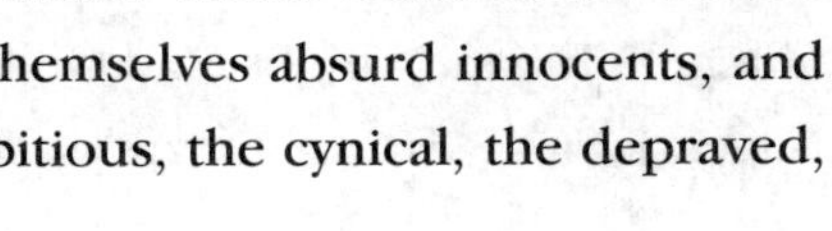

http://en.wikipedia.org/wiki/Joseph_Heller, 2013-02-15.

Aldridge, John W. "The Deceits of Black Humor." *Harper's, Vol.258, No. 1546*, March, 1979.

Billson, Maecus K. III, "The Un-minderbinding of Ocarina: Genesis Inverted in 'Catch-22'." *Arizona Quarterly*, *Vol. 36, No. 4*, Winter, 1980.

Cockburn, Alex. "A Review of *Catch-22*." *New Left Review*, *No. 18*. January-February, 1963.

Dickstein, Morris. "Black Humor and History: The Early Sixties." *Gates of Eden: American Culture in the Sixties, 1977*, Reprint by Penguin Books, 1989.

Heller, Joseph. *Catch-22*. New York: Everyman's Library, 1995.

Hicks, Granville. "Medals for Madness." *Saturday Review*, *Vol. XLIV, No. 40*, October 7, 1961.

Kiley, Frederick and Walter McDonald. *A "Catch-22" Casebook*. New York: Crowell, 1973.

Lindberg, Gary. "Playing for Real." *The Confidence Man in American Literature*. Oxford: Oxford University Press, 1982.

Mailer, Norman. "Some Children of the Goddess." *Contemporary American Novelists*. Illinois: Southern Illinois University Press, 1964.

Meller, James M. "Heller's 'Catch-22'." *The Exploded Form: The Modernist Novel in America*. Urbana, Chicago, and London: University of Illinois Press, 1980.

Merrill, Robert. "The Structure and Meaning of *Catch-22*." *Studies in American Fiction*, *Vol.14, No.2*, Autumn, 1986.

Mitchell, Julian. "Under Mad Gods." *Spectator*, *Vol. 208, No. 6990*, June 15, 1962.

Nagel, James. *Critical Essays on Joseph Heller*. Boston: G. K. Hall, 1984.

Kurt Vonnegut

His Life and Writing Career

His Life

Kurt Vonnegut, Jr. (1922–2007) was an American novelist known for works blending satire, black comedy, and science fiction, such as *Slaughterhouse-Five* (1969), *Cat's Cradle* (1963), and *Breakfast of Champions* (1973). He was known for his humanist beliefs as well as being honorary president of the American Humanist Association.

Kurt Vonnegut was born to fifth-generation German-American parents (Kurt

Vonnegut, Sr., and Edith née Lieber), son and grandson in the Indianapolis firm Vonnegut & Bohn. He attended Cornell University, where he served as assistant managing editor and associate editor for the student newspaper, the *Cornell Daily Sun*, and majored in chemistry. While attending Cornell, he was a member of the Delta Upsilon Fraternity, following in the footsteps of his father. While at Cornell, Vonnegut enlisted in the U.S. Army. The army sent him to the Carnegie Institute of Technology and the University of Tennessee to study mechanical engineering. On May 14, 1944, Mothers' Day, his mother committed suicide.

Kurt Vonnegut's experience as a soldier and prisoner of war had a profound influence on his later work. As a private with the 106th Infantry Division, Vonnegut, along with five other battalion scouts, wandered behind enemy lines for several days. They were cut off from their battalion and captured by Wehrmacht troops on December 14, 1944. Imprisoned in Dresden, Vonnegut was chosen as a leader of the POWs because he spoke some German. After insulting some German soldiers that were guarding him he was beaten and had his position as leader taken away. While a prisoner, he witnessed the fire bombing of Dresden in February 1945 which destroyed most of the city.

Vonnegut was one of a group of American prisoners of war to survive the attack in an underground slaughterhouse meat locker used by the Germans as an ad hoc detention facility. The Germans called the building *Schlachthof Fünf* (Slaughterhouse Five) which the Allied POWs adopted as the name for their prison. Vonnegut said the aftermath of the attack was "utter destruction" and "carnage unfathomable." This experience was the inspiration for his famous novel, *Slaughterhouse Five*, and is a central theme in at least six of his other books. In *Slaughterhouse Five* he recalls that the remains of the city resembled the surface of the moon, and that the Germans put the surviving POWs to work, breaking into basements and bomb shelters to gather bodies for mass burial, while German civilians cursed and threw rocks at them. Vonnegut eventually remarked, "There were too many corpses to bury. So instead the Germans sent in troops with flamethrowers. All these civilians' remains were burned to ashes."

Vonnegut was repatriated by Red Army troops in May 1945 at the Saxony-Czechoslovakian border. Upon returning to America, he was awarded a Purple Heart for what he called a "ludicrously negligible wound," later writing in *Timequake* that he was given the decoration after suffering a case of "frostbite."

After the war, Vonnegut attended the University of Chicago as a graduate student in anthropology and also worked at the City News Bureau of Chicago. Vonnegut admitted that he was a poor anthropology student, with one professor remarking that some of the students were going to be professional anthropologists and he was not one of them. According to Vonnegut in *Bagombo Snuff Box*, the university rejected his first thesis on the necessity of accounting for the similarities between Cubist painters and the leaders of late 19th Century Native American uprisings, saying it was "unprofessional." He left Chicago to work in Schenectady, New York, in public relations for General Electric, where his brother Bernard worked in the research department. The University of Chicago later accepted his novel *Cat's Cradle* as his thesis, citing its anthropological content and awarded him the M.A. degree in 1971.

In the mid 1950s, Vonnegut worked very briefly for *Sports Illustrated* magazine, where he was assigned to write a piece on a racehorse that had jumped a fence and attempted to run away. He refused and left. On the verge of abandoning writing, Vonnegut was offered a teaching job at the University of Iowa Writers' Workshop. While he was there, *Cat's Cradle* became a best-seller, and he began *Slaughterhouse-Five*, now considered one of the best American novels of the 20th Century, appearing on the 100 best lists of *Time* magazine and the Modern Library.

The author's name appears in print as "Kurt Vonnegut, Jr." throughout the first half of his published writing career; beginning with the 1976 publication of *Slapstick*, he dropped the "Jr." and was simply billed as Kurt Vonnegut. His older brother, Bernard Vonnegut, was an atmospheric scientist at the University at Albany, SUNY, who discovered that silver iodide could be used for cloud seeding, the process of artificially stimulating precipitation.

On November 11, 1999, the asteroid 25399 Vonnegut was named in Vonnegut's honor. On January 31, 2001, a fire destroyed the top story of his home. Vonnegut suffered smoke inhalation and was hospitalized in critical condition for four days. He survived, but his personal archives were destroyed. After leaving the hospital, he recuperated in Northampton, Massachusetts.

Vonnegut smoked unfiltered Pall Mall cigarettes, a habit he referred to as a "classy way to commit suicide."

Vonnegut died on April 11, 2007, in Manhattan, following a fall at his Manhattan home several weeks earlier which resulted in irreversible brain injuries.

His Writing Career

Vonnegut's first short story, "Report on the Barnhouse Effect" appeared in the February 11, 1950 edition of *Collier's* (it has since been reprinted in his short story collection, *Welcome to the Monkey House*). His first novel was the dystopian novel *Player Piano* (1952), in which human workers have been largely replaced by machines. He continued to write short stories before his second novel, *The Sirens of Titan*, was published in 1959. Through the 1960s, the form of his work changed, from the relatively orthodox structure of *Cat's Cradle* (which in 1971 earned him a Master's Degree) to the acclaimed, semi-autobiographical *Slaughterhouse-Five*, given a more experimental structure by using time travel as a plot device.

These structural experiments were continued in *Breakfast of Champions* (1973), which included many rough illustrations, lengthy non-sequiturs and an appearance by the author himself, as a *deus ex machina*.

> "This is a very bad book you're writing," I said to myself.
> "I know," I said.
> "You're afraid you'll kill yourself the way your mother did," I said.
> "I know," I said.

Deadeye Dick (1982), although mostly set in the mid-twentieth century, foreshadows the turbulent times of contemporary America; it ends prophetically with the lines "You want to know something? We are still in the Dark Ages. The Dark Ages — they haven't ended yet." The novel explores themes of social isolation and alienation that are particularly relevant in the postmodern world. Society is seen as openly hostile or indifferent at best and popular culture as superficial and excessively materialistic.

Vonnegut attempted suicide in 1984 and later wrote about this in several essays. *Breakfast of Champions* became one of his best-selling novels. It includes, in addition to the author himself, several of Vonnegut's recurring characters. One of them, science fiction author Kilgore Trout, plays a major role and interacts with the author's character.

In much of his work, Vonnegut's own voice is apparent, often filtered through the character of science fiction author Kilgore Trout (whose name is based on that of real-life science fiction writer Theodore Sturgeon), characterized by wild leaps of imagination and a deep cynicism, tempered by humanism. In the foreword to *Breakfast of Champions*, Vonnegut wrote that as a child, he saw men with locomotor ataxia, and it struck him that these men walked like broken machines; it followed that healthy people were working machines, suggesting that humans are helpless prisoners of determinism. Vonnegut also explored this theme in *Slaughterhouse-Five*, in which protagonist Billy Pilgrim "has come unstuck in time" and has so little control over his own life that he cannot even predict which part of it he will be living through from minute to minute. Vonnegut's well-known phrase "So it goes," used ironically in reference to death, also originated in *Slaughterhouse-Five* and became a slogan for anti-Vietnam War protestors in the 1960s. "Its combination of simplicity, irony, and rue is very much in the Vonnegut vein."

With the publication of his novel *Timequake* in 1997, Vonnegut announced his retirement from writing fiction. He continued to write for the magazine *In These Times*, where he was a senior editor, until his death in 2007, focusing on subjects ranging from contemporary U.S. politics to simple observational pieces on topics such as a trip to the post office. In 2005, many of his essays were collected in a new bestselling book titled *A Man Without a Country*, which he insisted would be his last contribution to letters.

The April 2008 issue of *Playboy* featured the first published excerpt from *Armageddon in Retrospect*, the first posthumous collection of Vonnegut's work. The book itself was published in the same month. It included never before published short stories by the writer and a letter that was written to his family during WWII when Vonnegut was captured as a prisoner of war. The book also contains drawings that Vonnegut himself drew and a speech he wrote shortly before his death. The introduction of the book was written by his son, Mark Vonnegut.

Vonnegut was deeply influenced by early Socialist labor leaders, especially Indiana natives Powers Hapgood and Eugene V. Debs, and he frequently quotes them in his work. He named characters after both Debs (Eugene Debs Hartke in *Hocus Pocus* and Eugene Debs Metzger in *Deadeye Dick*) and Russian Communist leader Leon Trotsky (Leon Trotsky Trout in *Galápagos*). He was a lifetime member of the American Civil Liberties Union and was featured in a print advertisement for them.

Vonnegut frequently addressed moral and political issues but rarely dealt with specific political figures until after his retirement from fiction. (Although the downfall of Walter Starbuck, a minor Nixon administration bureaucrat who is the narrator and main character in *Jailbird* (1979), would not have occurred but for the Watergate scandal, the focus is not on the administration.) His collection *God Bless You, Dr. Kevorkian* referenced controversial assisted suicide proponent Jack Kevorkian.

With his columns for *In These Times*, he began a blistering attack on the Bush administration and the Iraq war. "By saying that our leaders are power-drunk chimpanzees, am I in danger of wrecking the morale of our soldiers fighting and dying in the Middle East?" he wrote. "Their morale, like so many bodies, is already shot to pieces. They are being treated, as I never was, like toys a rich kid got for Christmas." *In These Times* quoted him as saying "The only difference between Hitler and Bush is that Hitler was elected."

In *A Man Without a Country*, he wrote that "George W. Bush has gathered around him upper-crust C-students who know no history or geography." He did not regard the 2004 election with much optimism; speaking of Bush and John Kerry, he said that "no matter which one wins, we will have a Skull and Bones President at a time when entire vertebrate species, because of how we have poisoned the topsoil, the waters and the atmosphere, are becoming, hey presto, nothing but skulls and bones."

Vonnegut was descended from a family of German freethinkers, who were skeptical of "conventional religious beliefs." His great-grandfather Clemens Vonnegut had authored a free thought book entitled *Instruction in Morals*, as well as an address for his own funeral in which he denied the existence of God, an afterlife, and Christian doctrines about sin and salvation. Kurt Vonnegut reproduced his great-grandfather's funeral address in his book *Palm Sunday* (1981), and identified these free thought views as his "ancestral religion," declaring it a mystery as to how it was passed on to him.

Vonnegut described himself variously as a skeptic, freethinker, humanist, Unitarian Universalist, agnostic, and atheist. He disbelieved in the supernatural, considered religious doctrine to be "so much arbitrary, clearly invented balderdash," and believed people were motivated by loneliness to join religions.

Vonnegut considered humanism to be a modern-day form of free thought, and advocated it in various writings, speeches and interviews. His ties to organized humanism included membership as a Humanist Laureate in the Council for Secular Humanism's International Academy of Humanism. In 1992, the American Humanist Association named him the Humanist of the Year. Vonnegut went on to serve as honorary president of the American Humanist Association (AHA), having taken over the position from his late colleague Isaac Asimov, and serving until his own death in 2007. In a letter to AHA members, Vonnegut wrote: "I am a humanist, which means, in part, that I have tried to behave decently without expectations of rewards or punishments after I am dead."

Vonnegut's views on religion were unconventional and nuanced. While rejecting the divinity of Jesus, he was nevertheless an ardent admirer, and believed that Jesus' Beatitudes informed his own humanist outlook. While he often identified himself as an agnostic or atheist, he also frequently spoke of God and despite describing free thought, humanism and agnosticism as his "ancestral religion," and despite being a Unitarian, he also spoke of himself as being irreligious. In a press release by the American Humanist Association he was claimed to have been "completely secular."

He had published 14 novels such as *Player Piano* (1952), *The Sirens of Titan* (1959), *Mother Night* (1961), *Cat's Cradle* (1963), *God Bless You, Mr. Rosewater; or, Pearls before Swine* (1965), *Slaughterhouse-Five; or, The Children's Crusade* (1969), *Breakfast of Champions; or, Goodbye Blue Monday* (1973), *Slapstick; or, Lonesome No More* (1976), *Jailbird* (1979), *Deadeye Dick* (1982), *Galápagos* (1985), *Bluebeard* (1987), *Hocus Pocus* (1990), *Timequake* (1997).

Analysis of and Comment on His Representative Novel

Slaughterhouse-Five (1969)

Plot Summary

The narrator opens with an elaborate hyperbole of a subtitle for the book, explaining that he is a veteran living in easy circumstances, who witnessed the bombing of Dresden, Germany as a prisoner of war and survived to tell the tale in the manner of the planet of Tralfamadore where the flying saucers come from. He went back to Dresden with a war buddy years later. He ends the first chapter saying that his war novel, his novel of looking back is over since there is nothing intelligent one can say about a massacre.

He then tells the story of Billy Pilgrim, who is unstuck in time—he uncontrollably gets flung around the scenes of his life. He was a prisoner of war, became an optometrist, and married a rich girl who died of carbon monoxide poisoning. He was the only survivor of a plane crash. He was abducted and kept in a zoo on the planet Tralfamadore, where he was mated with movie star Montana Wildhack.

With every mention of death in the book, the narrator says, "So it goes," Tralfamadorians believe that time exists all at once and not moment-by-moment like beads on a string. So a person is never dead, because he is still alive in the past. Billy's daughter Barbara is furious at him for trying to tell people his crazy notions.

He wandered behind enemy lines with a fat, sadistic soldier named Roland Weary and two scouts, who ditched them. Weary got so mad at Billy for this that he beat him and when they were captured by German soldiers, he convinced many others that it was Billy's fault when he died. Pre-capture, Billy also traveled to, among other places, his mother's nursing home, where she asks him weakly how she got old, and to the YMCA where his father taught him to swim by throwing him into the deep end. He also goes back to the night of his abduction.

Everyone at the prison camp was shocked to see how weak the Americans were. Billy was delirious, and he flipped out and was hospitalized. Edgar Derby, an older soldier who would be shot for plundering a teapot, stayed with him. Paul Lazzaro, a weak, hateful man, told Billy he had sworn to avenge Roland Weary by shooting him. Billy was not worried; he had seen when he would die. He traveled in time to his second hospitalization during his last year of optometry school. There he met Eliot Rosewater, who introduced him to the science fiction works of Kilgore Trout.

While there, Billy traveled back to Tralfamadore. When he told the crowd at the zoo to fear the power of Earthlings, they thought he was stupid; they knew it would be them, experimenting with a new jet fuel, who would destroy the universe.

Billy and the other soldiers were transferred to Dresden, which was a beautiful city. Billy traveled to the airplane crash, where he mistook the people who rescued him for German soldiers. During surgery, he traveled back to Dresden. In Dresden, he worked at a factory that made malt syrup with vitamins, which everyone illegally spooned. They were kept in slaughterhouse number five. About a month later, the city was bombed, and the prisoners survived in an underground bunker.

At his eighteenth wedding anniversary party, to which he invited Trout after they met in an alley, Billy flipped out; the barbershop quartet reminded him of the Dresden guards.

Years later, in the hospital after the plane crash, Billy met Air Force Historian and war-hawk Bertram Copeland Rumfoord, who told him that the bombing of Dresden was necessary and had to be kept a secret because of all the American "bleeding hearts."

After the crash, Billy escaped to New York, where he snuck onto a radio show to preach his Tralfamadorian wisdom.

In the last chapter, the narrator tells of how he traveled back to Dresden, and how Billy and the other prisoners had been made to dig up corpses from the ruins.

Themes

Fate and Free Will and the Illogical Nature of Human Beings *Slaughterhouse-Five* explores Fate and Free Will and the illogical nature of human beings. Protagonist Billy Pilgrim is unstuck in time, randomly experiencing the events of his life, with no idea of what part he next will visit (relive)—so, his life does not end with death; he re-lives his death, *before* its time, an experience often mingled with his other experiences.

Billy Pilgrim says there is no free will; an assertion confirmed by a Tralfamadorian, who says, "I've visited thirty-one inhabited planets in the universe ... Only on Earth is there any talk of free will." The story's central concept: most of humanity is inconsequential; they do what they do, *because* they must.

To the Tralfamadorians, everything simultaneously exists, therefore, everyone is always alive. They, too, have wars and suffer tragedies (they destroy the universe whilst testing spaceship fuels), but, when Billy asks what they do about wars, they reply that they simply ignore them. The Tralfamadorians counter Vonnegut's true theme: life, as a human being, is only enjoyable with unknowns. Tralfamadorians do not make choices about what they do, but have power only over what they think (the subject of *Timequake*). Vonnegut expounds his position in Chapter One, "that writing an anti-war book is like writing an anti-glacier book," both being futile endeavors, since both phenomena are unstoppable. This concept is difficult for Billy to accept, at first.

Author Vonnegut's other novels, e.g. *The Sirens of Titan*, suggest that the Tralfamadorians, in *Slaughterhouse-Five*, satirize Fatalism. The Tralfamadorians represent the belief in war as inevitable. In their hapless destruction of the universe, Vonnegut does not sympathize with their philosophy. To human beings, Vonnegut says, ignoring a war is unacceptable when we have free will.

This human illogicality appears in the climax that occurs, not with the Dresden fire bombing, but with the summary execution of a man who committed a petty theft. Amid all that horror, death, and destruction, *time* is taken to punish one man. Yet, the time is taken, and Vonnegut takes the outside opinion of the bird asking, "Poo-tee-weet?" The same birdsong ends the novel *God Bless You, Mr. Rosewater*, as the protagonist gives away his fortune to the plaintiffs of hundreds of false paternity suits brought against him—a Dada observation of human absurdity.

Slaughterhouse-Five is framed with chapters in the author's voice, about his experience of war, indicating the novel is intimately connected with his life and convictions. That established, Vonnegut withdraws from the unfolding of Billy Pilgrim's story, despite continual appearances as a minor character: in the POW camp latrine, the corpse mines of Dresden, when he mistakenly dials Billy's telephone number. These authorial appearances anchor Billy Pilgrim's life to reality, highlighting his existential struggle to fit in the human world.

Literary Techniques

Black Humor Like *Catch-22* by Joseph Heller, *Slaughterhouse-Five* is also considered a representative work of black humor. It is generally acknowledged that with the publication of novels of black humor such as *Catch-22* (1961), *Cat's Cradle* (1962) and *Slaughterhouse-Five* (1969) that American postmodernist literature formally appeared in the 1960s. The story in *Slaughterhouse-Five* continually employs the refrain "So it goes" when death, dying, and mortality occur, as a narrative transition to another subject, as a *memento mori*, as comic relief, and to explain the unexplained. It appears one hundred and sixteen times.

Metafiction As a postmodern metafictional novel, the first chapter of *Slaughterhouse-Five* is an author's preface about how he came to write *Slaughterhouse-Five*, apologizing, because the novel is "so short and jumbled and jangled," because "there is nothing intelligent to say about a massacre." As in *Mother Night* (1961), but more extensively, Vonnegut manipulates fiction and reality. The first sentence says: "All this happened, more or less," then appears in Billy Pilgrim's WWII, then followed by the narrator's note: "That was I. That was me. That was the author of this book."

The story repeatedly refers to real and fictional novels and fiction; Billy reads *The Valley of the Dolls* (1966), and skims a Tralfamadorian novel, and participates in a radio talk show, part of a literary expert panel discussing "The Death of the Novel."

The narrator introduces *Slaughterhouse-Five* with the novel's genesis and ends discussing the beginning and the end of the Novel. The story proper begins in Chapter Two, although there is no reason to presume that the first chapter is not fictional. This is a technique common to postmodern meta-fiction. The story purports to be a disjointed, discontinuous narrative, of Billy Pilgrim's point of view, of being unstuck in time. Vonnegut's writing usually contains such disorder.

The narrator reports that Billy Pilgrim experiences his life discontinuously, wherein he randomly experiences (relives) his birth, youth, old age, and death, not in (normal) linear order. There are two narrative threads, Billy's experience of War (itself interrupted with experiences from elsewhere in his life) is mostly linear; and his discontinuous pre-war and post-war lives. Billy's existential perspective was compromised in witnessing Dresden's destruction, although he had come unstuck in time before arriving to Dresden. *Slaughterhouse-Five* is told in short, declarative sentences that impress the sense of reading a report of facts.

The narrator begins the novel telling his connection to the Dresden bombing, why he is recording it, a self-description (of self and book), and of the fact that he believes it is a desperate attempt at scholarly work. He then segues to the *story* of Billy Pilgrim: "Listen: Billy Pilgrim has come unstuck in time," thus, the transition from the writer's perspective to that of the third-person, omniscient Narrator.

Kilgore Trout, whom Billy Pilgrim meets, operating a newspaper delivery business, can be seen as Vonnegut's alter ego, though the two differ in some respects. For example, Trout's career as a science fiction novelist is checkered with thieving publishers, and the fictional author is unaware of his readership.

Slaughterhouse-Five is structured like a Tralfamadorian novel, the literature Billy Pilgrim encounters on Tralfamadore. The only Earth reading available to Billy is a popular novel, *Valley of the Dolls* (1966); asking his captors what they read, he is handed thin booklets with symbols. The Tralfamadorians tell him the symbols represent pleasing thoughts and events. When they are all simultaneously read, as do the Tralfamadorians, it creates an emotion in the reader's mind. Billy's time-tripping juxtaposes his life's events—war, wedding night, travel to father's funeral—mixing black humor, tragedy, and happiness in few paragraphs.

Bibliography

http://en.wikipedia.org/wiki/Kurt_Vonnegut, 2013-02-15.

http://en.wikipedia.org/wiki/Slaughterhouse-Five, 2013-02-15.

Chen, Shidan. *Vonnegut's Art of Postmodernist Fiction*. Beijing: Foreign Languages Teaching and Research Press, 2010.

Chen, Shidan. *A Study of American Postmodernist Fiction*. Beijing: Foreign Languages Teaching and Research Press, 2010.

John Barth

His Life and Writing Career

His Life

John Barth (1930–1999), called "Jack," was born in Cambridge, Maryland. Barth has an older brother, Bill, and a twin sister, Jill. He briefly studied "Elementary Theory and Advanced Orchestration" at Juilliard before attending Johns Hopkins University, from which he received a B.A. in 1951 and an M.A. in 1952 (for which he wrote a thesis novel, *The Shirt of Nessus*). Barth was a professor at The Pennsylvania State University from 1953 to 1965. During the "American high Sixties," he moved to teach at University at Buffalo, The State University of New York from 1965 to 1973. In that period he came to know "the remarkable short fiction" of the Argentine Jorge Luis Borges, which inspired his collection Lost in the Funhouse. He then taught at Boston University (visiting professor, 1972–1973) and Johns Hopkins University (1973–1995) before retiring in 1995.

John Barth is the author of *Giles Goat-Boy* (1966), *The Sot-Weed Factor* (1960), and *Chimera* (1972), among many others. His short story collection *Lost in the Funhouse* (1968) and his essay "The Literature of Exhaustion" (1967) have been required reading on college campuses since the '70s. Barth is widely considered to be among the most important American novelists of the 20th century and one of the foremost practitioners of postmodernism and metafiction. He was born in Cambridge on the eastern shore of Maryland, the grandson of nineteenth-century German immigrants on May 27, 1930. After graduating from high school, Barth briefly attended the Julliard School of Music before enrolling as a scholarship student at John Hopkins University. While an undergraduate, he published two stories in the student literary magazine and "Lilith and the Lion" in the *Hopkins Review*. He married Harriete Anne Strickland on January 11, 1950. He received his B.A. in creative writing from Hopkins and enrolled in the institution's graduate writing program in 1951. He received a B.A. in 1951 and an M.A. in 1952 in Johns Hopkins University. After the birth of his son John in 1952, Barth had to leave graduate school for financial reasons. He accepted a position as an instructor in the English Department at Pennsylvania State University in 1953, and the next year saw the birth of his second son, Daniel. Barth spent the first part of *The Floating Opera* (1956), the next three months revising it for his publisher, and the last three months of the year writing *The End of the Road* (1958). Once upon a time, Barth was the hippest writer in America. Nowadays many consider his concerns with the mythical story cycle and the mechanics of storytelling relics from the '60s. While college students still read stories from Lost in the Funhouse in literature classes, his works do not seem to maintain the same kind of cultural resonance as, say, those of Thomas Pynchon or Don DeLillo. It doesn't help that Barth's novels are almost entirely unfilmable, rarely touch on current affairs, and don't trade in self-pity or ingratiating sarcasm or apocalyptic pessimism.

His Writing Career

Barth began his career with *The Floating Opera* (1956). He is also the author of *The End of the Road* (1958), *The Sot-Weed Factor* (1960), *Giles Goat-Boy* (1966), *Lost in the Funhouse: Fiction for Print, Tape, Live Voice* (1968), *Chimera* (1972), *LETTERS: A Novel* (1979), *Sabbatical: A Romance* (1982), *Tidewater Tales: A Novel* (1987), *The Last Voyage of Somebody the Sailor* (1991), *Once upon a Time: A Floating Opera* (1994), *On with the Story* (1996), *Coming Soon!!!: A Narrative* (2003), *The Book of Ten Nights and a Night: Eleven Stories* (2004), and *Where Three Roads Meet: Novellas* (2005). *The Floating Opera* and *The End of the Road* are two short "realist" novels that deal wittily with controversial topics, suicide and abortion respectively. They are straightforward realistic tales; as Barth later remarked, they "didn't know they were novels." *The Sot-Weed Factor*, was initially intended as the completing novel of a trilogy comprising his first two "realist" novels, but, as a consequence of Barth's maturation as a writer, it developed into a different project. The novel is significant as it marked Barth's discovery of Postmodernism. Barth's next novel, *Giles Goat-Boy* (about 800 pages), is a speculative fiction based on the conceit of the university as universe. A boy raised as a goat discovers his humanity and becomes a savior in a story presented as a computer tape given to Barth, who denies that it is his work. In the course of the novel Giles carries out all the tasks prescribed by Joseph Campbell in "The Hero with a Thousand Faces." Barth kept a list of the tasks taped to his wall while he was writing the book. The short story collection *Lost in the Funhouse* and the novella collection *Chimera* are even more metafictional than their two predecessors, foregrounding the writing process and presenting achievements such as a seven-deep nested quotation. Chimera shared the U.S. National Book Award for Fiction. In the novel *LETTERS* (1979), Barth interacts with characters from his first six books. His 1994 *Once upon a Time: A Floating Opera* reuses stock characters, stock situations and formulas, styles, approaches and artistic criteria. Barth's work is characterized by a historical awareness of literary tradition and by the practice of rewriting typical of postmodernism. He said: "I don't know what my view of history is, but insofar as it involves some allowance for repetition and recurrence, re-orchestration, and reprise [...] I would always want it to be more in the form of a thing circling out and out and becoming more inclusive each time." In Barth's postmodern sensibility, parody is a central device. Around 1972, in an interview, Barth declared that "The process [of making a novel] is the content, more or less."

Barth's fiction continues to maintain a precarious balance between postmodern self-consciousness and wordplay and the sympathetic characterization and "page-turning" plotting commonly associated with more traditional genres and subgenres of classic and contemporary storytelling. While writing these books, Barth was also pondering and discussing the theoretical problems of fiction writing. In 1967 he wrote a highly influential and to some controversial essay considered a manifesto of postmodernism, "The Literature of Exhaustion" (first printed in *The Atlantic*, 1967). It depicts literary realism as a "used-up" tradition; Barth's description of his own work, which many thought illustrated a core trait of postmodernism, is "novels which imitate the form of a novel, by an author who imitates the role of author." The essay was widely considered a statement of "the death of the novel" (compare with Roland Barthes' "The Death of the Author"). Barth has since insisted that he was merely making clear that a particular stage in history was passing, and pointing to possible directions from there. He later (in 1980) wrote a follow-up essay, "The Literature of Replenishment," to clarify the point.

Barth's novel *The End of the Road* was published in 1958 and nominated for the National Book Award. Barth's awards and honors include National Book Award nominations for *The Floating Opera and Lost in the Funhouse*, and the Award itself for *Chimera*. He also won a Brandeis University Creative Arts Award in 1965, a Rockefeller Foundation grant for 1965–1966, a National Institute of Arts and Letters grant in 1966, and an honorary LittD degree from Johns Hopkins in 1973. Barth is widely considered to be among the most important American novelists of the 20th century and one of the foremost practitioners of postmodernism and metafiction.

Analysis of and Comment on His Representative Novel

The Sot-Weed Factor (1960)

Plot Summary

The Sot-Weed Factor was initially intended as the completing novel of a trilogy comprising his first two "realist" novels, but, as a consequence of Barth's maturation as a writer, it developed into a different project. The novel is significant as it marked Barth's discovery of Postmodernism. The novel is a satirical epic of the colonization of Maryland based on the life of an actual poet, Ebenezer Cooke, who wrote a poem of the same title. The book is a bare-knuckled satire of humanity at large and the grandiose costume romance, done with meticulous skill in imitation of such eighteenth-century picaresque novelists as Fielding, Smollett and Sterne.

The novel is set in the 1680s and 90s in London and on the eastern shore of the colony of Maryland. It tells the story of an English poet named Ebenezer Cooke who is given the title "Poet Laureate of Maryland" by Charles Calvert. He undergoes many adventures on his journey to Maryland and while in Maryland, all the while striving to preserve his innocence (i.e. his virginity). The book takes its title from the grand poem that Cooke composes throughout the story, which was originally intended to sing the praises of Maryland, but ends up being a biting satire based on his disillusioning experiences. *The Sot-Weed Factor* was initially intended, with Barth's first two, as the concluding novel on a trilogy on nihilism, but the project took a different direction as a consequence of Barth's maturation as a writer. The novel takes its title from a poem of the same name published in London in 1708 and signed Ebenezer Cooke. "Sot-weed" is an old term for the tobacco plant. A "factor" is a middleman who buys something to resell it. The novel parodies, mimics, recuperates and rewrites the forms of the 18th century genre of the Bildungsroman (formation novel) and Künstlerroman (novel on the formation of an artist), and in particular Henry Fielding's *Tom Jones* (1749), Laurence Sterne's *Tristram Shandy* (1759–1767), and Samuel Richardson's three epistolary novels. The narrative presents Ebenezer as a Künstlerroman hero. The novel is also a parody of the picaresque genre, in particular of *Tristram Shandy* and *Tom Jones*. *The Sot-Weed Factor* is ushered into a special category of literature: it is seemingly received into that hall of infamy, barred to the ordinary reader by the champions of prudishness, and thrown open only by future enlightened generations—the rogue's gallery inhabited by, for example, D. H. Lawrence and *Lady Chatterley's Lover* (1928), and Vladimir Nabokov and *Lolita* (1955). The first edition was written during four years, and published by Doubleday in 1960, consisting of about 800 pages. Barth revisited the text for a new edition issue in 1967 by another publisher, dried off by 60 pages. In 1987, the revised edition was reissued by the original publisher, in the Doubleday Anchor Edition series, with an added foreword. The novel has been translated to several languages, including Italian, Japanese and others. *TIME* included it in its TIME 100 Best English-language Novels from 1923 to 2005.

In *The Sot-Weed Factor*, born in America, with a twin sister Anna, Ebenezer is raised in England towards the close of the seventeenth century and tutored by one Henry Burlingame III. Subconsciously living with his sister, Ebenezer decides to become a poet and remain a virgin for the rest of his life, thus devoting himself to the sublimation of sex through words. He rejects the advances of the whore Joan Toast, offering her his pure love instead. Named Poet Laureate of Maryland by Lord Baltimore, the proprietor of the province, who happens to be Henry Burlingame in disguise, he sets out for America in order to sing the New World's praise in a long epic poem which he intends to call Marylandiad. Yet after his encounters with life in an American colony, he writes a satiric poem entitled *The Sot-Weed Factor* instead. Unbeknownst to him, Ebenezer has been followed by Joan Toast, who has fallen in love with him. She ultimately becomes his wife, after enduring every sort of physical illness and psychic humiliation imaginable. Through a string of unforeseen occurrences she can re-bestow on her husband the title to Malden, his father's former estate in Maryland, which Ebenezer, through inexperience and wrongheaded idealism, had lost shortly after his arrival in America. However, Joan insists that he first consummate their marriage despite the fact that she suffers from syphilis. Thus, Ebenezer loses his innocence, if not his health. When Joan Toast dies shortly after wedding, Ebenezer, disillusioned, lives out his life together with his twin sister Anna. Together they raise Anna's son, Henry Burlingame's child. Following his successful sexual union with Anna, Burlingame, the "anti-hero" of the novel, who is as many-faced in attitude and appearance as Ebenezer is single-minded and constant, disappears from history, civilization, and the novel's plot, although Barth's later novels will be haunted by his descendants. Ebenezer Cooke's *The Sot-Weed Factor* is published and later revised.

Themes

The Sot-Weed Factor pretends to "re-write" the satirical poem, first published in 1780, of one Ebenezer Cooke, poet Laureate of Maryland. Cooke and his poem in fact existed, and the sot-weed of the title is tobacco, in which the factor traded. Since it is only through words that the historical eighteenth-century Ebenezer Cooke can be revived, the fictional twentieth-century Ebenezer Cooke must pay the price for this revival by remaining within the realm of words, and becoming the plaything of Barth's fiction. This is not just the condition, but the principle of his existence. When Ebenezer, who has vowed to remain a virgin, eventually breaks his vow in order to consummate his marriage with the former whore Joan Toast, he and his author must both lay down their pens, for "pen" and "penis," both tools of productivity, cannot be employed at the same time. Thus, in *The Sot-Weed Factor*, Sigmund Freud's notion that literature is a sublimation of unfulfilled sexual desire is taken literally and consequently parodied; for whereas words flow seemingly without difficulty, sex is their ultimate "end." When physical and spiritual productivity become severed from one another, when, that is, one is but delimited by the other, then both are reduced to a quantitative measure, and values are leveled. This applies particularly t the genre of Bildungsroman, since the idea of Bildung is dependent on individual advancement through conscious choice, the preference of one set of rules over another. *The Sot-Weed Factor* can indeed be described as Bildungsroman, a description of the character development of the protagonist Ebenezer Cooke, whose unfounded idealism, after being thwarted time and again by his harsh encounters with reality, is ultimately replaced with a pragmatic attitude towards life. Thus, Ebenezer seems to pursue the well-trodden path of the American youth's initiation into life, originating in innocence and terminating in experience.

Literary Techniques

Wordplay *The Sot-Weed Factor* (which means "tobacco salesman") introduces Barth's penchant for fancy wordplay, ontological tricks, historical parody, and existential games. The novel takes its title from a poem of the same name published in London in 1708 and signed Ebenezer Cooke. "Sot-weed" is an old term for the tobacco plant. A "factor" is a middleman who buys something to resell it. As Barth explained: "*The Sot–Weed Factor* began with the title and, of course, Ebenezer Cooke's original poem... Nobody knows where the real chap is buried; I made up a grave for Ebenezer because I wanted to write his epitaph."

Historical parody Barth also makes extensive use of the few pieces of information known at the time about the historical Cooke, his assumed father and grandfather, both called Andrew Cooke, and his sister, Anna. The novel parodies, mimics, recuperates and rewrites the forms of the 18th century genre of the Bildungsroman (formation novel) and Künstlerroman (novel on the formation of an artist), and in particular Fielding's *Tom Jones*, Sterne's *Tristram Shandy*, and Samuel Richardson's three epistolary novels. The narrative presents Ebenezer as a Künstlerroman hero. The novel is also a parody of the picaresque genre, in particular of *Tristram Shandy* and *Tom Jones*.

Bibliography

http://en.wikipedia.org/wiki/John_Barth, 2013-02-15.

http://www.dave-edelman.com/barth/, 2013-02-15.

Betts, Richard A. "The Joke as Informing Principle in *The Sot-Weed Factor*." *College Literature 10, No.1* (1983): 38-49.

Bowen, Zack. *A Reader's Guide to John Barth*. London: Greenwood Press, 1994.

Dippie, Brain. "'His Visage Wild; His Form Exotick': Indian Themes and Cultural Guilt in John Barth's *The Sot-Weed Factor*." *American Quarterly* 21 (1969): 113-121.

Diser, Philip. "The Historical Ebenezer Cooke." *Critique* 10, no. 3 (1968): 48-59.

Fiedler, Leslie. "John Barth: An Eccentric Genius." *On Contemporary Literature*. Ed.

Richard Kostelanetz. New York: Avon Books, 1964.

Gladsky, Thomas S. "*The Sot-Weed Factor* as Historiography." *Arkansas Philological Association 7, No. 2* (1981): 37-47.

Kostelanetz, Richard. *The New American Arts*. New York: Horizon Press, 1965.

Miller, Russsell H. "*The Sot-Weed Factor*: A Contemporary Mock-Epic." *Critique: Studies in Modern Fiction 8, No. 2* (Winter 1965-1966): 88-100.

Puetz, Manfred. "John Barth's *The Sot-Weed Factor*: The Pitfalls of Mythopoesis." *Critical Essays on John Barth*. Ed. Joseph J. Waldmeir. Boston: G. K. Hall, 1980.

Ziegler, Heide. *John Barth*. New York: Methuen Co. Ltd, 1987.

Donald Barthelme

His Life and Writing Career

His Life

Donald Barthelme (1931–1989) was born on April 7 in Philadelphia in 1931. His parents had attended the University of Pennsylvania. His father was a noted architect, who was trained in the beaux arts tradition of meticulous draftsmanship, soon moved the family to Houston, where, much in advance of his time, he developed an interest in the modernism of Le Corbusier, Mies van der Rohe, and Alvar Aalto, who, Barthelme noted, were interested not only in aesthetics but in the possibility of improving human existence. Their influence, which Barthelme acknowledges as visually and spiritually important to him, was felt most immediately in the home his father designed for the family. Barthelme describes it as somewhat weird, although beautiful and similar to Mies van der Rohe's Tugendhat House. Barthelme was interested not only in aesthetics but in the possibility of improving human existence. Though he contends there is very little autobiography in his work, Barthelme acknowledges the influence of his mother, who he describes as a "wicked wit." Barthelme's association with contemporary painters and his interest in contemporary painting and literature did not so much serve to provide models for his own writing as a sense of the possibilities open to a writer. He received his education in Texas, where he attended the University of Houston as a journalism major and worked for the *Houston Post*. He founded the University of Houston *Forum*, a literary journal. In 1974–1975, Barthelme served as a Distinguished Visiting Professor of English at the City College of the City University of New York. He has been placed in the front rank of postmodernist writers along with John Barth, John Hawkes, Thomas Pynchon, and Italo Calvino. Donald Barthelme died of cancer in Houston on July 23, 1989. He was 58 years old. Barthelme fondly recalled childhood visits with his grandfather, a rancher and lumber dealer in Galveston, whose home on the Guadalupe River not far from San Antonio the writer described as "a wonderful place to ride and hunt, talk to catfish and try to make the windmill run backward." With the appropriate changes, those encounters with the windmill at times appear to reflect the way in which much of his fiction is written.

In 1951, as a student, he wrote his first articles for the *Houston Post*. Two years later, Barthelme was drafted into the U.S. Army, arriving in Korea on July 27, 1953, the day of the signing of the Korean Armistice Agreement, which ended the Korean War. He served briefly as the editor of an Army newspaper before returning to the U.S. and his job at the *Houston Post*. Once back, he continued his studies at the University of Houston, studying philosophy. Although he continued to take classes until 1957, he never received a degree. He spent much of his free time in Houston's Black jazz clubs, listening to musical innovators such as Lionel Hampton and Peck Kelly, an experience that influenced his later writing.

Barthelme's relationship with his father was a struggle between a rebellious son and a demanding father. In later years they would have tremendous arguments about the kinds of literature in which Barthelme was interested and which he wrote. While in many ways his father was avant-garde in art and aesthetics, he did not approve of the post-modern and deconstruction schools. Barthelme's attitude toward his father is delineated in the novels *The Dead Father* and *The King* as he is pictured in the characters King Arthur and Lancelot. Barthelme's independence also shows in his moving away from the family's Roman Catholicism (his mother was especially devout), a separation that troubled Barthelme throughout his life as did the distance with his father. He seemed much closer to his mother and agreeable to her strictures.

Barthelme went on to teach for brief periods at Boston University, University at Buffalo, and the College of the City of New York, where he served as Distinguished Visiting Professor from 1974 to 1975. His brothers Frederick (born 1943) and Steven (born 1947) are also respected fiction writers.

His Writing Career

Barthelme would go on to write over a hundred more short stories, first collected in *City Life* (1970), *Sadness* (1972), *Amateurs* (1976), *Great Days* (1979), and *Overnight to Many Distant Cities* (1983). Many of these stories were later reprinted and slightly revised for the collections *Sixty Stories* (1981), *Forty Stories* (1987) and, posthumously,

Flying to America (2007). Though primarily known for these stories, Barthelme also produced four novels characterized by the same fragmentary style: *Snow White* (1967), *The Dead Father* (1975), *Paradise* (1986), and *The King* (1990, posthumous). In 1971, he won the National Book Award in the juvenile literary category for his book *The Slightly Irregular Fire Engine; or the Hithering Thithering Djinn*, which he also illustrated. Donald Barthelme died of cancer in Houston on July 23, 1989.

In 1961, Barthelme became director of the Contemporary Arts Museum in Houston; he published his first short story the same year. His *New Yorker* publication, "L' Lapse," a parody of Michelangelo Antonioni's film *L'Eclisse*, followed in 1963. The magazine would go on to publish much of Barthelme's early output, including such now famous stories as "Me and Miss Mandible," the tale of a 35-year old sent to elementary school by either a clerical error or failing at his job as an insurance adjuster and failing in his marriage, and "A Shower of Gold," in which a sculptor agrees to appear on the existentialist game show "Who Am I?" In 1964, Barthelme collected his early stories in Come Back, Dr. Caligari, for which he received considerable critical acclaim as an innovator of the short story form. His style (fictional and popular figures in absurd situations, e.g., the Batman-inspired "The Joker's Greatest Triumph"), spawned a number of imitators and would help to define the next several decades of short fiction.

Barthelme continued his success in the short story form with "Unspeakable Practices" and "Unnatural Acts" (1968). One widely anthologized story from this collection, "The Balloon," appears to reflect on Barthelme's own intentions as an artist. The narrator of the tale inflates a giant, irregular balloon over most of Manhattan, causing widely divergent reactions in the populace. Children play across its top, enjoying it quite literally on a surface level; adults attempt to read meaning into it, but are baffled by its ever-changing shape; the authorities attempt to destroy it, but fail. Only in the final paragraph does the reader learn that the narrator has inflated the balloon for purely personal reasons, and sees no intrinsic meaning in the balloon itself, a metaphor for the amorphous, uncertain nature of Barthelme's fiction. Other notable stories from this collection include "The Indian Uprising," a mad collage of a Comanche attack on a modern city, and "Robert Kennedy Saved From Drowning," a series of vignettes showing the difficulties of truly knowing a public figure; the latter story appeared in print only two months before the real Kennedy's 1968 assassination.

Barthelme also wrote the non-fictional *Guilty Pleasures* (1974). His other writings have been posthumously gathered into two collections, "The Teachings of Don B.: Satires," "Parodies," "Fables, Illustrated Stories," and "Plays of Donald Barthelme" (1992), and "Not-Knowing: The Essays" and "Interviews" (1997). With his daughter, he wrote the children's book *The Slightly Irregular Fire Engine*, which received the 1972 National Book Award in category Children's Books. He was also a director of PEN and the Author's Guild, and a member of the American Academy and Institute of Arts and Letters.

Analysis of and Comment on His Representative Novel

Snow White (1965)

Plot Summary

Snow White, published first in *The New Yorker* in 1965 and then in hard cover in a slightly different novel. The plot of *Snow White* follows the broad outline of the fairy tale of that name, and the characters are vaguely analogous to the characters in the fairy tale. A consideration of Barthelme's treatment of character and plot in *Snow White* will reveal how far Barthelme departs from the conventional treatment of these elements and how well *Snow White* operates within the formula that we have defined. *Snow White* opens with what can only be called a map: "She is a tall dark beauty containing a great many beauty spots: one above the breast, one above the belly, one above the knee, one above the ankle, one above the buttock, one on the back of the neck. All of these are on the left side, more or less in a row as you go up and down." What follows are six printer's bullets, set in a straight vertical line that leads to a single sentence: "The hair is black as ebony, the skin white as snow" (*SW* 3). Snow White, 22, is a college graduate. A section describing her education, which she later refers to as her training in "the finest graces and arts" (102), reveals a conscious attempt to fashion herself in the image of a Renaissance woman: "She studied *Modern Woman, Her Privileges and Responsibilities*: the nature and nurture of women and what they stand for, in evolution and in history, including house holding, upbringing, peacekeeping, healing and devotion, and how these contribute to the re-humanizing of today's world." And in typical Barthelme anticlimactic juxtaposition: "Then she studied *Classical Guitar I*, utilizing the models and techniques of Sor, Tarrega, Segovia, etc." This is followed by: "Then she studied *English Romantic Poets II*: Shelley, Byron, Keats" (25). Continuing on page 25: "Then she studied *Theoretical Foundations of Psychology*: mind, consciousness, unconscious mind, personality, the self, interpersonal relations, psychosexual norms, social games, groups, adjustment, conflict, authority, individuation, integration and mental health. Then she studied *Oil Painting I*...," followed b a list of the 12 paints she was told to bring to the first class. It goes on: "*Personal Resources I and II*: self-evaluation, developing the courage to respond to the environment, opening and using the mind, individual experience, training, the use of time, mature redefinition of goals, action project," and, finally, "*Realism and Idealism in the Contemporary Italian Novel*" with a list of 17 Italian writers, and ending at a stroke with the fragment "Then she studied—" (25-26). The eclecticism of all this reflects her superficiality. The original *Schneewittchen* or her Disney counterpart would never give a thought to being a Renaissance woman. This is a setup for failure, not only of imagination, as she says, but a failure of quest.

These old and often funny juxtapositions of Barthelme's have a disjunctive function, quite the opposite of Hawthorn's embroidery of paranormal events onto history. Mentioned on page 41 are the following: a horror film, a sexual advance, a dry martini garnished with a picked onion, a trout garnished with almonds, God, a Polish film, Snow White's reputation, and the name of an esoteric religious philosopher read by Snow White when she sulks in her room. Rather than flowing with the narrative, each of these stands apart, and with the appearance of a name like Teilhard de Chardin, impedes it. The jackdaw again, a glittering accretion. Snow White's seven housemates manufacture and distribute Chinese-style baby food with labels like *Baby Dow Shew*, bean curd stuffed with ground pike; *Baby Gai Goon*, chicken, bean sprouts and cabbage; and *Baby Pie Guat*, pork and oysters in soy sauce (18). Despite occasional ups and downs—"The grade of pork ears we are using in the Baby Ding Sam Dew is not capable of meeting U.S. Govt. standards, or indeed, any standards" (119)—the business has been lucrative: "It is amazing how many mothers will spring for an attractively packed jar of Baby dim Sum, a tasty-looking potlet of Baby Jing Shar Shew Bow. Heigh-ho" (18). The recipes came from their father, who had always told them, "Try to be a man about whom nothing is known." Such a man was their father: "Nothing is known about whom nothing is known." Such a man was their father: "Nothing is known about him still. He gave us the recipes. He was not very interesting" (19).

Themes

The theme of *Snow White* focuses on the vanished love. It shows that love, sympathy, and satisfactoriness all have disappeared in the postmodern world. The seven wonder how life would be if they got into another line of work: "God know what. We do what we do without thinking. One tends the vats and washes the buildings and carries the money to the vault and never stops for a moment to consider that the whole process may be despicable." Before Snow White entered their lives, "There was equanimity for all. We washed the buildings, tended the vats, wended our way to the county cathouse once a week (heigh-ho). Like everybody else. We were simple bourgeois. We knew what to do." But everything has changed since the day came upon her wandering in the forest, hungry and distraught, and gave her food. "Now we do not know what to do. Snow White has added a dimension of confusion and misery to our lives. Whereas once we were simple bourgeois who knew what to do, now we are complex bourgeois who are at a loss. We do not like this complexity" (87-88). It is on a Monday that Snow White "let[s] down her hair black as ebony form the window." She says, "This motif, the long hair streaming from the high window, is a very ancient one I believe, found in many cultures, in various forms. Now I recapitulate it, for the astonishment of the vulgar and the refreshment of my venereal life" (80). The hair generates public reaction. Two old men remark, "'You need a Paul or Paul-figure for that sort of activity. Probably Paul is even now standing in the wings, girding his pants for his entrance'" (89). Actually, Paul is in his bath, trying to get over a case of nerves caused by seeing the hair black as ebony on his way back from the Unemployment Office (94).

Snow White, meanwhile, becomes agitated by the 200 people watching her. She wishes she were on the beach at St. Tropez, "surrounded by brown boys without a penny. Here everyone has a penny. Here everyone worships the almighty penny." She laments: "O Jerusalem, Jerusalem! Thy daughters are burning with torpor and a sense of immense wasted potential, like one of those pipes you see in oil fields, burning off the natural gas that it isn't economically rational to ship somewhere!" (102). Although this passage could be one of the targets of Barthelme's self-accusation, one joke too many (O'Hara 205), it does make the point that real men are in short supply for the daughters.

As more is revealed about Snow White—she's alternately bored, unpredictable, compulsive, narcissistic, and without "a pinch of emotion coloring the jet black of her jet-black eyes" (10)—a fine tension is set up between what she's supposed to be and what she is here. Certainly, she's physically similar to the Disney version, and to the original *Schneewittchen* in the German tale of the Brothers Grimm collection. What happens in Barthelme's novel is that the *Schneewittchen* becomes the *doppelganger*, the ghostly double haunting and weaving a spell over her postmodern counterpart, who knows the old story and the role she's supposed to play. The contrarieties at work here—the impostor, her hoax and pretenses, and the other characters with their consciousness of self and awareness of the story on which they are based, each trying to play the role of their counterpart in the original—generate disharmony and greater tension. And they're all double minded. If only we make a little contrast between it and the original "Snow White" in *Grimm's Fairy Tales*, we can go beyond its own surface layer without depths and obtain such a new meaning: in the postmodern world, love, sympathy, and satisfactoriness all have disappeared and similarly morality and even logic do not exist any more.

Literary Techniques

Short-Short Story Barthelme's short stories are often exceptionally compact (a form sometimes called "short-short story," "flash fiction," or "sudden fiction"), often focusing only on incident rather than complete narratives. (He did, however, write some longer stories with more traditional narrative arcs.) At first, these stories contained short epiphanic moments. Later in his career, the stories were not consciously philosophical or symbolic. His fiction had its admirers and detractors, being hailed as profoundly disciplined or derided as meaningless and academic postmodernism. Barthelme's thoughts and work were largely the result of 20th-century angst as he read extensively, for example in Pascal, Husserl, Heidegger, Kierkegaard, Ionesco, Beckett, Sartre, and Camus.

Collage Barthelme's stories typically avoid traditional plot structures, relying instead on a steady accumulation of seemingly-unrelated details. By subverting the reader's expectations through constant non sequiturs, Barthelme creates a hopelessly fragmented verbal collage reminiscent of such modernist works as T. S. Eliot's *The Waste Land* and James Joyce's *Ulysses*, whose linguistic experiments he often challenged. However, Barthelme's fundamental skepticism and irony distanced him from the modernists' belief in the power of art to reconstruct society, leading most critics to class him as a postmodernist writer. Literary critics have noted that Barthelme, like the French poet Stéphane Mallarmé, whom he admired, plays with the meanings of words, relying on poetic intuition to spark new connections of ideas buried in the expressions and conventional responses.

Illustrations Another Barthelme device was breaking up a tale with illustrations culled from mostly 19th century popular publications, collaged, and appended with ironic captions; Barthelme called his cutting up and pasting together pictures "a secret vice gone public." One of the pieces in the collection Guilty Pleasures, called "The Expedition," featured a full-page illustration of a collision between ships, with the caption "Not our fault!"

Accumulation of Seemingly-Unrelated Detail Barthelme's stories typically avoid traditional plot structures, relying instead on a steady accumulation of seemingly-unrelated detail. He maintains words are not inert, but furiously busy. In that moment, fiction does not so much provide a compensatory or even distractive balance to the inadequacy of experience—sexual, marital, filial, even, it turns out, linguistic. Rather it immerses the reader directly in that experience. Accordingly readers have difficulty identifying in his work a narrative voice outside the action which connects it to a system of values or beliefs, even to a designated set of attitudes or feelings that would allow them to interpret a story or indicate how they are expected to react to it. His prescription for fiction can't be read literally. What his fiction draws upon most of all is the ability of language to look both ways—transparently toward the world and self, apparently toward the mediating function of other words upon each other. What emerges as a defining element of Barthelme's fiction is a tendency which, like abstract painting, is significant for what it subtracts form conventional form. There is no linear development (beginning, middle, and end) either within his stories or from one collection to the next. Motivation remains unclear or, at best, arbitrary. Within the narrative there is no focus which allows for development, no clear indication of an agent whose purpose generates the action, an antagonist or natural force who opposes this purpose, a deepening or complication of the circumstances, and a final confrontation followed by a resolution which points up or explains the significance of what has happened. Irony is very much a tonal element in his fiction; but it is an element which itself proves subject to ironic challenge and which finally gives way to appreciation of the sensuous moment whose transient quality at once occasions pain and is a cause for celebration. For Barthelme, the joke occurs, if anywhere, in the disparity between the response the reader is prepared to make and the one the text actually invites.

Drawing upon Common Art Forms Barthelme's fiction, especially in its approach to language, has much in common with the cultural tendency to draw upon common art forms—the Wild West show, the music hall tradition, the comic strip—that Pauline Kael points to in her celebrated essay "Trash, Art and the Movies." The enjoyment of these films, Kael argues, comes often despite the audience's knowledge of the actors and of the circumstances in which the films are made, often, in fact, as a result of the presence created by the actor in a series of roles in previous movies. Accordingly, she concludes, unlike pure art, movies may be enjoyed for many reasons that have little to do with the story or the subtleties of theme or character, and so are more open and unlimited. In Barthelme's fiction, the catalog neither nostalgically commemorates the objects or events that evoke a historical moment nor plays with the seemingly infinite elaborations of reality that present themselves to the literary imagination. Its intent, in fact, is not so much illustration or expansion at all as it is the celebration of reality through repetition. Unlike those found in Whitman, Barthelme's catalogs do not name things which, almost mystically, exist by virtue of an incantatory act that demonstrates a unity in time and space. That unity does inform Barthelme's enumeration, but it does not call things into being or magically summon their presence; it reminds the reader of their unique and unknowable nature.

Bibliography

http://en.wikipedia.org/wiki/Donald_barthelme, 2013-02-15.

Arnason, H. H. *History of Modern Art*. New York: Harry N. Abrams, 1986.

Barth, John. "Thinking Man's Minimalist: Honoring Barthelme." *The New York Times Book Review*, 3 September 1989: 9.

Bartheleme, Donald. "Not-Knowing." *Major Writers of Short Fiction: Stories and Commentaries*. Ed. Ann Charters, Boston: Bedford Books of St. Martin's Press, 1993: 113-24.

——. *Snow White*. New York: Atheneum, 1972.

Bernhard, Thomas. *The President & Eve of Retirement*. Trans. Gitta Honegger. New York: Performing Arts Journal Publications, 1982.

Handke, Peter. *Kaspar and Other Plays*. Trans. Michael Roloff. New York: Farrar, Straus and Giroux, 1969.

Hern, Nicholas. *Peter Handke*. New York: Frederick Ungar Publishing Co., 1972.

Herzinger, Kim, ed. *The Teachings of Don B: Satires, Parodies, Fables, Illustrated Stories, and Plays of Donald Barthelme*. New York: Turtle Bay Books, 1992.

Hudgens, Michael Thomas. *Donald Barthelme Postmodernist American Writer*. New York: The Edwin Mellen Press, 2001.

Kael, Pauline. "Trash, Art, and the Movies." *Going Steady*. Boston: Little, Brown, 1970. 85-129.

McCaffery, Larry. "An Interview with Donald Barthelme." *Anything Can Happen: Interview with Contemporary American Novelists*. Eds. Thomas LeClair and McCaffery. Urbana: U of Illinois P, 1983: 32-44.

O'Hara, J. D. "Donald Barthelme: The Art of Fiction LXVI." *The Paris Review*, 1981: 180-210.

Schlueter, June. *The Plays and Novels of Peter Handke*. Pittsburgh: University of Pittsburgh Press, 1981.

Trachtenberg, Stanley. *Understanding Donald Barthelme*. Columbia: University of South Carolina Press, 1990.

Venturi, Robert. *Complexity and Contradiction in Architecture, 2nd Ed*. New York: Museum of Modern Art, 1977.

Thomas Pynchon

His Life and Writing Career

His Life

Perhaps the most acclaimed and the most elusive of the postmodernists, Thomas Pynchon (1937–) is generally regarded as a figure whose writing is unprecedented yet somehow entirely representative of the fiction of a particular age. It is often remarked that Pynchon is to postmodernism what James Joyce to modernism. Pynchon's work, *Gravity's Rainbow* (1973), which was a co-winner of the National Book Award, is regarded as the model for postmodern fictions and has spawned a vast industry of interpreters and devoted students, determined to pursue every lead in the text and decode every reference.

Thomas Ruggles Pynchon, Jr. was born on May 8, 1937, in Glen Cove, New York, one of three children of Thomas Ruggles Pynchon, Sr., and Katherine Frances Bennett Pynchon. The family moved when Pynchon was a child. His father became town supervisor of Oyster Bay, New York, and later an industrial surveyor. Pynchon graduated from Oyster Bay High School in 1953 at age 16 with distinction in English. He received a scholarship to Cornell University and took engineering and physics classes until he left school during his sophomore year, in 1955, for service in the navy. He returned to Cornell two years later and took classes in English, including a course taught by Vladimir Nabokov (who did not remember him). Pynchon was on the editorial staff of the *Cornell Writer*, which published his first short story, "The Small Rain," in 1959. He graduated with distinction that year.

Pynchon had several options after graduating, including pursuing a number of fellowships, teaching creative writing at Cornell, becoming a disk jockey, or working as a film critic for *Esquire*. He published many short stories, including "Mortality and Mercy in Vienna" in *Epoch* (Spring 1959), "Low-lands" in *New World Writing* (1960), and "Under the Rose" in *The Noble Savage* (May 1961). He also began work on his first novel, *V.* (1963), while in New York and in Seattle, where he worked writing technical documents for the Boeing Company until 1962. He finished *V.* in California and Mexico and in 1963. *V.* was published and won the William Faulkner Foundation Award for the best first novel of the year. *V.* is a whimsical, cynically absurd tale of a middle-aged Englishman's search for an elusive, adventuresome, supernatural woman. The object of the Englishman's search appears in various guises at critical periods in European history. Of his few short stories, most notable are "Entropy" (1960), a neatly structured tale in which Pynchon first used extensive technical language and scientific metaphors, and "The Secret Integration" (1964), a story in which Pynchon explored small-town bigotry and racism.

His second novel, *The Crying of Lot 49* (1966), won the Richard and Hilda Rosenthal Foundation Award of the National Institute of Arts and Letters. In the book, Pynchon described a woman's quest to discover the mysterious, conspiratorial Tristero System in a futuristic world of closed societies. The novel served a condemnation of modern industrialization. Pynchon wrote "A Journey into the Mind of Watts" for the *New York Times Magazine* (June 12, 1966). He worked on *Gravity's Rainbow* for several years and in 1974 that novel shared the National Book Award for fiction with Issac Bashevis Singer's *Crown of Feathers*. *Gravity's Rainbow* was set in an area of post-World War Ⅱ Germany called "the Zone." It centered on the wanderings of a U.S. soldier who is one of many odd characters looking for a secret V-2 rocket that will supposedly break through the Earth's gravitational barrier when launched. The narrative is filled with descriptions of obsessive and paranoid fantasies, grotesque imagery, and esoteric mathematical and scientific language. Many critics deemed *Gravity's Rainbow* a visionary apocalyptic masterpiece. Judges unanimously selected *Gravity's Rainbow* for the Pulitzer Prize in literature, but the Pulitzer advisory board overruled the selection, saying the book was "unreadable," "turgid," "overwritten," and "obscene." No prize was given that year. *Gravity's Rainbow* was also awarded the William Dean Howells Medal of the American Academy of Arts and Letters in 1975, but Pynchon declined the award, suggesting that it be given to another author. In a letter, he wrote, "The Howells Medal is a great honor, and being gold, probably a good hedge against inflation, too. But I don't want it. Please don't impose on me something I don't want. It makes the Academy look arbitrary and me look rude.... I know I should behave with more class, but there appears to be only one way to say no, and that's no."

Pynchon has remained elusive to his fans—his 1953 high school yearbook still provides his most recent photographic portrait. He has done best to make himself "disappear" as a biographical persona (no mean feat in the era of mass media) in order to speak only through his art. Pynchon's only deliberate emergence into public world (aside from his publications) was his 2004 "appearance" in *The Simpsons* episode "Diatribe of a Mad Housewife," where he stood outside his house with a paper bag over his head with holes cut out for the eyes, before a flashing neon sign declaring "Thomas Pynchon's House—Come on In" (Season 15, episode 10).

Many of Pynchon's early short stories were collected in 1984 under the title *Slow Learner* (1984) with the autobiographical notes by the author. Pynchon was awarded the John D. and Catherine T. MacArthur Foundation Fellowship in 1989. His novel *Vineland* was published in 1990 and *Mason and Dixon*, another novel, appeared in 1997. In recent years, two other novels of Pynchon were published, *Against the Day* (2006) and *Inherent Vice* (2009).

His Writing Career

Pynchon has been his own fiercest critic. In an introductory essay to his early stories, *Slow Learner* (1984), he has said that his fundamental problem when he began writing was an inclination "to begin with a theme, symbol or other unifying agent, and then try to force characters and events to conform to it." His books are this self-criticism or not, it is clear that Pynchon laid down his intellectual cards early. This very important postmodernist novelist expresses complicated and profound ideas by his language games such as black humor, outlandish puns, slapsticks, running gags, parodies, and ridiculous names. The protagonists in Pynchon's novels all live in the confusion of postmodern existence reflected by the structure of fictional fragments and they undertake vague but very conscientious quests, attempting to discover their own identities and find out meaning and order in their life.

The title of his first important short story is "Entropy" (1960). It contains specific references to Henry Adams; and it follows carefully the Adams formulation, "Chaos was the law of nature; Order was the dream of man". The use of entropy as a figure for civilization running down was to become structurally formative in his later fiction. So was his use of two kinds of characters, alternative central figures first sketched out here. The situation in "Entropy" is simply and deliberately schematic. There is a downstairs and upstairs apartment. Downstairs, a character called Meatball Mulligan is holding a lease-breaking party, which moves gradually towards chaos and consequent torpor. Upstairs, another character, an intellectual called Callisto, is trying to warm a freezing bird back to life. In his room he maintains a small hothouse jungle, referred to as a "Rousseau-like fantasy". "Hermetically sealed, it was a tiny enclave in the city's chaos," the reader is told, "alien to the vagaries of the weather, national politics, of any civil disorder." The room is a fantasy, a dream of order, in which Callisto has "perfected its ecological balance". But the room leaves him in paralysis, the dream does not work; the bird dies, and Callisto's girlfriend, realizing that he is "helpless in the past", smashes the window of their hermetically sealed retreat, breaking the shell surrounding his fantasy life. Meatball Mulligan, meanwhile, does what he can to stop his party "deteriorating into total chaos" by tidying up, calming his guest, getting things mended.

"Entropy," in this way, mediates between binary opposites: which are the opposites of modern consciousness and culture. There is the pragmatist, active to the point of excess, doing what he can with the particular scene, working inside the chaos to mitigate it. And there is the theorist, passive to the point of paralysis, trying to shape and figure the cosmic process, standing outside as much as he can, constructing patterns for the chaos to explain it. Meatball is immersed, drowning in the riotous present; Callisto is imprisoned in the hermetically sealed glasshouse of the past. The text, which here and later is the dominant presence in Pynchon's writing, is the interface between these two figures, these two systems or levels of experience. As such, it sketches out human alternatives in a multiverse where mind and matter are steadily heading for extinction. Or, it may be, the alternatives of hyperactivity and containment, the open and the closed, between which the individual consciousness constantly vacillates. The two are not, in any event, mutually exclusive. To an extent, what Pynchon does in his work is to give a decidedly postmodernist spin to perennial American preoccupations. In the tradition of the American jeremiad, he presents a culture, if not bound for heaven, then bent towards hell, its own form of apocalypse or heat death. And in the grain American writing structured around the figures of the wilderness and the clearing, he develops a sometimes bewildering series of systems, human and non-human, built around the fundamental, formative principles of spatial openness and closure, immersion and separation, the flexible and the fixed, the signified and the signifier—a world that is a totality of things, data, and a world that is totality of fact, signs.

In his first novel, *V.* Pynchon returned to two formative characters recalling Callisto and Meatball in the shape of Hubert Stencil and Benny Profane. The book confirms its author's sense of the modern world as an entropic wasteland, inhabited by men and women dedicated to the annihilation of all animatedness. It is bounded by dead landscapes, urban, mechanical, underground. A populous narrative, it is also packed with characters who are ciphers: seeing others and themselves not as people but as things, objects, they lapse into roles, masquerade and cliche. Blown along the mean streets, and even meaner sewers, of this story, Benny Profane is a schlemiel, the suffering absurd comedian of Jewish lore. A faded copy of a picaro, he drifts through life in such enterprises as hunting alligators underneath New York City; it is there, in fact, in the darkness and oblivion of the sewers, that he finds his greatest comfort and peace. Hubert Stencil, on the other hand, searches the world for V., the mysterious female spy and anarchist who is by turns Venus, Virgin and Void and seems to be everywhere and nowhere. Stencil appears to be on a significant quest. Described as "a century's child" and born in 1901, he is pursuing the remnants of the Virgin in the world of the Dynamo. His father, a former British spy, has left behind enigmatic clues pointing to a vast conspiracy in modern history. So, whereas Profane lives in a world of sightlessness without signs or discernible patters, Stencil enters a world of elusive signs and apparent patterns, all gravitating towards an absent presence, the lady V. His quest is for a fulcrum identity. In a sense, he is given an outline identity by his search, since he thinks of himself as "quite purely He who looks for V. (and whatever impersonations that might involve)" It is also for the identity of modern times. Using the oblique strategy of "attack and avoid," Stencil moves through many of the major events of the twentieth century, seeking to recover the master plot, the meanings of modern history and this book. The only meaning found, however, is the erasure of meaning: the emptying of a significant human history and its sacrifice to mechanism and mass. The purposiveness of Stencil, it turns out, and the purposelessness of Profane are both forms of "yo-yoing"; movement, often violent oscillation, bereft of all significance except the elemental one of postponing inanimatedness.

Almost the last reported words of *V.* are "How pleasant to watch Nothing". In his subsequent fiction, Pynchon has continued this watching, and searching, the boundlessness of "Nothing" in a variety of fictional guises. In his second novel, *The Crying of Lot 49* (1966), the main character, Oedipa Mass, learns that her onetime lover, Pierce Inverarity, has made her an executor of his estate. Now he is dead, she sets out to investigate Inverarity's property: an investigation that leads to the discovery of what she takes to be a conspiratorial underground communications system dating back to the sixteenth century. Following the clues, she finally believes she will solve the enigma through a mysterious bidder keen to buy Inverarity's stamp collection. But the novel ends with the enigma unsolved, the plot and its meaning unresolved, as Oedipa awaits the crying out at the auction of the relevant lot number 49. The subject and its significance still wait to be located. So do they in *Gravity's Rainbow* (1973), Pynchon's third novel. Set in the closing years of the Second World War, the story here, a complex web of plots and counterplots, involves a Nazi Lieutenant Weissman, disguised as a mysterious Captain Blicero, and an American sleuth, Lieutenant Tyrone Slothrop, while V-2 rockets rain down London. Weissman, it appears, was once the lover of V.: in this elaborately intertextual world, Pynchon's texts echo his own as well as the texts of others. The gravitations of mood are characteristic: from black humor to lyricism to science fiction to fantasy. So is the feeling the reader experiences, while reading this book, that he or she is encountering not so much different levels of meaning or reality as different planes in fictive space, with each plane in its shadow box proving to be a false bottom, in an evidently infinite regression. So also, finally, is the suspicion of conspiracy: *Gravity's Rainbow* explores the possibility that, as one character puts it, "war was never political at all, the politics was all theatre, all just to keep the people distracted."

Since *Gravity's Rainbow*, Pynchon has moved forwards to the landscape of the 1980s and, through ample reminiscence, the 1960s in *Vineland* (1990). Then, he has moved back to the early republic in *Mason and Dixon* (1997), to the days when men like the two famous surveyors mentioned in the title were trying to establish boundaries in the boundlessness of America, in order to appropriate it. America is memorably described in this novel as "a very Rubbish-Tip for subjunctive Hopes, for all that *may yet be true.*" It is the realm, the landscape that inhabits all Pynchon's fiction: the realm of measurelessness and dream, the indicative and the subjunctive, the closed and appropriated and the open. And it is typical of the author that he should weave his speculations on legends, the rich "Rubbish-Tip" of dreams ("Does Britannia when she sleeps, dream?" one character asks, "Is America her dream?"), into a densely populated social fabric and a meditation on historical decline. The fictive energy of Pynchon seems inexhaustible, not least because it careers with tireless energy between contraries. But to an extent, what drives it is summed up in one simple question one central character asks the other in his novel: "Good Christ, Dixon. What are we about?"

Analysis of and Comment on His Representative Novel

Gravity's Rainbow (1973)

Plot Summary

Gravity's Rainbow is a novel of such vastness and range that it defies—with a determination unusual even in this age of "difficult" books—any inclusive summary. There are over 400 characters—we should perhaps say "names", since the ontological status of the figures that drift and stream across the pages is radically uncertain. There are many discernible, or half-discernible plots. These plots touch and intersect, or diverge and separate, involving characters who don't appear until the closing pages of the novel or who are introduced into the plot and then don't appear again at all. The following is only a very brief, elliptical summary trying to get the gist of the book.

Gravity's Rainbow is composed of four parts: "Beyond the Zero," "Un Perm' au Casino Hermann Goering," " In the Zone," and "The Counterforce."

In "Beyond the Zero," the opening pages of the novel follow Pirate Prentice, first in his dreams, and later around his house in wartime London. Pirate then goes to work at ACHTUNG, a top-secret military branch, with Roger Mexico and Pointsman, who both worked there at the time. It is here the reader is introduced to the possibly promiscuous US Army lieutenant named Tyrone Slothrop, whose erratic story becomes the main plot throughout most of the novel. It is noted that each of Slothrop's sexual encounters in London precedes a V-2 rocket hit in the same place by several days. Both Slothrop's encounters and the rocket sites match the Poisson Distributions calculated by Roger Mexico, leading into reflections on topics as broad as Determinism, the reverse flow of time, and the sexuality of the rocket itself. Slothrop meets a woman named Katje, and they fall in love, maintaining a relationship until Slothrop's sudden removal to Germany in part three.

In Part Two, "Un Perm' au Casino Hermann Goering", Slothrop is studied covertly and sent away by superiors in mysterious circumstances to the Hermann Goering casino in recently liberated France, in which almost the entirety of Part Two takes place. There he learns of a rocket, with the irregular serial number 00000, and a component called the S-Gerät (short for Schwarzgerät, which translates to black device) which is made out of the hitherto unknown plastic Imipolex G. Early in Part Two, the octopus attacks Katje on the beach, and Slothrop is "conveniently" at hand to rescue her. Their romance begins here, extending into Part Three and the events that follow. It is hinted at that Slothrop's prescience of rocket hits is due to being conditioned as an infant by the creator of Imipolex G, Laszlo Jamf. Later, the reality of this story is called into question in a similar fashion as the existence of Slothrop's original sexual exploits was. After getting this information, Slothrop escapes from the casino into the coalescing post-war wasteland of Europe, "the Zone," searching for the 00000 and S-Gerät. In the closing of Part Two, Katje is revealed to be safe in England, enjoying a day at the beach with Roger Mexico and Jessica, as well as Pointsman, who is in charge of Slothrop's furtive supervision. While unable to contact Slothrop (or prohibited from contacting him), Katje continues to follow his actions through Pointsman.

In Part Three "In the Zone," Slothrop's quest continues for some time as he is chased by other characters. Slothrop meets and has an extended relationship with Margherita Erdman, a pornographic film actress and masochist. Originally meeting her in an abandoned studio in the Zone, it is she who leads him on to the Anubis, a ferry on which many different characters travel at various times. Here, Slothrop later also has extended encounters with her twelve-year-old daughter Bianca, though it is unclear whether or not he has stopped his casual relationship with Margherita by this time. Towards the end of this section, several characters not seen since early in the novel make a return, including Pirate Prentice, in his first appearance since the novel's very start. "In the Zone" also contains the longest episode of the book, a lengthy tale of Franz Pökler, a rocket engineer unwittingly set to assist on the S-Gerät's production. The story details Pökler's annual meetings with his daughter Ilse, and his growing paranoia that Ilse is really a series of impostors sent each year to mollify him. The story ultimately reveals that the 00000 was fired in the spring of 1945, close to the end of the war. Slothrop spends much of the time as his invented alter-ego Rocketman, wearing an operatic Viking costume with the horns removed from the helmet, making it look like a rocket nose-cone. Rocketman completes various tasks for his own and others' purposes, including retrieving a large stash of hashish from the centre of the Potsdam Conference. This continues until he leaves the region for northern Germany, continuing his quest for the 00000, as well as answers to his past. It becomes steadily apparent that Slothrop is somehow connected to Dr. Laszlo Jamf, and a series of experiments performed on him as a child.

Slothrop later returns to the Anubis to find Bianca dead, a possible trigger for his impending decline. He continues his pilgrimage through northern Germany, at various stages donning the identities of a Russian colonel and mythical Pig Hero in turn, in search of more information on his childhood and the 00000. Unfortunately, he is repeatedly sidetracked until his persona fragments totally in Part Four, despite the efforts of some to save him. Throughout "The Counterforce," there are several brief, hallucinatory stories, of superheroes, silly Kamikaze pilots, and immortal sentient light bulbs. These are presumed to be the product of Slothrop's finally collapsed mind. At the same time, other characters' narratives begin to collapse as well, with some characters taking a bizarre trip through Hell, and others flying into nothingness on Zeppelins. Slothrop's narrative ends a surprisingly long time before the novel's end, which focuses more on the 00000, and the people associated with its construction and launch.

Towards the end of "The Counterforce," it transpires that the S-Gerät is actually a capsule crafted by Blicero to contain a human. The story of the 00000's launch is largely told in flashbacks by the narrator, while in the present Enzian is constructing and preparing its successor, the 00001 (which isn't fired within the scope of the novel), though it is unknown who is intended to be sacrificed in this model. In the flashbacks, the maniacal Captain Blicero prepares to assemble and fire the 00000, and asks Gottfried to sacrifice himself inside the rocket. He launches the rocket in a pseudo sexual act of sacrifice with his bound adolescent sex slave Gottfried, captive within its S-Gerät. At the end of a final episode, told partially in second person, the rocket descends upon Britain. The text halts, in the middle of a song composed by Slothrop's ancestor, with a complete obliteration of narrative as the 00000 lands (or is about to land) on a cinema. Thus the novel opens and closes in wartime Britain, and opens and closes with the landing of a V-2 rocket.

Themes

An Expanded Thinking about Death One theme of the novel is considered to be an expanded thinking about death. Pynchon mixes up true details and fantastic events, contains comic and cruel scenes, evolves extensive and symbolic deducibilities and offers several perspectives about historical events. Pynchon implies that the Western society, by perfecting destructive weapons like the German rocket bomb V-2, actively accelerates the death culture. He also hints that the progress of science and technology is wrongly used in historical patterns, politics, economy, social values, and especially the war effort in human world.

Continual Returns to Ideas Related to Metaphysics Another theme is his continual returns to ideas related to metaphysics, a branch of philosophy that studies fundamental questions of reality and existence. The novel questions what is real, how one is able to discern reality, and whether there actually is any reality at all. Its complex plot can be seen as a search for causes of death and a quest to discover who or what it is (if anything) that controls the world.

Paranoia Paranoia, "the onset, the leading edge, of the discovery that everything is connected," is also emphasized in *Gravity's Rainbow*. Slothrop's paranoia appears in various guises, ranging from his suspicion that the rock-bombs falling on London have his name written on them to his fantasy that he is the intended victim of a Father Conspiracy. According to Richard Locke, megalomaniac paranoia is the "operative emotion" behind the novel, and an increasingly central motivator for the many main characters. In many cases, this paranoia proves to be vindicated, as the many plots of the novel become increasingly interconnected, revolving around the identity and purpose of the elusive 00000 Rocket and Schwarzgerät.

Literary Techniques

Symbolism Symbolism is richer in *Gravity's Rainbow* than in Pynchon's other novels, all of it coming together around the image of the V-2 rocket, which was the German weapon against which there was no defense, just as the American apocalyptic threat was the atomic bomb. All of the themes, characters and episodes of the novel coalesce around the frightening missile which is a symbol simultaneously of science and technology triumphant even while reason has utterly fled, since the device has no purpose but mass destruction. At the end of the book, Pynchon tightens the screw by not merely giving the reader a questing main character to identify with, but also by placing the reader in the novel as part of an audience in a theater waiting while the rocket descends on their helpless heads.

Encyclopedic Fantasy Pynchon's encyclopedic fantasy operates through mixed styles and breaks the boundaries between high culture and pop culture by utilizing brilliant improvisations, tall talks, obscene parables, and burlesque stage routines, all of which work together into a story of supersonic capabilities and annihilative retributions. As the four main and the countless subsidiary plots take shape, characters—and the reader as well—attempt to "read" the messages flickering, the dumb intent to communicate, in the most casual as well as the most portentous sign. Pynchon's knowingness and fascination with popular culture are overwhelmingly evident in *Gravity's Rainbow* as is his preoccupation with the lore of theoretical science, of obscure historical tales, and of contemporary comic books. No one denies the formidably encyclopedic nature of this astonishing effort.

Actual Events and Locations Additionally, the novel uses many actual events and locations as backdrops to establish chronological order and setting within the complex structure of the book. Examples include the appearance of a photograph of Wernher Von Braun in which his arm is in a cast. Historical documents indicate the time and place of an accident which broke Von Braun's arm, thereby providing crucial structural details around which the reader can reconstruct Slothrop's journey.

Parable The novel's title is a reference to the parabolic trajectory of a V-2 rocket: the "rainbow-shaped" path created by the missile as it moves under the influence of gravity, subsequent to the engine's deactivation; it is also thought to refer to the "shape" of the plot, which many critics such as Weisenburger have found to be cyclical or circular, like the true shape of a rainbow.

Flashbacks The story of the rocket is told in flashbacks, along with the revelation that it was fired in 1945. The Schwarzgerät is revealed to have been a capsule designed to contain a human being. The novel ends mid-sentence as the rocket is about to hit its target, raising the possibility that the reader themselves is killed in the blast. The novel also opens with the striking of a V-2 rocket, forming a narrative circle of "rainbow" that mimics the arc of the V-2 rocket in flight.

An Omniscient Narrator Pynchon employs an omniscient narrator as a consciousness that interprets and recreates experiential reality. The consciousness of the narrator of *Gravity's Rainbow* is the screen on which the action of the novel is flashed as he tries to comprehend the apparent chaos of his time and to create an interpretive historical and cultural overview of it. *Gravity's Rainbow* revels in the juxtaposition of different voice. Steven Weisenburger's *A Gravity's Rainbow Companion* lists the "formal discourses" we encounter in the book: Hebrew, German, Kazkh, Russian, Spanish, French, Japanese and Herero, mixed with "informal discourses" as "popular slang" (jokes, song lyrics, street speech), "ethnic usage" (black English) and "folk usage" (folktales, children's games) etc. Reading Pynchon, then is a matter of being immersed in a constant stream of different voices, an impression deepened by his characteristic long, rhythmical, parenthetical sentences.

Gravity's Rainbow is engaged with Europe at the end of the Second World War and just after. In choosing to situate his novel at this point in time, Pynchon is concentrating on a crucial moment when a new transpolitical order began to merge out of the ruins of old orders that could no longer maintain themselves. At one point he describes the movements of displaced people at the end of the war, "a great frontierless streaming." The sentences that follow mime out this "frontierless" condition in an extraordinary flow of objects and people, and conclude: "so the populations move, across the open meadow, limping, marching, shuffling, carried, hauling along the detritus of an order, a European and bourgeois order they don't yet know is destroyed forever." A later passage suggests what is taking the place of this vanished order. "Oh, a State begins to take form in the stateless German night, a State that spans oceans and surface politics, sovereign as the International or the Church of Rome, and the Rocket is its soul."

Bibliography

Baym, Nina, ed. *The Norton Anthology of American Literature, Shorter Fifth Edition*. New York & London: W. W. Norton & Company, 1999: 2476-2478.

Chambers, Judith. *Thomas Pynchon*. New York: Twayne Publishers, 1992: 2-13, 123-183.

Chen, Shidan. *A Study of American Postmodernist Fiction*. Tianjin: Nankai University

Press, 2010: 153-181.

Geyh, Paula, et al. ed. *Postmodern American Fiction: A Norton Anthology.* New York and London: W. W. Norton & Company, 1997: 4.

Gray, Richard. *A History of American Literature*. Cornwall: Blackwell Publishing Ltd., 2004: 728-733.

Newman, Robert D. *Understanding Thomas Pynchon.* Columbia, S.C.: University of South Carolina Press, 1986: 1-11, 89-137.

Nicol, Bran. *The Cambridge Introduction of Postmodern Fiction.* Cambridge U.K. and New York: Cambridge University Press, 2009: 89-98.

Oakes, Elizabeth H. *American Writers.* New York: Facts on File, Inc., 2004: 284-286.

Sanders, Scott. "Pynchon's Paranoid History." *Twentieth Century Literature, May 75, Vol. 21*, Issue 2: 177-192.

Siegel, Mark R. "Creative Paranoia: Understanding the System of *Gravity's Rainbow*." *Critique*, *Vol. 18,* Issue 3 (1977): 39-54.

Tanner, Tony. *Thomas Pynchon.* London and New York: Methuen, 1982: 11-19, 74-91.

http://en.wikipedia.org/wiki/Gravity%27s_rainbow, 2013-02-15.

http://www.bookrags.com/shortguide-gravitys-rainbow/techniques.html, 2013-02-15.

http://en.wikipedia.org/wiki/Gravity%27s_rainbow, 2013-02-15.

http://www.bookdrum.com/books/gravitys-rainbow/9780099533214/summary.html, 2013-02-15.

Vladimir Nabokov

His Life and Writing Career

His Life

Best known as the author of *Lolita* (1955), one of the most controversial novels of the 20th century, Vladimir Nabokov (1899–1977) wrote dozens of novels, as well as several collections of poetry, which were highly praised for their eloquence and stylistic innovations. Also revered as the preeminent postmodern writer due to his metafiction *Pale Fire* (1962), his work influenced the development of postmodernism in American literature.

Vladimir Nabokov was born in St. Petersburg, Russia, on (or about) April 23, 1899, into a prominent and well-to-do, educated family. He was the oldest of five children born to his father, a distinguished liberal aristocratic jurist and member of Kerensky's government, and his mother, Elena Ivanovna, a wealthy member of the Russian nobility whose family was noted for its artistic achievements. He is said to have inherited his sensitive and artistic nature from his mother and his work ethic and love of butterflies from his father.

Nabokov's family routinely spoke French, Russian, and English around the house, which had a great effect on the development of Nabokov's linguistic talents. The tutors who assisted with his education at home instructed him and his siblings in all three languages. In 1911, he began attending the highly respected Tenishev School.

When the Bolshevik revolution broke out, the Nabokov children and their mother left St. Petersburg for Yalta, in the Crimea, where a friend had an estate. Nabokov's father remained in St. Petersburg and accepted a position in the provisional government following Czar Nicholas Ⅱ's abdication, but after his imprisonment by the Bolsheviks, the senior Nabokov fled to Crimea, as well, where the family remained for approximately 18 months, at which time they went into exile in Europe.

Nabokov went to school in England, attending Trinity College, Cambridge, from 1919 to 1922. He originally studied zoology but eventually switched to Romance and Slavic languages. He wrote two volumes of poetry in Russian during these years, which were published in 1923. In 1922, he moved to Berlin, Germany, where his family now resided. That same year, his father was murdered by a reactionary White Russian who later became a Nazi official. Nabokov married Vera Slonim in 1925 and lived in Berlin with her and their son, Dimitri, who was born in 1934, until 1937, writing for the Russian newspaper his father had founded under the pseudonym of Vladimir Sirin. He also coached tennis and boxing and composed chess problems and crosswords. Many of his early Russian novels were published during these years in Berlin including *Mashen'ka* (1926; Mary, 1970), *Korol', dama, valet* (1928; *King, Queen, Knave,* 1968), *Zashchita* (1930; *The Defense,* 1964), *Podvig* (1933; *Glory,* 1972), and *Camera Obscura* (1933; revised and translated as *Laughter in the Dark,* 1938). Other Russian works were *Otchayaniye* (1936; *Despair,* 1937), *Dar* (1937; *The Gift,* 1963), and *Priglashenie na kazn* (1938; *Invitation to a Beheading,* 1959).

With the Nazi regime's rise to power, Nabokov became disgusted with Germany and fearful due to his wife's Jewish heritage. The family moved to Paris, where Nabokov met the Irish writer James Joyce, wrote several books in French, and wrote his first novel in English, *The Real Life of Sebastian Knight,* which was published 1941. It concerns a young Russian in Paris, the narrator, who discovers the true nature of his half-brother, an English novelist, while writing his biography. Nabokov decided at around this time that English was the language in which he should write in order to have the best prospects in publishing, but when he was unable to secure a position teaching in an English university, the Nabokov family moved once again, this time to the United States.

Nabokov settled with his family in 1940 in Boston and worked as a professor of English literature at Wellesley College from 1941 to 1948. In 1948, he took a position as a professor of Russian literature at Cornell University, where he remained until 1959, and became a research fellow in entomology at Harvard, pursuing his lifelong interest in butterflies. In all, Nabokov wrote 18 papers on entomology, some of which deal with his discovery and description of new species.

In 1945, Nabokov became a U.S. citizen. His novel, *Bend Sinister,* was published in 1947, about a politically uncommitted professor in a totalitarian state who tries to maintain personal integrity. Many of his short stories and poems appeared in the *New Yorker* during this period. His next novel, *Lolita*, which established his fortune, his reputation for some and his notoriety for others, was originally denied publication in the United States and Britain and so was first published in Paris in 1955. After censorship problems were resolved, the American publication appeared in 1958, which brought Nabokov instant fame and wealth. A film version (the first of two) was made of *Lolita* in 1962, directed by Stanley Kubrick. Within a few years, Nabokov gave up his teaching position at Cornell to focus entirely on his writing. He moved to Montreux, Switzerland, and lived the rest of his life at the Montreux Palace Hotel.

Nabokov's other novels written in English include *Pnin* (1957), *Pale Fire* (1962), *Ada, or Ardor: A Family Chronicle* (1969), *Transparent Things* (1972), and *Look at the Harlequins* (1974). His books of short stores include *Nabokov's Dozen* (1958), *Tyrants Destroyed* (1975), and *The Stories of Vladimir Nabokov* (1955), a posthumous collection that includes 13 previously unpublished stories. In addition to the two books of poetry he published in Russian, Nabokov wrote one book of poems in English, entitled simply *Poems.* It appeared in 1959. He also wrote several scholarly works of nonfiction—*Nikolai Gogol* (1944), a critical study of the 19th-century Russian writer; *Strong Opinions* (1973), a collection of his answers to questions about himself, art and public issues; *Lectures on Literature* (1980); and *Lectures on Russian Literature* (1981). He translated the novel *Eugene Onegin* by Alexander Pushkin and published the four-volume work with commentaries in 1964. He also wrote two autobiographical works. *Speak, Memory* (1966) is a compelling account of his childhood in Russia. It originally appeared under the title *Conclusive Evidence* in a shorter form in 1951.

Nabokov received the American National Medal for Literature in 1977, but enjoyed few other awards during his lifetime. He declined election to the National Institute of Arts and Letters, preferring a quiet life of writing and studying butterflies. Vladimir Nabokov died on July 2, 1977, in Montreux of a mysterious lung ailment.

His Writing Career

Nabokov first treaded into the literary field with the aid of his native language, Russian. Critics generally consider that his early novels written in Russian are more autobiographical but less significant compared with his later ones written in English, which brought him international distinction. *Lolita* was controversial for its explicit portrayal of a sexual relationship between a pathetic middle-aged professor Humbert Humbert and his 12-year-old step-daughter. It became a classic postmodern novel because it expertly weaves numerous well-known literary devices in creating a parody of the romance novel. Critics have generally read the book as a satire, though Nabokov himself rejected the label. In *Lolita*, Nabokov exhibits the love of intricate word play and synaesthetic detail that characterized all his works. The novel was ranked at No. 4 in the list of the Modern Library 100 Best Novels. *Pale Fire* (1962) was ranked at No. 53 on the same list. His memoir, *Speak, Memory,* was listed No. 8 on the Modern Library nonfiction list.

As a novelist of formidable erudition, Nabokov's fictions are informed by clever wordplay, descriptive detail, multilingual puns, anagrams, and coinages of terms. He combined satire and social commentary with complex explorations of time and memory.

Nabokov embraced the view that would become increasingly popular in twentieth-century art and fiction, namely the self-referential nature of the literary text, its "extract of personal reality," and the inherently collaborative role of the reader. Writing in *Lectures on Literature*, Nabokov said that "the good reader is one who has imagination, memory, a dictionary, and some artistic sense—which sense I propose to develop in myself and in others whenever I have the chance."

All of the work by Nabokov reflects, in some way, his aesthetic of subjective idealism. All of it plays variations on the observation made by the academic commentator Kinbote in *Pale Fire*: "'reality' is neither the subject nor the object of true art," he observes, "which creates its own special reality having nothing to do with the average 'reality' perceived by the communal eye." "To be sure, there is an average reality, perceived by all of us," Nabokov admits in *Strong Opinion*. "But that is not true reality: it is only the reality of general ideas, conventional forms of humdrum, current editorials." "Average reality," Nabokov insists, "begins to rot and stink as soon as the act of individual creation ceases to animate a subjectively perceived texture." Any book he makes, any art anyone makes that is worth reading, is "a subjective and specific affair", Nabokov suggests. It is the creative act that effectively maintains reality just as—and the analogy is his—electricity binds the earth together. As a writer, a creator, he has "no purpose at all when composing the stuff except to compose it." "I work long, on a body of words," as Nabokov puts it, "until it grants me complete possession and pleasure." According to this subjective idealist creed, there can be no totalizing, totalitarian reading of experience, no monolithic entity entitled "life." There is only the "manifold shimmer" of separate, specific lives, *my* life, *your* life, *his* life or *her* life. As Nabokov has it, "life does not exist without a possessive epithet." Nor is there some kind of absolute truth or absolute morality disclose. "Reality is an infinite succession of stops, levels of perception, false bottoms, and hence unquenchable, unattainable," Nabokov argues. "You can never get near enough"; and so "whatever the mind grasps it does so with the assistance of creative fancy, that drop of water on a glass slide which gives distinction and relief to the observed organism." There is no place here for naturalism or didacticism. "I am neither a reader nor a writer of didactic fiction," Nabokov confesses. "Why do I write books, after all? For the sake of pleasure, for the sake of the difficulty." "*Lolita* has no moral in tow," he adds. "For me a work of fiction exists only insofar as it affords me what I bluntly call aesthetic bliss." That bliss is the triumph of art, for Nabokov. Its tragedy is suggested by an anecdote Nabokov tells about the original inspiration for *Lolita*, which is a story about an ape who, after months of coaxing, produced the first ever drawing by an animal. "This sketch showed the bars of the poor creature's cage."

In *Lolita*, Humbert, the narrator, is constantly teasing and eluding his audience by using a style both outrageously lyrical and outrageously jokey, He tells his reader "I shall not exist if you do not imagine me." Undercutting what might seem predictably valid responses, he plays on the whole literary history of dubious anti-heroes and duplicitous first-person protagonist from Diderot to Dostovesky. "I am writing this under observation," Humbert admits. Within the narrative, this is literal, since he is in the psychiatric ward of the prison waiting for his trial for murdering Lolita's new lover. But Humbert is, additionally acutely aware of being under our observation as well. That helps to make his story slippery, his character protean, and his language radically, magically self-referential. Like all Nabokov's novels, but even more than most, *Lolita* is a verbal game, a maze: what one character in *Pale Fire* christens a "lexical playfield."

Analysis of and Comment on His Representative Novel

Pale Fire (1962)

Plot Summary

Pale Fire is written in very strange form. It consists of four parts: an allegedly posthumous autobiographical poem "Pale Fire" in heroic couplets of 999 lines by a fictional professor and poet John Shade and Foreword, Commentary and Index by another fictional figure, the self-appointed editor, Charles Kinbote.

Shade's poem consists of four cantos full of reminiscences in which the prominent 61-year-old poet and professor tells in detail his trivial matters in his life: his parents who were both ornithologists, brought him up and lived in the house in New Wye where he has lived all his life; his special sensitivity that he has had from his childhood and accompanies him even when he is in a fitful state of unconsciousness; his gentle and soft emotions to his wife who was his high school sweetheart; his deep love for his fat but intelligent daughter who committed suicide; his methods of writing poems and his philosophical thinking of life, death and afterlife.

Charles Kinbote, the refugee professor who is a neighbor of Shade, is given permission by Shade's wife Sybil to be in charge of annotating and editing the poem. He adds Foreword, Commentary and Index to the poem. In Kinbote's editorial contributions, he tells three stories intermixed with each other. One is his own story, notably including what he thinks of as his friendship with Shade. After Shade was murdered, Kinbote acquired the manuscript, including some variants, and has taken it upon himself to oversee the poem's publication, telling readers that it lacks only line 1000. Kinbote's second story deals with King Charles II, "The Beloved," the deposed king of Zembla. King Charles escaped imprisonment by Soviet-backed revolutionaries, making use of a secret passage and brave adherents in disguise. Kinbote repeatedly claims that he inspired Shade to write the poem by recounting King Charles's escape to him and that possible allusions to the king, and to Zembla, appear in Shade's poem, especially in rejected drafts. However, no explicit reference to King Charles is to be found in the poem. Kinbote's third story is that of Gradus, an assassin dispatched by the new rulers of Zembla to kill the exiled King Charles. Gradus makes his way from Zembla through Europe and America to New Wye, suffering comic mishaps. In the last note, to the missing line 1000, Kinbote narrates how Gradus killed Shade by mistake.

The reader soon realizes that Kinbote is King Charles, living incognito—or, though Kinbote builds an elaborate picture of Zembla complete with samples of a constructed language, that he is insane and that his identification with King Charles is a delusion, as perhaps all of Zembla is.

Themes

The Artist, Art, and Criticism Perhaps even more dynamic than the conflict between Gradus and King Charles is the inherent conflict between John Shade, the author of the poem "Pale Fire," and Charles Kinbote, the expert who writes extensive commentary on the poem. In terms of volume, it is immediately obvious to the reader that the critic's commentary is far longer and far more involved than the actual poem.

Kinbote really ceases to be a critic and he creates his own work of creative literature, presenting a romantic portrait of an exiled king and a crystal land. The question remains as to which work of art is true; this is complicated because both the poem and the commentary follow the conventions of their respective genre. The poem "Pale Fire" is "art about art." We find that the artist John Shade primarily defines himself in terms of his artistic and aesthetic experiences. Likewise, the use of the written text in Kinbote's hands is much like Humbert Humbert in Nabokov's *Lolita*, who writes as a means of immortalizing himself and his love.

Reality, Disguise, and Delusion Charles Kinbote is really at the center of this theme, as one of the novel's plot elements forces the question of whether or not Charles Kinbote is really King Charles the Beloved of Zembla. Either reality has been seriously disrupted and Kinbote is the exiled king of Zembla or else Kinbote is dangerously delusional. Kinbote's descriptions of his rival critics and professors have a way of making him seem less honest and less professional. For that matter, Sybil states that Kinbote is deranged. The difference between the poem and the biography that Kinbote produces also suggests that reality is difficult to understand in a comprehensive, satisfying way.

Besides the disguise of Charles the Beloved as Charles Kinbote of New Wye, there is the red-clad escape from the Zemblan palace and the one hundred Royalists. Gradus, the incompetent assassin is nonetheless, a man full of disguises and pseudonyms. D'Argus, Gradus, Degre become disguises that also refer to the meaning of disguise. Not mere pseudonyms, D'Argus and Gradus are anagrams. Gradus and Degre refer to gradations of change, from one identity to another. Gradus' disguises meet with varying degrees of success in New Wye. The irony of all of the efforts to disguise oneself is the fact that Gradus makes his way to New Wye quite by accident. When Gradus has the opportunity to kill Charles Kinbote (who may or may not be the exiled king of Zembla), he accidentally kills John Shade (who is definitely not the exiled king of Zembla). In the end, none of Kinbote's commentary can be assumed to be "true."

Exile and Memory Exile is one of the autobiographical themes that dominate the body of Nabokov's major work. There is, of course, a major parallel between Nabokov who left Russia and Charles the Beloved/ Charles Kinbote, who flees Zembla (a Russia-like place, whose name is, in fact, derived from that of a Russian island Novaya Zemlya). There is generally a combination of nostalgia and memory-loss in addressing one's homeland. Kinbote remains full of nostalgia to the point that he sees Zembla, his "crystal land" in John Shade's descriptions of the wintry New England landscape. It is also worth noting that Kinbote is double-exiled, for after leaving Zembla, he moves to New Wye only to be ostracized after the events surrounding John Shade's death. He is literally writing the commentary from some hideout among the desolate caves of the American West.

Fate and Destiny The idea of fate and destiny is challenged throughout Nabokov's novel. The underlying argument that Nabokov essentially makes is that there are so many accidents (so much chaos) that it is difficult to thread a direct connection between "act" and "consequence." The most dramatic example of this is the murder of John Shade by Gradus, an assassin who intended to kill the disguised exiled king of Zembla. If fate does exist, Nabokov shows that it is not determined by intention, but can be foiled by disguises and by human error. The idea of destiny is related to "purpose." In one sense, the exiled king represents the idea of destiny (dynasty) gone awry; on the other hand, Gradus, the assassin, is described as a man who is inept but full of purpose. His trajectory goes from Zembla, through Europe, across the Atlantic and deep into New England, and it is described as the workings of fate to bring murderer to victim. Logically, the concept of "fate" cannot really be proven or denied.

Literary Techniques

In *Pale Fire*, Nabokov constructs a complicated and labyrinthine narrative by using a game of worlds including multilingual puns, anagrams, wordplay (containing palindrome, the alphabetic games, and word golf), and language games. His purpose is to invite the reader to perform and participate in his games and make the reader feel pleased in the course of trying to go out of the labyrinth. The following are two notable techniques he utilizes as a preeminent postmodernist.

Intertextuality In writing *Pale Fire*, Nabokov blows up the previous unification of poetry and fiction, turns his fictional world inside out, pours out all the fragmented contents in it on the table top, leaving the work of integrating poetry and narration to the reader to do as well as possible. The intertextual characteristics are very obvious in the correlative relationship between Shade's poem and Kinbote's commentary, which are basically not related to each other in contents, forming a juxtaposition of two texts of different genres and embodying hybridization, one of the characteristics of the reconstructive tendency of postmodernism. Kinbote annotates the poem in such a way that he just extends a word or a phrase mentioned in Shade's poem to narrate his own story. By unfolding the three stories such as the escape of Charles the Second, the friendship of Kinbote and Shade, and Gradus's hunting down the disguised King in the sequence of time, Nabokov invites even the most conservative reader to find the comic nature of the novel produced by the inconsistency between the poem and the commentary. The special aesthetic effect produced by the poem and the commentary lies where they associate each other: they intertextualize and intercross each other from the beginning to the end, expressing a common theme: the awful solitude of the self and the attempt to crush it; it is just from these two texts that are seemingly unrelated to each other but actually interdependent in existence that the reader spells over the moral of the pale fire: between different lonely people, between a poet and a critic, between a realist and a romanticist, between people living in different conditions or working in different fields, even if they speak different languages, they may still interplay and communicate with each other.

Parody Nabokov creates not only the "correlated pattern in the game" but also "pleasure" for the reader by cleverly and fully using parody and many kinds of implications in *Pale Fire*. By reading Kinbote's "Commentary," the reader gradually becomes aware that he is in the face of an unreliable, stupid, pedantic, demure, especially infinitely arrogant editor. The image of Kinbote seems to embody all the worst shortcomings that an editor may have.

Shade's poem is also an obvious parody of Pope's poem *An Essay on Man* (1734). There are quotations from Pope's poem and similar to Pope's poem, Shade's "Pale Fire" is also written in heroic couplets and discusses the meaning of life. The difference between them lies in that Pope enters the general philosophical discussion about the meaning of life while Shade as a post-romantic poet would rather solve the problem in the subjective way of looking back on his personal life and the things that he has experienced in his life. However, Shade's systematic thinking does not lead him to penetrate the essence and the aim of life but on the contrary the essence and aim of life are exposed to him through his accidental discovery of the similarity between the structure of life and that of art, which is "…not text, but texture; not the dream / But topsy-turvial coincidence, / Not flimsy nonsense, but a web of sense." Even like Pope, Shade also ironically and satirically discusses the attempt to have a more precise picture of the otherworldliness in his poem. With the method of parody, Nabokov denies the philosophical discussion about the meaning of life that is considered meaningless in the postmodern times.

Metafiction As a typical metafiction, *Pale Fire* focuses more on the fictionality rather on following a clear plot and the usual development of traditional novels. To initial appearances, *Pale Fire* is the final, unfinished poem by renowned poet John Shade, with a forward and commentary by fellow university instructor Charles Kinbote. The poem is clear and simple and orderly from its form to its contents but it is only a small part of the whole book. Kinbote's "Commentary," however, is a peritext which explicates the poem surprisingly little. Focusing instead on his own concerns about the "distant northern land" Zembla, he divulges what proves to be the plot piece by piece, some of which can be connected by following the many cross-references, and the reader must attempt to discern the layers of illusive truth behind the tale. Thus the novel is a mixture of poetry and commentary, fiction and facts, reality and history with fragments and collages.

Unreliable Narrator *Pale Fire* magnifies vastly the effects of *Lolita*'s unreliable narrator. The convention of the "unreliable narrator" is when an account is demonstrably erroneous or biased, not necessarily because the narrator is lying but because something—such as age, vanity, spite, questionable sanity, etc.—causes his or her presentation of "the facts" to be distorted. While modernist fictionists can determine in what ways and the degree to which a narrator is being unreliable, the unreliable narration in *Pale Fire*, by contrast, is much more destabilizing. In the end, the reader's option is to accept that a number of possibilities have equal validity.

The first impression on encountering the novel is not of being immersed in a fully realized world, but that the reader must come to this world through a collection of different texts. The main text, the poem "Pale Fire" is framed by texts written by the critic, Charles Kinbote. The structure of book can be illuminated by Gérard Genette's theory of "paratexts," his term for the various kinds of texts which supplement a "main" text, such as the dedication, the preface or postscripts in the work, or an interview with the author, letters or diaries by the author. The function of Kinbote's paratexts conforms to Genette's theory, only more obviously so—their explicitness about their purpose expressing what most "real" paratexts keep implicit. Kinbote is trying deliberately to steer the reader towards a particular reading of the poem. In his Foreword he writes: "Let me state that without my notes Shade's text simply has no reality at all since the human reality of such a poem as his...has to depend entirely on the reality of its author and his surroundings, attachments and so forth, a reality that only my notes can provide". "For better or worse," the "Foreword" concludes, "it is the commentator who has the last word." He insists that the poem is a meditation on the land of Zembla and that his own friendship with Shade and his tales of the exiled king of Zembla "Charles the Beloved" have inspired the poet to write this veiled tribute to the King. Given that Zembla and Charles are never mentioned directly in the poem, swallowing this reading takes some persuasion. In his efforts to persuade, Kinbote's reading of specific images and lines stretch credibility. The words "that crystal land," for example, are interpreted by Kinbote as being "Perhaps as allusion to Zembla, my fair country."

Nabokov does not provide linear and hierarchical narrative for one single truth of the story, instead, he gives the reader many plausible texts—each story, each reading of the text is potentially as valid as the other. Not even the "real, real story," "the plane of ordinary sanity and common sense" can be considered final. This means that even Kinbote's "Zemblan" reading of the poem does have certain validity, even though it appears untenable because these are no direct references to the country anywhere. The interpretive gymnastics *Pale Fire* invites is a way of asking readers not to solve the mysteries of the text so much as to consider what a legitimate reading of the text is. Kinbote's narration is undoubtedly partial, even delusive, but just in this way, Nabokov exposes the partiality of all narration.

Bibliography

Chen, Shidan. *A Study of American Postmodernist Fiction*. Tianjin: Nankai University Press, 2010: 227-264.

Gray, Richard. *A History of American Literature*. Cornwall: Blackwell Publishing Ltd., 2004: 768-771.

Nicol, Bran. *The Cambridge Introduction of Postmodern Fiction.* Cambridge U.K. and New York: Cambridge University Press, 2009: 83-86.

Oakes, Elizabeth H. *American Writers.* New York: Facts on File, Inc., 2004: 252-253.

Yang, Renjing & Chen Shidan, eds. *Selected Readings in American Postmodernist Fiction.* Beijing: Foreign Languages Teaching and Research Press, 2009: 49-51.

http://en.wikipedia.org/wiki/Vladimir_Nabokov, 2013-02-15.

http://en.wikipedia.org/wiki/Pale_Fire, 2013-02-15.

http://www.newworldencyclopedia.org/entry/Vladimir_Nabokov, 2013-02-16.

http://www.novelguide.com/PaleFire/index.html, 2013-02-16.

http://www.gradesaver.com/pale-fire/study-guide/major-themes/, 2013-02-16.

Toni Morrison

Her Life and Writing Career

Her Life

Considered one of the foremost figures in contemporary American fiction, Toni Morrison (1931–) has won international acclaim for works in which she examines the role of race in American society. Her novels are known for their epic themes, vivid dialogue, and richly detailed characters. Her novels explore issues of African-American female identity in stories that integrate elements of the oral tradition, postmodern literary techniques, and magical realism to give voice to the experiences of women living on the margins of white American society. Among her best known novels are *The Bluest Eye* (1970), *Sula* (1974), *Song of Solomon* (1977) and *Beloved* (1987). As a best-selling African-American female author, Morrison represented a breakthrough for other black women novelists to succeed in the mainstream publishing industry. But Morrison's work does not only focus on black experience of white racism. There is a recurring interest in black people who have acquired social status through accommodating themselves to white society and by approaching white values. Of course, Morrison herself has been very successful as a writer and as a university teacher.

Morrison once received the Pulitzer Prize, the National Book Critics Circle Award and in 1993, she became the first African-American writer to receive the Nobel Prize in Literature. The citation for the award reads: "Toni Morrison, who in novels characterized by visionary force and poetic import, gives life to an essential aspect of American reality." In 1996, she received National Book Foundation Medal for Distinguished Contribution to American Letters. In April 2012, it was announced she would be awarded the Presidential Medal of Freedom, and on 29 May 2012, she received the award.

Toni Morrison was born Chloe Anthony Wofford in Lorain, Ohio. Her parents had moved to the North to escape the problems of southern racism and she grew up relatively unscarred by racial prejudices. Hers was a family of migrants, sharecroppers on both sides. She spent her childhood in the Midwest and read voraciously, from Jane Austen to Tolstoy.

From her farther, Chloe gained a Marcus-Garvey-like perspective on whites, one that left her with distrust for them all. In 1949 she entered Howard University in Washington, D.C., America's most distinguished black college. There she changed her name from "Chloe" to "Toni," explaining once that people found "Chloe" too difficult to pronounce. After obtaining a degree in English and in the classics, Morrison enrolled in graduate school at Cornell University where she wrote her master's thesis on the works of William Faulkner and Virginia Woolf, and received her M.A. in 1955.

In 1955, Morrison began her teaching career at the Texas Southern University. She returned to Howard in 1957 as an English instructor and began working on her own writing. It was there that she met and married Harold Morrison, a Jamaican architect. They divorced in 1964, and Morrison moved to Syracuse, New York to become an editor for Random House. There she edited books by such black authors as Toni Cade Bambara and Gayl Jones. She also continued to teach at two branches of the State University of New York. In 1984 she was appointed to an Albert Schweitzer chair at the University of New York at Albany, where she nurtured young writers through two-year fellowships.

Her Writing Career

While teaching at Howard University and caring for her two children, Morrison wrote her first novel, *The Bluest Eye* (1970). With the publication of the book, Morrison also established her new identity, which she later in 1992 rejected: "I am really Chloe Anthony Wofford. That's who I am. I have been writing under this other person's name. I write some things now as Chloe Wofford, private things. I regret having called myself Toni Morrison when I published my first novel, *The Bluest Eye*. " The story is set in the community of a small, Midwestern town. Its characters are all black. The book was partly based on a story Morrison wrote for a writers' group in 1966, which she had joined after the break-up of her six-year marriage with the Jamaican architect Harold Morrison. Pecola Breedlove, the central character, is a black girl, who prays each night for the blue-eyed beauty of Shirley Temple. She believes everything would be all right if only she had beautiful blue eyes. The narrator, Claudia MacTeer, tries to understand the destruction of Pecola. Although *The Bluest Eye* received scant notice at first, Morrison's career as a nationally recognized author was launched with the success of *Sula* (1974), her second novel, after which *The Bluest Eye* was retrospectively given renewed consideration as an important work of fiction. *Sula* depicts two black women friends and their community of Medallion, Ohio. It follows the lives of Sula, considered a threat against the community, and her cherished friend Nel, from their childhood to maturity and to death. The novel won the National Book Critics Award.

With the publication of *Song of Solomon* (1977), a family chronicle comparable to Alex Haley's *Roots*, Morrison gained international attention. *Song of Solomon* won the National book Critics Circle Award. It was the main selection of the Book-of-the-Month Club, the first novel by a black writer to be chosen since Richard Wright's *Native Son* in 1949. Morrison wrote the book from a male point of view. The story dealt with Milkman Dead's efforts to recover his "ancient properties," a cache of gold. After the success of *Song of Solomon* Morrison bought a four-story house near Nyack, N.Y. Since 1989, she has maintained a post as professor of Humanities at Princeton University.

Morrison published her next novel, *Beloved*, in 1987. A central incident in the work involves a fugitive slave who murders her infant daughter to spare her a life in bondage. Morrison based this scenario on an article she read in a nineteenth-century magazine while editing *The Black Book* (1974), and unconventional history of blacks in America, for Random House. Like Sethe, the protagonist of *Beloved*, Margaret Garner was a runaway slave who was tracked by her owner to Cincinnati, where she sought refuge with her freed mother-in-law. Faced with imminent capture, Garner attempted to murder her four children, succeeding in killing one. "I just imagined the life of a dead girl which was the girl that Margaret Garner killed," Morrison explained. "And I call her *Beloved* so that I can filter all these confrontations and questions that she has...and then to extend her life...her search, her quest." In *Beloved*, Sethe's daughter returns from the grave after twenty years, seeking revenge for her death. The highly acclaimed novel became a source of controversy several months after publication. When *Beloved* failed to win National Book Award in 1987, forty-eight prominent black writers and critics signed a tribute to Morrison's career and published it in the January 24, 1988, edition of the *New York Times Book Review*. The writers' statement promoted heated debate within the New York literary community, and some critics charged Morrison's supporters with racist manipulation. In 1988, *Beloved* received the Pulitzer Prize.

Beloved was adapted into the 1998 film of the same name starring Oprah Winfrey and Danny Glover. Morrison later used Margaret Garner's life story again in the libretto for a new opera, *Margaret Garner*, with music by Richard Danielpour. In May 2006, *The New York Times Book Review* named *Beloved* the best American novel published in the previous twenty-five years.

Although her novels typically concentrate on black women, Morrison does not identify her works as feminist. She has stated that she thinks "it's off-putting to some readers, who may feel that I'm involved in writing some kind of feminist tract. I don't subscribe to patriarchy, and I don't think it should be substituted with matriarchy. I think it's a question of equitable access, and opening doors to all sorts of things."

Morrison's overarching thematic concern throughout her oeuvre is with issues of African-American female identity in the contemporary world. Her novels offer complex examinations of problems within the African-American community, power dynamics between men and women, and issues of racism in relations between black and white America. Morrison's primary interest lies with the experiences of African-American women, whose quests for individual identity are integrally intertwined with their community and their cultural history.

Toni Morrison has published 10 main masterpieces as follows: *The Bluest Eye* (1970), *Sula* (1974), *Song of Solomon* (1977), *Beloved* (1987), *Tar Baby* (1981), *Jazz* (1992), *Paradise* (1997), *Love* (2003), *A Mercy* (2008), *Home* (2012).

Analysis of and Comment on Her Representative Novel

Song of Solomon (1977)

Plot Summary

Song of Solomon is based around the search of a young black man, Milkman Dead, for his legacy. He has been brought up in a family where his father has shunned his own community whilst striving to become a small businessman represented by white people. His mother has been ostracized by her husband because he believed he had discovered her in a Negrophile relationship with her father. Milkman's adolescence and early adulthood are years of irresponsibility and of indifference to the emerging civil rights movement of the time. But his quest for the lost family gold eventually a search for spiritual values and for the black ancestry in which he had previously shown no interest and which had also been denied by his father. His spiritual mentor in this search and the guardian of the lore he hopes to find his aunt, Pilate, another member of the family disowned by his father because she is not respectable enough for him.

Macon Dead is the only father in the novel who is physically present with his children, but his presence is so overpowering that it appears to do more harm than good. Cold, controlling, and domineering, Macon rules his household like a tyrant. With a wife who is "stunned into silence" by his rejection, two "half-grown" daughters, and a son who refuses to accept responsibility for his life, Macon exemplifies the western patriarch whose penchant for order and discipline provides him with the illusion of being in control.

Milkman's mother (Ruth Foster Dead) is the daughter of the town's only black doctor; she makes her husband feel inadequate, and it is clear she idolized her father, Doctor Foster, to the point of obsession. After her father dies, her husband claims to have found her in bed with the dead body, sucking his fingers. Ruth later tells Milkman that she was kneeling at her father's bedside kissing the only part of him that remained unaffected by the illness from which he died. These conflicting stories expose the problems between his parents and show Milkman that "truth" is difficult or impossible to obtain. Macon (Jr.) is often violently aggressive towards Ruth because he believes that she was involved sexually with her father and loved her father more than her own husband. On one occasion, Milkman punches his father after he strikes Ruth, exposing the growing rift between father and son.

In contrast, Macon Dead Jr.'s sister, Pilate, is seen as nurturing—an Earth Mother character. Born without a navel, she is a somewhat mystical character. It is strongly implied that she is Divine—a female Christ-in spite of her name. Macon (Jr.) has not spoken to his sister for years and does not think highly of her. She, like Macon, has had to fend for herself from an early age after their father's murder, but she has dealt with her past in a different way than Macon, who has embraced money as the way to show his love for his father. Pilate has a daughter, Reba, and a granddaughter named Hagar. Hagar falls desperately and obsessively in love with Milkman, and is unable to cope with his rejection, attempting to kill him at least six times.

Hagar is not the only character who attempts to kill Milkman. Guitar, Milkman's erstwhile best friend, tries to kill Milkman more than once after incorrectly suspecting that Milkman has cheated him out of hidden gold, a fortune he planned to use to help his Seven Days group fund their revenge killings in response to killings of blacks.

Searching for the gold near the old family farm in Pennsylvania, Milkman stops at the rotting Butler Mansion, former home of the people who killed his ancestor to claim the farm. Here he meets Circe, an almost supernaturally old ex-slave of the Butlers. She tells Milkman of his family history and this leads him to the town of Shalimar. There he learns his great-grandfather Solomon was said to have escaped slavery by flying back to Africa, leaving behind twenty-one children and his wife Ryna, who goes crazy with loss. Returning home, he learns that Hagar has died of a broken heart. He accompanies Pilate back to Shalimar, where she is accidentally shot and killed by Guitar, who had intended to kill Milkman.

Themes

The Acceptance and Return to African American Culture In *Song of Solomon*, Macon Dead is the epitome of the black man who has acquiesced to the white capitalist system. Estranged from his family, his community, and his African heritage, Macon is hated and feared by blacks, who detest his arrogance, and ignored and ostracized by whites, who use him primarily to keep black tenants in their place. A fervent believer in the mythological American Dream, Macon prizes his ring of keys, which distinguishes him as a man of property. Convinced that his wealth will compensate for his race, Macon has no time for lower-class blacks, whom he considers beneath him socially and economically. As a result, he finds himself spiritually and psychologically estranged from himself and others, desperately clinging to the illusion that material success is all he needs to make his life worthwhile.

Pilate is the ancestor who, as the critic Stelamaris Coser notes, represents "the only sign of a vital black tradition surviving in the urban industrial environment." Milkman's "pilot" on his "flight" home, she defies virtually every stereotype of a black woman and exemplifies Morrison's rejection of binary thinking. Just as Milkman fails to recognize Pilate's innate beauty and dignity until he sees it reflected in the women of Shalimar, we may fail to recognize her courage and power until we place it within the context of African history and classical mythology. Viewed from these perspectives, we find that Pilate is both a storyteller and village elder, charged with preserving the cultural memory of her people, and a wise, moral teacher who offers a new vision of the future. A conjurer and root woman skilled in the art of voodoo, she is a healer and peacemaker who has no qualms about resorting to any means necessary to protect those she loves.

Even according to conventional Eurocentric standards, Pilate is the true hero: Odysseus wanders for ten years; Pilate wanders for twenty years and experiences a series of adventures that shape her character and free her to make hard choices concerning her role in society. From the moment she emerges from her mother's womb, she creates herself, improving her situation by working her way up from washerwoman to entrepreneur. Unlike her brother, Macon, who inherits his wealth from Ruth, Pilate creates her own way. And unlike Odysseus, whose journey is aided by gods and goddesses with supernatural powers, Pilate herself is endowed with supernatural powers; she completes her journey without the help of others' magic or divine intervention. She is a courageous woman who assumes full responsibility for her life and meets life head on, but because she is neither white and male nor young and beautiful, her accomplishments are discounted and her wisdom discredited—even by the black community.

Song of Solomon explores the quest for cultural identity. Based on the African-American folktale about enslaved Africans who escape slavery by flying back to Africa, it tells the story of Macon "Milkman" Dead, a young man alienated from himself and estranged from his family, his community, and his historical and cultural roots. Milkman is mentally enslaved and spiritually dead, but with the help of his eccentric aunt, Pilate, and his best friend, Guitar Bains, he embarks on a physical and spiritual journey that enables him to reconnect with his past and realize his self-worth.

Through Milkman's quest, this novel introduces an important theme: the acceptance and return to African American culture. It is the return that helps Milkman find his root and acquire his maturity and identity. The novel also depicts the alienating effects of racism. Racism is the central cause of suffering in the novel. It has long-lasting damaging effects on the community, the knowledge that his father died because of his white employers' negligence made guitar especially sensitive to the injustices perpetrated against African-American, and transformed him into a ruthless, vengeful murder. Guitar's story shows that racism alienates its victims from their native communities and causes them to lose touch with their own humanity.

With the help of Pilate and Guitar, Milkman eventually discovers the secret of Solomon's song once he recognizes the vital link between the past and the future. His mission to find Pilate's gold takes him back to his ancestral roots, enabling him to learn the origin of his name and to reconnect with the black community—his "tribe."

Flight The concept of flight is clearly addressed in the beginning of the novel with Mr. Smith's jump—his attempt to fly. Although flight may have positive attributes of the possibility of escape, it also contains negative connotations. Escape suggests leaving behind one's old world and thus pain for those left behind. Solomon, who flew back to Africa, leaves behind his wife Ryna and their twenty-one children. Solomon's departure, although happy in the face of his struggle with slavery, is disastrous for Ryna, who goes mad with grief. Milkman's escape from Not Doctor Street, a relief from his daily unhappiness, is devastating for Hagar, who eventually dies from heartbreak. The overall theme of flight, therefore, is associated with abandonment. Although it is an impossible feat, flight is regarded as natural in the novel. It is believed that Milkman's great-grandfather, Solomon, literally flew away by simply spinning around with his arms spread out until he elevated. Milkman, at the beginning of the novel, spiritually dead and mentally enslaved by apathy and materialism, embarks on a quest for his inheritance, which he initially believes to be Pilate's gold. Instead, through a series of mishaps and coincidences, he finds himself on a spiritual quest for his identity. Eventually he learns the meaning of grace and mercy, and he inherits the gift of flight.

The community's acceptance of flight as normal highlights Morrison's use of magical realism in her writing. Even the novel's epigraph, "The fathers may soar and the children may know their names," references the theme of flight.

Allusions in Characters' Names Names hold a special significance in regard to each character. Pilate, a biblical reference to the Roman governor who allowed the execution of Jesus Christ, shares some similar traits with her namesake, such as strength and power. Although she is not cruel in her authority, Pilate is a male name suggesting that she bears the stereotypical characteristics of a man, at least as perceived by society at the time. Circe's name bears homage to the enchantress in Homer's *Odyssey*, who provides Odysseus with crucial information on how to end his voyage. In *Song of Solomon*, Circe supplies Milkman with segments of his family history, so that he may end his search for his family heritage. Hagar, a biblical name, is a direct explanation of her strained and desperate relationship with Milkman, who abandons her, as can be predicted through the Bible.

The family surname of Dead is a spiritual wordplay. Milkman's family accidentally received the name from white oppressors, thus suggesting that their real name died, and at that point, so did their family history. The importance of names relates to a sense of belonging, to being able to trace one's roots through the ages. Throughout the entire novel, there are continuous references to Milkman being Dead, both in terms of name and character. Upon Milkman's rebirth, he no longer can be called Dead, neither by name nor by personality.

Singing The theme of singing and songs is a reference not only to the African oral tradition but also to the days of slavery. Slaves, as means of getting through their work on the plantation, sang spirituals. Such songs talked of faith and hope, and how to live with the spirit of God. Singing was a way in which slaves could express their personal feelings, and it was also a means of cheering one another up. Many songs also contained "secret messages," for instance making indirect references to the Underground Railroad.

The act of singing communicates the importance of the oral tradition, demonstrated through Pilate's "Oh Sugarman done fly away..." The song, originally a reference to Solomon, tells the tale of Milkman's great-grandfather. It is this song that transmits Milkman's family history, and steers him towards his spiritual rebirth. Overall, songs underline the rebuilding of a spiritual and emotional bond. In the novel, Pilate, Hagar and Reba all bond through the act of singing. And, after Hagar's death, Reba and Pilate comfort one another through a song.

Racial Injustice As a black man, Macon's lack of compassion is illustrated in his treatment of Porter and Mrs. Bains, both tenants of his, but it is especially evident in his treatment of his sister, Pilate, whom he despises for refusing to conform to his rigidly defined standards of correct behavior. His disdain and lack of respect for other blacks are also evident in his speech, which echoes the beliefs and stereotypes of racist whites—he is the first one in the novel to use the word "nigger" to refer to Porter, Pilate, and Guitar.

Toni Morrison emphasizes the country's state of racial injustice. Chapter One mentions racial uplift groups and makes note of segregated hospitals to create a focus on race. Further emphasis is placed on white oppression in regards to race as Guitar remembers that his mother received four ten dollar bills for his father's body. The reasons for Guitar's anger towards whites are reemphasized in his unfair treatment by a white nurse. His hatred grows to transform him into a revengeful fiend who loses his humanity. The Seven Days society, of which Guitar is a member of, takes justice into their own hands.

Wealth The pursuit of money and property is a struggle for which Macon Dead II has sacrificed his humanity. Macon inherited his initial wealth through Ruth. Not satisfied with his wife's inheritance, his insatiable greed prompts him to try to steal his sister's inheritance—gold—as well. The gold further accents his greed, and his desire for monetary objects consumes Milkman as well. Although Macon's longing to accumulate worldly goods is a sign of bereavement for his father, his manner of mourning soon turns against him. Milkman's search for the gold becomes a search for his identity, his real inheritance.

The Color White Throughout the novel, black and white colors are used to differentiate between good and evil. Stereotypically, society associates white with good and black with evil. *Song of Solomon*, on the other hand, presents the color white as a symbol of malevolence. All the white characters as well as white symbols represent wrongdoing and/or violence. Guitar's father's employer, who is white, gives his mother forty dollars for his father's dead body, a suggestion of how much a black man is thought to be worth. Corinthian's employer, white as well, also does not regard her employee as an equal, although she claims her views are liberal. Freddie's description of his mother's death involves a white bull. And the white peacock that Milkman and Guitar chase represents greed.

Literary Techniques

Quality of Speech Morrison's prose has the quality of speech. She deliberately strives for this effect, which she calls "aural literature." She hears her prose as she writes, and during the revision process she cuts phrasing which sounds literary or written rather than spoken. She rejects critics' assertions that her prose is rich; to those who say her prose is poetic, she responds that metaphors are natural in black speech.

Morrison wants readers to participate in her novels, to be involved actively. Readers are encouraged to create the novel with her and to help construct meaning.

Postmodern Meta-Narratives Morrison's fictions are self-consciously concerned with myth, legend, storytelling, and the oral tradition, as well as with memory, history, and historiography, and have thus been recognized as postmodern meta-narratives. Morrison's stories are conscious of African cultural heritage as well as African-American history, thus demonstrating the importance of the past to the struggles of contemporary African-Americans. She employs strong elements of Black English in her dialogue and narration to express the importance of language in the formation of identity.

One of the most important concerns in her writing is the "use value" of narrative. Storytelling is historiography in Morrison's fiction, and in most novels she carefully examines the role of narrative in the reconstitution of both the individual self and society at large.

Magical Realism Morrison uses fantasy, folktales, supernatural and mythic elements along with realistic depiction of racial, gender and class conflict. Her style combines these unrealistic elements with a realistic presentation of life and characters. This mixture has been called "magical realism."

Bibliography

Bouson, J. Brooks. *Quiet As It's Kept.* Albany: State University of New York Press: 1999: 75-98.

Gunton, Sharon R. & Jean C. Stine, eds. *Contemporary Literary Criticism (Vol.22).* Detroit, Michigan: Gale Research Company, 1982: 314-320.

Hunter, Jeffrey W. ed. *Contemporary Literary Criticism (Vol.194).* Farmington Hills: Thomson Gale, 2005: 150-160.

Peach, Linden. *Toni Morrison.* New York: St. Martin's Press, 2000: 65-101.

Samuels, Wilfred D. & Celnora Hudson-Weems. *Toni Morrison.* Boston: Twayne Publishers, 1990: 58-78.

http://en.wikipedia.org/wiki/Toni_Morrison, 2013-02-15.

http://www.newworldencyclopedia.org/entry/Toni_Morrison, 2013-02-15.

常耀信 . 美国文学简史（第二版）. 天津：南开大学出版社，2006: 541-545.

后　记

《美国文学史（上、下）》的编写分工如下：陈世丹、屈晓丽担任主编，负责全书内容、体例、规模设计，陈世丹负责第一、第二、第三、第六部分的统稿工作，屈晓丽负责第四、第五部分的统稿工作，最后由陈世丹统合成书、修改、定稿。

全书各章节编写分工如下：

PART I　AMERICAN LITERATURE IN THE COLONIAL PERIOD (1607–1700)

史岩林：Historical Introduction
American Puritanism
Early New England Literature
John Smith
John Cotton
Roger Williams
Anne Bradstreet
Edward Taylor

PART II　AMERICAN LITERATURE IN THE AGE OF REASON AND REVOLUTION (1700–1800)

张东芹：Historical Introduction
Neoclassicism
Benjamin Franklin
Thomas Paine
Thomas Jefferson
Philip Freneau

PART III　AMERICAN LITERATURE IN THE ROMANTIC PERIOD (1800–1865)

赵　丽：Historical Introduction

陈世丹：Romanticism
American Romanticism
American Transcendentalism

赵　丽：Washington Irving
James Fenimore Cooper
William Cullen Bryant

张东芹：Edgar Allan Poe
Ralph Waldo Emerson

Henry David Thoreau
史岩林：Nathaniel Hawthorne
Herman Melville
Henry Wadsworth Longfellow

PART IV AMERICAN LITERATURE IN THE REALISTIC PERIOD (1865–1900)

苏　凤：Historical Introduction
Realism
Psychological Realism
Naturalism
王桃花：Walt Whitman
Emily Dickinson
Harriet Beecher Stowe
苏　凤：Mark Twain
Henry James
李金云：Edith Wharton
苏　凤：Jack London
李金云：Theodore Dreiser
Willa Cather

PART V AMERICAN LITERATURE IN THE MODERN PERIOD (1900–1945)

屈晓丽：Historical Introduction
The Development of Literature
Modernism
Terms of Modernist Literature
吴银燕：Ezra Pound
Robert Lee Frost
Wallace Stevens
Thomas Stearns Eliot
尹　宇：F. Scott Fitzgerald
屈晓丽：Ernest Hemingway
William Faulkner
王阿芳：Eugene O'Neill
Arthur Miller

PART VI AMERICAN LITERATURE IN THE POSTMODERN PERIOD (1945–)

陈世丹：Historical Introduction
Postmodernism
Postmodernist Fiction
Metafiction
Terms of Postmodernist Literature

吴泽庆：Robert Lowell
　　　　Charles Olson
张丽秀：Joseph Heller
陈世丹：Kurt Vonnegut
张丽秀：John Barth
　　　　Donald Barthelme
尹　宇：Thomas Pynchon
　　　　Vladimir Nabokov
王阿芳：Toni Morrison

主 编
2019 年 3 月 30 日

图书在版编目（CIP）数据

美国文学史：全2册：英文/陈世丹，屈晓丽主编. —2版. — 北京：中国人民大学出版社，2019. 3
中国人民大学“十三五”规划教材
ISBN 978-7-300-26773-9

Ⅰ. ①美… Ⅱ. ①陈… ②屈… Ⅲ. ①英语–阅读教学–高等学校–教材 ②文学史–美国–高等学校–教材 Ⅳ. ①H319. 4: I

中国版本图书馆 CIP 数据核字（2019）第 032481 号

中国人民大学“十三五”规划教材
美国文学史（第二版）
主　编　陈世丹　屈晓丽
编　者（以姓名拼音首字母为序）
陈世丹　李金云　屈晓丽　史岩林　苏　凤
王阿芳　王桃花　吴银燕　吴泽庆　尹　宇
张东芹　张丽秀　赵　丽
Meiguo Wenxueshi (Di-er ban)

出版发行	中国人民大学出版社		
社　址	北京中关村大街 31 号	邮政编码	100080
电　话	010–62511242（总编室）		010–62511770（质管部）
	010–82501766（邮购部）		010–62514148（门市部）
	010–62515195（发行公司）		010–62515275（盗版举报）
网　址	http:// www. crup. com. cn		
	http:// www. ttrnet. com（人大教研网）		
经　销	新华书店		
印　刷	北京鑫丰华彩印有限公司		
规　格	185 mm × 260 mm 16 开本	版　次	2019 年 3 月第 1 版
印　张	30.25	印　次	2019 年 3 月第 1 次印刷
字　数	705 000	定　价	68.00 元

中国人民大学出版社外语出版分社读者信息反馈表

尊敬的读者：

感谢您购买和使用中国人民大学出版社外语出版分社的 ______________ 一书，我们希望通过这张小小的反馈卡来获得您更多的建议和意见，以改进我们的工作，加强我们双方的沟通和联系。我们期待着能为更多的读者提供更多的好书。

请您填妥下表后，寄回或传真回复我们，对您的支持我们不胜感激！

1. 您是从何种途径得知本书的：

   □书店　□网上　□报纸杂志　□朋友推荐

2. 您为什么决定购买本书：

   □工作需要　□学习参考　□对本书主题感兴趣　□随便翻翻

3. 您对本书内容的评价是：

   □很好　□好　□一般　□差　□很差

4. 您在阅读本书的过程中有没有发现明显的专业及编校错误，如果有，它们是：

   ____

   ____

   ____

5. 您对哪些专业的图书信息比较感兴趣：

   ____

   ____

   ____

6. 如果方便，请提供您的个人信息，以便于我们和您联系（您的个人资料我们将严格保密）：

您供职的单位：______________________________

您教授的课程（教师填写）：______________________________

您的通信地址：______________________________

您的电子邮箱：______________________________

请联系我们：贾乐凯　黄婷　程子殊　鞠方安

电话：010-62515580，62512737，62513265，62515576

传真：010-62514961

E-mail：jialk@crup.com.cn　huangt@crup.com.cn　chengzsh@crup.com.cn　jufa@crup.com.cn

通信地址：北京市海淀区中关村大街甲 59 号文化大厦 15 层　邮编：100872

中国人民大学出版社外语出版分社